Contemporary Business Law in a Global Economy

Nancy Kubasek, Dan Herron,
Dan Ostas, Neil Browne, and
Andrea Giampetro-Meyer

The University of Oklahoma
Legal Studies 3323
Professor Dan Ostas

Crown Custom Publishing Inc.
Brunswick, Ohio

Contemporary Business Law in a Global Economy

Printed in the United States of America

B C D E F G E

ISBN 1-983403063

This publication is designed to provide accurate and authoritative information with regard to the subject matter involved. It is sold with the understanding that the publisher is not engaged in rendering legal, accounting or other professional advice. If legal advice or other expert assistance is required, the services of a qualified professional person should be sought.

—From: *A Declaration of Principles*, jointly adopted by a Committee of the American Bar Association and a Committee of Publishers and Associations.

Visit our home page at: http://www.crowncustompublishing.com

CONTENTS

Custom Edition Table of Contents

CONTENTS
Global Context Listing

CONTENTS

Technology Listing

PREFACE
To the Instructor

We are all fortunate to teach business law; its relevance is not difficult to portray to business students. The cases have enough human interest to fascinate almost all students; the laws themselves are both fluid enough to fascinate those who yearn for a better world and, at the same time, are stable enough to provide a body of knowledge needed by all those who intend to be business managers. As your colleagues, we believe we can help you provide an even more exhilarating course by creating a text that is readable and contemporary.

Something Very Special For The Business Law Market

We formed a partnership with Lakeshore Communications to produce this text because they promised to address the two major complaints we heard from those who teach business law: the soaring prices of the texts and the disappointing service provided by the remaining players in the Business Publishing field.

We are especially proud to be able to say we are not only producing a less expensive book, but a **better** book in many ways. Suffice it to say, we have infused a global approach throughout the text, selected cases that are more recent and appealing than those of competing books, and integrated AASCB concerns about ethics and critical thinking into each chapter. To summarize, our book is a better book that, as a bonus, is much cheaper to the student.

With respect to the **price**, we and Lakeshore agreed that we did not want to merely produce a cheaper book; instead, what we have done is to provide a guarantee that our book is and will continue to be priced 20% below the price of comparable books. This lower price permits you to justifiably claim that you are concerned about the extraordinarily high prices of your students' textbooks and have decided to do something about it.

Lakeshore and we wanted to directly address the second major complaint of those teaching Business Law: the disappointing **service** often experienced by those of us who need materials from the publishers, but find their bureaucratic layers serving all too frequently as obstacles to our teaching. When we negotiated our

agreement with Lakeshore, we insisted that our adopters be treated as the professionals they are. We expect telephone calls and web site solicitations about our text to be answered promptly. Furthermore, we sought promises that text materials would be sent immediately to those who needed them.

Lakeshore has complied with all our requests in this regard. Our text has a dedicated 800 number (800-537-7054) to ensure that you can receive the service you need. In addition, Lakeshore guarantees a 72-hour response time to any requests for ancillaries and desk copies from either prospective or existing adopters. Lakeshore also is an experienced provider of local campus customization options and will work with you, if you wish, to develop a version of our text that is more focused on the needs of your local situation.

If for any reason there is a breakdown in these pledges, we want to hear from you. We have all been the victims of poor service from book publishers; and, consequently, we are especially earnest about wishing to make certain that the needs of your students are being met expeditiously and proficiently.

Special Features

Prefaces are notorious for promising more than they deliver. But give our text a try, and you will see that we provide the significant inclusions we pledge to incorporate. The authors have a collective experience of 120 years as business professors, and we have tried to distill that experience in determining the major constitutive elements of this text.

Before we enumerate the special features of our text, we want to highlight one aspect of the text that has received universal acclaim from the numerous business law professors and students with whom we have piloted early versions of *Contemporary Business Law in a Global Economy*. The cases we have selected are especially current and compelling.

One of the advantages of our text is that a smaller publisher can move more nimbly to assure that, in an area like business law where contemporaneity is crucial, a text like ours includes incredibly current cases. We have taken full advantage of that capability, as evidenced by our frequent allusions to Enron's problems in the appropriate chapters. Hence, you can assure your students that you have chosen a text for them that is fresh and up-to-date.

To give you a sense of how current *Contemporary Business Law in a Global Economy* is, we wanted to list just a few of the cases discussed or excerpted in the text:

- *A & M Records, Inc. v. Napster, Inc.*, 239 F.3d 1004 (2001)
- *Equal Employment Opportunity Commission. v. Waffle House, Inc.*, 2002 WL 6763 (2002)
- *Hunt v. Nebraska Power District*, 282 F.3d 1021 (8th Cir. 2002)
- *Solid Waste Agency of Northern Cook County, Petitioner, v. United States Army Corps of Engineers, et al.*, 531 U.S. 159 (2001)
- *Christy Brzonkala v. Antonio J. Morrison et al.*, 120 S. Ct. 1740 (2000)
- *Lorillard Tobacco Co. v. Reilly*, 533 U.S. 525 (2001)
- *Kyllo v. U.S.*, 523 U.S. 27 (U.S. 2001)
- *TrafFix Devices Inc. v. Marketing isplays Inc.*, 532 U.S. 23 (2001)
- *Circuit City v. Saint Clair Adams*, 121 S. CT. 1302 (2001)

The agility with which we can continue to keep the text current for you and your students is an especially valuable aspect of our partnership with Lakeshore Publications.

Following are the special features that we believe will make this book one your students will read and learn from:

A. **Global Emphasis**: Each chapter has one or more Global boxes that remind readers that business managers must now be prepared to be familiar with business laws that are not necessarily similar to American business law. The method behind these Global boxes is to not only prepare students for a global marketplace, but also to make them aware that American business law can sometimes profit from studying how other commercial communities encourage and regulate business practice. If law is to evolve with the help of our students, their study of legal practices among our trading partners should yield them a rich source of possibilities.

Allusions to business law in other economies is also integrated in several places throughout the book. We did not want the Global boxes to just

make their appearance in each chapter without our having reinforced the global approach in the remainder of the chapter as well. So we tried to interweave references to non-American law into the general flow of the chapters to reinforce our belief in the importance of this dimension of business school education for modern managers.

B. **Integrated Chapters**: Each chapter begins with an actual business scenario that presents a problem elucidated by the chapter contents. Multiple times in each chapter, the text returns to the opening scenario to provide continuity and purpose to the chapter. Finally, at the conclusion of the chapter, the text reminds the reader of the usefulness of what has been learned in the chapter for situations like the one introduced in the opening scenario.

The objective of these opening scenarios is to tie the chapter to real business dilemmas that have been faced by actual commercial entities, many of them recognizable by the readers. The hope of these inclusions is to make certain that our students can see business law in action.

C. **Critical Thinking Framework**: The opening chapter presents a critical thinking approach created for this text by a prominent critical thinking educator. Many texts claim to be encouraging critical thinking; ours is designed by a co-author of what is perhaps the most successful critical thinking text in the country especially for *Business Law in a Global Economy*. Consequently, those who use this text can correctly argue that they are making a contribution to the general education mission of their schools, as well as responding to AACSB mandates that critical thinking be taught in the business school curriculum. This element of the book should be particularly valuable to those who find themselves needing to defend the importance of business law in the business school curriculum.

The questions following each case contain one question earmarked as a critical thinking question. To answer those questions, students can use the critical thinking framework provided in the initial chapter.

D. **Practical Business Ethics Protocol**: Business law teachers are increasingly the primary source of what business students learn about business ethics.

As if the business law course were not already bursting at the seams with content, we business law professors have absorbed this additional responsibility because we believe it to be crucial to the forms of business management that promise a better economic future, not only in the sense of greater material abundance, but also with respect to the need for businesspeople to do the good or the right, not just the effective.

But we will not be effective in this objective unless we provide a protocol that our students will be able to apply when they are in the midst of contemporary business pressures. While philosophers can and should think deeply about ethical dilemmas, the speed of commercial transactions requires businesspeople to have a series of protocols that they can use on a regular basis without taking an ethical reflection break from their jobs. Our text attempts to explain one set of possible approaches that can be used as part of the ordinary problem-solving approach used by any active manager.

Chapter 2 sets out a series of logical steps for ethical decision making in a business enterprise. It encourages the learning and use of a mnemonic device that is referenced in the ethical questions raised after the legal cases in each chapter. While ethics is much more complicated than this practical approach to ethics suggests, we wanted to give students an approach that they could use in their careers, an approach that promises to make a visible improvement in business conduct if it is followed.

E. **Technology Boxes**: Cyberlaw is highlighted in every chapter where the burgeoning implications of emerging computer and Internet technology have surfaced. The Tech Boxes reinforce our belief that this area of business law is an essential dimension of modern business practice. By our making it a regular feature of our text, we send students the message that they will need to stay informed about legal developments surrounding technology because there are so many new legal questions suggested by new forms of information transfer.

F. **Assignments on the Internet**: Every chapter contains assignments requiring students to develop proficiency with the Internet. In addition, Contemporary Business Law in a Global Economy will have a special password-protected web site where users of our text will receive new Internet assignments and teaching suggestions as they are developed for each chapter.

****

We want to create a textbook that you will be proud to use. We are open to all suggestions about how we make the book more effective for learning business law. We cannot promise we will follow all your suggestions, but we are genuine in our openness to considering whatever you propose. We have written the best book we know how to produce, but we know it can be better with your assistance. We and future readers can only benefit from your contributions. Please feel free to contact any of the authors about your concerns.

Write us at nkubase@cba.bgsu.edu; herrondj@muohio.edu; dostas@ou.edu; nbrown2@cba.bgsu.edu; and agiampet@loyola.edu with any of these concerns.

PREFACE

To the Student

Your instructor chose this textbook after looking at many alternatives. There are many strong business law texts, and your instructor selected this one. We want to prove to you that the choice was a wise one—a decision focusing on your future. As a prospective business manager, you need to appreciate the role of business law in shaping the range of socially acceptable business decisions.

Let us explain. Businesspeople cannot do whatever they please. They function in a social world, where the interests of consumers, suppliers, distributors, shareholders, employees, and lenders rarely are identical. Business laws provide a guidebook of evolving boundaries within which these conflicting interests are acknowledged and distributed. Your task in this course is to familiarize yourself with the realm of acceptable behavior within which the general community expects businesses to operate. Go outside those boundaries, as Enron recently did, and the community imposes a harsh judgment, seeing you as having violated the community's trust.

This text was written because the authors respect business law and its role in guiding a successful economy. If we can get you to share in our admiration for the essential nature of business law as a lubricant for commercial life, you will be more engaged in improving it. And it's the excitement of making business law even better than it is that energizes all of us who find this area of study so fulfilling. We do not want to simply accept existing business law as a final word about the correct interests of commercial stakeholders. Rather, we want to learn what business law is and then assist in some small way in making it what it should be.

We know you are busy, but we are always open to your suggestions about how to make this textbook a better tool for your learning. The following are Special Features that we believe will make this book one you will enjoy reading and learning from:

A. **Global Emphasis**: Each chapter has one or more Global boxes that remind readers that business managers must now be prepared to be familiar with business laws that are not necessarily similar to American business law. The method behind these Global boxes is to not only prepare you for a global marketplace, but also to make you aware that American business law can sometimes profit from studying how other commercial communities encourage and regulate business practice. If law is to evolve with the help of students such as yourselves, your study of legal practices among our trading partners should yield you a rich source of possibilities.

B. **Integrated Chapters**: Each chapter begins with an actual business scenario that presents a problem elucidated by the chapter contents. Multiple times in each chapter, the text returns to the opening scenario to provide continuity and purpose to the chapter. Finally, at the conclusion of the chapter, the text reminds the reader of the usefulness of what has been learned in the chapter for situations like the one introduced in the opening scenario.

The objective of these opening scenarios is to tie the chapter to real business dilemmas that have been faced by actual commercial entities, many of them recognizable by yourselves. The hope of these inclusions is to make certain that you can see business law in action.

C. **Critical Thinking Framework**: The opening chapter presents a critical thinking approach created for this text by a prominent critical thinking educator.

The questions following each case contain one question earmarked as a critical thinking question. To answer those questions, you will find yourself using the critical thinking framework provided in the initial chapter.

D. **Practical Business Ethics Protocol**: We believe the study of Business Ethics to be crucial to the forms of business management that promise a better economic future, not only in the sense of greater material abundance, but also with respect to the need for businesspeople to do the good or the right, not just the effective.

But we will not be effective in this objective unless we provide a protocol that you will be able to apply when you are in the midst of contemporary business pressures. While philosophers can and should think deeply about ethical dilemmas, the speed of commercial transactions requires businesspeople to have a series of protocols that they can use on a regular basis without taking an ethical reflection break from their jobs. Our text attempts to explain one set of possible approaches that can be used as part of the ordinary problem-solving approach used by any active manager.

Chapter 2 sets out a series of logical steps for ethical decision making in a business enterprise. It encourages the learning and use of a mnemonic device that is referenced in the ethical questions raised after the legal cases in each chapter. While ethics is much more complicated than this practical approach to ethics suggests, we wanted to give you an approach that you can use in your careers, an approach that promises to make a visible improvement in business conduct if it is followed.

E. **Technology Boxes**: Cyberlaw is highlighted in every chapter where the burgeoning implications of emerging computer and Internet technology have surfaced. The Tech Boxes reinforce our belief that this area of business law is an essential dimension of modern business practice. By our making it a regular feature of our text, we send to you and future generations the message that you will need to stay informed about legal developments surrounding technology because there are so many new legal questions suggested by new forms of information transfer.

F. **Assignments on the Internet**: Every chapter contains assignments requiring you to develop proficiency with the Internet, if you have not already done so. In addition, *Contemporary Business Law in a Global Economy* will have a special password-protected web site where users of our text will receive new Internet assignments and teaching suggestions as they are developed for each chapter. See: www.cont-businesslaw.com.

If you have seen features in a text in another discipline that were especially effective in assisting your learning, do a favor for future readers of this book; pass the suggestions along to us. We are relatively humble textbook authors, and as such we would welcome your suggestions. Send them to Neil Browne at nbrown2@cba.bgsu.edu. He will respond to all suggestions, regardless of how small or huge they are.

In conclusion, we hope your business law course is not just another course. We want it to open your eyes to the concepts, rules, and methods of persuasion that together make up business law. If the course and this text are a success, you should finish the course and wonder to yourself: how could anyone possibly be a successful business manager without a thorough understanding of business law?

Again, let us know if you believe you have a better idea for achieving this objective.

Acknowledgments

The authors wish to acknowledge the several individuals who helped in the creation of this book. First, we would like to acknowledge a large cadre of research assistants who helped us at various stages of this project. Carrie Williamson, currently a third year law student at the University of California at Berkeley Law School, who aspires toward becoming a Business Law professor herself in the near future, and has assisted in various aspects of this project from its inception. Much of the research for the global boxes was done by Kathleen Hale, currently a law student at the University of Arizona. Melissa Hinds, Anne Hardenbaugh, and Chaz Giles helped by finding interesting case problems. Finally, the following assistants helped with a wide variety of essential tasks: Elizabeth Barre, Steve Weigand, Emily Coplin, Jason Slobe, Modesto Rosado, Mohamed Smaidi, Kevin Minnick and Brandi Buettner.

We would also like to thank Elizabeth Cameron, Joseph Petrick, and Linda Christianson for their thoughtful comments as to how to improve the manuscript. And, of course, we were delighted to have Sheryl Kaiser's special feature on the Enron debacle.

The book would never have been completed on time if it were not for the careful word processing of Karen Masters, who typed most of the manuscript. Her colleague in the BGSU word processing department, Tami Thomas, typed the remainder of this manuscript.

Finally, we want to thank the team at Lakeshore Communications, beginning with the Publisher, Roger Williams, who was has taken a genuine interest in the project from the moment we approached him about it, and has worked very hard to make sure that the authors' expectations were met. We also want to thank Judy Neal, the copyeditor; Jim Fedor, who designed the layout and cover; and all of those involved in the production of the book: Nick Connavino, Travis Hessman, Sue Henderson, Tia Andrako, of L.A. graphics, Elena Mussari and Jeff Howe, Webmaster.

CHAPTER 1

An Introduction to Law and Legal Reasoning

- **Effective Managers and Business Law**
- **Sources of Business Law**
- **The Purpose of Business Law**
- **Learning from Business Law in Other Countries**
- **Critical Thinking and Legal Reasoning**
- **The Role of Ethics in Legal Reasoning**

Effective Managers and Business Law

This book is for future business managers. Part of the preparation for that career requires an awareness of the legal issues arising in business. While it is tempting to leave legal questions to the lawyers, such an approach will create unnecessary business problems. Once a person is familiar with legal terminology, legal issues, and rules of law as they pertain to particular business decisions, that future businessperson can ask better questions of those with more extensive legal training. Those thoughtful questions are the product of training in business law.

Business managers will face daily encounters with business law, the rules of conduct that legislatures, regulatory bodies, and courts have spelled out to provide order and a degree of certainty to the practice of business. It is unreasonable to expect that a business manager can seek legal advice every time he or she needs to interpret or predict the legal status of a prospective business decision. Business managers need to have their own understanding of the legal system governing their business conduct. This book and your professor can assist in developing this understanding.

The law has its own language and style of reasoning. Thus, prospective business managers need to spend some time acquiring the basics of that language, as well as an appreciation for the form of legal reasoning. Aided by that knowledge, they will be better prepared to absorb and then evaluate what the lawyers are saying.

Finally, the study of business law is necessary because there simply is no market transaction that occurs apart from legal guidelines. All contracts, employment decisions, and payments to a supplier are limited and protected by business law. The law is the framework for business decisions. It just would not make sense to work so hard to train to be a business manager and then overlook the framework that provides a structure for all the various kinds of decisions businesses must make.

Even a quick glance at some business newspaper headlines during the time this book was being written should convince you that this book may become one of those textbooks you will want to keep long after graduation:

"Court Boosts Workers' Rights Against Retaliation"—*Arizona Business Gazette*

"Buyer Circles North Face, Makes Buyout Offer"—*San Francisco Business Times*

"New Owner to Beef Up Arby's, Add 26 Stores"—*St. Louis Business Journal*

"American Axle Forges Deal with Nissan"—*Buffalo Business First*

"Atlanta Lawyer Untangles Internet Laws for E-Commerce"—*High Tech Journal*

"Energy Firm Seeks Permits to Reopen Mothballed Liquid Natural Gas Plant"—*Savannah Business Report*

Each story that follows these headlines raises questions about what business managers can legally do.

Study this textbook, and you will see such business decisions with new eyes and a more thoughtful mind.

Sources of Business Law

Once convinced that you need to learn about business law, where exactly would you look to find those laws?

Constitutions

The first source that should come to mind is the various constitutions of the federal government and the states. **Constitutional law** refers to the general limits and powers of these governments as stated in their written constitutions. The U.S. Constitution is the major authority to study when trying to identify the relationship between business organizations and government.

Statutes

Legislative actions, called statutes, provide one more important source of law. The assortment of rules and regulations put forth by legislatures are what we call **statutory law**. These legislative acts can be found in The United States Code when they are passed by Congress, or in the various state codes when they are enacted by state legislatures. The codes are a collection of all the laws in one convenient location.

Because so much business activity must make its peace with local rules, we must not forget that there is one more element of statutory law that business managers must study—the local ordinances that cities and counties set forth to govern matters not covered by federal or state codes. Important business considerations such as local taxes, environmental standards, zoning ordinances, and building codes are addressed in these local ordinances.

While they are not exactly a source of law in the same sense as constitutions and statutory law, **model** or **uniform laws** serve as a basis for some statutory law at the state level. Business activity is made more difficult when state laws vary. To prevent these problems, a group of legal scholars and lawyers formed the National Conference of Commissioners on Uniform State Laws (NCC). The NCC regularly urges states to enact model laws. The response is entirely in the hands of the state legislatures. They can ignore the suggestion or adopt part or all of the proposed model law.

The proposals of the Conference, while not laws themselves, have been adopted on more than 200 occasions by state legislatures. Thus, businesspeople pay close attention to the proposals for uniform laws that emerge frequently from the NCC. The NCC is an especially important influence on business law. Paired with the publications of the American Law Institute, NCC became the source of the Uniform Commercial Code (UCC). The UCC is a body of law so significant for business activities that it will be the focus for intensive study in portions.

Administrative Law

Constitutions and statutes are never complete in the sense that they cover all the detailed rules that affect government and business relations. The federal, as well as state and local governments, have dozens of administrative agencies, whose task is to perform a particular governmental function. For example, the Environmental Protection Agency (EPA) has broad responsibilities to enforce the federal statutes in the area of environmental protection.

Administrative law is the collection of rules and decisions made by all these administrative agencies. Glance at Exhibit 1-1 to get a sense of the scope of a few of the major federal administrative agencies.

EXHIBIT 1-1

Independent Agencies

Commodity Futures Trading Commission (CFTC)
Consumer Product Safety Commission (CPSC)
Equal Employment Opportunity Commission (EEOC)
Federal Trade Commission (FTC)
Federal Communications Commission (FCC)
Interstate Commerce Commission (ICC)
National Labor Relations Boards (NLRB)
National Transportation Safety Board (NTSB)
Nuclear Regulatory Commission (NRC)
Securities and Exchange Commission (SEC)

Executive Agencies

Federal Deposit Insurance Corporation (FDIC)
Occupational Safety and Health Administration (OSHA)
General Services Administration (GSA)
National Aeronautics and Space Administration (NASA)
Small Business Administration (SBA)
International Development Cooperative Agency (IDCA)
National Science Foundation (NSF)
Veterans Administration (VA)
Office of Personnel Management (OPM)

Business functions within the framework of rules established by these agencies. Multiply that scope by all the other federal, state, and local administrative agencies, then you will begin to grasp the importance of administrative law as a source of business law.

Cases

Constitutions, legislatures, and administrative agencies decide that business law will look this way and not that way. The resulting laws will encourage certain behavior and will prevent other actions. But the boundaries of these laws are never self-explanatory. Consequently, law must be interpreted.

Case law is the collection of legal interpretations made by judges. An alternative name for case law is the **common law**. These interpretations are law unless they are revoked later by new statutory law.

Case law is especially significant for businesses because a modern business often operates in multiple legal jurisdictions. Because statutory laws are not self-explanatory, courts may have interpreted particular laws one way at one of your business locations and quite differently in a second business location. A thoughtful manager will know that constitutional, statutory, and administrative law may, thus, be only a small part of the various legal and regulatory environment that the business must understand.

Just as state statutes have been strongly influenced by the suggestions of the NCC, common law evolves with the assistance of a mechanism called **Restatements of the Law**. These **Restatements** are summaries of the common law rules in a particular area of the law that have been enacted by most states. The American Law Institute prepares these *Restatements* for contracts, agency, property, torts, and many other areas of law that affect business decisions. While the *Restatements* are not themselves a source of business law, judges frequently use them to guide their interpretations in a particular case. For that reason, an alert manager is very observant when a new *Restatement* appears.

In addition to the Restatements, many influences are at work in the minds of judges when they interpret constitutions, statutes, and regulations. For example, the values and social background of the judges function as lights and shadows, moving the judges toward particular legal decisions.

One especially important influence on judicial interpretation is a body of law known as **equity**. This law consists of rulings that represent an attempt by courts to use principles of justice to reduce any rigidity and consequent unfairness in previous common law decisions. When courts make a decision guided by equity, they do so by reference to a set of moral maxims that summarize our sense of social justice.

Exhibit 1-2 should give you a strong sense of the flavor of these maxims.

EXHIBIT 1-2

Equitable Maxims

Equity will not suffer a wrong to be without a remedy.

Equity follows the law.

Equity is equality and equality is equity.

Equity regards that as done as ought to be done.

Equity regards substance as intent rather than form.

Equity aids the vigilant and the diligent, not those who slumber on their rights.

Equity will leave parties to illegal transactions where they find themselves.

Equity imputes an intention to fulfill an obligation.

One who seeks equity must do equity.

Equity is a form of law representing our recognition that we are in part a community whose self-concept depends, in part, on a sense that justice has been done. For example, a court might issue an **injunction**—an order requiring or forbidding a party to act in a particular way—because some other party requires the order for our sense of justice to be upheld.

The Purposes of Business Law

Before we begin to study the many specifics of business law, it is useful to consider its purpose. By thinking about this, we are better able to evaluate the law. One of our standards for supporting a particular business law should be that it fulfills an important purpose.

Business Law is OUR Business Law

Law is a tool for us to use; we are not its slaves. We create laws, and we can reconstruct them as well. Whenever some aspect of business law is not contributing to the type of economy we wish to nurture, we are free to change that law. As a future business manager, you should be excited by the prospect that you can help create a better community of buyers and sellers by contributing to a new, improved business law.

But how do we change the law? Here, the previous section can be very useful. Constitutions, statutes, regulations, ordinances, and the common law are not etched in stone. When we find any of them to be inappropriate for the kinds of business activities that we want to encourage, we can work to change them.

However, we do not want to give you the reader, that changing the law is simple. None of us would want to live in a society where a law could be changed whenever by whomever and for whatever reason.

Part of what we want from law is a sense of stability. The very existence of constitutions, statutes, and regulations gives us greater predictability. We can go to the legal codes and find the rules of the game. Nevertheless, each source of law contains steps by which concerned citizens can repair existing law.

Basic Functions of the Law

The previous section urged you to think about our freedom to construct the law we want. However, to build something requires a plan. What, exactly, can law do for us? What specific use does it have?

There are many social functions that laws encourage. As you read a list of those functions, resist the temptation to see them as simple or clear-cut. Indeed, the tensions between them provide much of the importance and excitement that this text contains. Each purpose is far from being self-explanatory. But knowing the identity of the primary functions of law can open up many possibilities about new directions for the law. [See Exhibit 1-3].

When judges and legislatures attempt to use the law to achieve these purposes, they run into repeated difficulties. First, these purposes each have multiple definitions. Some people gain from the use of one of the definitions of "efficiency" for instance; others, understandably, want a very different concept of efficiency to be implemented by legislatures and courts. In addition, the purposes conflict. The legal system provides a forum where these tensions are resolved. But what guides the legal process as it grinds through the conflicting arguments surrounding our attempts to create a better business law?

Alternative Guides for Designing Legal Change

When legislators or courts make law, they do so guided by certain habits of mind, particular understandings about the best way to determine wisdom, and specific beliefs about human nature. These views guide

EXHIBIT 1-3

The Purposes of Business Law

1. **Order and predictability:** When buyers and sellers get together in a market economy, they are bargaining over price, quantity, and the quality of the goods or services they hope to exchange. Many of the decisions made by these parties are dependent on the assumption that the rules by which they are playing will not be altered. What will a buyer want to pay? The answer will depend in large part on a reliance on today's rules being those that apply tomorrow as well. No small wonder that businesses usually seek predictability!

2. **Flexibility:** The business environment is not stable. The excitement of entrepreneurial activity and the demands of global competition require a legal system that can adjust to the changing needs of those who must obey it. Businesses, thus, expect the law to provide a lubricant of *flexibility* that will smooth the path toward their growth and achievement.

3. **Efficiency:** Successful business activity often depends on economic growth. This economic growth or economic efficiency guarantees that there will be more demand for the goods and services that businesses hope to sell. Law can advance the likelihood that efficiency will occur when it encourages competition and certain kinds of investment activities.

4. **Social Justice:** Business affects many individuals. Some of those individuals are better equipped to take care of themselves than others who are more vulnerable to abuses of power. Many laws are enacted to protect those whose needs exceed their ability to provide for themselves. For example, we have laws against sex discrimination in employment because the vulnerability of certain employees and their consequent treatment disturbs us enough that we request legal protection on grounds of social justice.

them toward particular legal solutions and away from others. This section briefly describes several of the more common guides to legal change. As you study them, we recommend two things:

1. Think about the rules that existed in your own home as an analogy to the laws in a society. Then ask yourself, how would those rules have been different had they been shaped by each of these various guides to legal change.

2. *Decide for yourself which of the guides is best in terms of creating the kind of legal system that you believe our society needs.*

Tradition

One of the most often used guidelines to legal change is **tradition**, or **custom**. When we follow tradition, we attempt to link our future behavior to the behavior of those who faced similar problems in earlier historical periods. The logic of the approach is that we need not reinvent the wheel each time a legal problem arises. Past practice is assumed to have been the product of careful thought.

From inside this particular perspective, it just makes sense for us to strive to benefit by following the advice contained in tradition. For example, you will see as we study the common law that courts are often guided by the doctrine of **stare decisis**, or following precedent. The court makes a particular decision and supports that decision by pointing to its similarity to previous court decisions. Judges are thereby indicating their respect for tradition.

Legal Positivism

This guide urges us, as followers of **legal positivism**, to design our legal system on the basis of the belief that legitimate political authority deserves our obedience when it issues a rule. This idea stresses that society requires authority and the hierarchy that such authority demands. When a branch of government that is duly authorized issues a law, our proper role is to obey. The law is then a set of appropriate commands.

This view sees law as something quite distinct from morality. Moral questions about the law should not interfere with our inclination to obey it. A judge with leanings in the direction of legal positivism, for example, might write that she is deciding to enforce the law in question, but that her decision does not necessarily mean that she sees the law as the morally correct rule.

Cost-benefit Analysis

Suppose that we could attach a monetary figure to the benefits of a particular law or legal decision; then, we next look at all the costs of that same law or decision and place a monetary value upon it. Wouldn't it make good sense to choose those legal alternatives that maximized the ratio of benefits to costs? Those who use **cost-benefit analysis** as a guide to legal change believe it does. So, for instance, in a contract dispute someone using this approach would attempt to attach responsibility for the problem in such a way that total benefit is maximized in relation to costs.

This approach to legal change is tied closely to the pursuit of efficiency. If the law to be applied yields more benefits than costs, then we have saved resources. Those resources can, in turn, be used to provide us with more goods and services. Our economy is, thus, more efficient in the sense of producing more for less.

Identification with the Vulnerable

Some members of our society are able to take care of themselves in terms of most life situations. Others, especially the ill, children, the aged, the disabled, and the poor, require assistance to meet their fundamental needs of life, health, and education. The law can be used to assist those with whom we empathize. Legal change to address the needs of these people is based on **identification with the vulnerable**.

This guide to legal change is tied closely to the pursuit of fairness in our society. The metaphor of a level playing field is linked with some higher law or body of moral principles that links all of us in the human community. We might look at a particular employment contract, for example, and react by observing that "it is just not fair." Our caring impulse as a human feels outrage at that legal arrangement. That outrage can be a stimulus for legal change.

To review, modern business managers must have an ongoing fascination with the law to function effectively. Business law tells business managers the basic rules of the business game. Play any game without having first studied the rules, and you will not have given yourself a chance to compete.

But, unlike an ordinary game, the business game has a rulebook that is changing on a daily basis. Constitutions, statutes, regulations, and ordinances change while the game is being played. Consequently, this book wants not only to describe business law for you, but also motivate you to study it regularly. If you pledge to yourself to make the study of business law an ongoing part of your continuing education as a business manager, the benefits for your career will be tremendous.

But your study needs a plan. That is what we are developing in this chapter. While there is a body of current business law, we as a society are not stuck with the law as it is. The law is our tool. When it does not work well, we can change or trade it in for a better tool. So the major theme of our plan is *change*.

We will learn business law with one part of our brain focusing on how the law might change to create a better business community. As you begin your study of business law, it makes sense to think about the purpose of that law. What needs of a market economy does this law supposedly fulfill? While these purposes may be numerous, predictability, flexibility, efficiency, and social justice are four of the most common purposes. They represent values that the law can assist us in achieving.

The next step in our plan is becoming aware of the legal perspectives that guide us as the society creates its laws. As the law evolves, it does so through debate and struggle. The participants in that debate are guided by different understandings of the standards a good law should reflect. Tradition, legal positivism, cost-benefit analysis, and identification with the vulnerable—all direct legal development in different directions. These perspectives give us a framework for thinking about legal change.

The rest of this chapter completes our plan. First, we want to study business law from a global perspective. The law in other countries gives us a valuable picture of *what the law could be*. Second, we need some evaluation tools to sharpen our ability to see where business law might be failing us. Thus, our plan requires critical thinking skills and attitudes. Then, the final component of our plan highlights the role of ethics as the basis for both existing business laws, as well as for legal change.

Learning from Business Law in Other Countries

Each chapter in this book contains brief discussions of business law in other countries. As you use this text, you will learn about American business law by contrasting the concepts of our business law system with those of our primary trading partners. Just as learning Spanish helps us to better understand English, learning how other countries handle business transactions will help you to better understand how our system handles these same transactions.

Several times in each chapter we will pause to consider how other countries treat a particular business problem within their legal system. Especially valuable for this purpose will be the "Global Boxes", where we will take a break in the flow of the chapter to look at the business law of one of our trading partners. We will typically use Canada, Japan, China, Russia, Mexico, and the European Union for our comparisons because modern business managers will be more likely be interacting with the law in those particular jurisdictions.

Critical Thinking and Legal Reasoning

Success in the modern business firm requires the development of **critical thinking skills**—the ability to understand the structure of what someone is saying and then to apply a set of evaluative criteria to determine the worth of what was said. In other words, you need to be able to sort sense from nonsense by developing attitudes and abilities that help you evaluate the law.

Any critical thinking includes the application of evaluative standards to assess the quality of the reasoning being offered to support the conclusion. And there is no better context in which to develop critical thinking skills than the study of the laws that affect business. Critical thinking skills learned in the study of business law will be easily transferred to your eventual role as a manager, entrepreneur, or other business professional.

As you learn about our legal system and how its evolution affects the legal environment of business, you will also be developing your critical thinking skills. As critical thinking skills develop, your understanding of the law will be enhanced. Learning business law and critical thinking are mutually reinforcing.

Legal reasoning is like other reasoning in some ways and different in others. When people, including lawyers and judges, reason, they do so for a purpose. Some problem or dilemma bothers them. The stimulus that gets them thinking is an ISSUE. It is stated as a question because it is a call for action. It requires us to do something, to think about answers.

For instance, we are all interested in such issues as the following:

- *When are union organizers permitted under the National Labor Relations Act to trespass on an employer's property?*
- *Do tobacco manufacturers still have liability for the deaths of smokers?*
- *Must a business fulfill a contract when the contract is made with an unlicensed contractor in a state requiring all contractors to be licensed?*

These questions have several different answers. Which one should you choose as your answer? Here is where critical thinking is essential to your business success. Some of the answers can get you into trouble; others will advance your purpose. Each answer is called a CONCLUSION.

Business firms come into contact with these conclusions in the form of laws or court decisions. Business managers are therefore both consumers of and contributors to these legal conclusions. As business people learn about and react to decisions or conclusions made by courts, they have two primary methods of response:

1. Memorizing the conclusions or rules of law as a guide for future business decisions and

2. Making judgments about the quality of the conclusions.

This book encourages you to do both. There are many forms of critical thinking, but they all share one characteristic—they focus on the quality of someone's reasoning. Critical thinking is active; it challenges each of us to form judgements about the quality of the link between someone's reasons and their conclusion. In particular, we will be focusing on the link between a court's reasons and conclusions.

Our reactions to legal arguments shape our efforts to either support the *status quo* in the legal environment of business or offer support for particular changes. Why are we even curious about the legal environment? The answer is we want it to be the best we can create. But improvement requires our very best critical thinking.

While you will develop your own workable strategies for legal reasoning, we urge you to start by following our structure. Every time you read a case, follow the pattern described below.

First find the facts.

Facts

Here we are looking for the most basic building blocks in a legal decision or argument. These building blocks, or facts, provide the environment or context in which the legal issue is to be resolved. Certain events occurred; certain actions were or were not taken; particular persons behaved or failed to behave in specific ways. All of these and many more possibilities together make up the intricate setting for the playing out of the issue in question. We always wonder, what happened in this case?

Now look for the issue.

Issue

In almost any legal conflict, finding and expressing the issue is an important step in forming our reaction. The issue is the question that caused the lawyers and

their clients to enter the legal system. Usually, there are several reasonable perspectives concerning the correct way to word the issue in dispute.

Don't let the possibility of *multiple* useful ways to word the issue cause you any confusion. The issue is certainly not just anything that we say it is. If we claim something is an issue, our suggestion must fulfill the definition of an issue *in this particular factual situation*.

Next identify the judge's reasons and conclusion.

Reasons and Conclusions

Judges do not form legal conclusions based on whim. They have support for their decisions. That support consists of their reasons. When we ask someone *why* a judge formed a particular conclusion, we are showing our respect for reasons as the proper basis for any assertion. We want a world rich with opinions so we can have a broad field of choice. But we should agree with only those legal opinions that have convincing reasons supporting the conclusion. To ask "why?" is our way of saying, "I want to believe you, but you have an obligation to help me by sharing the reasons for your conclusion."

Locate in the decision the rules of law that govern the judge's reasoning.

Rules of Law

Judges cannot offer just any reasoning that they please. They must always look back over their shoulders at the laws and previous court decisions that together provide an anchor for current and future decisions. What makes legal reasoning so complex is that statutes and legal findings are never *crystal* clear. They may seem very clear, but judges and businesspeople have room for interpretive flexibility in their reasoning.

Evaluation of the Reasoning

A judge's reasoning, once it has been laid before us by following the steps discussed here, is a message that we may either accept or reject. One of the most exciting things about our legal system is its potential for change. Critical thinking in the legal context consists of examining the legal opinion in search of potential problems in the reasoning.

Here is a small sample of some especially useful critical thinking tools for business managers when thinking about business law:

- Look for potential ambiguity in the reasoning. Ambiguity refers to a lack of clarity in a word or phrase in the reasoning. Many words have multiple meanings, and until the intended meaning is discovered, we cannot tell whether we wish to agree or disagree with the reasoning.

- Ask whether the analogies used in the decision are strong. When judges follow particular precedents, they are saying that the key similarities between the facts in the precedent and those in the case at hand are so similar that it makes sense to apply the same rule of law in both. Are there key differences in the factual situations that raise questions about the quality of that analogy?

- Check the quality of the judge's reasoning. Does the judge use evidence to support the opinion that is both abundant enough and reliable enough that we should agree with the reasoning?

- Think about the extent to which important missing information prevents you from being totally confident about the judge's reasoning. Is there important missing information that you would need to have before making up your mind?

- Consider the possibility of rival causes. When the judge claims that one action caused another, think about whether some alternative cause may not have been responsible.

By applying these standards to legal reasoning, you will establish a logical basis for either agreeing with the court's decision or, alternatively, seeing this decision as something you want to work to change. After each case in this text, the first question will be a critical thinking question to provide practice in the development of this important skill.

The Role of Ethics in Legal Reasoning

When you evaluate business law, you have in mind what you expect the law to accomplish. One fundamental way to think about our expectations is captured in our conversation about **ethics**. Ethics are the guidelines we use to shape the world we wish to create. As such, they provide guidance for the kind of business behavior we want to reinforce. After each case, we pause to think about the ethics of business law by asking a question derived from the practical approach to business ethics developed in Chapter Two.

Ethical discussion focuses on the basic observation that we are socially and globally interdependent as workers, businesspeople, and consumers. Our inescapable contact with one another requires our aspirations to be defined, at least in part, by their impact on others.

> Most of us do not need to be taught to reflect about how a decision will affect our own interests. But what makes ethics so compelling an inclusion in business decision making is its mandate that other people and their desires count too. Ethics is, thus, the study of what we owe one another.

To summarize this last section of the chapter, we have explained the importance of (1) an awareness of the global context of business law, (2) critical thinking, and (3) sensitivity to ethics. This completes our plan for studying business law. If you apply yourself to learning the content and purposes of business law by using these three active learning approaches, your career as a manager will be accelerated.

Questionable Conduct by Nike and Reebok

Nike, Reebok, and other shoe manufacturers can reduce costs by having their shoes made in countries where wages are lower than they are in the United States. A worker in Indonesia or Vietnam is willing to work long hours for significantly less than is demanded by American workers. For example, after a recent wage increase, Indonesian workers in Nike and Reebok plants made the rough equivalent of twenty cents per hour. In one sense, what Nike and Reebok want to do is just smart business. By reducing labor costs, they can make more profits.[1] In addition, Nike, by employing these workers, is giving them employment opportunities that would otherwise not be available.

Yet, this situation is even more complicated than it first appears. In the late 1990s Nike and Reebok's profits dropped by as much as forty percent. Why? Industry leaders reported that a major cause was the negative publicity they received from the production of their shoes in foreign "sweatshops." Typical of the criticisms was a student letter in the Brown University Daily Herald:

> [S]weatshops do not exist to promote economic development. They exist to MAXIMIZE PROFITS at the expense of human dignity. What little investments that companies do put into the local economy do not even come close to compensating for what they reap through disgustingly low wages and slave-like working conditions. The bottom line is that it is in the companies' best interests to keep workers poor and powerless....Ending sweatshop labor will not solve the problem of poverty overnight, but it is an important step in the right direction.[2]

In addition, UNITE, an organization that includes union, church, and college student groups reports that Nike is rapidly moving its production facilities to China where in factory/ dormitory complexes, labor is regulated in military fashion. For example, young migrant women who work for Nike in China are allegedly restricted from leaving company grounds or quitting their jobs.[3]

1. What would you do if you were in a position at Nike or Reebok to decide whether to continue or revise your labor practices in foreign countries?

2. Would it change your mind once you learned that since 1992, Nike has implemented a code of conduct that insisted on the enforcement of all child labor, fair wage, and health laws in their foreign plants?

---

[1] Robert Collier, *"U.S. Firms Reducing Sweat Shop Abuses But Wages Still at Poverty Level,"* SAN FRANCISCO CHRONICLE, April 17, 1999, at A1.

[2] Vinay Ravi, *"Sweatshop Labor Deters Economic Growth,"* BROWN DAILY HERALD, October 8, 1998, at p. 2.

[3] http://www.uniteunion.org/pressbox/nike-report.html, April 25, 2000 (July 20, 2000).

CHAPTER 2
Business Ethics

Business Ethics and Social Responsibility

Business Law and Business Ethics

Theories of Business Ethics

The WPH Framework for Business Ethics

What you should do as a manager in the situation described in the opening scenario is not altogether clear. Ethical conversation is less about finding the one and only right thing to do than it is about finding the better thing to do. Whatever you choose to do, certain people will be hurt and others will benefit. Similarly, any decision you make will be both potentially risky, as well as potentially beneficial, for the firm.

This chapter tries to provide some assistance in thinking systematically about issues of right and wrong in business conduct. Initially, we need to sort through the meaning of key terms like "business ethics" and "social responsibility." Then, because it is helpful to have an approach to these decisions that business managers can actually use, we provide a practical method by which future business managers can think more carefully about the ethical dilemmas they will face during their career.

Business Ethics and Social Responsibility

Ethics is the study and practice of decisions about what is good or right. Ethics guide us when we are wondering about what we should be doing in a particular situation. **Business ethics** is an application of ethics to the special problems and opportunities experienced by businesspeople. For example, as a business manager, you might some day be in the position of the Nike decision-makers who must decide what is best for Nike and the various people affected by decisions at Nike. Are they doing the right thing when they attempt to reduce costs of production by having their shoes assembled in countries where the working conditions are very substandard compared to those in the United States?

These types of questions present businesses with ethical choices, each of which has advantages and disadvantages. An **ethical dilemma** is a dilemma or choice concerning what is right or good for which no clear right decision is available. The dilemma has multiple potential solutions, none of which is altogether superior.

For example, imagine yourself in the position of a business manager at Wells Fargo Bank. You know that providing bank accounts for customers has a cost attached to it. You want to cover those costs by charging the customers the cost of their checking accounts. By doing so, you can preserve the bank's revenue for shareholders and employees of Wells Fargo. So far, the decision seems simple. But an ethical dilemma soon appears.

You learn from recent government reports that 12 million families cannot afford to have bank accounts when they are charged a fee to maintain one. You want to do the right thing in this situation. But what would that right thing be? The study of business ethics can help you resolve this dilemma.

Making these decisions would be much easier if managers could focus only on the impact of decisions on the firm. If, for example, a firm had as its only objective the maximization of profits, the "right thing" to do would be that option that had the largest positive impact on the firm's profits.

But businesses operate in a community. The community has expectations of businesses. Trying to identify what those expectations are and deciding whether to fulfill them complicates business ethics. The community often expects firms to do much more for them than just provide a useful good or service at a reasonable price. For example, they may expect firms to resist paying bribes, even when the payment of such fees is an ordinary cost of doing business in certain global settings. Alternatively, the community may expect businesses to refuse to sell unsafe products in foreign countries even when the laws of that country permit the sale of those products.

The **social responsibility of business** consists of the collection of expectations that the global community imposes on its firms. These expectations must be honored to a certain extent, even when the firm wishes to ignore them, because firms are always subject to the implicit threat that legislation will impose social obligations on the firm. So, if the community intends for businesses to obey certain standards of fairness even when they interfere with profit maximization, firms ignore those expectations at their peril. Laws imposing these expectations will interfere with the firm's economic freedom.

Business Law and Business Ethics

As with all business decisions, business managers need to gather all the relevant facts. Nike's and Reebok's decision about where and how to manufacture their shoes depends on a huge array of facts: alternative costs, the legal framework in each relevant country, the social responsibilities of firms in the various jurisdictions, unemployment rates, and levels of literacy among potential workers, just to name a few. Business ethics affect even this first step of business decision making. For example, if the firm's ethical stance focuses primarily on the impact of alternatives on their economic bottom line, then facts about the social responsibilities of business, in particular cultural contexts, may not be regarded as valuable facts.

But experienced managers know that assembling the facts is just the beginning of a thoughtful business decision. Next, it makes sense to ask:

Is it legal to go forward with this decision?

The legality of the decision is the minimal standard that must be met. But the existence of that minimum standard is essential for the development of business ethics. To make this point, let us a look at certain con-

temporary attributes of commercial activity in Russia.

Russian tax laws are now in flux, and no clear bookkeeping standards exist. Consequently, Russian businesses often choose to not file any financial reports for fear of violating a rule they did not know existed. These common business practices in Russia are considered unethical in the United States b*ecause they are illegal.*

Another illustration of the need for legal standards for business ethics is the growing practice of bribery in the absence of those legal standards. Businesses must, in some countries, pay bribes to receive legitimate supplies. Though the businessperson may be morally opposed to paying the bribes, the supplies are necessary to stay in business and there may be no other means of obtaining them.

Foreign companies must decide whether to pay bribes or find alternative sources of supplies. For instance, when McDonald's opened its doors in Moscow, they made arrangements to receive their supplies from foreign providers. These arrangements ensured that the franchise did not have to engage in questionable business practices.

Look at the following case as an exercise in comparing what is legal with what is ethical. Business law affects ethics because it provides a basis for managerial ethics. However, the law does even more. Discussions about the desirability of particular business laws require us to examine our sense of what managers and owners should be doing in their interactions with consumers, workers, and the general community.

As you review the *Kipps* case, consider the relationship between law and ethics.

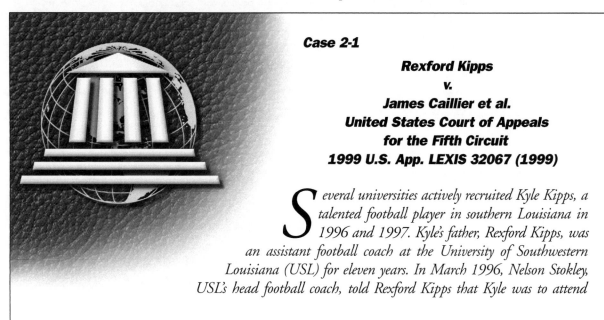

Case 2-1

Rexford Kipps
v.
James Caillier et al.
United States Court of Appeals
for the Fifth Circuit
1999 U.S. App. LEXIS 32067 (1999)

Several universities actively recruited Kyle Kipps, a talented football player in southern Louisiana in 1996 and 1997. Kyle's father, Rexford Kipps, was an assistant football coach at the University of Southwestern Louisiana (USL) for eleven years. In March 1996, Nelson Stokley, USL's head football coach, told Rexford Kipps that Kyle was to attend either LSU or a college or university outside of Louisiana. When Kyle notified Stokley that he had orally committed to play at Louisiana State University (LSU) on a football scholarship, Stokley told Rexford Kipps to forbid his son to play football for LSU. Rexford Kipps argued that he could not and would not force his son to refuse to play for LSU. Consequently, Stokley terminated Kipps' employment with USL. Both Nelson Schexnayder, Jr., USL Director of Athletics, and Ray Authement, President of USL, approved Kipps' termination. The President of the Board of Trustees, James Caillier, also approved Kipps' termination.

Rexford Kipps brought constitutional and state law claims against defendants Caillier, Schexnayder, Authement, and Stokley. These defendants filed for summary judgment, arguing that the at-will employment status of Kipps precluded any wrongful termination action. Furthermore, they claimed that they were entitled to qualified immunity and Kipps's termination was justified because Kyle's choice would affect USL's ability to recruit athletes. The district court granted Stokley, Schexnayder, and Authement's motion for summary judgment on qualified immunity grounds. Kipps appealed.

JUDGE PARKER

Public officials acting within the scope of their official duties are shielded from civil liability by the qualified immunity doctrine. Government officials are entitled to qualified immunity "insofar as their conduct does not violate clearly established statutory or constitutional rights of which a reasonable person would have known."

In order to establish that the defendants are not entitled to qualified immunity, plaintiffs must satisfy a three-part test. First, "[a] court evaluating a claim of qualified immunity must first determine whether the plaintiff has alleged the deprivation of a constitutional right at all." Second, the court must "determine whether that right was clearly established at the time of the alleged violation." Finally, the court "must determine whether the record shows that the violation occurred, or at least gives rise to a genuine issue of material fact as to whether the defendant actually engaged in the conduct that violated the clearly-established right." If it is determined that the official's conduct was unconstitutional, then the court must decide whether the conduct was nonetheless "objectively reasonable."

Assuming arguendo that defendants violated Kipps's clearly established constitutional liberty interest in familial association, the resolution of this issue turns on whether the defendants' actions were "objectively reasonable." Because we find that defendants' actions were objectively reasonable, we affirm the district court's dismissal of Kipps's 1983 claim on the basis of qualified immunity.

Even if defendants violated Kipps's clearly established constitutional right, they are still entitled to qualified immunity if their actions were objectively reasonable. . . . The record indicates that Kipps was fired because his son chose to play football for a Louisiana school other than USL. Notwithstanding the defendants' subjective motivation and belief as to the lawfulness of their conduct, we find the defendants' motivation for terminating Kipps was objectively reasonable. Defendants' motivation, according to the record in this case, was to mitigate the damage that Kyle's attendance at LSU as opposed to USL would have on alumni relations and recruiting efforts.

The summary judgment record of this appeal contains no facts upon which we could find that defendants' actions were objectively unreasonable.

AFFIRMED.

> Critical Thinking: Why did the judge conclude that Kipps' termination was legal? Do you
> agree with the argument?

The *Kipps* case provides a snapshot of the complexity of the link between ethics and the law. Do you believe that some conception of what it means to do the right thing is responsible for the legal decision in this case? Business managers must sometimes decide whether to hire and fire particular employees. Their decisions will be guided by legal rules that have ethical foundations. These same decisions raise in our minds the potential need for creation of a better law.

At the same time, ethics in general helps guide the law. In this manner, law and business ethics serve as an interactive system—informing and implicitly assessing each other. For example, our inclination to encourage dependability and efficiency in market exchanges shapes the boundaries of many of our business laws. The principles of contract law, for instance, facilitate market exchanges and trade because the parties to an exchange can count on the enforceability of agreements. Legal rules that govern the exchange have been shaped in large part by our sense of commercial ethics. Consider the role of ethics in contract law in Japan by studying the global box below.

In addition, the definition of business ethics refers to *standards* of business conduct. *It does not offer a set of correct decisions.* Business ethics can improve business decisions by serving as a reminder not to choose the first business option that comes to mind or the one that enriches us in the short run. But business ethics can never produce a list of correct business decisions that all ethical businesses will make.

Well-managed firms try to provide ethical leadership by establishing codes of ethics for the firm. For example, the Exhibit 2-1 addresses the attempt by the Halliburton Company, a major energy services corporation, to make a statement about the importance of business ethics to its firm. However, notice that this corporate code can never do more than provide guidance. The complications associated with managerial decisions do not permit any ethical guide to provide definitive lists of right and wrong decisions. In addition, a code of business conduct is much easier to create than to obey.

Global Context: Contractual Relationships and Ethics in Japan

In the United States, business contracts are extensive and lengthy. They stipulate action for nearly every possible situation that may arise between parties. Lawyers direct the process of creating and agreeing to a contract. Most American businesspersons would not think of drawing up a contract without legal assistance.

In Japan, however, the idea of involving lawyers in contractual relationships is quite upsetting. The Japanese are disturbed that American contracts discuss what would happen if one party in the contract cheated, lied, or wished to terminate. Such discussion is seen as a sign of distrust between the parties. Japanese contracts are based on trust. Often the relationship is finalized verbally rather than by a signature. These verbal agreements are called *yakusoku*.

Because contracts are founded on mutual trust between parties, the contents are open and flexible in comparison to the painstakingly rigid American contracts. This structure allows Japanese businesspersons to deal with problematic issues between the parties as they arise. The Japanese also prefer to solve contract problems through arbitration or compromise rather than through the legal system. Executives will go to great lengths to avoid involving lawyers and the court system with their business.

EXHIBIT 2-1

Ethical Business Practices

Halliburton Company

Company policy requires employees to observe high standards of business and personal ethics in the conduct of their duties and responsibilities. Employees must practice honesty and integrity in every aspect of dealing with other Company employees, the public, the business community, stockholders, customers, suppliers and government authorities.

Company policy prohibits unlawful discrimination against employees, stockholders, directors, officers, customers or suppliers on account of race, color, age, sex, religion or national origin. All persons shall be treated with dignity and respect and they shall not be unreasonably interfered with in the conduct of their duties and responsibilities.

No employee should be misguided by any sense of loyalty to the Company or a desire for profitability that might cause him or her to disobey any applicable law or Company policy. Violation of Company policy will constitute grounds for disciplinary action, including, when appropriate, termination of employment.

Theories of Business Ethics

One source of assistance business managers can use in thinking about ethical business decisions come from the general theories or perspectives about ethics. One of the eternal human quests is to find a better way of organizing our living. Ethics plays a major role in shaping that vision.

Those who have thought deeply about ethics have noted that it is possible to generalize about broad theoretical approaches to pursuing ethics. We will discuss a few such theories in this section. Those students who wish a more robust treatment of the theories of business ethics can consult either a business ethics text or one of the websites we recommend at the end of this chapter.

These theories are important and complex. They represent the mental efforts of those who have thought deeply about how we go about justifying particular decisions as "Ethical." They are the approaches we would rely on were we to have large amounts of time to reflect about the ethics of individual business ethics dilemmas.

Consequentialism

The first major ethical theory we will discuss is consequentialism. As the very look of the word suggests, this ethical approach "depends on the consequences." **Consequentialism** is a theoretical approach to ethical dilemmas that requires us to inquire about the consequences to relevant people of our making a particular decision.

Utilitarianism is one form of consequentialism that business managers may find useful. As with any consequentialist theory of ethics, **utilitarianism** urges managers to take those actions that provide the greatest pleasure after having subtracted the pain or harm associated with the action in question. One form of utilitarianism is **cost-benefit analysis**. When a business makes decisions based on cost-benefit analysis, it is comparing the pleasure and pain of its optional choices, when that pleasure and pain are measured in monetary terms.

Let us apply consequentialism to the opening story for this chapter. Someone using consequentialism to decide what Nike and Reebok should do with respect to foreign wage rates would first attempt to make a list of all the consequences of each available option. If you will imagine yourself following this framework, you will realize just how tough a task the potential manager faces. First, there are huge groups of people affected in so many different ways by whether the shoes are produced in the U.S. or abroad. Second, you need to think through not only the more immediate and thus noticeable short run costs, but also the long-run effects of the decision. But who among us has a very good grasp of the long-run consequences of even our most simple decisions! Third, you must face the difficult problem of trying to decide how to weigh the various consequences.

Especially troublesome is our realization that any of us is tempted to weigh very heavily the impacts on our immediate family and ourselves. For example, if one option that Nike or Reebok faces is to build a production plant in a town where we have unemployed family members, the decision has definite and potentially huge financial impacts on those closest to us. But would that approach be *right*? How would a decision to build the plant in the U.S. affect others?

As we have shown, consequentialism is not altogether helpful because of the extreme difficulty in making the required calculations about consequences. But this last question raises an important additional objection to consequentialist thinking. Where does the important social value of justice fit into consequentialist reasoning? Many business decisions could be beneficial in their consequences for a majority of the population. But is it just to require a few to be harmed so that the majority can be improved? In a related fashion, for a decision like Nike's, how do we rank the consequences to those in the United States, compared to the consequences for the people in other countries who will be affected by the decision?

Deontology

An alternative theoretical approach to consequentialism is deontology. When you see references to **Kantian ethics**, the analysis to follow will be a discussion of the most famous of the deontological approaches to business ethics. Unlike consequentialism, a person using a deontological approach will not see the relevance of making a list of harms and benefits that result from a particular decision. Instead, **deontology** consists of acting on the basis of the recognition that certain actions are right or wrong, regardless of their consequences. For example, a business leader might consider it wrong to terminate a person whose spouse has terminal cancer because a firm has an obligation to support its employees when they are vulnerable, *period*.

From the deontological viewpoint the duties or obligations that we owe one another as humans are much more ethically significant than are measurements of the impacts of business decisions. For example, a person using a deontological theory of ethics may see any business behavior that violates our duty of trust to be wrong. To sell a car that one knows will probably no longer work after four years is, from this perspective, unethical. No set of positive consequences that might flow from the production decision can overcome the certainty of the deontological recognition that the sale is wrong.

Just as consequentialism is incredibly complicated, deontology is difficult to apply because people disagree about what duties we owe to one another and which duties are more important than others when they conflict. For example, imagine the dilemma of a scientist working for a tobacco firm who discovers that cigarettes are carcinogenic. She owes a duty of loyalty to her employer, but she also has a conflicting duty to the community, to do no harm. Where would a business manager find a list of relevant duties, under the deontological framework, and why should we accept and act on any particular list?

In addition, the absolute nature of many deontological lists of duties and rights seems overly rigid when applied to a wide variety of contexts. For instance, saying that we owe a duty to respect human life sounds absolute. But in application, we might be forced to harm one life to preserve another life.

Virtue Ethics

Virtue ethics is a theoretical approach in which the development of virtues, or positive character traits like courage, justice, and truthfulness, is the basis for morality. A morally excellent (and thus good) person develops virtues and distinguishes them from vices, or negative character traits like cowardice and vanity. This development of virtues occurs through practice. Virtues are those habits of mind that move us toward excellence, the good life, or human flourishing.

As a guide to business ethics, virtue ethics would require managers to act in such a way that they would become better persons. They would follow the character traits that, upon introspective reflection, the business manager would see as consistent with virtue. Identifying the relevant virtues and vices requires reasoning about the kind of human behavior that moves us toward the good, successful, or happy life.

A difficulty with the application of virtue ethics is the lack of agreement about the meaning of "the good life." Without that agreement, we are not able to agree about what types of behavior are consistent with our achievement of that goal. But virtue ethics is useful in reminding us that ethics is grounded in a sense of what it means to be virtuous. We need some moral beacon to call us toward a more morally excellent condition.

Ethics of Care

A related theory of business ethics is the ethics of care. The **ethics of care** argues that the right course of action is the option most consistent with the building and maintenance of human relationships. Those who adhere to an **ethic of care** argue that traditional moral hierarchies ignore an important element of life: relationships. Care for the nurturing of our many relationships serves as a reminder of the importance of responsibility to others.

According to someone who adheres to an ethic of care, when one person cares for another person, the first person is acting morally. When other ethical theories emphasize different moral dimensions as a basis for resolving ethical dilemmas, they rarely consider the

EXHIBIT 2-2

Johnson & Johnson's Credo

THE CREDO

We believe our first responsibility is to the doctors, nurses and patients, to mothers and fathers and all others who use our products and services. In meeting their needs everything we do must be of high quality. We must constantly strive to reduce our costs in order to maintain reasonable prices. Customers' orders must be serviced promptly and accurately. Our suppliers and distributors must have an opportunity to make a fair profit.

We are responsible to our employees, the men and women who work with us throughout the world. Everyone must be considered as an individual. We must respect their dignity and recognize their merit. They must have a sense of security in their jobs. Compensation must be fair and adequate, and working conditions clean, orderly and safe. We must be mindful of ways to help our employees fulfill their family responsibilities. Employees must feel free to make suggestions and complaints. There must be equal opportunity for employment, development and advancement for those qualified. We must provide competent management, and their actions must be just and ethical.

We are responsible to the communities in which we live and work and to the world community as well. We must be good citizens—support good works and charities and bear our fair share of taxes. We must encourage civic improvements and better health and education. We must maintain in good order the property we are privileged to use, protecting the environment and natural resources.

Our final responsibility is to our stockholders. Business must make a sound profit. We must experiment with new ideas. Research must be carried on, innovative programs developed and mistakes paid for. New equipment must be purchased, new facilities provided and new products launched. Reserves must be created to provide for adverse times. When we operate according to these principles, the stockholders should realize a fair return.

harm they might do to relationships; thus, from the perspective of the ethics of care, alternative theories of business ethics often encourage unethical behavior.

Ethics-of-care theorists argue that when one individual, the *caregiver*, meets one other person's needs, the *cared-for* party, the caregiver is actually helping to meet the needs of all of the individuals who fall within the cared-for party's *web of care*. Thus, by specifically helping one other individual, the caregiver is assisting numerous people.

The strength of this theoretical approach is that it focuses on the basis of ethics in general, the significance of the interests of other people. The urging to care for relationships speaks to the fundamental basis why we are concerned about ethics in the first place. Most of us do not need any encouragement to think about how a decision will affect us personally. But ethical reasoning requires us to weigh the impact of decisions on the larger community.

However, as with any ethical theory, the application to a business setting is difficult. Suppose Nike and Reebok were to emphasize the ethics of care as they decide where and how to manufacture their shoes. What exactly would they do? Which relationships should they weigh and by how much? They have relationships with workers, shareholders, customers and the general public *in various countries*. On what grounds do they emphasize care for certain relationships and not others?

To practice thinking in terms of these ethical theories, study Exhibit 2-2, an abbreviated version of the Johnson & Johnson *Credo*, or statement of shared corporate values. General Robert Wood Johnson, who guided Johnson & Johnson from a small, family-owned business to a worldwide enterprise, believed the corporation had social responsibilities beyond the manufacturing and marketing of products. He wrote and published the Johnson & Johnson Credo, a document outlining those responsibilities, in 1943. Does the credo depend more on consequentialism, deontology, virtue ethics, or an ethics of care for its ethical vision?

The following Global Box's present one more complication for managers who wish to be more ethical. They must be alert to different concepts of ethics among our trading partners. The global box's provides additional opportunities to practice applying the alternative ethical theories. From the evidence of these global box's does Korea appear to have business laws drawn from a particular ethical theory?

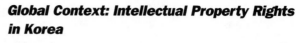

Global Context: Intellectual Property Rights in Korea

In most Western nations, laws protecting intellectual property are common. Violation of these laws is thus viewed as unethical behavior. Westerners take for granted that similar standards exist in other countries and may be surprised to learn that in some countries, Korea, for instance, protecting intellectual property is an unfamiliar notion.

The Chamber of Commerce in Korea reports that currently "There is no effective protection" for intellectual property. Such protection does not exist in Korea because the people of the country have no sense that the creator has a right to the intellectual property. They believe it belongs to the community as a whole and not to an individual.

Foreign companies are advised to register trademarks in Korea before relations with Korean companies are confirmed. For purposes of clarity, the trademark should be registered in the language of the foreign investor and in Korean.

Considering these ethical theories is an appropriate place to begin "thinking beyond the law." They point to considerations that an ethical manager would want to consider. But none of them permits the manager to make the kinds of rapid ethical judgments that competitive business requires. Hovering in the background of a thoughtful business ethic are these abstract formulations of ethics known as ethical theories.

In the interest of providing future business managers with an approach to business ethics *that they can use*, we suggest a three-step process, the WPH approach. While anchored to one or more ethical theories, this approach provides future business managers with some **ethical guidelines,** or practical steps that provide a dependable stimulus to moral reasoning in a business context. We urge the reader to return periodically to these ethical theories and to revisit the anchors to which ethical guidelines are attached.

The WPH Framework for Business Ethics

A useful framework for business ethics requires recognition that ethical managerial decisions must meet the following primary requirements:

1. They self-consciously affect particular groups of people. The pertinent question is, thus, **Whom** would this decision affect?
2. They are made in pursuit of a particular **Purpose**. Business decisions are instruments toward an ethical end.
3. They must meet the standards of practical, action-oriented business behavior. Managers need a doable set of guidelines for **How** to make decisions that are more ethical.

The remainder of this chapter attempts to explain and illustrate that framework.

Global Context: Business Ethics and Italian Taxes

When Italian corporations file their tax returns, the tax authorities assume that the corporations are underestimating their profits by thirty to seventy percent. This assumption proves to be true, yet the Italian Revenue Service does not press charges. In fact, purposely understating profits is the accepted practice within Italy.

Knowing the faulty nature of the tax return, the Revenue Service sends an "invitation to discuss" about six months after a corporation has filed. The parties agree on a meeting date. At the meeting, the corporation's executives do not attend. Instead, they send a *commercialista* whose "function exists for the primary purpose of negotiating corporation tax payments."

Several rounds of bargaining take place between the *commercialista* and the tax authorities. Based on the corporation's taxes the previous year and the estimation of the current return, the two parties agree upon a payment that is usually much higher than the original estimation, but still less than face value.

This negotiating process, while it may seem foreign to Americans, is a common business practice in Italy. In the early 1980's, an American banker learned the difficult lesson that, while doing business in a foreign country, local custom has a significant impact on ethical practice. The banker refused to underestimate profits on the tax return on ethical grounds. The Italian Revenue Service suggested several times that he hire a *commercialista* and resubmit his tax return.

The American banker refused all such suggestions. Finally, the Revenue Service sent the American a notice that demanded payments fifteen times larger than what he owed. The banker immediately arranged an appointment to express his outrage. When he arrived at the meeting, the Italian tax authorities were pleased to see him and said, "Now we can begin our negotiations."

EXHIBIT 2-3

The WPH Process of Ethical Decision Making

1. W—Who	2. P—Purpose	3. H—How
Shareholders:	Values:	Guidelines:
Consumers	Freedom	Universalization Test
Owners	Security	Public Disclosure
Managers	Justice	Golden Rule
Employees	Efficiency	
Community		

Who are the relevant stakeholders?

The **stakeholders** of a firm refer to the assorted groups of people affected by the firm's decisions. Any given managerial decision affects in varying degrees the following stakeholders:

1. Owners or shareholders,
2. Employees,
3. Customers,
4. Management,
5. The General Community where the firm operates, and
6. Future generations.

Exhibit 2-4 gives a portrait of Nortel Networks' commitments to its primary stakeholders and demonstrates that Nortel is aware of the people involved in its various decisions.

When considering the relevant stakeholders, try to go beyond the obvious. Maria's encounter with her company's vice president in Case 2-2 below certainly highlights certain common interests of management and its employees. However, a useful exercise for all of us is to force ourselves to think more broadly about additional stakeholders who may be affected just as much in the long run. Then, we will be less likely to make decisions that have unintended negative ethical impacts.

EXHIBIT 2-4

Commitments to Nortel Networks Stakeholders

To Employees

Nortel Networks commits to treating individuals with respect, following fair and equitable employment practices, and protecting and enhancing employee health and safety.

To Shareholders

Nortel Networks seeks to provide value to shareholders, while maintaining financial prudence.

To Customers

Nortel Networks maintains high ethical standards in all its customer relationships, and upholds the Core Value: "We fulfill our commitments and act with integrity."

To Suppliers

Nortel Networks is fair in its choice of suppliers and honest in all business interactions ith them.

Case 2-2

Maria Lopez

*M*aria recently became the purchasing manager of a small, lawnmower manufacturing firm. She is excited about the opportunity to demonstrate her abilities in this new responsibility. She is very aware that several others in the firm are watching her closely because they do not believe she deserves the sales manager position.

Her new job at the firm requires her to interact with several senior managers and leaders. One vice president in particular, Brian O'Malley, was someone she admired because he had earned the respect of the CEO on the basis of his success at making profits for the firm. Again and again, he just seemed to know how to discover and take advantage of competitive opportunities that ended up paying off royally for the firm.

Maria's first responsibility is to buy the motors for the assembly line. The motors constitute thirty percent of the total construction cost of the lawnmowers. Consequently, even a small error on Maria's part would have huge implications for the firm's profitability. The bids from the motor suppliers are required *to be secret in order to maximize competition among the suppliers. The bids are due at 5 p.m. today.*

At 3 p.m., Maria accidentally sees Brian returning the submitted bids to the locked safe where they are to be stored, according to company policy, until all bids have been submitted at 5 p.m. Then ,at 4:45 p.m., she notices a postal delivery of a bid from Stein's Motor Company. Her head buzzes as it hits her that Stein's President is one of Brian O'Malley's cousins.

She has no idea what to do. However, she knows she has to decide quickly.

Critical Thinking: Suppose that you believe that Maria should open the bids at 5 p.m. and forget about what she had seen. Generate two reasons in support of this conclusion.

Maria's ethical dilemma is complex. Many of the issues in the dilemma pertain to her career and the welfare of her firm. But consider the many stakeholders whose interests were not brought into the conversation. When we overlook important relevant stakeholders, we are ignoring an important component of ethical reasoning.

The interests of these various groups will sometimes be held in common and will sometimes conflict. Getting into the habit of thinking about the stakeholders affected by a decision places business ethics on the human level, where it belongs. Ethics is *our* attempt to create a better world for ourselves. There is elementary good sense at work when a firm concerns itself with the well-being of those whose space it shares and affects.

Consider the negative impact when a firm fails to show adequate respect for a major stakeholder. On December 3, 1984, a horrible catastrophe occurred at a chemical plant in Bhopal, India. The plant was a subsidiary of Union Carbide.

Damage to some equipment resulted in the emission of the deadly gas, methyl isocyanate, into the atmosphere. The emission of the gas caused injuries to more than 200,000 workers and Indian citizens in the neighborhood of the chemical plant. Several thousand people died.

Many factors, including worker error, faulty management decisions, equipment failures, and poor safety standards combined to cause the accident. Union Carbide was accused of not demanding the same rigorous safety standards in India as it had in the U.S. Citizens of both India and the United States demanded the corporation be held responsible for its evident neglect of safety. Union Carbide argued that it could not operate the plant if it were required to obey rigid Indian safety standards and that the economic benefits of the plant to India outweighed the risks of not following these standards. After years of litigation in both U.S. and Indian courts, Union Carbide was eventually ordered to monetarily compensate the victims of the accident. The costs of not paying attention to who is affected by business decisions can often be huge.

What are the Ultimate Purposes of the Decision?

The next step in the WPH framework is to consider the purpose of business decisions. We look first at the parties involved; next, we want to think about the purposes that bring these various parties together in common effort.

When we think about the ultimate reason or purpose as to why we make decisions in a business firm, we turn to the basic unit of discourse about business ethics, values. **Values** are positive abstractions that capture our sense of what is good or desirable. They are *ideas* that underlie conversations about business ethics. We derive our ethics from the interplay of values. Values represent our understanding of the purposes we will fulfill by making particular decisions.

For example, we value honesty. We want to live in communities where the trust that we associate with honesty prevails in our negotiations with one another. Business depends on the maintenance of a high degree of trust. No contract can protect us completely against every possible contingency. So we need some element of trust in one another when we buy and sell.

If one thinks about the definition of values for a moment, one realizes two things immediately. First, there are a huge number of values that pull and push on our decisions. Second, to state that a value is important in a particular situation is to start a conversation about what is meant by that particular value.

Because we want WPH to be useful for you as a manager, we present Exhibit 2-5. What we have done in this table is present you with an efficient way to use this second step in the WPH framework considering the Purpose of a business decision. We identify four of the most important values influencing business ethics, as well as presenting alternative meanings for each. This table should not only help clarify the importance of values in your own mind, but also enable you to question others who claim to be acting in an ethical fashion.

Just to make certain that you are comfortable with the idea of values, take this opportunity to jot down a few more values that might affect financial and trade decisions.

1._____

2._____

3._____

If you need some help, just think about what positive abstractions you intend to emphasize to your children. If that vision is not helpful, imagine what you would want your friends to list as your special qualities as a person. What positive abstractions would be responsible for those qualities?

Values are the mental abstractoions we need to consider when we make daily business decisions. For instance, a manager might ask whether they should fire an employee whose performance is less than impressive. In making this decision, the manager explores alternative visions of key values such as justice and efficiency and then makes choices about which action to take.

Exhibit 2-6 contains a statement of Nortel's core or primary values. They identify for its stakeholders what positive abstractions guide Nortel's business decisions. A useful exercise might be to compare Exhibits 2-5 and 2-6. See whether you can take the elements in Nortel's list and translate them into the primary values of business ethics.

EXHIBIT 2-5

Primary Values and Business Ethics

VALUE	ALTERNATIVE FORMS
FREEDOM	To act without restriction from rules imposed by others.
	To possess the capacity or resources to act as one wishes.
SECURITY	To possess a large enough supply of goods and services that basic needs are met.
	To be safe from those wishing to interfere with your property rights.
	To achieve the psychological condition of self-confidence such that risks are welcome.
JUSTICE	To receive the products of your labor.
	To treat all humans identically, regardless of race, class, gender, age, and sexual preference.
	To provide resources in proportion to need.
	To possess anything that someone else was willing to grant you.
EFFICIENCY	To maximize the amount of wealth in society.
	To get the most from a particular output.
	To minimize costs.

EXHIBIT 2-6

Nortel Networks Core Values

Core Values: A Guide to Ethical Business Practice

1. We create superior value for our customers.
2. We work to provide shareholder value.
3. Our people are our strength.
4. We share one vision. We are one team.
5. We have only one standard—excellence.
6. We embrace change and reward innovation.
7. We fulfill our commitments and act with integrity.

New ways of organizing people and work within the corporation are giving each of us more decision-making responsibility. Given the complexity and constantly changing nature of our work and our world, no book of hard-and-fast rules—however long and detailed—could ever adequately cover all the dilemmas people face. In this context, every Nortel Networks' employee is asked to take leadership in ethical decision making.

In most situations, our personal values and honesty will guide us to the right decision. But in our capacity as employees and representatives of Nortel Networks, we must also always consider how our actions affect the integrity and credibility of the corporation as a whole. Our business ethics must reflect the standard of conduct outlined in this document—a standard grounded in the corporation's values and governing Nortel Networks's relationships with all stakeholders.

Review the list of a firm's major stakeholders on page 21 and Exhibit 2-3 before you think about the ethical issue in Case 2-3.

Case 2-3

International Union, United Automobile, Aerospace and Agricultural Implement Workers of America, UAW

v.

Johnson Controls
United States Supreme Court
111 S. Ct. 1196 (1991)

*B*efore the Civil Rights Act of 1964 became law, Johnson Controls did not employ any women in a battery-manufacturing job. After passage of that law, they began to allow women in such jobs, but warned them of the potential dangers of the job to unborn fetuses and made them sign a statement acknowledging that they knew of the dangers of the job. But after five years of operating with this warning policy, they adopted a "fetal protection policy" that barred all women, except those whose infertility was medically documented, from jobs involving actual or potential lead exposure exceeding the Occupational Safety and Health Administration (OSHA) standard.

The UAW filed a class action challenging Johnson Controls' policy. Among the individual named plaintiffs were petitioners Mary Craig, who had chosen to be sterilized in order to avoid losing her job, Elsie Nason, a 50-year-old divorcee, who had suffered a loss in compensation when she was transferred out of a job where she was exposed to lead, and Donald Penney, who had been denied a request for a leave of absence for the purpose of lowering his lead level because he intended to become a father. The United States District Court granted summary judgment for employer. The Court of Appeals affirmed, and certiorari was granted.

JUSTICE BLACKMUN

In this case we are concerned with an employer's gender-based fetal-protection policy. May an employer exclude a fertile female employee from certain jobs because of its concern for the health of the fetus the woman might conceive?

Respondent, Johnson Controls, Inc., manufactures batteries. In the manufacturing process, the element lead is a primary ingredient. Occupational exposure to lead entails health risks, including the risk of harm to any fetus carried by a female employee. In June 1977, however, it announced its first official policy concerning its employment of women in lead-exposure work: "[P]rotection of the health of the unborn child is the immediate and direct responsibility of the prospective parents. While the medical profession and the company can support them in the exercise of this responsibility, it cannot assume it for them without simultaneously infringing their rights as persons." The company also required a woman who wished to be considered for employment to sign a statement that she had been advised of the risk of having a child while she was exposed to lead. The statement informed the woman that although there was evidence "that women exposed to lead have a higher rate of abortion," this evidence was "not as clear...as the relationship between cigarette smoking and cancer," but that it was, "medically speaking, just good sense not to run that risk if you want children and do not want to expose the unborn child to risk, however small...." Five years later, in 1982, Johnson Controls shifted from a policy of warning to a policy of exclusion. Between 1979 and 1983, eight employees became pregnant while maintaining blood lead levels in excess of thirty micrograms per deciliter. This appeared to be the critical level noted by the Occupational Safety and Health Administration (OSHA) for a worker who was planning to have a family. The company responded by announcing a broad exclusion of women from jobs that exposed them to lead:

"...[I]t is [Johnson Controls'] policy that women who are pregnant or who are capable of bearing children will not be placed into jobs involving lead exposure or which could expose them to lead through the exercise of job bidding, bumping, transfer or promotion rights." The policy defined "women...capable of bearing children" as "[a]ll women except those whose inability to bear children is medically documented."

The District Court granted summary judgment for defendant-respondent Johnson Controls.

The bias in Johnson Control's policy is obvious. Fertile men, but not fertile women, are given a choice as to whether they wish to risk their reproductive health for a particular job. Respondent's fetal-protection policy excludes women with childbearing capacity from lead-exposed jobs and so creates a facial classification based on gender. Respondent assumes as much in its brief before this Court.

Respondent does not seek to protect the unconceived children of all its employees. Despite evidence in the record about the debilitating effect of lead exposure on the male reproductive system, Johnson Controls is concerned only with the harm that may befall the unborn offspring of its female employees. The beneficence of an employer's purpose does not undermine the conclusion that an explicit gender-based policy is sex discrimination.

It is no more appropriate for the courts than it is for individual employers to decide whether a woman's reproductive role is more important to herself and her family than her economic role. Congress has left this choice to the woman as hers to make. The case is remanded for further proceedings consistent with this opinion.

IT IS SO ORDERED.

1. Critical Thinking: One of the most valuable steps in critical thinking involves our trying to squeeze as many facts out of a situation as we can **before we make a decision**. In this particular case, what additional information would you like to have before you decided about the most ethical course of action for Johnson Controls?

2. Ethical Decision Making: If the Supreme Court were guided just by ethical considerations, what do you believe it should have decided in this case? Which stakeholders do you see as having the major interests in this situation? Which value is most prominent in your argument about what Johnson Controls should have done with respect to its conditions of employment?

The third and final step of the WPH approach to business ethics is more action-oriented than the first two steps appear to be. The first two steps, by themselves, do not explain **How** to use our consideration of stakeholders and primary values to make the better managerial decision. The third step, however, uses the first two steps in combination with three ethical guidelines to move us towards that decision. An **ethical guideline** is a pathway to ethical conduct.

Using Classical Ethical Guidelines for Understanding How to Make Ethical Decisions

Bright and upstanding people have long struggled with ethical decisions. Their hard work and thought has been distilled into a few general, classical guidelines that move us further toward our goal of making more ethical business decisions.

The Golden Rule

When you were a child, you probably heard your mother or father say, "Don't hit your sister! How would you like it if she hit you?" This interaction might have been the first time you encountered the Golden Rule. Alternatively, you might have heard about the Golden Rule in the course of religious training, "Do unto other as you would have done unto you." Confucius and Aristotle offer similar messages.

Many different interpretations and variations of the Golden Rule have been offered. For example, one scholar has identified six ways the Golden Rule can be interpreted.

1. Do to others as you want them to gratify you.
2. Be considerate of others' feelings as you want them to be considerate of yours.
3. Treat others as persons of rational dignity like you.
4. Extend brotherly or sisterly love to others, as you would want them to do to you.
5. Treat others according to moral insight, as you would have others treat you.
6. Do to others as God wants you to do to them.[4]

These suggestions remind us that ethics requires some awareness that other humans matter. We are pretty definite that *we* matter, and because we see ourselves in others, we should strive to think long and hard about the impacts of our actions on those we see and also on those we cannot directly see. All persons, seen and unseen, matter as human beings.

Let's return to the ethical problem outlined at the beginning of this chapter. Using the Golden Rule as your ethical guideline, how you would you behave? Would you hide the information, or would you disclose the information? Put yourself into the consumers' posi-

---

[4] Jeffrey Wattles, *"Levels of Meaning in the Golden Rule,"* JOURNAL OF RELIGIOUS ETHICS, 15, (1987) 106-129, quoted in W. Patrick Cunningham, *"The Golden Rule as Universal Ethical Norm,"* JOURNAL OF BUSINESS ETHICS, 17, 1998, 105-109.

tion. As a consumer, would you want to know that a shoe was manufactured in another country? Are there other stakeholders in the organization whose interests should be the focus of your application of the golden rule? What values would be advanced by your following the Golden Rule?

Public Disclosure Test

Starting with the ethical dilemma faced by Nike and Reebok, suppose you decide to ignore the complaints about working conditions in your plants in foreign countries. Now, suppose that your decision to ignore the complaints is in the newspaper. How would the public react? How would you feel about the public's having full knowledge of what you intend to do?

We tend to care about what others think about us as ethical agents. For managers, this guideline provides a special light that illuminates the effects and implications of their decisions. Stop for a moment and think of corporations that failed to apply the public disclosure test and generated negative reactions as a result. For example, Dr. Hugh Davis, a professor at Johns Hopkins University, invented the Dalkon Shield birth control device. In the late 1960's and early 1970's, Dr. Davis was considered a rising star in the field of women's health and family planning. By the mid-1980's, Dr. Davis was known as an evil, dishonest man. A.H. Robins, the company that sold the Dalkon Shield, was bankrupt.

What caused the change in public opinion? Many women became infertile because of the device, and a few women died. The public learned that Dr. Davis—the man who was performing the apparently objective medical studies of the Dalkon Shield's safety—had a financial interest in the Dalkon Shield. Because of Dr. Davis' failure to disclose this interest, the birth control device was not tested appropriately, and many women were damaged as a result.

Dr. Davis is likely to have behaved differently if he had realized the public would eventually know of his financial interest in the Dalkon Shield. Presumably, he would have made sure that he took actions to protect his reputation and ensure the safety of women who used the Dalkon Shield.

Another way to think of the public disclosure test is to view it as providing sunshine that makes our actions open, rather than hidden. The premise of this Classical Guideline is that ethics is hard work, labor that we might resist if we did not have frequent reminders that we live in a community. As a member of that community, our self-concept is tied, at least in part, to how that community perceives us.

Universalization Test

A third Classical Guideline shares with the other two a focus on the other—the stakeholders whom our actions affect. Before we act, the universalization test asks us to consider what the world would be like were our decision emulated by everyone else. Applying the universalization test causes us to wonder aloud: Is what I am about to do the kind of action that, *were others to follow my example,* makes the world a better place for me and those I love?

Exhibit 2-7 summarizes the use of the Classical Ethical Guidelines in moving the ethical manager toward better decisions.

"In summary, business managers can apply the WPH approach to most ethical dilemmas. The WPH Framework provides a practical process that is suited to the frequently complex ethical dilemmas that business managers must address quickly in today's society."

In summary, business managers can apply the WPH approach to most ethical dilemmas. The WPH

EXHIBIT 2-7

Classical Guidelines

1. **Golden Rule Test:** Ask yourself: would you want other companies to withhold from you the kind of information you might be considering withholding from others.

2. **Public Disclosure Test:** Imagine how your company would be perceived by the public if the information you are considering withholding from them would be written up in the newspapers or reported on the nightly news.

3. **Universalization Test:** Ask yourself if withholding this information could hurt anyone. Would the world be better off following your example?

Framework—as we shall see in the Enron scenario—provides a practical process that is suited to the frequently complex ethical dilemmas that business managers must address quickly in today's society.

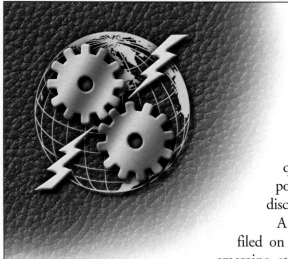

Technology: Computer Use and Ethics

The use of computers to store and transfer important business information has resulted in a new set of ethical concerns. How private is the computer screen? Who owns the information that is transferred electronically?

Computer law is gradually adjusting to such questions. But, as the beginning of this chapter pointed out, knowing the law is just the first step in discovery of the ethical business decision.

A recent Federal Trade Commission(FTC) complaint, filed on July 10, 2000, illustrates the importance of this emerging ethical dilemma. The FTC charged online retailer Toysmart.com with selling customer lists despite earlier privacy statements that their customers' personal data would never be shared with a third party. The customer lists were included as assets to be sold as part of the company's bankruptcy proceedings. On July 21, the FTC issued its settlement with Toysmart.com allowing the lists to be sold as long as the sale occurs before July 2001, a family-oriented company buys the customer lists, and the buyer agrees to abide by the original Toysmart.com privacy.

Contemporary Application

The ENRON disaster is a challenge to all future business managers. What went wrong? How could a group of talented businesspeople make the decisions that the following narrative details? Is ENRON a typical business organization, except for one small, but highly significant dimension—they got caught?

As they play themselves out in the ENRON story this fascinating set of questions present a laboratory for applying business ethics. As starters, you might find it a valuable review of the ethical theories presented in Chapter 2 to ask yourself how a consequentialist, a deontologist, a virtue ethicist, or an ethics of care perspective would analyze the decisions that led to the fall of ENRON.

But what would be especially useful for you to do is make your first stab at applying the WPH framework to an actual business setting. ENRON is no blackboard creation, but a flesh-and-blood global business nightmare. Walk yourself through the practical steps of the WPH process and try to envision yourself in the midst of the decisions that collectively led to the firm's downfall. What would you have done?

Corporation *n.* An ingenious device for obtaining individual profit without individual responsibility

Ambrose Bierce, THE DEVIL'S DICTIONARY (1909)

THE COLLAPSE OF ENRON
A Business Ethics Perspective

By Sheryl Kaiser, J.D.

The essential questions posed by business ethics ask: Who in the society is the corporation responsible to for its actions and activities? What are the purposes and goals of the entity? And, by what means, within what limits, may these goals be pursued?

Two main schools of thought on these questions have developed in the study of business ethics. The first approach, developed in the 19th century and in modern times championed most ardently by economist Milton Friedman, is known as the maximizing profits model. The maximizing profits model posits that the sole purpose of the corporation is to benefit its shareholders by maximizing their profits, and that the means to achieving that end may include any activities not prohibited by law. In his famous 1970 article, "The Social Responsibility of Business Is to Increase Its Profits" (*New York Times Magazine*, September 13, 1970), Friedman argued that corporate executives are employees of the owners of the business and have direct responsibility only to them. "That responsibility is to conduct the business in accordance with their desires, which generally means to make as much money as possible while conforming to the basic rules of society, both those embodied in law and those embodied in ethical custom."

Friedman goes so far as to assert that it is irresponsible for a corporation to act on social issues such as controlling pollution or training the unemployed, because these are political functions that should be left to the political processes of government. Corporations are simply not designed or equipped for such considerations. Hence, under the maximizing profits model, all areas of social concern and social responsibility should be left to governmental regulation. The sole corporate focus should be on making profits within the confines of these rules.

The second approach to corporate social responsibility is called the stakeholder interest model, and was developed in the mid- to late-20th century, partly in response to the harsh effects of the maximizing profit model. The stakeholder interest model recognizes that there are many constituencies with as great a stake in the effects of corporate activity as the shareholders, and that the shareholders are but one constituency to be considered in corporate decision making. Other stakeholder groups include the corporation's employees, management, customers, business partners, and the communities in which the corporation operates. The stakeholder interest model posits that the interests of and impact on these other groups should also be considered when determining how a corporation will go about achieving its goals and making its profits. This approach does not trust the political process and the enforcement of law exclusively to ensure socially responsible behavior in commerce. Instead, it looks to internal accountability and values within the corporation to protect the legitimate interests of those affected by corporate actions.

The swift and messy collapse of the Enron Corporation, at the time one of the largest corporations in the United States, represents a failure of corporate business ethics and corporate responsibility under either model. Enron not only failed to serve the interests of its shareholders, but it did so in a manner that exploited and harmed all of its stakeholders.

From Bricks and Mortar to a House of Cards

Enron was created in 1985, with the combination of two natural gas pipeline companies. With the deregulation of the industry, Enron executives developed a business in trading gas as well as being a gas supply company. As the profits from the trading business overtook that of the business of building pipelines and drilling wells, the company emphasis moved away from the nuts and bolts of providing the resource and into the realm of developing innovative financial devices and arrangements to buy and sell the product. Enron management adopted an "asset-light" strategy for the business, emphasizing intellectual capital over hard assets. Profits and revenues climbed steadily from the company's natural gas and electricity trading in financial instruments and derivatives (financial instruments that derive their value from another financial instrument or commodity such as interest rates, stock prices, precious metals or other resources). These revenues were bolstered significantly by utilities deregulation generally, and also by special regulatory exemptions for the types of derivatives Enron traded in. Enron had lobbied hard for these accommodations, giving substantial political contributions to the decision makers on those issues.

In the mid- to late-1990s, the company decided to expand its financial expertise to other diverse areas—water, coal, broadband, fiber-optic capacity, and several others. Enron's stock price rose steadily and it became a favorite with Wall Street as well as with its own employees, many of whom invested their entire retirement savings in company stock through the company-maintained 401(k) plan. For the most part, however, these new ventures were not profitable for the company, saddling it with vast quantities of debt; debt that would hurt the company's stock price if revealed to the public. Accordingly, the company took aggressive advantage of complicated loopholes in the accounting laws to keep these losses from public view. It engaged in questionable reporting practices including the utilization of a slush fund to shelter bad deals, the swapping of financial instruments to shift profits from one deal to another, and the use of unrealistic profit projections to mislead the markets as to the financial results of its trade deals.

Enron also embarked on a scheme to structure its riskier ventures in entities that would not have to be reported on its balance sheet (called "special purpose entities," or SPEs). These off-balance-sheet partnerships and subsidiaries permitted Enron to keep its mounting corporate debt off of its balance sheet, thus protecting its credit rating and its stock price from the losses. The problems with these off-balance-sheet entities were several. First, in simplified terms, any losses suffered by these entities were effectively guaranteed by Enron stock; meaning that Enron shareholders would be left holding the bag if the investment turned sour. As well, these guarantees were built on the assumption of Enron's stock price remaining high. Any drop in the stock price could trigger calls for repayment of the debt by these off-balance-sheet entities. The quest to keep the stock price high thus became essential not only to keep Wall Street impressed but, in fact, to prevent the entire financial edifice of Enron from collapsing. Indeed, it was just this mechanism that would ultimately bring down the entire house of cards and lead to the largest bankruptcy in US corporate history.

The other major issue with the off-balance-sheet entities was who invested in them and what they got. Many of the banks and investment houses that did business with Enron participated as venturers in the SPEs. Enron executives, as individuals, were partners in several of the entities, as well. Enron's Chief Financial Officer, Andrew Fastow, collected more than $30 million as a partner in SPEs that he himself had engineered. Michael Kopper, another Enron executive, garnered a return of more than $10 million. The fiduciary duty of a corporate executive is to act in the best interest of the corporation. The conflict of interest is clear where corporate executives partner with the very corporations they are bound to represent and negotiate with such corporations in their own interest. In the case of Enron's SPEs, Enron executives with a personal stake in the entities negotiated terms and conditions of the investment across the table from their corporate subordinates, obviating any chance of an arm's length transaction. When presented with these transactions, Enron's Board of Directors twice suspended the corporation's code of ethics in order to approve the self-dealing. The depth of the Board's understanding of the dubious accounting and financial practices of Enron management remains suspect. One thing is certain: no information regarding the existence of these entities, holding hundreds of millions of dollars of Enron debt, was made public to Enron's investors.

At the beginning of 2001, Enron's stock was trading in excess of $80 per share. Early in the year, an energy crisis in California and a serious downturn in the technology sector caused Enron's stock price to dip. By early summer, the stock price had fallen to the $50-$60-range, a point that would trigger the repayment provisions for several of the off-balance-sheet partnerships that were keeping hundreds of millions of dollars of debt off Enron's public books. In mid-August, Jeffrey Skilling, Enron's CEO of six months, abruptly resigned, citing personal reasons. Enron's Chairman of the Board, Kenneth Lay, who served as CEO prior to Skilling's appointment, resumed the CEO position. The day after Skilling's departure, Vice President Sherron Watkins sent a confidential memo to Lay outlining the problems with the off-balance-sheet financial structures and their imminent breakdown. The memo warned that the company would "implode in a wave of accounting scandals." Upon cursory review of Watkins' allegations, Enron's lawyers opined that there was no cause for concern.

Enron's stock continued to decline in the aftermath of the September 11 terrorist attacks, though Lay and other executives actively sought to reassure outside investors and the employees invested in the company stock that the company was in great shape and that "the third quarter is looking great." In October, Enron reported a third quarter loss of more than $600 million and the following day restated its balance sheet, reducing its reported assets by more than $1 billion. That same day, the company froze all assets in the employees' 401(k) plan, preventing employees from selling the company stock in their retirement portfolios. The employees would not regain the right to sell Enron stock until its value had fallen to pennies per share. Within days, the SEC initiated an investigation into Enron's accounting and financial practices, the CFO was fired, and Enron reported overstated profits of nearly $600 million in the previous financial statements. Further damaging financial revelations ensued. The stock plummeted to near zero and, at the beginning of December Enron filed for Federal bankruptcy protection from its creditors and investors.

The breadth and depth of the investigation into Enron's "implosion in a wave of accounting scandals" is considerable. Soon after opening its investigation of Enron, the SEC expanded its investigation to Enron's accountant and auditor, Arthur Andersen. Evidence of secret destruction of Enron financial records and documents by Andersen personnel has led to a criminal indictment of the accounting firm by the Justice Department. Enron executives and members of the Board of Directors are under investigation by a variety of Federal agencies and are named defendants in dozens of lawsuits by shareholders, employees, and creditors. Many of the executives refused to testify when called before Congress, invoking their Fifth Amendment right against self-incrimination. Banks and investment partners involved in Enron financing schemes not only face suits from Enron plaintiffs for their role in the arrangements, but also regulatory fallout from their own accounting improprieties and balance sheet problems arising from Enron's collapse. On the political front, the public call for legislative and regulatory reform to prevent another Enron has been met with unease and some trepidation by the many politicians who counted

Enron and its executives among their largest financial contributors.

The **ethical issues** that emerged from the Enron debacle are copious and relate not only to Enron itself, but also to the many businesses engaged with it. The demise of Enron not only reflects a failure of regulatory oversight, but also a failure of internal corporate governance and checks and balances. A few of these key business ethics issues are examined below.

Obligations to the Shareholders

Whether one embraces the maximizing profits model or the stakeholder interest model, the primary, if not exclusive, obligation of a corporation is to its owners, the shareholders. Corporate management, which consists of the company's directors and officers, are elected and appointed to represent the interests of the shareholders in running the company. These directors and officers, and the agents they hire, have a legal fiduciary duty to act prudently and in the best interests of the corporation and its owners and not in their own self-interest or for their own benefit.

In the case of Enron, officers of the corporation worked with the accountants and law firms hired to represent the company (and who were paid handsomely for such advice with corporate funds) to hide from the owners of the company the true status of the corporation's financial affairs. Grand and complex machinations between Enron executives, Arthur Andersen accountants, and Vinson & Elkins attorneys served to conceal from investors an accurate picture of the company's financial situation and how its business was being conducted. Further, many of these executives personally profited from the deception. The CFO and others involved in the off-balance-sheet partnerships profited by tens of millions of dollars. Similarly, top Enron executives cashed out of their Enron stock while continuing to publicly reassure investors of the soundness of the company. Between May 2000 and August 2001 when the company imploded, top Enron executives profited from the sale of more than $100 million of the company's stock. These insider trades were not reported to the public investors until long after the fact. Enron executives profited at the expense of those they were charged with representing and serving. Clearly, they breached their fiduciary duty.

There is plenty of blame to be spread. Gaping loopholes in the accounting rules permitted an opening for the chicanery; loopholes that business and industry and the accounting profession had fought hard to keep open. Internal controls that should have caught the problems did not. Enron's auditor, Andersen, and attorneys, Vinson & Elkins, helped to structure and then signed off on the questionable deals. Enron's Board of Directors failed to use the prudent care required of directors to inform itself about the transactions. The Board's audit committee failed to diligently examine the transactions and the full Board, when presented with transactions which clearly violated the company's policy on self-dealing by corporate officers, merely waived Enron's corporate code of ethics (not once, but twice).

In the absence of fraud, corporate directors and officers are generally indemnified and insured against personal liability for such negligence—a practice that raises ethical issues of its own, but is nonetheless necessary to attract people of means to serve on corporate boards. However, several of Enron's insurance carriers are exploring ways to rescind their policies on Enron directors and avoid their responsibility for paying legal judgments entered against the Enron directors. The enormous restatement of earnings by the company on account of the undisclosed partnerships (nearly $600 million and dating back several years), could serve to void the policies on the grounds of apparent fraud. If so, the Enron directors could be looked to individually for liability to creditors and shareholders.

The loss to Enron's shareholders from the beginning of 2001 to the bankruptcy filing in December of that year is estimated to be in excess of $60 billion.

Obligations to the Other Stakeholders

Perhaps the most negatively affected stakeholder group in the Enron scandal was its employees. Not only did some 5000 of them lose their jobs at the outset of the bankruptcy (and counting), but more than 20,000 employees, loyally trusting the assurances of upper management, lost their retirement savings in Enron stock. Employees participated in a company-managed 401(k) plan. Inspired by management optimism, many Enron employees invested their retirement savings heavily in their employer's stock. On the date that the company went public with the first of its financial revelations and restated its assets downward by more than $1 billion, the company froze the employees' plans, ostensibly for a change in fund managers, which prevented the employees from conducting any trades. By the time the ban was lifted, the value of a share of Enron stock had fallen to mere pennies, rendering the retirement accounts worthless.

The fallout from Enron affected many other constituencies as well. Enron's trading partners suffered several billions of dollars in losses on uncollateralized derivative contracts. Enron's bondholders also lost several billions of dollars. Suppliers large and small were not paid. A negative ripple effect was experienced by the energy sector generally. The City of Houston, already reeling from the economic downturn, lost not only one of the largest businesses in the United States and a major employer, but a city icon and the sponsor of its premier professional sports venue, Enron Field.

Enron's Corporate Culture from an Ethical Perspective

Enron's collapse was not the result of missteps by one rogue actor. Many within Enron's executive ranks, managers and directors, and many of Enron's advisors were privy to the trick accounting arrangements being used to cook the corporate books. Improbity to the degree exhibited in the Enron case requires a corporate environment that rewards results by any means necessary. Due to the fragile and complex nature of the company's off-balance-sheet financial structure, it was driven by the need to keep its stock price artificially high. Accordingly, as CEO, Jeffrey Skilling nurtured a corporate environment where risk-taking and creative, if shaky, deal-making that enhanced the immediate bottom line were rewarded with large bonuses and positive reviews, whereas concern for long-term growth and shareholder value were marginalized.

Skilling was reportedly a manager who surrounded himself with "yes men." In such an environment, the critical thinking required to sustain a multinational company such as Enron is absent. Lost is the key dialogic component that permits a company to realistically and effectively assess and react to the market and to its business exigencies. Alternative views and perspectives are essential for real growth in any organization. Moreover, bad news travels up the corporate ladder badly in the best of organizations. In an organization led by those who refuse to hear bad news, it doesn't travel at all. And in such circumstances, no one wants to be the messenger. It was said that raising a red flag at Enron was a "ticket to exile."

Nonetheless, there were a few heroic souls in Enron's corporate environment willing to point out the lack of Emperor's clothes. Enron's treasurer, Jeffrey McMahon (who took over as COO of the company in Enron's bankruptcy), was reported to have raised issues regarding the propriety of the partnerships when they were initially established. He was promptly transferred to London. In early spring 2001, Jordan Mintz, an in-house Enron lawyer, raised issues with the chief accounting officer and chief risk officer for the company regarding the propriety of the off-balance-sheet arrangements. He was told to stay out of it. Later that spring—Mintz would arrange for an independent review of some of the transactions by outside counsel. Sherron Watkins, Enron's vice-president of corporate development, submitted a powerful confidential memo to Kenneth Lay the day after CEO Skilling's resignation, outlining the nature of the off-the-books entities and the potentially devastating financial problems they presented. Presciently, she warned of the imminent "implosion" of Enron due to the accounting artifice. Watkins' memo was passed on to Enron's lawyers and promptly deemed to be of no real concern by them.

Business ethicist Joanne Ciulla has asserted that there is something wrong with an environment "where doing what is sensible or right takes an heroic gesture . . . morality in the workplace should not be that drastically different from the morality in the culture outside of it." (Joanne Ciulla, "Messages from the Environment: The Influence of Policies and Practices on Employee Responsibility", in Chimezie A.B. Osigweh, Yg., ed., *Communicating Employee Responsibilities and Rights: A Modern Management Mandate* New York: Quorum Books, 1987). A corporate culture that suppresses, frowns upon, or punishes sensible questions and concerns by loyal employees regarding transparency and accountability is doomed to fail by its own sensory deprivation.

(See no evil, hear no evil, speak no evil...).

The Use of Political Influence to Thwart Regulation

Political contributions on Enron's behalf to Federal candidates and parties totaled nearly $6 million in the decade from 1990 to 2000; $1.7 million was contributed in the 2000 election cycle alone. Hundreds of thousands of dollars were also contributed to state politicians, particularly in California and Texas. A substantial percentage of these contributions went to members of Congress holding powerful positions in the committees charged with oversight of Enron's business activities. Contributions to the parties generally and additional lobbying expenditures of $1-$2 million each year provided Enron access to all levels of the political process.

Throughout the 1990s, Enron lobbied hard for deregulation in the areas of its businesses, particularly

that of the wholesale electricity market. The Federal government began deregulation of these markets in 1992, California in 1996, and Texas in 1999. Beginning in 1992, Enron also worked with the Commodities Futures Trading Commission (CFTC), then chaired by Wendy Gramm, wife of Texas Senator Phil Gramm, to exempt from regulation futures trading in energy derivatives. The CFTC exempted such transactions and they soon became one of Enron's most profitable activities. In 1993, Wendy Gramm stepped down from the CFTC and became a member of Enron's Board of Directors, where she remained through the 2001 collapse. Efforts in 2001 by the CFTC to reassert control over the trading in these derivatives were defeated by Congress, hindered largely by the Senate Banking Committee, then-chaired by Senator Phil Gramm.

With respect to the accounting sleights performed so artfully by Enron's advisors, attempts to close such loopholes were thwarted by the financial industry throughout the 1990s. A forceful effort by the SEC in 2000 to separate audit and consulting practices by accounting firms was swiftly derailed. This was a major ethical issue in the Enron debacle, as Andersen served as both consultant and auditor to Enron—two roles often in conflict—and its consulting revenues were many times greater than its audit fees.

So, what is wrong with a corporation using money to exercise its First Amendment freedom of speech, and, in the process, gain access to the political decision makers that govern its activities? Well, it depends on what you do with the access.

In a stakeholder-interest approach to corporate responsibility, a corporation will take into account the effects of its actions on its various constituencies and self-regulate to ensure fairness to those interests. In making corporate decisions, it will take into consideration the social costs and social impact, as well as the effect on the bottom line.

In a maximizing-profits approach, a corporation need not take into account the effects of its actions on anyone save the shareholders, provided it is acting within the confines of the laws in effect at the time. As Friedman observed, the social costs and social impact on the rest of society are left to the protections of the government that enacts those laws. Accordingly, with this narrow focus of obligation to the shareholders only, there is a corresponding obligation on the part of corporations to stay out of, and certainly not to thwart, efforts at social protection by other institutions (the government). A Friedmanian who not only believes that the only social responsibility of a corporation is to make a profit for its shareholders, but who also acts to prevent political institutions from placing limits upon those activities in the interests of the good of the society, is not a Friedmanian but a Friedmaniac.

There is also a more profound ethical issue involved in efforts to deregulate a commodity that is a necessity, an "essential good" for the society, like natural gas and electricity. These commodities are in the nature of public goods—in limited supply, but necessary for the maintenance and progress of the society as a whole. Although the capitalist system permits private ownership of and profit from the sale of these kinds of goods, there is a paramount public interest in how and to whom these goods are distributed. Given the far-reaching social implications, the use of political influence to completely privatize the availability and cost of such an essential good as natural gas is dubious under any construct of corporate social responsibility.

Proposals for Reform—Averting Enron: The Sequel

Proposals for external regulation to prevent the recurrence of an Enron-type corporate collapse are wide-ranging. Among the submissions with strong support:

- Require that corporate executives disclose their transactions in the corporation's stock within forty-eight hours of the trade. This one has already been implemented—under the prior rules, up to thirteen months could pass before other shareholders were informed of the insider transactions.
- Require that the audit committee of the corporation's Board of Directors consist entirely of outside, independent members to ensure diligence and autonomy.
- Modify the standard for indemnification and insurance to hold board members and corporate executives personally liable for negligence in misleading investors.
- Require corporate CEOs to personally vouch for and be held personally liable for the veracity of the company's reported finances to ensure due diligence at the very top level of the corporation.
- Prohibit executive offenders from holding executive positions in the future, and disgorge their bonuses and stock options. There is currently nothing that prevents corporate wrongdoers

from continuing to serve in their positions and keeping ill-gotten corporate compensation.
- Bar accounting firms from selling other services, like consulting, to their audit clients to prevent conflicts of interest. Enron's fees to Andersen for consulting services dwarfed its revenues from auditing Enron.
- Bar audits by accounting firms with former employees serving as executives of the audit client. This response to the revolving-door problem is intended to ensure independence in the audit process. Many in Enron's management ranks were former Andersen partners.
- Impose independent oversight on the accounting profession generally. Presently, only a peer-review process provides checks on accounting excesses or irregularities.
- For company-sponsored 401(k) retirement plans, require diversity in the portfolio holdings. These proposals are varied but could include the imposition of a cap limiting the percentage of employer stock in the portfolio, or shortening the holding period during which an employee is prohibited from trading the stock after it is contributed.
- Ban unregulated, unlimited "soft money" contributions to political parties.

What form punishment will take for the Enron miscreants remains to be determined. Civil penalties are certain, criminal penalties are possible. The United States punishes white-collar crime under a scheme known as the Federal Sentencing Commission Guidelines. The Guidelines contain severe penalties for fraud, not only for individual wrongdoers within a corporate structure but also for the entity itself. Under principles of vicarious liability, a principal (here the business entity) is liable for the misdeeds of its agents acting on its behalf (employees, partners). Although Enron as an entity is bankrupt, many of the other major players in the scandal are not. The accounting firms, law firms, investment banks, and others who participated in the Enron transactions that led to its demise face the possibility of harsh and very expensive comeuppance. The Guidelines were amended to strengthen and increase fines and sentences, effective for fraudulent activities occurring after November 1, 2001. This date, and the activities that occurred after it, could well play a very significant role in the legal arguments of Enron defendants.

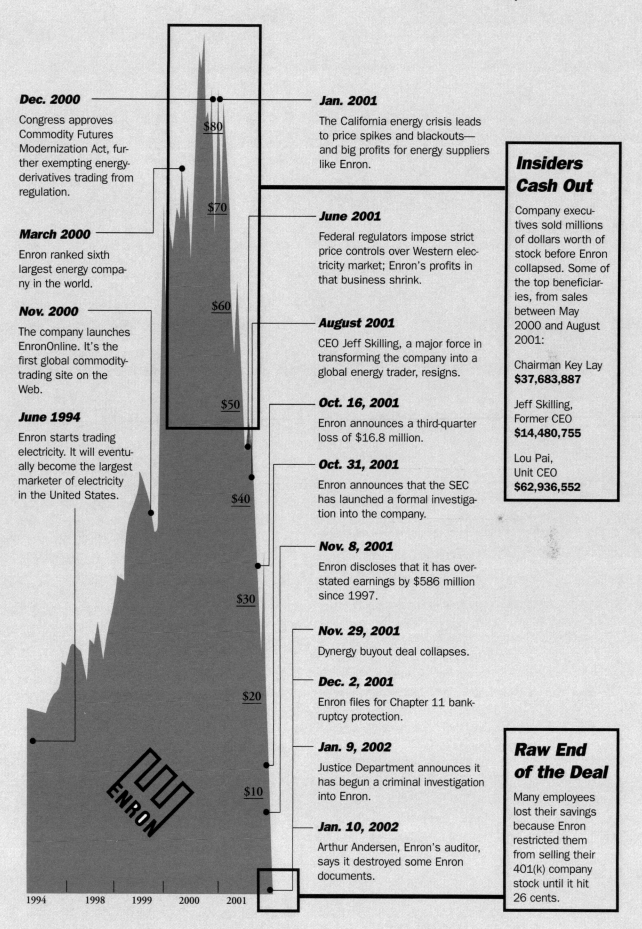

Dec. 2000

Congress approves Commodity Futures Modernization Act, further exempting energy-derivatives trading from regulation.

March 2000

Enron ranked sixth largest energy company in the world.

Nov. 2000

The company launches EnronOnline. It's the first global commodity-trading site on the Web.

June 1994

Enron starts trading electricity. It will eventually become the largest marketer of electricity in the United States.

Jan. 2001

The California energy crisis leads to price spikes and blackouts—and big profits for energy suppliers like Enron.

June 2001

Federal regulators impose strict price controls over Western electricity market; Enron's profits in that business shrink.

August 2001

CEO Jeff Skilling, a major force in transforming the company into a global energy trader, resigns.

Oct. 16, 2001

Enron announces a third-quarter loss of $16.8 million.

Oct. 31, 2001

Enron announces that the SEC has launched a formal investigation into the company.

Nov. 8, 2001

Enron discloses that it has overstated earnings by $586 million since 1997.

Nov. 29, 2001

Dynergy buyout deal collapses.

Dec. 2, 2001

Enron files for Chapter 11 bankruptcy protection.

Jan. 9, 2002

Justice Department announces it has begun a criminal investigation into Enron.

Jan. 10, 2002

Arthur Andersen, Enron's auditor, says it destroyed some Enron documents.

Insiders Cash Out

Company executives sold millions of dollars worth of stock before Enron collapsed. Some of the top beneficiaries, from sales between May 2000 and August 2001:

Chairman Key Lay
$37,683,887

Jeff Skilling,
Former CEO
$14,480,755

Lou Pai,
Unit CEO
$62,936,552

Raw End of the Deal

Many employees lost their savings because Enron restricted them from selling their 401(k) company stock until it hit 26 cents.

$80 $70 $60 $50 $40 $30 $20 $10

1994   1998   1999   2000   2001

There is no doubt that some measure of reform and some measure of retribution will be exacted in response to Enron's collapse; public outrage demands it. Accounting reforms, further securities regulation, and some protections for employee pension plans seem certain. But the underlying causes that fueled the scandal may go unheeded. "The climate of inadequate regulatory controls that fostered the Enron debacle in the first place is likely to weather this storm, as other wealthy corporate interests step into Enron's void to finance the next election season." (*Multinational Monitor*, January/February 2002.)

Discussion Questions

1. Identify the W, P, and H (as outlined in Chapter 2) of the two models of corporate responsibility described in the Enron case study.

2. Identify and discuss the W, P, and H in Enron's collapse. Who was affected? In pursuit of what ends? What values were at stake? How might responsible corporate management have responded differently?

3. Put yourself in the position of the various stakeholders and consider your rights and obligations:

    a. An Enron executive in the late 1990s. How might you have responded to the situation had you known of it?

    b. An Enron employee during the same time period. What are your expectations for management? What do you expect in return for your loyalty as an employee?

    c. A shareholder of Enron. What are your expectations of management? How much information is an owner of a public company entitled to receive?

    d. The other Enron stakeholders?

Sheryl Kaiser, J.D. teaches Business Law and Ethics and Corporate Social Responsibility

THE AFTERMATH OF ENRON AND WHAT LIES AHEAD

The swift and messy collapse of Enron, at the time one of the most admired companies in the world, was just the first wave in a tsunami of financial scandals that would deluge Wall Street in 2002 and beyond. Greater scrutiny of the books and records of public companies in the wake of its demise revealed that the accounting artifice and financial reporting chicanery employed by Enron and its accountants was common practice among large US companies; and that self-dealing and undisclosed self-enrichment was rife among corporate executives. Several of the largest, oldest, and most respected companies and firms revealed massive fraud—many of these resulting in the bankruptcy of the companies involved. Like Enron, most of these corporate disasters left employees, shareholders, and creditors holding the bag once again.

Among the more noteworthy scandals in the nearly 600 SEC investigations opened in 2002 (a record year):

Conflicts of Interest in Public Accounting

Along with the demise of Enron came the demise of Arthur Andersen, one of the oldest and most revered public accounting firms in the country. Andersen's dual role of auditor and consultant compromised its ability to provide independent judgment and an objective evaluation of the company for its public investors. Reports indicate that at the time of Enron's collapse, nearly three-quarters of the revenue generated by all of the largest public accounting firms consisted of fees for nonauditing services to their customers. Even with the passage of the Sarbanes-Oxley Act (discussed further below and see box), the largest firms continue to generate nearly half of their fees from nonauditing services.

Improper Accounting—Improperly Booking Expenses, Frontloading Income, Off-Balance Sheet Partnerships

Worldcom revealed that it had improperly booked close to $4 billion of routine expenses as capital expenditures, giving rise to a restatement of earnings and an Enron-like implosion of the company. The number was later adjusted upward to at least $8 billion. The company sought bankruptcy protection in late 2002, the largest

ever in US history. In 2003, it renamed itself MCI.

On the other side of the balance sheet, many companies used Enron's mark-to-market accounting approach to book uncertain revenues as current income. The practice was widespread throughout the energy sector. Halliburton, during the time the company was headed by Vice-President Dick Cheney, used this approach to report more than $100 million of frontloaded income. AOLTimeWarner was also forced into a major restatement of earnings on account of this practice.

The wide net of involvement in Enron's special purpose entities (SPEs), the off-balance-sheet partnerships, also revealed this practice to be commonplace. In addition, the involvement and complicity of the major banks in these transactions—JP Morgan, Citigroup, Merrill Lynch, Credit Suisse First Boston and others—has left them exposed to liability.

Insider Transactions

Insider trading was rampant at Enron and elsewhere at the turn of this century. At Imclone, a pharmaceutical manufacturer, CEO Sam Waksal and family and friends were indicted for selling company shares before announcing an adverse FDA ruling. Homemaking guru and Waksal buddy, Martha Stewart, was also implicated in insider transactions in Imclone stock. Insider trading investigations were legion in 2002 and reached the highest office in the land. President George W. Bush was investigated by the SEC for sales of more than 200,000 shares of Harken, where he served as a director. Company insiders had earlier been warned by Harken's outside attorneys to not sell given their inside negative information about the company.

Loans to corporate officers and directors also proliferated. More than three-quarters of the top 1500 companies engaged in the practice of providing insiders with interest-free or otherwise preferential loans from the corporate funds. Many of these were never repaid. At the time of Worldcom's implosion, CEO Bernie Ebbers had more than $400 million in outstanding company loans. Other companies that suffered financial disasters in 2002 had similar practices: at Adelphia,

CEO John Rigas and family borrowed more than $263 million from the company, and Dennis Kozlowski at Tyco had $120 million outstanding.

Other, subtler forms of self-enrichment by corporate management were also employed. A practice known as IPO "spinning" involved investment bankers giving preferential purchase options for lucrative initial public offerings to chief executives in exchange for their company's business. While the legality of such transactions is questionable, the ethics of it are not. Rewards or opportunities that derive from the company belong to and should accrue to the benefit of all of the shareholders, not the inside managers.

The foregoing examples uncover the mere tip of the iceberg of financial scandals occurring or investigated just in the year 2002. Further revelations regarding the Enron gang continue weekly and most of these financial disasters continue to be the subject of ongoing investigation and a multitude of civil litigation. And the investigatory net continues to widen. In 2003, New York Attorney General Eliot Spitzer and his small team of prosecutors charged an egregious abuse of trust by securities analysts in selling stocks they believed unworthy to unwitting clients (also known as "putting lipstick on this pig"). The case resulted in a landmark settlement by the securities industry of $1.4 billion in fines (a mere fraction of the profits they made on these transactions).

TIME Magazine declared 2002 as "The Year of the Whistleblower" and named three such women—Sherron Watkins of Enron, Cynthia Cooper of Worldcom, and Colleen Rowley of the FBI—as its Person of the Year. In the summer of 2002, Congress passed landmark legislation to regulate some of the areas of greatest corporate abuse in the Sarbanes-Oxley Act (aka "Sarbox" –see box for highlights of its provisions). Though well-intentioned, it is not yet clear how effective the legislation will be in curbing corporate abuses. The SEC is charged with promulgating the regulations to implement the Act, and its proposals have generally been weak interpretations of the legislative mandate. Much of the watering-down may be due to the practical limitations of the agency, which is generally underfunded, understaffed, and outgunned by those it is charged with overseeing.

You may be asking "Why are we reading about these securities law issues in Chapter Two on Business Ethics instead of Chapter 40 on Securities and Investor Protection?" (If you're paying attention, you should be asking that!). The discussion is here is because many of the corporate abuses that led to this avalanche of financial disasters were not technically prohibited by law at the time they were undertaken. They may not have been prudent or diligent and many of them were purely self-interested and disloyal to the company; nonetheless, tax and securities regulations, accounting standards, and other regulatory schemes did not specifically prohibit many of the actions taken. They were clearly unethical, but arguably legal. This is where business ethics and ethical dilemmas are most prevalent. Where the law ends or does not yet speak to regulate conduct is where ethics plays its most important role in corporate decision-making. If the players in these financial scams had considered their actions from an ethical perspective, many of them may not have occurred. Some of the largest corporate collapses can be attributed to departments and individuals within the organization pushing the legal envelope at each level of the process—not technically violating any written rule, but surely the violating the spirit of their fiduciary obligations to the corporation—with a cumulative result way beyond the bounds of law and ethics.

Discussion Questions

1. Revisit the discussion questions in the Enron case study. Consider them in the context of the other types of corporate abuse that occurred in 2002 and beyond.

2. How might an ethical business avoid these types of abuses?

SARBANES-OXLEY ACT OF 2002

Corporate Fraud Accountability Act of 2002
White-Collar Crime Penalty Enhancement
Act of 2002
Corporate and Criminal Fraud Accountability
Act of 2002

"To protect investors by improving the accuracy and reliability of corporate disclosures made pursuant to the securities laws, and for other purposes."

Summary of Key Provisions

Establishes the Public Company Accounting Oversight Board

Creates a 5-member board to oversee public accounting firms and audits of public companies, which will operate under the authority and supervision of the SEC. Heretofore, the accounting profession was essentially only self-policed. The Board is prohibited from having more than two CPAs as members; and all of its members serve full-time and exclusively on the Board. Board imposition of sanctions and penalties are limited to cases of intentional misconduct or repeated instances of negligent conduct

Bars auditors from performing consulting and other services for an audit client to ensure independence

Prohibits contemporaneous audit and non-audit representation; requires that all audit and non-audit services be pre-approved by independent audit committee (see below); and mandates audit partner rotation every five years. Requires proactive disclosure to the audit committee of all critical or controversial positions or practices used in the audit, and addresses the revolving door problem by prohibiting audits if former employees of auditor serve as senior executives of the issuer

Requires only independent members of the board of directors serve on the corporate audit committee

An independent director is defined as one who, other than in their capacity as a corporate director of the issuer, accepts no consulting, advisory, or other compensatory fee from the issuer, nor any affiliate or subsidiary of the issuer

Requires certification of financial statements and other financial filings by the corporate CEO and CFO

Certification includes statements regarding: the veracity of the report; that it fairly represents the financial condition and obligations of the company; that the certifiers are responsible for ensuring that they have received all material information to which they are certifying; and that they have disclosed to the auditors and audit committee any internal control deficiencies or potential fraud. The Act provides for criminal penalties including 10-20 years imprisonment for knowing violations of this provision [An attempt by the Senate to include Federal income tax returns among the reports requiring certification by the CEO failed]

Forfeiture of CEO and CFO compensation following violation of securities laws

Where the violation leads to an accounting restatement, CEO and CFO bonuses and compensation may be forfeited

Bars further service as officer or director by corporate wrongdoers

The standard is whether the person's conduct demonstrates "unfitness" to serve (the standard under prior law was "substantial unfitness")

Prohibits insider trades during pension fund blackout periods

Specifically in response to the Enron problem—if the pension plan cannot trade, then neither can corporate executives and board members. Provides for disgorgement of profits realized in such trades

Attorneys as internal whistle blowers

Requires the SEC to establish rules for attorneys who practice before the SEC to report securities or financial violations or breaches of fiduciary duty to:

first, the CEO or chief legal counsel of the company, then, failing a response, to the audit committee of the board of directors of the company

Requires enhanced disclosure of off-balance-sheet transactions

Standard for disclosure includes those items and relationships having a "material effect" on the financial status of an issue. Pro forma information must be reconcilable with the actual financial condition of the issuer under GAAP

Prohibits personal loans by corporation to its officers and directors

Addresses a rampant problem of corporate management self-dealing with corporate funds—from Bernie Ebbers at Worldcom ($400 million) to George W. Bush at Harkin (a couple hundred thousand dollars)

Requires immediate disclosure of insider trades by senior management, directors, and principal stockholders

Electronic notification of the trades must be made within two days of the transaction (previously, public disclosure could take up to 13 months)

Directs the establishment of regulatory control over securities analysts potential conflicts of interest

Requires the SEC to adopt rules to address the conflicts of interest inherent in firms that engage in both securities analysis and investment banking

Creates criminal penalties for the wrongful destruction of documents

Presumably, specifically in response to Arthur Andersen's actions in the Enron case. Imposes a five-year retention period for audit and work papers and directs the SEC to develop an industry-standard document retention policy.

Provides anti-retaliation protection for corporate whistle blowers

Prohibits retaliation against an employee who assists or participates in a regulatory investigation of corporate wrongdoing or a shareholder suit for corporate wrongdoing

Enhances criminal penalties for white-collar crimes, including conspiracy to commit fraud

A variety of enhancements and directions for other agencies to consider penalty and sanction enhancements are included in the Act.

Studies and reports inquiring into the cause and nature of corporate accountability and transparency problems

Primarily to be undertaken by the SEC and/or the GAO, the Act requires studies on, among other things: the consolidation of the accounting industry; the role of credit rating agencies in the securities market; the number and nature of securities laws violators active in the industry; and the role of investment banks and financial advisors in financial manipulation and misrepresentation—specifically with respect to Enron and Global Crossing, but not limited to those corporate frauds.

Summary	
Business Ethics And Social Responsibility	**Business ethics**—an application of ethics to the special problems and opportunities experienced by business people. **Social Responsibility of business** consists of the collection of expectations that the community imposes on its firms
Business Law And Business Ethics	Business ethics builds on business law. The law both affects and is affected by evolving ethical patterns. But business law provides only a floor for business ethics, communicating the minimally acceptable course of action.
Theories Of Business Ethics	**Consequentialism**—ethical approach that considers the consequences (i.e., harms and benefits) of making a particular decision. **Deontology**—ethical approach that recognizes certain actions as right or wrong, regardless of the consequences. **Virtue Ethics**—ethical approach that encourages individuals to develop virtues (e.g., courage, truthfulness, etc) that guide behavior. **Ethics of Care**—ethical approach that ethical behavior is determined by actions that care for and maintain human relationships.

The WPH Framework For Business Ethics	**Who are the relevant stakeholders?** Determines which interests (consumers, employees, managers, owners) are being pushed and prodded.
	
	What are the ultimate purposes of the decision? Determines which values (freedom, efficiency, security, and justice) are being upheld by the decision
	
	Using classical ethical guidelines for understanding how to make ethical decisions
	
	    The Golden Rule—Do unto others as you would have done unto you.
	
	    Public Disclosure Test—If the public knew about this decision, how would you decide?
	
	    Universalization Test—What the world would be like were our decision emulated by everyone else?

Review Questions and Case Problems

1. Aileen Morris was an employee at a Kauszer's convenience store. Convenience Management Services, Inc. (CMSI) own Krauszer's. While working at the store, Aileen, a mother of nine children, was shot to death by a robber. The store was located in a dangerous area and had a history of robberies and criminal attacks. Despite the dangerous location, the store did not have an alarm, a security camera, or an immediate connection to the police. According to the plaintiffs, the absence of these security precautions created a dangerous environment. CMSI argued that they had no duty to protect Morris because the robbery and shooting was unforeseeable. How far do you think a company should go to protect employees? Do you think that CMSI was responsible for the shooting? Why or why not? *Morris v. Krauszer's Food Stores,* 693 A. 2d 510 (1997).

2. Shiman and Krementz were both companies in the business of manufacturing jewelry. The companies merged, and Krementz agreed to take responsibility for all of Shiman's property, liabilities, and obligations. Shiman used a punch press machine to manufacture certain pieces of jewelry. While Arsenio Vega was using the machine, the belt on the machine broke, and Arsenio's fingers and hand were crushed. Vega argued that Shiman should have warned Krementz about the dangerous machine and that Shiman should have placed warning labels on the machine. Who do you think was responsible for Vega's injury? Did Shiman have a duty to warn Krementz about the potentially dangerous machine? *Vega v. Standard Mach. Co.,* 675 A. 2d. 1194 (1996).

3. Deborah Vargo-Adams was employed as a distribution clerk for the U.S. Postal Service. Adams was regularly absent from work and had been reprimanded and suspended several times. After receiving a notice of removal, Adams filed a grievance claiming that she suffered from migraine headaches and was frequently unable to go to work. The Postal Service reinstated Adams under the condition that she provide them with medical documentation of her illness and acceptable evidence for future absences when required. At first, Adams complied with the condi-

tions. During an eight-month period, Adams was absent without leave more than two days, was late to work seven times, and was absent nine days. On each of these occasions she provided notice and excuses for her absences. Seven of her notices were rejected because her supervisor claimed that they lacked the proper documentation. After receiving the rejections, Adams stopped submitting her written excuses, but continued to verbally notify her supervisor that the absences were related to her illness. She continued to have an attendance problem and was terminated in 1995. Do you think the Postal Services should have made a better attempt to accommodate her "serious health condition?" Did the termination constitute a "wrongful discharge?" *Vargo-Adams v. U.S. Postal Service,* 992 F. Supp. 939 (1998).

4. Grand Central Partnership Social Services Corporation is a not-for-profit organization. The organization provides counseling, referrals, clothing, showers, and mail access for the homeless. Additionally, the organization implemented a program known as Pathways to Employment (PTE), designed to assist in the development of vocational skills. The program provided workshops covering topics such as interviewing skills and resume writing. Participants in the PTE program were assigned to five areas: maintenance, food services, administration, outreach, and recycling. Each of these tasks related to the overall operation and goals of the Center. Individuals participating in the PTE program were required to participate forty hours per week and were paid between $40 and $60 dollars per week. The plaintiffs, predominantly homeless and jobless individuals, alleged that the wages paid by Grand Central were below minimum wage and therefore unlawful. Grand Central argued that participants in the PTE program were trainees, not employees, and that the participants were learning valuable job readiness skills. Do you think that this is an appropriate distinction? What ethical issues should be considered? *Archie v. Grand Central Partnership,* 997 F. Supp. 504 (1998).

5. Marilyn Engstrom had worked as a cashier at Kinney's garage since 1976. In 1993, the company implemented a policy requiring the cashiers to wear a uniform. As part of the uniform, employees were required to wear a bow tie. Kinney's vice-president, Michael Beck, noticed that Engstrom was not wearing the bow tie and sent her home from work. Engstrom, a Jehovah's Witness, said that her religious beliefs prevented her from wearing the bow tie. Beck informed Engstrom that she could substitute for the bow tie a sash, ribbon, or scarf. Though informed of the alternatives, Engstrom reported to work the next day wearing the bow tie. She was informed that her work hours, which had been 11:00 a.m. to 7 p.m. for the past three years, were changed to 12:30 p.m. to 8:30 p.m. She called in sick to work the next day and informed her supervisor that she could not work under the new schedule. Her schedule was not changed, and two days later Engstrom failed to show up for work. Beck notified Engstrom and her union that Kinney considered her position abandoned. Engstrom argued that her suspension and schedule change constituted religious discrimination.

Do you agree with her? Do you think that Beck "reasonably accommodated" her religious needs? Why or why not? *Engstrom v. Kinney System, Inc.,* 661 N.Y.S. 2d 610 (1997).

6. Donna Reeves began working for Dairy Queen in 1990. She was rewarded for good performance by pay raises and promotions. Donna had been diagnosed with high blood pressure in the early 1980s. Symptoms of her health condition included dizziness, shortness of breath, headaches, heat sensitivity, and flushing. Donna's co-workers informed her manager, Bill Barber, that Donna had experienced dizziness while climbing on a table to reach an item. Barber also noticed her frequent shortness of breath. Though he had never spoken with Reeves or her doctor about her medical condition, Barber terminated Reeves in 1994. He provided her with a reference letter and stated, "We had to terminate Donna Reeves employment at the Columbia Falls Dairy Queen due to health reasons. Donna worked here for 5-1/2 years and was an excellent employee, but we felt that it was for her own well-being that we let her go. Without going into great detail, it was a combination of having high blood pressure and working in a position as a fast order cook working under conditions of pressure, stress, and heat. We could see her health deteriorating and I decided this would be best for Donna." Do you agree with Barber's decision? Do you think that he could have accommodated her illness? *Reeves v. Dairy Queen, Inc.,* 953 P. 2d 703 (1998).

7. Doctors diagnosed Leo Guilbeault with lung cancer. He had been smoking the same brand, Camel cigarettes, since 1951. Guilbeault filed a complaint against the manufacturer of Camel cigarettes, R.J. Reynolds Tobacco Co. According to the Guilbeault, Reynolds failed to adequately warn consumers about the dangers of smoking. Prior to 1970, Camel cigarettes were sold without a warning label. After the Labeling Act of 1969, Reynolds began to put warning labels on packages of cigarettes. Guilbeault believes that Reynolds knew about the adverse health consequences of smoking before 1970, and therefore, Reynolds had a duty to warn consumers of these consequences. Do you agree with his argument? Should Reynolds have warned consumers earlier? *Guilbeault v. R.J. Reynolds Tobacco Co.,* 44 Fed. R. Serv. 3d 124 (1999).

8. Plaintiffs and providers of health care benefits, alleged that the defendants, manufacturers of cigarettes and smokeless tobacco, conspired, to market their products in such a way as to deceive the public about the addictive nature of their products. According to the plaintiffs, the defendants did not provide the public with adequate information about the adverse health problems associated with tobacco use. Further, the plaintiffs argued that the manufacturers actually intended to create and sustain cigarette addictions. Do you agree with the plaintiffs? Do you think that the cigarette companies had an ethical obligation to inform the public of the addictive nature of their product? Why or why not? *Oregon Laborers-Employers Health & Welfare Trust Fund v. Philip Morris Inc.,* 188 F.R.D. 365 (1998).

9. Erby Givens, the owner of a four-wheeled Honda all-terrain vehicle, allowed twelve-year-old Michael Ladd to drive the vehicle. Givens had seen children driving the vehicle in Honda advertisements, and he assumed that it was safe for children to drive the vehicle. While driving the vehicle in his parent's backyard, Michael lost control and crashed into a utility pole. He hit the pole head-on and was paralyzed. Michael's parents brought a suit against Mr. Givens and Honda. They argued that the vehicle was unreasonably dangerous, that the safety warnings for the vehicle were inadequate, and that Honda had misrepresented the vehicle through advertising. Do you think Honda's decision to use children in advertisements was irresponsible and unethical? Should they have used stronger safety warnings? *Ladd v. Honda Motor Co.,* 939 S.W. 2d 83 (1996).

10. Gordon Gundaker owned a real estate company. He worked on commission and sold homes in a new subdivision, Turnberry Place. Directly adjacent to Turnberry Place was an area known as Bliss Ellisville site. The site was listed on the Missouri Department of Natural Resource's confirmed Abandoned or Uncontrolled Hazardous Waste Sites Registry and also on the Federal Superfund National Priorities List. Fences with warning signs surrounded the area, but the landscaping in Turnberry Place kept these signs from being visible. When potential buyers asked about the presence of toxic chemicals, Gundaker presented them with scientific reports that contained the results of chemical hazard testing. The results were difficult for a lay person to understand, but Gundaker explained that Turnberry Place had been given "a clean bill of health." The brochure described Turnberry Place as "a park-like setting or rolling streets, woods, and dramatic privacy." Those who purchased lots in Turnberry Place were not aware of the neighboring hazardous waste sites until after purchasing their homes. One resident recalled seeing people walking through the site wearing full body suits and helmets and wearing air breathing equipment. The residents filed an action against Gundaker for fraudulent concealment, fraudulent misrepresentation, and negligent misrepresentation. Gundaker stated that an attorney advised him that he was not obligated to disclose information to potential buyers about the sites. Do you think that Gundaker's actions were ethical? What information do you think should have been provided to potential buyers? *Haberstick v. Gordon,* 921 S.W. 2d 104 (1996).

11. Jana Battistoni suffered serious injuries and was paralyzed after diving into the shallow end of a friend's pool during a pool party. The pool did not contain any permanent warning labels or depth markers. Jana had been in the pool before and was familiar with the shallow and deep ends. However, she did not know that diving in the shallow end could result in serious injuries. Jana believed that a broken nose or chipped tooth were the worst injuries she could receive. Jana and her family brought suit against the manufacturers of the pool, Weatherking Products. Weatherking argued that the danger was open and obvious, and therefore, that they were not under any duty to warn potential pool users of the specific dangers associated with diving in the shallow end. Do you think that Weatherking should have provided more information and warnings? Did their decision not to provide warning labels or depth markers cause Jana's injuries? *Battistoni et al. v. Weatherking Products, Inc. et al.,* 676 A. 2d 890 (1996).

Assignment on the Internet

Many sites on the Internet provide ethical guidance for business managers. Many of them develop techniques and strategies for ethical reasoning that go beyond the scope of this single chapter on business ethics. The first part of your assignment is to find something on the Internet that goes beyond this chapter in terms of providing a new direction to your consideration of the ethics of a particular managerial decision. The second part of your assignment is in the spirit of critical thinking pervasive in this text. Explain how the information you found on the Internet would have been a worthwhile addition to this chapter, if only it absent length considerations.

On the Internet

http://www.depaul.edu/ethics/ & http://www.ethics.ubc.ca/resources/business/ *Provides a huge number of sites and suggestions about the pertinent issues in business ethics and the places where one can find answers to managerial ethical dilemmas.*

http://condor.depaul.edu/ethics/bizethics.html *Serves as an online magazine for those interested in business ethics. Each issue contains interviews with major business leaders, news features, and timely stories about business ethics in action. The magazine covers issues such as personnel management, truth in marketing, employee ownership, and environmental protection.*

http://www.nlx.com/journals/beq.htm *Provides full-text articles in the journal, Business Ethics Quarterly*

http://www.latinsynergy.org/latameri.htm *Considers the challenges of business ethics in Latin America.*

CHAPTER 3

Questionable Jurisdiction over Caterpillar

James Lewis, a resident of Kentucky, was injured while operating a bulldozer manufactured by Caterpillar, Inc. He filed suit against Caterpillar, a company incorporated in Delaware, with its principal place of business in Illinois, and also against the supplier of the bulldozer, Whayne Supply Company, which has its principal place of business in Kentucky. Lewis filed his case in the Kentucky state court on the following claims: defective manufacture, negligence, failure to warn, and breach of warranty. Lewis then entered into a settlement agreement with Whayne Supply Company, subject to acceptance by Wayne County's insurance carrier. Thereafter, Caterpillar filed a motion to exercise its right of removal (its right to move the case from the state to the federal court system), arguing that the federal court had jurisdiction over the case because Caterpillar and Lewis were from different states. Lewis disagreed with Caterpillar's contention. Instead, Lewis claimed that because he had not completed his settlement with Whayne, and since one of the defendants (Whayne) was also from the plaintiff's state of Kentucky, the federal courts did not have jurisdiction over the case.

The case was moved to the federal district court. Shortly thereafter, Lewis and Whayne finalized their settlement agreement, and the district court dismissed Whayne from the lawsuit. The trial was held and Caterpillar received a favorable judgment in the federal court. However, Lewis appealed the district court's decision on grounds that the district court did not have jurisdiction over the case. The Court of Appeals agreed with Lewis that Whayne was a defendant in the case at the time that Caterpillar moved the case from state to federal court, and therefore, the dispute should have been resolved in a state court because there was no diversity of citizenship to give the federal court jurisdiction over the case. Consequently, the appellate court vacated the decision made by the District Court. Caterpillar then appealed to the Supreme Court, asking the high court to overturn the appellate court's ruling and reinstate the decision made by the District Court.

1. *What factors determine whether a case is heard in the state or federal court system?*
2. *If you were a businessperson with Caterpillar, why would you prefer that a federal court have jurisdiction over the dispute with Lewis as opposed to a state court?*

The U.S. Legal System

Jurisdiction

Venue

The Structure of the Court System

Threshold Requirements

Steps in Civil Litigation

As the opening scenario illustrates, when a dispute arises, parties in this country do not simply go "to court." They sometimes have the right to choose between the state and the federal court systems. This chapter examines these two systems, as well as the procedures that must be followed when a civil case is tried.

Jurisdiction

The word "jurisdiction" comes from the Latin terms *juris*, which means law, and *diction,* which means to speak. So, the term can be literally translated to mean "to speak the law." You can think of the term as referring to the power of the courts to hear a case and render a decision that is binding on the parties before it. As you will soon learn, there are several types of jurisdiction a court must have to decide any particular case.

Original Versus Appellate Jurisdiction

Some courts have the power to hear and decide cases when they first enter the legal system. These courts are called "courts of **original** jurisdiction," or trial courts. These courts are places where the evidence is presented and witnesses testify. In the state court system, these courts are often called "courts of common pleas" or county courts. In the federal system, they are called district courts.

Courts that have the power to review previous judicial decision to determine whether the trial court erred in its decision are called courts of **appellate** jurisdiction. In these courts, there are no trials. Appellate judges will review transcripts of trial court proceedings, and may consider oral and written arguments from each side.

Jurisdiction over Persons and Property

In personam jurisdiction, or **jurisdiction over the person**, is the power of the court to render a decision affecting the rights of the specific person(s) before it. Generally, a court's power to exercise in personam jurisdiction is limited to a specific geographic region. In the state court system, a court's jurisdiction is usually limited to its borders, while the federal system, described in a later section, is divided into geographic districts, with each court's jurisdiction limited to the district in which it is located.

The court automatically acquires in personam jurisdiction over the party filing the lawsuit, the **plaintiff**, when that party files the case. The court acquires jurisdiction over the party being sued, the **defendant**, by giving them a copy of the complaint and a summons. The **complaint** contains the factual and legal basis for the lawsuit and the relief being sought. The **summons** is a court order that notifies the defendant of the lawsuit and how and when to respond to the complaint. The process of giving these documents to the defendant is called **service of process**.

The traditional method of service is **personal service**, which occurs when an officer of the court hands the summons and complaint to the defendant. Other types of service that are more common today include **residential service**, which occurs when the court representative leaves the summons and complaint with a responsible adult at the defendant's home, or service by certified or ordinary mail.

If the defendant is a corporation, service will generally be made to either the president of the corporation or to an agent of the corporation who has been appointed specifically to receive service. Most states require that corporations appoint an *agent* for service when they are incorporated. Once either the president or the agent has been served, the corporation is served.

The corporation is subject to personal jurisdiction in three locations: the state of its incorporation, where its main office is located, and where it conducts business.

As previously explained, a court's in personam jurisdiction is limited to those within a specific geographic region. Traditionally, courts from one state could not acquire in personam jurisdiction over out-of-state defendants unless those defendants could be served within the state in which the court was located. This restriction imposed a hardship on plaintiffs injured by out-of-state defendants who never returned to the plaintiff's state. To alleviate this problem, most states enacted *long-arm statutes* that enable the court to serve the defendant outside the state, as long as the defendant has sufficient minimum contacts within the state. The contacts required to grant jurisdiction vary from state to state, but most statutes deem acts such as committing a tort, or doing business in the state, as sufficient to allow the state to serve the defendant. In the Caterpillar case described in the opening scenario, the company's selling of a product in Kentucky that caused an injury in that state provided sufficient minimum contacts to allow the out-of-state company to be served by the Kentucky court.

Technology: The Internet and in Personam Jurisdiction

If a website can be visited from every state, is its sponsor subject to in personam jurisdiction in every state? As long as the sponsor is not conducting any business or trying to reach customers in a state, many courts have held that access to the website alone does not constitute sufficient contacts to grant in personam jurisdiction

A recent case that illustrating this point involved a lawsuit filed against an Indiana financial services company with a website that allowed customers in Illinois to access financial planning information from the company and contact it via e-mail. In that case, First Financial Resources (FFR), a California financial services organization with 150 offices located in twenty-eight states, filed an action in the federal district court in Indiana against First Financial Resources Corp. (FFRC), an Indiana corporation licensed to do business in Indiana and Kentucky.

Defendant FFRC filed a motion to dismiss, arguing that the court in Indiana did not have personal jurisdiction over it. The court dismissed the case for lack of personal jurisdiction, stating that even though the website could be contacted from anywhere, the company does not accept orders or requests for financial planning services directed to its site and does not enter into contracts on the site.[1] Thus, the defendant did not have the "continuous and systematic" contacts with the forum state sufficient to allow the court to exercise jurisdiction.[2] Merely providing information was not enough to subject the defendant to in personam jurisdiction.

However, the outcome of a case may be different if the potential defendant is actively trying to do business in multiple states via a website, as in *Minnesota v. Granite Gate Resorts*.[3] In that case a Minnesota Court of Appeals found a Nevada provider of Internet gaming services subject to in personam jurisdiction in Minnesota in an action for consumer fraud. The website of the Nevada firm claimed to "provide sports fans with a legal way to bet on sporting events from anywhere in the world…24 Hours a Day!" The website provided consumers a toll-free number to call for more information. The phone contact said it was legal for Minnesota residents to place bets with the service. This active solicitation of Minnesota consumers was found by the court to be sufficient minimum contacts for in personam jurisdiction.

[1] *First Financial Resources v. First Financial Resources Corp.,* 2000 WL 1693973 (ND Ill.).

[2] *Id.*

[3] 568 N.W. 2d 715 (1997).

If a defendant has property in a state, the plaintiff may bring action against the property instead of the owner. For example, if a Utah defendant owned land in Idaho on which taxes had not been paid, an Idaho court would have **in rem jurisdiction** over the property, and an in rem proceeding could order the property sold to pay the taxes.

Subject Matter Jurisdiction

Subject matter jurisdiction is the power of the court to hear certain kinds of cases. The United States has a dual court system comprised of both a state and a federal system. Subject matter jurisdiction determines which court system may hear the case. When asking which court system has subject matter jurisdiction, there are three possible answers. The case may fall under state jurisdiction, exclusive federal jurisdiction, or concurrent jurisdiction. Subject matter jurisdiction is an issue in the United States because of its unique dual court system. In most industrialized countries there is a unitary system, with courts located all over the country that hear cases arising under both national and local laws.

Exclusive Federal Jurisdiction

A very limited number of cases fall exclusively within the jurisdiction of the federal system and, therefore, must by heard in a federal court. The subject matter of these cases includes admiralty, bankruptcy, federal criminal prosecutions, lawsuits by one state against the other, claims against the United States, and claims arising under federal statutes that specify exclusive federal jurisdiction.

State Jurisdiction

The state court system has the broadest range of jurisdiction, as it has the power to hear all cases not within the exclusive jurisdiction of the federal court system. Most cases, therefore, fall under the state court's jurisdiction. Notice that the Caterpillar case described in the opening scenario fell under the state court's jurisdiction because its subject matter—product liability and negligence—did not fall under the exclusive jurisdiction of the federal courts.

Concurrent Federal Jurisdiction

Concurrent federal jurisdiction means that both the state and federal court systems have jurisdiction. Two types of cases have concurrent jurisdiction: *federal*

question and diversity of citizenship cases. Federal question cases require an interpretation of the United States Constitution, a federal statute, or a federal treaty. For example, a case in which the plaintiff alleges that a state's new campaign financing law violates her First Amendment free speech rights raises a federal question, and thus it falls under concurrent jurisdiction and could be filed in either state or federal court.

A *diversity of citizenship* case is one in which the plaintiff(s) and defendant(s) reside in different states. When the basis for federal jurisdiction is diversity of citizenship, there must also be an amount in excess of $75,000 in controversy. To determine the residence of a person for the purpose of establishing diversity of citizenship, courts consider the location of the party's home or residence. A business may be a resident of two states: the state of its incorporation and its principal place of business. So, in the opening scenario, Caterpillar was a resident of Delaware, where it was incorporated, and of Illinois, which is its primary place of business.

Diversity must be complete. In the opening scenario, Lewis argued that diversity was not complete because the supply company, the second defendant originally sued, was a resident of Kentucky, as was Lewis. The appellate court agreed with this argument, which is why they overturned the district court's decision for a lack of subject matter jurisdiction.

When a case involving concurrent jurisdiction is filed in state court, the defendant has a *right of removal*, which means that he is entitled to have the case transferred to federal court. Once the defendant files a motion with the state court asking to exercise his right of removal, the case must be transferred to federal court. Thus, if either party wants the case in federal court, it will be heard there. The plaintiff puts it in federal court by initially filing it there, and the defendants can move it there using the right of removal. Remember that Caterpillar used its right of removal to have the case against it moved to the federal district court.

When one party wishes to have the case tried in federal court and the other prefers state court, the issue of whether the case is within the concurrent jurisdiction of the federal courts may arise, as we see in the Gafford case.

Case 3-1

Gafford
v.
General Electric Co.
United States Court of Appeals
997 F. 2d 150 (1993)

*P*laintiff Carol Gafford filed a gender discrim-ination action in state court against defendant General Electric Co. The defendant filed a motion to exercise its right of removal based on diversity of citizenship and the case was transferred to the federal district court over the plaintiff's objection. The trial was held and plain-tiff lost. She appealed, arguing that the case should not have been tried in federal court because there was insufficient evidence of the complete diversity of citizenship.

JUDGE JONES

Gafford takes issue with the district court's determination that diversity of citizenship among the par-ties was complete. Gafford is a citizen of Kentucky. For purposes of determining diversity jurisdiction, a corporation can be a citizen of two states: (1) its state of incorporation; and (2) the state of its principal place of business. GE is incorporated in New York.

What is disputed is whether GE's principal place of business is in Kentucky. Gafford basically argues that, given the size of the GE facility in Kentucky which encompasses over 9,000 employees, "[i]t would be reasonable to conclude that Jefferson County, Kentucky is a principal place of business for General Electric."

By common sense and by law, a corporation can have only one principal place of business for pur-poses of establishing its state of citizenship. GE submitted evidence to the court that Schenectady, New York, is its principal place of business, where basic corporate and personnel records are maintained.

"The question of a corporation's principal place of business is essentially one of fact, to be determined on a case-by-case basis, taking into account such factors as the character of the corporation, its purposes, the kind of business in which it is engaged, and the situs of its operations."

In making this determination, courts have followed various approaches, or "tests." The "nerve center" test emphasizes the situs of corporate decision-making authority and overall control. The "corporate activ-ities"/"place of activity" test emphasizes the location or production activities or service activities. These tests are not mutually exclusive.

Where a corporation carries on its business in a number of states and no one state is clearly the state in which its business is principally conducted, the state in which the substantial part of its business is trans-acted and from which centralized general supervision of its business is exercised is the state in which it has its principal place of business.

Since General Electric is neither incorporated nor has its principle [sic] place of business in Kentucky, it is not a citizen of the state for the purposes of diversity.

AFFIRMED IN FAVOR OF THE DEFENDANT.

1. Critical Thinking: Why did the court not find Kentucky to be GE's principal place of busi-ness, despite the fact that approximately 9,000 workers were employed there?

2. Ethical Decision Making: The Court in this instance may appear to be making a decision with no ethical content. However, ask, yourself: What stakeholders in GE would prefer that Kentucky be deemed the principal place of business for General Electric?

Venue

Once a case is in the proper court system, **venue** determines which of the trial courts in that system can hear the case. Venue, prescribed by statute in each state, is a matter of geographic location. It is typically appropriate in the county in which the plaintiff or defendant resides. If the case involves property, venue is also appropriate in the county where that property is located. Finally, if some incident is the focus of the case, venue exists in the county where the dispute occurred. The plaintiff initially chooses from among the courts where venue is appropriate.

When the location of the court in which the plaintiff filed the case is a hardship or inconvenience to one of the parties, or the defendant believes it will be difficult to select an unbiased jury in that county, the defendant may request that the case be moved by filing a motion for a change of venue. The judge has the discretion to grant or deny the motion.

Now that we have explained the legal definitions of jurisdiction and venue, we will examine the structure of the state and federal court systems. In examining these structures, remember that not all countries have a dual court system, as the global context box at the end of this section illustrates.

The Structure of the Court System

The U.S. legal system has two parallel court structures, one federal and one state system. Once a case is filed in a system, it will stay in that system, except for appeals to the United States Supreme Court.

The Federal Court System

The federal court system consists of three main parts: the trial courts, intermediate appellate courts, and the court of last resort. This system is diagrammed in Exhibit 3-1.

EXHIBIT 3-1

The Courts of the Federal System

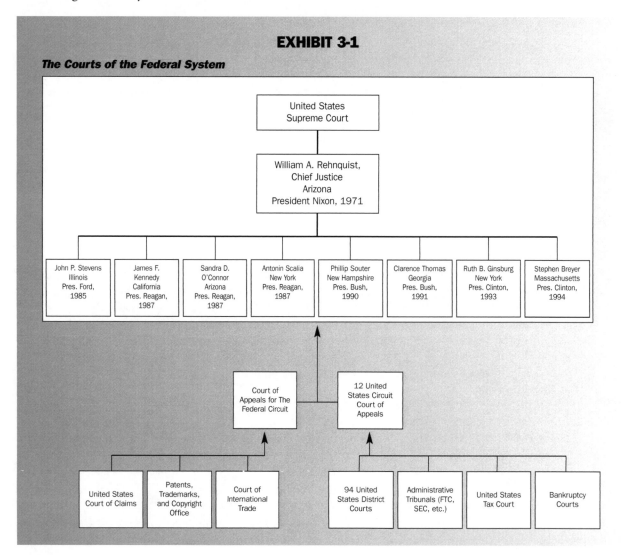

Federal Trial Courts

In the federal court system, the trial courts, or courts of original jurisdiction, are the *United States District Courts*. The United States is divided into ninety-six districts and each district has at least one *trial court of general jurisdiction*. Courts of *general jurisdiction* have the power to hear a wide range of cases and are not limited in the types of remedies they can grant. All cases heard in the federal system are filed in these courts, except those cases for which Congress has established special *trial courts of limited jurisdiction.*

These trial courts are limited by the subject matter of cases they can hear. The types of cases for which these special trial courts have been established include: bankruptcy cases, claims against the U.S. government, and copyright, patent, and trademark cases. In an extreme-ly limited number of cases, the U.S. Supreme Court also functions as a trial court of limited jurisdiction. Such cases include controversies between two or more states and suits against foreign ambassadors.

Intermediate Courts of Appeal

The *U.S. Circuit Courts of Appeal* constitute the second level of courts in the federal system. The United States is divided into twelve geographic areas, including the District of Columbia, each of which has a circuit court of appeals. Each circuit court of appeals hears appeals from all of the district courts located in its geographic area. There is also a Federal Circuit Court of Appeals, which hears appeals from the administrative agencies. Exhibit 3-2 illustrates where the district and circuit court borders are drawn.

EXHIBIT 3-2

The Districts and Circuits of the Federal Court System

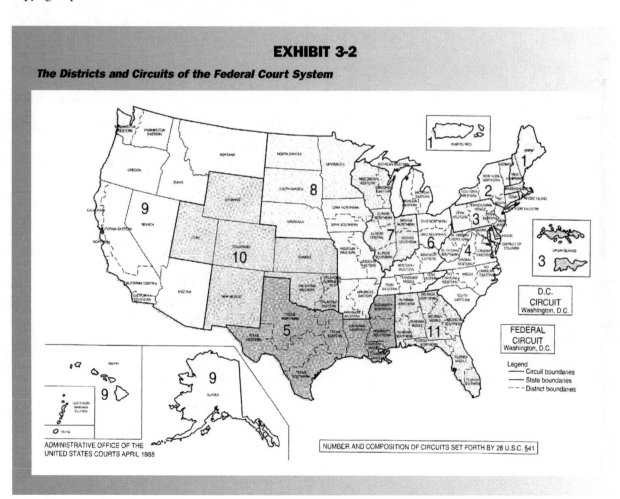

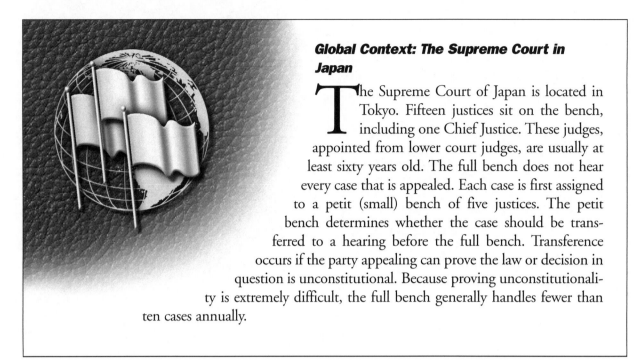

Global Context: The Supreme Court in Japan

The Supreme Court of Japan is located in Tokyo. Fifteen justices sit on the bench, including one Chief Justice. These judges, appointed from lower court judges, are usually at least sixty years old. The full bench does not hear every case that is appealed. Each case is first assigned to a petit (small) bench of five justices. The petit bench determines whether the case should be transferred to a hearing before the full bench. Transference occurs if the party appealing can prove the law or decision in question is unconstitutional. Because proving unconstitutionality is extremely difficult, the full bench generally handles fewer than ten cases annually.

The Court of Last Resort

The U.S. Supreme Court is the final appellate court in the federal system. The high court is made up of nine justices, all of whom have lifetime appointments. In a limited number of instances, the U.S. Supreme Court also hears cases from the court of last resort in a state system, and occasionally functions as a trial court. The structure and functioning of the U.S. Supreme Court system differs from those in other countries, as the above Global Context box illustrates.

State Court Systems

There is no uniform state court structure because each state has devised its own court system. Most states, however, follow a general structure similar to that of the federal court system.

State Trial Courts

In state court systems, most cases are originally filed in the *trial court of general jurisdiction*. As in the federal system, state trial courts of general jurisdiction are those that have the power to hear all the cases that would be tried in the state court system, except those cases for which special trial courts of limited jurisdiction have been established. Trial courts of general jurisdiction are distributed throughout each state, usually by county. The names of these courts vary by state, but are usually called *courts of common pleas* or *county courts*. In some states, these courts may have specialized divisions, such as domestic relations or probate.

Most states also have trial courts of limited jurisdiction. These courts are usually limited in the remedies that they may grant. A common court of limited jurisdiction in most states is the small claims court, which may not grant damage awards in excess of specified amounts. Some courts of limited jurisdiction are limited to certain types of cases, such as traffic cases. It is difficult to generalize about these courts because they vary so much from state to state. The main distinction between trial courts of general and limited jurisdiction, however, is that the former hear almost all types of cases that are filed in the state system and are unlimited in the remedies they can provide; whereas the latter hear only a particular type of case or may award only limited remedies.

Intermediate Courts of Appeal

Intermediate courts of appeal, analogous to the federal circuit courts of appeal, exist in approximately half the states. These courts usually have broad jurisdiction, hearing appeals from courts of general and limited jurisdictions, as well as from state administrative agencies. The names of these courts also vary by state. They may be called *courts of appeal* or *superior courts*.

Courts of Last Resort

In almost all cases filed in the state court system, the last appeal is to the state court of last resort. This court is frequently called the *supreme court*, although in some states it is called the *court of appeals*. In approximately half of the states, it is the second court to which an appeal can be made; in the remaining states, it is the only appellate court.

Now that we have explored the structure of the federal and state court system, we want to examine the civil litigation process. Before tracing the steps of the litigation process, however, we need to examine the threshold requirements that cases must meet before being litigated.

Threshold Requirements

There are three threshold requirements that a case must meet before it can be litigated. The purpose of these requirements is to ensure that only cases that really require adjudication come before the courts. The three requirements are: standing; case or controversy; and ripeness.

Standing

One who has standing is the person who has the legal right to bring the action. To have standing, one needs to be personally affected by the outcome of a case. Thus, if your uncle has a contract with a landscaper to mow his grass every week, and he fails to show up half the time or does a poor job, only your uncle has standing to sue the landscaper. You cannot sue on behalf of your uncle because you do not have a personal stake in the outcome.

A personal stake in the outcome is thought to be necessary to stimulate the plaintiff to put forth the best possible case. One area where standing requirements

Global Context: Federal and Cantonal Law in Switzerland

Switzerland is one of the many countries that has a unitary rather than a dual court system. Switzerland is a confederation of twenty-three individual entities, like states, that are called cantons. These cantons all apply their individual cantonal law, but they also apply the federal laws and codes.

Swiss cantons differ not only in the local laws they apply, but also in the official language of the court. Sixteen are predominantly German-speaking. Six are French-speaking and one is mostly Italian. Each state has developed its own judicial structure and procedures.

The German-speaking cantons have the most extensive court structure. Justices of the peace preside with limited jurisdiction. Each canton has a court that is overseen by five judges. Appellate courts also have five judges, but there is only one court per canton. These cantons also have commercial courts with two professional judges and three "business" judges (individuals with professional business careers selected by the government to serve). Finally, there is the Court of Cassation, whose seven judges hear appeals from all sixteen German cantons.

The French- and Italian-speaking court structure is more simplified. Each canton has a justice of the peace, a court of first instance with a single judge and general jurisdiction, and one court of appeals. French-speaking cantons have a Court of Cassation, but the Italian one does not. Any appeals in the Italian-speaking canton are sent back to the appellate court and tried by a different panel of judges.

have been subject to frequent litigation has been when citizens groups have sued to enforce environmental laws. We can see how courts examine the standing issue by looking at the recent Supreme Court decision in *Friends of the Earth (FOE) v. Laidlow Environmental Services*[4]. In that case, FOE filed a lawsuit against Laidlow, alleging that the defendant had violated the Clean Water Act by discharging excessive amounts of pollutants into the river. The defendants lost and were assessed a penalty of $405,800, payable to the U.S. Treasury.

In addressing the standing issue when this case was ultimately appealed to the Supreme Court, Justice Ginsburg cited three factors that were needed for standing: (1) the plaintiff had an injury in fact that is concrete and actual or imminent; (2) the injury is fairly traceable to the challenged action of the defendant; and (3) it is likely that the injury will be redressed by a favorable decision.[5] In applying those criteria to the Laidlaw case, the court found that the first two criteria were satisfied by the members' testimony that they were now afraid to fish and swim in the river they used to enjoy. The final criteria was satisfied because even though they would not receive the money from the penalties themselves, they would benefit because the penalties would serve to deter the company and others from polluting the river in the future.[6]

Case or Controversy

The case or controversy requirement is another way of saying that the court will not render advisory opinions. Three criteria are considered necessary for a case or controversy to exist. First, there must be an adverse relationship between the parties. Second, actual or threatened actions of at least one of the parties must give rise to an actual legal dispute. Third, the courts must have the ability to render a decision that will resolve the dispute. In other words, the courts can only give final judgments that solve existing problems; they cannot provide rulings about hypothetical situations.

[4] 120 S. Ct. 923 (2000).
[5] *Id.*
[6] *Id.*

Ripeness

Closely linked to the case or controversy requirement is that of ripeness. This requirement means that the judge's decision must be capable of affecting the parties immediately. Usually ripeness arises when one party claims that the case is moot. In other words, there is no point in the court's hearing the case because no judgment can affect the situation between the parties.

In the Laidlaw case described in the section about standing, the defendants had also argued that the case was moot because by the time the case went to trial, the defendants had come into compliance with the requirements of its discharge permits. Therefore the only remedy left to the courts—imposition of a penalty to be paid to the government—would not affect the plaintiffs. The high court disagreed, and said that the fact that a defendant voluntarily ceases a practice once litigation has commenced does not deprive a federal court of its power to determine the legality of the practice; such a ruling would leave the defendant free to return to his old unlawful practices. Thus, the court found the case was not moot because imposing a penalty on the defendant would have an important deterrent effect.[7]

Steps in Civil Litigation

The U.S. litigation system is an adversary system, which means that a neutral fact finder—a judge—hears evidence and arguments presented by opposing sides and then makes an objective decision based on the facts and the law presented. Strict rules govern the types of evidence that the fact-finder may consider. Theoretically, the truth emerges in an adversary system because each side has an incentive to find all relevant evidence and make the strongest possible arguments supporting its position. Critics of this system, however, point out several drawbacks: the time and expense of a lawsuit, the damage a suit may cause to the litigating parties' relationship, and the unfair advantage to those with wealth and experience using the court system. As we examine the litigation process, consider the validity of these criticisms.

[7] *Id.*

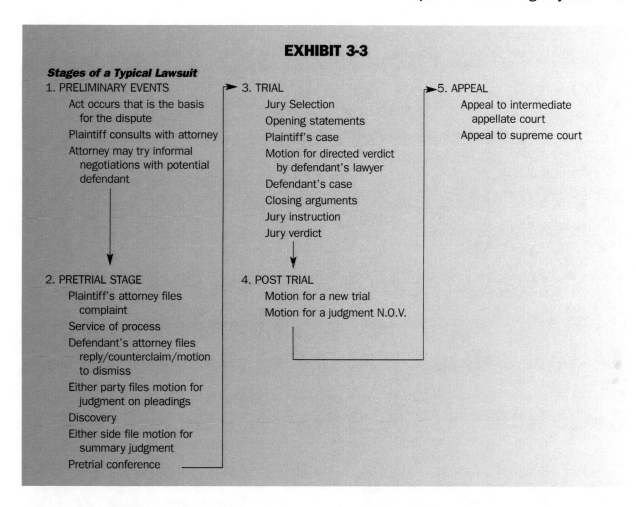

EXHIBIT 3-3

Stages of a Typical Lawsuit

1. PRELIMINARY EVENTS
   Act occurs that is the basis
   for the dispute
   Plaintiff consults with attorney
   Attorney may try informal
   negotiations with potential
   defendant

2. PRETRIAL STAGE
   Plaintiff's attorney files
   complaint
   Service of process
   Defendant's attorney files
   reply/counterclaim/motion
   to dismiss
   Either party files motion for
   judgment on pleadings
   Discovery
   Either side file motion for
   summary judgment
   Pretrial conference

3. TRIAL
   Jury Selection
   Opening statements
   Plaintiff's case
   Motion for directed verdict
   by defendant's lawyer
   Defendant's case
   Closing arguments
   Jury instruction
   Jury verdict

4. POST TRIAL
   Motion for a new trial
   Motion for a judgment N.O.V.

5. APPEAL
   Appeal to intermediate
   appellate court
   Appeal to supreme court

The Pretrial Stage

This section examines the procedure used in a civil case. The stages are outlined in Exhibit 3-3. The rules that govern such proceedings are called the *rules of civil procedure*. The Federal Rules of Civil Procedure apply in all federal courts. Each state has its own set of rules that are usually very similar to the Federal Rules of Civil Procedure. In addition, each court usually has its own set of local court rules that must be followed.

Informal Negotiations

The first stage in a business dispute is usually a discussion or negotiation among the parties to informally resolve the dispute. If the parties are unable to do so, one or the other(s) will seek the advice of an attorney.

Together, the attorney and the client may be able to resolve the dispute informally with the other party.

Pleadings

The first formal stage of a lawsuit is the *pleading stage*. Pleadings are papers filed in court and served on the opponent. The basic pleadings are the *complaint*, the *answer*, the *counterclaim*, and the *motion to dismiss*.

The plaintiff's attorney initiates a lawsuit by filing a *complaint* in the appropriate court. The complaint states the names of the parties to the action, the basis for the court's subject matter jurisdiction, the facts on which the party's claim is based, and the relief that the party is seeking. Exhibit 3-4 illustrates a typical complaint.

EXHIBIT 3-4

Complaint

THE COURT OF COMMON PLEAS
OF CLARK COUNTY, NEVADA

Bob Lyons and Sue Lyons, Plaintiffs

v.

Christine Collins, Defendant

COMPLAINT FOR NEGLIGENCE
Case No. _____

Now come the plaintiffs, Bob Lyons and Sue Lyons, and, for their complaint, allege as follows:

1. Plaintiffs, Bob Lyons and Sue Lyons, both of 825 Havercamp Street, are citizens of Clark County, in the state of Nevada, and defendant, Christine Collins, 947 Rainbow Ave., is a citizen of Clark County in the state of Nevada.
2. On May 1, 2001, the Defendant built a wooden hanging bridge across a stream that runs through the plaintiffs' property at 825 Havercamp Street.
3. Defendant negligently used ropes in the construction of the bridge that were not thick enough to sustain human traffic on the bridge.
4. At approximately 4:00 P.M., on May 20, 2001, the plaintiffs were attempting to carry a box of landscaping stones across the bridge when the ropes broke, and the bridge collapsed, causing plaintiffs to fall five feet down into the stream.
5. As a result of the fall, plaintiff, Bob Lyons, suffered a broken arm, a broken leg, and a skull fracture, incurring $160,000 in medical expenses.
6. As a result of the fall, plaintiff, Sue Lyons, suffered two broken cervical vertebrae and a skull fracture, incurring $300,000 in medical expenses.
7. As a result of the fall, the landscaping stones, which had cost $1200, were destroyed.
8. As a result of the foregoing injuries, plaintiff Bob Lyons, was required to miss eight weeks of work, resulting in a loss of $2,400 in wages.
9. As a result of the foregoing injuries, plaintiff Sue Lyons, was required to miss twelve weeks of work, resulting in a loss of $3,600 in wages.
   WHEREFORE, Plaintiffs demands judgment in the amount of $467,200, plus costs of this action.

Harlon Elliot
Attorney for Plaintiff
824 Sahara Ave.
Las Vegas, Nevada, 89117

JURY DEMAND
Plaintiff demands a trial by jury in this matter.

Service of Process

In order to obtain in personam jurisdiction over the defendant, and to satisfy due process, the court must notify the defendant of the pending lawsuit. As explained in the section on jurisdiction, service of process occurs when the representative of the court *serves* (delivers) a copy of the complaint and a summons to the defendant.

The complaint explains the basis of the lawsuit to the defendant. The summons tells the defendant to either respond to the lawsuit within a certain period of time, or face the plaintiff's receiving a *default judgment*. A default judgment is a judgment in favor of the plaintiff that occurs when the plaintiff's complaint alleges facts that would support such a judgment and the defendant fails to answer the complaint.

Defendant's Response

The defendant's response to the complaint is called the answer. In this document, the defendant denies, affirms, or claims no knowledge of the truth of the plaintiff's allegations.

The answer may admit that the facts contained in the complaint are true, but provide additional facts that would justify the defendant's actions and provide a legally sound reason to deny relief to the plaintiff. Such justifications for the defendant's conduct are called "affirmative defenses." For example, if a man was sued for battery for punching a woman in the face, he might raise as an affirmative defense that he hit her only because she was aiming a gun at him and threatening to shoot, and he was therefore acting in self-defense. Affirmative defenses must be raised in the answer to give the plaintiff adequate notice of them. If they are not raised in the answer, the judge will most likely not allow them to be raised during the trial.

Upon receiving the complaint, if the defendant believes that all of the plaintiff's factual allegations are true, but wants to deny the plaintiff a favorable judgment, the defendant may file a **motion to dismiss**. (A *motion* is a request by a party for the court to do something—in this instance; the request is to dismiss the case.) In deciding such a motion, the judge accepts the facts as stated by the plaintiff and makes a ruling on the legal issues in the case. Judges are generally not receptive to such motions, granting them only when it appears beyond a doubt that the plaintiff can prove no set of facts that would justify granting the judgment sought in the case.

If the defendant believes he or she has a claim against the plaintiff, this clause of action will be included with the answer as a *counterclaim*. As Exhibit 3-5 shows, the form of a counterclaim is just like that of a complaint. The defendant states the facts supporting the claim and asks for relief.

If the defendant files a counterclaim, the plaintiff generally files a *reply*. A reply is an answer to a counterclaim. In the reply, the plaintiff admits, denies, or claims a lack of knowledge as to the truth of the facts asserted by the defendant in the counterclaim. Any appropriate affirmative defenses to the counterclaim must be raised in the reply.

EXHIBIT 3-5

Defendant's Answer and Counterclaim

THE COURT OF COMMON PLEAS
OF CLARK COUNTY, NEVADA
Bob Lyons and Sue Lyons, Plaintiffs v. Christine Collins, Defendant
ANSWER AND COUNTERCLAIM FOR BREACH OF CONTRACT
Case No. _____

Now comes the defendant, Christine Collins, and answers the complaint of plaintiff herein as follows:
FIRST DEFENSE
1. Admits the allegations in paragraphs 1 and 2.
2. Denies the allegation in paragraph 3.
3. Is without knowledge as to the truth or falsity of the allegations contained in paragraphs 4, 5, 6, 7, 8, and 9.
SECOND DEFENSE
4. If the court believes the allegations contained in paragraph 3, which the defendant expressly denies, plaintiffs should still be denied recovery because they were informed prior to the construction of the bridge that there should be no more than one person on the bridge at one time, and that no individual weighing more than 200 pounds should be allowed to walk on the bridge.
COUNTERCLAIM
5. On April 15, the parties agreed that Defendant would build a wooden hanging bridge across a stream that runs through the defendants' property at 825 Havercamp Street, in exchange for which plaintiffs would pay defendant $2,000 upon completion of construction.
6. On May 1, 2001, the Defendant built the agreed upon ornament, wooden, hanging bridge across a stream that runs through the defendants' property at 825 Havercamp Street, but Plaintiffs failed to pay the agreed upon price for the bridge.

7. By their failure to pay, plaintiffs breached their contract and are liable to defendant for the contract price of $2,000.

WHEREFORE, defendant prays for a judgment dismissing the plaintiffs' complaint, and granting the defendant a judgment against plaintiff in the amount of $2,000 plus costs of this action.

Melissa Davenport
Attorney for Defendant
777 Decatur Ave.
Las Vegas, Nevada 89117

Pretrial Motions

The early pleadings just discussed establish the legal and factual issues of the case. Once established, the plaintiff or defendant may file a motion designed to conclude the case early, eliminate some claims, or gain some advantage. A party may request—or "move"— that the court do almost anything pertaining to the case. For example, if a suit is brought over the right to a piece of property, the court may grant a motion prohibiting the sale of the land by the current possessor.

When a party files a motion with the court, a copy is always sent to the opposing attorney. That attorney may respond to the motion, usually by requesting that the judge deny the motion. In many cases, the judge will rule on the motion, either granting or denying it. In some cases, the judge may hold a hearing at which the two sides orally present their arguments as to how the judge should decide the motion.

The two major pretrial motions are the **motion for judgment on the pleadings** and a **motion for summary judgment**. A motion for judgment on the pleadings can be made by either party once the pleadings have been filed. The party making the motion is claiming that if all the facts presented in the pleadings are considered to be true, when applying the law to those facts, the only way the court could decide the case would be in favor of the party filing the motion.

After the discovery process described in the next section occurs, the motion for a summary judgment can also be filed by either party. The party filing the motion asserts that there are no factual disputes that need to be decided by a jury, and that if the judge applies the law to the undisputed facts, the case would have to be decided in favor of the party filing the motion. This motion may be supported by affidavits, relevant documents, and depositions or interrogatories. If the judge examines all the documents and finds that in fact there are no factual disputes, he will grant the motion. But if he finds that there are some factual issues about which the parties disagree, the motion will be denied and the case will go to trial.

Discovery

Once the initial pleadings and motions have been filed, the parties gather information from each other through **discovery**. The discovery process enables each party to gather knowledge about the facts surrounding the case and is designed to prevent surprises from occurring in the courtroom. Three common discovery tools are **interrogatories**, **requests to produce documents**, and **depositions**.

Interrogatories are a series of written questions sent to the opposing party that must be answered under oath. Interrogatories are frequently accompanied by a *request to admit certain facts.* The attorney works with the client to answer interrogatories and requests for admission of facts.

A *request to produce documents* or other items forces the opposing party to produce (turn over) the requested information, unless it is privileged or irrelevant to the case. Photographs, contracts, written estimates, medical records, and government documents such as tax forms are among items that may be requested. One party may also request that the other party submit to a *mental* or *physical examination.*

Finally, testimony before trial may be obtained by the taking of a *deposition.* At a deposition, attorneys examine a witness who is under oath. A court reporter (stenographer) records every word spoken by the attorneys and witnesses. The testimony is usually transcribed into document form so that both parties have a written copy of the proceeding. The deposition provides information and may also set up inconsistencies between a person's testimony at the deposition, trial, or at some other time in the legal proceedings. If such inconsistencies exist, they will be brought to the fact finder's attention and may cause diminished credibility for the witness. Depositions may also be used when a potential witness is elderly, moving, or so ill they may be unavailable at the time of the trial.

Parties must comply with requests for discovery, or the court may order that the facts sought to be discovered be deemed to be admitted. Thus, business people involved in litigation should produce all requested discovery material. An attorney who feels that certain material should not be discovered makes arguments about its lack of relevance to the case. However, if the court disagrees, the information must be supplied. Although these discovery tools are important in the United States, many countries, including Japan, do not have a discovery process.

Pretrial Conference

The trial is preceded by a pretrial conference, an informal meeting of the judge with the lawyers representing the parties. During this conference, they try to narrow the legal and factual issues and possibly work out a settlement. Before the conference, business people should determine the limits of a settlement they are willing to agree to and should communicate those limits to their attorney, who may be able to reach a settlement at the conference. If no settlement can be reached, the attorneys and the judge discuss the administrative details of the trial, its length, the witnesses, and any pretrial stipulations of fact or law to which the parties can agree.

The Trial

A plaintiff seeking a legal remedy (money damages), is usually entitled to a jury trial. However, the jury must be demanded in the complaint. If an equitable remedy (an injunction or other court order) is being sought, or the parties have waived their right to a jury, a judge will be the fact finder in the case.

There are six stages to a trial: jury selection, the opening statements, the examination of the witnesses, closing agreements, the conference on jury instructions, and post-trial motions. These stages are described in the following sections and listed in Exhibit 3-3.

Jury Selection

Many lawyers believe that the most important part of a jury trial is the selection of the jury. The clerk of the courts randomly selects a number of potential jurors from the citizens within the jurisdiction of the court. The source of citizens' names varies depending on the court system, but typically they will come from lists of registered voters or residents to whom drivers' licenses have been issued. Once the potential jurors have been notified and have reported for jury duty, the *voir dire*, or jury selection process begins. This process is used to select the jurors who will actually decide the case, as well as two or three "alternate jurors," who will watch the actual trial, and be available to replace any juror who, for some legitimate reason, must leave jury duty before the case is decided.

During *voir dire,* the judge, the attorneys, or both, question potential jurors to determine whether they will be able to render an unbiased opinion in the case. Any time a juror's response to a question indicates that the individual will be biased, the attorney may challenge, or ask the court to remove, that potential juror "for cause." For example, in a securities fraud case, a lawyer could challenge for cause a potential juror who responds that he has been the victim of securities fraud or says that he was a college roommate of the defendant. In most states, each attorney is allowed to challenge a small number of potential jurors without giving a reason. These rejections are called **peremptory challenges**.

Peremptory challenges allow lawyers to rely on their instincts to challenge a potential juror who does not say anything that technically reveals a bias, but may have one. However, such challenges may lead to abuse, such as selecting juries to eliminate a certain class, ethnic group, or gender.

In the 1986 case of *Batson v. Kentucky,*[8] the United States Supreme Court ruled that race-based peremptory challenges in criminal cases violated the equal protection clause. The Supreme Court later extended the ban to the use of race-based challenges in civil cases. Finally, in the following case, the court extended the equal protection guarantee to cover gender-based challenges.

---

[8] 476 U.S. 79 (1986).

Case 3-2

J.E.B.,
v.
Alabama, EX. REL. T.B.
United States Supreme Court
114 S. Ct. 1419 (1994)

*T*he State of Alabama filed a complaint for paternity and child support against J.E.B on behalf of T.B, the unwed mother of a minor child. The court called a panel of twelve males and twenty-four females as potential jurors. Only ten males remained after three individuals were removed for cause. The state used its peremptory challenges to remove nine male jurors, and J.E.B. removed the tenth, resulting in an all female jury. The court rejected J.E.B.'s objection to the gender-based challenges and the jury found J.E.B. to be the father. J.E.B. appealed, and the court of appeals affirmed the trial court's ruling that the Equal Protection Clause does not prohibit gender-based challenges. The Alabama Supreme Court denied certiorari and J.E.B. appealed to the U.S. Supreme Court.

JUSTICE BLACKMUN

Discrimination in jury selection, whether based on race or on gender, causes harm to the litigants, the community, and the individual jurors who are wrongfully excluded from participation in the judicial process. The litigants are harmed by the risk that the prejudice which motivated the discriminatory selection of the jury will infect the entire proceedings. The community is harmed by the State's participation in the perpetuation of invidious group stereotypes and the inevitable loss of confidence in our judicial system that state-sanctioned discrimination in the courtroom engenders.

As with race-based *Batson* claims, a party alleging gender discrimination must make a *prima facie* showing of intentional discrimination before the party exercising the challenge is required to explain the basis for the strike. When an explanation is required, it need not rise to the level of a "for cause" challenge; rather, it merely must be based on a juror characteristic other than gender and the proffered explanation may not be pretextual.

Equal opportunity to participate in the fair administration of justice is fundamental to our democratic system. It reaffirms the promise of equality under the law—that all citizens, regardless of race, ethnicity, or gender, have the chance to take part directly in our democracy. When persons are excluded from participation in our democratic processes solely because of race or gender, this promise of equality dims, and the integrity of our judicial system is jeopardized.

REVERSED AND REMANDED IN FAVOR OF J.E.B.

1. Critical Thinking: The defendant was contesting the removal of males from the jury. Does this fact weaken the court's reasoning? Explain.

2. Ethical Decision Making: Which ethical norm does the decision in this case serve?

The *voir dire* process has become much more sophisticated over the years. In many of today's cases that involve significant amounts of money, rather than relying on their instinct or experience during jury selection, lawyers use a professional jury selection service to identify demographic data to help build a profile of the ideal juror and to provide assistance during the *voir dire* itself.

Jury selection firms also provide additional services, such as **mock trials** and **shadow juries**. A mock trial occurs when a group of individuals, who match the demographics of the real jury, listen to mock arguments of the lawyers and questioning of witnesses to give the lawyers a sense of how the planned approach to the case will appear to the actual jurors. If the mock jury does not seem receptive to a particular argument, it can be modified before trial.

A shadow jury is likewise composed of individuals who match the demographics of the actual jurors, but the shadow jury sits inside the courtroom and watches the trial. At the end of each day, the shadow jury "deliberates," giving the lawyers an idea of how the actual jurors are likely to be reacting to the case. If the other side appears to be winning, the lawyers may decide to modify their strategy.

The lawyers using these services believe that their use significantly increases a client's chances of winning the case. However, many people believe that use of jury selection services gives an unfair advantage to one side when that party is the only one wealthy enough to afford to hire such a service

Opening Statements

Once a jury has been impaneled, or selected, the case begins with the opening statements. Each party's attorney explains to the judge and the jury what facts the attorney intends to prove, the legal conclusions to which these facts will lead, and how the case should be decided based on those facts.

The Examination of Witnesses and Presentation of Evidence

Following their opening statements, the plaintiff and defendant, in turn, each presents his or her case, which consists of examining witnesses and presenting evidence. The plaintiff has the burden of proving the case, so must go first. The procedure for each witness is the same. First, the plaintiff's attorney questions the witness in what is called *direct examination*. The plaintiff's lawyer asks questions designed to elicit from the witness facts that support the plaintiff's case. Questions must relate to matters about which the witness has direct knowledge. The lawyers are not allowed to elicit "hearsay" from the witnesses. Hearsay occurs when a party testifies as to something that they heard someone else say. Hearsay is not allowed because the opposing party would not be able to question the person who made the statement that is being introduced in court. This would be unfair because that statement was not made under oath and the jury has no basis for determining whether it is a true statement.

The lawyer is also prohibited from asking leading questions, that is, questions where the lawyer suggests the answer. Another way to think of leading questions is that they are questions that can be answered with a simple, Yes, or No. An example of a leading question would be, "Did the defendant come to your office and ask you to purchase stock from him?" Instead, the lawyer would have to ask a question like, "What was your first encounter with the defendant?"

After direct examination, the opposing counsel may then *cross-examine* the witness, but may ask only questions related to the witness' direct examination. However, on cross-examination, the lawyer is allowed to ask leading questions. The primary purpose of cross-examination is to show inconsistency in the witness' testimony or cast doubt on the claims of plaintiff's case.

After cross-examination, the plaintiff's attorney may conduct a redirect examination, which is a series of questions designed to repair any damage done by the cross-examination. At the judge's discretion, opposing counsel has an opportunity to cross-examine the witness to address facts brought out in redirect examination. This procedure is followed for each of the plaintiff's witnesses.

Immediately following the plaintiff's presentation of their case, the defendant may ask the court to direct a verdict for the defendant on grounds that even if all of the evidence and testimony presented by the plaintiff were accepted as true, there would still be no legal basis for a decision in favor of the plaintiff. This request is called a *motion for a directed verdict* in most state courts, and a *motion for a judgment as a matter of law* in the federal court. Motions for a directed verdict are rarely granted because the plaintiff will almost always present at least some minimal amount of evidence to support each element of the cause of action.

If the defendant's motion for directed verdict is denied, the defendant then presents his case. The defendant's witnesses are questioned in the same manner as the plaintiff's, except that the defendant's attorney conducts direct and redirect examination and the plaintiff's attorney cross-examines the witnesses.

Closing Arguments

After the defendant's case is finished, the attorneys present their closing arguments. The lawyers attempt to summarize the evidence presented at trial in a manner that is consistent with their client's winning the case. The plaintiff presents first, followed by the defendant, and the plaintiff is then entitled to a rebuttal of closing arguments.

Jury Instructions

In a jury trial, the judge instructs the jury on how the law applies to the facts of the case. This process is sometimes referred to as "charging the jury." Prior to writing the jury instructions, the judge will have received both lawyers' statements of how they believe the jury should be charged. The judge's instructions are usually a combination of the suggestions submitted by both sides. After the jurors have been instructed, they retire to the jury room to deliberate. Once they reach a decision, they return to the courtroom, where their verdict is read, and they are then discharged from their duty and free to go home. Note how different our trial procedures are from those in Japan, as described in the Global Context box entitled "Trials in Japan."

Post-trial Motions

Once the trial is over, the party who received the favorable verdict will generally file a motion for a judgment in accordance with the verdict. Until the judge enters the judgment, there is no legally binding decision in the case.

The party who loses at trial has a number of available options. One option is to file a *motion for a judgment notwithstanding the verdict*, or *judgment non obstante verdicto*, asking the judge to issue a judgment that is contrary to the jury's verdict. To grant the motion, the judge must find that when the evidence is viewed in the light most favorable to the non-moving party, a reasonable jury could not have found in favor of that party. In other words, as a matter of law, there simply was not sufficient evidence to support the jury's verdict. In the federal court system, this motion is called *a motion for a judgment as a matter of law.*

A second option is to file a *motion for a new trial.* This motion will be granted only if the judge believes that the decision by the jury was clearly erroneous, yet it is not clear that the other side should necessarily have won the case. A motion for a new trial is often granted when there is new evidence discovered, or there was some kind of erroneous ruling made by the judge, or there occurred misconduct during the trial that may have prevented the jury from reaching a fair decision.

Appellate Procedure

Either party may appeal the decision of the judge on the post-trial motions or on his final judgment. Sometimes, both parties may appeal the same decision. For example, if a jury verdict were for the defendant, but the judge entered a directed verdict in favor of the plaintiff, the defendant may appeal the overruling of the jury's verdict, while the plaintiff may appeal the amount of the judgment.

To appeal a case, the losing party must allege that a *prejudicial error of law* occurred during the trial. A prejudicial error is a mistake that is so significant that it was likely to have affected the outcome of the case. For example, a prejudicial error could occur if the judge improperly refuses to allow the plaintiff to introduce a certain piece of evidence that is crucial to the plaintiff's being able to prove one of the elements of the case.

When a case is appealed, the attorney for the appealing party (the appellant) must file a notice of appeal with the clerk of the trial court within a prescribed time. The clerk will then forward the record of appeal to the court that will hear the appeal. The record of appeal will typically contain: the pleadings; a transcript of the trial and copies of the exhibits; copies of the judge's rulings on any motions made by the parties; arguments of the attorneys; jury instructions; the verdict; post-trial motions; and the judgment order from which the appeal is being taken.

The attorney for the appellant will then file a brief, or written argument, with the court, that will attempt to explain why the judgment in the lower court was erroneous and should be reversed. The attorney for the party who won in the lower court (the appellee) will file an answering brief. The appellant may then file a reply brief in response to the appellee's brief, but generally does not do so.

The lawyers are then usually, but not always, provided the opportunity to present oral arguments before the appeals court. The court considers these arguments, reviews the record of the case, and renders a decision.

There are four basic decisions an appellate court may render. The court **affirms** the decision of the lower court, meaning they accept its judgment. Alternatively, the appellate court may conclude that the lower court's decision was correct, but the remedy was inappropriate, so it will **modify** the remedy. If the appellate court decides that the lower court was incorrect in its decision, that decision will be **reversed**. Finally, the appeals court may feel that an error was committed, but it does not know how that error would have affected the outcome of the case, so it will **remand** the case to the lower court for a new trial.

Appellate courts are usually composed of a bench with at least three judges. There are no juries. The majority of the judges decide the case. One of the judges who votes with the majority records the court's decision and its reasons in what is called the *majority opinion*. These decisions have precedential value—that is, they are used by judges in later cases to make decisions and by attorneys in advising their clients in similar situations. If any of the judges in a case agrees with the ultimate decision of the majority, but for different reasons, that judge may write a *concurring opinion*, stating how this conclusion was reached. Finally, the judge or judges disagreeing with the majority may write a *dissenting opinion*, giving the reasons for reaching a contrary conclusion. Attorneys arguing that the law should be changed may cite dissenting opinions in briefs. An appellate judge who decides to change the law may also cite dissenting opinions.

For most cases, only one appeal is possible. In some states, where there is both an intermediate and a final court of appeals, a losing party may appeal from the intermediate appellate court to the state supreme court. In a limited number of cases, a losing party may be able to appeal from a state supreme court or a federal circuit court of appeals to the U.S. Supreme Court.

Appeal to the U.S. Supreme Court

Every year thousands of individuals attempt to have their appeals heard by the U.S. Supreme Court. But the court hears, on average, only about 80 to 90 cases every year. A party wishing to have his or her case heard by the highest court in the nation files a petition with the court, asking it to issue a *writ of certiorari*, which is an order to the lower court to send to the Supreme Court the record of the case. Few writs are issued.

The justices review the petitions they receive and issue a writ only when at least four justices vote to hear the case. The court is most likely to issue a writ in four instances: (1) the case presents a *substantial federal question* that has not yet been addressed by the Supreme Court; (2) the case involves a matter that has produced

Global Context: Trials in Japan

Civil procedure is very different in Japan. There are no juries and no separate pretrial stage. Trials are a series of discrete meetings with the judge. At the first meeting with the judge, the parties identify the most critical and contested issues. They choose one and recess to gather evidence and marshal arguments on the issue.

At the next meeting, that issue is decided. If the issue is decided against the plaintiff, the case is over. If the plaintiff wins, the process continues with the next issue. The process continues until either the plaintiff loses an issue, or all issues are decided in the plaintiff's favor, resulting in a verdict for the plaintiff. In addition, the discovery process in the Japanese court system is not as simple as it is in the United States. To obtain evidence, parties must generally convince the judge to order others to testify or produce documents. A party who refuses the judge's order can be fined, jailed, or the fact sought to be discovered is considered proven in favor of the party seeking discovery.

conflicting decisions from the various circuit courts of appeal and is therefore in need of resolution; (3) a state court of last resort holds that a federal law is invalid or upholds a state law that has been challenged as violating federal law; or (4) a federal court has ruled that an act of Congress is unconstitutional.

Caterpillar Wrap-Up

The timing of events was crucial to the outcome of the Caterpillar case. At the time the case was filed in the state court, there was no basis for concurrent jurisdiction because one of the defendants and the plaintiff were both from the same state. Once the supply company reached an agreement with the plaintiff, the other defendant, Caterpillar, filed his motion to exercise his right of removal, on the grounds that diversity jurisdiction would exist in the absence of the Kentucky defendant. The problem with the reasoning used by Caterpillar and adopted by the district court, was that the agreement was not final at the time of the motion because the agreement was subject to the insurer's approval. Thus, as the appellate court recognized in overturning the district court decision, at the time the case was removed, the supply company was still a party to the agreement, so the district court could not exercise jurisdiction over the case.

The U.S. Supreme Court, however, chose to overrule the appellate court because even though the initial motion to remove the case should not have been granted, shortly after the motion was granted and before the trial commenced, the settlement agreement was accepted by the insurer, and the supply company was dropped from the case; thereby, making the diversity complete. Because the jurisdictional requirements had been met by the time the decision was made, the high court ruled that the district court's error in not sending the case back when it was initially moved to the federal system would not be fatal. The court felt that to require the case to be sent back to the state system, when in fact all of the jurisdictional requirements had been met by the time of the trial and judgment, would be an undue waste of judicial resources. It is important to recognize, however, that if the requirements of complete diversity had not been met by the time the judgment was rendered, the district court's judgment would have had to have been vacated, because a court cannot render a judgment when it does not have subject matter jurisdiction.

Obviously, we cannot know for certain why Caterpillar wanted to have this particular case heard in federal district court, but there are some general considerations that might cause a businessperson in a similar situation to prefer the federal system. First, the case involves product liability claims, and if we look at the average awards in such cases brought in both federal and state courts, the awards in the state courts tend to be higher. So, Catepillar might have thought that if they lost, they might end up with less liability in a federal court.

Another reason might be a fear of local prejudice. State court judges are elected from the state and subject to re-election, whereas federal court judges are appointed for life. While all judges are supposed to be neutral, the out-of-state defendant might be fearful that an elected judge might be slightly biased in favor of the in-state party.

Thus, we can see that an important consideration any time a businessperson is involved in litigation is whether the case should be held in a state or federal choice, if there is concurrent jurisdiction.

	Summary
Jurisdiction	**In personam jurisdiction**—the power of the court to render a decision affecting that person's legal rights. **Subject matter jurisdiction**—the power of the court to render a decision in a particular type of case. The three forms of subject matter jurisdiction are state, exclusive federal, and concurrent.
Venue	**Venue**—the geographic location for the trial. It is the county where the plaintiff or defendant resides, where the property that is the subject matter of the dispute is located, or where the incident that gave rise to the case took place.

	Summary (continued)
Threshold Requirements	**Standing**—party must be personally affected by the outcome of a case. **Case or controversy**—there must be an issue before the court that is capable of resolution by a decision; parties cannot ask the judge for an "advisory opinion." **Ripeness**—The case cannot be moot; it must be ready for a decision to be made.
Structure of the Court System	The United States has two parallel court structures—the state and federal systems. The **federal system** is composed of the **District Courts** (trial courts), the **Circuit Courts of Appeal**, and the **United States Supreme Court**. The **state court systems** vary by state, but generally consist of trial courts called courts of common pleas, state courts of appeal, and a state supreme court.
Steps in a Civil Proceeding	The stages of a civil trial can be divided into the pre-trial, trial, post-trial and appellate stages. **Pretrial**—includes the consultation with the attorney, the pleadings stage, discovery process, and the pretrial conference. **The trial**—begins with the jury selection and is followed by the opening statements, presentation of the plaintiff's case, presentation of the defendant's case, closing arguments, jury instructions, jury deliberations, the jury verdict, and the judgment. **Post-trial motions**—including a motion for a new trial, may be filed. **Appeals**—may then be made to the appropriate appellate court, and in some cases, ultimately to the United States Supreme Court.

Review Questions and Case Problems

1. Explain the two types of jurisdiction that a court needs to hear a case and render a binding decision over the parties.

2. Explain the differences between trial courts and appellate courts.

3. Identify and define the alternative tools of discovery.

4. Explain the three threshold requirements that must

5. The Robinsons lived in New York, and bought a new Audi from Seaway Volkswagon Corp., a retailer that is incorporated in New York and also has its principal place of business there. World-Wide Volkswagon, incorporated in New York, and doing business in New York, New Jersey, and Connecticut, distributed the Audi to Seaway. Neither company does any business in Oklahoma, nor ships any cars there. The Robinsons were driving their Audi through Oklahoma, on their way to their new home in Arizona, when they were struck in the rear by another vehicle. The gas tank of the Audi exploded, injuring the members of the family in the car. The Robinsons brought a product liability suit against the manufacturer, distributor, and retailer of the Audi in the state court of Oklahoma. Seaway and World-Wide argued that the Oklahoma state court could not have in personam jurisdiction over them. After the state's trial court and supreme court held that the state did have in personam jurisdiction over the parties, they appealed to the United States Supreme Court. What do

you believe the outcome was, and why? *World-Wide Volkswagen Corp. v. Woodson*, 444 U.S. 286 (1980).

6. Flanagan's is a New Jersey company that installs irrigation systems. The company ordered an irrigation pump from another New Jersey corporation, Aquarius, and paid a $3,500 down payment for the product. The pump was manufactured by Watertronics, a Wisconsin Corporation. Flanagan's had no direct contact with Watertronics, other than a four minute telephone conversation in which Flanagan's attempted to find out whether they could get a better price on a pump. After receiving and installing the pump, Flanagan's was unhappy with its performance, and so refused to pay the balance due on the pump of $34,000. Watertronics sued Flanagan's in the state court in Wisconsin. Flanagan's argued that the court could not exercise in personam jurisdiction over it. Explain why you believe that the Wisconsin state court either could or could not exert in personam jurisdiction over *Flanagan's. Watertronics, Inc. v. Flanagan's Inc.,* __N.W. __ (2001 WL 42639, Ct. App. Wisc., 2001).

7. Conseco Inc. filed suit against Hickerson, a Texas resident, in Indiana alleging trademark dilution and infringement, commercial disparagement, defamation, and tortious interference with contractual relationships. These claims all involved an Internet website published by Hickerson that mentioned Conseco and one of its subsidiaries, Philadelphia Life Insurance Company. Hickerson's website sought information concerning fraud or other evidence of unfair treatment by Philadelphia Life

or any of Conseco's other insurance subsidiaries. The website explained that Hickerson sought this information to aid in a lawsuit he had filed against Philadelphia Life as the trustee of his father's estate. To help gather information, the site included a mail-to link enabling the reader to send Hickerson e-mail. Hickerson's website did not advertise, offer any product, or seek any money. Conseco's suit was based on Hickerson's use of Conseco's trademarked name, "Conseco Inc.," in the text of his website. The trial court dismissed the case, finding that the defendant did not have sufficient minimum contacts to allow Indiana to exercise personal jurisdiction over him. Explain why you believe that the Indiana Court of Appeals either agreed or disagreed with the trial court decision. *Conesco v. Hickerson*, 698 N.E. 2d 816 (1998).

8. THI, a Louisiana home health care agency, sued TGMC in Louisiana state court for alleged violations of Louisiana antitrust and unfair competition laws. TGMC removed the case to federal court on the grounds that the antitrust claims were federal in nature because they involved interstate commerce. The plaintiff, however, had not filed any claims based on federal antitrust law. *Terrebonne Homecare, Inc. v. SMA Health Plan, Inc.*, 271 F.3d 186 (5th Cir., 2001)

9. Athena Automotive, Inc., a corporation incorporated in Georgia, conducted an automobile repair business under the trade name "Brakes for Less" in Silver Spring, Maryland, until August 10, 1994. Even though it ceased its business operations at that time, Athena Automotive continued to maintain its corporate charter in good standing with the Georgia Secretary of State. On August 8, 1997, Athena Automotive filed an action in federal court in Maryland against John DiGregorio and J & D Automotive, Inc., a Maryland corporation. In the suit, Athena Automotive alleged that J & D breached its agreement to purchase the assets of Athena Automotive and that, through fraud, both DiGregorio and J & D obtained and converted to their own use Athena Automotive's assets, demanding $270,000 in compensatory damages and $1 million in punitive damages. Defendants filed a motion to dismiss, claiming a lack of subject matter because the plaintiff was a citizen of Georgia for purposes of the question of whether diversity of citizenship existed between the parties. The district court denied the defendants' motion, and reasoning that complete diversity existed because the three years that elapsed between Athena Automotive's last business activity in Maryland and the date it filed this action was "sufficient to shed Athena Automotive of its local character." How do you think the appellate court ruled in this case? Why? *Athena Automotive v. John J. Digregorio; J & D Automotive, Inc.*, 166 F. 3d 288 (1999)

10. The Fish and Wildlife Service proposed limiting the release of water from an irrigation project to protect two endangered species of fish. Ranchers whose access to water would be reduced by the FWS's proposed action filed a lawsuit to challenge the restriction. The district court dismissed their case for lack of standing. The ranchers appealed on grounds that they would suffer direct economic loss from the enforcement of the Endangered Species Act in the manner proposed by the FWS, and

therefore they had standing to challenge the FWS's actions. How do you think the Supreme Court ruled in this case? Why? *Bennett v. Spear*, 115 S. Ct. 1154 (1997).

Assignment on the Internet

While most long-arm statutes are similar, managers faced with a particular situation need to know whether a defendant's actions will subject that party to a state's long-arm jurisdiction. To find a state's specific long-arm statute, visit the legal database called Findlaw, located at **findlaw.com/casecode** or through Lexis-Nexis. Using either of these databases, find the long-arm statutes of your state and one other state. Write a brief memo explaining how the two statutes are similar and how they differ.

On the Internet

http://www.uscourts.gov *The Federal Judiciary Home Page is located at this address. From this site, you can find a significant amount of information about the federal court system.*

www.ncse.dni.us *The National Center for State Courts' home page is located at this site, which is perhaps one of the best resources for information about our state courts.*

http://courts.state.wy.us/rules.htm *Here you can find the Wyoming Rules of Civil Procedure, which are a typical illustration of the rules a state would establish to govern court procedures.*

http://www.lawresearch.com/v2/statute/ statstat.htm *This site contains links to all of the state constitutions, statutes, and rules of civil procedure.*

http://www.lexisone.com/legalresearch/ legalguide/codes_statutes/federal_rules_ of_civil_procedure.htm *This location will lead you to a number of sites that contain the federal rules of civil procedure in a variety of formats.*

http:www.martindale.com *This is the site of the Martindale-Hubble Law Directory, which provides information about lawyers and law firms. Typical entries would include area of special expertise, address, and telephone number.*

http://www.litigationlaw.com *This site provides a collection of litigation resources, including judicial news, decisions, employment listings, and information about federal practice and trial technology.*

Mandatory Arbitration at Hooters

In 1994, Hooters Restaurant in Myrtle Beach, South Carolina, implemented an alternative dispute resolution program, which is a program to resolve disputes outside the traditional court system. Employees had to sign an "agreement to arbitrate employment-related disputes" to be eligible for raises, transfers, and promotions. The agreement provided that Hooters and the employee each agreed to resolve all disputes arising out of employment, including "any claim of discrimination, sexual harassment, retaliation, or wrongful discharge, whether arising under federal or state law," through a specific form of alternative dispute resolution, arbitration.

In a separate policy document not shared with employees until after they had signed the agreement, Hooters set forth the rules and procedures of its arbitration program, which included the following:

• The employee had to provide notice of the specifics of the claim but Hooters did not need to file any type of response to these specifics or notify the claimant of what kinds of defenses the company planned to raise.

• Only the employee had to provide a list of all fact witnesses and a brief summary of the facts known to each.

• Although the employee and Hooters could each choose an arbitrator from a list, and those arbitrators would then select a third to create the arbitration panel that would hear the dispute, Hooters alone selected the arbitrators on the list.

• Only Hooters had the right to widen the scope of arbitration to include any matter, whereas the employee was limited to those raised in its notice.

• Only Hooters had the right to record the arbitration.

• Only Hooters had the right to sue to vacate or modify an arbitration award because the arbitration panel exceeded its authority.

• Only Hooters could cancel the agreement to arbitrate or change the arbitration rules.

Annette Phillips had been a bartender at Hooters restaurant in Myrtle Beach since 1989. When Hooters adopted its new arbitration policy, she was given a copy of the agreement to look at for five days and then sign. She signed the agreement.

In June of 1996, a Hooters official sexually harassed her by grabbing and slapping her buttocks. After appealing to her manager for help and being told to "let it go," she quit her job. When she threatened to file a lawsuit against them, Hooters filed an action in federal district court to compel arbitration of the issue.[1]

1. *Should Phillips be forced to settle her claim through arbitration?*
2. *Assume your company's arbitration policy was exactly like Hooters'. Which aspects would you retain and which might you change?*

---

[1] *Hooters of America, Inc. v. Phillips*, 79 Fair Empl.Prac.Cas. (BNA) 629 (4th Cir.1999).

CHAPTER 4
Alternative Dispute Resolution

Primary Forms of Alternative Dispute Resolution

Other ADR Methods

Court Annexed ADR

Use of ADR in International Disputes

Many firms, like Hooters, find themselves desirous of taking advantage of the many benefits of using **alternative dispute resolution** methods, or ADR, to resolve their legal problems. The term ADR refers to resolving legal disputes through methods other than litigation, such as negotiation, mediation, arbitration, summary jury trials, minitrials, neutral case evaluations, and private trials. Many organizations often use a form of ADR to resolve disputes involving contracts, insurance, labor, the environment, securities, technology, and international trade.

Not only are businesses increasingly turning to ADR, but courts are generally quite supportive of ADR methods, which alleviate some of the pressure on the overwhelming court dockets. Congress has recognized the benefits of ADR methods through its enactment of the Alternative Dispute Resolution Act of 1998. This act requires federal district courts to have an ADR program along with a set of rules regarding this program. Additional evidence of Congressional support for ADR comes from their passage of the Administrative Dispute Resolution Act, which mandated that federal agencies create internal ADR programs.

This chapter will explain the various ADR methods, as well as the advantages and disadvantages of each. ADR is becoming more favored internationally, and the latter portion of this chapter discusses its use in other countries.

Primary Forms of Alternative Dispute Resolution

Negotiation

The oldest, and perhaps most commonly used, method of dispute resolution is **negotiation**, the bargaining process in which disputing parties come together informally, either with or without lawyers, to attempt to resolve their dispute. A neutral third party, such as a judge or jury, is not involved. Thus, negotiation differs from other methods of dispute resolution because the parties maintain high levels of autonomy. Some courts require that parties engage in negotiation before they bring their dispute to trial.

Before negotiation begins, each side must determine its goals for the negotiation. Lawyers can enter negotiations with one of two approaches: adversarial or problem solving. In adversarial negotiation, each party seeks to maximize its own gain. In contrast, in problem solving negotiation, the parties seek joint gain. Typically, however, to reach a successful settlement, each party must give up something in exchange for getting something from the other side. Because negotiation generally occurs in every case before a more formal dispute resolution method is chosen, negotiation is not necessarily considered an alternative to litigation.

Mediation

An extension of negotiation is mediation. In **mediation**, the disputing parties select a neutral party to help them reconcile their differences by facilitating communication and suggesting ways for the parties to solve their dispute. Therefore, the distinguishing feature of mediation is that the parties voluntarily select a neutral third party to help them work together to resolve the dispute. The neutral third party frequently has expertise in the area of the dispute.

Mediation begins when parties select a mediator. An important feature of mediation is that it allows multiple parties to participate in a dispute. Typically, when the disputing parties meet with the mediator, the mediator first assures the parties that the proceedings are confidential. Second, the parties take turns explaining the dispute. One of the mediator's main goals is to help each party listen carefully to the opposing party's concerns. Third, the mediator asks the parties to identify any additional concerns. This discussion is an attempt to identify underlying circumstances that might have contributed to the dispute. A dispute typically arises after various problematic incidents; mediation permits the parties to address the various incidents, as well as the underlying circumstances leading to those incidents. After concerns have been highlighted, the mediator emphasizes areas of agreement and reframes the disputed points.

Fourth, the parties begin generating alternatives or solutions for the disputed points. The mediator helps the parties evaluate the alternatives by comparing the alternatives with the disputed points and interests identified earlier. Finally, the mediator assists the parties in agreeing to a solution. Because the mediator's role is

Global Context: Mediation in Sweden

Beginning in the 1960's, Sweden began expanding urban housing with the construction of large-scale, multiple occupant buildings (more commonly known as "flats"). While these buildings did fill the need for urban housing, they soon fell into disrepair. Only those without the means to choose their housing occupied the rather unpleasant flats. With the degradation of the flats, relations between tenants and landlords became strained. Tenants, desperate to have rent lowered, utilities fixed, and defacing of the property stopped, began bringing suits against the housing companies.

Recognizing the potential overload on the courts in having tenants sue the housing companies, the government took action. They implemented a program to improve the physical environment of the flats with the intention of making the areas safer and more attractive. However, this program provided for improvements such as the planting of gardens, which did little to control rent or fix the tenants' broken showers.

The government then ordered housing companies to alter the structure of their companies so greater attention could be given to the upkeep of the flats. The housing companies responded by using the concept of mediation. One particular company, SABO, divided its flats geographically into areas of about 1,000 residents. A local mediator was named to each area. The mediator's duties primarily involve keeping the lines of communication open between the tenants, the employees, and the superiors.

At its inception, the concept of mediation appeared ineffective. However, the problem did not lie in mediation itself, but in the individuals hired to be mediators. Most companies hired males with administrative and technical education who eventually proved to be ineffective mediators. Today, most mediators for the flat disputes are women with a socially-oriented education. The companies discovered that women had more applicable social and communicative skills, which are key to the process of mediation. While the adoption of area mediators has not eliminated the problems with the flats completely, tenants now have more direct and personable access to the housing companies.

that of a facilitator of an agreement, the mediator will often need to use persuasion to help the parties concede certain points so that agreement can be reached. The mediation concludes when the agreement between the parties is reached. The agreement is then usually put into the form of a contract and signed by the parties. The agreement generally does not assign blame to one of the parties; instead, it simply reflects the agreements made in the mediation session. If one of the parties does not live up to the agreement, that party can be sued for breach of contract. However, parties typically abide by the agreement because they helped to form that agreement.

If mediation is not successful, the parties can turn to litigation or arbitration to resolve their dispute. However, nothing that was said during the mediation can be used in another dispute resolution method; the mediation process is confidential.

Selecting A Mediator

Parties can find mediators from nonprofit sources as well as private companies, such as Judicial Arbitration and Mediation Services (JAMS). When selecting a mediator, parties should be aware that mediators come from a variety of backgrounds: experts in the area of the dispute, lawyers, judges, psychologists, and sociologists. While judges are often a popular choice for a mediator, they might be more likely to attempt to make the decision for the parties, instead of facilitating their discussion to reach a decision.

Uses Of Mediation

Mediation is probably most commonly used to resolve collective bargaining disputes. Because workers and employers must continue to work together, mediation typically helps preserve the relationship between the workers and employers. Under the National Labor Relations Act (NLRA), a union must contact the Federal Mediation and Conciliation Services to attempt to mediate their demands before beginning a strike to achieve higher wages or better working hours.

Mediation is also commonly used in environmental disputes. Japan has created a committee, the Environmental Pollution Disputes Committee, devoted solely to the resolution of environmental disputes. This committee may use mediation or arbitration. Why is mediation particularly useful for environmental disputes? First, mediation allows for creative solutions and compromises, which are often needed in environmental disputes. Suppose an endangered species makes its home on land that an entrepreneur recently purchased with the intention of building a bed and breakfast facility. Now, the entrepreneur cannot build on the land because the Endangered Species Act prohibits landowners from destroying an endangered species' habitat. Using mediation can help the landowner come to some kind of compromise to still use the land. For example, there might be a way to preserve a portion of the land so that the species may thrive, yet the business could still be operated, although perhaps in a smaller facility.

Second, multiple parties are often involved in environmental disputes. Because mediation serves to facilitate communication between various parties, numerous parties can participate in the mediation. Finally, those involved in environmental disputes will often become involved in future disputes. Thus, it is important that the parties maintain a good relationship.

In Germany, mediation has a special use by the parliamentary groups, the Bundestag and the Bundesrat, similar to Congress. These two groups must reach a majority consensus on all pieces of federal legislation in Germany. A Mediation Committee was formed for the purpose of reaching such consensus on bills being debated by the two groups. The Mediation Committee is composed of sixteen members from each group. The meetings of the mediation committee are confidential to prevent outside political pressures from barring consensus. Free of unwanted pressures, the Committee creates a proposal for the disputed bill.

The frequency of the meetings of the Mediation Committee depends upon the political atmosphere of the time. Between 1972 and 1976, when rival majorities held the Bundestag and the Bundesrat, the Mediation Committee convened ninety-six times. Yet between 1983 and 1987, the committee met only six times.

Current Status Of Mediation

While mediation is one of the more common alternatives to litigation, a primary purpose of mediation is to keep disputes out of the court system. However, sometimes litigation results from mediation. In 1998, approximately twenty-two cases were filed in federal and state courts regarding mediation issues.[2] One of the most important mediation-related cases decided in 1998 was the following *Folb* decision, which held that there is a mediation privilege under the Federal Rules of Evidence.

---

[2] Michael M. Bowden, *More Lawsuits are Being Filed Over Mediation*, Lawyers Weekly USA, 1999.

Case 4-1

Scott Folb

v.

Motion Picture Industry Pension & Health Plans, et al.
District Court For the Central District Of California
16 F. Supp. 2d 1164 (C.D. Cal. 1998)

*S*cott Folb was fired from his position as Administrative Director at the Motion Picture Industry Pension & Health Plans (the "Plans"). Folb argued that the directors at the Plans fired him in retaliation for various whistle-blowing activities in which he was involved. Folb objected to and reported various misbehaviors by the Plans. The Plans argued that Folb was fired for sexually harassing another employee, Vivian Vasquez.

Vasquez had filed a sexual harassment complaint against Folb, her manager. In February 1997, Vasquez and the Plans engaged in formal mediation to settle Vasquez's sexual harassment claims. Vasquez and the Plans signed an agreement ensuring the confidentiality of the mediation. Vasquez's counsel prepared a mediation brief and provided copies of this brief to the Plans' attorney as well as the mediator. Vasquez and the Plans did not reach an agreement during the mediation; however, they settled the claim during later negotiations.

Earlier, the Plans had hired Deborah Saxe, an outside attorney, to investigate Vasquez's sexual harassment claim. At some point, the lawyer for the Plans gave Saxe a copy of the mediation brief prepared by Vasquez's attorney, who did not authorize the Plans to give this brief to Saxe.

Folb, in his own claim against the Plans, wanted the Plans to produce (1) Vasquez' mediation brief; (2) correspondence between Vasquez' attorney and counsel for the Plans regarding mediation or other settlement discussions; and (3) notes prepared by Vasquez' attorney regarding settlement communications. Folb argued that the Plans claimed that they legitimately fired Folb because of the sexual harassment. Yet, Folb argues that in the mediation and negotiations, the Plans may have argued that Vasquez was never sexually harassed at all. The Plans refused to produce the information because they asserted that the documents were confidential. Magistrate Judge Woehrle denied Folb's motion to compel production of the documents, and Folb filed the pending Objections.

JUDGE PAEZ

[T]he Court must decide whether to adopt a federal mediation privilege under FED. R. EVID. 501….To determine whether an asserted privilege constitutes such a public good, in light of reason and experience, the Court must consider (1) whether the asserted privilege is "rooted in the imperative need for confidence and trust[;]" (2) whether the privilege would serve public ends; (3) whether the evidentiary detriment caused by exercise of the privilege is modest; and (4) whether denial of the federal privilege would frustrate a parallel privilege adopted by the states.

a. Need for Confidence and Trust

The proliferation of federal district court rules purporting to protect the confidentiality of mediation and the ADR Bill now pending before the United States Senate indicate a commitment to encouraging confidential mediation as an alternative means of resolving disputes that would otherwise result in protracted litigation. [M]ost federal courts considering the issue have protected confidential settlement negotiations and mediation proceedings, either by relying on state law or by applying the confidentiality provisions of federal court ADR programs. [T]he Court concludes that the proposed blanket mediation privilege is rooted in the imperative need for confidence and trust among participants.

b. Public Ends

A new privilege must serve a public good sufficiently important to justify creating an exception to the "general rule disfavoring testimonial privileges." . . . The proposed blanket mediation privilege would serve public ends by encouraging prompt, consensual resolution of disputes, minimizing the social and individual costs of litigation, and markedly reducing the size of state and federal court dockets.

c. Evidentiary Detriment

...[T]here is very little evidentiary benefit to be gained by refusing to recognize a mediation privilege.

d. Mediation Privilege in the 50 States

[S]tate legislatures and state courts have overwhelmingly chosen to protect confidential communications in mediation proceedings in order to facilitate settlement of disputes through alternative dispute resolution. "Denial of the federal privilege ... would frustrate the purposes of the state legislation that was enacted to foster these confidential communication." Accordingly, this Court finds it is appropriate, in light of reason and experience, to adopt a federal mediation privilege applicable to all communications made in conjunction with a formal mediation.

e. Contours of the Privilege

The mediation underlying the instant dispute was a formal mediation with a neutral mediator, not a private settlement discussion between the parties. Accordingly, the mediation privilege adopted today applies only to information disclosed in conjunction with mediation proceedings with a neutral.

On the facts presented here, the Court concludes that communications to the mediator and communications between parties during the mediation are protected. In addition, communications in preparation for and during the course of a mediation with a neutral must be protected. Subsequent negotiations between the parties, however, are not protected even if they include information initially disclosed in the mediation. To protect additional communications, the parties are required to return to mediation. A contrary rule would permit a party to claim the privilege with respect to any settlement negotiations, so long as the communications took place following an attempt to mediate the dispute.

III.

For the foregoing reasons, plaintiff's Objections to the Magistrate Judge's order are SUSTAINED with respect to the underlying legal reasoning and OVERRULED with respect to the magistrate judge's ultimate decision to deny plaintiff's motion to compel production of the mediation brief and communications between counsel privy to the mediation, at least to the extent that those communications were made in anticipation of or during the course of the mediation. Plaintiff may seek, by renewed motion before the Magistrate Judge within fifteen days of entry of this order, to compel production of any documents relating to communications between Vasquez and the Plans that were not made in conjunction with, or pursuant to, the formal mediation proceeding.

1. Critical Thinking: What was the judge's logic in distinguishing between facts discussed during the mediation and facts discussed in negotiations outside of mediation? Do you agree with his reasoning?

2. Ethical Decision Making: Explain which of the two primary parties in this case might change their behavior if their actions were subjected to the public disclosure test.

Advantages And Disadvantages of Mediation

For those disputes in which the parties must maintain a working relationship, mediation is popular because it allows parties to preserve their relationship throughout the dispute. The idea behind mediation is to get parties to work together to reach a consensus. Because parties are encouraged to communicate openly, they usually do not experience bitterness toward the opposing parties. Furthermore, parties typically leave mediation with a better understanding of the opposing party; consequently, this better understanding may actually facilitate a better working relationship between the parties. Therefore, the first advantage of mediation is that it helps disputing parties to preserve their relationships.

The second advantage to mediation is the potential for creative solutions. The parties are responsible for offering alternatives to solve problems. A party to mediation is often not necessarily looking for a money award. Instead, that party may be trying to find a solution so that both parties can benefit from the resolution of the dispute.

Third, parties to mediation have a high level of autonomy. Unlike litigation or arbitration, where a neutral third party makes a decision that resolves the dispute, mediation allow parties the opportunity to take control of the process and resolve the dispute together. The parties seem to have more dedication to the agreement because they helped make the decision. Finally, mediation, like other methods of alternative dispute resolution, is less costly, less time consuming, and less complicated than litigation.

The aforementioned benefits can obviously be very worthwhile. However, we need to pay attention to the critics of the mediation process. They argue that the informal mediation process creates an image of equality between the parties; consequently, we assume that the resulting agreement between the parties is also equal. However, if one party has more power than the other, the agreement is not necessarily fair or equal. Thus, the image of equality in mediation can be misleading. Furthermore, a party who knows that he or she has no chance of winning a case could enter the mediation process in bad faith, with no intention of making an agreement. Therefore, some people may abuse the mediation process in an attempt to simply draw out the dispute.

Arbitration

One of the most frequently used methods of dispute resolution is **arbitration**, the resolution of a dispute by a neutral third party outside the judicial setting. Arbitration is often a voluntary process in that parties have a contractual agreement to arbitrate any disputes. This agreement may stipulate how the arbitrator will be selected and how the hearing will be administered.

If a party wanted to begin arbitration, it would send the other party a written demand for arbitration. This demand would identify the parties involved, the dispute issue, and the type of relief claimed. The opposing party typically responds to the demand in writing, indicating agreement or disagreement with the claim that the dispute is arbitrable.

Selecting An Arbitrator

If disputing parties have not made an earlier agreement about how to select an arbitrator, they typically use either the Federal Mediation and Conciliation Services (FMCS), a government agency, or the American Arbitration Associa-tion (AAA), a private, nonprofit organization whose purpose is to "foster the study of arbitration in all its aspects, to perfect its techniques under arbitration law, and to advance generally the science of arbitration for prompt and economical settlement of disputes." The AAA helps arbitrate more than 50,000 disputes a year.

When a party contacts one of the agencies, the party receives a list of potential arbitrators. This list includes biographical information about the potential arbitrators, and both parties examine the list and jointly select an arbitrator. While most arbitrations are conducted by one arbitrator, panels of three arbitrators are becoming more frequent. Typically, each party will choose one arbitrator. Then, those two arbitrators would select an additional arbitrator.

Once the parties agree on an arbitrator, the parties and arbitrator agree on the location and time of the arbitration. Additionally, they determine which procedural and substantive rules will be followed during the arbitration.

Lawyers, professors, or other professionals typically serve as arbitrators. The general qualifications to be an arbitrator are honesty, impartiality, and subject matter competence. Additionally, arbitrators are expected to follow the Arbitrator's Code of Ethics.

The Arbitration Hearing

The arbitration hearing is quite similar to a trial. Both parties present their case to a neutral third party. Through this presentation, parties may introduce witnesses and documentation. Parties may represent themselves or use legal counsel. The parties may cross-examine the witnesses, and the parties offer closing statements. The fact finder offers a legally binding decision. In these ways, a trial and an arbitration hearing are similar.

However, arbitration is also different in several ways. First, the arbitrator often takes a much more active role in an arbitration hearing, in the sense that the arbitrator is more likely than a judge to question a witness. Second, no official written record of the hearing is kept. Third, the rules of evidence applicable in a trial are typically relaxed in arbitration. Fourth, the arbitrator is not as constrained by precedent as are judges.

The Arbitrator's Award

The arbitrator typically provides a decision within thirty days of the arbitration hearing. The arbitrator's decision is called an award, even if no monetary compensation is awarded. The arbitrator's decision differs from a judge's decision in several ways. The arbitrator

does not have to state any findings of fact, conclusions of law, or reasons to support the award, and is not as bound by precedent as a judge. Because the arbitrator was hired to resolve a dispute between two parties, the arbitrator is more likely to make a compromise ruling instead of a win-lose ruling. After all, if the parties are satisfied with the ruling, they will probably be more likely to use that arbitrator again to resolve future disputes.

The arbitrator's decision is legally binding. In certain cases, a decision may be appealed to the district court. However, few of these cases are appealed. For example, of approximately 25,000 labor cases arbitrated each year, fewer than 200 cases are appealed. The courts give extreme deference to arbitrators' decisions. Unless a party can clearly demonstrate that an arbitrator's decision was contrary to law, or that there was a defect in the arbitration process, the decision will be upheld. The Federal Arbitration Act (FAA), the federal law enacted to encourage the use of arbitration, explic-

Technology: Dispute Resolution on the Internet

If you have an Internet-related dispute, you have the opportunity to resolve that dispute online. The Online Ombuds Office offers mediators with experience in law and in Internet use. Ombuds mediators have resolved disputes between webmasters as well as persons who have bought or sold items on online auction sites. Online dispute resolution can be even less expensive and time consuming than other methods of ADR.

To request that your dispute be heard by online mediators, go to the website of the Ombuds Office, **http://aaron. sbs.umass.edu/center/ombuds**, to fill out an online request form. Once the organization receives your information, it assigns a mediator who then e-mails you. Parties typically communicate through electronic mail or conferencing software. The Ombuds Office helped mediate 175 disputes online during Spring of 1999.

Various websites are springing up for the purpose of helping individuals and firms resolve any type of dispute. In other words, the dispute does not have to relate to the Internet. For example, ClickNSettle, **http://www.clickNsettle.com**, a subsidiary of a private firm, allows any two parties with Internet access to resolve their dispute online through a form of negotiation. Each party must pay $20 to begin the negotiations. Each time the party enters an offer or demand, that party must pay $10. Parties are charged a settlement fee according to the settlement amount. If the parties settle for less than $1,000, each party must pay $50. However, if the case settles for $250,000 or above, each party must pay $500.

itly lists four grounds on which an arbitrator's award may be set aside:

1. The award was the result of corruption, fraud, or other undue means.
2. The arbitrator displayed bias or corruption.
3. The arbitrator refused to postpone the hearing despite sufficient cause, refused to hear relevant evidence, or otherwise misbehaved to prejudice the rights of one of the parties.
4. The arbitrator exceeded his or her authority or failed to use that authority to make a mutual, final, and definite award.

Consequently, in the United States, arbitration decisions are generally upheld. Other countries are taking actions to increase the number of arbitrations, while reducing the need to appeal the arbitration decisions. For example, Brazilian lawmakers reformed several articles in the Brazilian Civil Code to increase the practice of arbitration. These reforms mandate that parties sign an "arbitration commitment" during arbitration proceedings. This commitment states the disputed issue, the venue of the arbitration, and the parties involved. The "arbitration commitment" renders the outcome of the arbitration comparable to a decision handed down by the judiciary branch. Consequently, parties no longer need to appeal to the judiciary branch after an arbitration hearing.

Advantages And Disadvantages Of Arbitration

Arbitration may be preferable to litigation for several reasons. First, arbitration is more efficient and less expensive than litigation. Second, parties have more control over the process of dispute resolution through arbitration. They choose the arbitrator and determine how formal the process will be. Third, the parties can choose someone to serve as the arbitrator who has expertise in the specific subject matter. Because the arbitrator has expertise, parties often believe the arbitrator will be able to make a better decision. Fourth, the arbitrator has greater flexibility in decision making than a judge has. Unlike judges, who are bound by precedent, arbitrators generally do not have to offer reasons for their decisions.

However, arbitration is not without its critics. First, arbitration panels are being used more frequently, resulting in a loss of some of the prior advantages of arbitration. For example, using a panel, as opposed to one arbitrator, causes greater scheduling difficulties because of the number of people involved, consequent-

ly negating some of the efficiency associated with arbitration. Along the same lines, paying an arbitration panel is more costly than paying one arbitrator.

Second, because appealing an arbitration award is so difficult, some scholars argue that injustice is more likely to occur. Third, some individuals are concerned that by agreeing to give up one's right to litigate, one may be losing important civil rights or giving up important potential remedies without really understanding what rights are being given up. And, especially in an employment context, they may not really want to give up such rights, but they have no choice if they want the job.

Fourth, some scholars are afraid that if more and more employers and institutions turn to mandatory arbitration, it will become more and more like litigation. More and more people will be forced to arbitrate their disputes; consequently, the efficiency associated with arbitration will start to erode.

Finally, some scholars are concerned about the privacy associated with arbitration. Companies and employers are able to "hide" their disputes through arbitration. Suppose a credit card company is charging greater amounts of money than their posted finance charge. If an individual arbitrates her claim, other customers might not know to check their credit card statement to ensure that they are being charged the correct amount. If the claim went to court, the publicity surrounding the case would probably better educate the public to pay more attention to their statements. Thus, the confidentiality associated with an arbitration proceeding may be harmful in some cases.

Methods of Securing Arbitration

Arbitration can be mandated, or it can be secured voluntarily. Mandated arbitration is not very common. However, sometimes state law does mandate arbitration. For example, some states require that disputes involving less than $10,000 be arbitrated.

Most arbitration, however, is voluntary. The two primary means of voluntarily securing arbitration are through a binding arbitration clause and a submission agreement. A **binding arbitration clause** is a provision in a contract that mandates that all disputes arising under the contract must be settled by arbitration. The clause also typically states how the arbitrator will be selected. Exhibit 4-1 provides an example of a binding arbitration clause that could be included in almost any business contract.

EXHIBIT 4-1

Sample Binding Arbitration Clause

Any controversy, dispute, or claim of whatever nature arising out of, in connection with, or in relation to the interpretation, performance, or breach of this agreement, including any claim based on contract, tort, or statute, shall be resolved, at the request of any party to this agreement, by final and binding arbitration conducted at a location determined by the arbitrator in (City, State) administered by and in accordance with the existing Rules of Practice and Procedure of Judicial Arbitration & Mediation Services, Inc. (JAMS) and judgment upon any award rendered by the arbitrator may be entered by any state or federal court having jurisdiction thereof.

If a contract does not contain a binding arbitration clause, parties may secure arbitration by entering into a **submission agreement**, a contract providing that a specific dispute will be resolved through arbitration. The submission agreement will typically state the following: the nature of the dispute; how the arbitrator will be selected; the place of the arbitration; and any limitations on the arbitrator's authority to remedy the dispute.

If parties have a binding arbitration agreement or entered into a submission agreement, the parties *must* resolve the dispute through arbitration. Both federal and state courts must uphold agreements to arbitrate. The Supreme Court has, in several opinions, held that courts must enforce such agreements.

While courts must uphold binding arbitration clauses, courts have recently been finding specific reasons why a binding arbitration clause might not be upheld. For example, the following case provides an illustration of how, when the arbitration of federal statutory rights are at issue, employers must make "clear and unmistakable" arbitration agreements.

Case 4-2

Jerome Brown

v.

ABF Freight Systems, Inc.
U.S. Court of Appeals, 4th Circuit
U.S. App. LEXIS 15582 (1999)

*J*erome Brown, a diabetic commercial truck driver, claimed that ABF Freight Systems violated the Americans with Disabilities Act and the Virginians with Disabilities Act when it informed him that ABF would no longer accept his bids for yard and dock jobs. He filed his claim in a district court in Virginia. However, ABF argued that its collective bargaining agreement ("CBA") with Brown's union, the International Brotherhood of Teamsters, required Brown to submit his ADA claim to arbitration in accordance with the agreement. The District Court ruled that Brown would have to submit his claim to arbitration, and Brown appealed.

CIRCUIT JUDGE LUTTIG

Because we conclude that the collective bargaining agreement in question does not clearly and unmistakably require the arbitration of statutory discrimination claims, we reverse the judgment of the district court.

In reviewing Brown's claims, we write on a slate that is far from clean. After Brown had filed a timely notice of appeal and an opening brief in this court, we held the case in abeyance pending the Supreme

Court's review of our decision in *Wright v. Universal Maritime Serv. Corp*....In *Wright v. Universal Maritime Serv. Corp*..., the Court established that a union-negotiated waiver of employees' right to a federal judicial forum for statutory employment-discrimination claims must be clear and unmistakable. Because the asserted waiver did not meet that standard, the Court expressly declined to reach the question whether even a waiver that did would be enforceable. In addition, after briefing in this appeal was completed—but before oral argument was heard—we applied the Universal Maritime standard in *Carson v. Giant Food, Inc.* ...concluding that under the Supreme Court's newly announced standard, the CBA in question did not compel arbitration of appellee's statutory discrimination claims. It is with the benefit of the decisions in these two recent cases, *Universal Maritime* and *Carson*, that we consider this appeal.

... The question whether the parties to a CBA agreed to arbitrate discrimination claims arising under the ADA—or any other federal statutory antidiscrimination law—is one of contract interpretation. In making that determination, however, we do not apply the usual interpretive presumption in favor of arbitration. . . . Rather, under the rule of *Universal Maritime*, we will not find an intent to arbitrate statutory claims absent a "clear and unmistakable" waiver of an employee's "statutory right to a judicial forum for claims of employment discrimination."

In *Carson*, a panel of this court explained that the requirement of a "clear and unmistakable" waiver can be satisfied through two possible means. First, and most obviously, such intent can be demonstrated through the drafting of an "explicit arbitration clause" pursuant to which the union agrees to submit all statutory employment-discrimination claims to arbitration. Second, where the arbitration clause is "not so clear," employees might yet be bound to arbitrate their federal claims if "another provision, like a nondiscrimination clause, makes it unmistakably clear that the discrimination statutes at issue are part of the agreement."

With respect to the first of these means, there is no doubt that the arbitration clause contained in Article 37 of the CBA in this case is insufficiently explicit to pass muster under *Universal Maritime*. The clause is a standard one, submitting to arbitration "all grievances or questions of interpretation arising under . . . this Agreement." Because the arbitration clause refers only to grievances arising under the Agreement, it cannot be read to require arbitration of those grievances arising out of alleged statutory violations.

Under *Carson's* second means, however, even such a "broad but nonspecific" arbitration clause may, nonetheless, require arbitration of statutory discrimination claims if another provision of the agreement has, of the ADA (or any other federal antidiscrimination statute). Rather, it merely adds disability, as defined by the ADA, to the list of grounds established with the "requisite degree of clarity" that the "discrimination statute at issue is part of the agreement." Because the only provision that might even arguably qualify—Article 37, the nondiscrimination clause—does not make it "unmistakably clear" that it is incorporating federal statutory employment discrimination law, we hold that the argument grounded in this alternative of *Carson* is also unavailing.

Article 37 begins with an explicit agreement between the Employer and the Union that neither will discriminate against any individual "with respect to hiring, compensation, terms or conditions of employment" or "limit, segregate or classify employees in any way to deprive any individual employee of employment opportunities" because of that individual's "race, color, religion, sex, age, or national origin." While the language of this contractual agreement not to discriminate on certain specified bases in certain specified ways may parallel, or even parrot, the language of federal antidiscrimination statutes and prohibit some of the same conduct, none of those statutes is thereby explicitly incorporated into the agreement, by reference or otherwise. As a result, the contractual rights the agreement creates "cannot be said to be congruent with," those established by statute or common law, and an arbitrator in interpreting the scope of those rights pursuant to the general arbitration clause will be bound to interpret the explicit terms of the agreement rather than of any federal statutory antidiscrimination law.

ABF argues that the catch-all concluding clause of the first sentence of Article 37, by which the Employer and Union agree not to "engage in any other discriminatory acts prohibited by law," constitutes the explicit incorporation of federal statutory discrimination law contemplated by *Carson*. We disagree. There is a significant difference between an agreement not to commit discriminatory acts that are prohibited by law and an agreement to incorporate the antidiscrimination statutes that prohibit those acts. . . . Rather, the parties must make "unmistakably clear" their intent to incorporate in their entirety the "discrimination statutes at issue," as we said in *Carson*. This, these parties have not done.

Finally, we reject appellee's argument that the second sentence of the nondiscrimination provision alone constitutes the "explicit incorporation of statutory antidiscrimination requirements" that *Carson* held could establish a waiver. This second sentence does not purport to incorporate any requirements which the parties in the previous sentence have agreed not to discriminate.

Accordingly, because we cannot say that the intent of the union to waive its employees' statutory right to a federal forum has been clearly and unmistakably established, we reverse the district court's order dismissing Brown's ADA claim.

REVERSED.

1. Critical Thinking: Why does the court say that in determining whether the CBA constituted a waiver of an employee's right to file a discrimination claim, the usual interpretive presumption in favor of arbitration does not apply? Why do you agree or disagree with the court's interpretation that the union did not clearly and unmistakably give up union members' rights to file discrimination claims?

2. Ethical Decision Making: Based on the judge's decision, which values do you think are most important to him?

Another constraint on binding arbitration clauses is that they must be drafted in such a way as to ensure that the courts do not see them as being unconscionable. An unconscionable contract provision has been defined as one in which the terms are "manifestly unfair or oppressive and are dictated by a dominant party."[3] The doctrine has been used most often to strike down binding arbitration clauses in consumer and employment contracts.

For example, in the Hooters illustration at the beginning of the chapter, the court refused to uphold the contract because of a number of provisions it found to be unconscionable, including: requiring employees to provide notice of the specifics of the claim, but not making the company file any type of response to these specifics or notify the claimant of what kinds of defenses the company planned to raise; making only the employee provide a list of all fact witnesses and a brief summary of the facts known to each; allowing the company to widen the scope of arbitration to include any matter, whereas the employee was limited to those raised in its notice; giving only the company the right to record the arbitration; allowing only the company to sue to vacate or modify an arbitration award because the arbitration panel exceeded its authority; and allowing only the company to cancel the agreement to arbitrate or change the arbitration rules. Provisions found to be unconscionable in other binding arbitration clauses included provisions that: mandated cost sharing for hiring a three-member arbitration panel;[4] limited available damages;[5] adopted unreasonably short time periods for filing claims; and limited the amount of discovery available.[6] Exhibit 4-2 offers tips on creating a binding arbitration clause.

[3] *Farris v. County of Camden*, 61 F. Supp. 2d 307, 341 (D. N.J. 1999).

[4] *Maciejewski v. Alpha Systems Lab Inc.*, 87 Cal. Rptr. 2d 390 (Cal. Ct. App. 1999).
[5] *Johnson v. Circuit City Stores, Inc.* 203 F. 3d 821 (4th Cir. 2000).
[6] *Geiger v. Ryan's Family Steak House and Employment Dispute Services Inc.*, 2001 WL 278120 (S.D. Ind. 2001).

EXHIBIT 4-2

Tips for Creating a Binding Arbitration Clause

Overall, make sure the clause treats both parties fairly.

1. **Be clear and unmistakable.** If you wish to arbitrate employment disputes or discrimination claims, make sure that you explicitly state "employment disputes and discrimination claims" in the binding arbitration clause.

2. **The arbitration clause must be bilateral.** If the arbitration clause requires one party only to arbitrate but does not spell out the same requirement for the other party, the clause will probably not be upheld. This agreement would be asking one party to give up its right to have a claim before a jury while the other party retains that right. The courts are concerned about fairness. This bilateral consideration must extend to damages. For example, both parties must able to get the same damages.

3. **State explicitly which party will pay the arbitrator's fees, and make sure that it will not cost the employee more to arbitrate than it would have cost to litigate.** Courts have refused to enforce arbitration agreements that require the plaintiff to pay the costs of the arbitration. Some courts have refused to enforce agreements requiring the employee to pay a pro rata share of arbitration expenses.[7] Furthermore, a court recently refused to enforce an agreement that did not specify who would pay the arbitrator's fees along with other costs. For ease and assurance that the agreement will be enforced, companies might consider stating that they will pay the costs of the arbitration.

4. **Specify how the arbitrator will be selected.**

5. **Spell out the costs associated with the arbitration.**

6. **Avoid limitations on the remedies available to the parties.** Limitations on punitive damages or attorney fees are likely to be causes for refusing to uphold cases.

7. **Consider other potential parties when determining where to hold the arbitration.** If a credit card company states in its arbitration clause that all disputes will be arbitrated in its state of incorporation, a court might be more likely to not enforce the agreement. Requiring consumers to travel far distances may be perceived as an unfair burden on the consumer.

---

[7] See, e.g., *Shubin v. William Lyon Homes, Inc.,* 84 Cal. App. 4th 1041 (2000) and *Cole v. Burns Internal Security Services,* 105 F. 3d 1465 (D.C.Cir. 1997).

Common Uses of Arbitration

Arbitration is used in a variety of situations. Arbitration is so commonly used in labor disputes that it is frequently referred to as the primary method of resolving labor disputes. And just like the management of Hooters, employers are often eager to resolve all employment-related disputes through arbitration. Before the following case occurred, employers and employees were extremely uncertain as to whether employees could be required to resolve all employment disputes through arbitration, especially those involving discrimination claims.

Gilmer upheld the validity of the of the National Association of Securities Dealers' policy of requiring all employees who execute, buy, or sell orders at brokerages or investment banks to arbitrate all employment disputes as a condition of their employment. Immediately following this case, the use of mandatory arbitration agreements in employment contracts increased significantly.

Case 4-3

Robert Gilmer

v.

Interstate/Johnson Lane Corporation
United States Supreme Court
111 S. Ct. 1647 (1991)

*P*laintiff Robert Gilmer filed a charge with the Equal Employment Opportunity Commission (EEOC) and sued his employer, defendant Interstate/Johnson Lane Corporation. Gilmer alleged that his employer violated the Age Discrimination in Employment Act (ADEA). When the defendant hired him as a registered securities dealer, Gilmer had signed an agreement to settle by arbitration any disputes arising out of that employment. The employer therefore filed a motion to compel arbitration. The trial court denied the defendant's motion and defendant appealed to the circuit court. The circuit court reversed in favor of the defendant and the plaintiff appealed to the U.S. Supreme Court.

JUSTICE WHITE

The question presented in this case is whether a claim under the Age Discrimination in Employment Act of 1967 (ADEA) can be subjected to compulsory arbitration pursuant to an arbitration agreement in a securities registration application.

...It is by now clear that statutory claims may be the subject of an arbitration agreement, enforceable pursuant to the FAA.... In [recent] cases we recognized that "by agreeing to arbitrate a statutory claim, a party does not forgo the substantive rights afforded by the statute; it only submits to their resolution in an arbitral, rather than a judicial, forum."

Although all statutory claims may not be appropriate for arbitration, "[h]aving made the bargain to arbitrate, the party should be held to it unless Congress itself has evinced an intention to preclude a waiver of judicial remedies for the statutory rights at issue." The burden is on Gilmer to show that Congress intended to preclude a waiver of a judicial forum for ADEA claims.... Throughout such an inquiry, it should be kept in mind that "questions of arbitrability must be addressed with a healthy regard for the federal policy favoring arbitration."

Gilmer concedes that nothing in the text of the ADEA or its legislative history explicitly precludes arbitration. He argues, however, that compulsory arbitration of ADEA claims pursuant to arbitration agreements would be inconsistent with the statutory framework and purposes of the ADEA. Like the Court of Appeals, we disagree.

We also are unpersuaded by the argument that arbitration will undermine the role of the EEOC in enforcing the ADEA. An individual ADEA claimant subject to an arbitration agreement will still be free to file a charge with the EEOC, even though the claimant is not able to institute a private judicial action. Indeed, Gilmer filed a charge with the EEOC in this case.

Gilmer also argues that compulsory arbitration is improper because it deprives claimants of the judicial forum provided for by the ADEA. Congress, however, did not explicitly preclude arbitration or other nonjudicial resolution of claims, even in its recent amendments to the ADEA. Moreover, Gilmer's argument ignores the ADEA's flexible approach to resolution of claims. The EEOC, for example, is directed to pursue "informal methods of conciliation, conference, and persuasion," which suggests that out-of-court dispute resolution, such as arbitration, is consistent with the statutory scheme established by Congress.

In arguing that arbitration is inconsistent with the ADEA, Gilmer also raises a host of challenges to the adequacy of arbitration procedures. Such generalized attacks on arbitration "res[t] on suspicion of arbitration as a method of weakening the protections afforded in the substantive law to would-be complainants," and as such, they are "far out of step with our current strong endorsement of the federal statutes favoring this method of resolving disputes."

Gilmer also complains that the discovery allowed in arbitration is more limited than in the federal courts, which he contends will make it difficult to prove discrimination. It is unlikely, however, that age discrimination claims require more extensive discovery than other claims that we have found to be arbitrable, such as RICO and antitrust claims. Although those procedures might not be as extensive as in the federal courts, by agreeing to arbitrate, a party "trades the procedures and opportunity for review of the courtroom for the simplicity, informality, and expedition of arbitration."

It is also argued that arbitration procedures cannot adequately further the purposes of the ADEA because they do not provide for broad equitable relief and class actions. As the court below noted, however, arbitrators do have the power to fashion equitable relief. Indeed, the NYSE rules applicable here do not restrict the types of relief an arbitrator may award, but merely refer to "damages and/or other relief."

AFFIRMED, in favor of Defendant, Johnson/ Lane Interstate Corp.

1. Critical Thinking: What ambiguity led to this case going to court?
2. Ethical Decision Making: What group of stakeholders would be most happy with the outcome of this case? Which would be the least happy?

However, the EEOC became concerned about whether arbitration agreements that had to be accepted as a condition of employment were actually voluntary. In July 1997, the EEOC issued a statement regarding arbitration agreements, stating that arbitration of discrimination claims as a condition of employment was in conflict with the fundamental principles of employment laws.

While the EEOC strongly supported agreements to arbitrate once a dispute has arisen, they did not support inclusion of arbitration agreements as an unconditional element of employment. In response to the EEOC's statement, the National Association of Securities Dealers created a policy that allowed employees to choose between entering into a private arbitration agreement with the employer, and reserving the right to file suit in a federal or state court for discrimination claims.

Gilmer did not end the questions about whether binding arbitration contracts in the employment area should be enforced. Two subsequent United States Supreme Court decisions, however, have clarified the impact of the Federal Arbitration Act on binding arbitration clauses in employment contracts. Perhaps the most significant ruling was that in the 2001 case of *Circuit City v. Saint Clair Adams*.[8] In that case, the plaintiff, an employee of Circuit City, had signed a binding arbitration agreement that had specifically

included claims based on discrimination, but two years later he brought an employment discrimination case against his employer in state court. Circuit City filed suit in federal district court to enjoin the state case and compel arbitration. The District Court issued the order.

On appeal of the District Court's order, the Circuit Court of Appeals held that the Federal Arbitration Act did not apply to employment contracts. This ruling was contrary to all other appellate rulings, and the U.S. Supreme Court heard the case. The high court overruled the Circuit Court's ruling, clearly setting forth the rule that the Federal Arbitration Act does apply to employment contracts, thereby making binding arbitration agreements in employment contracts enforceable, a decision giving much relief to employers. Many commentators forecast that this decision will lead to an even greater number of employers putting binding arbitration clauses in their employment contracts.

A subsequent decision by the high court, however, was not viewed quite so favorably by many employers. In the following case, the court went back to a situation similar to that in *Gilmer*, but in this case, it was not the employee seeking to bring a discrimination claim; rather, it was the EEOC. While this case involved the ADA, the high court stated that the analysis was applicable to all of the civil rights statutes used to eradicate discrimination in the workplace.

[8] 121 S. CT. 1302 (2001).

Case 4-4

Equal Employment Opportunity Commission

v.

Waffle House, Inc.

Supreme Court of the United States

2002 WL 6763 (January 15, 2002)

*A*ll employees of respondent Waffle House had to sign an agreement requiring employment disputes to be settled by binding arbitration. After Eric Baker suffered a seizure and was fired by respondent, he filed a discrimination charge with the Equal Employment Opportunity Commission (EEOC) alleging that his discharge violated the Americans with Disabilities Act of 1990 (ADA). The EEOC subsequently filed an enforcement suit, to which Baker is not a party, alleging that respondent's employment practices, including Baker's discharge "because of his disability," violated the ADA, and that the violation was intentional and done with malice or reckless indifference. The EEOC sought the following: an injunction to "eradicate the effects of [respondent's] past and present unlawful employment practices"; specific relief designed to make Baker whole, including back pay, reinstatement, and compensatory damages; and punitive damages for malicious and reckless conduct.

Respondent sought to dismiss the EEOC's suit and compel arbitration because of the binding arbitration clause signed by Baker. The District Court denied the motion, so respondent appealed. The Fourth Circuit agreed with the District Court that the arbitration agreement between Baker and respondent did not foreclose the enforcement action because the EEOC was not a party to the contract, but had independent statutory authority to bring an action to enforce the statute. However, the appellate court held that the EEOC was limited to injunctive relief and precluded from seeking victim-specific relief because the FAA policy favoring enforcement of private arbitration agreements outweighs the EEOC's right to proceed in federal court when it seeks primarily to vindicate private, rather than public, interests. EEOC appealed to the United States Supreme Court.

JUSTICE STEVENS

When Title VII was enacted in 1964, it authorized private actions by individual employees and public actions by the Attorney General in cases involving a "pattern or practice" of discrimination...

In 1972, Congress amended Title VII to authorize the EEOC to bring its own enforcement actions; indeed, we have observed that the 1972 amendments created a system in which the EEOC was intended "to bear the primary burden of litigation..."

In 1991, Congress again amended Title VII to allow the recovery of compensatory and punitive damages by a "complaining party." The term includes both private plaintiffs and the EEOC... Thus, these statutes unambiguously authorize the EEOC to obtain the relief that it seeks in its complaint if it can prove its case against respondent.

The Court of Appeals based its decision on its evaluation of the "competing policies" implemented by the ADA and the FAA.... It recognized that the EEOC never agreed to arbitrate its statutory claim...and that the EEOC has "independent statutory authority" to vindicate the public interest, but opined that permitting the EEOC to prosecute Baker's claim in court "would significantly trample" the strong federal policy favoring arbitration, because Baker had agreed to submit his claim to arbitration. To effectuate this policy, the court distinguished between injunctive and victim-specific relief, and held that the EEOC is barred from obtaining the latter, because any public interest served when the EEOC pursues "make whole" relief is outweighed by the policy goals favoring arbitration. Only when the EEOC seeks broad injunctive relief, in the Court of Appeals' view, does the public interest overcome the goals underpinning the FAA.

If it were true that the EEOC could prosecute its claim only with Baker's consent, or if its prayer for relief could be dictated by Baker, the court's analysis might be persuasive. But once a charge is filed, the exact opposite is true under the statute—the EEOC is in command of the process. The EEOC has exclusive jurisdiction over the claim for 180 days. During that time, the employee must obtain a right-to-sue letter from the agency before prosecuting the claim. If, however, the EEOC files suit on its own, the employee has no independent cause of action, although the employee may intervene in the EEOC's suit. In fact, the EEOC takes the position that it may pursue a claim on the employee's behalf even after the employee has disavowed any desire to seek relief. The statute makes the EEOC the master of its own case and confers on the agency the authority to evaluate the strength of the public interest at stake. Absent textual support for a contrary view, it is the public agency's province—not that of the court—to determine whether public resources should be committed to the recovery of victim-specific relief. And if the agency makes that determination, the statutory text unambiguously authorizes it to proceed in a judicial forum.

The Court of Appeals…simply sought to balance the policy goals of the FAA against the clear language of Title VII and the agreement. While this may be a more coherent approach, it is inconsistent with our recent arbitration cases. The FAA directs courts to place arbitration agreements on equal footing with other contracts, but it "does not require parties to arbitrate when they have not agreed to do so."… Here there is no ambiguity. No one asserts that the EEOC is a party to the contract, or that it agreed to arbitrate its claims. It goes without saying that a contract cannot bind a nonparty. Accordingly, the proarbitration policy goals of the FAA do not require the agency to relinquish its statutory authority if it has not agreed to do so.

Even if the policy goals underlying the FAA did necessitate some limit on the EEOC's statutory authority, the line drawn by the Court of Appeals between injunctive and victim-specific relief creates an uncomfortable fit with its avowed purpose of preserving the EEOC's public function while favoring arbitration. For that purpose, the category of victim-specific relief is both overinclusive and underinclusive. For example, it is overinclusive because while punitive damages benefit the individual employee, they also serve an obvious public function in deterring future violations.… Punitive damages may often have a greater impact on the behavior of other employers than the threat of an injunction, yet the EEOC is precluded from seeking this form of relief under the Court of Appeals' compromise scheme. And, it is underinclusive because injunctive relief, although seemingly not "victim-specific," can be seen as more closely tied to the employees' injury than to any public interest…

[T]he statutory language is clear; the EEOC has the authority to pursue victim-specific relief regardless of the forum that the employer and employee have chosen to resolve their disputes. Rather than than attempt to split the difference, we are persuaded that, pursuant to Title VII and the ADA, whenever the EEOC chooses from among the many charges filed each year to bring an enforcement action in a particular case, the agency may be seeking to vindicate a public interest, not simply provide make-whole relief for the employee, even when it pursues entirely victim-specific relief. To hold otherwise would undermine the detailed enforcement scheme created by Congress simply to give greater effect to an agreement between private parties that does not even contemplate the EEOC's statutory function.

It is true… that Baker's conduct may have the effect of limiting the relief that the EEOC may obtain in court. If, for example, he had failed to mitigate his damages, or had accepted a monetary settlement, any recovery by the EEOC would be limited accordingly.

But no question concerning the validity of his claim or the character of the relief that could be appropriately awarded in either a judicial or an arbitral forum is presented by this record. Baker has not sought arbitration of his claim, nor is there any indication that he has entered into settlement negotiations with respondent. It is an open question whether a settlement or arbitration judgment would affect the validity of the EEOC's claim or the character of relief the EEOC may seek. The only issue before this Court is whether the fact that Baker has signed a mandatory arbitration agreement limits the remedies available to the EEOC. The text of the relevant statutes provides a clear answer to that question. They do not authorize the courts to balance the competing policies of the ADA and the FAA, or to second-guess the agency's judgment concerning which of the remedies authorized by law that it shall seek in any given case.

Moreover, it simply does not follow from the cases holding, that the employee's conduct may affect the EEOC's recovery, that the EEOC's claim is merely derivative. We have recognized several situations in which the EEOC does not stand in the employee's shoes. See Occidental, (EEOC does not have to comply with state statutes of limitations); General Telephone, (EEOC does not have to satisfy Rule 23 requirements); Gilmer, (EEOC is not precluded from seeking classwide and equitable relief in court on behalf of an employee who signed an arbitration agreement). And, in this context, the statute specifically grants the EEOC exclusive authority over the choice of forum and the prayer for relief once a charge has been filed. The fact that ordinary principles of res judicata, mootness, or mitigation may apply to EEOC claims, does not contradict these decisions, nor does it render the EEOC a proxy for the employee.

REVERSED, in favor of petitioner EEOC.

1. Critical Thinking: How would you criticize the reasoning of the Supreme Court in this decision?

2. Ethical Decision Making: Which values are being furthered by this decision?

Arbitration is also used in medical malpractice cases, environmental disputes, commercial contract disputes, and insurance liability claims. However, no area uses arbitration in as great a percentage of cases as does the employment area.

Other ADR Methods

Several other methods of ADR are used less frequently. Some of these methods are similar to negotiation, involving the assistance of a neutral third party. It will be clear after finishing this section that today's manager really does have a variety of options to choose from when a dispute arises. Exhibit 4-3, provides some key questions for a manager to consider when trying to choose from among this array of dispute resolution options.

Summary Jury Trial

The summary jury trial began in 1983, when a court in Cleveland attempted to relieve pressure on an overloaded docket. A summary jury trial is an abbreviated trial that leads to a nonbinding jury verdict. Two advantages are inherent in this method of dispute resolution. First, it is quick; a summary jury trial lasts only a day. Second, because a jury offers a verdict, both parties would get a chance to see how their case would fare before a jury of their peers.

The process of the summary jury trial is similar to a regular trial, but there are some important differences. First, a judge advises a jury on the law. Second, each party's lawyer presents an opening statement along with

EXHIBIT 4-3

Questions to Ask When Selecting a Dispute Resolution Method

If you are party in a dispute, you would want to ask yourself the following questions to determine which dispute resolution method would be best.

1. How concerned are you about keeping costs low?
2. How quickly do you want to resolve the dispute?
3. Do you want to keep the dispute private?
4. Do you want to protect the relationship between the disputing parties?
5. Are you concerned about vindication?
6. Do you want to set a precedent with the resolution of your dispute?

a limited amount of evidence before the jury. Two key differences here are that the lawyers have a limited amount of time for this presentation, and there are no witnesses. All the evidence is presented by the lawyers. The jury then reaches a verdict. While this verdict is only advisory, the jury is not aware that the verdict is not binding. After the jury provides the verdict, the parties enter into a settlement conference, where they decide to accept the jury verdict, to reject the verdict, or to settle on some compromise. Approximately ninety-five percent of cases are settled at this time. However, if the case is not settled, it will go to

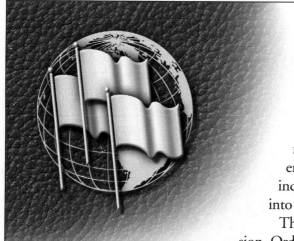

Global Context: Arbitration in Australia

In preparation for the 2000 Olympics in Sydney, Australia established a unique forum of arbitration: The Court of Arbitration for Sport. CAS was created in 1996 to assist individuals and sporting associations involved in sport-related disputes, from disciplinary measures to endorsement contracts. CAS is accessible to any individual or sporting association capable of entering into a legal transaction.

There are two divisions within CAS. The first division, Ordinary Arbitration, focuses on disputes arising from legal relations. For example, two television stations vying for coverage of the Indy 500 could settle the matter in the Ordinary Arbitration division. The second division is the Appeals Arbitration Division. Here, disputes over qualifications and disciplinary decisions of sports federations or associations are heard. A swimmer who tests positive for steroids, but denies the charge, could bring suit against the federation for the accusation in Appeals Arbitration Division.

Athletes and sports federations may find several advantages to using CAS over a traditional court system. CAS is suitable for international disputes because it allows the parties to choose the applicable law. The Code of Sports-Related Arbitration, which governs CAS, is a flexible code designed to be expeditious and efficient.

---

trial. At trial, nothing from the summary jury trial is admissible as evidence.

Minitrial

A minitrial is similar to arbitration and mediation because it involves a neutral third party. However, despite the presence of a neutral third party, the senior executives of the disputing corporations retain settlement authority. Lawyers for each side present their arguments before a corporate executive from each of the disputing companies and the neutral advisor, who would then offer an opinion as to what the verdict would be if the case went to trial. The neutral advisor's opinion, like the jury's verdict in the summary jury trial, is not binding. Next, the corporate executives discuss settlement options. If they reach an agreement, they enter into a contract that reflects the terms of the settlement.

A minitrial may be preferred to arbitration for three reasons. First, a minitrial is less costly than arbitration. Second, in the typical minitrial, the corporate executives, who presumably understand the complex matters of the dispute better than an outside arbitrator, have settlement authority. Third, the procedures of the minitrial can be modified to meet more precisely the needs of the parties. For example, parties may give the neutral advisor the authority to settle the case if the executives cannot come to a settlement agreement after a certain period of time.

Early Neutral Case Evaluation

Another form of ADR where the role of the neutral is advisory is early neutral case evaluation. In this form of ADR, parties select a neutral third party and explain their respective positions to this neutral, who evaluates the strengths and weaknesses of the case. The parties use this evaluation to reach a settlement.

Private Trials

Several states now allow **private trials**, trials where a referee is selected and paid by the disputing parties to offer a legally binding judgment in a dispute. These referees do not have to have any specific training;

Global Context: ADR in Japan

Some judges, lawyers, and politicians in the United States advocate the adoption of Japan's ADR techniques into the U.S. judiciary system. The techniques come in three forms: compromise, conciliation, and arbitration.

Compromise (wakai) is defined as a contractual agreement between parties that becomes the basis for a voluntary settlement. Due to the voluntary nature, no compromise is possible if one party does not wish to settle. Compromise may be proposed at three distinct times. First, a simple compromise may be reached before the initiation of a suit. Second, after initiation, but before litigation, the parties may appear in court and present a compromise. Such a compromise is legally binding on both parties. Finally, parties may compromise during litigation. This form of compromise is the most popular form. It has been estimated that nearly one-third of all disputes are settled using this technique.

The second ADR technique used in Japan is conciliation (chotei). Conciliation, reaching compromise through a third party's intervention, has been a part of Japanese culture for hundreds of years. In modern times, conciliation committees consist of one judge and two appointed members of the community. Acceptance of the committee's recommendation is not necessary, but if the parties wish to concede, the recommendation has the force of a judgment.

The final type of ADR is arbitration. Japanese arbitration is markedly similar to the United States' procedures. A two or three judge panel reaches a recommendation that is a binding decision.

The success and popularity of all three types of ADR in Japan is attributed to the attitudes of citizens. People in Japan are reluctant to bring a lawsuit against a fellow citizen. To them, ADR is a less brash way to resolve a dispute than suing someone outright. Obviously, this attitude is quite distinct from that of the American legal culture.

however, because retired judges often serve as referees, this method is often referred to a "rent-a-judge."

The case is often heard in private to ensure confidentiality. The disputing parties determine the time and place of the trial. The referee writes a report stating the findings of fact and the conclusions of the law. This report is filed with the trial judge; however, if any party is dissatisfied with the resolution of the case, they can request a new trial before a trial court judge. If this request is denied, they can appeal the decision of the referee.

Recently, private firms have started to offer private jury trials. The jurors are often better educated and have served in multiple private jury trials. Many scholars criticize the typical jury because they believe that the jury is unable to accurately fulfill its role as fact finder. Thus, offering a better educated, experienced jury helps to assuage these criticisms of the jury, yet offers the advantage of being judged by a jury of peers.

The private trial has been criticized for several reasons. First, scholars argue that use of the private trial could lead to a two-tiered system of justice. Those who have financial resources can afford a private trial that is much faster and cheaper than litigation, while those who are lacking resources are forced to use the slower public system. Second, private trials, like arbitration, have been criticized because they allow disputing parties to "hide" the dispute from the public.

Court Annexed ADR

The 1998 Alternative Dispute Resolution Act required that all district courts "consider the use of an alternative dispute resolution process at an appropriate stage in the litigation." Since that time, many federal and state jurisdictions have been mandating that parties use some form of ADR before they bring a dispute to trial. Some courts mandate certain forms of ADR, while other courts make ADR voluntary. Some simply mandate that all potential litigants be informed about alternatives to litigation. Some courts refer almost all civil cases to ADR, while others refer cases according to subject matter.

Mediation is the primary ADR process used in federal district courts. Arbitration is the next most frequently authorized program. In the federal system, more than 40 of the 94 district courts and almost all the circuit courts have mediation programs using judges or lawyers as mediators. Mediation programs are also underway in more than one-third of the state courts and in many bankruptcy courts. However, the "mandatory" component is not necessary to move cases to arbitration or mediation; 580 cases were voluntarily mediated in the Northern District of Texas in 1996.

The district courts vary greatly in terms of what ADR methods are approved. For example, in the Northern District Court of Alabama, each judge conducts an ADR evaluation conference to determine whether a case would be appropriate for ADR. The case could be either arbitrated or mediated. In contrast, in the Southern District of California, mediation, early neutral evaluation, minitrial, summary jury trial, and arbitration have been approved for use. The judicial officer may order a nonbinding arbitration to all simple contract and tort cases under $100,000.

Appellate courts also use ADR techniques. All thirteen appellate courts have created programs to help parties resolve issues on appeal. These programs typically encourage mediation. For example, the Tenth Circuit's Mediation office may schedule a mandatory settlement conference for any civil case on its docket. Once the conference is scheduled, the parties are required to participate. The purpose of the conference is to explore the possibility of settlement.

Use of ADR in International Disputes

Think for a moment how difficult litigation would be for an international dispute. Where would the case be heard? Who would decide the case? What kinds of awards would be offered? Because these questions are difficult to answer in the global context, ADR is favored.

Over 100 countries now belong to the United Nations Convention on the Recognition and Enforcement of Foreign Arbitral Awards, otherwise known as the New York Convention. This treaty ensures that an arbitration award will be enforced by countries that are parties to the treaty. There are three defenses to lack of enforcement of the arbitration award. First, the arbitrator acted outside the scope of their authority when making the decision. Second, one of the parties to the agreement did not have the authority to enter into a legal contract. Finally, the losing party did not receive notice of the arbitration.

Various organizations offer dispute resolution methods for international companies. These organizations include the American Arbitration Association, the International Chamber of Commerce, the United Nations Commission of International Trade Law, and the London Court of International Arbitration. The number of arbitration cases they hear each year is not insubstantial; the Arbitration Court of the International Chamber of Commerce alone heard 541 arbitration cases in 2000.[9]

The United States favors arbitration for resolution of international disputes. The Mitsubishi case illustrates this U.S. policy.

---

[9] Emmanuael Galliard, *The New ADR Rules of the International Chamber of Commerce*, NEW YORK UNIVERSITY LAW JOURNAL, October 10, 2001, at 3.

Case 4-5

Mitsubishi Motors Corporation

v.

Soler Chrysler-Plymouth
United States Supreme Court
473 U.S. 614 (1985)

*P*laintiff Mitsubishi Motors was a joint venture company formed by a Swiss and a Japanese firm to engage in the worldwide distribution of motor vehicles manufactured in the United States and bearing Mitsubishi and Chrysler trademarks. Defendant Soler Chrysler-Plymouth, a dealership incorporated in Puerto Rico, entered into a distributorship agreement with Mitsubishi that included a binding arbitration clause. Defendant Soler began to have difficulty selling the requisite number of cars, so it asked Mitsubishi to delay shipment of several orders. Thereafter, Defendant refused to accept liability for its failure to sell vehicles under the contract.

In accordance with a binding arbitration clause in the distribution agreement, Plaintiff Mitsubishi filed an action to compel arbitration. The district court ordered arbitration of all claims, including defendant's allegations of antitrust violations. The court of appeals reversed in favor of the defendant. Plaintiff Mitsubishi, appealed to the U.S. Supreme Court.

JUSTICE BLACKMUN

We granted certiorari primarily to consider whether an American court could enforce an agreement to resolve antitrust claims by arbitration when that agreement arises from an international transaction. Soler reasons that because it falls within a class of whose benefit the federal and local antitrust laws were passed, the clause cannot be read to contemplate arbitration of these statutory claims.

We do not agree, for we find no warrant in the Arbitration Act for implying in every contract a presumption against arbitration of statutory claims. The "liberal federal policy favoring arbitration agreements," manifested by the Act as a whole, is at bottom a policy guaranteeing the enforcement of private contractual arrangements: the Act simply "creates a body of federal substantive law establishing and regulating the duty to honor an agreement to arbitrate."

There is no reason to depart from these guidelines where a party bound by an arbitration agreement raises claims founded on statutory rights. Of course, courts should remain attuned to well-supported claims that the agreement to arbitrate resulted from the sort of fraud or overwhelming economic power that would provide grounds "for the revocation of any contract." But, absent such compelling considerations, the Act itself provides no basis for disfavoring agreements to arbitrate statutory claims.

By agreeing to arbitrate a statutory claim, a party does not forgo the substantive rights afforded by the statute, it only submits to their resolution in an arbitral, rather than a judicial, forum. It trades the procedures and opportunity for review in the courtroom for the simplicity, informality, and expedition of arbitration.

We now turn to consider whether Soler's antitrust claims are nonarbitrable even though it agreed to arbitrate them. . . . [W]e conclude that concerns of international comity, respect for the capacities of foreign and transnational tribunals, and sensitivity to the need of the international commercial system for predictability in the resolution of dispute, require that we enforce the parties' agreement, even assuming that a contrary result would be forthcoming in a domestic context.

There is no reason to assume at the outset of the dispute that the international arbitration will not provide an adequate mechanism. To be sure, the international arbitral tribunal owes no prior allegiance to the legal norms of particular states; hence, it has no direct obligation to vindicate their statutory dictates. The tribunal, however, is bound to effectuate the intentions of the parties. Where the parties have agreed that the arbitral body is to decide a defined set of claims that includes, as in these cases, those arising from the application of antitrust law, the tribunal therefore should be bound to decide that dispute in accord with the national law giving rise to the claim.

As international trade has expanded in recent decades, so, too, has the use of international arbitration to resolve disputes arising in the course of that trade. The controversies that international arbitral institutions are called upon to resolve have increased in diversity, as well as in complexity. Yet the potential of these tribunals for efficient disposition of legal disagreements arising from commercial relations has not yet been tested. If they are to take a central place in the international legal order, national courts will need to "shake off the old judicial hostility to arbitration" and also their customary and understandable unwillingness to cede jurisdiction of a claim arising under domestic law to a foreign or transnational tribunal. To this extent, at least, it will be necessary for national courts to subordinate domestic notions of arbitrability to the international policy favoring commercial arbitration.

Accordingly, we "require this representative of the American business community to honor its bargain,"...by holding this agreement to arbitrate "enforce[able] in accord with the explicit provisions of the Arbitration Act."

REVERSED AND REMANDED IN FAVOR OF THE PLAINTIFF, MITSUBISHI (on the issue of arbitrability).

1. Critical Thinking: Why did the court enforce the agreement?
2. Ethical Decision Making: Are there any important stakeholders whose interests are significantly harmed by this decision?

Hooters Case Wrap-up

The District Court of Virginia initially denied Hooters' petition to compel arbitration. The company appealed to the 4th Circuit Court of Appeals, which likewise ruled in Ms. Phillips' favor. The court held that although a predispute agreement to arbitrate Title VII claims is enforceable as a general matter, the employer in this particular case materially breached the agreement to arbitrate by promulgating "egregiously unfair" arbitration rules that called into question its contractual obligation to draft the arbitration rules in good faith.[10] The court found the arbitration rules so one-sided that it concluded, "their only possible purpose is to undermine the neutrality of the proceeding."

Although the procedures that turned the arbitration proceeding into a one-sided affair clearly need to be redrafted, Hooters management did do some things well. For example, it clearly stipulated in the agreement exactly which claims were going to be arbitrated, thereby giving employees full notice of the rights they were giving up. It also gave employees five days to think about signing the agreement. Had they provided full details of the arbitration procedures, employees would have had time to review and consider the contents of the agreement.

---

[10] *Hooters of America, Inc. v. Phillips,* 79 Fair Empl. Prac. Cas. (BNA) 629 (4th Cir. 1999).

	Summary
Primary Alternative Dispute Resolution Methods	**Negotiation**—an informal bargaining process, with or without lawyers, to try to solve a dispute. **Arbitration**—an ADR method in which a neutral third party (known as the arbitrator) hears both parties cases and renders a binding decision. **Summary jury trial**—an abbreviated trial that leads to a nonbinding jury verdict **Minitrial**—an ADR method in which a neutral advisor oversees presentation of the dispute, with the settlement authority residing with the senior executives of the disputing corporations.
Other ADR Methods	**Early neutral case evaluation**—an ADR method in which parties independently explain their positions to a neutral third party who evaluates the strengths and weaknesses of the case. This evaluation guides them in their settlement. **Private trials**—trials in which the disputing parties select and pay a referee to provide a legally binding judgment in a dispute
Court Annexed ADR	**Court Annexed ADR**—programs whereby courts encourage or mandate that parties use some form of ADR before they bring a dispute to trial.
Use of ADR in International Disputes	ADR is favored in international disputes.

Review Questions and Case Problems

1. What are the advantages and disadvantages of ADR?

2. How is mediation similar to arbitration?

3. When will a court overturn an arbitrator's decision?

4. How do you secure arbitration as a means of resolving a dispute?

5. Why is a minitrial sometimes described as a combination of other forms of ADR?

6. What type of ADR is preferred for resolving international disputes?

7. Plaintiffs, members of the International Brotherhood of Teamsters, Local 30 sued the Turnpike Commission, arguing that the commission was violating the Fair Labor Standards Act ("the FLSA"), by imposing a fluctuating hours method of compensation on the Plaintiffs. The grievance first went to mediation, but when this process was unsuccessful, the lawsuit was filed. Plaintiffs sought to introduce evidence of a statement made by one of the commissions' attorneys during depositions taken for and introduced in the mediation. Plaintiffs sought to introduce the evidence on the grounds that it was necessary for them to establish their retaliation claim under the FLSA. Defendants argued that these statements, which were made for the purpose of furthering the mediation process, should not be admissible in court. How do you believe the court ruled in this case, and why? *Patsy B. Sheldone, et al. v. Pennsylvania Turnpike Commission*, 48 Fed. R. Serv. 3d 943 (2001).

8. Adams, an African American, applied for a position with Frank's as an Executive Assistant in the company's Detroit, Michigan facility. Before it would consider Adams for the position, however, Frank's required Adams to complete and sign an application form that provided for compulsory arbitration of any and all employment claims. Specifically, by signing the form, applicants averred: I understand and agree that any claim I may wish to file against the Company or any of its employees or agents relative to my employment or termination of employment (including but not limited to any claim for any tort, discrimination, breach of contract, violation of public policy or statutory claim) must be filed no more than six months after either occurrence of which I am complaining or the termination of my employment, whichever occurs first. I specifically agree not to commence any claim more than six months after the date of termination of my employment and waive any statutes of limitation to the contrary. Any and all claims will be submitted for binding and final arbitration before the American Arbitration Association; arbitration will be the exclusive remedy for any and all claims unless prohibited by applicable law.

Frank's hired Adams as an Executive Assistant to Cohen. Five months later Frank's replaced Cohen with Carol Cox, who is white. Cox created an Executive Administrative Assistant position and did not hire Adams for the position, claiming that she needed to hire a more highly qualified individual for the job. Cox hired Lorraine Kryszak, an outside applicant, who is also white. Adams filed a complaint with the EEOC alleging that Frank's bypassed her for promotion to Executive Administrative Assistant because of her race. She subsequently resigned.

The EEOC investigated the matter and issued a determination that concluded that Frank's bypassed Adams for promotion because of her race. The EEOC subsequently filed suit in the district court, alleging that Frank's had engaged in unlawful employment practices by (1) bypassing Adams for promotion to Executive Administrative Assistant because of her race; and (2) requiring Adams and other applicants to sign and comply with an application for employment that requires arbitration of statutory rights afforded them by Title VII.

In its complaint, the EEOC requested (1) a permanent injunction enjoining Frank's from engaging in employment discrimination on the basis of race; (2) a permanent injunction enjoining Frank's from requiring prospective applicants or employees to sign an arbitration agreement limiting the right to sue under Title VII; (3) an order requiring Frank's to institute and carry out policies, practices, and programs providing equal employment opportunities to African Americans.

The district court declared the arbitration provision in the employment application enforceable, in light of *Gilmer v. Interstate/Johnson Lane Corp.*; held that the EEOC was bound by Adams' agreement to arbitrate in its effort to bring an employment discrimination claim on her behalf; and concluded that while, as a general principle, the EEOC could sue for injunctive relief on behalf of a class of individuals, but not in this case because it had not identified a class of individuals that suffered discrimination on the basis of race under Frank's' employment. The EEOC appealed. What do you think the outcome of their appeal was, and why? *EEOC v. Frank's Nursery & Crafts*, 79 Fair Emp. Cases (BNA) (1999).

9. The Sacharow brothers were the executors of their deceased father's estate. The brothers filed a statement of claim with the National Association of Securities Dealers (NASD) against Smith Barney in 1994. They alleged that Smith Barney, through one of its brokers, made risky and speculative investments that resulted in significant losses in their father's investment account. The brothers argued that their father was unable to monitor his account because of his health status.

The father's customer agreement with Smith Barney contained a clause that mandated arbitration. While Smith Barney agreed that there originally was an agreement to arbitrate, they argued that because the transactions that the Sacharow brothers disputed occurred six years prior to the filing of the claim, their claims were ineligible according to the six-year eligibility provision of the arbitration codes of the National Association of Securities Dealers and the New York Stock Exchange. The brothers argued that arbitrators, instead of courts, should determine whether potential claims are eligible for arbitration. Smith Barney highlighted the fact that many securities firms have been receiving injunctions to prevent customers from arbitrating claims older than six years from the date of filling.

Why did the New York Court Appeals rule in favor of the brothers? In the Matter of *Smith Barney Shearson, Inc. et. al. v. Jeffrey S. Sacharow et. al.*, 91 N.Y. 2d 39 (1997).

10. Miller injured her arm while at work at Public Storage Mangement. She took a medical leave for eight months. At the end of the leave, she was unable to return to work and was fired. Miller filed suit against Public Storage Management for violation of the Americans with Disabilities Act. Miller's employment contract included an arbitration clause mandating that any controversy over employment discrimination be resolved through arbitration. How did the court of appeals rule? Why? *Miller v. Public Storage Management, Inc.*, 121 F. 3d 215 (5th Cir., 1997).

11. When Matthew Shankle was hired by B-G Maintenance Management (B-G), he signed an employment agreement that included a binding arbitration clause. This clause stated that any disputes between Shankle and B-G were to be resolved through arbitration, and Shankle would "be responsible for one-half of the arbitrator's fees, and the company is responsible for the remaining half." Shankle was fired, and he brought suit against B-G for employment discrimination. B-G moved to mandate arbitration. The arbitrator required a $6,000 deposit. The district court ruled in Shankle's favor by refusing to compel arbitration because the fee-splitting requirement was held to be unenforceable. B-G appealed. Did the appellate court agree with Shankle? Why or why not? *Shankle v. B-G Maintenance Management of Colorado*, 163 F. 3d 1230 (10th Cir., 1999).

12. Rainbow Investments, which owned a motel in Alabama, signed an agreement to become a Super 8 Motel. Rainbow had to pay $21,000 to become a franchise. Additionally, they were required to make various repairs to the motel to achieve Super 8 standards. Rainbow argued that they signed the agreement with an oral understanding that Super 8 would return the $21,000 if the repairs were too expensive. When Rainbow discovered that they would have to pay $168,000 for repairs, they requested their money back from Super 8 to cancel the deal. Super 8 responded, claiming that the money was nonrefundable. When Rainbow brought suit against Super 8, Super 8 argued that the court should compel arbitration because the original contract contained a binding arbitration clause. Rainbow argued that Super 8 used fraud to convince Rainbow to sign the agreement; thus, Rainbow suggested that the arbitration clause is unenforceable. How did the district court rule? Why? *Rainbow Investments v. Super 8*, 1997 WL 464509 (M.D. Ala., 1997).

13. The Fair Labor Standards Act (FLSA) requires payment of overtime to employees who work more than 40 hours a week, unless the employee is in an "administrative" or "executive" position. Delfina Montes worked more than 40 hours a week for Shearson Lehman, and the firm did not pay her overtime on the grounds that she held an administrative or executive position that was exempt from the FLSA overtime requirement. An arbitrator hearing this case decided in favor of Shearson Lehman. Montes peti-

tioned the district court to vacate the arbitration board's decision because Shearson's attorney made the following statements before the arbitration board: "you as an arbitrator are not guided strictly to follow case precedent"; "You have to decide whether you're going to follow the statutes that have been presented to you, or whether you will do. . . what is right and just and equitable in this case." Montes argued that the arbitrator could not simply ignore the law when arbitrating a case, which was what she felt Shearson's attorneys had asked the arbitrator to do.

Montes' petition was denied by the District Court. How do you believe the Court of Appeals ruled in this case? Why? *Delfina Montes v. Shearson Lehman Brothers, Inc.*, 128 F. 3d 1456 (11th Cir. 1997).

14. Plaintiffs Armendariz and Olague-Rodgers were employed by defendant Foundation Health Psychcare Services, Inc. On June 20, 1996, they were told they were being terminated because their positions were being eliminated. They sued the defendant for wrongful termination, arguing that they had been fired because of their perceived and/or actual sexual orientation.

Both had signed employment agreements that contained binding arbitration clauses that required them to submit all employment disputes to binding arbitration, and limited their remedies related to employment claims to "a sum equal to the wages I would have earned from the date of any discharge until the date of the arbitration award." The agreement further provided that the plaintiff would not be entitled to any other remedy at law or equity.

On what grounds do you believe that the California State Supreme Court ultimately refused to enforce the binding arbitration clause? *Marybeth Amendariz et al. v. Foundation Health Psychcare Services, Inc.*, P.3d 669 (2000).

15. Mr. Gibbs and a termite exterminator entered into termite control contract in which they agreed that all disputes would be settled by arbitration. Dobson purchased Mr. Gibbs and took over the contract with the exterminator. When Allied-Bruce-Termix did not meet the terms of the contract, Dobson filed suit in court. The state court ruled in favor of Dobson, stating that the Federal Arbitration Act did not apply to the contract because the contract did not involve an interstate transaction. The case was appealed to the Supreme Court. Why did the court overrule the state supreme court? *Allied-Bruce-Termix Cos. v. Dobson*, 513 U.S. 265 (1995).

16. Correll entered into an employment agreement with Distinctive Dental Service (DDS). This agreement stated that Correll could not directly or indirectly engage in business with any competitor located within seven miles of DDS. Furthermore, the employment agreement included a clause providing that any dispute between Correll and DDS should be settled by arbitration. When Correll's wife, who was also a dentist, went to work for a competitor within seven miles of DDS, Corell was fired. Corell filed a suit against DDS for marital status discrimination, but DDS demanded arbitration. The District Court ruled in Corell's favor by refusing to enforce the arbitration clause. DDS appealed. What did the appellate court decide? *Correll v. Distinctive Dental Services*, 594 N.W. 2d 222 (Ct. App., Minn., 1999).

Assignment on the Internet

This chapter has briefly discussed several websites that offer dispute resolution for a fee. For example, ClickNSettle allows disputing parties to quickly settle their disputes through negotiation on the Internet. Look at the ClickNSettle website. Try to find at least one other website that provides the opportunity for online dispute resolution. Look carefully at the website's steps for dispute resolution. What kinds of problems might be associated with this process? Use your knowledge of the advantages and disadvantages of ADR to make a list of potential problems with the website's process.

Next, find a website that provides a listing of mediators or allows you to search for a mediator. Explain how you would go about selecting a mediator based on the information provided. In other words, what qualifications do you consider necessary for a mediator? Furthermore, is there any information missing about your potential mediator you would like to know?

On the Internet

http://adrr.com *Offers many online materials for ADR, specifically mediation.*

http://www.adr.org *Home page of the American Arbitration Association.*

http://www.internationalADR.com/ *Provides information about aspects of international mediation and arbitration.*

http://www.pon.harvard.edu *Home page of the Harvard Program on Negotiation, which is dedicated to improving the theory and practice of negotiation and dispute resolution.*

Regulation of Wetlands: A Job for the Federal or State Governments?

In 1972, using the power it was given by the Commerce Clause to regulate interstate commerce, Congress passed the Clean Water Act (CWA) to reduce the pollution of United States waters. Congress gave the Army Corps of Engineers (Corps) the power to approve or deny permits to discharge dredged or fill materials into navigable waters, and Congress gave the Environmental Protection Agency (EPA) the power to veto the Corps' permits. In 1975, a federal judge decided that this provision also applied to wetlands that were adjacent to navigable waters. Subsequent regulatory and court decisions further expanded federal power through the adoption of the "migratory bird rule" in 1986, which gave the Corps the authority to also issue permits for the filling of isolated wetlands if those wetlands were used by migratory birds.

In 1994, a consortium of suburban Chicago municipalities selected as a solid waste disposal site an abandoned sand and gravel pit with excavation trenches that had evolved into permanent and seasonal ponds. Because the operation called for filling in some of the ponds, the consortium contacted the Corps to determine whether they needed a permit. Because the ponds were used as habitat for migratory birds, the Corps required them to apply for a permit. When the Corps refused to grant the permit, the consortium challenged both the denial of the permit on its merits, and the authority of Congress to regulate bodies of water that were not interstate. In other words, they argued that the migratory bird rule was beyond the scope of the federal government's authority.[1]

1. *Do you believe that Congress has exceeded the scope of its authority under the Commerce Clause? Why or why not?*
2. *If the court ruled in favor of the consortium and struck down Congressional authority to protect isolated wetlands, what would prevent all such wetlands from eventually being developed and destroying significant amounts of migratory birds' habitat?*

---

[1] Sources: James Bovard, *Bloody Nose for Petty Tyrants*, THE WASHINGTON TIMES, January 14, 2001 at __; Jo Sandin, *McCallum Promises to Safeguard Wetlands*, THE MILWAUKEE JOURNAL & SENTINEL, January 12, 2001 (2001 WL 9332869); *Solid Waste Agency Of Northern Cook County, Petitioner, v. United States Army Corps Of Engineers, et al.*, 120 S.Ct. 2711 (2000).

CHAPTER 5

Constitutional Principles

The U.S. Constitution

The Commerce Clause

Taxing and Spending Powers of the Federal Government

The Bill of Rights

Other Constitutional Restrictions on Government

The framework of our nation is set forth in the U.S. Constitution, which established a system of government that divides power between the federal government and the states. This system of government provides the initial focus for this chapter.

In this chapter we examine the Constitutional provisions that affect business, beginning with the Supremacy Clause, and then turn our focus to the Commerce Clause, mentioned in the opening scenario, which is the primary source of the federal government's authority to regulate business. We next examine the federal government's authority to tax and spend. Finally, in the latter part of the chapter we focus on how several amendments to the Constitution affect business.

The U.S. Constitution

Although we think of a constitution as providing the foundation for every country's system of government, not every nation has a written constitution. Great Britain, for example, does not have such a document. In fact, it was England's lack of a formal document containing fixed constitutional protections that helped convince the founders of the United States to establish a written constitution.

The U.S. Constitution establishes a system of government that is based on the principle of **federalism**, under which the authority to govern is divided between the federal and the state governments. Under the principle of federalism embodied in our Constitution, all powers not given exclusively to the federal government nor taken from the states are reserved to the states. Because the federal government has only those powers

granted to it by the Constitution, federal legislation that affects business must be based on an expressed constitutional grant of authority.

In addition to allocating authority between the state and federal governments, the Articles of the Constitution allocate the power of the federal government among the three branches of government. The first three Articles establish three independent branches of the federal government: the legislative, executive, and judicial branches. The Constitution ensures that each independent branch is given a separate sphere of power to prevent any one branch from obtaining more power than the others and taking control of the government.

In addition to creating this **separation of powers**, the Constitution also set up a system of *checks and balances*. The powers given to each branch operate as a check to keep the other branches from being able to seize enough power to dominate the government. For example, Congress, the legislative or lawmaking branch, has the power to enact legislation, but the President can veto a law that Congress passes. However, the legislature could then overturn the President's veto with a vote of two-thirds of the members of Congress. And even if Congress passes a bill and the President signs it, the judiciary may strike it down as being unconstitutional. Exhibit 5-1 illustrates this system in more detail.

While there is usually not a lot of conflict among the branches of government about the powers each has, as this book goes to press, an interesting dispute is developing between the legislative and executive branches that may end up being settled by the judiciary. Fairly soon after taking office, Vice President Cheney established a task force to help him draft an energy policy. The task force allegedly held a number of meetings with executives and lobbyists from a number of energy concerns. When the draft energy policy was released, Congress, in an attempt to exercise its oversight authority, asked for information about whom the vice presidential task force met with as it was formulating its energy policy. The Vice President refused to turn the information over to Congress or to the General Accounting Agency, the agency used by Congress to conduct investigations of how the government is functioning. While it first appeared that the executive branch's stonewalling tactics were going to be successful, once one of the primary energy companies the task force was alleged to have conferred with, Enron, filed bankruptcy, Congressional interest in investigating the task force activities was renewed. While the executive branch claims the information is protected by executive privilege, Congress insists that details of how the policy was crafted are crucial to their debate over the policy. If some sort of compromise is not reached, the courts may decide the issue.[2]

[2] *GAO Brandishes Lawsuit in Energy Task Force Probe*, FINDLAW LEGAL NEWS AND COMMENTARY <wysiwyg://2/http://news.findlaw.com/scr...s/s/20020125/enroncongresscheneydc.html> (January 27, 2002).

EXHIBIT 5-1

The System of Checks and Balances

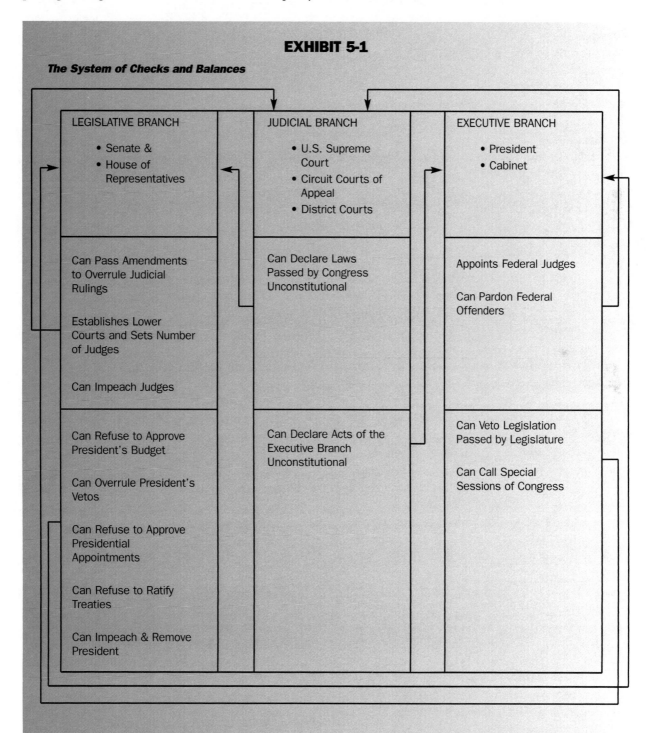

LEGISLATIVE BRANCH	JUDICIAL BRANCH	EXECUTIVE BRANCH
• Senate & • House of Representatives	• U.S. Supreme Court • Circuit Courts of Appeal • District Courts	• President • Cabinet
Can Pass Amendments to Overrule Judicial Rulings Establishes Lower Courts and Sets Number of Judges Can Impeach Judges	Can Declare Laws Passed by Congress Unconstitutional	Appoints Federal Judges Can Pardon Federal Offenders
Can Refuse to Approve President's Budget Can Overrule President's Vetos Can Refuse to Approve Presidential Appointments Can Refuse to Ratify Treaties Can Impeach & Remove President	Can Declare Acts of the Executive Branch Unconstitutional	Can Veto Legislation Passed by Legislature Can Call Special Sessions of Congress

The Supremacy Clause and Federal Preemption

The **Supremacy Clause**, Article V of the U.S. Constitution, provides that the Constitution, laws, and treaties of the United States constitute the supreme law of the land, "any Thing in the Constitution or Laws of any State to the Contrary notwithstanding." This Article is based on the principle of **federal supremacy**, which means that any state or local law that directly conflicts with the U.S. Constitution or federal laws or treaties is void. Federal laws include rules promulgated by federal administrative agencies.

The United States is not alone in holding that its Constitution is the supreme law of the land. Section 52(1) of the Constitution Act of Canada, passed in 1982, states that "the Constitution of Canada is the supreme law of Canada, and any law that is inconsistent with the provisions of the Constitution is, to the extent of the inconsistency, of no force or effect."

In some areas, the state and federal governments have **concurrent authority**; that is, both governments have the power to regulate the same subject matter. In such cases, the states may regulate in the area as long as a party's compliance with the state regulation would not cause that party to be in violation of a federal regulation. For example, Congress has established a number of environmental standards, but some states have chosen to promulgate even more protective standards.

Sometimes, however, in areas where the state and federal governments have concurrent authority, the federal government expresses the intent to provide the exclusive regulation of that area. In such a situation, under the doctrine of **federal preemption**, the state law will be struck down. To determine Congressional intent, the court will look to the language of the statute and the transcripts of the hearings that took place when the law was being considered. It is often difficult to know when the courts will find that Congress intended to preempt the area. For example, in many instances the federal government will establish product safety standards. If a plaintiff is injured, the question often arises as to whether the federal government intended to preempt regulation of that product, thereby preventing injured parties from bringing lawsuits against the manufacturers under state laws that would otherwise give them the right to sue. Cases of federal preemption are especially likely to arise in matters pertaining to interstate commerce (discussed in the next section), where a local regulation imposes a substantial burden on the flow of interstate commerce through a particular state.

The Commerce Clause

The primary source of authority for the federal regulation of business is the Commerce Clause, Article I, Section 8 of the U.S. Constitution. This clause states that the U.S. Congress has the power to "regulate Commerce with foreign Nations, and among the several States, and with the Indian Tribes." This allocation of authority gives power to the federal government, while at the same time, effectively restricts the power of the state governments.

The Commerce Clause as a Source of Authority for the Federal Government

Today, most federal regulations are justified as being exercises of congressional authority under the Commerce Clause. As long as a law can be shown to somehow affect commerce among the states, or interstate commerce, the regulation will generally be upheld. The interpretation of the phrase "among the several states" has been subject to changing interpretations throughout our history. Prior to the 1930's, the clause was interpreted very strictly, or narrowly, to require that the regulated activity actually involve trade between states. Such an interpretation authorized only a limited number of federal regulations of business.

But in the 1930's, after the Great Depression indicated to some a need for greater federal regulation of economic matters, the Supreme Court began to broaden its interpretation of the Commerce Clause. A turning point in the Supreme Court's interpretation of the Commerce Clause was their decision in the 1937 case of *NLRB v. Jones & Laughlin Steel Corp.*, a case in which the Supreme Court ruled that Congress could regulate labor relations at a manufacturing plant because a work stoppage at such a plant would have a serious impact on interstate commerce. In that case, the Court stated, "[a]lthough activities may be intrastate in character when separately considered, if they have such a close and substantial relationship to interstate commerce that their control is essential or appropriate to protect that commerce from burdens or obstructions, Congress cannot be denied the power to exercise that control."[3] Since that case, a broad range of business activities have been regulated under the authority of the Commerce Clause. Statutes as diverse as the Federal Mine Safety and Health Act, which sets standards for safety in coal mines; the Americans with Disabilities Act, which prohibits firms from discriminating against employees and

---

[3] *NLRB v. Jones & Laughlin Steel Corp.*, 301 U.S. 1 (1937).

potential employees who have disabilities; and the Consumer Protection Act, which criminalizes certain "loan sharking" activities, have all been challenged as being beyond the scope of Congressional power, but have been upheld as valid exercises of Commerce Clause authority.[4]

However, beginning with the 1995 case of *United States v. Lopez,*[5] the U. S. Supreme Court seems to be giving less deference to Congressional attempts to pass legislation based on the Commerce Clause. In *Lopez,* the U.S. Supreme Court found that Congress had

[4] See *U.S. v. Lake,* 985 F. 2d 265 (1995); *International House of Pancakes v. Theodore Pinnock,* 844 F. Supp. 574 (1993); and *Perez, Petitioner, v. United States,* 402 U.S. 146 (1971).
[5] 514 U.S. 549 (1995).

exceeded its authority under the Commerce Clause when it passed the Gun-Free School Zone Act, a law that banned the possession of guns within one thousand feet of any school. In finding the statute unconstitutional, the high court said that Congress was attempting to regulate in an area that had "nothing to do with commerce, or any sort of economic enterprise." While some initially thought that the *Lopez* case was an anomaly, the following case indicates that the court was serious in its intent to scrutinize the basis for federal laws more carefully. The court's ruling in these commerce clause cases seems to be consistent with what many legal scholars see as a willingness of the current Supreme Court to increasingly shift the balance of power away from the federal governments to the state governments.

Case 5-1

Christy Brzonkala
v.
Antonio J. Morrison et al.
Supreme Court of the United States
120 S. Ct. 1740 (2000)

*P*etitioner Christy Brzonka and respondents Antonio Morrison and James Crawford were students at Virginia Polytechnic Institute (Virginia Tech). Brzonkala met the respondents at a campus party, where they allegedly assaulted and raped her. According to Brzonkala, during the months following the rape, Morrison made boasting, debasing, and vulgar remarks in the dormitory's dining room about what he would do to women. Brzonkala claimed that this attack, and Morrison's subsequent behavior, caused her to become severely, emotionally disturbed and depressed. She sought assistance from a university psychiatrist, who prescribed antidepressant medication. Shortly after the rape Brzonkala stopped attending classes and withdrew from the university.

Brzonkala filed a complaint against respondents under Virginia Tech's Sexual Assault Policy. Morrisson was initially found guilty and suspended for two semesters, but his punishment was ultimately set aside.

Brzonkala subsequently sued Morrison, Crawford, and Virginia Tech in federal court, alleging, among other claims, that Morrison's and Crawford's attack violated the Violence Against Women Act. Morrison and Crawford moved to dismiss this complaint on the grounds that it failed to state a claim and that the Act's (§ 13981's) civil remedy was unconstitutional.

The District Court found that Brzonkala's complaint stated a claim against Morrison and Crawford under § 13981, but dismissed the complaint because it concluded that Congress lacked *authority to enact the section. The United States Court of Appeals, by a divided vote, affirmed the District Court's conclusion that Congress lacked constitutional authority to enact § 13981's civil remedy.*

CHIEF JUSTICE REHNQUIST

…Section 13981 was part of the Violence Against Women Act of 1994,…It states that "[a]ll persons within the United States shall have the right to be free from crimes of violence motivated by gender." To enforce that right, subsection (c) declares:

"A person…who commits a crime of violence motivated by gender and thus deprives another of the right declared in subsection (b) of this section shall be liable to the party injured, in an action for the recovery of compensatory and punitive damages, injunctive and declaratory relief, and such other relief as a court may deem appropriate."…

Every law enacted by Congress must be based on one or more of its powers enumerated in the Constitution….[W]e turn to the question whether § 13981 falls within Congress' power under Article I, § 8, of the Constitution. Brzonkala and the United States rely upon the third clause of the Article, which gives Congress power "[t]o regulate Commerce with foreign Nations, and among the several States, and with the Indian Tribes."

As we discussed at length in *Lopez,* our interpretation of the Commerce Clause has changed as our Nation has developed…*Lopez* emphasized, however, that even under our modern, expansive interpretation of the Commerce Clause, Congress' regulatory authority is not without effective bounds.

…[M]odern Commerce Clause jurisprudence has "identified three broad categories of activity that Congress may regulate under its commerce power." …"First, Congress may regulate the use of the channels of interstate commerce." …"Second, Congress is empowered to regulate and protect the instrumentalities of interstate commerce, or persons or things in interstate commerce, even though the threat may come only from intrastate activities." …"Finally, Congress' commerce authority includes the power to regulate those activities having a substantial relation to interstate commerce,…i.e., those activities that substantially affect interstate commerce."

Petitioners…seek to sustain § 13981 as a regulation of activity that substantially affects interstate commerce. Given § 13981's focus on gender-motivated violence wherever it occurs…we agree that this is the proper inquiry.

Since *Lopez* most recently canvassed and clarified our case law governing this third category of Commerce Clause regulation, it provides the proper framework for conducting the required analysis of § 13981. In *Lopez,* we held that the Gun-Free School Zones Act of 1990, which made it a federal crime to knowingly possess a firearm in a school zone, exceeded Congress' authority under the Commerce Clause. Several significant considerations contributed to our decision.

First, we observed that § 922(q) was "a criminal statute that by its terms has nothing to do with 'commerce' or any sort of economic enterprise, however broadly one might define those terms." …[T]he pattern of analysis is clear. "Where economic activity substantially affects interstate commerce, legislation regulating that activity will be sustained."

Both petitioners and Justice Souter's dissent downplay the role that the economic nature of the regulated activity plays in our Commerce Clause analysis. But a fair reading of *Lopez* shows that the noneconomic, criminal nature of the conduct at issue was central to our decision in that case…*Lopez's* review of Commerce Clause case law demonstrates that in those cases where we have sustained federal regulation of intrastate activity based upon the activity's substantial effects on interstate commerce, the activity in question has been some sort of economic endeavor.

The second consideration that we found important in analyzing § 922(q) was that the statute contained "no express jurisdictional element which might limit its reach to a discrete set of firearm possessions that additionally have an explicit connection with or effect on interstate commerce." Such a jurisdictional element may establish that the enactment is in pursuance of Congress' regulation of interstate commerce.

Third, we noted that neither § 922(q) "'nor its legislative history contain[s] express congressional findings regarding the effects upon interstate commerce of gun possession in a school zone.'"…While "Congress normally is not required to make formal findings as to the substantial burdens that an activity has on interstate commerce," the existence of such findings may "enable us to evaluate the legislative judgment that the activity in question substantially affect[s] interstate commerce, even though no such substantial effect [is] visible to the naked eye."

Finally, our decision in *Lopez* rested in part on the fact that the link between gun possession and a substantial effect on interstate commerce was attenuated.…The United States argued that the possession of guns may lead to violent crime, and that violent crime "can be expected to affect the functioning of the national economy in two ways. First, the costs of violent crime are substantial, and, through the mechanism of insurance, those costs are spread throughout the population. Second, violent crime reduces the willingness of individuals to travel to areas within the country that are perceived to be unsafe." The Government also argued that the presence of guns at schools poses a threat to the educational process, which in turn threatens to produce a less efficient and productive workforce, which will negatively affect national productivity and thus interstate commerce.

We rejected these "costs of crime" and "national productivity" arguments because they would permit Congress to "regulate not only all violent crime, but all activities that might lead to violent crime, regardless of how tenuously they relate to interstate commerce." We noted that, under this but-for reasoning: "Congress could regulate any activity that it found was related to the economic productivity of individual citizens: family law (including marriage, divorce, and child custody), for example. Under the[se] theories…, it is difficult to perceive any limitation on federal power, even in areas such as criminal law enforcement or education where States historically have been sovereign. Thus, if we were to accept the Government's arguments, we are hard pressed to posit any activity by an individual that Congress is without power to regulate."

With these principles underlying our Commerce Clause jurisprudence as reference points, the proper resolution of the present cases is clear. Gender-motivated crimes of violence are not, in any sense of the phrase, economic activity. While we need not adopt a categorical rule against aggregating the effects of any noneconomic activity in order to decide these cases, thus far in our Nation's history our cases have upheld Commerce Clause regulation of intrastate activity only where that activity is economic in nature.

Like the Gun-Free School Zones Act at issue in *Lopez*, § 13981 contains no jurisdictional element establishing that the federal cause of action is in pursuance of Congress' power to regulate interstate commerce.

In contrast with the lack of congressional findings that we faced in *Lopez*, § 13981 is supported by numerous findings regarding the serious impact that gender-motivated violence has on victims and their families.…But the existence of congressional findings is not sufficient, by itself, to sustain the constitutionality of Commerce Clause legislation. As we stated in *Lopez*, "'[S]imply because Congress may conclude that a particular activity substantially affects interstate commerce does not necessarily make it so.'" …Rather, "'[w]hether particular operations affect interstate commerce sufficiently to come under the constitutional power of Congress to regulate them is ultimately a judicial rather than a legislative question, and can be settled finally only by this Court.'"

In these cases, Congress' findings are substantially weakened by the fact that they rely so heavily on a method of reasoning that we have already rejected as unworkable if we are to maintain the Constitution's enumeration of powers. Congress found that gender-motivated violence affects interstate commerce "by deterring potential victims from traveling interstate, from engaging in employment in interstate business, and from transacting with business, and in places involved in interstate commerce;…by diminishing national productivity, increasing medical and other costs, and decreasing the supply of and the demand for interstate products." Given these findings and petitioners' arguments, the concern that we expressed in _Lopez_ that Congress might use the Commerce Clause to completely obliterate the Constitution's distinction between national and local authority seems well founded.

The reasoning that petitioners advance seeks to follow the but-for causal chain from the initial occurrence of violent crime (the suppression of which has always been the prime object of the States' police power) to every attenuated effect upon interstate commerce. If accepted, petitioners' reasoning would allow Congress to regulate any crime as long as the nationwide, aggregated impact of that crime has substantial effects on employment, production, transit, or consumption. Indeed, if Congress may regulate gender-motivated violence, it would be able to regulate murder or any other type of violence since gender-motivated violence, as a subset of all violent crime, is certain to have lesser economic impacts than the larger class of which it is a part.

We accordingly reject the argument that Congress may regulate noneconomic, violent criminal conduct based solely on that conduct's aggregate effect on interstate commerce. The Constitution requires a distinction between what is truly national and what is truly local.…In recognizing this fact we preserve one of the few principles that has been consistent since the Clause was adopted. The regulation and punishment of intrastate violence that is not directed at the instrumentalities, channels, or goods involved in interstate commerce has always been the province of the States.

AFFIRMED, IN FAVOR OF RESPONDENTS.

DISSENT

JUSTICE SOUTER, with whom Justice Stevens, Justice Ginsberg, and Justice Breyer join

…Congress has the power to legislate with regard to activity that, in the aggregate, has a substantial effect on interstate commerce. The fact of such a substantial effect is not an issue for the courts in the first instance, but for the Congress, whose institutional capacity for gathering evidence and taking testimony far exceeds ours. By passing legislation, Congress indicates its conclusion, whether explicitly or not, that facts support its exercise of the commerce power. The business of the courts is to review the congressional assessment, not for soundness but simply for the rationality of concluding that a jurisdictional basis exists in fact. Any explicit findings that Congress chooses to make, though not dispositive of the question of rationality, may advance judicial review by identifying factual authority on which Congress relied.

One obvious difference from _United States v. Lopez_ is the mountain of data assembled by Congress, here showing the effects of violence against women on interstate commerce. Passage of the Act in 1994 was preceded by four years of hearings, which included testimony from physicians and law professors; from survivors of rape and domestic violence; and from representatives of state law enforcement and private business. The record includes reports on gender bias from task forces in twenty-one states, and we have the benefit of specific factual findings of the eight separate reports issued by Congress and its committees over the long course leading to enactment.

Having identified the problem of violence against women, Congress may address what it sees as the most threatening manifestation…Congress found that "crimes of violence motivated by gender have a substantial adverse effect on interstate commerce, by deterring potential victims from traveling interstate, from engaging in employment in interstate business, and from transacting with business, and in places involved, in interstate commerce…[,] by diminishing national productivity, increasing medical and other costs, and decreasing the supply of and the demand for interstate products.…"

Congress thereby explicitly stated the predicate for the exercise of its Commerce Clause power. Is its conclusion irrational in view of the data amassed? True, the methodology of particular studies may be challenged, and some of the figures arrived at may be disputed. But the sufficiency of the evidence before

Congress to provide a rational basis for the finding cannot seriously be questioned…Indeed, the legislative record here is far more voluminous than the record compiled by Congress and found sufficient in two prior cases upholding Title II of the Civil Rights Act of 1964 against Commerce Clause challenges.

The fact that the Act does not pass muster before the Court today is therefore proof, to a degree that *Lopez* was not, that the Court's nominal adherence to the substantial effects test is merely that. Although a new jurisprudence has not emerged with any distinctness, it is clear that some congressional conclusions about obviously substantial, cumulative effects on commerce are being assigned lesser values than the once-stable doctrine would assign them. These devaluations are accomplished not by any express repudiation of the substantial effects test or its application through the aggregation of individual conduct, but by supplanting rational basis scrutiny with a new criterion of review.

Thus the elusive heart of the majority's analysis in these cases is its statement that Congress's findings of fact are "weakened" by the presence of a disfavored "method of reasoning." This seems to suggest that the "substantial effects" analysis is not a factual enquiry, for Congress in the first instance with subsequent judicial review looking only to the rationality of the congressional conclusion, but one of a rather different sort, dependent upon a uniquely judicial competence.

This new characterization of substantial effects has no support in our cases (the self-fulfilling prophecies of *Lopez* aside), least of all those the majority cites.

1. Critical Thinking: The fate of the Migratory Birds rule discussed in the opening of this chapter was determined after the decision was handed down in this challenge to the Violence Against Women Act. Explain why you believe the decision in this case is or is not relevant to the court's determination of whether the Migratory Bird rule was beyond the scope of federal authority.

2. Ethical Decision Making: Explain how different stakeholders would be the primary beneficiaries of the majority and minority decisions.

The Commerce Clause as a Restriction on State Authority

Because the Commerce Clause grants authority to regulate commerce to the federal government, a conflict sometimes arises over the extent to which granting such authority to the federal government restricts the states' authority to regulate commerce. Courts have attempted to resolve the conflict over the impact of the Commerce Clause on state regulation by distinguishing between regulations of commerce and regulations under the state *police power*. **Police power** means the residual powers retained by the state to enact legislation to safeguard the health and welfare of its citizenry. Typical exercises of a state's police power would include not only state criminal laws, but also laws such as building codes, zoning laws, sanitation standards for restaurants, and regulations for the practice of medicine within a state.

Sometimes, when a state exercises its police power, the law has an impact on interstate commerce. If the court finds that the *purpose* of a state law is to regulate interstate commerce, or to discriminate against interstate commerce, this law will usually be struck down. Likewise, if a law *substantially* interferes with interstate commerce, it will generally be struck down.

Most cases are not so simple, however, and the court must apply a balancing test, weighing the states' interest in protecting its citizens and the regulatory scheme used to further that interest, against the impact on interstate commerce. In attempting to balance the competing interests, the court will generally begin by asking *whether the state regulation is rationally related to a legitimate state end.* If it is, the court may then ask *whether the regulatory burden imposed on interstate commerce is outweighed by the state interest in enforcing the legislation.* They may additionally inquire as to *whether there is some less drastic alternative available to attain the legitimate state purpose.* Although there is generally a presumption of validity given to laws adopted pursuant to a state's police powers, it is not always easy to know whether a law will be upheld. One example of a challenged piece of state legislation that was eventually upheld by the U.S. Court of Appeals was an ordinance passed by the city of Chicago to ban spray paint in the city as a means of fighting graffiti that was springing up all over.[6]

[6] http://www.lawyersweeklyusa.com:8000/signup/archives.cfm? articledate=95&articlestate=USA&articleid==View&VdkVgwKey =95002648%&page=/archives/usa/95/95002648.htm (March 23, 2001).

The following case provides an illustration of an attempt to challenge a state regulation on grounds that it places an undue burden on interstate commerce. Notice that in this case, we do not actually have a final outcome on the matter. In this case, the plaintiffs asked for a preliminary injunction prohibiting the state from enforcing the law because they believed that they would have a good chance of ultimately winning the case on its merits. So the issue on appeal was technically whether the plaintiffs were likely to win the case.

Case 5-2

National Electrical Manufacturers Association
v.
William H. Sorrell, Attorney General of the State of Vermont, John Kassel, et al
Second Circuit Court of Appeals
53 ERC 1385 (2001)

In 1998, the Vermont Legislature enacted a statute that requires manufacturers of certain mercury-containing products (including thermostats, batteries, and lamps) to label their products and packaging to inform consumers that; (1) the products contain mercury and (2) on disposal, should be recycled or disposed of as hazardous waste. The trade association of manufacturers of mercury-containing light bulbs (NEMA) brought action against state officials, seeking to have the law declared unconstitutional, and asking for a preliminary injunction to prohibit enforcement of the law. The United States District Court granted the preliminary injunction, and officials appealed.

CHIEF JUDGE JOHN M. WALKER, JR.

[1] A statute may violate the well-established "dormant" aspect of the Commerce Clause in one of two ways: it may clearly discriminate against interstate commerce, in which case it is virtually invalid per se, or even if it does not evince such discriminatory effect, it may still be unconstitutional if it imposes a burden on interstate commerce incommensurate with the local benefits secured…

[2] NEMA argues that section 6621d violates the Commerce Clause in the latter manner. We disagree and thus conclude that NEMA cannot show likely success on the merits of its Commerce Clause claim.

In *Pike*, the Supreme Court adopted a balancing test to determine whether state statutes that incidentally burden interstate commerce violate the Commerce Clause. The Court held that [w]here the statute regulates even-handedly to effectuate a legitimate local public interest, and its effects on interstate commerce are only incidental, it will be upheld unless the burden imposed on such commerce is clearly excessive in relation to the putative local benefits. If a legitimate local purpose is found, then the question becomes one of degree. And the extent of the burden that will be tolerated will of course depend on the nature of the local interest involved, and on whether it could be promoted as well with a lesser impact on interstate activities.

For a state statute to run afoul of the Pike standard, the statute, at a minimum, must impose a burden on interstate commerce that is qualitatively or quantitatively different from that imposed on intrastate commerce. Under Pike, if no such unequal burden be shown, a reviewing court need not proceed further.

[3] The focus of our disparate burden analysis is a state's shifting the costs of regulation to other states.…Such circumstances raise the risk that state policymakers will not bear the true political costs of their decisions, because those costs will fall in some measure on the residents of other political jurisdictions.…

While several types of burdens on interstate commerce would qualify as "disparate" to trigger Pike balancing, NEMA cites two in particular in this case: (1) control of commerce that occurs wholly beyond the state's borders and (2) risk of imposing regulatory requirements inconsistent with those of other states. Regulations that fall into the first category may be said to have extraterritorial operation, while those in the second may be said to create interstate regulatory conflicts.

[4] A regulation may disproportionately burden interstate commerce if it has the practical effect of requiring out-of-state commerce to be conducted at the regulating state's direction.

[5] Given the manufacturing and distribution systems used by its members, NEMA argues that, if its members continue selling in Vermont, they would also be forced as a practical matter to label lamps sold in every other state.…We disagree.…

NEMA's extraterritoriality contention fails because the statute does not inescapably require manufacturers to label all lamps wherever distributed.…To the extent the statute may be said to "require" labels on lamps sold outside Vermont, then, it is only because the manufacturers are unwilling to modify their production and distribution systems to differentiate between Vermont-bound and non-Vermont-bound lamps. To avoid the statute's alleged impact on other states, lamp manufacturers could arrange their production and distribution processes to produce labeled lamps solely for the Vermont market and then pass much of the increased costs along to Vermont consumers in the form of higher price.…To be sure, manufacturers will rarely be able to fully pass through to consumers the costs of a new tax or regulation. A lamp manufacturer's ability to pass costs along depends on the price elasticity of demand for lamps: the more responsive demand is to changes in price, the more added costs the manufacturer will be forced to absorb. But that manufacturers must bear some of the costs of the Vermont regulation in the form of lower profits does not cause the statute to violate the Commerce Clause. Such a burden is simply attributable to legitimate intrastate regulation.

NEMA's lament that Vermont's labeling requirement violates the Commerce Clause because it effectively forces manufacturers not to sell lamps in Vermont is nonetheless unpersuasive for three reasons. First, it is axiomatic that the increased cost of complying with a regulation may drive up the sales price of the product and thus erode demand for the product such that production becomes unprofitable. Consequently, any regulation may drive some or all producers or distributors from the regulating state. But in every such case, a decision to abandon the state's market rests entirely with individual manufacturers based on the opportunity cost of capital, their individual production costs, and what the demand in the state will bear. Because none of these variables is controlled by the state in this case, we cannot say that the choice to stay or leave has been made for manufacturers by the state legislature, as the Commerce Clause would prohibit. Although a regulation might violate the Commerce Clause by creating market incentives that encourage out-of-state manufacturers to abandon a state market while encouraging in-state manufacturers to pick up the slack, the instant regulation is evenhanded such that lamp producers both inside and outside Vermont would face the same putative need to develop separate production and distribution systems to accommodate simultaneously the Vermont market and other state markets.

Second, the manufacturers' choice to discontinue Vermont sales would not amount to a special, disproportionate injury to interstate commerce of the sort required by our precedents. If lamp manufacturers were to withdraw from the Vermont market, only Vermont residents would feel any appreciable effect, in the lost utility of mercury-bearing bulbs. Any loss felt by residents of other states would be minor by comparison.

[6][7] NEMA also contends that the statute burdens interstate commerce by exposing its members to the possibility of multiple, inconsistent labeling requirements imposed by other states. A state regulation might impose a disproportionate burden on interstate commerce if the regulation is in substantial conflict with a common regulatory scheme in place in other states....It is not enough to point to a risk of conflicting regulatory regimes in multiple states; there must be an actual conflict between the challenged regulation and those in place in other states....No such conflict has been shown here. NEMA concedes that no other state even regulates the labeling of mercury-bearing bulbs, much less does so in conflict with Vermont's approach. Indeed, there is record evidence that the Vermont statute is consistent with regimes under consideration by other states. While the scope of conflict required to state a dormant Commerce Clause claim is somewhat unclear, it is clear that the present case involves no conflict whatsoever.

REVERSED, IN FAVOR OF DEFENDANT STATE OF VERMONT.

1. Critical Thinking: Explain why you agree or disagree with the reasoning of the court in this case.

2. Ethical Decision Making: Identify the primary stakeholders helped and hurt by the outcome of this case.

Taxing and Spending Powers of the Federal Government

Obviously, no government can function without a source of revenue. Article 1, Section 8, of the Constitution gives the federal government the "Power to lay and collect Taxes, Duties, Imports and Excises." The taxes laid by Congress, however, must be uniform across the states. In other words, the U.S. government could not impose higher taxes on residents of one state than another.

Although the collection of taxes is essential for the generation of revenue needed to provide essential government services, taxes can be used to serve additional functions. For example, the government may wish to encourage the development of certain industries and discourage the development of others, so it may provide tax credits for firms entering the favored industries. As long as the "motive of Congress and the effect of its legislative action are to secure revenue for the benefit of the general government,"[7] the tax will be upheld as Constitutional. The fact that it also has what might be described as a regulatory impact will not affect the validity of the tax.

Article 1, Section 8, also gives Congress its spending power, by authorizing it to "pay the Debts and provide for the common Defence and general Welfare of the United States." Just as Congress can indirectly use its power to tax to achieve certain social welfare objectives, it can do the same with its spending power. For example, the U.S. Supreme Court in 1987 upheld the right of Congress to condition the states' receipt of Federal highway funds on their passing state legislation making twenty-one the legal drinking age.

The Bill of Rights

The first ten amendments to the U.S. Constitution, known as the Bill of Rights, have a substantial effect on governmental regulation of business. These amendments prohibit the federal government from infringing on certain individual freedoms. The Fourteenth Amendment extends most of the provisions in the Bill of Rights to the states, prohibiting state interference in its citizens' exercise of these rights. Thus, the federal and state governments must refrain from depriving individuals of the freedoms protected by the Bill of Rights.

In contrast, many countries do not have Constitutional provisions designed to protect individual citizens from the government. The Australian Constitution, for example, simply creates the framework for establishing the government of Australia. In countries that do have individual protections in their Constitution, these protections may be recent, as we see in the Global Context feature on Canada's Constitution. Many citizens of the United States are surprised

---

[7] *J.W. Hampton Co. v. United States*, 276 U.S. 394 (1928).

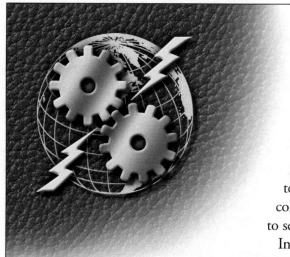

Technology: Internet and Taxation

As Internet commerce began to increase; many states became concerned about how to collect their fair share of sales taxes from online retailers. Sales taxes are a large source of revenue for state governments, but states are only allowed to require business to submit sales tax payments if the business has a store or distribution center in the state. Otherwise, states are prohibited from collecting sales taxes, although residents are supposed to send in the taxes.

Increased access to the Internet led some to advocate a use tax on Internet access, in addition to a sales tax on Internet purchases. However, because of the myriad of state tax jurisdictions, with greatly varying rules and procedures, the federal government passed a moratorium on Internet taxes until October 21, 2001, while a panel discussed what would be the best approach to taxing the Internet.

That panel, the Advisory Commission on Electronic Commerce, submitted its recommendations to Congress. Its recommendations included: examining the difference in computer access between the rich and the poor; examining the privacy implications of Internet taxation; and implementing a moratorium on international taxes and tariffs. The Commission also reported majority policy proposals, which included: extending the sales tax moratorium for five years to allow states to collaborate further on implementing a sales tax regime, implementing a permanent moratorium on Internet access taxes, and eliminating the three percent federal excise tax on communications.*

Just before the ban on Internet purchases expired, Congress passed a law extending the moratorium for two more years, giving states time to find a non-burdensome way for online sellers to collect sales tax from consumers of multiple states. Tax administrators from 33 participating states and five observer states have now formed the Streamlined Sales Tax Project (SSTP) to work with the private sector to design, test, and implement a simplified sales tax system that can be implemented by all participating states. You can keep up to date about the progress being made by the SSTP by periodically going to **http://www.ecommercetax.com/doc/070900. htm** or **www.streamlinedsalestax.org**.

Source: Advisory Commission on Electronic Commerce. Report to Congress, April 2000
http://www.ecommercecommission.org/acec_report.pdf (May 25, 2001) 4-6. [This site went offline in June of 2001.]

to find that some other countries' constitutions actually provide some rights that citizens of this country do not have. The constitution of Belarus, featured later in this chapter, includes some of these additional rights.

In addition, courts have held that many amendments to the Constitution apply to corporations because corporations are treated, in most cases, as "artificial persons." The amendments in the Bill of Rights that apply to corporations have the most significant impact on the regulatory environment of business, as we see in the remainder of this chapter. A summary of the first ten amendments is found in Exhibit 5-2, which you may want to review before reading about some of our protected rights in more detail. In reading about the impact of the amendments on business and citizens, it is important to keep in mind that the rights are not absolute.

EXHIBIT 5-2

Summaries of the Amendments Contained in the Bill of Rights

Amendment 1
   Protects freedom of religion, press, speech, peaceable assembly.
   Assures that people have the right to ask the government to redress grievances.

Amendment 2
   Finds that a well-regulated militia is necessary for security.
   States that the right of people to bear arms should not be infringed.

Amendment 3
   Provides that soldiers will not be housed in private residences during peacetime, nor during war except for provisions in the law.

Amendment 4
   Protects people from unreasonable search and seizure.
   Ensures that warrants are issued only with probable cause.

Amendment 5
   Ensures that people are not put on trial except by the indictment of a grand jury.
   Gives people the right not to testify against themselves.

Prevents people from being tried twice for the same crime.
   Creates due process rights.
   Provides that private property cannot be taken for public use without just compensation.

Amendment 6
   Provides the right to a speedy public trial with an impartial jury, the right to know what one is accused of, the right to have witnesses both against and for the accused, and the right to have an attorney.

Amendment 7
   In common law suits where the monetary value exceeds $20, the right to a trial by jury is preserved.

Amendment 8
   Provides that bail will not be excessive.
   Prohibits the imposition of excessive fines.
   Prohibits cruel and unusual punishment.

Amendment 9
   Although the Bill of Rights names certain rights, such naming does not remove other rights retained by people.

Amendment 10
   Provides that powers not given to the federal government are given to the state.

Global Context: Constitution Act of Canada

The Constitution Act of Canada (1982) established the Canadian Charter of Rights and Freedoms, which superceded the Bill of Rights Canada had established in 1960. Their Bill of Rights, however, had applied only to the Canada government at the national level, not to the provincial governments. Like the Fourteenth Amendment of the U.S. Constitution, Section 32(1) of the Charter states that the Charter applies to the Parliament and government of Canada and to the legislature and government of each province of Canada. The Charter is similar to the U.S. Bill of Rights in that it protects rights and fundamental freedoms such as the freedom of conscience and of religion, the freedom of peaceful assembly and of association, the right to be secure against unreasonable search and seizure, and the right to equal protection of the law. However, these rights and freedoms are qualified. The Charter states in Section 1 that "The Canadian Charter of Rights and Freedoms guarantees the rights and freedoms set out in the subject only to such reasonable limits prescribed by law as can be demonstrably justified in a free and democratic society."

Freedom of Speech and Assembly

The First Amendment guarantees freedom of speech and of the press. It also prohibits the abridgment of the right to assemble peacefully and to petition for redress of grievances. Finally, it prohibits the government from aiding the establishment of a religion and from interfering with the free exercise of religion. We highly value our first amendment freedoms, but emphasizing these freedoms means that we must sacrifice what important value to a greater degree? Examining the attitude toward free speech in China, as discussed in the following Global Box may help us answer this question.

Global Context: Free Speech in China

The Chinese Constitution does not provide guarantees of freedom of speech or assembly that compare to those protected in the First Amendment to the U.S. Constitution. The Chinese Constitution does not recognize any form of natural rights or human rights, but recognizes only citizens' rights, which are those specifically enumerated in the Chinese Constitution or laws. With regard to speech, not only does the Chinese Constitution not provide any protections for expressive activity, but numerous Chinese laws directly prohibit citizens from engaging in political acts directed against the regime that would be protected in a country like the United States. For example, Article 25 of the Publishing Control Act prohibits the publishing of anything that opposes the basic rules of the Constitution. Articles 7 and 12 of the Law on Assemblies, Processions and Demonstrations prohibit any assemblies, processions, and demonstrations that oppose these basic rules.

Like other rights, our First Amendment rights are not absolute. Most people would agree that a person does not have the right to yell "Fire!" in a crowded theater. Nor does one's right of free speech extend to making false statements about another that would be injurious to that person's reputation. Because of the difficulty of determining the boundaries of individual rights, the courts have decided a large number of First Amendment cases.

Corporate Speech. The protections of the First Amendment are given to corporations. However, not all corporate speech is treated the same. Corporate commercial speech, speech designed to convey information related to the sales of goods and services, is analyzed today under a four-part test set forth in the case of *Central Hudson*. In Case 5-2, the Supreme Court affirmed the continuing viability of this test, as it applied it to a number of regulations promulgated by the state of Massachusetts.

Case 5-3

Lorillard Tobacco Co.
v.
Reilly
United States Supreme Court
533 U.S. 121 (2001)

*A*fter the Attorney General of Massachusetts promulgated comprehensive regulations governing the advertising and sale of tobacco products, a group of tobacco manufacturers and retailers filed suit, asserting, among other claims, that the regulations violated the First and Fourteenth Amendments to the U.S. Constitution. The District Court upheld most of the regulations, finding that neither the regulations prohibiting outdoor advertising within 1,000 feet of a school or playground, nor the sales practices regulations restricting the location and distribution of tobacco products violated the First Amendment. The court ruled, however, that the point-of-sale advertising regulations requiring that indoor advertising be placed no lower than five feet from the floor are invalid because the Attorney General had not provided sufficient justification for that restriction.

The First Circuit affirmed the District Court's rulings that the outdoor advertising regulations and the sales practices regulations did not violate the First Amendment, but reversed the lower court's invalidation of the point-of-sale advertising regulations, concluding that the Attorney General is better suited than courts to determine what restrictions are necessary. The tobacco groups appealed the decision to the U.S. Supreme Court.

JUSTICE O'CONNOR

For over twenty-five years, the Court has recognized that commercial speech does not fall outside the purview of the First Amendment. In recognition of the distinction between speech proposing a commercial transaction, which occurs in an area traditionally subject to government regulation, and other varieties of speech, we developed a framework for analyzing regulations of commercial speech that is substantially similar to the test for time, place, and manner restrictions. The analysis contains four elements:

At the outset, we must determine whether the expression is protected by the First Amendment. For commercial speech to come within that provision, it at least must concern lawful activity and not be misleading. Next, we ask whether the asserted governmental interest is substantial. If both inquiries yield positive answers, we must determine whether the regulation directly advances the governmental interest asserted, and whether it is not more extensive than is necessary to serve that interest.

Petitioners urge us to reject the *Central Hudson* analysis and apply strict scrutiny...we see no need to break new ground. *Central Hudson*, as applied in our more recent commercial speech cases, provides an adequate basis for decision.

Only the last two steps of *Central Hudson*s four-part analysis are at issue here. The Attorney General has assumed for purposes of summary judgment that petitioners' speech is entitled to First Amendment protection. With respect to the second step, none of the petitioners contests the importance of the States interest in preventing the use of tobacco products by minors.

The third step of *Central Hudson* concerns the relationship between the harm that underlies the States interest and the means identified by the State to advance that interest. It requires that the speech restriction directly and materially advanc[e] the asserted governmental interest. This burden is not satisfied by mere speculation or conjecture; rather, a governmental body seeking to sustain a restriction on commercial speech must demonstrate that the harms it recites are real and that its restriction will in fact alleviate them to a material degree.

We do not, however, require that empirical data come accompanied by a surfeit of background information. [W]e have permitted litigants to justify speech restrictions by reference to studies and anecdotes pertaining to different locales altogether, or even, in a case applying strict scrutiny, to justify restrictions based solely on history, consensus, and simple common sense.

The last step of the *Central Hudson* analysis complements the third step, asking whether the speech restriction is not more extensive than necessary to serve the interests that support it. We have made it clear that the least restrictive means is not the standard; instead, the case law requires a reasonable fit between the legislature's ends and the means chosen to accomplish those ends, a means narrowly tailored to achieve the desired objective.

Focusing on the third and fourth steps of the *Central Hudson* analysis, we first address the outdoor advertising and point-of-sale advertising regulations for smokeless tobacco and cigars.

The outdoor advertising regulations prohibit smokeless tobacco or cigar advertising within a 1,000-foot radius of a school or playground. The District Court and Court of Appeals concluded that the Attorney General had identified a real problem with underage use of tobacco products, that limiting youth exposure to advertising would combat that problem, and that the regulations burdened no more speech than necessary to accomplish the States goal. The smokeless tobacco and cigar petitioners take issue with all of these conclusions....

Our review of the record reveals that the Attorney General has provided ample documentation of the problem with underage use of smokeless tobacco and cigars. In addition, we disagree with petitioners claim that there is no evidence that preventing targeted campaigns and limiting youth exposure to advertising will decrease underage use of smokeless tobacco and cigars.

Whatever the strength of the Attorney Generals evidence to justify the outdoor advertising regulations, however, we conclude that the regulations do not satisfy the fourth step of the *Central Hudson* analysis. The final step of the *Central Hudson* analysis, the critical inquiry in this case, requires a reasonable fit between the means and ends of the regulatory scheme. The Attorney General's regulations do not meet this standard. The broad sweep of the regulations indicates that the Attorney General did not carefully calculat[e] the costs and benefits associated with the burden on speech imposed by the regulations.

The outdoor advertising regulations prohibit any smokeless tobacco or cigar advertising within 1,000 feet of schools or playgrounds. In the District Court, petitioners maintained that this prohibition would prevent advertising in 87% to 91% of Boston, Worchester, and Springfield, Massachusetts. Thus, the Court of Appeals concluded that the regulations prohibit advertising in a substantial portion of the major metropolitan areas of Massachusetts.

In some geographical areas, these regulations would constitute nearly a complete ban on the communication of truthful information about smokeless tobacco and cigars to adult consumers. The breadth and scope of the regulations, and the process by which the Attorney General adopted the regulations, do not demonstrate a careful calculation of the speech interests involved.

First, the Attorney General did not seem to consider the impact of the 1,000-foot restriction on commercial speech in major metropolitan areas....[T]he effect of the Attorney General's speech regulations will vary based on whether a locale is rural, suburban, or urban. The uniformly broad sweep of the geographical limitation demonstrates a lack of tailoring.

Similarly, a ban on all signs of any size seems ill suited to target the problem of highly visible billboards, as opposed to smaller signs. To the extent that studies have identified particular advertising and promotion practices that appeal to youth, tailoring would involve targeting those practices while permitting others. As crafted, the regulations make no distinction among practices on this basis...

The States interest in preventing underage tobacco use is substantial, and even compelling, but it is no less true that the sale and use of tobacco products by adults is a legal activity. We must consider that tobacco retailers and manufacturers have an interest in conveying truthful information about their products to adults, and adults have a corresponding interest in receiving truthful information about tobacco products.

In addition, a retailer in Massachusetts may have no means of communicating to passersby on the street that it sells tobacco products because alternative forms of advertisement, like newspapers, do not allow that retailer to propose an instant transaction in the way that on-site advertising does. The ban on any indoor advertising that is visible from the outside also presents problems in establishments like convenience stores, which have unique security concerns that counsel in favor of full visibility of the store from the outside. It is these sorts of considerations that the Attorney General failed to incorporate into the regulatory scheme.

We conclude that the Attorney General has failed to show that the outdoor advertising regulations for smokeless tobacco and cigars are not more extensive than necessary to advance the States substantial interest in preventing underage tobacco use.

A careful calculation of the costs of a speech regulation does not mean that a State must demonstrate that there is no incursion on legitimate speech interests, but a speech regulation cannot unduly impinge on the speaker's ability to propose a commercial transaction and the adult listeners opportunity to obtain information about products. After reviewing the outdoor advertising regulations, we find the calculation in this case insufficient for purposes of the First Amendment.

We conclude that the point-of-sale advertising regulations fail both the third and fourth steps of the *Central Hudson* analysis. A regulation cannot be sustained if it provides only ineffective or remote support for the government's purpose, or if there is little chance that the restriction will advance the States goal. As outlined above, the States goal is to prevent minors from using tobacco products and to curb demand for that activity by limiting youth exposure to advertising. The five foot rule does not seem to advance that goal. Not all children are less than five feet tall, and those who are certainly have the ability to look up and take in their surroundings.

Massachusetts may wish to target tobacco advertisements and displays that entice children, much like floor-level candy displays in a convenience store, but the blanket height restriction does not constitute a reasonable fit with that goal.

The Attorney General also promulgated a number of regulations that restrict sales practices by cigarette, smokeless tobacco, and cigar manufacturers and retailers. Among other restrictions, the regulations bar the use of self-service displays and require that tobacco products be placed out of the reach of all consumers in a location accessible only to salespersons.

Two of the cigarette petitioners challenge the sales practices regulations on First Amendment grounds. The cigar petitioners additionally challenge a provision that prohibits sampling or promotional giveaways of cigars or little cigars.

...As we read the regulations, they basically require tobacco retailers to place tobacco products behind counters and require customers to have contact with a salesperson before they are able to handle a tobacco product.

The cigarette and smokeless tobacco petitioners contend that the same First Amendment principles that require invalidation of the outdoor and indoor advertising restrictions require invalidation of the display regulations at issue in this case.

We conclude that the sales practices regulations withstand First Amendment scrutiny. The means chosen by the State are narrowly tailored to prevent access to tobacco products by minors, are unrelated to expression, and leave open alternative avenues for vendors to convey information about products and for would-be customers to inspect products before purchase.

AFFIRMED IN PART AND REVERSED IN PART.

1. Critical Thinking: Using the four-part system of analysis derived from the *Central Hudson* case, explain why the high court struck down regulations banning outdoor advertising within 1,000 feet of a school and prohibiting displays or advertisements of tobacco products, yet upheld regulations that would bar the use of self-service displays of these products? In light of the way the court responded to these regulations, can you draft a regulation that would meet the state's goal of reducing teenage smoking, yet would not violate the tobacco companies' First Amendment rights?

2. Ethical Decision Making: Could you make an argument that even though the regulations were struck down, the companies that would have been affected by them should go ahead and act as if the regulations had been upheld?

Corporate Political Speech. Sometimes corporations choose to engage in political speech; that is, they choose to spend money to support political candidates or referenda. At one time, states restricted the amount of political advertising firms could engage in because they feared that corporations, with their huge assets, would speak out on behalf of a particular candidate or issue and drown out other voices. However, in the 1978 *First National Bank of Boston v. Bellotti* case,[8] the U.S. Supreme Court struck down a state law that prohibited certain corporations from making contributions or expenditures influencing voters on any issues that would not materially affect the corporate assets or business. The court stated, "The concept that the government may restrict speech of some elements of our society in order to enhance the relative voice of others is wholly foreign to the First Amendment." The high court ruled that corporate political speech should be protected to the same extent as the ordinary citizen's political speech.

Unprotected Speech. Some speech is unprotected. For example, speech that harms the reputation of another is not only unprotected, but, as discussed in Chapter 6, may lead to the speaker's being required to pay compensation to the person whose reputation was harmed by the speech.

Obscenity is another form of speech that is not protected, although, there have been numerous cases trying to distinguish when something crosses the line from being protected free expression to being unprotected

obscenity. Although the standard is not easy to apply, courts have ruled that material is obscene if it: (1) appeals to a prurient or sordid and perverted interest in sex; (2) has no serious literary, artistic, political, or scientific merit; and (3) is on the whole offensive to the average person in the community. A recent illustration of the court's application of this test can be found in *Bad Frog Brewery v. New York State Liquor Authority.*[9] In that case, the state liquor control board argued that the Bad Frog Beer label, which featured a frog with its middle finger raised, was obscene. The appellate court stated that the label might be in bad taste, but it was not obscene.

So called "fighting words," words that are said to incite violence are also not protected. An interesting issue that has arisen on many campuses is whether so called "hate speech," derogatory speech directed at members of another group, such as another race, is unprotected speech that can be banned. Thus far, hate speech codes on campuses that were challenged as unconstitutional have been struck down by state courts or federal appeals courts, though the issue has not yet reached the Supreme Court. Hate speech is a serious issue that affects more than one million students every year; prompting 60 percent of universities to ban verbal abuse and verbal harassment and 28 percent of universities to ban advocacy of an offensive viewpoint.[10] Because universities are often viewed as breeding grounds for ideas and citizen development, courts have

---

[8] 435 U.S. 765 (1978).

[9] 134 F. 3d 87 (2d Cir. 1998).

[10] Timothy C. Shiell, *Campus Hate Speech on Trial* (Lawrence, KS: University Press of Kansas), 1998, pp. 2, 49.

not looked favorably upon limits to speech on campuses. The international community has been more willing to call hate speech unprotected speech, with a declaration from the United Nations and laws in several countries.[11]

Freedom of Religion

The first amendment prohibits the government from aiding the establishment of a religion and from interfering with the free exercise of religion. These two elements are known as, respectively, the "establishment clause" and the "free exercise clause." The government must remain neutral in matters of religion, but it is often difficult to determine whether an action by the government is advancing religion or merely allowing the free exercise of religion. Likewise, other actions can easily be seen, depending on one's perspective, as either aiding in the establishment of religion, or simply not interfering with free exercise.

In governmental workplaces, this conflict sometimes raises difficult issues. For example, in 1966, Tucker, an employee of the California Department of Education, insisted on signing office memos with his name and the acronym "SOTLJC," which stood for "Servant of the Lord Jesus Christ." His supervisor, in an attempt to avoid workplace disruptions and the appearance of government support for religion, prohibited all displays of religious symbols and all religious advocacy in the workplace. Tucker was suspended for refusing to comply with the restrictions, and when he challenged the suspension on grounds that the rules interfered with his free exercise of religion, the appellate court agreed.[12] In private workplaces, issues related to free exercise of religion most often arise under Title VII, the federal law designed to prohibit discrimination in employment. This important legislation is discussed in greater detail in Chapter 42.

Freedom from Unreasonable Searches and Seizures

The Fourth Amendment guarantees the right of individuals to be "secure in their persons, their homes, and their personal property." It therefore prohibits the government from conducting unreasonable searches of individuals and seizing their property to use as evidence against them.

A search is unreasonable if it is conducted without the government official first obtaining a search warrant from the court. A search warrant is a court order that allows law enforcement agents to search for or seize items specifically described in the warrant. Government officials are able to obtain such warrants only when they can show probable cause to believe that the search will turn up the specified evidence of criminal activity. Showing probable cause means that the official must have a sufficient reason based on known facts to obtain a warrant.

The Supreme Court, however, has ruled that there are certain circumstances in which no search warrant is needed. For example, warrantless searches of automobiles, under certain circumstances, are allowed. In May of 2001, the state ACLU and a college professor filed a lawsuit seeking preliminary and permanent injunctions to invalidate a recently passed Ohio law that the plaintiffs claim is an attempt to restrict people's Fourth Amendment rights by requiring individuals to consent in advance to what might be an otherwise unreasonable, warrantless search.[13] The law at issue requires buyers of five or more beer kegs to provide the address of the party to the beer distributor and to sign a form allowing police and liquor agents to enter their property without a warrant to search the premises for the purpose of enforcing the state liquor laws. While opponents of the law see it as forcing them to sign away their constitutional rights, the local police see it as a proactive approach to the problem of parties getting out of control and the police finding out about these situations after it is too late. The police also said that the party host could always refuse to honor the affidavits when the police showed up, and the police would then have to get a warrant. While representatives of the state Attorney General's Office have not commented publicly on the lawsuit, a representative of the ACLU has said that she hopes a reasonable compromise can be negotiated.[14]

Improvements in technology have also caused problems in the application of the Fourth Amendment because it is now simpler to eavesdrop on people and to engage in other covert activities. One such case was decided by the United States Supreme Court in mid-2001.[15] In that case, the police had information from

---

[11] *Id* at 32.
[12] *Tucker v. State of Cal. Dep't of Ed.*, 97 F. 3d 1204 (9th Cir. 1996).

[13] Robert Ruth, *Lawsuit Challenges Restrictions on Beer Buyers,* Columbus Dispatch, May 26, 2001, at 1B.
[14] Hillary Copsey, Ohio State U: *Ohio Professor Sues State Over Keg Law,* u-Wire, May 31, 2001, (2001 WL 20502730).
[15] *Kyllo v. U.S.,* 533 U.S. 27 (2001).

informants that led them to believe that Danny Kyllo was growing marijuana in his home. Kyllo also had unusually high electricity bills, common when you are using heat lamps to grow the plant indoors. The police used a thermal imager, an instrument that can detect unusually high levels of heat emissions and translate them into an image, to provide them with the evidence necessary to get a warrant to physically search his house. The question the court had to address was whether the use of the thermal imaging instrument on the property constituted a "search." Or, if we think of the case as judges do, by comparing it to past precedents, it is a question of whether thermal imaging is more like going through someone's garbage, or is it more like using a high-powered telescope to look through someone's window? If the former situation is more analogous, then the behavior does not constitute a search. But if the case is more analogous to the latter scenario, then using thermal imaging on a home is a search that requires a warrant. The Ninth Circuit, examining the use of this technology for the first time, found that using thermal imaging was not a search that was prohibited by the fourth amendment without a warrant.

The United States Supreme Court, however, in a 5-4 decision, ruled that the use by the police of a thermal imaging device to detect patterns of heat coming from a private home is a search that requires a warrant. The court said, further, that the warrant requirement would apply not only to the relatively crude device at issue, but also to any "more sophisticated systems" in use or in development that let the police gain knowledge that in the past would have been impossible without a physical entry into the home. In explaining the decision, Justice Scalia wrote that in the home, "all details are intimate details, because the entire area is held safe from prying government eyes." He went on to add that the court's precedents "draw a firm line at the entrance to one's house."[16]

While many were happy with the Supreme Court's decision in this case, some were quick to point out that this case is not necessarily the final word when it comes to the use of technology. They noted that Scalia seemed to rely heavily on the fact that the thermal imaging was used to see inside one's *home*. It is, therefore, not clear whether thermal imaging of some other locale would be upheld.

The Fourth Amendment protects corporations as well as individuals, and places of business as well as homes. This protection is generally applicable, as noted earlier, in criminal cases. However, Fourth Amendment issues also arise when government regulations authorize warrantless searches by administrative agencies.

Although administrative searches are presumed to require a search warrant, courts have carved out an exception to this rule. If an industry is one that has been subject to a long history of pervasive regulation, a warrantless search is not considered unreasonable. In such industries, warrantless searches are required to make sure that regulations are being upheld.

The "pervasive regulation" exception as it applies to businesses is difficult to interpret. Warrantless searches authorized by the Federal Mine Safety and Health Act have been held to be legal because the federal regulatory presence is sufficiently comprehensive and defined that the owner of commercial property cannot help but be aware that his property will be subject to periodic inspections undertaken for specific purposes.[17] A warrantless search under the Occupational Safety and Health Act (OSHA), however, might violate the Fourth Amendment, because there is no significant legislation of working conditions before OSHA was passed in 1970, and therefore no reason for a businessperson covered by the law to anticipate being subject to warrantless searches. Case 5-4 illustrates how the Supreme Court of Michigan treated one city's attempt to authorize warrantless administrative searches.

---

[16] *Ibid.*

[17] *Raymond J. Donovan, Secretary of Labor, United States Department of Labor v. Douglas Dewey et al.*, 452 U.S. 594, 101 S.Ct. 2534 (1981).

Case 5-4

Hildegard Gora, et al.

v.

City of Ferndale
Supreme Court of Michigan.
551 N.W. 2d 454 (1998)

*I*n November 1990, the city of Ferndale enacted a comprehensive ordinance regulating massage parlors. The regulations, among other things, established the procedures and educational requirements for obtaining a city license or permit to own, operate, or work in a massage parlor, and prescribed necessary facilities, hours of operation, and employee conduct and dress. The ordinance also provided for periodic inspections of massage parlor establishments by the chief of police or other authorized inspectors. The failure of any licensee to allow an inspection officer access to the premises, or hinder such officer in any manner was designated as a misdemeanor punishable by a fine of up to $500 or ninety days in jail.

The plaintiffs challenged the constitutionality of a number of the provisions of the ordinance, including the provision for searches without a warrant. Initially, the court found that several sections of the ordinance violated the state and federal constitutions. The Court of Appeals eventually found that two provisions were unconstitutional, including the provision for a search without a warrant. It reached this conclusion reasoning that the administrative search exception to the warrant requirement was inapplicable because the State of Michigan did not pervasively regulate the massage parlor industry. The city appealed.

JUSTICE TAYLOR

…While it is well established that the Fourth Amendment's prohibition of unreasonable searches and seizures applies to administrative inspections of private commercial property, an exemption from the search warrant requirement exists for administrative inspections of closely regulated industries. Whether the exemption applies is primarily determined by "'the pervasiveness and regularity of the…regulation' and the effect of such regulation upon an owner's expectation of privacy." When a person chooses to engage in a "pervasively regulated business…he does so with the knowledge that his business…will be subject to effective inspection." …In part, the justification for this is that, unlike under general inspection schemes, the person in the pervasively regulated business "is not left to wonder about the purposes of the inspector or the limits of his task" as long as the regulations provide notice of and implicitly restrict the scope of the inspection to those areas of the business that must be examined to enforce the regulations.…

We are unpersuaded by plaintiffs' contention that there can be no finding that the massage parlor trade is a pervasively regulated industry in the absence of a history of regulation by the City of Ferndale. The United States Supreme Court expressly rejected an approach that relied exclusively on historical factors…stating that "if the length of regulation were the only criterion, absurd results would occur." Rather, "it is the pervasiveness and regularity of the…regulation that ultimately determines whether a warrant is necessary to render an inspection program reasonable under the Fourth Amendment".…Moreover, the goal of the ordinance is primarily to prevent massage establishments from being used as a front for prostitution, which, as "the oldest profession," historically has been subject to pervasive regulation for perhaps longer than any other industry.

While regulation of massage parlors has not been as extensive as that of some other enterprises, such as the liquor or firearms industries, it has nonetheless been held to be a pervasively regulated industry....[I]n *Indianapolis v. Wright*...the Indiana Supreme Court upheld a local massage parlor inspection ordinance similar to the one at issue in this case...[T]he court concluded that this was a pervasively regulated enterprise and that the massage parlor inspection scheme authorized by the ordinance was reasonable and permissible under the administrative search exception to the warrant requirement. When appealed, the United States Supreme Court dismissed the appeal for want of a substantial federal question....[T]he Supreme Court's disposition of a case in this manner is a decision on the merits that is *stare decisis* with regard to the issues presented, including, of course, the question of pervasive regulation....Thus, we conclude that the United States Supreme Court has determined that the massage parlor industry is a pervasively regulated business and that inspections of massage parlors conducted without warrants pursuant to a comprehensive licensing and regulation ordinance are permissible under the administrative search exception to the warrant requirement of the Fourth Amendment.

REVERSED, IN FAVOR OF DEFENDANT.

1. Critical Thinking: What ambiguous term is the focus of the court's opinion? Why do you believe the court does or does not satisfactorily resolve the ambiguity of the term?

2. Ethical Decision Making: Even if an agency is not successful as the City of Ferndale was in arguing that a warrant is unnecessary, it is still easier to obtain a warrant in a commercial context because the courts require a slightly lower standard of probable cause in a business context. An agency can generally obtain a search warrant by demonstrating that they wish to search a business under a general and neutral enforcement plan. Should the city have been required to obtain a search warrant on ethical grounds? Why or why not?

Due Process

The Fifth Amendment contains a number of important protections. For example, it protects against self-incrimination and against *double jeopardy*, that is, being tried twice for the same crime. For the businessperson, and the corporation, one of the most important aspects of the Fifth Amendment is the due process clause. This clause states that one cannot be deprived of life, liberty, or property without *due process of law.*

There are two types of due process: *procedural and substantive.* **Procedural due process** requires that the government uses fair procedures when an individual or corporation's life, liberty, or property may be taken. At minimum, due process entitles one to notice of a legal action and a hearing in front of an impartial tribunal. Originally, courts interpreted the due process clause of the Fifth Amendment to protect an individual's right of procedural due process in federal criminal proceedings only. Subsequently, passage of the Fourteenth Amendment made the requirement of due process applicable to criminal proceedings by state governments. Today, the Due Process Clause has been applied to such diverse situations as the termination of welfare benefits,[18] the discharge of a public employee from their job, and the suspension of a student from school.

The procedures that the government must follow when there may be a taking of an individual's life, liberty, or property vary according to the nature of the taking. In general, as the magnitude of the potential deprivation increases, the extent of the procedures required also increases.

Substantive due process, which refers to the basic fairness of laws that may deprive an individual of his or her liberty or property, requires the government to have a proper purpose for enacting a law that will restrict individuals' liberty or the use of their property. The standard for determining whether a law violates substantive due process depends on the nature of the

---

[18] *Goldberg v. Kelly*, 90 U.S. 101 (1970). In this case, the U.S. Supreme Court stated that the termination of a welfare recipient's welfare benefits by a state agency without affording the person the opportunity for an evidentiary hearing before termination violates the recipient's procedural due-process rights.

potential deprivation. If the governmental action in question affects a *fundamental right,* then the restriction in question must bear a *substantial relationship* to a *compelling* governmental purpose. Fundamental rights entitled to this higher level of scrutiny generally include the rights protected by our Constitution. Examples of fundamental rights include the right to vote, the right to travel freely from state to state, and the emerging right to privacy. *Compelling state interests* would include, for example, public safety or national security.

If an affected interest is not considered a fundamental right, the government must only prove that its action bears a rational relationship to a legitimate state interest. Under this "rational basis" test, most governmental regulations will be upheld. Examples of laws upheld under this standard include minimum wage laws, rent control laws, banking regulations, environmental laws, and regulations prohibiting unfair trade practices.

The Prohibition against Uncompensated Takings

The Fifth Amendment further provides that if the government takes private property for public use, it must pay the owner just compensation. This provision is referred to as the *Takings Clause,* and is applicable to corporations. This provision has caused considerable litigation recently. One significant issue that has arisen is the question of what constitutes a "public use," for which the government can take property. This issue is discussed in greater detail in Chapter 48.   .

A second issue under the Takings Clause is the question of when a government regulation can become so onerous as to constitute a taking for which just compensation is required. Environmental regulations, because they often have an affect on the way landowners may use their property, have been increasingly challenged as unconstitutionally violating the takings clause. In the following case, the Supreme Court examined a state regulation challenged as violating the Fifth Amendment, as applied to the state by the Fourteenth Amendment.

Case 5-5

Lucas
v.
South Carolina Coastal Commission
Supreme Court of the United States
112 U.S. 2886 (1992)

*I*n *1986 plaintiff David Lucas purchased two beachfront lots on the South Carolina Coast. He paid $975,000 for the lots, intending to build a home for himself on one and sell the other to a wealthy buyer. Nineteen months after his purchase, South Carolina passed a Beachfront Management Act, which banned construction close to the shore to prevent flying debris and other environmental damage from Atlantic storms. The new law prevented Lucas from constructing either house, which he believed rendered his land "valueless." So he sued the state, seeking "just compensation" under the Takings Clause of the Fifth Amendment. The trial court found in favor of Lucas and awarded him $1.2 million. On appeal, the state argued successfully that a landowner had no right to harm his land, which Lucas would be doing by constructing the homes, and reversed the trial court's decision. Lucas appealed to the U.S. Supreme Court.*

JUSTICE SCALIA

Prior to Justice Holmes' exposition in *Pennsylvania Coal Co. v. Mahon,* it was generally thought that the Takings Clause reached only a "direct appropriation" of property, or the functional equivalent of a "practical ouster of [the owner's] possession."

…We have, however, described at least two discrete categories of regulatory action as compensable without case-specific inquiry into the public interest advanced in support of the restraint. The first encompasses regulations that compel the property owner to suffer a physical "invasion" of his property. In general (at least with regard to permanent invasions), no matter how minute the intrusion, and no matter how weighty the public purpose behind it, we have required compensation.

The second situation in which we have found categorical treatment appropriate is where regulation denies all economically beneficial or productive use of land. As we have said on numerous occasions, the Fifth Amendment is violated when land-use regulation "does not substantially advance legitimate state interests or *denies an owner economically viable use of his land.*"

Affirmatively supporting a compensation requirement is the fact that regulations that leave the owner of land without economically beneficial or productive options for its use—typically, as here, by requiring land to be left substantially in its natural state—carry with them a heightened risk that private property is being pressed into some form of public service under the guise of mitigating serious public harm…

[P]etitioner "concede[d] that the beach/dune area of South Carolina's shores is an extremely valuable public resource; that the erection of new construction contributes to the erosion and destruction of this public resource; and that discouraging new construction in close proximity to the beach/dune area is necessary to prevent a great public harm." In the [state] court's view, these concessions brought petitioner's challenge within a long line of this Court's cases, sustaining against Due Process and Takings Clause challenges against the State's use of its "police powers" to enjoin a property owner from activities akin to public nuisances, [e.g., order to destroy diseased cedar trees to prevent infection of nearby orchards].

It is correct that many of our prior opinions have suggested that "harmful or noxious uses" of property may be proscribed by government regulation without the requirement of compensation. For a number of reasons, however, we think the South Carolina Supreme Court was too quick to conclude that principle decides the present case. The "harmful or noxious uses" principle was the Court's early attempt to describe in theoretical terms why government may, consistent with the Takings Clause, affect property values by regulation without incurring an obligation to compensate—a reality we nowadays acknowledge explicitly with respect to the full scope of the State's police power.…

Where the State seeks to sustain regulation that deprives land of all economically beneficial use, we think it may resist compensation only if the logically antecedent inquiry into the nature of the owner's estate shows that the proscribed use interests were not part of his title to begin with…

The "total taking" inquiry we require today will ordinarily entail analysis of, among other things, the degree of harm to public lands and resources, or adjacent private property, posed by the claimant's proposed activities, the social value of the claimant's activities and their suitability to the locality in question, and the relative ease with which the alleged harm can be avoided through measures taken by the claimant and the government (or adjacent private landowners) alike. The fact that a particular use has long been engaged in by similarly situated owners ordinarily imports a lack of any common-law prohibition (though changed circumstances or new knowledge may make what was previously permissible no longer so). So also does the fact that other landowners, similarly situated, are permitted to continue the use denied to the claimant.

It seems unlikely that common-law principles would have prevented the erection of any habitable or productive improvements on petitioner's land. We emphasize that to win its case…South Carolina must identify background principles of nuisance and property law that prohibit the uses he now intends in the circumstances in which the property is presently found. Only on this showing can the State fairly claim that, in proscribing all such beneficial uses, the Beachfront Management Act is taking nothing.

REVERSED AND REMANDED, IN FAVOR OF PLAINTIFF.

1. Critical Thinking: The Court outlines two instances in which compensation is required, one being that the landowner has lost all economically beneficial productive use of the land. What are the descriptive assumptions underlying the decision to require compensation in this instance?

2. Ethical Decision Making: Many people very passionately support expanding the concept of regulatory takings to a multitude of laws. Opponents of this group feel equally as strong that the use of the concept of regulatory takings should be extremely limited. The strong feelings of both groups have been influenced by the conflicting value preferences of those in each group. Can you identify which strong held values would be influencing each group's positions?

Many commentators believed that the fact that the law that prohibited construction on Lucas' property had been enacted after Lucas had acquired the land was a critical factor in the outcome of the case. However, in the 2001 case of *Palazzolo v. Rhode Island*,[19] the U.S. Supreme Court held by a 5-4 decision that someone who bought property after restriction on development were in place could still challenge the restrictions as an unconstitutional "taking" of private property, leading some to speculate that there will be an increasing number of similar challenges.

The Privilege against Self-Incrimination

Although most provisions of the Fifth Amendment apply to corporations, protection against self-incrimination does not. Because of this limitation, when someone has a business, it is important to know whether that business is a sole proprietorship or a corporation. A businessperson who is a sole proprietor is entitled to Fifth Amendment rights that an agent of a corporation would not have.

In the case of *Braswell v. United States*,[20] the U.S. Supreme Court clearly distinguished between the role of a custodian of corporate records and a sole proprietor. In *Braswell*, the defendant operated his business as a corporation, with himself as the sole shareholder. When a grand jury issued a subpoena requiring him to produce corporate books and records, Braswell argued that to do so would violate his Fifth Amendment privilege against self-incrimination. The high court denied Braswell's claim and said "clearly, subpoenaed business records are not privileged, and as a custodian for the

records, the act of producing the records is in a representative capacity, not a personal one, so the records must be produced."[21]

The court stated that had the business been a sole proprietorship, Braswell would have had the opportunity to show that the act of production would have been self-incriminating. Because his business was a corporation, he was acting as a representative of a corporation, and regardless of how small the corporation, he could not claim a privilege.

Equal Protection

The Equal Protection Clause, which prevents the states from denying "the equal protection of the laws" to any citizen, is contained in the Fourteenth Amendment. This clause, a useful tool in fighting discrimination, is applicable any time a government attempts to treat some individuals differently than others, generally by using some sort of classification scheme.

As we saw with the application of the Due Process Clause, the standards courts use in determining whether a governmental action violates the equal protection clause is determined by the nature of the right that is going to be affected by the classification. Under this classification system, there are three different standards of scrutiny that apply: strict scrutiny, intermediate scrutiny, and the rational basis test.

If a government action is going to prevent some people from exercising a *fundamental right*, or if the classification involves what we have come to refer to as *suspect classifications*, then the action will be subject to

---

[19] WL 721005 (USRI 2001).
[20] 487 U.S. 99 (1988).

[21] *Ibid.*

strict scrutiny. Suspect classifications that we generally recognize today include classifications based on race, national origin, and citizenship.

As with the due process analysis, courts will only uphold the classification if it is necessary to promote a *compelling state interest,* so few laws will pass this standard. Courts, however, have held that in some cases remedying past illegal discrimination against a group may be compelling interest. This issue is discussed in greater detail in Chapter 42.

If the classification is based on gender or whether one is a legitimate or illegitimate child, courts apply an intermediate level of scrutiny. Under this standard, the government action must be *substantially related* to an *important government objective.* As a result, it is more difficult to predict whether a particular regulation will be upheld.

When the classification at issue involves any other matters, the court applies a rational basis test. According to this test, the court simply looks to see whether there is any justifiable reason to believe that the classification advances a legitimate government interest. Under such a test, almost all government regulations are upheld.

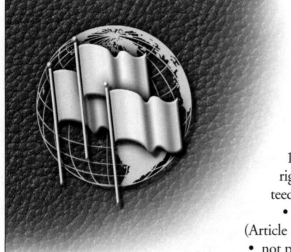

Global Context: Protections under the Constitution of the Republic of Belarus

While we are justifiably proud of the protections guaranteed by our Bill of Rights, our Constitution does not provide the greatest number of protections of any nation. The Constitution of Belarus, adopted in 1994, provides one of the most exhaustive set of rights of any constitution. Some of the rights guaranteed by their Constitution include the right to:

• be presumed innocent until proven guilty (Article 26).

• not provide evidence against one's self or one's close family relations (Article 27).

• move freely and choose their place of residence within the Republic of Belarus, to leave it, and to return to it without hindrance (Article 30).

• profess any religion individually or jointly with others, or to profess none at all, to express and spread beliefs connected with his attitude towards religion, and to participate in the performance religious rituals (Article 31).

• freedom of thoughts and beliefs and their free expression (Article 33).

• hold assemblies, rallies, street marches, demonstrations, and pickets that do not disturb law and order or violate the rights of other citizens (Article 35).

• the right to work as the worthiest means of an individual's self-assertion, that is, the right to choose a profession, type of occupation, and work in accordance with one's vocation, capabilities, education, and vocational training, and having regard to social needs, and the right to healthy and safe working conditions. The State shall create the conditions necessary for full employment of the population. Where a person is unemployed for reasons which are beyond his control, he shall be guaranteed training in new specializations and an upgrading of his qualifications having regard to social needs, and to unemployment benefit in accordance with the law (Article 41).

• a working week of no more than forty hours, shorter working hours at night, and the provision of annual paid leave and weekly rest days (Article 43).

• health care including free treatment at state health-care establishments (Article 45).

Other Constitutional Restrictions on Government

We have examined most of the aspects of the Constitution that impact business. However, there are three additional clauses that deserve our attention.

The Privileges and Immunities Clause

Closely related to the Equal Protection Clause of the Fourteenth Amendment is the Privileges and Immunities Clause (Article IV, Section 2). The clause provides that "Citizens of each State shall be entitled to all Privileges and Immunities of Citizens in the several States." This provision prohibits a state from discriminating against citizens of other states when those non-residents are engaging in ordinary and essential activities such as buying or selling property, seeking employment, or using the court system. A state may treat non-residents different from residents only when it has a substantial reason for doing so.

Because of the Equal Protection Clause, it would be unconstitutional for a state to prohibit nonresidents from opening restaurants in the state. However, states can pass legislation allowing state universities to charge higher tuition to out-of-state students. The reason this law is not unconstitutional is that residents pay a significant amount of taxes used to fund the state universities, which the out-of-state students do not pay.

The Full Faith and Credit Clause

Article IV, Section 1, of the Constitution contains the Full Faith and Credit Clause, which states: "Full Faith and Credit shall be given in each State to the public Acts, Records, and Judicial Proceedings of every other State." Because of this provision, which has been held to apply to only civil matters, rights that have been established by documents such as wills, contracts, marriage and divorce decrees, and judgments in civil cases will be upheld by courts in all states. Imagine the chaos that would exist if not for this clause. A debtor could evade responsibility for his debts simply by moving to another state.

The Contract Clause

Article 1, Section 9 contains the contract clause, which provides that the government may not pass any "Law impairing the Obligation of Contract." In application, this clause has been interpreted to mean that no law can be passed that will *unreasonably* interfere with

existing contracts. For example, in *Home Building and Loan Association v. Blaisdell*, Minnesota's Mortgage Moratorium Act was challenged under the Contract Clause. The act was temporarily implemented during the Great Depression and authorized the courts to extend the redemption periods of mortgages. Its intent was to delay foreclosures of mortgages on real estate. The Supreme Court decided that the Minnesota statute was within the state's police powers to protect its citizens and did not violate the Contract Clause. A contractual obligation existed and was clearly impaired by the statute, but the court decided that even a substantial impairment must be balanced with the state's interest in protecting the welfare of its people.

Wetlands Protection Wrap-Up

The District Court initially granted the Corps summary judgment on the jurisdictional issue. The Seventh Circuit Court of Appeals subsequently held that Congress has authority under the Commerce Clause to regulate intrastate waters and that the Migratory Bird Rule is a reasonable interpretation of the Clean Water Act (CWA). But after seven years of court battles, the Supreme Court reversed two lower court rulings and said the CWA does not give the federal government jurisdiction over the site. Many commentators saw this decision as another illustration of the court's growing tendency to shift power from the federal to the state governments.

A day after the U.S. Supreme Court ruled that federal regulators did not have the authority to stop the landfill, the state waste agency asked staff members to draft a strategic plan that will list the steps the group must take to complete the project, thereby making it clear that they did, in fact, intend to build a regional landfill near Bartlett, Illinois.[22]

Officials eager to build the landfill, however, were not the only ones who swung into action after the court's decision was handed down. Groups in states such as Washington, where there were a significant number of wetlands that suddenly appeared to no longer be under federal protection, immediately began looking for ways to protect these resources at the state level.[23] Under the police power, states can pass legislation prohibiting the filling of a wetlands as a means of

---

[22] Matt Arado, *Agency Acts Quickly After Landfill Court Wins*, Chicago Daily Herald, January 11, 2001 (2001 WL 3786983).
[23] *Supreme Court Ruling—Corps' Wetlands Oversight Weakened*, The Columbian, January 11, 2001, (2001 WL 6276888).

protecting the welfare of the citizens of the state. The first state to enact a comprehensive set of wetlands protections in response to the Supreme Court's ruling was Wisconsin. Fearing that 4.2 million acres of wetlands had lost protection, the state quickly passed legislation, giving the State Department of Natural Resources (DNR) the responsibility for issuing permits for filling in wetlands, and giving the DNR authority to inspect private property if they have "reason to believe" a wetlands had been filled in without a permit. Whether many states take on this responsibility remains to be seen.

	Summary
The United States Constitution Establishes our System of Government	**Federalism**—the authority to govern is divided between two sovereigns, or supreme lawmakers. **Separation of Powers**—our system of checks and balances under which the powers given to each branch operate to keep the other branches from being able to seize enough power to dominate the government.
Impact of the Supremacy Clause	**Federal Supremacy**—any state or local law that directly conflicts with the U.S. Constitution or federal treaties is void. **Concurrent Authority**—both state and federal governments have the power to regulate the matter; generally, the federal government defers to the state **Federal Preemption**—a doctrine used to strike down a law that does not directly conflict with a federal law but attempts to regulate a solely federal area.
The Effects Of The Commerce Clause On Business	**The Commerce Clause is a Source of Federal Authority** The Commerce Clause gives the federal government the authority to pass regulations that have a significant impact on interstate commerce. Today, the Commerce Clause provides the basis for most federal government regulations. In the 1930's, the Supreme Court gave a broad interpretation to the clause; today, some see the Supreme Court giving a more narrow interpretation. **The Commerce Clause Restricts State Authority** **Police Powers**—the residual powers retained by the state to enact legislation to safeguard the health and welfare of its citizenry. If a statute is a legitimate exercise of the state's police power, but it also interferes with interstate commerce, the court will have to weigh the benefit to the state with the burden on interstate commerce. If the burden on interstate commerce outweighs the benefit to the state, the law will be struck down. It will also make sure that the state law is carefully drafted to minimize impacts on interstate commerce.
Taxing and Spending Powers of the Federal Government	Taxes created by Congress must be uniform across all states. Taxes may have effects other than to raise revenue; thus, taxing power can be used indirectly to promote social goals. The same is true of spending power.
The Impact of the Amendments to the Constitution on Business and Citizens	**Freedom of Speech and Assembly** Corporate speech may be protected by the First Amendment. Regulations may be instituted if they pass a four-pronged test: It must be protected by First Amendment. The asserted government interest must be substantial. The regulation must directly advance the government interest. The regulation must not be more extensive than is necessary to serve that interest.

	Summary (continued)
The Impact of the Amendments to the Constitution on Business and Citizens (continued)	**Freedom of Religion** **Establishment Clause**—Congress may not make laws respecting an establishment of religion. **Free Exercise Clause**—Congress may not make laws prohibiting the free exercise of religion. **Freedom from Unreasonable Searches and Seizures** The Fourth Amendment provides protection to both corporations and individuals. However, although administrative searches generally require a warrant, some industries may be inspected without a warrant to insure compliance with the regulation. **Due Process** **Procedural Due Process**—focuses on rules for enforcing laws; entitles a person to notice of legal action **Substantive Due Process**—requires the government to have a proper purpose for enacting a law that will restrict individuals' liberty or the use of their property. **The Prohibition against Uncompensated Takings** If the government takes private property for public use, it must compensate the owner. However, much litigation occurs over the extent to which some government regulations constitute takings. **The Privilege against Self Incrimination** The privilege against self incrimination does not apply to business. Only businesses that operate as sole proprietorships may claim this right. **Equal Protection** Three different standards of scrutiny may be used in an equal protection case: **Strict Scrutiny**—actions preventing fundamental rights or including suspect classifications. **Intermediate Scrutiny**—classification based on gender or on legitimacy of a child. **Rational Basis**—classification involving other matters.
Other Constitutional Restrictions on Government	**The Privileges and Immunities Clause** This clause prohibits states from discriminating against citizens of other states. **The Full Faith and Credit Clause** In civil matters, courts in all states must uphold rights that have been established by legal documents. **The Contract Clause** No law can be passed that would unreasonably interfere with existing contracts.

Review Questions and Case Problems

1. Explain how each branch of the government controls the other branches.

2. How could both Sue and Sam be correct when Sue claims the Commerce Clause increases the government's power and Sam claims the Commerce Clause reduces the government's power?

3. What is the purpose of the Contract Clause?

4. What impact does the Contract Clause have on state regulation?

5. How does the First Amendment protection of corporate political speech differ from the protection of corporate commercial speech?

6. The state of Oklahoma required that all coal-burning power plants in the state purchase at least ten percent of the coal they burned from coal mines in the state of Oklahoma. The state of Wyoming challenged the legislation. On what Constitutional basis did Wyoming bring its

action? Why do you believe the state's challenge was either successful or unsuccessful? *Wyoming v. Oklahoma,* 502 U.S. 437 (1992).

7. Eric King was allegedly $300,000 past due on child support payments to his child and her mother. King, living in Texas, had been ordered by the court to pay $3,000 a month to his child and her mother, who lived in New York. King, being remiss on his payments, was charged with violating the Child Support Recovery Act of 1992 (CRSA), as amended by the Deadbeat Parents Punishment Act of 1998. These acts made it a federal crime to willfully neglect to make child support payments to a child who resides in another state. King moved to have the charges dismissed claiming that, in light of *U.S. v. Morrison,* Congress had exceeded its congressional authority under the Commerce Clause by passing the CRSA. Remembering that the Commerce Clause allows congress to regulate three specific areas, please explain why or why not you feel this is a justified exercise of the commerce clause, citing the specific ways it complies with or violates the commerce clause. *United States v. King,* U.S. App. Lexis 54 (2002).

8. Deputy Catherine Hedges stopped Allan K. Hollowell on November 14, 1998 for going 56 m.p.h. in a 35 m.p.h. zone. When she neared the truck she observed Hollowell removing his hands from his pocket and called for backup. Once backup arrived, they discovered Hollowell had a suspended license and placed him under arrest. Searching Hollowell, Deputy Bennett found marijuana and crack cocaine. Upon searching the truck, the officers discovered a set of scales, plastic bags, a laptop computer, and a large quantity of cocaine. Hollowell was found guilty of two felonies and misdemeanors. The Defendant appealed, contending, "the trial court committed reversible error by refusing to exclude the evidence police discovered searching the Defendant's person and his truck." If you were the prosecutor in this case, what would your arguments be? What do you think the Supreme Court of Indiana found? *Hollowell v. Indiana,* 753 N.E. 2d 612 (Sup. Ct. IN., 2001).

9. Kevin Murphy was incarcerated in a Montana State Correctional facility. During his incarceration he was trained by the prison to be a law clerk. After learning a fellow inmate had been charged with assaulting a correctional officer, he decided to attempt to assist this inmate with his legal defense. Because inmate-to-inmate contact was prohibited by the prison administration, Murphy sent the inmate a letter offering his assistance. The letter, according to prison guidelines, was intercepted and read. Based on this interception, the prison sanctioned Murphy for interference with hearing procedures and insolence. Murphy filed suit against the prison administration alleging that the disciplinary action violated his First Amendment rights, including a right to provide legal assistance to other inmates. The District Court reviewed the connection between impinging a prisoner's First Amendment rights with the overall interest in preserving the safety and order within the prison system. The District Court, finding a balance between the impingement and interests, rejected his

claim. The Ninth Circuit Court of Appeals reversed this decision claiming the "balance should tip in the favor of Murphy." The case was appealed the to Supreme Court. Explain how you think the Supreme Court ruled and what values are implicit in this ruling. *Robert Shaw v. Kevin Murphy,* 532 U.S. 223; 121 S. Ct. 1475 (2001).

10. City officials of Dallas, Texas, passed a local ordinance restricting admission to so-called "Class E" dance halls to persons between the ages of fourteen and eighteen. The ordinance did not impose similar age restrictions at other kinds of establishments where teenagers seemed to congregate. Charles Stanglin operated both a Class E dance hall and a roller skating rink in the same building. He sued to have the ordinance struck down as an unconstitutional violation of the Equal Protection Clause. The trial court upheld the ordinance, but a higher Texas court overturned the decision. The city appealed to the United States Supreme Court. Explain what standard the United States Supreme Court would apply to the case and why. What would be the result of an equal protection analysis according to that standard? *City of Dallas v. Stanglin,* 490 U.S., 19 (1989).

11. The Federal Alcohol Administration Act prohibited beer labels from disclosing the beer's alcohol content. Coors Brewing Company challenged the regulation. The government argued that it had a substantial interest in suppressing "strength wars" among beer producers, and the Act was tailored to further that interest. Use the *Central Hudson* test to explain how you believe the U.S. Supreme Court ruled in this case. *Rubin v. Coors Brewing Co.,* 115 S. Ct. 1585 (1995).

12. In 1987, the Department of Transportation (DOT) passed the Federal Motor Vehicle Safety Standards 208 (FMVSS 208). This administrative order was promulgated in order to give automobile manufacturers a choice of passive safety devices to install in their cars. The order required auto manufacturers "to equip some but not all of their 1987 vehicles with passive restraints." The order was not required for all vehicles for several reasons. First, the DOT was intentionally trying to gain acceptance from auto manufacturers for the restraints systems by introducing them gradually. Second, the DOT was trying to help reduce the cost through gradual introduction and finally, they were trying to win widespread consumer acceptance for the devices. The DOT had defined objectives for the order and specifically designated that not all cars be fit with the same devices.

In 1992, Alexis Geier was driving her 1987 Honda Accord and was seriously injured when she collided with a tree. The car was not equipped with any passive restraint devices, including airbags. Geier filed suit against the car's manufacturer, American Honda Motors, under the District of Columbia tort law, claiming Honda had negligently designed the vehicle without airbags. The Court reviewing the objectives of FMVSS 208 found that Geier's suit sought to set a new safety standard, opposed to the one proscribed in FMVSS 208. Thus, the Court found the claim to be preempted by the FMVSS 208. The Court of

Appeals affirmed this decision. The United States Supreme Court granted *certiorari*, noting that many state courts have found differently than the two courts in this case. Several state courts have held that FMVSS 208 does not preempt "no air bag" state torts. The United States Supreme Court is looking to unify the case law in this area. Explain how you believe they will rule and why. *Geier v. American Honda Motor,* 529 U.S. 861; 120 S. Ct. 1913 (2000).

13. In April of 1986 Larry Dean Dusenbery was arrested in his home by the FBI. After Dusenbery was removed from the premises and in custody, the FBI obtained and executed a search warrant for his property. During the execution of this warrant the agents seized drugs, drug paraphernalia, weapons, an automobile, and $21,939 in currency. In the coming months, Dusenbery plead guilty to a possession with intent to distribute charge. For this charge he received twelve years imprisonment and a six year special parole. Two years after Dusenbery was imprisoned the FBI began the process of administratively forfeiting the seized possessions. This process required the agency, attempting to conduct the forfeiture, to send written notice of the forfeiture procedures "to the each of the parties who appeared to have an interest in the property." This process is meant to allow all interested parties to be able to speak up for the property. The FBI, in accordance with this policy, drafted and sent letters to Dusenbery by certified mail to the Federal Corrections Institution where he was incarcerated. In addition to Dusenbery, the FBI sent letters to his home address as well as his mother's address. They received no response and, thus, proceeded with the forfeiture of his assets.

Roughly five years later Dusenbery filed a motion seeking to have his property returned to him. He received a response from the United States that all property not used in the drug business had been returned and the rest had been forfeited. Dusenbery then filed a civil suit claiming he had been denied his right of due process in the forfeiture of his property because he had never received the letter from the FBI. The District Court ruled that his right to due process had not been violated and had been satisfied when the FBI sent the notice. The Sixth Circuit Court of Appeals affirmed the lower court's decision. To provide a definitive answer, where the Court of Appeals have reached differing conclusions concerning, "what the Due Process Clause requires of the United States when it seeks to provide notice to a federal inmate of its intention to forfeit property in which the inmate appears to have an interest, the United States Supreme Court granted *certiorari*." The case was decided in a 5-4 decision. What do you think the Court found? What do you think the majority opinion was? What arguments do you believe were made

by the majority and the dissent? *Dusenbery v. United States,* 2002 U.S. LEXIS 401; 70 U.S.L.W. 4044; 15 Fla. L. Weekly Fed. S 48

14. Congress, in 1996, enacted the 505 of the Telecommunications Act (47 USCS 561). This piece of legislation stemmed from growing public concern that sexually oriented programming, such as the Playboy Channel, could be accessed, at least in part, by children. The concern was based on a phenomenon called signal bleed. Signal bleed occurs when audio or visual portions of the programs can be seen or heard despite the cable providers attempt to scramble the program. The act required the cable providers to: "(1) fully scramble or otherwise fully block those channels, or (2) "time channel," that is, limit transmission to hours when children were unlikely to be viewing." In an effort to comply with these regulations most cable operators adopted the time channeling, resulting in programming that was unavailable for roughly two-thirds of the day. Playboy Entertainment Group, one of the firms that owned and prepared and transmitted this type of programming to cable television operators filed suit against the Federal Government. The suit claimed that 505 violated the First Amendment and wanted an injunction prohibiting its enforcement. The District Court found that 505 imposed a content-based restriction on speech and concluded that although the State interests were compelling, the government might further those interests in a less restrictive way. The case was appealed to the United States Supreme Court. Noting that content-based regulation receives a strict scrutiny review by the court and that commercial speech is different than individual speech, explain how you believe the Supreme Court ruled in this case. *United States v. Playboy Entertainment Group,* 529 U.S. 803; 120 S. Ct. 1878 (2000)

15. The City Council of Bloomington, Indiana, passed a zoning ordinance limiting occupancy of dwellings in certain neighborhoods to a maximum of three unrelated adults. Property that was rented to more than three unrelated adults at the time the ordinance was passed was protected by a grandfather clause. A grandfather clause means that when ordinances are passed, uses of land that existed before the new ordinance may continue even though the old use is forbidden in the new ordinance. The Leiszes later bought some grandfathered rental property that lost its protection because it had not been properly registered with the city, thereby limiting the number of renters they could have on the property. They were convicted of violating the ordinance, and contested the ordinance as a takings. The appeals court held that the zoning ordinance to be a takings. The City appealed. Explain why you believe the State Supreme Court either upheld or overturned the decision of the appellate court. Board of Zoning Appeals, *Bloomington, Ind. v. Leisz,* 702 N.E. 2d 1026 (Sup. Ct., Ind., 1998).

Assignment on the Internet

In the Global Context sections of this chapter you have learned about the constitutions and legal systems of other countries. To find out more about constitutional law in other countries, visit the International Constitutional Law homepage at **http://www.uni-wuerzburg.de/law/index.html**. Examine the constitutions or legal systems of two countries other than those discussed in this chapter. What features make these constitutions more or less desirable than that of the United States? Can you note any strong similarities or differences? Using the information you have gathered and the information provided in this chapter, explain what you think are the most important features of a constitution.

On the Internet

http://www.supremecourtus.gov *Official website of the U.S. Supreme Court, including the docket, rules and opinions of the Court.*

http://www.law.cornell.edu/focus/bulletins. html *Subscribe via E-mail to receive the syllabi of recent Supreme Court Decisions.*

http://oyez.nwu.edu/cases/cases.cgi? command=search_by_title *To hear oral arguments in selected United States Supreme Court cases, visit this website.*

http://www.findlaw.com/casecode/supreme. html *This website will allow you to search a database of Supreme Court opinions.*

http://legalnews.findlaw.com/LegalNews/SC/ index.html *To read the latest Supreme Court news, go to this location.*

http://www.findlaw.com/11stategov/ *To read the constitutions of most of the states, go to this site.*

http://www.uni-wuerzburg.de/law/home.html *Constitutions from over eighty countries mainly in Europe, Africa, and the Middle East.*

http://www.georgetown.edu/LatAmerPolitical /Constitutions/constitutions.html *Constitutions from the Americas.*

http://www.law.emory.edu/FEDERAL/ *If interested in U.S. Constitutional history, go to this site to view early U.S. documents, including the original Constitution and Bill of Rights.*

Criminal Charges against Royal Caribbean Cruise Line

In October 1993, the Coast Guard noticed an oil slick behind a Royal Caribbean cruise ship that was heading for San Juan, Puerto Rico.[1] The Coast Guard, and later the Environmental Protection Agency (EPA), began investigating the water dumping practices of the Royal Caribbean Cruise ships. Over the next few years, the U.S. government discovered that the ships kept false logbooks regarding their dumping activities and secretly dumped huge amounts of oil and polluted water in the ocean. Moreover, Royal Caribbean employees lied to the Coast Guard about their dumping; some higher-ranking employees even ordered lower-ranking employees to destroy evidence regarding the dumping.[2] Royal Caribbean had originally argued that the dumping was the act of employees who were violating company policy.

The cruise company eventually pled guilty to twenty-one felony counts for dumping oil and hazardous chemicals from their cruise ships and agreed to pay an $18 million fine.[3] However, the EPA is continuing to investigate cruise ship dumping practices. In an attempt to change their polluting practices, Royal Caribbean has been testing a new water filtration system on some of their ships.[4]

1. *Suppose you are a manager for Royal Caribbean. What can you do to ensure that you no longer have a problem with dumping polluted water and oil?*
2. *Now suppose you were an employee who was told to destroy evidence of the dumping of polluted water and oil. How would you respond to your supervisor? Why?*

---

[1] Dave Bryan, *Cruise Line To Pay Fine of $18 Million For Polluting*, THE SEATTLE TIMES, July 22, 1999 at A1.

[2] *United States v. Royal Caribbean Cruise Lines*, No. 98-103CR (S.D. Fla. June 2, 1998), 13 NATIONAL ENVIRONMENTAL ENFORCEMENT JOURNAL 19 (August 1998).

[3] Laurie Asseo, *Cruise Line is Fined $18 Million For Dumping at Sea*, THE SEATTLE TIMES, July 21, 1999 at A3.

[4] Paul Queary, *Cruise Line Ships Cleaning Up Their Act*, THE SEATTLE TIMES, July 31, 2000 at A1.

CHAPTER 6

Crime and the Business Community

Elements of a Crime

Criminal Procedure

Major Defenses to Crimes

Liability for Crimes

Common Crimes Affecting Business

Tools for Fighting Business Crime

As the Royal Caribbean case shows, when a company commits a crime, the crime can lead to severe penalties and costs to the company. Royal Caribbean's $18 million dollar fine is quite large, but there was likely also some change in customers' attitudes toward Royal Caribbean. These customers were angry at the environmental harm caused by Royal Caribbean's dumping. The polluted water and oil clearly prevent individuals from safely consuming the water. Thus, in addition to causing significant environmental harm, Royal Caribbean suffered a serious financial blow because of the company's criminal activities.

In this chapter, we introduce the elements of criminal law and explain criminal procedure. We also identify the characteristics of crimes affecting business. Finally, we discuss types of business-related crimes, including computer crime.

Elements of a Crime

The purpose of criminal law is to punish an offender for causing harm to public health, safety, or morals. Criminal laws usually define criminal behavior and set guidelines for punishment. To punish an individual for criminal behavior, the government must demonstrate the two elements of a crime:

1. wrongful behavior, that is, **actus reus** (guilty act), and
2. wrongful state of mind, also known as **mens rea** (guilty mind).

The government, then, must show that a defendant committed a prohibited act with a wrongful intent.

Note that in a criminal proceeding, the *government* files the charges against the defendant. Thus, the government is always a party to a criminal action. This involvement of the government distinguishes criminal trials from civil proceedings. For civil actions an individual person or corporation can file a suit.

To prove the state-of-mind element, the government must prove the defendant acted with purpose, knowledge, recklessness, or negligence, depending upon which of these states of mind is required by the law of the relevant offense. The defendant's type of wrongful state of mind helps determine the seriousness of the punishment for the crime. First, a defendant can *purposefully* commit a crime by engaging in a specific wrongful behavior to bring about a specific wrongful result. Second, a defendant can *knowingly* commit a wrongful act if the person knows a wrongful act has occurred and believes or suspects that an act is wrongful, yet does nothing to confirm the belief that the act is wrongful. Third, a defendant is *reckless* if a criminal act occurs when the individual consciously ignores substantial risk. Finally, defendants are *negligent* if they do not meet a standard of care that the reasonable person would use in the context that led to the criminal act.

Classifications of Crimes

Crimes are divided into categories based on the seriousness of the offense. These categories are felonies, misdemeanors, or petty crimes. **Felonies** include serious crimes, such as murder, that are punishable by imprisonment for more than one year or death. **Misdemeanors** are less serious crimes punishable by fines or imprisonment for less than one year. A **petty offense**, such as violating a building code, is a minor misdemeanor, and is usually punishable by a jail sentence of less than six months or a small fine The statute defining the crime usually establishes whether the crime is a felony, misdemeanor, or petty offense.

Criminal Procedure

Criminal procedure differs from civil procedure in several key ways. First, the government, referred to as the prosecutor, always brings the criminal case, whereas in a civil case, the plaintiff filing the case can be an individual, business, or government entity. Second, the outcome of each is different. In the criminal case, the objective is punishment, so the defendant may be fined or imprisoned, whereas in a civil case the objective is to remedy a wrong done to the plaintiff, so the defendant will either have to provide compensation to the plaintiff or may be subject to an equitable remedy such as an injunction or order for specific performance. Other differences will become clear as you read the following sections describing the pretrial, trial, and posttrial procedures in a criminal case.

Pretrial Procedures

Prior to an arrest, grand juries may conduct criminal investigatory proceedings or issue a grand jury subpoena for company records. Criminal proceedings generally begin when an individual is **arrested** for a crime. A law enforcement officer, who is often a police officer, but may also be from another government agency—such as the Bureau of Alcohol, Tobacco and Firearms; the Federal Bureau of Investigation; or the Immigration and Naturalization Service—must perform the arrest. A law enforcement officer should obtain an arrest warrant before an individual is taken into custody. In certain circumstances, however, courts have recognized that law enforcement agents can arrest a suspect without a warrant if the officer believes there is probable cause, but not enough time to obtain the warrant. Ordinarily, to obtain an arrest warrant, the police or other law enforcement agents must demonstrate that there is **probable cause**, or a likelihood, that a suspect committed or is planning to commit a crime. A *magistrate,* the lowest ranking judicial official, issues the arrest warrant on the basis of probable cause.

When law enforcement agents arrest individuals, the officers must inform the individuals of their **Miranda rights**. If they fail to do so, any information a defendant offers at the time of the arrest is not admissible at trial. To comply with the Supreme Court's requirements for protecting a citizen's rights, a law enforcement officer must inform the defendant of the following facts before questioning:

1. "You have the right to remain silent and refuse to answer any questions."

2. "Anything you say may be used against you in a court of law."

3. "You have the right to consult an attorney before speaking to the police and have an attorney present during any questioning now or in the future."

4. "If you cannot afford an attorney, one will be appointed for you before the questioning begins."

5. "If you do not have an attorney available, you have the right to remain silent until you have had an opportunity to consult with one."

6. "Now that I have advised you of your rights, are you willing to answer any questions without an attorney present?"

After being arrested and read their Miranda rights, defendants are taken to the police station for **booking**, a procedure during which the name of the defendant and the alleged crime are recorded in the investigating agency or police department's records. After the prosecutor files the complaint, the defendant makes the **first appearance**, which is the appearance before a magistrate who determines whether there was probable cause for the arrest. If the magistrate ascertains that probable cause did not exist, the individual is freed.

If the defendant committed a minor offense and pleads guilty, the magistrate will sentence the individual. However, if the defendant claims innocence, the magistrate will ensure that the defendant has a lawyer, or appoint one, if necessary for an indigent defendant, and set **bail**, which is the amount of money defendants pay to the court on release from custody as security that they will return for trial.

Next, the prosecutor has a choice: Should the case be prosecuted? The *Principles of Federal Prosecution*, established by the U.S. Department of Justice, suggest that at the federal level the decision to prosecute depends on two primary factors: (1) whether the evidence is sufficient to obtain a conviction, and (2) whether prosecuting the case serves a federal interest. If the prosecutor decides not to go forward with the case, defendants may still be liable for their actions in civil court.

If the prosecutor chooses to proceed with a criminal action, the prosecutor must demonstrate the likelihood that the defendant's actions and intent meet the elements of a crime by charging the defendant with a crime through an *information* or an *indictment*. For a misdemeanor, the prosecutor must present to the magistrate evidence sufficient to justify prosecution of the defendant. The result would be a written document called information, a formal accusation stating the facts and specifying the violation of criminal law. However, for a felony, the prosecutor must present evidence adequate to justify bringing the defendant to trial to a grand jury. If the grand jury agrees that the evidence is adequate, it issues an **indictment**, a written accusation of the crime allegedly committed by the defendant.

Note that the grand jury does not determine guilt. It is simply a group of citizens who consider evidence of criminal conduct presented by the prosecutor and then determine whether the accused should be required to stand trial for a criminal offense. Unlike the petit jury, whose function is to decide facts, the grand jury merely determines whether there is enough evidence to try the defendant for the crime.

For example, on March 14, 2002, the U.S. Justice Department issued an indictment against Arthur Andersen, the accounting firm that was accused of obstruction of justice in Enron's collapse. Enron, once a multi-billion dollar corporation involved in energy trading, filed for bankruptcy in early December 2001. Following Enron's collapse, the U.S. Securities and Exchange Commission (SEC) stated that it would widen its investigation into Enron by considering whether Arthur Andersen, Enron's chief auditor, destroyed documents while an investigation was underway. Allegedly, the massive shredding stopped around November 8, 2001 after the SEC issued Andersen a subpoena. The grand jury indicted Andersen for ordering its employees to intentionally destroy documents that included information about official proceedings and criminal investigations.

In federal cases, a defendant accused of a felony has a constitutional right to a prosecution by grand jury indictment. However, felony prosecution may proceed by information if the defendant waives that right. For instance, in a high-profile case in which the defense attorney is trying to work out a deal with the prosecution, the defendant may ask that the case proceed by information. Federal misdemeanor cases may proceed by indictment or information.

If the criminal trial takes place in state court, the defendant may or may not have access to a grand jury. The United States Supreme Court has held that a grand jury trial is not a fundamental right, and thus states are not required to offer grand juries.[5] About half the states still require that felony prosecutions be initiated by

grand jury indictments; most of the rest use information as the method for commencing prosecution.

If the grand jury issues an indictment, the defendant appears in court to answer the indictment by entering a plea of guilty or not guilty. A defendant may also enter a plea of **nolo contendere**, a plea in which the defendant does not admit guilt, but agrees not to contest the charges. The advantage of a nolo contendere plea over a plea of guilty is that the former cannot be used against the defendant in a civil suit. This post-indictment appearance in court is called the **arraignment**. If the defendant pleads not guilty, his case will be heard before a **petit jury**, which is a fact-finding jury.

At any time, the prosecutor and defendant can make a **plea bargain**, an agreement in which the prosecutor agrees to reduce charges, drop charges, or recommend a certain sentence if the defendant pleads guilty. Plea-bargaining benefits both parties: the defendant gets a lesser sentence and the prosecution saves time and resources by not trying the case. Business people who commit crimes that affect business often engage in plea bargaining to avoid the publicity associated with a trial and the risk of a severe sentence.

Trial Procedure

If the case goes to trial and the crime is a felony or a misdemeanor punishable by six months or more in prison, the defendant has a constitutional right to a jury trial. In most states, if the defendant waives the right to a jury trial, the judge will hear the case. When a judge is the fact finder in a case, the trial is called a **bench trial**.

In a criminal trial, the prosecutor has the burden of proof and the defendant does not have to prove anything. The **burden of proof** has two elements: the *burden of production of evidence* and the *burden of persuasion*. To meet the burden of production of evidence, the prosecution must produce any tangible evidence and testimony that prove the elements of the crime that the defendant allegedly committed. Along with producing evidence, the prosecution also has the burden of persuasion; the prosecutor must persuade the jury *beyond reasonable doubt* that the defendant committed the crime. The burden of proof, then, is higher in a criminal case than in a civil case, because in a civil case the burden of persuasion requires only that the claim be supported by a preponderance of the evidence.

Unlike a civil case, a defendant cannot be forced to testify at a criminal trial. The Fifth Amendment guarantees the defendant freedom from self-incrimination.

---

[5] See *Hurtado v. California*, 110 U.S. 516 (1884).

After the jury hears the case, it deliberates and tries to reach a verdict. A jury that is unable to reach a verdict is known as a "hung jury." If the jury finds the defendant not guilty, the accused is acquitted and released. If the jury returns a guilty verdict, the judge will set a date to sentence the criminal.

Post-Trial Procedure

If the petit jury returns a verdict of not guilty, the government cannot appeal the acquittal. However, if the verdict is guilty, the defendant may appeal the verdict by claiming that a prejudicial error of law occurred at the original trial.

If there is no appeal, the defendant will be sentenced after the judge has received additional information relevant to sentencing. Federal sentences are determined largely by the guidelines set forth by the 1991 Sentencing Guidelines. These guidelines shift some of the authority to sentence away from the judges by prescribing a specific range of possible penalties for each crime.

In determining the precise sentence within that range, judges are given certain factors to consider, such as the defendants criminal record. Guidelines have also been established for white-collar crimes, once again allowing judges to consider individual factors such as the company's history of past violations and the firm's cooperation with federal investigators. Although some people criticize the Sentencing Guidelines as harsh, the next Global Context box demonstrates that they are rather tame compared to some of the punishments handed down in Dubai.

EXHIBIT 6-1

Steps of a Criminal Procedure

ARREST

↓

BOOKING

↓

FIRST APPEARANCE

INFORMATION (FOR MISDEMEANOR)   INDICTMENT BY A GRAND JURY (FOR FELONY)

↓

ARRAIGNMENT

↓

TRIAL

↓

APPEAL

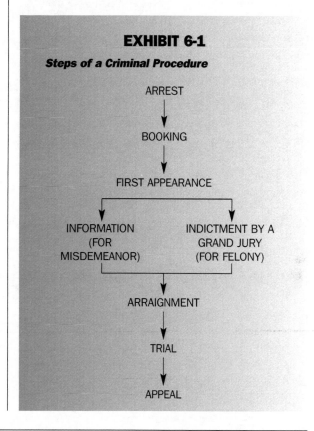

Global Context: First-Class Jails in Dubai

Dubai, the second largest emirate in the United Arab Emirates (UAE), takes a novel approach to criminals convicted of business crimes. In 1998 Dubai began construction on a multi-million dollar jail for elite white-collar criminals. Prisoners will have double rooms with air-conditioning, television, and beds. Along with Internet access, the inmates will have access to secretarial services.

In sharp contrast, consider how Dubai punishes other criminals. In 1997 two individuals were crucified as punishment for their crimes. Why is there such a distinction between the treatment of "common" criminals compared to white-collar criminals? Dubai is trying to attract global business and is thus willing to accommodate criminal business people to prevent financial losses.

Source: *Executive-Class Jail Cells*, THE NEW YORK TIMES, Oct. 11, 1998, at Section 6, p. 21.

Major Defenses to Crimes

In addition to claiming the defendant is innocent, or that the prosecution did not follow proper procedures, the defense may use several **affirmative defenses**, which are excuses for unlawful behavior. Some of the most common defenses include mistake of fact, intoxication, insanity, duress, and entrapment.

Mistake

With a **mistake of fact** defense, the defense tries to prove a defendant made an honest and reasonable mistake that negates the "guilty mind" element of a crime. For example, if the Royal Caribbean Cruise employees who dumped the toxic substances into the ocean thought they were actually dumping clean water into the ocean, they could claim mistake of fact.

On the other hand, mistake of law is generally not a legitimate defense. For example, the Royal Caribbean employees could not escape conviction by claiming they did not know that dumping toxic substances into the ocean is against the law. While initially these rules may seem contradictory (because in both cases, the defendant seems to lack a "guilty mind"), the mistake of law rule serves a policy goal. Courts have refused to recognize mistake of law as a defense because they fear that doing so would create a disincentive for people to learn basic tenets of law.

Intoxication

If a person has been forced to ingest an intoxicating substance or involuntarily ingests an intoxicating agent, that person can claim **involuntary intoxication**. This defense only applies if the person was unable to understand that the act committed was wrong because of the intoxication. However, in most states, a defendant cannot claim voluntary intoxication as a defense when the defendant knowingly chose to become intoxicated.

Insanity

Although a claim of insanity is a well-known criminal defense, it is not used as often as the public believes. A person cannot simply claim he or she is or was crazy; psychiatrists usually testify to the defendant's mental state at the time of the crime. Although the standards vary from state to state, in general defendants can claim **insanity** when their mental condition at the time the crime was committed was so impaired that they could not (1) understand the wrongful nature of the specific act or (2) distinguish between right and wrong in a general sense.

When the insanity defense is used, there is often a "battle of the experts." The psychiatrist testifying on behalf of the defense claims the accused was insane and the psychiatrist for the prosecution refutes the first psychiatrist's diagnosis. Furthermore, legal scholars debate whether psychiatrists who apply the tests of legal insanity are able to determine whether an individual is or was insane at the time of the criminal act. The complexity of the insanity standards almost guarantees that psychiatric experts will disagree about the application of the standards.

Most people have become very aware of the defense of insanity because of its use in the highly publicized case brought against Andrea Yates for the murder of her five children. In raising the insanity defense, Andrea's lawyer argued that his client believed killing her children was the right thing to do. In support of this claim, he offered evidence that she had said that her children were "going to be tormented the rest of their lives, and they were going to perish in the fires of hell," and so she killed them to save them.

Duress

If Greg threatened Bill with immediate bodily harm or loss of life unless Bill performed a wrongful act, Bill can use the **duress** defense. However, to claim duress, Bill must establish the following three elements:

Greg threatened Bill with *serious bodily harm or loss of life*. Threatening to take Bill's money would not be considered duress.

Greg's threat of harm must be *more serious* than the harm caused by Bill's crime. If Greg threatened to injure Bill's daughter seriously unless Bill handed over the $5,000 in the company cash register, duress would apply.

Greg's threat of harm must be *immediate and inescapable*. If Greg threatened to kill Bill in a year if Bill did not comply with Greg's order, Bill could not use the duress defense.

Entrapment

A relatively common defense for white-collar crime is entrapment. A defendant can use the **entrapment** defense if the idea for a crime did not originate with the defendant, but a police officer or other government official suggested it to the defendant and the defendant would not otherwise have committed the crime. The purpose of this defense is to prevent law enforcement officials from instigating crime.

Typically, a defendant claims an undercover government official suggested that a crime be committed and pressured the defendant into performing that crime. To refute the defense, the prosecution must demonstrate either that the defendant was not induced by government agents to commit the crime, or that the defendant was predisposed to commit the crime. In other words, a long-term drug dealer could not use the entrapment defense to claim that the undercover agent who offered to buy the dealer's drugs was the one who gave the dealer the idea to sell drugs.

Liability for Crimes

An individual or a corporation can be charged with and convicted of a crime. However, there has been much debate over whether corporations should be held criminally responsible.

Corporate Criminal Liability

Under the common law, a corporation could not be considered a criminal because it was not an actual person and thus did not have a "mind." Consequently, it could not meet the *mens rea* (guilty mind) requirement for a crime. Slowly, however, courts began to impose liability on corporations for **strict liability offenses**, those offenses that do not require state of mind. Next, courts imposed liability on corporations by imputing the state of mind of the employee to the corporation. Currently, corporations can be held criminally accountable for almost any crime. However, they cannot be held liable for those crimes that are punishable only by a prison sentence. Case 6-1 was instrumental in establishing corporate criminal liability.

Case 6-1

New York Central & Hudson River Railroad Company

v.

United States
United States Supreme Court
212 U.S. 481 (1909)

Sugar manufacturers in the early 1900's had to transport their sugar from New York to Detroit. Railroads had a published tariff rate on sugar at twenty-three cents per 100 pounds of sugar transported. To encourage sugar manufacturers to use railroads instead of water routes between New York and Detroit, the New York Central & Hudson River Railroad Company agreed to give companies shipping sugar, and those, later, legally holding the sugar, a rebate of five cents per 100 pounds shipped by their railroad company, which reduced the tariff to eighteen cents per 100 pounds. This agreement violated the Elkins Act, which prohibited a person or corporation from granting or receiving rebates related to the transportation of property in interstate commerce by common carrier.

The railroad company and assistant traffic manager were convicted of violating the Elkins Act, and the assistant traffic manager was sentenced to pay a fine of $1,000 for each violation of the act. The New York Central & Hudson River Railroad Company was to pay a fine of $18,000 on each count, for a total of $108,000. The corporate defendant argued that a corporation should not be subject to criminal liability and appealed the decision.

JUSTICE O'CONNER

The principal attack in this court is upon the constitutional validity of certain features of the Elkins Act. It is contended that these provisions of the law are unconstitutional because Congress has no authority to impute to a corporation the commission of criminal offenses, or to subject a corporation to a criminal prosecution by reason of the things charged. The argument is that to thus, punish the corporation, is in reality to punish the innocent stockholders, and to deprive them of their property without opportunity to be heard, consequently without due process of law.

…In considering the subject [of corporate criminal liability], Bishop's New Criminal Law states the law to be: 'Since a corporation acts by its officers and agents, their purposes, motives, and intent are just as much those of the corporation as are the things done. If, for example, the invisible, intangible essence or air which we term a corporation can level mountains, fill up valleys, lay down iron tracks, and run railroad cars on them, it can intend to do it, and can act therein as well viciously as virtuously.' *Telegram Newspaper Co. v. Com.* held that a corporation was subject to punishment for criminal contempt; and the court, speaking by Mr. Chief Justice Field, said: 'We think that a corporation may be liable criminally for certain offenses of which a specific intent may be a necessary element. There is no more difficulty in imputing to a corporation a specific intent in criminal proceedings than in civil. A corporation cannot be arrested and imprisoned in either civil or criminal proceedings, but its property may be taken either as compensation for a private wrong or as punishment for a public wrong.'

In this case we are to consider the criminal responsibility of a corporation for an act done while an authorized agent of the company is exercising the authority conferred upon him.…Applying the principle governing civil liability, we go only a step farther in holding that the act of the agent, while exercising the authority delegated to him to make rates for transportation, may be controlled, in the interest of public policy, by imputing his act to his employer and imposing penalties upon the corporation for which he is acting on the premises.

It is true that there are some crimes which, in their nature, cannot be committed by corporations. But there is a large class of offenses, of which rebating under the Federal statutes is one, wherein the crime consists in purposely doing the things prohibited by statute. In that class of crimes we see no good reason why corporations may not be held responsible for and charged with the knowledge and purposes of their agents, acting within the authority conferred upon them. If it were not so, many offenses might go unpunished and acts be committed in violation of law where, as in the present case, the statute requires all persons, corporate or private, to refrain from certain practices, forbidden in the interest of public policy.

We see no valid objection in law, and every reason in public policy, why the corporation, which profits by the transaction, and can only act through its agents and officers, shall be held punishable by fine because of the knowledge and intent of its agents to whom it has entrusted authority to act in the subject-matter of making and fixing rates of transportation, and whose knowledge and purposes may well be attributed to the corporation for which the agents act.

AFFIRMED.

1. Critical Thinking: What evidence does Justice O'Conner offer to support her conclusion? Does this evidence persuade you?

2. Ethical Decision Making: What is the ultimate purpose of the court's decision? In other words, what values are reflected in the court's decision?

Although the *Central Hudson* case is over ninety years old, it remains significant because it was the first case in which criminal liability was assigned to a corporation for a crime other than a strict liability offense. Over the years, the courts have refined the standards required for finding a corporation criminally liable for the acts of one of its employees or agents. Today, for a corporation to be held criminally liable for the acts of an agent, it must be shown that: (1) the individual was acting within the scope of her employment; (2) the individual was acting with the purpose of benefiting the corporation; and (3) the act was imputed to the corporation.[6]

---

[6] Matthew E. Beck & Matthew E. O'Brien, *Corporate Criminal Liability*, 37 AM. CRIM. L. REV. 261 (2000).

Liability of Corporate Executives

In addition to corporate criminal liability, corporate executives may also be personally liable for a business crime. As Case 6-2 demonstrates, corporate executives sometimes have the responsibility and power to ensure the company's compliance with the law. If the executive fails to meet this responsibility, the executive can be held criminally liable.

Case 6-2

United States

v.

Park

United States Supreme Court

421 U.S. 658 (1975)

*D*efendant Park, the president of a national food-chain corporation, was charged, along with the corporation, with violating the Federal Food, Drug, and Cosmetic Act by allowing food in the warehouse to be exposed to rodent contamination. Park had conceded that his responsibility for the "entire operation" included warehouse sanitation, but claimed that he had delegated the responsibility for sanitation to dependable subordinates. He admitted at trial that he had received a warning letter from the Food and Drug Administration regarding the unsanitary conditions at one of the company's warehouses. The trial court found the defendant guilty. The court of appeals reversed. The case was appealed to the U.S. Supreme Court.

CHIEF JUSTICE BURGER

The question presented was whether "the manager of a corporation, as well as the corporation itself, may be prosecuted under the Federal Food, Drug, and Cosmetic Act of 1938 for the introduction of misbranded and adulterated articles into interstate commerce. In *Dotterweich*, a jury had disagreed as to the corporation, a jobber purchasing drugs from manufacturers and shipping them in interstate commerce under its own label, but had convicted *Dotterweich*, the corporation's president and general manager.

Central to the Court's conclusion that individuals other than proprietors are subject to the criminal provisions of the Act was the reality that "the only way in which a corporation can act is through the individuals who act on its behalf." The Court also noted that corporate officers had been subject to criminal liability under the Federal Food and Drugs Act of 1906, and it observed that a contrary result under the 1938 legislation would have been incompatible with the expressed intent of Congress to "enlarge and stiffen the penal net" and to discourage a view of the act's criminal penalties as a "license for the conduct of illegitimate business."

The rationale of the interpretation given the Act in *Dotterweich*, as holding criminally accountable the persons whose failure to exercise the authority and supervisory responsibility reposed in them by the business organization, resulted in the violation complained of, has been confirmed in our subsequent cases. Thus, the Court has reaffirmed the proposition that "the public interest in the purity of its food is so great as to warrant the imposition of the highest standard of care on distributors." In order to make "distributors of food the strictest censors of their merchandise," the Act punishes "neglect where the law requires care, and inaction where it imposes a duty." The accused, if he does not will the violation, usually is in a position to prevent it with no more care than society might reasonably expect and no more exertion than it might reasonably extract from one who assumed his responsibilities."

Thus, *Dotterweich* and the cases which have followed reveal that in providing sanctions which reach and touch the individuals who execute the corporate mission—and this by no means necessarily confined to a single corporate agent or employee—the Act imposes not only a positive duty to seek out and remedy violations when they occur, but also, and primarily, a duty to implement measures that will insure that violations will not occur. The requirements of foresight and vigilance imposed on responsible corporate agents are beyond question demanding, and perhaps onerous, but they are not more stringent than the public has a right to expect of those who voluntarily assume positions of authority in business enterprises who services and products affect the health and well-being of the public that supports them.

The Act does not, as we observed in *Dotterweich*, make criminal liability turn on "awareness of some wrongdoing" or "conscious fraud." The duty imposed by Congress on responsible corporate agents is, we emphasize, one that requires the highest standard of foresight and vigilance, but the Act, in its criminal aspect, does not require that which is objectively impossible. The theory upon which responsible corporate agents are held criminally accountable for "causing" violations of the Act permits a claim that a defendant was "powerless" to prevent or correct the violation to "be raised defensively at a trial on the merits."

...[I]t is equally clear that the Government established a prima facie case when it introduced evidence sufficient to warrant a finding by the trier of the facts that the defendant had, by reason of his position in the corporation, responsibility and authority either to prevent in the first instance, or promptly to correct, the violation complained of, and that he failed to do so. The failure thus to fulfill the duty imposed by the interaction of the corporate agent's authority and that statute furnishes a sufficient causal link. The considerations, which prompted the imposition of this duty, and the scope of the duty, provide the measure of culpability.

REVERSED, IN FAVOR OF THE GOVERNMENT.

1. Critical Thinking: The Court relies heavily on the *Dotterweich* decision in coming to its present conclusion. Why does the Court use *Dotterweich* to come to its conclusion? Do you think the court should have relied so heavily on *Dotterweich*?

2. Ethical Decision Making: Suppose you were in Park's position in this case. You allegedly allowed food in your warehouse to be exposed to rodent contamination. If you were guided by the public disclosure test, what would you decide to do?

Since *U.S. v. Park*, the general rule that corporate executives may be held accountable for the crimes arising from their failure to meet their responsibility has remained intact. The rule has, in fact, broadened such that now, executives can be held criminally liable for crimes that we generally do not think of as crimes. For example, in *United States v. Iverson*, 162 F. 3d 1015 (1998), a corporate officer of a waste treatment facility was convicted and sentenced for violating the Clean Water Act after he ordered employees to illegally dispose of wastewater. This case demonstrates that corporate executives can be sentenced for not only the common-law crimes that we have traditionally understood to be criminal offenses, but also for violating provisions of regulatory statutes that permit criminal sanctions.

Crimes Occurring in the Business Context

When people hear the word "crime," they often think of homicide. In this section, we will not examine violent crimes; instead, we will focus on those crimes that occur in a business context. As a future business manager, you should become familiar with the following crimes that could affect your company.

Property Crimes against Business

We now examine three criminal acts: robbery, burglary, and larceny. Certainly, these three crimes do not occur solely in the business context; however, these are crimes that could be committed against your future business. We distinguish these three crimes from white-collar crime, for three reasons. First, individuals who are not employees often commit these three crimes, while employees often commit white-collar crimes. Second, these three crimes are committed against the business, while white-collar crimes are usually committed against society. Third, these three crimes may involve violence, while white-collar crime usually does not involve violence.

Robbery

Robbery is defined as the forceful and unlawful taking of personal property. If force or fear is absent, the crime is not robbery. It is theft. An example of theft would be someone stealing your wallet undetected while you are walking down the street. However, if that person tackled you, pinned you down, and wrested your wallet from you, you were robbed. If someone threatened you with a deadly weapon while taking your property, that person would likely be charged with *aggravated robbery*, which carries a more severe penalty.

Burglary

A **burglary** occurs whenever someone unlawfully enters a building with the intent to commit a felony.

Although the words "breaking and entering" usually come to mind, an individual does not have to break anything. If the person enters the building unlawfully with intent to commit a wrongful act, the requirement is met.

Larceny

Although the definition may vary slightly state-by-state, **larceny** is the secretive and wrongful taking and carrying away of the personal property of another with the intent to permanently deprive the rightful owner of its use or possession. Unlike robbery, larceny does not require force or fear. In the business context, larceny occurs for example, when an employee takes office supplies, such as paper or floppy disks, for their personal use.

States generally make a distinction between grand *larceny and petty larceny*. Grand larceny involves items of greater value; thus, it is a felony and carries more severe penalties. As the following Global Context reveals, other nations distinguish between different degrees of larceny in different ways, and sometimes these distinctions reflect a particular aspect of a nation's culture.

Global Context: Larceny in Spain

Laws governing the crime of larceny in Spain differ from U.S laws in several ways. The frequent legal definition of larceny in the United States is the fraudulent intent to deprive an owner *permanently* of the property without threat or force. Therefore, if one's intent is to return the property, one can not be convicted of larceny. In Spain, an individual can be convicted of this crime despite an intent to return the property. Spanish laws lack specification about the time period that the defendant may keep the property before becoming criminally liable. The crime constitutes larceny if the property is taken without the owner's consent.

Once convicted, the punishment for larceny in Spain is relatively minor with the one exception. If the stolen property is 1) that which is used in religious services, 2) stolen during a religious service, or 3) from a religious building, the fine and potential jail time immediately increase. This concern about the location of the larceny differs from U.S. law where location is immaterial for the conviction of larceny. While location of the crime in the United States may dictate whether the crime is tried in federal or state court, a crucifix stolen from a Catholic Church and a rake stolen from someone's garage would be treated equally under the law.

White-Collar Crime

White-collar crime, a phrase coined by Edward Sutherland in 1939, originally distinguished white-collar crimes from other crime according to the social status of the offender. The more modern approach is to define white-collar crime as a variety of nonviolent illegal acts against society that occur most frequently in the business context. In this sense, the environmental crimes committed by Royal Caribbean can be deemed white-collar crimes, even if blue-collar workers committed them. Clearly, this definition is broad.

Mail fraud, bribery, embezzlement, and computer crimes are example of offenses typically classified as white-collar crimes. These crimes occur more frequently than you might think. According to the 1997 Annual Report of the Attorney General, U.S. Attorneys filed 6,312 white-collar crime cases against 8,839 defendants in fiscal year 1997.[7]

The consequences of white-collar crimes are far-reaching. First, the cost of white-collar crimes can be tremendous. It is estimated that fraud in the health care industry alone costs society over $100 billion each year.[8] Second, in cases where company employees commit the crime, many companies fail to report the crime to avoid publicity. In fact, in a 1998 survey, 84% of companies who had identified employees who committed some type of theft did not prosecute the employee.[9] In such instances, companies do not recover the costs of the crime, whether it is money or property, and must pass the costs on to consumers or absorb the loss, thus affecting employees and shareholders. Third, white-collar crimes can be costly to the environment. For example, improper disposal of chemicals, such as dumping chemicals in a stream, has long-term repercussions for marine life, the surrounding ecosystem, and any humans who may come into contact with the contaminated water source.

Of course, the amount of money collected in fines from corporate executives engaged in criminal activity has not been insignificant either. For example, in 1999,

the government won over $490 million in fines, judgments, and settlements from health care fraud cases alone.[10] Fines, however, are only one way that those found guilty of fraud and other white-collar crimes might be punished.

There are at least four alternative ways to punish white-collar criminals. First, confinement has been mandated for certain types of white-collar crimes. As the prevalence of white-collar crime has increased, so too, has the number of white-collar offenders who are in jail. A second type of punishment that white-collar criminals receive is mandated community service, such as giving speeches about business crime. For instance, junk-bond king Michael Milliken was compelled to give speeches on corporate crime after he was convicted of insider trading. Third, judges may disqualify the individual from employment. For instance, the judge may prohibit the offender from engaging in an occupation where the same or a similar criminal act could occur again. Finally, the offender can be placed under house arrest. Individuals must wear a sensor so that the government can monitor whether they have left their houses.

Bribery

One of the better known white collar crimes is bribery. **Bribery** is the offering, giving, soliciting, or receiving of money or any object of value for the purpose of influencing the judgment or conduct of a person in a position of trust. Bribery of a public official is a statutory offense under federal law. The purpose of this law against bribery is to maintain the integrity of the government. This statute also covers bribes offered to witnesses in exchange for testimony. Perhaps one of the most publicized recent examples of bribery was the 2002 Winter Olympics bribery scandal in Salt Lake City, Utah. The Salt Lake City Olympics Bid Committee allegedly gave International Olympic Committee members between $4 million and $7 million in cash and other benefits.[11] These benefits included college tuition assistance payments, shopping trips for bathroom fixtures and doorknobs, and trips to the

---

[7] FY 1997 Annual Report of the Attorney General of the United States, U.S. Department of Justice: Office of the Attorney General, at p.23.

[8] James K. Robinson, Assistant U.S. Attorney General, Criminal Division, speech presented to the Sponsoring Partner Forum of the Ethics Officer Association in Scottsdale, AZ, April 6, 2000, < http://www.usdoj.gov/criminal/fraud/speech/ethics.htm> (December 13, 2000).

[9] *Collared: White-Collar Crime Hits More Wallets Than Muggers Do*, THE HOUSTON CHRONICLE, August 15, 1998, at A38.

[10] U.S. Department of Health and Human Services (HHS) and U.S. Department of Justice (DOJ). January 2000. *Health Care Fraud and Abuse Control Program Annual Report for FY 1999*. Washington, D.C.: Authors, cited at <http://www.ojp.usdoj.gov /ovc/assist/ nvaa2000/academy/P-16-FIN.htm> (December 12, 2000).

[11] Gregory J. Wallace, *Of Doorknobs and a Pistol: The Olympics Scandal and Commercial Bribery*, 6 BUSINESS CRIMES BULLETIN 1, (March 1999).

Super Bowl. The bid committee members could have been charged with bribery.

To demonstrate bribery under this statute, the government must show three elements: 1) something of value was offered, given, or promised to 2) a federal public official with 3) intent to influence that person's judgment or conduct. The "thing of value" element has been construed very liberally; actual commercial value is not necessary. For instance, had the Salt Lake City Olympics Bid Committee given a member of the International Olympic Committee shares of stock in a new Silicone Valley start-up called BellyUp.com, but the shares turned out to be worthless because the start-up never was established, this act may constitute bribery even though the stock is commercially worthless.

Additionally, the definition of a "public official" is also expansive. The statute defines "public official" as members of Congress, government officers, and employees, anyone "acting for or on behalf of" the federal government "in any official function, under or by authority of" a federal government department or agency. For example, individuals who work for private corporations that have some degree of responsibility for carrying out federal programs or policies are considered public officials.[12] The following is an example of a successful bribery case against an Immigration and Naturalization Service (INS) agent, demonstrating the three criteria.

---

[12] *Dixson v. United States*, 465 U.S. 482 (1984).

Case 6-3

**United States of America,
Plaintiff-Appellee,
v.
Ralph Leyva, Jr., Defendant-Appellant.
United States Court of Appeals
for the Ninth Circuit
2002 U.S. App. LEXIS 2868**

Cesar Gonzalez, an immigrant from Nicaragua, was denied asylum after informing the INS that he had executed prisoners while severing as a Sandinista soldier. Ralph Leyva, an INS asylum officer, offered to help Gonzalez for $1,500. Gonzalez reported the incident to the government authorities, and agreed to help in the investigation. Gonzalez gave Leyva the money, and Leyva arranged for another interview. Leyva changed information in the files from the first hearing, and wrote an officer assessment omitting the references to Gonzalez's killings as a Sandinista soldier. Government agents arranged for an informant to pose as Gonzalez's uncle, "Julio Boza." Boza went to Leyva requesting assistance in obtaining asylum. Boza provided an outline of his background to support his application. For $1,500 in cash and approximately $1,100 in services, Leyva filed applications for asylum and employment for Boza. Leyva even backdated the date of entries for Boza so he could bypass an INS interview.

Leyva was indicted on two counts of bribery, two counts of immigration document fraud, and one count of causing a false statement to be made to the INS. The jury found Leyva guilty on all five accounts. He appealed claiming the district court erroneously rejected his proposed jury instructions on count two, which charged Leyva with violating § 201(b)(2)(B) by submitting Boza's falsified asylum and employment authorization applications in return for cash and services.

JUDGE WARDLAW

Subsection 201(b)(2)(B) makes it unlawful for any

> public official…[to] directly or indirectly, corruptly demand, seek, receive, accept, or agree to receive or accept anything of value personally or for any other person or entity, in return for being influenced to commit or aid in committing, or to collude in, or allow, any fraud, or make opportunity for the commission of any fraud, on the United States.

Leyva contests, because § 201 criminalizes bribery, the term "corruptly" must refer to illegal use of an official position. Leyva asserts that without this distinction, it is a general statement of fraud, and not bribery. The appeal claims, because Leyva did not use his official position to submit Boza's application, this does not constitute bribery.

Leyva, during his first trial, made two requests regarding jury instructions. The first request asked the judge to instruct the jury, with regards to count two, the government was required to prove:

> the defendant acted corruptly in that he received, accepted, or agreed to receive or accept the approximately $1,500 in cash payments, and services valued at approximately $1,100 in return for using his official position as an asylum officer to knowingly commit and aid in committing a fraud on the Immigration and Naturalization Service….

The second request asked that "corruptly" be defined as:

> A public official acts corruptly when he accepts a thing of value in return for knowingly violating his official duty.…The public official must use his official position to commit or aid in the commission of the fraud.

Leyva contests his conviction because the judge did not use these instructions.

It is the opinion of this court that the district court did not err in refusing to use these instructions. The distinction that Leyva makes based on "use of official position" is not supported in the text of the statute, or in case law regarding bribery. Statutory construction deems that the court should not look beyond the plain meaning of the statute, unless its application will lead to unreasonable results. The plain meaning did not lead to unreasonableness in this case; furthermore, the plain meaning only required that a public official accept something of value for the committing of a fraud. The use of official position is not required, and the fact that the act was committed with the intent to influence an official act meets a subsection of the statute.

The jury instructions used by the district court read:

> a public official acts corruptly when he accepts or receives, or agrees to accept or receive a thing of value, in return for being influenced with the specific intent that, in exchange for the thing of value, some act would be influenced. This is known as the quid pro quo in Count Two.

These instructions comply with the decision made in *United States v. Strand*. This decision stated that "corruptly," with regards to bribery, refers to the defendant's intent to be influenced to commit an unlawful act for financial gain. Also, because "official position" is not a factor, these instructions were more than adequate to properly instruct the jury. Therefore, the district court did not err in rejecting the proposed instructions, nor did they err in using the previously stated jury instructions. Furthermore, the court finds that the rest of Leyva's claims are meritless, and we therefore find no error in the previous trial.

AFFIRMED.

1. Critical Thinking: Central to Leyva's argument is the use of the words "corruptly" and "official position." Does the reasoning persuade you that the court was correct in rejecting Leyva's definition of "corruptly"? Why or why not?

2. Ethical Decision Making: Think carefully about the reasons offered by the court for its decision. Did Leyva act unethically by offering to help Gonzalez receive asylum, for the price of $1,500? Should the government have used an undercover agent to pretend to be Gonzalez's uncle?

Recently, a new question regarding bribery has been raised in the courts. If Jessica and Michael are charged with a crime, a prosecutor might offer to give Jessica leniency in her case if she offers truthful testimony against Michael. However, some defendants who are in Michael's position have raised the argument that such prosecutor plea deals are bribes and thus violate federal bribery law, which prohibits the exchange of anything of value for testimony. They argue that because such bargains pin leniency to Jessica's trial performance, they tempt Jessica to embellish her testimony. Prosecutors argue that such deals are necessary to try white-collar crimes and drug cases. The following case addressed such an argument.

Case 6-4

United States of America, Plaintiff-Appellee,

v.

Sonya Evette Singleton, Defendant-Appellant
Circuit Court of Appeals for the Tenth Circuit
165 F. 3d 1297 (1999)

*S*onya Singleton was charged with money laundering and conspiring to distribute cocaine. Her co-conspirator, Napoleon Douglas, entered into a plea agreement with the prosecuting attorney under which he agreed to testify truthfully. In exchange, the prosecuting attorney promised leniency; the government would not prosecute him for related offenses, and the attorney would advise the sentencing court of Douglas' cooperation. Singleton argued that such an agreement violated the "antigratuity" statute, U.S.C. § 201(c)(2). The District Court allowed Douglas' testimony and convicted Singleton. A panel of the Tenth Circuit Court reversed the conviction, arguing that the attorney's promise for leniency did violate federal bribery law. The full circuit voted to rehear the case.*

JUDGE PORFILIO

The question before us is whether section 201(c)(2) applies to the government in the prosecution of criminal offenses. Ms. Singleton argues the plain language of the statute permits no answer but that it does. As expected, the government counters such a reading is beyond the intent of Congress and clearly wrong.

(c) Whoever—

(2) directly or indirectly, gives, offers, or promises anything of value to any person, for or because of the testimony under oath or affirmation given or to be given by such person as a witness upon a trial…before any court …shall be fined under this title or imprisoned for not more than two years, or both. 18 U.S.C. § 201(c)(2) (1994).

Viewing the statute on its face, it is apparent the dispute revolves about the word "whoever." As correctly argued by Ms. Singleton, "whoever" is a broad term that by its ordinary definition would exclude no one. However, the defendant's approach, while facially logical, ignores a crucial point that must be considered in any attempt to apply the statute to the issues of this case. She argues the breadth of the word "'whoever' includes within its scope the assistant United States attorney who offered Douglas something of value in exchange for his testimony." To begin the parsing of the statute with this assumption, however, ignores a fundamental fact: the capacity in which the government's lawyer appears in the courts.

Only officers of the Department of Justice or the United States Attorney can represent the United States in the prosecution of a criminal case. Therefore, the government's sovereign authority to prosecute and conduct a prosecution is vested solely in the United States Attorney and his or her properly appointed assistants. Of course, it cannot be otherwise because the government of the United States is not capable of exercising its powers on its own; the government functions only through its officers and agents. We thus infer in criminal cases that an Assistant United States Attorney, acting within the scope of authority conferred upon that office, is the alter ego of the United States exercising its sovereign power of prosecution. Hence, in the attempt to apply section 201(c)(2), the United States and the Assistant United States Attorney cannot be separated.

Put into proper context, then, the defendant's argument is: in a criminal prosecution, the word "whoever" in the statute includes within its scope the United States acting in its sovereign capacity. Extending that premise to its logical conclusion, the defendant implies Congress must have intended to subject the United States to the provisions of section 201(c)(2), and, consequently, like any other violator, to criminal prosecution. Reduced to this logical conclusion, the basic argument of the defendant is patently absurd.

The next question, then, is whether applying the statute to the government would deprive the sovereign of a recognized or established prerogative, title, or interest. The answer to that question is, inescapably, yes.

From the common law, we have drawn a longstanding practice sanctioning the testimony of accomplices against their confederates in exchange for leniency. This ingrained practice of granting lenience in exchange for testimony has created a vested sovereign prerogative in the government. It follows that if the practice can be traced to the common law, it has acquired stature akin to the special privilege of kings. However, in an American criminal prosecution, the granting of lenience is an authority that can only be exercised by the United States through its prosecutor; therefore, any reading of section 201(c)(2) that would restrict the exercise of this power is surely a diminution of sovereignty not countenanced in our jurisprudence.

Moreover, in light of the longstanding practice of leniency for testimony, we must presume if Congress had intended that section 201(c)(2) overturn this ingrained aspect of American legal culture, it would have done so in clear, unmistakable, and unarguable language.

AFFIRMED.

1. Critical Thinking: The outcome of this case hinges on the definition of an ambiguous word. Explain how the different meanings of that word would lead to different results in their case.

2. Ethical Decision Making: Think carefully about the reasons offered by the court for its decision. What value seems to be guiding the reasoning? What value does the court's reasoning diminish?

Before this case was decided, two district court judges agreed with the district court's ruling in *Singleton*.[13] They were persuaded by the argument that such deals would encourage fabrication and exaggeration by the person engaged in the deal. More importantly, a multitude of motions was made to reverse previous convictions in light of the original *Singleton* decision. In an attempt to end the controversy, two senators introduced bills that explicitly allowed deal making by prosecutors.[14] However, those bills died, and the full circuit court offered its ruling in January 1999.

Another type of bribery is commercial bribery, which includes a bribe in exchange for new information or payoffs. For example, Dell Computer is looking for a company that manufactures a certain type of computer part. Jane Devlon owns such a company, and realizes that if Dell gets the computer parts from her, she will potentially make a lot of money. When Dell sends

---

[13] *United States v. Lowery*, 1999, 166 F. 3d 1199; *U.S. v. Fraguela* 1998, 162 F. 3d 308.

[14] S.2314 , 105th Cong., 2d. Sess. (1998); S.2311, 105th Cong., 2d Sess. (1998).

its contractor to the Devlon factory, Ms. Devlon offers the contractor $500,000 in exchange for the contractor's promise that Dell will buy all such parts from only her factory for the next year. Alternatively, she might offer the contractor $5,000 to disclose the dollar amounts of the competing bids so that she can offer a better bid to earn the contract [hypothetical, of course].

One final type of bribery is the bribery of foreign officials. The purpose of the Foreign Corrupt Practice Act (FCPA) serves to combat such bribery. The FCPA prohibits payments to foreign officials to corruptly influence an official act or decision or to influence a foreign government. You might think of the FCPA as an extension of the law to prevent bribery of a public official. The FCPA allows the government to prosecute those who bribe foreign officials.

Congress amended the FCPA in 1998 to conform to the anti-bribery convention adopted by the Organization for Economic Cooperation and Development (OECD). The amendments broaden the scope of actions covered by the act and the definition of a public official. As of this writing, it is expected that 30 OECD countries—such as Japan, South Korea, and Brazil—will adopt similar anti-bribery statutes. Before the amendment, U.S. companies complained that anti-bribery laws disadvantaged them because many European and Asian competitors were not subject to similar laws. Between May 1994 and April 1998, bribes were allegedly used to influence the outcomes of 239 international contract competitions.[15]

Fraud

Criminal fraud encompasses a variety of means by which an individual intentionally uses some sort of misrepresentation to gain an advantage over another person. Most fraud statutes require the following three elements: (1) an intent or scheme to defraud; (2) the commission of a fraudulent act; and (3) the accomplished fraud. The scheme to defraud includes a multitude of frauds, including, for example, credit card fraud, insurance fraud, and securities fraud.

In June 2000, the FBI achieved its largest securities fraud crackdown in history when it arrested a group of Mafia leaders for a series of scams that cost investors an estimated $25 million. Government officials claimed that the Mob bought large stakes in small companies and then bribed and coerced brokers to promote the stocks to other investors at inflated prices.[16]

The Enron scandal also involves securities fraud with Enron's top executives allegedly overstating its earnings to maintain high stock prices. Complex accounting methods were used to hide the corporation's debt. Enron's top executives and big investors sold their stocks, while encouraging employees to continue buying company stocks. With the drastic decline in the company's stock value, many Enron employees lost much of their 401k investments.

Forgery, the fraudulent making or altering of any writing in a way that changes the legal rights and liabilities of another, is another type of fraud. If you sign your colleague's name to the back of a check made out to your colleague, you have committed forgery.

One of the most frequently prosecuted frauds is mail fraud, which is the use of mails to defraud the public. The Mail Fraud Act of 1990 makes mail fraud a federal crime. To prove mail fraud, the government must demonstrate two elements: (1) an intent to defraud, and (2) the use of or causing the use of mails to further the fraudulent scheme. The following case demonstrates the consideration of these two elements.

---

[15] Glenn R. Simpson, *Foreign Deals Rely on Bribes, U.S. Contends*, WSJ, February 23, 1999, at A3.

[16] Noelle Knox, *FBI Swoops Down on Wall Street Mob Authorities, Arrest 120 in Farthest-Reaching Securities Fraud Yet*, USA Today, June 15, 2000, at 1B.

Case 6-5

United States of America

v.

Gerson Cohen
Court of Appeals for the Third Circuit
171 F. 3d 796 (1999)

*G*erson Cohen, a meat salesperson for Butler foods, made illegal cash payments to supermarkets' meat managers in an attempt to persuade them to buy their meat from Butler Foods. If the customer bought at least 10,000 pounds of meat per week, the cash payments usually amounted to one penny per pound of meat purchased. After a customer made the minimum purchase, Larry Lipoff, part owner of Butler Foods, would give the cash payment to the salespeople who then gave the cash to the customer. Over a period of three years, Cohen made payments totaling $111,548.21 to managers for Thriftway Food Stores. The District Court convicted Cohen on twenty-five counts of mail fraud, in violation of 18 U.S.C. § 1341. Cohen appealed his conviction.

JUDGE NYGAARD

Cohen argues that the Government's evidence was insufficient to prove that he used the U.S. mail. We disagree. An essential element of mail fraud is "the use of the United States mails in furtherance of the fraudulent scheme"—*United States v. Hannigan*, 27 F. 3d 890, 892 (3d Cir. 1994). This element requires some competent evidence that, as a routine business practice or office custom, the type of document at issue in the case was sent through the U.S. mail. As we indicated in Hannigan, "the prosecution need not affirmatively disprove every conceivable alternative theory as to how the specific correspondence was delivered," but "some reference to the correspondence in question is required."

Cohen himself need not have placed the particular documents into the U.S. mail. A mailing is knowingly caused within the terms of the statute "where one does an act with knowledge that the use of the mails will follow in the ordinary course of business." *Pereira v. United States*, 347 U.S. 1, 8-9, 74 S. Ct. 358, 363, 98 L. Ed. 435 (1954). Here, the bookkeeper for Butler Foods, who supervised the clerical workers who were responsible for generating and mailing invoices, testified extensively about the company's standard business practice for billing its customers. She testified that after the meat invoices were prepared, they were placed in envelopes, run through the postal meter, and put in a U.S. mail bin which Lipoff took to the post office in his car. She testified that Butler Foods never used any delivery method other than the U.S. mail for any of its invoices, and that the Thriftway invoices at issue in this case were handled in the normal manner.

A manager at the company testified that it was standard practice to pick up the invoices in the U.S. mail bin and drop them off at the post office, and that he himself did this on occasion. Finally, an accountant for the Thriftway stores testified that it was normal business practice for his company to receive Butler Foods' invoices through the U.S. mail. This testimony provides sufficient evidence that Butler routinely delivered its invoices through the U.S. mails.

AFFIRMED.

1. Critical Thinking: Are you persuaded that Thriftway was using the mails to perpetuate a fraudulent scheme? Why or why not? What part of the opinion supports your conclusion?

2. Ethical Decision Making: Return to the WPH Process of Ethical Decision Making. Whom does this decision affect? In other words, who are the stakeholders in this decision?

Congress amended the mail fraud statute in 1994 to include commercial carriers and courier services as substitutes for the United States Mail. In other words, using FedEx or UPS to further a fraudulent scheme can be prosecuted as mail fraud. Similarly, the wire fraud statute attempts to prevent the use of wire, radio, or television transmissions to defraud the public.

Other types of fraud include health care fraud, telemarketing fraud, and bankruptcy fraud. The Department of Justice recently named *health care fraud* its top priority after violent crime. An example of health care fraud is the submission of false claims to insurance plans such as Medicare or Medicaid. Additionally, some doctors prescribe unneeded equipment to patients and then receive kickbacks from the manufacturers of the equipment. In 1992, there were 343 criminal investigations pending in health care fraud cases; this number leaped to 1,866 in 1998.[17] In 1999 alone, the FBI's investigations of various parties within the health care industry led to Medicare cost savings of over $1.16 billion.[18] The Department of Justice's emphasis on health care fraud has had other important consequences; the number of health care lawyers has increased enormously.

Telemarketing fraud has also gained much attention recently. The National Fraud Information Center reported that telephone cramming was the top telemarketing fraud of 1998.[19] *Cramming* is a scheme in which companies bill consumers for optional services that the consumers did not order. Another frequent telemarketing scheme is *slamming*, in which consumers are tricked into changing their phone service to another carrier without their consent.

The elderly, who have been more susceptible to telemarketing fraud, are often the specific targets of telemarketing schemes. Thus, the Department of Justice and the FBI have been collaborating on various undercover operations, such as Operation Senior Sentinel, to investigate and prosecute fraudulent telemarketers.

Finally, in 1999, more than 1.3 million bankruptcy filings occurred.[20] An individual can file for bankruptcy to be relieved of oppressive debt. Yet claims need to be carefully reviewed to prevent *bankruptcy fraud*. For example, an individual might hide some assets so that they will not be considered during the proceedings. Conversely, a creditor (a party to whom another owes money) might file a false claim against a debtor (the party who owes money to a creditor). Thus, bankruptcy fraud can occur on the part of the debtor or the creditor. From 1996 through fall 1997, U.S. Attorneys considered 1,400 cases of bankruptcy fraud.[21] Exhibit 6-2 lists other fraudulent acts that might occur in the corporate setting.

EXHIBIT 6-2

Types of Fraudulent Crimes

1. FORGERY: The fraudulent making or altering of any writing in a way that changes the legal rights and liabilities of another
2. DEFALCATION: The misappropriation of trust funds or money held in a fiduciary capacity.
3. FALSE ENTRIES: The making of an entry into the books of a bank or corporation that is designed to represent the existence of funds that do not exist.
4. FALSE TOKEN: A false document or sign of existence used to perpetrate a fraud, such as making counterfeit money.
5. FALSE PRETENSES: A designed misrepresentation of existing facts or conditions by which a person obtains another's money or goods, such as the writing of a worthless check.
6. FRAUDULENT CONCEALMENT: The suppression of a material fact that the person is legally bound to disclose.
7. MAIL FRAUD: The use of mails to defraud the public
8. HEALTHCARE FRAUD: Any fraudulent act committed in the provision of healthcare products or services.
9. TELEMARKETING FRAUD: Any scheme, including cramming and slamming, by using the telephone to commit a fraudulent act.

---

[17] Peter Aronson, *Health Law Boom*, NATIONAL L.J., May 17, 1999, at A1, A10.
[18] *Fiscal Year 1999 Accountability Report*, U.S. DEPT. OF JUSTICE, at p. I-23.
[19] National Fraud Information Center, *Top Ten Telemarketing Scams Fact Sheet*, http://www.fraud.org/info/special/top10tele.htm (July 22, 1999).
[20] *Bankruptcy Statistics from American Bankruptcy Institute*, http://www.abiworld.org/stats/newstatsfront.html (December 15, 2000).

[21] *FY 1997 Annual Report of the Attorney General of the United States*, U.S. DEPARTMENT OF JUSTICE: OFFICE OF THE ATTORNEY GENERAL, at p. 26.

Sometimes fraud cases can be very complex and involve multiple types of fraud. For example, a Beverly Hills lawyer was recently convicted of three counts of mail fraud, seven counts of wire fraud, and five counts of lying in a court hearing in an elaborate fraudulent scheme in which he purchased a yacht for $1.9 million, sold it to two other partners to drive up its insurance value, and then had a company he owned repurchase the yacht and then insure it for $3.5 million. Finally, he and his partners sunk the yacht and tried to collect the insurance.[22]

Embezzlement

Joe is Kathleen's attorney. Kathleen gave Joe $5,000 to put in escrow, an account where Joe will have access to the money, although the money is not his to use as he pleases. Suppose Joe takes some of that money out of the account and uses it to gamble. Yet, he "fixes" the records to cover up the fact that he has used some of the money for his personal use. He has committed the crime of **embezzlement**, the wrongful conversion of another's property by one who is lawfully in possession of that property. Embezzlement is distinguished from larceny because the individual did not take the property from another; he was already in possession of the property.

Embezzlement usually occurs when an employee steals money. Thus, employees in banks often commit the crime. However, as the recent embezzlement of $6.9 million from the American Cancer Society demonstrates, even nonprofit organizations are vulnerable to the crime of embezzlement.[23] The Chinese government, which has been focusing on economic crimes, caught employees in three major Chinese banks altering deposit slips and bank orders to direct the money to

---

[22] *Beverly Hills Lawyer Convicted of Sinking Luxury Yacht to Collect Millions*, <http:www.kfwb.com/news/local/1030114.html> (March 4, 2002).

[23] *U.S. v. Fraguela*, 162 F. 3d 208 (1998).

Global Context: Embezzlement and Bribery in China

Between 1981 and 1982, The People's Republic of China witnessed a dramatic rise in white-collar crimes. Chinese officials were alarmed by the increase and sought to severely punish all economic offenders, regardless of political or social rank. On March 8, 1982, a resolution entitled "Severely Punishing Criminals Who Do Great Damage to the Economy" was added to the Chinese Criminal Code. The provision targeted top-ranking officials by stating that any state functionaries who extort, accept bribes, or exploit their office would no longer receive the fix-term punishment (usually 10 years) allocated for bribery and extortion. Instead, those officials found guilty of extortion and accepting bribes would be sentenced to life imprisonment or possibly put to death.

Such punishments may seem extreme, but the reaction of the Chinese to this increase in white-collar crime reflects the culture's unusually great concern for social harmony.

personal accounts throughout China.[24] Those employees received death sentences for embezzlement, as we see in the Global Context feature.

Computer Crimes

Computer crime refers broadly to any wrongful act that: (1) is directed against computers, (2) uses computers to commit a crime, or (3) involves computers. Computer crime is not necessarily a new kind of crime, but is instead a new way of committing traditional crimes. Consider fraud, a crime that has existed for centuries. Today, online auctions, such as eBay, are the top source of fraud in the United States.[25] Indeed, some statistics suggest that using computers is a more profitable method of committing crimes. According to federal officials, the average loss in a nonelectronic embezzlement is $23,500. In contrast, in a computer fraud case, the average loss is $500,000.

Computer crimes are often difficult to prosecute, in large part because they are difficult to detect. An insider, such as an employee, or an outsider, such as a hacker (a person who illegally accesses or enters another person's or company's computer system to obtain information or to steal money), could commit the crime. However, computer systems are quite open to attack. The American Society for Industrial Security has reported that the losses from computer crimes were more than $250 billion for U.S. companies.[26] Furthermore, the attacks are frequent. The IRS alone detects between 800 to 1,200 cases of computer system misuse annually.[27]

In an attempt to aid prosecutions of computer crimes, Congress passed the Counterfeit Access Device and Computer Fraud and Abuse Act of 1984. The Act prohibited the unauthorized, knowing use of, or access to computers in six broad categories:

- unauthorized use of or access to a computer to obtain classified military or foreign policy information with the intent to harm the United States or to benefit a foreign country;

- unauthorized use of a computer to collect financial or credit information protected under federal privacy law;
- unauthorized access to a federal computer and the use, modification, destruction, or disclosure of data it contains or the prevention of authorized person's use of such data;
- alteration or modification of data in financial computers causing a loss of $1,000 or more;
- modification of data that impedes medical treatment to individuals; and
- fraudulent transfer of computer passwords or other similar data that could aid unauthorized access that either: (a) affects interstate commerce or (b) permits access to a government computer.

Computer crimes falling into the first category are felonies, whereas the others are misdemeanors.

The National Information Infrastructure Protection Act of 1996 amended the Computer Fraud and Abuse Act. Some major changes to the act include the substitution of the term "protected computers" in place of "federal interest computers" so that the statute now protects any computer attached to the Internet.

In a further attempt to aid prosecution of computer crimes, the U.S. Department of Justice formed the Computer Crime and Intellectual Property Section (CCIPS) in its Criminal Division. Attorneys in this division prosecute only federal computer crimes. They also coordinate their activities with numerous government entities, the private sector, scholars, and foreign representatives in an attempt to develop a global response to computer crime.

Destruction of Computer Data

Destruction of data is one of the most serious problems facing companies today. A **virus** is a computer program that rearranges, damages, destroys, or replaces computer data. Thus, if an employee or a hacker creates and releases a virus, a company can easily lose vital information.

The most economically destructive computer crime to date was the creation of the "love bug" virus. In May 2000, the virus spread rapidly across the globe by e-mail. Once the e-mail was opened, it destroyed files on the user's computer, and then the virus sent itself to every address in the computer's e-mail address book. In the end, the virus caused over $10 billion in damages, and halted computers in major companies and government agencies all across the world.[28]

---

[24] Mitchell A. Silk, *Cracking Down On Economic Crime*, 21 THE CHINA BUSINESS REVIEW 21, 26 (May/June 1994).

[25] Noelle Knox, *Online Auctions Top List of Internet Fraud*, USA TODAY, August 29, 2000, at 1A.

[26] Joe D. Whitley & William H. Jordan, *Increasing Reliance on Computers Has Captured Attention of Criminal and Congress*, LEGAL TIMES, September 28, 1998, at S40.

[27] *IRS Tracks Computer Crime*, FEDERAL HUMAN RESOURCES WEEK, Vol.5, July 6, 1998, at 16.

[28] Mark Landler, *A Filipino Linked to 'Love Bug' Talks About His License to Hack*, NEW YORK TIMES, October 21, 2000, at C1.

Companies can try to prevent the destruction of data by installing virus detection programs on their computers. However, the detection programs recognize only previously existing harmful files. As a result, if an employee creates a new virus, the detection program is useless.

Unlawful Appropriation of Data or Services

When an employee uses a computer in a manner not authorized by the employer, the employee has committed a crime. Employers, then, must clearly communicate with employees about authorized versus unauthorized behavior. For example, if an employee uses a work computer to run a personal business on the side, the employer may argue that the employee is engaging in theft because the employee is not using the computer in an authorized manner.[29] Thus, when you become a business manager, you will want to make sure that you explicitly list acceptable computer uses along with the penalties associated with unauthorized use.

Tools for Fighting Business Crime

While there are clearly a significant number of business related crimes that can be committed, there are certain federal laws that help fight such crime. Two federal laws that have been somewhat successful in this battle are RICO and the False Claims Act. While these laws are currently extremely powerful white-collar crime laws, both laws were created with different purposes in mind.

The Racketeer Influenced and Corrupt Organizations Act (RICO)

One of the most important tools for fighting white-collar crime is in Title IX of the Organized Crime Control Act of 1970, the Racketeer Influenced Corrupt Organizations Act (RICO). Although the statute was originally enacted to combat organized crime, its effect is to prevent legitimate businesses from serving as covers for racketeering. This statute prohibits persons employed by or associated with an enterprise from engaging in a pattern of racketeering activity. Anyone whose business or property has been damaged by this pattern of racketeering activity can sue to recover treble damages and attorney's fees in a civil action.

Demonstrating a claim under RICO requires proof of a pattern of racketeering. Courts have defined a pattern as more than one action. Thus, a one-time violator could not be prosecuted under RICO because there could be no pattern as yet. Some courts additionally have found that a pattern requires continued criminal activity over a "substantial" period of time. Although "pattern" is restricted to more than one act, racketeering has been defined broadly to include almost all criminal actions, including acts of violence, fraud, bribery, securities fraud, and the provision of illegal goods and services. Therefore, RICO is an extremely effective tool in combating white-collar crimes.

In addition to being held civilly liable under RICO, a violator may also be subject to RICO's criminal penalties. A person found to have violated the act may be subject to a fine of up to $25,000 per violation, imprisonment for up to twenty years, or both.

The False Claims Act

Since 1986 private citizens have been using the False Claims Act to sue employers on behalf of the government for fraud against the government. For example, an employee in a healthcare facility might realize that his employer is submitting fraudulent claims to Medicare. The employee can bring a suit against the employer on behalf of the government for fraud against the government.

If the employee realizes that his employer is committing fraud against the government, he must first notify the government of his intent to file the case on behalf of the government. If the government chooses to intervene and prosecute the case itself, with the help of the employee, the citizen would receive twenty-five percent of the amount recovered. If the government opts to not get involved, the citizen receives thirty percent.

Certainly, an employee who brings a suit against her employer might be worried about retaliation, such as being fired or demoted. Thus, the Act provides protection for those employees who use the law. If an employer is found guilty of retaliation, the employer may be forced to pay the employee twice the amount of back pay plus special damages.

The biggest reward thus far under the act has been the $40 million share that Zachary Bentley and his partners received for blowing the whistle on a Massachusetts based company that was defrauding Medicare. The government settled the case against the company for $385 million. The reward in *Bentley* case, however, is far above the norm. The Justice

---

[29] See e.g. *State v. McGraw*, 459 N.E. 2d 61 (1984).

Department estimates that the median award in all the 425 cases settled between the act's inception and July of 2001 is around $150,000.[30]

Despite the fact that some of these cases might not have been pursued had it not been for the False Claims act, there are many who are opposed to the act. Some argue that the whistleblowers are receiving money that should belong to the taxpayers, while others say that the Act prompts people to not report fraud right away, but wait until the value of the case grows. Still others complain that the act results in frivolous lawsuits as employees try to find an "easy" way to make money.

Defenders of the act point out that the act has led to some significant cases of fraud being reported that otherwise might have cost the government millions of dollars. They point out that when an employee does report a fraudulent employer, it is going to be very difficult for that employee to get a job in that field in the future, and thus you need to offer a significant incentive to get employees to report fraud by their employers.

Royal Caribbean Wrap-Up

The EPA continues to investigate Royal Caribbean, along with other cruise lines, to monitor their dumping practices, particularly in Alaskan waters. If you were a business manager for Royal Caribbean, what would you do to ensure that the dumping problems didn't recur? Perhaps you might suggest a training course regarding the harmful effects of dumping polluted water and oil for all ship employees who might come into contact with the water filtration systems. Alternatively, Royal Caribbean has placed an environmental officer on each of its sixteen ships to monitor the treatment of polluted water.[31]

If you were told to destroy evidence of dumping polluted water and oil, how would you respond to your supervisor? One way to answer this question is to turn to the three ethical approaches you have already learned. For example, you could ask yourself, "What would happen if everyone in the world followed the order to destroy the evidence?" Alternatively, you could ask yourself what values are reflected in the dilemma, and you can select your response to the order based on those values with which you are most comfortable. While you may be concerned about the security of your job, there are a variety of statutory protections that would protect you from being fired for refusing to commit a crime. Finally, you might ask yourself how you would feel if your friend opened the Sunday newspaper and read about your being found guilty of illegally dumping untreated waste into the ocean. Thinking about what you would do as an employee can help you to better anticipate what kinds of orders you, a future business manager, may give your employees.

[30] Alice Dembner, *Lawmakers Justice Department Officials Question Whistle-Blower Windfalls*, KNIGHT-RIDDER TRIBUNE BUSINESS NEWS, July 29, 2001, 2001 WL 25947333 (page numbers not available).

[31] Dave Bryan, *Cruise Line To Pay Fine of $18 Million For Polluting*, THE SEATTLE TIMES, July 22, 1999, at A1.

	Summary
Elements of a Crime	**Actus reus**—wrongful behavior (guilty act). **Mens rea**—wrongful state of mind or intent (guilty mind).
Types of Crimes	**Felonies**—serious crimes punishable by imprisonment or death. **Misdemeanors**—less serious crimes punishable by fines or imprisonment for less than one year. **Petty crime**—minor misdemeanor punishable by fine or short imprisonment.
Criminal Procedure	**Pre-trial procedure**—the arrest, the booking, the first appearance, indictment, and arraignment **Trial procedure**—jury selection, trial with burden of proof on prosecution, jury deliberations, jury verdict, (if guilty) sentencing hearing **Post-trial procedure**—appeal

	Summary (continued)
Defenses to Crimes	**Mistake of fact**—the defense tries to prove a defendant made an honest and reasonable mistake that negates the "guilty mind" element of a crime. **Involuntary intoxication**—Defendant was forced or tricked into ingesting intoxicating substance, and as a result of being intoxicated was unable to understand that the act committed was wrong. **Insanity**—defendant's mental condition at the time the crime was committed was so impaired that the defendant could not (1) understand the wrongful nature of the specific act or (2) distinguish between right and wrong in a general sense. **Duress**—defendant committed the crime only because the defendant was 1. threatened with serious bodily harm or loss of life., 2. by a threat of harm must be more serious than the harm caused by the crime, and 3) was immediate and inescapable. **Entrapment**—the idea for a crime did not originate with the defendant, but rather a police officer or other government official suggested it to the defendant and the defendant would not otherwise have committed the crime.
Liability for Crimes	Both corporations, as legal entities, and the corporate officers and managers can be held liable for crimes committed on behalf of the corporation.

Common Crimes Affecting Business	**Property Crimes against the Business**
	1. Robbery
	2. Burglary
	3. Larceny
	White Collar Crime
	1. Bribery
	2. Fraud
	3. Embezzlement
	4. Computer Crimes
	   a. Destruction of computer data
	   b. Unlawful appropriation of data or services

Tools to Fight Business Crime	**RICO**—prohibits persons employed by or associated with an enterprise from engaging in a pattern of racketeering activity. Anyone whose business or property has been damaged by this pattern of racketeering activity can sue under RICO to recover treble damages and attorney's fees in a civil action. **False Claims Act**—allows employees to sue employers on behalf of the federal government for fraud against the government. The employee retains a share of the recovery as a reward for his efforts.

Review Questions and Case Problems

1. How does criminal law differ from civil law, both in terms of their purposes and in terms of the procedures used in each type of case?

2. Explain how crimes are classified.

3. List and define the primary affirmative defenses used in criminal cases.

4. Explain the federal laws that are currently being used to try to fight white-collar crime.

5. Robert Morris, a Ph.D. student in computer science at Cornell University, designed and released a computer program known as a "worm" onto the Internet. The "worm" spread and multiplied and eventually caused computers at various educational and military institutions to "crash." Morris argued that he released the worm to demonstrate to fellow graduate students the lack of security protecting computer networks. With what crime was he most likely charged? Was this prosecution successful? *United States v. Robert Tappen Morris*, 928 F. 2d 504 (1991).

6. Wayne T. Schmuck was a used car distributor who purchased used cars, rolled back their odometers, and sold them to Wisconsin retail dealers at prices artificially inflated by the low mileage readings. Those dealers, not knowing about the false odometers and inflated prices, resold the cars to customers and finished the transaction by mailing title application forms to the State on behalf of the customers. Schmuck was charged with twelve counts of mail fraud. The District Court convicted and the Circuit Court affirmed. How did the Supreme Court rule? Why? *Schmuck v. United States*, 109 S. Ct. 1443 (1989).

7. Attorney Maylon K. London represented clients being sued on contract for the installation of steam units in a motel. London presented to his clients a falsified court order with the supposed signature of the district judge, requiring the clients to pay $27,000. The district judge's signature had been photocopied on this falsified court order. The clients were supposed to write the check in London's name so that London could hold the amount in escrow. When London accepted the check from his clients, he was arrested, prosecuted, and convicted of forgery. On appeal, London argued that forgery did not occur because he unofficially reproduced the judge's signature by a copy machine. Did the court decide that London committed forgery? Why or why not? *United States v. London*, 714 F. 2d 1558 (11th Cir., 1983).

8. Thomas Faulkner, a truck driver for North American Van Lines, was supposed to ship 105 refrigerators from San Diego to Hartford, Connecticut. Faulkner stopped in Las Vegas, Nevada, to call appliance store owner Richard Urbauer and offered to sell the refrigerators. After Faulkner and Urbauer debated the sale of the refrigerators, Faulkner broke the truck's seals and opened two cartons to show Urbauer the refrigerators. While Urbauer examined the refrigerators, Faulkner began to rearrange the cartons. They began to discuss the deal again, but could not reach an agreement. When Faulkner left the store, he was arrested. He was prosecuted and convicted of embezzlement. Faulkner appealed, arguing that the evidence failed to establish embezzlement because he never physically removed goods from the truck and never sold the goods. What did the appellate court decide? *United States v. Faulkner*, 638 F. 2d 129 (9th Cir. 1981).

9. Two campus security officers questioned Michael Jensen when they saw him walking across campus with a dormitory lounge chair propped on his head at 3:13 A.M. Jensen refused to identify himself to the officers, but claimed he was simply playing a prank by carrying the chair from one residence hall to another residence hall across campus. The officers repeatedly asked him for identification, which he refused repeatedly to provide. When the officers told him that they would remove his identification from his jean pocket, he began to comply. When the officers told Jensen that he was under arrest, Jensen ran away. Later, he was caught and indicted by a grand jury for petit larceny. Jensen claimed that there was no evidence that he did not intend to return the chair, so the indictment was flawed. Why did the court of appeals affirm the indictment? *People of New York v. Jensen*, 86 N.Y. 2d 248 (1995); 1995 N.Y. LEXIS 2230.

10. Dotterweich, the general manager of a pharmaceutical company, was charged with violating the Food, Drug, and Cosmetics Act because he shipped misbranded drugs to a physician. Dotterweich argued that he had no personal contact with the shipments, so he should not be held responsible. However, he was responsible for overseeing the company's business and instructed employees to fill orders received by physicians. Was he held criminally responsible for violating the Act? *United States v. Dotterweich*, 320 U.S. 277 (1943); 1943 U.S. LEXIS 1100.

11. Bernadette Sablan was fired from her job at the Bank of Hawaii for circumventing security procedures when retrieving files. One night after drinking at a bar with a friend, she entered an unlocked door at the bank. She went to her old workstation and logged on to the mainframe by using an old password. She contends that she simply accessed several files and logged out. The government argued that she changed and deleted several files. Regardless, her actions damaged several bank files.

Sablan was charged with computer fraud. She argued that the government had to establish the *mens rea* element of the crime—that is, the government had to prove she intentionally tried to damage the files. The district court ruled that the intention element applied only to accessing the files. Sablan argued that the legislation in question was intended to apply only to those who intentionally damage computer data and appealed. How did the court of appeals rule? Why? *United States v. Sablan*, 92 F. 3d 865, 866 (9th Cir. 1996).

Assignment on the Internet

This chapter described various types of fraud. Search on the Internet for a type of fraud that was not discussed in this chapter. Why is this type of fraud a problem? How can you protect yourself from this type of fraud? Be prepared to discuss your findings in class.

On the Internet

http://www.usdoj.gov/criminal/cybercrime
The Computer Crime and Intellectual Property Section (CCIPS) provides general information as well as legal examination of computer crime.

http://www.nw3c.org/home.htm The National White Collar Crime Center is a support organization for enforcement agencies and conducts research on white-collar crime. For example, read about their recent survey on citizens' attitude regarding white-collar crime.

http://www.oecd.org/puma/gvrnance/ethics/
At "Ethics and Corruption in the Public Sector," read about the anti-corruption measures in OECD countries.

http://fraud.org/welcome.htm The National Fraud Information Center provides numerous fact sheets explaining types of fraud as well as ways to combat fraud.

Rubin v. U.S. News

Richard Rubin, chief executive of Republic Metals, a gold refining company, agreed to be interviewed and photographed for a *U.S. News and World Report* article.[1] Rubin argued that he was told that the article was about the Peruvian value tax, a rebate given to those who export gold from Peru. However, when the article appeared in the magazine, the article was titled, "The Golden Age of Crime: Why International Drug Traffickers are Invading the Global Gold Trade." The author of the article explained how the gold trade is used as a tool for money laundering, and Rubin, also pictured, was quoted as saying, "There's a dual economic system. There's on the books and there's off the books."

When Rubin discovered that the article was about money laundering, he brought suit against *U.S. News and World Report*. Rubin argued that the story implies that he is or has been involved in money laundering through his gold refining business, and this implication hurt his reputation. *U.S. News* issued a clarification stating that the purpose of the article was not to imply that Rubin was involved in illegal activity.

1. *Suppose you are Rubin. You are concerned that the article has damaged your gold refining business. What do you do? Why?*
2. *Now suppose you are a manager at a company that does business with Rubin's refining company. You read the story in U.S. News. Does the story lead to any change in your business with Rubin? Why or why not?*

---

[1] See Susan R. Miller, *U.S. News Sued By Gold Trader quoted in Money Laundering Story,* BROWARD DAILY BUSINESS REVIEW, May 25, 2000, at p. A1; *News Magazine Sued,* THE NATIONAL LAW JOURNAL, June 12, 2000, at p. B2.

CHAPTER 7

Tort Law

Introduction fo Tort Law

Damages Available in Tort Cases

Classifications of Torts

Intentional Torts

As a future business manager, you will likely be involved in a situation where one party believes he or she has been injured by the actions of another party, in the same way that Rubin believes he has been injured by the *U.S. News and World Report* article. The purpose of this chapter is to examine common wrongs that might occur in the workplace. We first examine the goals of tort law and the types of damages awarded in these cases. Then we spend the rest of the chapter considering the different types of torts. We conclude by considering how tort law is treated throughout the world.

Introduction to Tort Law

The previous chapter focused on criminal law and the punishment individuals may receive for committing crimes. When a person commits a crime, the victim of that crime will frequently be able to bring a tort action against the criminal, because many times the same actions that constitute a criminal offense often constitute a tort, or personal injury.

While criminal law has as its primary objective punishment of wrongdoers and preservation of order in society, tort law's primary objective is providing compensation for injured parties. It also contributes to our maintaining order in society by discouraging private retaliation by injured persons and their friends. After all, we do not want to live in a community where vigilantes with tempers are roaming about righting some harm they believe has occurred to them.

A third objective of tort law is to give citizens a sense that they live in a just society. Our collective sense of right and wrong suggests that someone who creates harm should make things right by compensating those who were harmed. This recognition that one will have to pay for the personal injuries they cause may also serve to deter the commission of torts.

Although this chapter discusses torts as if they are the same everywhere, tort law is state law, so states may have slightly different definitions of each tort. In describing torts, this chapter will use the definitions common in most states, noting those instances where there seems to be a significant difference in the way certain states define the tort.

Despite the public impression of a litigation explosion, tort litigation has been declining slightly since 1990.[2] The National Center for State Courts compiled statistics on tort filings in 28 states, representing 68% of the population, and in 1990, there were 667,477 cases filed. During the next nine years, the number of filings fluctuated from a high of 716,300 in 1996 to a low of 629,251 in 1999, the last year for which they have data available.[3] Thus, even if the number of tort cases is not increasing, there are still enough cases filed each year that tort liability should still concern a competent business manager.

Damages Available in Tort Cases

There are three types of damages available in tort cases: **compensatory**, **nominal**, and **punitive**. You will see this system of classifying damages again when we talk about damages in other contexts, such as in cases involving the breach of a contract.

---

[2] National Center for State Courts <http:www.ncsc.dni.us/divisions/ research/csp/csp-frd.html> (January 31, 2002).

[3] *Ibid.*

EXHIBIT 7-1

Types Of Tort Damages

TYPE	PURPOSE	AMOUNT
Compensatory	To make the plaintiff whole again.	An amount equivalent to all losses caused by the tort, including compensation for pain and suffering, but not attorney fees.
Nominal	To recognize that the defendant committed a tort against the plaintiff.	A nominal amount—typically $1.00-$5.00.
Punitive	To punish the defendant and deter future wrongdoers.	Based upon two factors: the severity of the wrongful conduct and the wealth of the defendant.

Compensatory Damages

As the primary objective of tort law is to compensate victims, the primary type of damages are compensatory damages, damages designed to compensate the victim for all of the harm caused by the person who committed the tort, often referred to as the **tortfeasor**. According to a survey by the Jury Verdict Research, compensatory damage awards in personal injury cases have been relatively stable in the United States over the past several years. The median award in 1999 was $50,000, the same as it was in 1993.[4]

Medical bills, lost wages, property repair bills, and compensation for pain and suffering are examples of the typical items covered by compensatory damages. For example, suppose Rubin could demonstrate that he and his company lost money because of the *U.S. News and World Report* article. He might be able to recover those lost damages from *U.S. News*. Surprisingly, attorneys' fees are *not* recoverable as compensatory damages, despite the fact that most plaintiffs could not bring an action against the tortfeasor without hiring an attorney. Because the plaintiffs in personal injury cases must usually pay their attorneys anywhere from one-third to one-half of their recovery, some people argue that compensatory damages do not fully compensate tort victims. Others point out that one of the ways plaintiffs can, in essence, recover their attorney fees is by increasing their pain and suffering damages enough to pay their lawyers' fees.

[4] Ted Rohrlich, *We Aren't Seeing You in Court*, Los Angeles Times, February 1, 2001.

Nominal Damages

Nominal damages are a small amount of money that are given to recognize that a defendant did indeed commit a tort, but there were no compensable damages suffered by the plaintiff. A plaintiff may receive nominal damages by simply failing to prove actual damages.

Punitive Damages

Punitive damages are damages that are awarded to punish the defendant. They are given only when the defendant's conduct is extremely outrageous. The purposes of punitive damages are to both punish the defendant, and to deter him and others who are similarly situated, from engaging in that kind of activity again. In awarding punitive damages, juries usually consider the egregiousness or willfulness of the tort and the wealth of the defendant. Obviously, the more wrongful the nature of the defendant, the greater the desire to send a message that such behavior will not be tolerated. And the greater the wealth of the defendant, the higher the damages must be in order to hurt the defendant.

While the threat of large punitive damages are seen by many groups, including consumer advocates, as a good method for encouraging manufacturers to produce the safest possible products, others disagree. They believe that no threat beyond compensatory damages is required, and that the main effect of punitive damages is to discourage innovation, because manufacturers will be afraid of the risk of producing a defective product that could cost them millions in punitive damages.

Since the late 1970's, insurance companies and "tort reform" groups have been trying to limit the amount of punitive damages that can be assessed. These advocates of tort reform have tried repeatedly to get the courts to strike down punitive damages as unconstitutional violations of the due process rights of defendants.

The 1994 case of *Honda Motor Company v. Oberg*,[5] provided tort reformists with their first judicial victory. In this case, the United States Supreme Court finally struck down a punitive damages award as being a violation of due process. *Oberg*, however, was a limited victory because of two unique aspects of the case. First, the punitive damages were over five hundred times the amount of the compensatory damages, which is extraordinarily rare. Second, the state law under which the damages were awarded was the only state law in the country that had no provision for judicial review of the amount of the punitive damage awards. And it was the denial of judicial review of the amount of punitive damages that violated the Due Process Clause. Because of its unusual facts, *Oberg* did not provide much guidance as to when punitive damages were so excessive as to violate due process.

A few years later, however, in *BMW v. Gore*,[6] the Supreme Court set forth a test that a number of commentators thought would substantially curb punitive damages awards. The court said that three factors should be considered in determining whether an award was grossly excessive: "the degree of reprehensibility of the nondisclosure; the disparity between the harm or potential harm suffered by [the plaintiff] and his punitive damages award; and the difference between this remedy and the civil penalties authorized or imposed in comparable cases." However, a 1999 study found that the year after *BMW v. Gore*, punitive damages awards across the country were not reduced any more frequently than they had been the year before the decision.[7]

And while the Ninth Circuit Court of Appeals overturned the highest punitive damages verdict in history—$5 billion against Exxon—as unconstitutionally excessive, other punitive damage awards that were not quite as high have been upheld recently. For example, in October of 2001, the Utah State Supreme Court actually reinstated a $145 million punitive damages award that had been reduced by the trial court judge to $25 million. In that case, the compensatory damages award had been only $1 million. The largest multiple ever upheld was $100,000, in a punitive damage award

of $100,000 in a landowner's trespass case against a mobile home company where the compensatory damages were only $1.[8]

A United States Supreme Court case, handed down in 2001, is again expected to encourage courts to view punitive damages awards more closely. In the case of *Cooper Industries, Inc. v. Leatherman Tool Group, Inc*,[9] the high court ruled that appellate courts must review the trial court's decision on the constitutionality of an award *de novo*, meaning that they should no longer give deference to the trial court's determination that the jury award was not unconstitutionally excessive and uphold it, unless there was a clear abuse of discretion on the part of the trial court judge. Whether this case will have any long run impact or not remains to be seen.

Attempts to curb punitive damages awards are not only being made in the courts, but also in the legislatures with so-called tort reform legislation. The closest such legislation has come to becoming law at the federal level was a relatively weak law limiting punitive damages that was passed in 1996, but was vetoed by President Clinton in May of that year. There was not enough Congressional support to override the veto. Subsequent proposals for federal tort reform legislation have met with even less success, although the reformers keep trying. Bills unsuccessfully considered by Congress in 1998 would have not only placed caps on punitive damages, but would have also placed upper limits on pain and suffering awards, forced the losing party to pay all the court costs and attorney fees of the losing party, and abolished the current contingency fee system. (The contingency fee system is the system whereby plaintiffs' lawyers do not receive an hourly fee for their services. Instead, they receive a percentage of the amount the plaintiff recovers. If the plaintiff receives no recovery, the attorney receives no compensation.)

Despite the reformers' failure thus far at the national level, tort reform is an issue likely to be debated repeatedly by Congress. But Congress is not alone in looking at such measures. State legislatures are also working on so-called tort reform.

By August of 1997, almost every state had enacted some sort of tort reform law. These reforms have taken various approaches from placing a cap on punitive damages, to setting evidentiary standards to restrict their availability, and to capping noneconomic damages such as pain and suffering. However, while tort reform-

---

[5] 114 S. Ct. 2331 (1994).

[6] *BMW of North America v. Ira Gore, Jr.*, 116 S. Ct.1589 (1995).

[7] James Dam, *Large Punitives Mostly Upheld, But $5B Award Overturned*, LAWYER'S WEEKLY, November 12, 2001, at A1.

[8] *Jacque v. Steenberg Homes, Inc.*, 563 N.W. 2d (1997).

[9] 532 U.S. 424 (2001).

ers have met with success in the state legislatures, they have not been as successful in the state courts. By the end of 1998, over seventy courts had struck down various provisions of state tort reform acts as unconstitutional. Thus the state of tort reform at both the state and federal levels is extremely uncertain.

EXHIBIT 7-2

Some Major Punitive Damages Awards in Recent Years

CASE	JURY AWARD	ULTIMATE RESOLUTION
Fugua v. Horizon/ CMS Healthcare Corporation (2001)	A jury awarded $2.8 million in compensatory damages and $310 million in punitive damages to the family of an elderly woman whose neglect in a nursing home was so severe that her bones were poking through her bedsores.	The plaintiffs settled for $20 million to prevent an appeal.
Ernst v. Horizon/ CMS Healthcare Corp. (2001)	In a second case that year against a nursing home the family of a patient who was neglected and died in horrendous pain with thirteen bedsores and skin in many places rotted off, received an award of $7 million in compensatory damages and $75 million in punitive damages.	Plaintiffs settled for $20 million, after refusing early settlement offers of $15, 17, and 19 million.
Liebeck v. McDonald's, 787 A.2d 443 (1994)	A jury awarded Stella Liebeck $2.9 million in damages, including $2.7 million in punitive damages for extensive burns she received when she spilled 170 degree coffee on her legs. McDonald's having known that prior customers had received severe burns from the coffee influenced jurors.	The trial court reduced the award by 75% to $640,000. The parties subsequently settled the case for an undisclosed amount.
Wal-Mart Stores Inc. v. Goodman, 789 So. 2d 166 (S. Ct. Ala. 2000)	A woman who was improperly detained for shoplifting at Wal-Mart was awarded $3,000,000 in punitive damages, but only $200,000 in compensatory damages.	The Alabama Supreme Court found that the punitive damages were so excessive that they violated the due process clause, and consequently the state's highest court reduced the punitive damage award to $600,000.
Robinson v. State Farm Idaho, 2000 WL 1877745	A plaintiff's insurance company, State Farm, was found to have acted in bad faith when it refused to cover the injuries she sustained in an auto accident by claiming that her injuries must have been caused by something other than the accident. The company's refusal had ostensibly been based on a recommendation from an independent company that had reviewed her medical records, but she demonstrated that State Farm had a practice of referring claims to that company knowing that no payment would be recommended. The jury awarded her punitive damages of $9,500,000, which was 95 times the amount of the compensatory damages.	The award was appealed and subsequently upheld by the Idaho Supreme Court.

EXHIBIT 7-2 (continued)

CASE	JURY AWARD	ULTIMATE RESOLUTION
Axen v. American Home Products Corp., 981 P. 34d 340 (1999)	A jury awarded Axen and his wife $23 million in damages, including $20 million punitive damages, after he became blind as a result of the drug he had taken for a heart condition. The drug was known to be linked to vision loss, but the package insert did not list vision loss as a possible risk. It listed only optic nerve inflammation as a risk.	In 1999, the Appeals court upheld $20 million punitive damages award, finding that the drug maker's actions were "reprehensible" given its knowledge and duty under FDA regulations. Therefore, the damages were not unconstitutionally excessive.
Anderson, et al. v. Islamic Republic of Iran 2001, 90 F Supp. 107 (D.C. May 2001)	Anderson filed suit against Iderzbollah, and the nation of Iran that funded the group, for damages suffered during his slightly less than seven year's captivity. The jury awarded him $41.7 million in compensatory damages and $300 million in punitives.	Anderson settled for the award of $41 million compensatory, plus an additional $4.1 million for agreeing not to attempt to collect the punitive damages award. He was able to collect this award from Iranian assets frozen in the U.S. by a special Act of Congress.

Global Context: Punitive Damages in Canada

Those who believe that the United States tort system is in need of reform with respect to its treatment of punitive damages may look to their Canadian neighbors with envy. Punitive damages awards in Canada are both rare and small.

A study in 1990 reported on punitive damages awards in Ontario. The researchers found that the highest award was $50,000. The majority of punitive damages awards were for less than $25,000; the median award was approximately twenty percent of the compensatory damage award in the particular case.

Following English common law, Canadian courts have traditionally restricted punitive damages to two situations: cases involving oppressive, arbitrary, or unconstitutional actions by government servants and those where the defendant's conduct was calculated to have made a profit in excess of compensatory damages. In 1989, the Canadian Supreme Court recognized that punitive damages could also be awarded for conduct deserving punishment because of its "harsh, vindictive, reprehensible, and malicious manner."

Two reasons seem to explain the differences in Canadian and American treatment of punitive damages. First, Canadians see something undignified about the flamboyant punitive damages awards in the United States. Second, civil juries are much less common in Canada, and, in general, judges tend to be much more conservative than juries in making punitive damages awards.

Classifications of Torts

Torts are most commonly classified as intentional, negligent, or strict liability torts. Each category differs in terms of the elements needed to prove the tort, the available damages, the available defenses, and the degree of willfulness of the actor. **Intentional torts** occur when the defendant takes an action intending that certain consequences will occur or knowing that certain consequences are likely to occur. **Negligent torts** occur when the defendant fails to act in a way that subjects other people to an unreasonable risk of harm. In other words, the defendant is careless to someone else's detriment. Finally, **strict liability torts** occur when the defendant takes an action that is inherently dangerous, and cannot ever be undertaken safely, no matter what precautions the defendant takes. It is important to remember that when we discuss these classifications, we are referring to their use in the United States. The Chinese legal system, for example, narrowly defines the activities actionable under tort law.

In this chapter, we will focus on intentional torts. Negligence and Strict Liability will be discussed in greater detail in Chapter 8.

Intentional Torts

Intentional torts, the most "willful" torts, include a substantial number of carefully defined wrongful acts. What each has in common is the element of intent. *Intent* here does not mean a specific determination to cause harm to the plaintiff; rather, it means the determination to do a specific physical act that may lead to harming the plaintiff's person, property, or economic interests.

Intentional torts are divided into the following three categories: (1) torts against persons; (2) torts against property; and (3) torts against economic interests.

The following sections discuss a number of specific torts that fall into each category, along with the defenses for each.

Intentional Torts against Persons

Torts against persons are intentional acts that harm an individual's physical or mental integrity. As you might imagine, there are a significant number of these torts. We will discuss five that a businessperson is most likely to either commit or be a victim of: assault and battery, defamation, privacy torts, false imprisonment, and intentional infliction of emotional distress.

Assault and Battery

Assault and battery are two of the most common torts. Imagine, after searching for a parking space for twenty minutes, you finally pull into a spot. However, as soon as you turn off your car, a man who looks like Mike Tyson pounds on your car window, claiming that you took his spot. He angrily yells, "You just took my spot! If you don't move your car now, I'm going to hit you so hard that you won't remember what your car looks like!" The man has just assaulted you.

An **assault** occurs when one person places another in fear or apprehension of an immediate, offensive bodily contact. Therefore, in the above example, if you think that the man is just joking, and you start laughing, no assault has taken place. There is no assault because the element of apprehension is missing. Likewise, if the man had called you on the telephone and threatened to come over and break your nose, it is not an assault because there is no question of *immediate* bodily harm.

An assault is often followed by a **battery**, an intentional, unwanted, offensive bodily contact. To return to the earlier example, if the man actually hit you, his action would constitute a battery. On the other hand, if you both happened to be getting out of your respective cars at the same time, and you consequently bumped into each other, no battery would have occurred because there was no intentional *bodily* contact.

There are a limited number of defenses available to an action for a battery. *Self-defense*, responding to the force of another with comparable force in order to defend yourself, is the most common defense. In our earlier example, if the man took a swing at you, and you shoved him to try to keep him from hitting you, and if your push caused him to fall backward and hit his head on the street, when he sued you for battery and attempted to get compensation for the concussion you gave him, you would be able to escape liability by arguing that you were acting in self-defense. In terms of the degree of force you may use, you cannot respond with greater than is being used against you. You may use deadly force, but only to defend against another's deadly force.

A second defense, defense of others, is just what it sounds like. If a large man were pummeling you, your brother could use his fists and try to hit the man in an attempt to get him to quite hitting you. The degree of force that your brother can use in defending you is limited to the degree of force that you could use yourself.

A final defense to a claim of battery is defense of property. You can use *reasonable force* to defend your property from an intruder. The use of deadly force in defense of property is rarely, if ever, considered justified.

Defamation

The tort alleged in the opening scenario was **defamation**, which is the intentional publication (communication to a third party) of a false statement that is harmful to the plaintiff's reputation. If the defamation is published in a permanent form, such as printed in a magazine or newspaper, it is known as libel. Television and radio broadcasts are also considered libel, since they are permanently recorded. In the case of libel, "general damages" are presumed. Thus, the victim would be entitled to compensation for the damages that are presumed to flow from defamation, yet are hard to prove, such as the humiliation the party would feel.

If the defamation is made orally, then it is slander. In order to recover damages in a case of slander, the plaintiff must prove "special damages," that is, the plaintiff must show specific monetary loss that resulted from the defamatory statements. One exception to the requirement of special damages is if the false statements constitute *slander per se*. Slander per se statements are considered to be so inherently harmful that again, general damages are presumed. The kinds of statements that are considered slander per se are claims that the plaintiff: (1) has a loathsome, communicable disease (traditionally venereal disease or leprosy); (2) has committed a crime for which imprisonment is a possibility; (3) is professionally incompetent; or (4) if a woman, has engaged in sexual misconduct.

Chinese law treats defamation in a similar manner. First, the Chinese courts determine whether there was a defamatory statement (i.e., if derogatory words are used to insult another person). Second, the statement must be published in writing, orally, or by gestures or signs. Third, the statement must clearly identify a particular person. However, in China, defamation can be a civil or criminal action.

If you say that your boss is a tyrant, or your roommate is a slob, are you in danger of being sued for defamation? One of the important elements of defamation is that the defamatory statement must be a statement of fact, not merely opinion, as the following case illustrates.

Case 7-1

Carl Sagan
v.
Apple Computer, Inc.
United States District Court, D.D. California
874 F. Supp. 1972 (1994)

*D*efendant Apple Computer Inc. used 'Carl Sagan' as the code name for a new personal computer. After this use was publicized in computer publications, Plaintiff requested that Defendant cease using his name. Defendant complied and changed the code name to 'Butt-head Astronomer,' which was published by the Defendant in numerous newspapers and in other media. Plaintiff consequently filed suit against Apple Computers for libel, among other claims. Defendant Apple Computer Company filed a motion to dismiss.

DISTRICT JUDGE BAIRD

Defendant argues that the statement "Butt-Head Astronomer" cannot be the basis of a libel action because such a statement is an opinion, which is nonactionable under the First Amendmen.....

In the Ninth Circuit, courts analyze the following conditions…

(1) whether the defendant used figurative or hyperbolic language that would negate the impression

that he was seriously maintaining an assertion of fact;

(2) whether the general tenor of the communication negated the assertion of fact; and

(3) whether the assertion is susceptible of being proved true or false.

…There can be no question that the use of the figurative term "Butt-Head" negates the impression that Defendant was seriously implying an assertion of fact. It strains reason to conclude that Defendant was attempting to criticize Plaintiff's reputation or competency as an astronomer. One does not seriously attack the expertise of a scientist using the undefined phrase "butt-head." Thus, the figurative language militates against implying an assertion of fact.

Furthermore, the tenor of any communication of the information, especially the phrase "Butt-Head Astronomer," would negate the impression that Defendant was implying an assertion of fact.…Any reader exposed to such a publication would likely have knowledge of the context in which the language was used. A reader aware of the context would understand that Defendant was clearly attempting to retaliate in a humorous and satirical way against Plaintiff's reaction to Defendant's use of his name.

A reasonable reader would further conclude that the use of the term "astronomer" did not imply that Plaintiff was a less than able astronomer, but that the word was merely a means of identifying Plaintiff. Finally, a reasonable reader would conclude that the phrase "Butt-Head Astronomer" did not imply that Plaintiff was legally wrong in asking Defendant to cease using his name. After all, by ceasing use of Plaintiff's name, Defendant's actions spoke louder than words. Thus, the tenor of the communication militates against implying an assertion of fact.…

Based on an analysis of the factors identified…, the Court has no reason to conclude that the statement made by Defendant implies an assertion of objective fact. Therefore, the statement is protected under the First Amendment and cannot form the basis of a claim for libel.…

Plaintiff cites *Gill v. Hughes*…in support of his position. However, in Gill the following statement was found to be actionable: "He is an incompetent surgeon and needs more training."….Such a statement is clearly distinguishable from the statement made here.

Therefore, the statement made by Defendant is protected under California law and cannot form the basis of a claim for libel.

MOTION DISMISSED.

1. Critical Thinking: Carl Sagan used an analogy to try to persuade the court to rule in his favor. Why was the court not persuaded by this analogy? Do you agree with the court's reason to reject the analogy?

2. Ethical Decision Making: What value is the court emphasizing in its opinion?

Technology: Defamatory Statements

The increase in communication over the Internet has presented new questions for the law of defamation to answer. First, does a false statement made over this information network constitute defamation? Second, who can be held liable if defamation does exist?

The court first attempted to answer these issues in the case of *Cubby v. CompuServ*,[10] In that case, CompuServ was sued because of defamatory statements published on one of the forums available through its online information service. In holding that CompuServ could not be held liable, the court made an analogy between an online information service provider such as CompuServ and bookstores, saying that 'CompuServ's CIS product is in essence an electronic, for profit library...' The court went on to say that once CompuServ decides to carry a given publication such as a news forum, it has little or no editorial control over that forum. It would therefore be no more feasible for CompuServ to examine every publication it carries for defamatory material, than it would for libraries or booksellers to do so.

Since *Cubby v. CompuServ* was decided, the Communications Decency Act of 1996 was passed. One section of this act gives immunity to providers of interactive computer services for liability they might otherwise incur on account of material disseminated by them, but created by others. This act, and its impact on online service providers is discussed in more detail in Chapter 11.

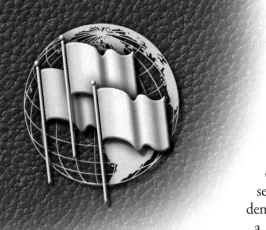

Global Context: Liability of Online Service Providers (OSPs) in Canada

In Canada, there have not yet been any landmark cases nor any legislation to clearly establish the liability of online service providers for content they disseminated, but did not originate. Currently, an OSP being sued under such circumstances in Canada would have to rely on the existing Canadian libel code's defense of innocent dissemination, which will succeed if the defendant demonstrates that:

a. The defendant does not know of the libel contained in the work published or authored by him;

b. There was no reason for the defendant to suppose that the work he or she authored or published would be libelous; and;

c. It was not negligence on the defendant's part that he or she did not know that the work contained libelous material.

---

[10] 77 F. Supp. 135 (1991).

A person who is accused of defamation can raise two defenses: truth and privilege. It is often stated that *truth* is an absolute defense. In other words, if I make an honest statement that harms the reputation of the defendant, there has been no defamation. If I say that Bill is a convicted felon, and he is, I have not committed defamation. Under ordinary circumstances, the fact that you thought a statement was true is not a defense. So if I honestly believe Bill is a convicted felon, and I tell others that he is, then I have committed slander, despite my sincere belief in the truth of what I have said.

Privilege is an affirmative defense in a defamation action. An affirmative defense, as you may recall from Chapter 6, occurs when the defendant admits to the accusation, but argues that there is a reason why they should not be held liable.

A privilege is either absolute or conditional. When an **absolute privilege** exists, one can make any false statement, regardless of intent or knowledge of the falsity of the claim, and cannot be sued for defamation. Absolute privilege arises in only a limited number of circumstances. The speech and debate clause of the United States Constitution gives an absolute privilege to individuals speaking on the House and Senate floors during Congressional debate. This privilege exists because the House wants to get to the truth of matters before it. And if people testifying before Congress had to fear that they might be sued, they might be afraid to testify. Therefore, the law protects them from being sued for defamation because of anything they say on the floor of the House or Senate.

Absolute privilege also arises in the courtroom during a trial. Again, we do not want people to be afraid to testify in court, so we prohibit their being sued for whatever occurs within the courtroom.

Conditional privilege is the second type. Under a conditional privilege, a party will not be held liable for defamation unless the false statement was made with actual malice. A statement is made with **actual malice** if it is made with *either* knowledge of its falsity or reckless disregard for its truth.

Businesspersons should be most concerned about the conditional privilege that arises with respect to job recommendations. To encourage employers to give honest assessments of their former employees, an employer who makes a false statement about a former worker will not be held liable, as long as the statements were made in good faith, and were made only to those who had a legitimate interest in the information that was being communicated.

Another conditional privilege is the **public figure privilege**. Public figures are individuals who are in the public eye, typically politicians and entertainers. Because these individuals have a significant impact on our lives, we want to encourage free discussion about them, so we don't hold people liable for making false statements about them, as long as the statements were not made with malice. This privilege does not seem to place an unfair burden on the public figure because such an individual has access to the media, and so can easily respond publicly to any false claims.

Some people argue that a conditional privilege should apply when the defamatory statement is published over the Internet. The rationale for application of the privilege in this context is that the person who has been defamed over the Internet can respond to the defamatory remarks in the same forum with a few keystrokes. Thus, there is less need for the stronger legal protection we ordinarily give to private parties who are defamed.

Secondly, we want to encourage free expression and the exchange of ideas on the Internet. Requiring a plaintiff to prove malice when the defamation occurred over the Internet would encourage such free discussion, because people would not have to be worried about making errors when they communicate on the Internet.

Thus far, however, no such privilege has been established. And when one is found to have committed defamation on an online bulletin board or website, the damages can be significant. For example, a jury awarded $3 million to a university professor who sued a former student who accused him of being a pedophile on a website that she maintained.[11]

---

[11] Read about the case at Paul J. Martin, *North Dakota Jury Awards $3M for Internet Defamation*, Lawyers Weekly USA http://www.lawyersweeklyusa.com/usanews040802a.cfm (April 8, 2002).

Global Context: Defamation of Public Figures in the United Kingdom

As you know from your reading, the media in the United States has the ability to print false information about public figures without being liable if they can demonstrate that they did so without malice. Government officials, about whom false statements have been made in the United Kingdom, have a much easier time winning a libel case.

In the United Kingdom, all a public figure, or any other libel plaintiff, must do to win a case against the media is demonstrate that the defamatory statement was communicated in the United Kingdom, and that their reputation was damaged as a result. The only defenses available to the defendant media are that either: (1) the statements made were true or (2) the statements were made in either Parliament or court. The burden of proving the truth of the alleged defamatory statement is thus on the defendant.

If a statement was originally broadcast by a company in the United States, and was rebroadcast in the United Kingdom without the consent of the originator of the broadcast, the U.S. company may still be held liable in the U.K. court.

Privacy Torts

The fact that truth is an absolute defense to a defamation action does not mean that people are free to reveal everything they know. Four distinct torts, collectively referred to as invasion of privacy, protect the individual's right to keep certain things out of the public view, even if they are true. Each of the four privacy rights protects a slightly different aspect of one's right to privacy. The four privacy torts are: (1) **false light**; (2) **public disclosure of private facts**; (3) **appropriation for commercial gain**; and (4) **invasion of privacy**.

False light is closely related to defamation and occurs when publicity about a person creates an impression about that individual that is not valid. It could involve attributing characteristics or beliefs to a person that they do not possess, or creating the impression that an individual has taken certain actions that he or she has not taken. Sometimes tabloids publish articles that may lead to false light claims, as the following case illustrates.

Case 7-2

Nellie Mitchell
v.
Globe Inc. D/B/A 'Sun'
United States District Court, W.D. Arkansas
786 F. Supp. 791 (1992)

*N*inety-six-year-old Nellie Mitchell had operated a newsstand on the Mountain Home, Arkansas town square since 1963. Known to almost everyone in this small Ozark Mountain town, she cared for herself and raised a family as a single parent for all of these years on what must have been the meager earnings of a "paper girl."

The October 2 edition of the Sun contained a photograph of the plaintiff, Mrs. Mitchell in conjunction with a story entitled:

SPECIAL DELIVERY

World's oldest newspaper carrier, 101, quits because she's pregnant!

"I guess walking all those miles kept me young"

The "story" purported to be about "papergal Audrey Wiles" in Stirling, Australia, who had been delivering papers for ninety-four years. Readers were told that Ms. Wiles became pregnant by "Will" a "reclusive millionaire" she met on her newspaper route. "I used to put Will's paper in the door when it rained, and one thing just kind of led to another."

In words that could certainly have described Nellie Mitchell, the article, which was in the form and style of a factual newspaper account, said: "[S]he's become like a city landmark because nearly everyone at one time or another has seen her trudging down the road with a large stack of papers under her arm."

A photograph of Nellie, apparently "trudging down the road with a large stack of papers under her arm" was used in conjunction with the story. The picture used in the October 2 edition of the Sun had been used by the defendant in a reasonably factual and accurate article about Mrs. Mitchell published in another of the defendant's publications, the Examiner, in 1980.

The case was tried before a jury that found that the defendant's conduct had invaded Mrs. Mitchell's privacy by placing her in a false light and had amounted to an intentional infliction of emotional distress. The jury awarded the plaintiff $650,000 in compensatory damages and $850,000 in punitive damages.

Defendant filed a motion for judgment as a matter of law or, alternatively, for remittitur of the jury award, or alternatively for new trial.

CHIEF JUDGE H. FRANKLIN WATERS

Testimony at trial indicated that most of the defendant's articles are created "TOH" or "top of the head," in the words of John Vadar, editor of the *Sun*. That is, the authors, none of whom use their real name, are given a headline and a picture and then "make up" the accompanying stories. In fact, according to the evidence, the editor, and perhaps others, "make up" a series of headlines for stories to appear in each issue, and they are placed on a table. The "reporters" or perhaps, according to defendant's contentions at the trial, their "authors of fiction" select from this list the stories they wish to write....

In order to prevail on this claim [of false light], the plaintiff has the burden of proving by clear and convincing evidence the following:

One, that the false light in which she was placed by the publicity would be highly offensive to a reasonable person, and

Two, that the defendant acted with actual malice in publishing the statements at issue in this case. Actual malice means that Globe International intended, or recklessly failed to anticipate, that readers would construe the publicized matter as conveying actual facts or events concerning Mrs. Mitchell...

Defendant argues that there was no evidence of intentional conduct on the part of Globe. It is further argued that no one understood the story to state actual facts about Mrs. Mitchell...

The court cannot say as a matter of law that the article is incapable of being interpreted as portraying actual events or facts regarding the plaintiff. The "facts" conveyed are not so inherently impossible or fantastic that they could not be understood to convey actual facts. Nor can we say that no person could take them seriously. Moreover, even if the headline and certain facts contained in the article could not be reasonably believed, other facts e.g., the implication of sexual promiscuity, could reasonably be believed...

In making this determination we 'consider the surrounding circumstances in which the statements were made, the medium by which they were published and the audience for which they were intended.'...No distinction is made between those articles that are wholly fictional and the articles that are intended to be factual. Fictional articles are not denoted as such. The *Sun* apparently intends for the readers to determine which articles are fact and which are fiction or what percentage of a given article is fact or fiction...

[T]he court believes the jury could have, and apparently did, find that the defendant intended their readers to construe the article in question as conveying actual facts or events concerning Mrs. Mitchell, or at the very least that the defendant recklessly failed to anticipate that the article would be so construed. The court believes the publication methods utilized by the defendant make it reasonable for the jury to draw such a conclusion.

MOTION DENIED.

1. Critical Thinking: Why did the court conclude that the jury's award would stand? Do you agree with the reasons that led to the court's ruling? Why or why not?

2. Ethical Decision Making: Which stakeholders are affected by the court's ruling?

While the defendant's motion for a new trial was denied, and the court allowed the amount of punitive damages to stand, since they are within the jury's discretion, the appeals court did order the trial court to review and reduce the amount of the compensatory damages.

Public disclosure of private facts about a person occurs when a person publicizes a private fact about someone that the reasonable person would find highly offensive. The plaintiff must have not waived his or her right to privacy. Publication of information about someone's sex life or failure to pay debts would fall under this tort.

Appropriation for commercial gain occurs when a defendant uses another person's name, likeness, voice, or other identifying characteristics without that person's permission for commercial gain. If a company hired someone who sounded like former President Bill Clinton to endorse a product on the radio, the company could be found liable for this tort.

The final privacy tort is **invasion of privacy**, which occurs when someone invades another's solitude, seclusion, or personal affairs when they have the right to expect privacy. Some examples of invasion of privacy would include wiretapping and using people's password to gain access to their electronic mail message. Or, if a defendant operated an ice skating rink and installed two-way mirrors in the women's dressing room, this action would likewise constitute an invasion of privacy, because the skaters should be able to expect a certain

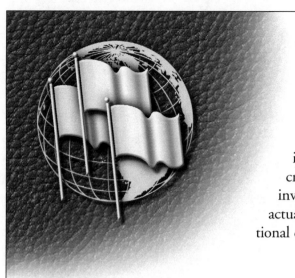

Global Context: Privacy in China

The Civil Code recognizes that a citizen has a right to definite remedies where a privacy violation occurs. While they constitute a small portion of the civil docket, defamation and invasion of privacy claims have been increasing in China. Unlike the United States, civil or criminal liability may be imposed for defamation or invasion of privacy in China. Plaintiffs may recover actual damages (i.e. lost income) or damages for emotional distress.

degree of privacy in a dressing room.

Entertainers often allege invasion of privacy claims. For example, Joan Collins recently sued the *Globe* for invasion of privacy when they took pictures of her and a male friend. However, editors and owners often claim that the public "demands" these invasions of privacy. As evidence of this "demand," they point out the higher circulation they have when they print sensational pictures.

False Imprisonment

False imprisonment is the intentional restraint or confinement of a person against their will for an appreciable period of time. This must be by either physical restraint, such as locking a door; physical force, such as holding someone down; threats of immediate physical force; or refusal to release the plaintiff's property. False imprisonment cases are so frequently brought against security guards and retailers, that it is known as the "shopkeeper's tort."

In most states, retailers who detain suspected shoplifters for questioning are entitled to raise the "shopkeepers' privilege." Under this privilege, a merchant who has reason to believe a person has shoplifted, may detain the person for questioning about the incident. The detention must be conducted in a reasonable manner, and the suspect can be held for only a reasonable time. The case below provides an illustration of a reasonable detention.

Case 7-3

Shirley Gordon
v.
May Dept. Store Company
New York Supreme Court,
Appellate Division
N.Y. Slip Op. 08712 (1998)

Plaintiff Shirley Gordon worked for Lord & Taylor Department Store. As she she was leaving work one day, she was stopped by store security personnel, who searched her bag. She did not object to the search. No stolen merchandise was found, and she left within a few minutes of being detained. She subsequently sued the store for false imprisonment. The trial court denied store's motion for summary judgment and appeal was taken.

JUDGES RITTER, SANTUCCI, ALTMAN and KRAUSMAN
MEMORANDUM BY THE COURT

…In order to sustain a claim for false imprisonment, the plaintiff must prove that: (1) the defendant intended to confine, (2) the plaintiff was conscious of the alleged confinement, (3) the plaintiff did not consent to the confinement, and (4) the confinement was not otherwise privileged.

The plaintiff admitted at her examination before trial that she was not under the impression that she was not free to leave the store at any point during the day in question. The affidavit that she submitted in opposition to the motion for summary judgment did not raise any genuine issue of fact in this regard. We find no merit to the plaintiff's contention that the brief search of her bag resulted in an unreasonable detention.

REVERSED IN FAVOR OF DEFENDANT.

1. Critical Thinking: The court made it's ruling by comparing the facts of the case with four elements needed to demonstrate false imprisonment. Carefully consider the four elements. Are there any ambiguous words in the four elements that might cause problems for a court in the future?

2. Ethical Decision Making: Which stakeholders were affected by this decision? In other words, which people should pay closer attention to this decision?

While many false imprisonment cases arise in conjunction with claims of shoplifting, cases of false imprisonment claims are not limited to suit against retailers or security guards. For example, three ambulance drivers recently filed a false imprisonment suit against a local psychiatric center because the crisis center locked them in and would not allow them to leave. The crisis center claimed that the drivers committed certain improprieties when delivering a violent girl to the crisis center.

Proving damages in a false imprisonment case is not easy. If the physical restraint caused harm requiring medical treatment, such damages would be clear, but most cases of false imprisonment do not involve physical harm. Typically, plaintiffs request compensation for lost time from work, and pain and suffering from the mental distress and humiliation.

Intentional Infliction of Emotional Distress

Sometimes called the tort of outrage, intentional infliction of emotional distress occurs when the defendant engages in outrageous, intentional conduct that is likely to cause extreme emotional distress to the party toward whom such conduct is directed. For example, if a debt collector calls a debtor and tells him that his son was just involved in a fatal car accident, most courts would find that behavior to be outrageous enough that it would satisfy the first element of the tort.

In some states, however, to recover damages for this tort, the plaintiff must demonstrate some physical symptoms caused by the emotional distress. For example, in the above example, if the plaintiff had fainted upon hearing the news, hitting his head on the table and cutting it as he passed out, he would have physical symptoms sufficient to justify a recovery. Other physical symptoms commonly arising from emotional distress include headaches, a sudden onset of high blood pressure, hives, chills, inability to sleep, or inability to get out of bed.

The following case provides an illustration of this tort.

Case 7-4

Irma White

v.

Monsanto Company and McDermott
Supreme Court of Louisiana
585 So. 2d 1205 (1991)

*P*laintiff Irma White, a woman in her late forties with grown children, was employed in the labor pool at Monsanto Company's refinery for several years. In the spring of 1986, she was working in the canning department under Defendant foreman, Gary McDermott. Plaintiff and three other employees were assigned at the beginning of the workday to transfer a certain chemical from a large container into smaller containers. When they arrived at their workstation and noticed that the container was marked "hazardous-corrosive," they requested rubber gloves and goggles before starting their assigned task. A supervisor sent for the safety equipment. While waiting for the gloves, Plaintiff started doing some cleanup work around the area and the two other employees sat around waiting. Someone reported to McDermott that the group was idle, causing him to become angry. He went to the workstation and launched a profane tirade at the three workers present, including plaintiff, referring to them as "mother f***ers," accusing them of sitting on their "f***ing asses," and threatening to "show them to the gate." The tirade lasted for about a minute, and then McDermott left the area.

Plaintiff was upset and began to experience pain in her chest, pounding in her head, and difficulty breathing. She went to McDermott's office to discuss the incident. He said he apologized to her; she said he did not. She went to the company nurse who suggested that plaintiff see a doctor. Plaintiff's family physician met her at the hospital, at which time plaintiff had chest pains, shortness of breath, and cold clammy hands. Fearing that she was having a heart attack, the doctor admitted her to the hospital. Plaintiff spent two days in the coronary care unit and another day in a regular room. Tests ruled out a heart attack, and the doctor's diagnosis was acute anxiety reaction, a panic attack. Plaintiff was released from the hospital after three days without restriction, but with medication to take if she had further trouble.

Ms. White returned to work within a week. She was paid her regular pay while off from work, and her medical bills, totaling about $3,200, were paid by the company's medical benefits program. Plaintiff continued to work at Monsanto, later transferring to McDermott's department at her own request. At the time of the lawsuit, she still occasionally became upset thinking about or dreaming about the incident, and has occasionally taken the prescribed medicine.

Employee-plaintiff Irma White brought this action against supervisor and employer to recover for intentional infliction of emotional distress. The trial court ruled in favor of the plaintiff, and awarded her $60,000 damages. Her supervisor and employer appealed. The Court of Appeals affirmed the lower court's judgment, and the supervisor and employer appealed to the State Supreme Court.

JUSTICE HALL

The particular intentional tort alleged in this case is the intentional infliction of emotional distress… in order to recover for intentional infliction of emotional distress, a plaintiff must establish: (1) that the conduct of the defendant was extreme and outrageous; (2) that the emotional distress suffered by the plaintiff was severe; and (3) that the defendant desired to inflict severe emotional distress or knew that severe emotional distress would be certain or substantially certain to result from his conduct.

The conduct must be so outrageous in character, and so extreme in degree, as to go beyond all possible bounds of decency, and to be regarded as atrocious and utterly intolerable in a civilized community. Liability does not extend to mere insults, indignities, threats, annoyances, petty oppressions, or other trivialities.

The distress suffered must be such that no reasonable person could be expected to endure it. Liability arises only where the mental suffering or anguish is extreme....

Liability can arise only where the actor desires to inflict severe emotional distress or where he knows that such distress is certain or substantially certain to result from his conduct....The conduct must be intended or calculated to cause severe emotional distress and not just some lesser degree of fright, humiliation, embarrassment, worry, or the like...

Applying these precepts of law to the facts of the instant case, we find that plaintiff has failed to establish her right to recover from the defendants for an intentional tort.

The one minute outburst of profanity directed at three employees by a supervisor in the course of dressing them down for not working as he thought they should, does not amount to such extreme and outrageous conduct as to give rise to recovery for intentional infliction of emotional distress. The vile language used was not so extreme or outrageous as to go beyond all possible bounds of decency and to be regarded as utterly intolerable in a civilized community. Such conduct, although crude, rough, and uncalled for, was not tortuous; that is, did not give rise to a cause of action for damages under general tort law. The brief, isolated instance of improper behavior by the supervisor who lost his temper, was the kind of unpleasant experience persons must expect to endure from time to time. The conduct was not more than a person of ordinary sensibilities can be expected to endure. The tirade was directed to all three employees and not just to plaintiff specifically.

The duty here was to not engage in extreme or outrageous conduct intended or calculated to cause severe emotional distress. The duty was not breached because the conduct was not extreme or outrageous to a degree calculated to cause severe emotional distress to a person of ordinary sensibilities, and the supervisor did not intend to inflict emotional distress of a severe nature, nor did he believe such a result was substantially certain to follow from his conduct...

REVERSED.

1. Critical Thinking: Consider the reasons that the court offered to support its conclusion. Are you persuaded by these reasons? Why or why not?

2. Ethical Decision Making: Suppose you were the accused supervisor at Monsanto Company. If the public disclosure test governed your ethical thought, how would you have behaved differently in this situation?

Intentional Torts against Property

Trespass to Realty

This tort, also called *trespass to real property,* occurs when a person intentionally: (1) enters the land of another without permission; (2) causes an object to be placed on the land of another without the landowner's permission; (3) stays on the land of another when the owner tells him to depart; or (4) refuses to remove something he placed on the property that the landowner asked him to remove.

It is no defense to argue that one thought he had a legal right to be on the property, or that he thought the land belonged to someone else. The intent refers to intentionally being on that particular piece of land. In a recent, unusual case heard in a small claims court in

Westchester County, a plaintiff sued the defendant for trespass to realty when the defendant entered the plaintiff's property to serve the plaintiff with a reply affidavit for another legal action. The defendant had previously been barred from entering the plaintiff's property. The plaintiff argued that the defendant could not dictate how legal papers are served. The plaintiff sued for $3,000 in compensatory, nominal, and punitive damages. While the court ruled that the defendant committed trespass to realty, they awarded only nominal damages in the sum of $1.00.

Private Nuisance

A private nuisance occurs when a person uses his property in an unreasonable manner that harms a neighbor's use and enjoyment of his property. Using one's property in a manner that caused the neighbor to be subjected to flooding, vibrations, excessive noise, or smoke could all lead to a nuisance claim.

Trespass to Personal Property

A person commits trespass to personal property, also called **trespass to personalty**, by temporarily exerting control over another's personal property or interfering with the true owner's right to use the property. The trespasser is liable for any harm caused to the property or any loss suffered by the true owner as a result of the trespasser having the property. For example, if I take someone's bike from their garage and use it for a week, I have committed trespass to personalty. If I return the bike after it has a flat tire, I will have to compensate the owner for the cost of repairing the tire and any expenses that resulted from my having the bike for a week.

Conversion

Conversion occurs when the defendant permanently removes the personal property from the owner's possession and control. When conversion occurs, the true owner can no longer regain the property. The owner usually recovers damages for the full value of the converted item, plus any additional damages that resulted from the loss.

An illustration of conversion comes from a recent case heard in the Westchester County Supreme Court. An amateur racecar driver left her racecar at a service station. While in the possession of the service station, an employee of the service station, with a known drinking problem, apparently drove the car, wrecked it, and totally destroyed it. It could never be returned in the original condition when it was taken. The driver sued for conversion and recovered the value of the car in damages.

Intentional Torts against Economic Interests

All businesspersons should be familiar with the torts against economic interest. The four most common torts against economic interests are disparagement, intentional interference with contractual relations, unfair competition, and misappropriation. The first tort, **disparagement**, is most easily understood as a form of defamation. It is the defamation of a business product or service.

The plaintiff in a disparagement case must prove that the defendant published a false statement of a material fact about the plaintiff's product or service that resulted in a loss of sales. When the statements are criticisms of the quality, honesty, or reputation of the business or product, the tort is sometimes called **slander of quality** (if spoken) or **trade libel** (if in printed form). If the statements relate to the ownership of the business property, then the term **slander of title** is used.

Damages for disparaging are ordinarily based on a decrease in profits that can be linked to the publication of the false statement. An alternative, although a less common way to prove damages, would be to demonstrate that the plaintiff had been negotiating a contract with a third party, but the third party lost interest shortly after the publication of the false statement. The profits the plaintiff would have made on the contract would be the damages.

Some interesting variations of the tort of disparagement have developed. For example, in thirteen states, courts now recognize the tort of **food disparagement**. These laws, sometimes referred to as "veggie libel" laws by their critics, provide ranchers and farmers a cause of action when someone spreads false information about the safety of a food product. The first major test of these laws came in a case filed by a cattle rancher against talk show host Oprah Winfrey and one of her guests. Oprah had said, during the broadcast at issue in the case, that the conversation they were having about the possibility of contracting disease from meat had stopped her from ever eating a burger again. Shortly after the show aired, the price of cattle futures fell.

Oprah and her guest were sued under the Texas veggie libel law, which says that anyone who knowingly makes a false claim that a perishable food product is unsafe, may be required to pay damages to the producer of the product. The jury in the case decided that their was no liability, because the statements were merely the parties' opinions, and were not statements of fact.

With the growing use of technology, it seems almost inevitable that a computer related disparagement tort would evolve, and it has. *Disparagement by computer* occurs when erroneous information from a computer about a business' credit standing or reputation impairs a business' ability to obtain credit, and the computer information's owner fails to correct the incorrect information in a timely manner.

Intentional Interference with Contract

Another tort against economic interests is the tort of *intentional interference with contract*. To successfully bring a claim of intentional interference with contract, the plaintiff must prove that: (1) a contract between the two parties existed; (2) the defendant party knew of the existence of the contract and its terms; (3) the defendant intentionally undertook steps to cause one of the parties to breach the contract; and (4) the plaintiff was injured as a result of the breach.

The most common situation involving intentional interference with a contract in the business context involves a situation where one employer tries to lure an employee away from another employer. Liability in such a situation, however, is limited to the case where the employee has a contract for a set period of time, and the employer actually knows of the contract.

Unfair Competition

Our legal system assumes that individuals go into business for the purpose of making a profit. Competition is supposed to drive inefficient firms out of business because the more efficient firms will be able to provide less expensive goods and services. For this system to work, however, firms must be in business to make a profit. Therefore, it is unlawful for a person to go into business for the purpose of causing a loss of business to another without regard for their own profit. For example, if there is only one jewelry store in town, Mark cannot come in and set up a store where he makes no profits, just to drive the other store out of business, so that an acquaintance of his can then move in and open up a legitimate jewelry store once the competition has been driven out of business.

Wrap-Up

Rubin is continuing with his suit against *U.S. News*. Will Rubin be able to demonstrate the elements of defamation? Under the elements of defamation, he must be able to demonstrate that he suffered financial loss because of the story.

Perhaps when the case is decided, we will know more about whether the reporter really told Rubin that he was writing an article about the Peruvian value tax or about money laundering in the gold trade. However, both parties could have worked to prevent the lawsuit by communicating more clearly. Perhaps Rubin and the author could have avoided this dispute, if they had learned a little more about tort law.

Summary	
Introduction to Tort Law	**Tort**—a civil wrong giving the injured party the right to bring a lawsuit against the wrongdoer to recover compensation for the injuries.
Goals of Tort Law	1. Compensate innocent persons who are injured. 2. Prevent private retaliation by injured parties. 3. Reinforce a vision of a just society. 4. Deter future wrongs.
Damages Available in Tort Cases	**Compensatory Damages**—an award that puts the plaintiff in the position he or she would have been in, had the tort not occurred. **Nominal Damages**—a minimal amount that signifies that the defendant's behavior was wrongful, but caused no harm. **Punitive Damages**—damages that punish the defendant and deter such conduct in the future.

	Summary (continued)
Classification of Torts	**Intentional Torts**—occur when the defendant takes an action intending that certain consequences will, or are likely to, occur.
	Intentional Torts against Persons
	Assault and Battery
	Defamation
	Privacy Torts
	False Imprisonment
	Intentional Infliction of Emotional Distress
	Intentional Torts against Property
	Trespass to Realty
	Trespass to Personalty
	Conversion
	Intentional Torts against
	Economic Interest
	Disparagement
	Intentional Interference with Contractual Relations
	Misappropriation
	Unfair competition

Review Questions and Case Problems

1. Distinguish the three types of damages available in tort cases.

2. Explain why some people see punitive damages as a necessary aspect of our tort system, while others want to restrict their availability.

3. List five intentional torts, and explain the elements needed to prove each.

4. Mr. Thomas Gottier was a regular patron at his local Denny's restaurant, typically spending long hours drinking coffee or tea and reading. On the day in question, Gottier became impatient with the service he was receiving. Gottier searched for a manager to convey his complaint. Unable to locate a manager, Gottier saw his waiter (Bruner) and approached him. Witnesses report that Gottier approached Bruner in a rude manner, instructing him to get out of his way. When Bruner did not comply, Gottier pushed him and "kind of slapped" him in the face. Bruner responded by striking Gottier across the head with a coffee pot, causing lacerations. Gottier sued Bruner and Denny's for negligence and battery. Bruner defended his actions by claiming self-defense. Explain why or why not you believe this defense will be successful. *Gottier v. Denny's Restaurant*, 2001 Cal. App. LEXIS 2880.

5. Levinsky's Inc., a family-owned business, competes in retail clothing sales with Wal-Mart in Portland, Maine. When Levinsky's began an intriguing advertising campaign, a writer for a Portland business magazine decided to write an article about Levinsky's reaction to Wal-Mart. While researching the article, the writer called the manager of an area Wal-Mart store. During this phone conversation, the manager described Levinsky's store as "trashy" and stated that when a person telephones Levinsky's, "you are sometimes put on hold for twenty minutes—or the phone is never picked up at all." The writer printed the manager's comments in his story, and Levinsky's sued Wal-Mart for defamation. Was their claim successful? Why or why not? *Levinsky's, Inc v. Wal-Mart Stores, Inc.* 127 F. 3d 122 (1st Cir. 1997).

6. Peter Kennedy, a long-distance truck driver, agreed to allow a *Dateline* news crew to accompany and film him on a coast-to-coast run. *Dateline* wanted to do a show that highlighted the pressures on truckers, the consequences of driver fatigue, and the violations of law truckers commit when reporting times. After the filming of the show, *Dateline* producers discovered that Kennedy was no longer driving for Veilleux, his employer at the time of the taping. After he was assured that his comments would be 'off the record,' Kennedy told *Dateline* producers that he had tested positive for amphetamines and marijuana in a random drug test. Kennedy was re-interviewed on camera, at which time he stated that he didn't want to discuss the drug test on camera. However, later in the interview, the producer asked him about the drug test, and Kennedy stated he did not take drugs. When the program was aired, it revealed the information regarding Kennedy's drug test. As a result of the publication of the drug test results, Kennedy brought a suit for public disclosure of private fact. Does Kennedy have a valid claim? Why or why not? *Raymond Veilleux, et al. v. National Broadcasting Company, Inc. et al.*, 8 F. Supp. 2d 23 (1998).

7. Jamie Messenger was an aspiring fourteen-year-old model. *Young and Modern (YM)* magazine hired

Messenger for a shoot in New York. At the shoot, she took a variety of photographs and gave consent for *YM* to use the photos, but never obtained written consent from a parent or guardian. *YM* used the photos of Messenger to illustrate a Love Crisis column. Her pictures were next to an article describing a young woman's sexual misfortunes. The article detailed an event where a fourteen-year-old got drunk and had sex with her boyfriend and two of his friends. Captions reading, "I got trashed and had sex with three guys" and "Afraid you are pregnant" accompanied her pictures. Messenger brought suit against *YM* for invasion of privacy, specifically false light. Does she have a compelling case? Why or why not? *Messenger v. Gruner*, 94 N.Y. 2d 436, 727 N.E. 2d 549 (2000).

8. In 1993, several Honda employees were working at their dealership in Santa Ana. In December of 1993, the employees watched in horror as an airliner plummeted from the sky toward the dealership. Fearing the airliner would hit them, they began to panic. The pilot of the plane was able to direct the airliner away from striking anyone. The employees, disregarding their fear, were among the first to arrive at the crash site. At the site they witnessed the crash and offered whatever aid they could. After the incident, Lawson, one of the employees, filed suit against the owners and operators of the airliner. The suit, joined by several other employees, alleged the crash had caused "serious, substantial and enduring mental anguish." The district court dismissed the case and Lawson et al. appealed. The appellants in this case are filing an intentional tort of emotional distress. What do you think the appellant court will find? How do you think the appellants could strengthen their case? *Lawson v. Management Systems Inc.*, 69 Cal. App. 4th 652, 1999 Cal. App. LEXIS 61 (1999).

9. Betty England worked at the Dairy Queen restaurant owned by S & M Foods. One day, while she was at work, several hamburgers were returned because they were incorrectly prepared. Her manager blamed her. He was so enraged at what he saw as her incompetence, that he yelled at her using profane language, and threw a hamburger at her, hitting her in the leg with it. She sued her manager and S & M Foods for battery, and received an award of $1,000. Explain why you believe this award was either upheld or overturned on appeal. *England v. S & M Foods, Inc.*, 511 S. 2d 1313 (1987).

10. Nuerotron Inc. manufactures medical testing devices known as the Nuerometer CPT. This device tests the patient's ability to feel electrical shocks delivered through the skin at a decreasing rate. Nuerotron filed suit against Highmark, an operator of nonprofit health care plans. The suit alleged disparagement of their Nuerometer in Highmark's company newsletter. The newsletter provides information about experimental services they will, or will not, cover for their members. Nuerotron requested that Highmark review its CPT. Based upon this review, Highmark concluded, "CPT was investigational and therefore not covered." Highmark wrote, "The neuro-selective current perception threshold test is performed to provide an objective measure of subjective sensation. It requires

the patient's conscious perception of the stimulation applied. The neuro-selective current perception threshold test has no proven clinical utility and is not eligible for payment, since it is considered to be investigational." Based on this statement, Nuerotron filed a disparagement suit. Though they were not specifically named, they claimed the reasonable reader would know Highmark was referring to CPT. Using your knowledge of what constitutes a tort of disparagement, predict the outcome of this case and explain your reasoning. *Nuerotron v. Medical Service Assoc.*, 254 F. 3d 44, 2001 U.S. App. LEXIS 13757.

11. In 1997 an Alaskan citizen contacted the Alaska Department of Health to inquire about the health implications for ozone-generating air purifiers. The health Department asked Dr. Lori Feyk to investigate the possible health risks and report back. After researching the topic she was asked to prepare a report of her findings as a health bulletin to distribute. The bulletin, entitled, "Ozone Generators—Warning—Not For Occupied Spaces," stated that ozone "is a potent lung irritant that can cause respiratory distress, and levels of ozone that clean air effectively are unsafe to human health." Further, the bulletin cited a Minnesota case where the state found Alpine Industries, an ozone-generator producer, "guilty of fraud and antitrust laws by making false and misleading claims about the efficacy and safety of ozone-generating Alpine purifiers." Alpine Industries filed suit against Feyk for libel. Create a defense for Feyk in this suit. *Alpine Industries v. Feyk*, 22 P. 3d 445 (2001).

12. When Outkast released its *Aquemeni* album, a debate was sparked between the rappers and Rosa Parks. Outkast produced a song titled, Rosa Parks, in which they refer to her 1956 refusal to move to the back of the bus. Her actions sparked the Montgomery bus boycott. Parks filed suit against Outkast and LaFace records for using her name without permission on an album that contained racial slurs, derogated women, and uses profane language. Parks sued alleging defamation as well as several other causes. Describe the strengths and weaknesses of her case. *Parks v. LaFace Records*, 76 F. Supp. 2d 775 (1999).

13. The plaintiff was ringing up Golden's purchases on the cash register at K-Mart. When plaintiff called out the price on a package of curtains, Golden told plaintiff the price was incorrect because the curtains were on sale. Plaintiff called a domestics department clerk for a price check. Upon hearing that the curtains in question were not on sale, Golden left her merchandise on plaintiff's counter and returned with the clerk to the domestics department to find the "sale" curtains.

The plaintiff moved Golden's merchandise to the service counter and began to check out other customers. When Golden returned, she asked what plaintiff had done with her money. When plaintiff replied, "What money?", Golden said that she had left four five-dollar bills on top of the merchandise she was purchasing. Plaintiff told Golden she had not seen any money. Golden continued in a loud, abrupt voice to demand her money from plaintiff and caused a general commotion.

The K-Mart manager, who had been observing the incident from nearby, walked over to plaintiff's counter. After conferring with Golden, he walked up to plaintiff, pulled out her jacket pockets, looked inside and found nothing. Then he and other employees searched the area for money. None was found, so the manager explained there was nothing more he could do except check out plaintiff's register. The register balanced perfectly.

Golden continued to insist loudly that the clerk took her money. The manager then told plaintiff to accompany a female assistant manager into the women's public restroom for the purpose of disrobing in order to prove to Golden that she did not have the money. The manager asked Golden if she wanted to watch the search; Golden replied: "You had better believe I do, it is my money." In the restroom, plaintiff took off all her clothes, except her underwear, while Golden and the assistant manager watched closely. When plaintiff asked Golden if she needed to take off more, Golden replied that it was not necessary because she could see through plaintiff's underwear anyway.

The plaintiff returned to work the next day, and was forced to work with another cashier on one register, a practice that the store had previously discontinued. The plaintiff consequently quit and filed suit. Thoroughly discuss whether you believe the plaintiff has a valid cause of action, and if so, against whom? *Bodewig v. K-Mart and Golden,* 635 P. 2d 657 (1981).

Assignment on the Internet

As you know from this chapter, tort reform is a hot issue today. Numerous groups have set up websites to publicize their view with respect to tort reform. Find two websites, other than the ones listed below, created by parties with opposing views toward tort reform. Explain the primary argument made on each website, and then evaluate the quality of each argument. Be sure to identify the full title and URL for each website you evaluate.

What is your position with respect to what the liability of online service providers should be? Why? Can you provide any additional arguments to strengthen either position?

On the Internet

http://law.house.gov/110.htm *The United States House of Representatives Internet Law Library has a collection of statutes, court decisions, and articles related to tort law.*

http://www.wwlia.org/tort2.htm *The worldwide Legal Information Association page provides information about tort law in the United States, Canada, Australia, and the United Kingdom.*

http://www.aaabiz.com/ATRA *The American Tort Reform Association provides a broad range of information on issues related to tort reform.*

http://www.cspinet.org/foodspeak *If you were bothered by the idea of "veggie libel laws," you will want to check out this site maintained by the Foodspeak Coalition.*

Tort Liability for the Boy Scouts of America?

Recently, numerous boys have brought suits against the Boy Scouts of America.[1] These boys had been sexually molested by their respective scout masters. These molestations occurred on officially sanctioned scouting events, like overnight camping trips or at week-long Boy Scout camps.

The boys argue that the Boy Scouts have a duty of care to protect its members from being molested by its scout leaders. In other words, they argue that the Boy Scouts, as an organization, should be aware that young scouts are vulnerable to molestation and should take some steps to protect the scouts. The organization's failure to do so is seen by the boys as negligence.

In response, Boy Scouts of America argues that molestation by particular scout leaders is not foreseeable; thus, they believe they should not be found to have a duty of care to protect scouts from molestation.

1. *Suppose you are the judge in this case. Do you think that Boy Scouts has a duty of care to protect its scouts from molestation by scout leaders? Why or why not?*
2. *Now suppose you are the manager of a day care facility. You hear about the cases against the Boy Scouts. Do you need to be concerned about similar charges against your day care facility? Why or why not?*

---

[1] Kevin Livingston, *Panel Oks Boy Scout Molest Suit*, THE RECORDER, May 15, 2000, at p.1; Theodore Postel, *Boy Scout Alleges Molestation*, CHICAGO DAILY LAW BULLETIN, Feb. 7, 2000, at p.1; *Doe v. Boy Scouts of America*, THE CONNECTICUT LAW TRIBUNE, Feb. 15, 1999.

CHAPTER 8

Negligence and Strict Liability

Introduction to Negligence And Strict Liability

In the previous chapter we discussed intentional torts, wrongs in which an individual took an action that he or she should have known would harm another person. In this chapter, we consider two other types of torts: negligent torts and strict liability torts. These torts are generally committed when an individual *fails* to maintain a duty of care to another individual. Thus, the Boy Scouts could potentially be liable if they owed a duty of care to the scouts.

Suppose Ross uses a piece of wood to smack Joey, the mailman, on the face. Ross has committed battery. However, if Ross is building a tree house in his yard and accidentally drops a piece of wood on Joey, who is delivering Ross' mail, Ross' action is missing intent, so there is no battery. Yet, he might be negligent.

One of the more notable situations in which people are attempting to use the tort of negligence is when teenage violence occurs. For example, the parents of Marcos Delgado Jr. filed a claim of negligence against a movie theater when it admitted thirteen-year-old Raymond Aiolentuna without an adult to the R-rated movie *Dead Presidents*. After the movie, Aiolentuna emerged from the theater, walked one block, and shot Delgado. Delgado's parents argued that the movie theater was negligent because it did not enforce the movie ratings system. However, the court ruled in favor of the movie theater. [2] Additionally, the families of the victims

of the 1999 Littleton, Colorado, school shootings sued the two alleged shooters and the gun manufacturer for negligence. What exactly is required to establish a successful negligence claim?

This chapter begins by examining the elements of negligence. Second, we consider the methods that courts have adopted to help plaintiffs make successful negligence claims. Next, we consider the defenses that defendants to a negligence claim can raise. Finally, we consider strict liability torts.

Elements of Negligence

Negligence describes behavior that creates an unreasonable risk of harm to others. In contrast to intentional torts, which result from a willful desire to cause injury, negligent torts involve the failure to exercise reasonable care to protect another's person or property.

Sometimes harm occurs because an individual suffers an **unfortunate accident**, an incident that simply could not be avoided, even with reasonable care. For example, Jonathan is driving on the highway when he suffers a stroke. Because of the stroke, he crashes into two other vehicles, but he is not liable for damages in the accident. Yet, if Jonathan had some type of warning that the stroke was going to occur, he might be liable for the accident.

The plaintiff in a negligence case must prove the presence of these four elements: (1) duty, (2) breach of duty, (3) causation, and (4) damages. A plaintiff who cannot establish all four of these elements will be denied recovery.

EXHIBIT 8-1

Elements of Negligence

To prove negligence, a plaintiff must demonstrate:

1. Duty
2. Breach of duty
3. Causation
4. Damages

---

[2] *Delgado v. American Multi-Cinema Inc.*, 99 C.D.O.S. 4772, Los Angeles Superior Court (1999).

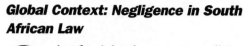

Global Context: Negligence in South African Law

South Africa's legal system is a collaboration of legal traditions—from Roman to Dutch to German. The Roman *actiones legis Aquiliae* influences South Africa's statues concerning liability. Under this Roman tradition, certain cases concerning liability mandate the presence of *culpa* or negligence. South African law defines negligence in three ways.

Negligence is first defined as a failure to observe the accepted standard of conduct. In other words, individuals should exercise care and foresight with regard for others. A failure to do so dictates negligent behavior. Second, negligence is determined by whether the defendant could have prevented the consequent damages. The law expects individuals to take the necessary precautions to avoid harm or damage. Finally, South African law outlines the extent to which one can be found negligent in a crisis situation. In such instances, individuals have a duty to do what is "reasonably" expected. Because of the obvious ambiguity associated with this definition, South African law cites the American 'doctrine of sudden emergency' as a standard for determining negligence in crisis situations. Encompassing all three of these definitions is an implicit duty of the individual to do all that is possible to prevent harm.

Duty

The duty the defendant owes to the plaintiff is the first element to be proved. For some particular parties, the law specifies the duty of care. In most cases, however, the courts use a "reasonable person" standard to determine the defendant's duty of care. This "reasonable person" is an objective measurement of the way members of society expect an individual to act in a given situation. To determine the defendant's duty of care, the judge or jury must determine the degree of care and skill a reasonable person would exercise under similar circumstances. This standard will then be used to evaluate the actions of the individual in the case. Going back to the Boy Scouts of America case, would a reasonable person owe the scouts a duty of care?

Businesses are generally considered by courts to have a duty of care to customers who enter the businesses' property. It is important, therefore, that future business managers are knowledgeable about this duty. Customers should be warned of any risk of harm they may encounter on business property.

Better yet, the business should ensure the customer's safety by removing such hazards. In *Haywood v. Baseline Construction Company*, a case recently decided in Los Angeles, a woman who tripped over lumber being stored on the front porch of the House of Blues restaurant sued for negligence. The business' attempt to warn customers by marking the lumber with yellow construction tape was insufficient to avoid the determination of negligence; the woman was awarded $91, 366 in damages.

The following case considers when a party has a duty to another party.

Case 8-1

Roland C. Feichtner

v.

City of Cleveland et al.,
Court of Appeals of Ohio, Eighth Appellate
District, Cuyahoga County
95 Ohio App. 3d 388 (1994)

*O*n April 13, 1991, Roland C. Feichtner was driving south on Interstate 77 in Cleveland, Ohio. This portion of I-77 was being resurfaced by Kenmore Construction Company. Traffic on I-77 South was diverted to the extreme right lane and the berm of the highway. Feichtner was driving on the berm of the highway. When he passed under an overpass on I-77, a fourteen-pound sandstone rock crashed through the windshield on the passenger side of the vehicle. Feichtner's wife was killed. When the police investigated the death, they discovered that Ronald Jackson had thrown a rock that he had obtained from a nearby construction site off the bridge, and this rock was the one that crashed through Feichtner's window. Jackson was indicted for the murder of Feichtner's wife.

During the Jackson's pending hearings, Feichtner filed a negligence claim against Cleveland and five construction companies. He argued that their negligence was the proximate cause of his wife's death. Feichtner claimed that the construction companies "knew or should have known" of the hazard of leaving debris near the bridge. The construction companies denied liability and filed motion for summary judgment. They argued that Feichtner could not demonstrate the element of duty. The trial court granted the construction company's motions for summary judgment, stating that Feichtner failed to establish a duty toward Feichtner's wife. Feichtner appealed.

JUDGE NAHRA

When the defendants furnish evidence which demonstrates the plaintiff has not established the elements necessary to maintain his negligence action, summary judgment is properly granted in favor of defendants.

"As to the elements of a cause of action in negligence it can be said that '[i]t is rudimentary that in order to establish actionable negligence, one must show the existence of a duty, a breach of the duty, and an injury resulting proximately therefrom.' Thus, the existence of a duty is fundamental to establishing actionable negligence. ' If there is no duty, then no legal liability can arise on account of negligence. Where there is no obligation of care or caution, there can be no actionable negligence.' Only when one fails to discharge an existing duty can there be liability for negligence."

A review of the evidence before the trial court in this case leads to the conclusion appellant did not establish the elements necessary to maintain his negligence action. The evidence reveals appellees owed no special duty toward appellant's wife and, furthermore, any negligence on their part was not the proximate cause of her death.

That conclusion is supported by a review of the Ohio Supreme Court's opinion in *Fed. Steel & Wire Corp. v. Ruhlin Constr. Co.* (1989. Ruhlin is particularly applicable to this case because of the similarity of certain facts.

In *Ruhlin,* a construction company had undertaken repairs of the Lorain-Carnegie bridge in Cleveland. The court noted that "[f]rom the very beginning of the project," Ruhlin was aware of "severe theft and vandalism problems," including specific instances of vandals throwing construction materials off the bridge....When work on the project was shut down for the winter,...Ruhlin left a quantity of construction materials on the bridge, stopped posting security guards, and replaced the barbed wire fencing with a simple barricade and a snow fence.

Over the winter, Federal, which occupied a building directly beneath the construction area, suffered significant damage to its building from vandals throwing Ruhlin's construction materials off the bridge. Federal instituted an action against Ruhlin; however, eventually, the trial court granted Ruhlin's motion for a directed verdict with a finding that Ruhlin owed no duty to Federal.

> "Ordinarily, there is no duty to control the conduct of a third person by preventing him or her from causing harm to another, except in cases where there exists a special relationship between the actor and the third person which gives rise to a duty to control, or between the actor and another which gives the other the right to protection. Thus, liability in negligence will not lie in the absence of a special duty owed by a particular defendant."

> ..."We recognize that there is no common-law duty to anticipate or [foresee criminal activity. Thus, the law usually does not require the prudent person to expect the criminal activity of others. As a result, the duty to protect against injury caused by third parties, which may be imposed where a special relationship exists, is expressed as an exception to the general rule of no liability."

The existence of such a "special" duty depends on the foreseeability of the injury....This court has held the foreseeability of criminal acts will depend upon the knowledge of the defendant-business, which must be determined from the totality of the circumstances. Only when the totality of the circumstances are "somewhat overwhelming" will a defendant-business be held liable for the criminal acts of a third party. The rationale for this rule is stated thus:

> "In delimiting the scope of duty to exercise care, regard must be had for the probability that injury may result from the act complained of. No one is bound to take care to prevent consequences, which, in the light of human experience, are beyond the range of probability."

It was this standard which led the Supreme Court in *Ruhlin* to conclude a special duty was owed by Ruhlin to Federal under the circumstances of that case. The court stated the rationale of its decision thus:

> "[I]f a person exercises control over real or personal property and such person is aware that the property is subject to repeated third-party vandalism, causing injury to or affecting parties off the controller's premises, then a special duty may arise to those parties whose injuries are reasonably foreseeable, to take adequate measures under the circumstances to prevent future vandalism."

In this case, however, no such "overwhelming" circumstances exist. Appellant presented no evidence from which to conclude that an exception to the general rule of no liability had been established which created a special duty on the part of appellees.

The evidence demonstrated the construction debris generated by the companies was not on the Fleet Avenue bridge as alleged in appellant's complaint. Rather, it was on a site at least twenty-five to thirty yards away from the bridge. The evidence further demonstrated that, contrary to the allegations of the complaint, prior to the incident there were no documented reports that persons were taking the construction debris and then transporting it to the bridge to throw it off. The only evidence on this point was a statement made in his deposition by one of the company owners that such a thing occurring was within the realm of possibility. This was insufficient to create a special duty on appellee's part.

Furthermore, there was no evidence that any of the appellees failed to comply with any safety regulations. Therefore, no liability in tort on this basis was established.

Accordingly, appellant's assignment of error is overruled. The judgment of the trial court is affirmed. AFFIRMED.

1. Critical Thinking: The court uses an analogy in this case to reach its conclusion. It compares the current case to the case of *Federal Steel & Wire Corp. v. Ruhlin Construction Company*. How strong is this analogy? Do you think there are any differences in the two cases that the court is ignoring? If so, why are these differences important?

2. Ethical Decision Making: Return to the WPH Process of Ethical Decision Making. Identify the purpose of the court's decision. What value are they particularly upholding in their decision that the City of Cleveland was not negligent?

Technology: Negligence on the Internet

A common explanation for the increased occurrence of violence is the increased violence portrayed in the media. As suggested earlier in the chapter, some plaintiffs are trying to hold owners of certain websites liable under negligence theories for violent acts committed by teenagers. For example, in *James v. Meow Media*, a 14-year-old school boy took six guns to school and shot three of his classmates to death.[3] The parents of the deceased classmates brought suit against various Internet websites and creators and distributors of various video games. The parents argued that these defendants had a duty of ordinary care to the slain girls.

However, the courts have been consistent in finding that it is not foreseeable that a boy who plays certain video games and views certain websites will murder three of his classmates. In similar cases, courts have ruled that defendants (such as website owners, creators and distributors of video games, and directors and producers of movies) do not have a duty to protect a person from the criminal acts of a third party, unless there is a special relationship that requires that the defendant owes that duty of harm.

While the issue appears settled that website owners, manufacturers, and producers will not be held liable, plaintiffs continue to bring suits against these groups of people. Can you think of an argument for why these groups of people would owe a duty of care to plaintiffs?

[3] *Internet Defamation Shooting Death Claims Against Internet, Video, Motion Picture Defendants are Dismissed.*, THE INTERNET NEWSLETTER, May 2000, at p. 4.

Breach of Duty

After the plaintiff has established that duty of care required of the defendant in the case, the plaintiff must prove that the defendant's conduct violated that duty. This violation is a breach of duty. For example, the driver of an automobile owes the other passengers in the car a duty of care to follow the traffic signs. If the driver runs a stop sign, that action puts the passengers at risk and is a breach of the driver's duty of care.

Causation

Causation has two separate elements: actual cause and proximate cause. The first element, **actual cause**, is simply the determination that the defendant's breach of duty resulted directly in the plaintiff's injury. A common procedure in determining whether the breach of duty was the actual cause of the plaintiff's injury is to ask, "Would the plaintiff have been injured if the defendant had fulfilled his or her duty?" If the answer is no, then the actual cause of the plaintiff's injury was the defendant's breach.

Proximate cause describes the extent of the defendant's liability. A person is not held legally responsible for all possible consequences of negligent conduct. The defendant is only liable for those consequences for which the negligent conduct was a proximate cause. In most states, proximate cause is determined by foreseeability.

For example, if a defective tire on a vehicle blows out, it is foreseeable that the driver will lose control and hit a pedestrian. It is not foreseeable, however, that the pedestrian is a scientist carrying a briefcase full of chemicals, which explode on impact, causing a third floor window to shatter, injuring an accountant at his desk. In most states, the accountant would not succeed if he sued the tire manufacturer for negligence. The tire failure is not considered a proximate cause of the accountant's injury, because the contents of the pedestrian's briefcase were highly unusual. The pedestrian, however, would not be prevented from recovering damages from the manufacturer on grounds of proximate cause. Hitting a pedestrian is a foreseeable consequence to tire failure; thus, the defect in tire manufacture is a proximate cause of the pedestrian's injury.

Let's return to the Boy Scout scenario. Do you think a scout's molestation is foreseeable? Boy Scouts of America believes that specific cases of molestation are not foreseeable. Do you agree?

Perhaps the most well-known case considering the issue of proximate cause is the *Palsgraf* case.

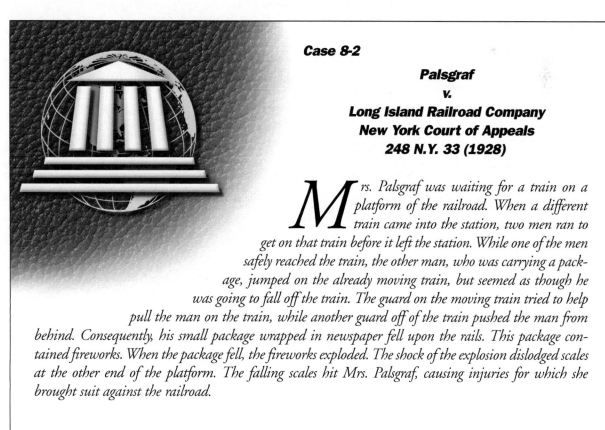

Case 8-2

Palsgraf
v.
Long Island Railroad Company
New York Court of Appeals
248 N.Y. 33 (1928)

*M*rs. Palsgraf was waiting for a train on a platform of the railroad. When a different train came into the station, two men ran to get on that train before it left the station. While one of the men safely reached the train, the other man, who was carrying a package, jumped on the already moving train, but seemed as though he was going to fall off the train. The guard on the moving train tried to help pull the man on the train, while another guard off of the train pushed the man from behind. Consequently, his small package wrapped in newspaper fell upon the rails. This package contained fireworks. When the package fell, the fireworks exploded. The shock of the explosion dislodged scales at the other end of the platform. The falling scales hit Mrs. Palsgraf, causing injuries for which she brought suit against the railroad.

JUDGE CARDOZO

Nothing in the situation gave notice that the falling package had in it the potency of peril to persons thus removed. Negligence is not actionable unless it involves the invasion of a legally protected interest, the violation of a right. "Proof of negligence in the air, so to speak, will not do." If no hazard was apparent to the eye of ordinary vigilance, an act innocent and harmless, at least to outward seeming, with reference to her, did not take to itself the quality of a tort because it happened to be a wrong, though apparently not one involving the risk of bodily insecurity, with reference to someone else. "In every instance, before negligence can be predicated of a given act, back of the act must be sought and found a duty to the individual complaining, the observance of which would have averted or avoided the injury" "The ideas of negligence and duty are strictly correlative" (Bowen, L. J., in *Thomas v. Quartermaine*, 18 Q. B. D. 685, 694).

The argument for the plaintiff is built upon the shifting meanings of such words as "wrong" and "wrongful," and shares their instability. What the plaintiff must show is "a wrong" to herself, i. e., a violation of her own right, and not merely a wrong to someone else, nor conduct "wrongful" because unsocial, but not "a wrong" to anyone. We are told that one who drives at reckless speed through a crowded city street is guilty of a negligent act and, therefore, of a wrongful one irrespective of the consequences. Negligent the act is, and wrongful in the sense that it is unsocial, but wrongful and unsocial in relation to other travelers, only because the eye of vigilance perceives the risk of damage. If the same act were to be committed on a speedway or a race course, it would lose its wrongful quality....[W]rong is defined in terms of the natural or probable, at least when unintentional (*Parrot v. Wells-Fargo Co.* [The Nitro-Glycerine Case], 15 Wall. [U.S.] 524)....Here, by concession, there was nothing in the situation to suggest to the most cautious mind that the parcel wrapped in newspaper would spread wreckage through the station. If the guard had thrown it down knowingly and willfully, he would not have threatened the plaintiff's safety, so far as appearances could warn him. His conduct would not have involved, even then, an unreasonable probability of invasion of her bodily security. Liability can be no greater where the act is inadvertent.

Negligence, like risk, is thus a term of relation. Negligence in the abstract, apart from things related, is surely not a tort, if indeed it is understandable at all (Bowen, L. J., in *Thomas v. Quartermaine*, 18 Q. B. D. 685, 694). Negligence is not a tort unless it results in the commission of a wrong, and the commission of a wrong imports the violation of a right, in this case, we are told, the right to be protected against interference with one's bodily security. But bodily security is protected, not against all forms of interference or aggression, but only against some. One who seeks redress at law does not make out a cause of action by showing without more, that there has been damage to his person. If the harm was not willful, he must show that the act as to him had possibilities of danger so many and apparent as to entitle him to be protected against the doing of it, though the harm was unintended. Affront to personality is still the keynote of the wrong.

The law of causation, remote or proximate, is thus foreign to the case before us. The question of liability is always anterior to the question of the measure of the consequences that go with liability. If there is no tort to be redressed, there is no occasion to consider what damage might be recovered if there were a finding of a tort.

The judgment of the Appellate Division and that of the Trial Term should be reversed, and the complaint dismissed, with costs in all courts.

REVERSED.

1. Critical Thinking: Why does the court believe that Mrs. Palsgraf should not be awarded damages? Are you persuaded by these reasons? Why or why not?

2. Ethical Decision Making: Think about the WPH Process of Ethical Decision Making. It may seem unfair that Mrs. Palsgraf was unable to collect damages for her injuries. Study the list of values or purposes for a decision. Which value do you think the court was upholding through its decision? Which value is in conflict with this favored value? With which value do you most agree?

Global Context: Negligence in Germany

German law is concerned with the defendant's ability to foresee, understand, and avoid danger. Both mental and physical capabilities are taken into account. For example, the standard "duty of care" stipulates that "physical and mental disabilities or defects, panic or confusion" exempt the defendant from being found negligent. Also, though not recognized by a statute, the courts distinguish between conscious and unconscious negligence. Conscious negligence requires knowledge that the offense is about to occur and that it is an actual offense. Unconscious negligence, on the other hand, is when the defendant is either unaware that the act constitutes an offense or unaware that it is occurring at all. If this is the situation, then the defendant is found not guilty by reason of unconscious negligence.

Courts in a minority of states do not distinguish actual cause from proximate cause; if the negligence is an actual cause, it is also judged to be a proximate cause. Therefore, in the minority of states, both the pedestrian-scientist and the third floor accountant would be able to recover damages in the previous example.

Damages

Damages are the final required element of a negligence action. The plaintiff must have sustained compensable injury from the defendant's actions. Remember, the purpose of tort law is to compensate individuals who suffer injuries as a result of another's action or inaction. Therefore, a party cannot bring an action in negligence seeking only nominal damages; the party *must* seek compensatory damages.

Courts rarely award punitive damages, damages imposed to punish the offender, in typical negligence cases. Instead, the court usually awards punitive damages in cases where the offender has committed **gross negligence**, an action of extreme recklessness or intent to injure.

Plaintiff's Doctrines

The plaintiff has the burden of proving all of the elements of the negligence case. However, direct evidence of negligence by the defendant is not always available—there may have been no witnesses to the

negligent conduct and other proof may have been destroyed. Therefore, two doctrines have been adopted by courts to aid plaintiffs in establishing negligence claims. These devices are *res ipsa loquitur* and **negligence per se**.

Res Ipsa Loquitur

Res ipsa loquitur literally means "the thing speaks for itself." The plaintiff uses this doctrine to allow the judge or jury to *infer* that the defendant's negligence was the cause of the plaintiff's harm when there is no direct evidence of the defendant's lack of due care. To establish *res ipsa loquitur* in most states, the plaintiff must demonstrate that:

1. The event was a kind that ordinarily does not occur in the absence of negligence.
2. Other responsible causes, including the conduct of third parties and the plaintiff, have been sufficiently eliminated.
3. The indicated negligence is within the scope of the defendant's duty to the plaintiff.

Proof of these elements does not *require* a finding of negligence; it merely permits it.

One of the earliest uses of *res ipsa loquitur* was the case of *Escola v. Coca Cola*[4]. In that case, the plaintiff, a waitress, was injured when a bottle of Coca Cola that she was removing from a case exploded in her hand.

---

[4] 150 P .2D 436 (1994)

From the facts that: (1) bottled soft drinks ordinarily do not spontaneously explode, and (2) the bottles had been sitting in a case, undisturbed, in the restaurant for approximately thirty-six hours before the plaintiff simply removed the bottle from the case, the jury reasonably inferred that the defendant's negligence in the filling of the bottle resulted in its explosion. The plaintiff therefore could recover without direct proof of the defendant's negligence. The doctrine has subsequently been used in numerous accident cases where there has been no direct evidence of negligence. Note that the jury does not have to infer negligence, but they may. The defendant's best response to the use of this doctrine is to try to demonstrate other possible causes of the accident.

The following case provides an illustration of the potential use of *res ipsa loquitur* by a plaintiff.

Case 8-3

Janet Kambat

v.

St. Francis Hospital et al.
Court of Appeals of New York
89 N.Y. 2d 489 (1997)

In August 1986, at St. Francis Hospital, Dr. Ralph Sperrazza performed an abdominal hysterectomy on Florence Fenzel. During the operation, ten laparotomy pads were available for use. Dr. Sperrazza placed several of these pads inside the defendant, next to the bowel. A few months following the operation, Fenzel began to complain of stomach pain. Approximately three months after the operation, x-rays of Fenzel's abdomen revealed a foreign object in her abdomen. A few days later, Dr. Robert Barone discovered that the foreign object partially or fully inside her bowel was a 18-by-18-inch laparotomy pad similar to the one used during Fenzel's hysterectomy. Barone removed the object. Fenzel's condition continued to worsen, and she died later that month due to infection-related illness.

Fenzel's family sued the hospital for negligence in leaving the laparotomy pad inside Fenzel. During the trial, Fenzel's family produced evidence that the abdominal pads were available only in operating rooms, where patients could not access them. Three experts testified for Fenzel's family, arguing about the precise location of the pad inside the bowel. In contrast, the hospital argued that standard procedures were followed during the operation and all pads and medical instruments were counted after the operation. Furthermore, the hospital argued that laparotomy pads were left in places accessible to plaintiffs. Thus, the hospital claimed that the defendant swallowed the pad.

The trial court refused to allow Fenzel's family to use res ipsa loquitur during the trial, and the jury ruled in favor of the hospital. The trial court argued that res ipsa loquitur was not applicable because lengthy and inconsistent expert testimony was not within the experience of a layperson. The appellate court agreed with the trial court's refusal to allow res ipsa loquituur.

JUDGE KAYE

Where the actual or specific cause of an accident is unknown, under the doctrine of res ipsa loquitur a jury may in certain circumstances infer negligence merely from the happening of an event and the defendant's relation to it. Res ipsa loquitur "simply recognizes what we know from our everyday experience: that some accidents by their very nature would ordinarily not happen without negligence."

Once a plaintiff's proof establishes the following three conditions, a prima facie case of negligence exists and plaintiff is entitled to have res ipsa loquitur charged to the jury. First, the event must be of a kind that ordinarily does not occur in the absence of someone's negligence; second, it must be caused by an agency or instrumentality within the exclusive control of the defendant; and third, it must not have been due to any voluntary action or contribution on the part of the plaintiff.

To rely on res ipsa loquitur, a plaintiff need not conclusively eliminate the possibility of all other causes of the injury. It is enough that the evidence supporting the three conditions afford a rational basis for concluding that "it is more likely than not" that the injury was caused by defendant's negligence otherwise, all that is required is that the likelihood of other possible causes of the injury "be so reduced that the greater probability lies at defendant's door." Res ipsa loquitur thus involves little more than application of the ordinary rules of circumstantial evidence to certain unusual events, and it is appropriately charged when, "upon 'a commonsense appraisal of the probative value' of the circumstantial evidence,...[the] inference of negligence is justified."

Submission of res ipsa loquitur, moreover, merely permits the jury to infer negligence from the circumstances of the occurrence. The jury is thus allowed—but not compelled—to draw the permissible inference. In those cases where "conflicting inferences may be drawn, choice of inference must be made by the jury."

In the typical res ipsa loquitur case, the jury can reasonably draw upon past experience common to the community for the conclusion that the adverse event generally would not occur absent negligent conduct. In medical malpractice cases, however, the common knowledge and everyday experience of lay jurors may be inadequate to support this inference....Courts in this State have differed as to whether expert testimony can supply the necessary foundation for consideration of res ipsa loquitur by a jury.

Widespread consensus exists, however, that a narrow category of factually simple medical malpractice cases requires no expert to enable the jury reasonably to conclude that the accident would not happen without negligence. Not surprisingly, the oft-cited example is where a surgeon leaves a sponge or foreign object inside the plaintiff's body. As explained by Prosser and Keeton in their classic treatise:

> "There are, however, some medical and surgical errors on which any layman is competent to pass judgment and conclude from common experience that such things do not happen if there has been proper skill and care. When an operation leaves a sponge or implement in the patient's interior,...the thing speaks for itself without the aid of any expert's advice." (Prosser and Keeton, Torts § 40 at 256-257 [5th ed]).

Manifestly, the lay jury here did not require expert testimony to conclude that an 18-by-18-inch laparotomy pad is not ordinarily discovered inside a patient's abdomen following a hysterectomy in the absence of negligence. Thus, plaintiffs' undisputed proof that this occurred satisfied the first requirement of res ipsa loquitur.

Turning to these remaining res ipsa loquitur conditions, plaintiffs' evidence that similar pads were used during decedent's surgery, that decedent was unconscious throughout the operation, that laparotomy pads are not accessible to patients, and that it would be anatomically impossible to swallow such pads sufficed to allow the jury to conclude that defendants had exclusive control of the laparotomy pad "at the time of the alleged act of negligence" and that it did not result from any voluntary action by the patient.

We agree with the Appellate Division dissenters, moreover, that defendants' evidence tending to rebut the three conditions did not disqualify this case from consideration under res ipsa loquitur. Plaintiffs were not obligated to eliminate every alternative explanation for the event. Defendants' evidence that they used due care and expert testimony supporting their competing theory that decedent might have had access to laparotomy pads and inflicted the injury upon herself by swallowing the pad, merely raised alternative inferences to be evaluated by the jury in determining liability. The undisputed fact remained in evidence that a laparotomy pad measuring 18 inches square was discovered in decedent's abdomen: "[f]rom this the jury

may still be permitted to infer that the defendant's witnesses are not to be believed, that something went wrong with the precautions described, that the full truth has not been told" (Restatement [second] of Torts § 328 D, comment n). Thus, the inference of negligence could reasonably have been drawn "upon 'a commonsense appraisal of the probative value' of the circumstantial evidence," and it was error to refuse plaintiffs' request to charge res ipsa loquitur. (George Foltis, Inc. v. City of New York, 287 U.S. at 115, supra).
REVERSED.

1. Critical Thinking: What evidence does the court give for its conclusion that the plaintiff could have used res ipsa loquitur? Are you persuaded by this evidence? Why or why not?

2. Ethical Decision Making: Suppose you were a business manager for the hospital when this case was first brought to the hospital's attention. The plaintiff's attorney has contacted you, claiming that the doctor in this case was negligent. The attorney argues that the hospital should pay the defendant's family in an attempt to compensate for the doctor's negligence. Suppose your actions are guided by the public disclosure test. What would your response to the plaintiff's family be?

Negligence Per Se

Negligence per se is also a helpful doctrine for the plaintiff. In a case where the defendant has violated a statute enacted to prevent a certain type of harm, and the violation causes that type of harm to befall the plaintiff, the violation is negligence per se; proof of the violation can be used to establish proof of the negligence. For example, if Ohio passes a statute prohibiting the sales of alcohol to minors, and a minor runs a red light and kills two pedestrians while driving under the influence of alcohol sold to him illegally, the liquor store's violation of the statute prohibiting the sale of alcohol to minors establishes *negligence per se* on the part of the store. Before examining the defenses to negligence, take a moment to compare the definition of negligence in this country with that in South Africa, as described in the Global Context box "Negligence in South Africa," found on page 170.

Defenses to Negligence

The plaintiff's case is helped by the courts' doctrines of *res ipsa loquitur* and *negligence per se*, but the courts also allow for certain defenses that relieve the defendant from liability, even where the plaintiff has proven all elements of negligence.

Contributory Negligence

Contributory negligence, a defense initially available in all states, is used when the plaintiff was also negligent. The defendant must prove that: (1) the plain-

tiff's conduct fell below the standard of care need to prevent unreasonable risk of harm, and (2) the plaintiff's failure was a contributing cause to the plaintiff's injury. How might contributory negligence be used in a case? Some lawyers have tried to argue that if an individual involved in an accident failed to wear his or her seatbelt, that failure constitutes contributory negligence because the individual has contributed to the injuries.

If contributory negligence is proven, no matter how slight the negligence is, the plaintiff will be denied any recovery of damages. Because this defense seemed so unfair, many states have adopted **the last-clear-chance doctrine**. This doctrine allows the plaintiff to recover damages despite proof of contributory negligence, if the defendant in the case had a last clear opportunity to avoid the action that injured the plaintiff.

For example, suppose that Samantha and Nicole's cars are facing each other while stopped at a red light. The light turns green, and Nicole starts to turn left at the intersection. Samantha sees Nicole start to turn, but she still continues to travel straight through the intersection and slams into Nicole's car. While Samantha had the right of way at the intersection, she could have avoided hitting Nicole's car by braking or swerving.

Comparative Negligence

The adoption of the-last-clear-chance doctrine, however, still left a lot of situations in which an extremely careless defendant caused a great deal of harm to a plaintiff, who was barred from recovery because of minimal contributory negligence. Thus, today, most states have replaced the contributory negligence defense with either pure or modified **comparative negligence**.

Under a **pure comparative negligence** defense, the court determines the percentage of fault of the defendant, and that is the percentage of damages for which the defendant is liable. Damages under **modified comparative negligence** are calculated in the same manner, except that the defendant must be more than fifty percent at fault before the plaintiff can recover. Twenty-eight states have modified comparative negligence, thirteen have pure comparative negligence, and nine have contributory negligence. Remember, every state adopts one of these three defenses. The parties do not get to pick from among them. However, if a party resides in a state that uses a defense that is not favorable to that party, he or she can always argue that the state should change its law to accept a different defense. For example, a plaintiff residing in a state that still allows the contributory negligence defense might try to argue that the state should follow the trend and modernize its law by moving to modified comparative negligence and abolishing the contributory negligence defense.

Assumption of the Risk

Another possible defense to negligence is that of **assumption of the risk**. A defendant, using this defense successfully, will prove that the plaintiff voluntarily and unreasonably encountered the risk of the actual harm that was caused by the defendant. In other words, the harm suffered by the plaintiff was willingly assumed as a risk.

The most difficult part of establishing this defense is showing that the harm suffered was indeed one that was assumed by the plaintiff. A good illustration of an unsuccessful attempt to use assumption of the risk as a defense comes from a 1998 case against the Family Fitness Center (FFC).[5] In that case, the plaintiff was injured when a sauna bench on which he was lying collapsed beneath him at the defendant's facility. The trial court granted a summary judgment in favor of defendant based on assumption of risk. The plaintiff had signed a contract that included the following provision: "Buyer is aware that participation in a sport or physical exercise may result in accidents or injury, and Buyer assumes the risk connected with the participation in a sport or exercise and represents that Member is in good health and suffers from no physical impairment which would limit their use of FFC's facilities." The appellate court overturned the trial court's decision because the type of injury suffered by the plaintiff was not the type of risk the plaintiff had assumed. The court said that anyone signing a membership agreement could be deemed to have waived any hazard known to relate to the use of the health club facilities, such as the risk of a sprained ankle due to improper exercise or overexertion, a broken toe from a dropped weight, injuries due to malfunctioning exercise or sports equipment, or from slipping in the locker-room shower. However, no patron could be charged with realistically appreciating the risk of injury from simply reclining on a sauna bench. Because the collapse of a sauna bench when properly used is not a 'known risk,' the court concluded that the plaintiff could not be deemed to have assumed the risk of this incident as a matter of law.

The following case illustrates the successful use of assumption of the risk as a defense. You may wish to compare this case to previous illustration to see whether you agree with different outcomes in the two cases.

---

[5] *Leon v. Family Fitness Center, Inc.*, 61 Cal. App. 4th 1227 (1998).

Case 8-4

Barran

v.

Kappa Alpha Order, Inc.
Supreme Court of Alabama
730 So. 2d 203 (1998)

When Jason Jones enrolled at Auburn University in 1993, he chose to become a pledge of the Kappa Alpha fraternity. Within two days, Jones began to experience hazing by fraternity members. Hazing activities included the following: 1) digging a ditch and jumping into it after it was filled with water, urine, feces, dinner leftovers, and vomit; 2) receiving paddlings to his buttocks; 3) eating foods such as peppers, hot sauce, and butter; 4) being pushed and kicked; 5) doing chores for fraternity members; 6) appearing at 2 a.m. "meetings" where pledges would be hazed for several hours; and 7) "running the gauntlet," in which pledges would run down a hallway and flight of stairs while fraternity members would push, kick, and hit them. Although Jones was aware that 20-40% of the pledges dropped out of the pledge program, Jones remained in the program until he was suspended from the university for poor academic performance. In 1995, Jones sued the national and local Kappa Alpha organization alleging negligence, assault and battery, negligent supervision, and various other claims. He argued that he suffered "mental and physical injuries" as a result of the hazing. For the negligence claims, the trial court granted summary judgment for Kappa Alpha. The trial court argued that Jones assumed the risk of hazing because he voluntarily entered the organization and could have quit at any time. Jones appealed, and the Court of Civil Appeals reversed the negligence ruling, reasoning that the peer pressure associated with fraternity life prevented Jones from voluntarily withdrawing from the pledge class. Kappa Alpha appealed.

JUSTICE SEE

Assumption of the risk has two subjective elements: (1) the plaintiff's knowledge and appreciation of the risk; and (2) the plaintiff's voluntary exposure to that risk....[I]n order to find, as a matter of law, that Jones assumed the risk, this Court must determine that reasonable persons would agree that Jones knew and appreciated the risks of hazing and that he voluntarily exposed himself to those risks.

First, KA and its members argue that Jones knew and appreciated the risks inherent in hazing....Jones's deposition indicates that before he became a KA pledge he was unfamiliar with the specific hazing practices engaged in at KA, but that the hazing began within two days of his becoming a pledge; that despite the severe and continuing nature of the hazing, Jones remained a pledge and continued to participate in the hazing activities for a full academic year; that Jones knew and appreciated that hazing was both illegal and against school rules; and that he repeatedly helped KA cover up the hazing by lying about its occurrence to school officials, his doctor, and even his own family. Given Jones's early introduction to the practice of hazing and its hazards, and in light of his own admission that he realized that hazing would continue to occur, the trial court correctly determined that reasonable people would conclude that Jones knew of and appreciated the risks of hazing.

Second, in addition to establishing that Jones both knew of and appreciated the risk, KA and the individual defendants argue that Jones voluntarily exposed himself to the hazing. Jones responds by arguing that a coercive environment hampered his free will to the extent that he could not voluntarily choose to leave the fraternity. The Court of Civil Appeals, in reversing the summary judgment as to KA and the individual defendants, stated that it was not clear that Jones voluntarily assumed the risk of hazing, because, that court stated:

"In today's society, numerous college students are confronted with the great pressures associated with fraternity life and…compliance with the initiation requirements places the students in a position of functioning in what may be construed as a coercive environment."

With respect to the facts in this case, we disagree.…The record indicates that Jones voluntarily chose to continue his participation in the hazing activities. After numerous hazing events, Jones continued to come back for more two o'clock meetings, more paddlings, and more gauntlet runs, and did so for a full academic year. Auburn University officials, in an effort to help him, asked him if he was being subjected to hazing activities, but he chose not to ask the officials to intervene. Jones's parents, likewise acting in an effort to help him, asked him if he was being subjected to hazing activities, but he chose not to ask his parents for help.

Moreover, we are not convinced by Jones's argument that peer pressure created a coercive environment that prevented him from exercising free choice. Jones had reached the age of majority when he enrolled at Auburn University and pledged the KA fraternity. We have previously noted: "College students and fraternity members are not children. Save for very few legal exceptions, they are adult citizens, ready, able, and willing to be responsible for their own actions." Thus, even for college students, the privileges of liberty are wrapped in the obligations of responsibility.

Jones realized that between 20% and 40% of his fellow pledges voluntarily chose to leave the fraternity and the hazing, but he chose to stay. See Prosser & Keeton, The Law of Torts 491 ("Where there is a reasonably safe alternative open, the plaintiff's choice of the dangerous way is a free one, and may amount to assumption of the risk.…"). As a responsible adult in the eyes of the law, Jones cannot be heard to argue that peer pressure prevented him from leaving the very hazing activities that, he admits, several of his peers left.

Jones's own deposition testimony indicates that he believed he was free to leave the hazing activities:

Q: You didn't have to let this [hazing] happen to you, did you?

A: No.

Q: And you could have quit at any time?

A: Yes.

Q: But yet you chose to go through with what you have described here in your complaint with the aspirations that you were going to become a brother in the Kappa Alpha Order? You were willing to subject yourself to this for the chance to become a member of the brotherhood…were you not?

A: Yes.

We conclude that Jones's participation in the hazing activities was of his own volition. The trial court correctly determined that reasonable people could reach no conclusion other than that Jones voluntarily exposed himself to the hazing.

REVERSED AND REMANDED.

1. Critical Thinking: Is there any important missing information that might influence your thinking about the court's conclusion that Jones participated in the hazing activities of his own volition? Why is this missing information important?

2. Ethical Decision Making: Return to the WPH Process of Ethical Decision Making. Which stakeholders are affected by the court's decision? Why are these people affected?

Strict Liability

Strict liability refers to liability without fault. We hold individuals liable without fault in this country when they engage in activities that are so inherently dangerous, that they cannot ever be safely undertaken. We could ban the performance of such activities, but instead, we allow people to engage in such activities, but hold them liable for all of the harm that results.

Inherently dangerous activities include blasting in a populated area and keeping nondomesticated animals. If an animal has shown a "vicious propensity," strict lia-

bility applies and the owner of the animal is responsible for any injuries suffered in an attack by the animal.[6] However, if an individual is injured by an animal who has not shown vicious propensity, the owner has a duty to warn and protect individuals who come into contact with the animal. The following case provides an example of the application of strict liability to injuries caused by animals.

_____

[6] _Schwartz v. Armand ERPF Estate_, 688 N.Y.S. 2d 55 (Sup. Ct., App. Div., N.Y., 1999).

Case 8-5

Gregory Scorza
v.
Alfredo Martinez and Worldwide Primates, Inc.
Court of Appeal of Florida, Fourth District
683 So. 2d 1115 (1996)

When Hurricane Andrew hit South Florida in August 1992, a number of primates whose cages were damaged escaped from Worldwide Primates, a breeder of monkeys and other primates. One of the escaped primates, a macaque monkey, was captured by Mr. Gomez, who then sold the monkey to Alfredo Martinez. Martinez sold the monkey to Gregory Scorza, who purchased the monkey for use in his business of photographing people with exotic animals. Martinez said that the monkey was a capuchin monkey and "a sweetheart." Scorza paid Martinez $500 and took the monkey home. However, when Scorza tried to remove the monkey from its cage, the monkey bit him. Scorza then took the monkey to a veterinarian, who told Scorza that the monkey was a macaque monkey, a breed of monkey known for carrying the hepatitis-B virus. The veterinarian notified the Florida Game and Fresh Water Fish Commission about the monkey. Later, the Commission returned the monkey to Worldwide.

Scorza brought a claim of negligence and strict liability against Worldwide. Scorza argued that Worldwide, as the owner of the monkey, was strictly liable for any injuries caused by the monkey. Worldwide argued that because Scorza purchased the monkey from Martinez, it was no longer the owner of the animal and not strictly liable for injuries. The trial judge ordered summary judgment in Worldwide's favor.

JUDGE STEVENSON

The owner, keeper, or possessor of a wild animal is strictly liable if the animal injures another. Furthermore, "if the animal is one of a class that is not indigenous to the locality, its escape does not prevent its possessor from being liable for the harm done by the animal no matter how long after its escape; in this case the risk of liability continues until some third person takes possession of the animal." Scorza had taken possession of the monkey at the time of the injury, and for the purposes of strict liability,

Worldwide was not responsible for the monkey at that time. Therefore, the trial court was correct in granting summary judgment in favor of Worldwide on the strict liability count.
AFFIRMED.

1. Critical Thinking: Are there any potentially ambiguous words or phrases used in the courts reasoning? How do these words or phrases affect the court's conclusion?

2. Ethical Decision Making: If you were a business manager at Worldwide Primates, you would be very happy with this decision. Which other stakeholders would be happy with this decision? Which stakeholders might be unhappy? Why?

As will be seen in the next chapter, in today's society, strict liability has had perhaps its greatest impact on cases involving products that are considered unreasonably dangerous.

Boy Scouts of America Wrap-Up

The courts have been divided in deciding whether the Boy Scouts have a duty of care to the scouts. At least two courts have ruled that Boy Scouts owe a duty of care to protect its scouts from sexual molestation. One of these courts cited the high incidence of sexual abuse in scouting as evidence for its conclusion that Boy Scouts has a duty of care. However, at least one court has disagreed, holding that there is no duty of care because the molestation was not foreseeable.

Which court is correct?

Because the courts disagree, the issue regarding duty of care could be heard by the Supreme Court. What can, and perhaps *should*, Boy Scouts, and similar groups, do to protect themselves from liability? Boy Scouts, and other groups, should likely conduct better screenings of those who wish to serve as scout leaders, or leaders of organizations. If a scout leader (or other organization leader) had a history of sexual misconduct and the Boy Scouts did not look at his background, the courts may be more likely to hold Boy Scouts liable. Until the courts reach a consensus as to whether Boy Scouts owe a duty of care to protect its scouts from sexual molestation, Boy Scouts and other organizations may wish to behave as though there *is* a duty of care.

	Summary
Introduction to Negligence and Strict Liability	When an individual fails to maintain a duty of care to protect other individuals, negligence and strict liability may occur.
Elements of Negligence	**Duty**—the standard of care that the defendant (i.e., a reasonable person) owes the plaintiff. **Breach of Duty**—the defendant's lack of maintaining the standard of care a reasonable person would owe the plaintiff. **Causation**—did the defendant's conduct (breach of duty) lead to the plaintiff's injury? **Damages**—is the plaintiff's injury compensable?
Plaintiffs' Doctrines	**Res Ipsa Loquitur**—doctrine that permits the judge or jury to infer that the defendant's negligence was the cause of the plaintiff's harm, when there is no direct evidence of the defendant's lack of due care. **Negligence Per Se**—doctrine that permits a plaintiff to use proof of defendant's violation of a statute, that has been enacted to prevent a certain type of harm, as proof of negligence.

Summary (continued)	
Defenses to Negligence	**Contributory Negligence**—a defense that allows the defendant to entirely escape liability by demonstrating any degree of negligence on the part of the plaintiff that contributed to the plaintiff's harm. **Comparative Negligence**—a defense that allow the liability to be apportioned between plaintiff and defendant in accordance with the degree of responsibility each bears for the harm suffered by the plaintiff. **Assumption of the Risk**—a defense that allows the defendant to escape liability by establishing that the plaintiff engaged in an activity fully aware that the type of harm he or she suffered was a possible consequence of engaging in the activity in question.
Strict Liability	Persons who engage in activities that are so inherently dangerous that no amount of due care can make them safe are strictly liable.

Review Questions and Case Problems

1. List and define the elements that are necessary to prove a case of negligence.

2. Explain the differences between contributory and comparative negligence.

3. Explain the relationship between *negligence per se* and *res ipsa loquitur*.

4. Susan Webstad was having an affair with her former coworker Joseph Stortini. She left her husband for Stortini, but Stortini did not leave his wife. Webstad was an alcoholic, and Stortini was well aware that she had been treated by alcoholic rehabilitation centers. She also took medication for a blood-pressure problem. Webstad was unhappy with the relationship, and one night she called Stortini to tell him she had taken an overdose of her pills. Stortini found her unconscious at her apartment, but he was able to revive her. Webstad continued to have suicidal tendencies and sought outpatient treatment. She frequently complained that her relationship with a married man left her feeling lonely and "jilted." Webstad and Stortini continued to date, and Stortini tried to explain to Webstad that he was not willing to divorce his wife. Upon hearing this, Webstad went into the kitchen and swallowed eight or ten pills. She told Stortini that she would be okay, and that she did not need to go to the doctor. When Webstad's condition worsened, Stortini called 911. Though the units were quick to respond, it was too late to save Webstad's life. Her son, Russell Webstad, brought an action against Stortini claiming that his negligent behavior caused Webstad's death. The trial court found that Stortini did not owe a duty of care to Webstad. Russell Webstad appealed the decision. How do you think the court decided? *Webstad v. Stortini*, 924 P. 2d 940 (1996).

5. James Napoli and Kurt Buckholz were both attending Camp Alvernia. The two boys were preparing for a game of baseball, and Buckholz was swinging a bat on the sidelines to warm up. He accidentally hit Napoli in the jaw with the bat. Napoli's mother brought an action against the camp to recover damages for Napoli's injuries. The defendants argued that by voluntarily allowing her son to participate in the camp's sporting activities, Napoli's mother assumed the risk of Napoli incurring an injury. Do you think that danger is inherent in the game of baseball? How would this affect the court's decision? *Napoli v. Mount Alvernia, Inc.*, 657 N.Y.S. 2d 197 (1997).

6. August 16, 1996, Billy Ezell was involved in a fatal accident in Christian County, Kentucky. The accident occurred when Ezell ran a stop sign and collided with another vehicle. Ezell's brother and executor of his estate brought suit against Chuck Chambers, the county director and engineer of public works, for negligence resulting in his brother's death. The suit claimed the stop sign was placed in a location that was not in conformance with Kentucky law and that the county failed to properly maintain the stop sign. The sign was obscured from the road by the overgrowth of bushes and weeds. Kentucky also has a statute stating, it is the county engineers' duty to "remove trees and other obstacles from the right of way" in order to avoid "a hazard to traffic," Kentucky Revised Statutes § 179.070, and another Kentucky statute provides that "a person injured by the violation of any statute may recover" damages, KRS § 446.070. What doctrine would the plaintiff use to try to prove his case? How do you believe the Court ruled? *Ezell v. Christian County, Kentucky*, 245 F. 3d 853 (6th Cir., 2001).

7. Eileen Hennessey resided in a condominium that bordered the Louisquisset Golf Club. Hennessey reported that golf balls pelted her home every year when the golf season resumed. On a Sunday afternoon, Hennessey was in her garden reading and enjoying the outdoors when a stray golf ball struck her. She was struck in the side of her head causing injury. Pyne, the golfer who hit the ball, was fully aware of the proximity of Hennessey's home to the course, as well as her usual presence on her property. Hennessey filed suit, claiming negligence on Pyne's behalf for failure to yell 'fore,' or any other warning, after seeing

his ball veer off course. Pyne filed a motion for summary judgment. Why is the defense of assumption of the risk relevant or irrelevant to this case? *Hennessey v. Pyne*, 694 A. 2d 691 (Sup. Ct. R.I., 1997).

8. While visiting a horse ranch with his parents a four-year-old boy crawled under an electric fence to see the horses. Once in the enclosure, the boy was kicked in the head by one of the horses causing severe brain damage. The boy's parents filed a negligence action against the owners of the horse and ranch. What rules of liability are applicable to this case? Construct an argument for both the plaintiff and defendants in this case. *Schwartz v. Armand ERPF Estate*, 255 A.D. 3d 35, 688 N.Y.S. 2d 55 (1999).

9. At 7:30 P.M. February 3, 1995 Mary Ann Eckstein was driving her vehicle along a windy, unlit stretch of road. Ahead of her, Joan Sandow had parked her car on the left side of the street to distribute materials into the mailboxes on the right. Sandow was wearing dark clothes and a black raincoat. Eckstein was driving down the roadway using her high beams and slowed down when she saw Sandow's car on the side of the road. Eckstein then felt her car hit something and stopped to investigate. Once she exited the car she saw Sandow in the road. Sandow filed a negligence claim against Eckstein, seeking compensatory damages. Eckstein responded to the suit by alleging contributory negligence. The plaintiff responded, arguing that motorists have an added duty of care for pedestrians. The trial court found for Sandow. How do you think the appellate court found? What is the basis for your decision? *Sandow v. Eckstein*, 67 Conn. App. 243 (2001).

10. Douglas Adams was traveling with his son on a Reno highway. While driving, he encountered a ladder blocking the left lane, his lane, and extending into the emergency shoulder. To avoid the ladder, he veered into the emergency lane where a utility truck was parked. Adams attempted to avoid the truck and unsuccessfully swerved back into the other lane. Adams collided with the truck and careened into the cement median. As a result of the accident Adams died. Adams' family filed for uninsured motorists benefits with State Farm, pursuant with their policy, to collect for the accident. They filed for this because the driver of the vehicle that the ladder fell from could not be identified. State Farm refused coverage. Adams' family then filed suit against State Farm for breach of contract, claiming that in using the doctrine of *res ipsa loquitur*, the owner of the ladder was the direct cause of the accident. The court agreed that if the owner could be determined to be the cause of the accident, State Farm would be responsible. During the trial, an officer testified that the ladder was the primary cause of the accident. However, he also testified that the ladder could be seen for a slight distance and several other cars had avoided it without incident. State farm argued that Adams' death was a result of his veering into the other lane. Explain why, or why not, you believe the court accepted the argument of *res ipsa loquitur*. *Woosley v. State Farm*, 18 P. 3d 317, 117 Nev. Adv. Op. No. 18 (2001).

11. Plaintiff Artlip was using the pool facility at her apartment. She was drinking a glass of wine when she noticed that a bee was flying too close to her. Artlip tried to avoid the bee by stepping back, and her foot was caught in a hole on the deck. The hole was intentionally made and allowed for a tree to grow through the deck. Artlip argued that the hole was a result of poor maintenance of the pool area and brought a suit against her landlord. She alleged that the landlord was negligent because the deck was not properly maintained and the hole was not clearly marked. The landlord demonstrated that Artlip was very familiar with the pool area. His maintenance supervisor testified that the deck was in good condition and had been inspected on many occasions by the county inspector. Do you think the court found the landlord's behavior to be negligent? *Artlip v. Queler*, 470 S.E. 2d 260 (1996).

12. Ginger Klostermeier was a regular customer of the In & Out Mart in Lucas County, Ohio. On May 29, 1998 she went into the store to purchase lottery tickets, but fell immediately upon entering the door. The clerk helped Klostermeier up and Klostermeier made her purchase. Klostermeier was later treated for injuries sustained to her upper body, including a broken left arm. Klostermeier suffered from multiple sclerosis, although it was in remission at the time of her fall. Examination of and research into the door revealed that the closer had been replaced on November 3, 1997, and that the door Klostermeier had used to enter the store took an average of 1.602 seconds to close. This is in noncompliance with the Americans with Disabilities Act, which states that doors must have a minimum closing time of three seconds to accommodate those with disabilities. Klostermeier sued the store and the installer of the door closer. One of Klostermeier's claims was *negligence per se*, because the door violated the Americans with Disabilities Act. The trial court and the court of appeals both ruled that the store was not guilty of *negligence per se*, though for different reasons. Can you articulate possible reasons why violation of the Americans with Disabilities Act does not constitute negligence per se? *Ginger R. Klostermeier v. In & Out Mart, Inc., et al.*, 2001 Ohio App. LEXIS 1499 (2001).

13. Paula Baddeaux was riding in a pickup truck with her fiancé Dave Zeringue. The rear tire on Zeringue's pickup truck blew out, and the poor road conditions resulted in the pickup truck flipping over. Both Baddeaux and Zeringue were seriously injured. They filed suit against the Department of Transportation and Development (DODT), and a trial judge found the DOTD 75% responsible for the accident. Baddeaux was awarded $308,825.85. The DODT appealed the trial judge's decision arguing that Baddeaux's overweight condition contributed to the costliness of her recovery. Baddeaux had a history of weight problems, and at the time of the accident she weighed over 200 pounds. She sustained serious knee injuries, and in failing to follow her doctor's recommendation to lose weight, Baddeaux made the knee injuries difficult and costly to treat. Do you think this was sufficient to warrant comparative negligence? Why or why not? *Baddeaux v.*

State of Louisiana Department of Transportation and Development, 690 So. 2d 203 (1997).

14. Danny and Kathy Ziegler owned an above-ground swimming pool. Six-year-old Rebecca Henson found her way into the pool and drowned. Rebecca's parents alleged that the Zieglers had a duty of care to protect Rebecca from the dangers of their above-ground swimming pool. The Zieglers maintained that the swimming pool was an open and obvious danger. They found it reasonable to assume that a six-year-old child would recognize the danger and avoid the pool. The trial court agreed with the Zieglers and denied the Henson's negligence suit. The Hensons appealed the decision. How do you think the court decided? *Henson v. Ziegler*, 665 N.E. 2d 877 (1996).

Assignment on the Internet

You learned about comparative negligence in this chapter. The Georgia House of Representatives considered a bill that would make joint tortfeasors comparatively liable for their torts. You can look at this bill at the following website: **http://www2.state.ga.us/Legis/1997_98/leg/fulltext/sb637.htm**. Make a connection between this bill and what you learned about comparative negligence in this chapter. Does it extend your knowledge about comparative negligence? Does it agree or disagree with what you learned? Now, ask the same questions of this Maryland House of Representatives bill: **http://mlis.state.md.us/1997rs/billfile/hb0846.htm**.

On the Internet

http://www.nwpr.com/neg.html   *For a discussion of how an employer could be held negligent in its hiring decisions, see this Negligent Hiring website.*

http://www.lexpert.ca/areas/medical.html   *For a consideration of the treatment of medical negligence in Canada, see this following website.*

http://www.tobacco.neu.edu/tot/Nov96/Wilks.htm   *For a brief discussion of a case in which plaintiffs argued that cigarette caused specific deaths and the manufacturers attempt to assert the "assumption of the risk" defense, see the following website.*

http://www.ljextra.com/practice/negligence/index.html   *To get information about current torts of national interest, go to the Law Journal Extra Torts Page.*

http://www.ll.georgetown.edu/lr/rs/torts.html   *Valuable links to primary legal materials, associations and organizations, journals and newsletters can be found at the Georgetown University Torts Page.*

http://ls.wustl.edu/WULQ/76-1/761-24.html   *To read more about comparative fault and suggested changes to statutes permitting comparative fault, see this following Washington University Law Quarterly article.*

Ford and Bridgestone/Firestone

Donna Bailey was paralyzed from the neck down after the tread from a Firestone tire separated and her friend's Ford Explorer, in which she was a passenger, rolled over. Bailey brought suit against both Ford and Bridgestone/Firestone after the March 2000 accident. In August of 2000, Bridgestone/Firestone recalled millions of its tires due to concerns of deaths following tread separations. Bailey's was not one of the tires named in the original Firestone recall.

Bailey was not the only injured party to file suit against Ford or Bridgestone/Firestone. In fact, several lawsuits against Ford and Bridgestone/Firestone are pending. One of Bailey's attorneys characterized the highly publicized problems as the "largest vehicular product liability crisis in the history of this country."[1] In June of 2001, a motion in a class action case filed by a number of owners of Explorers asked the judge to order a recall of all Explorers made between 1990, the first year that the model was produced, through 2000.

1. *What do you think the outcome of Bailey's case was?*
2. *What can Ford and Bridgestone/Firestone do about the other pending lawsuits?*
3. *How do product liability issues affect you?*

---

[1] MSNBC Staff and Wire Reporters. *"Settlement Reached in Lawsuit Against Ford and Bridgestone/Firestone."* January 8, 2001, FIRESTONE TIRES: IN THE NEWS, <http://www.elslaw.com/firestone_news_settlement.htm> (May 23, 2001).

CHAPTER 9

Product, Service, and Accountant's Liability

Theories of Liability in Product Liability Cases

Market Share Liability

Liability of Accountants and Other Professionals

Regardless of where you work in the distribution chain, if a product you are involved with causes harm to consumers, you may end up being liable. In 2000, 14,428 product liability cases were filed in the federal district courts alone.[2] There is no independent body that tracks the number of such cases filed in all state courts, but by looking at studies that have been done of groups of states, it is clear that at least as many cases are filed in state courts. Thus, being involved in a product liability, is a real possibility for any businessperson.

In this chapter, we are going to examine some the legal theories that are commonly used to bring product liability cases and some of the defenses that are used against these cases. Then, we are going to examine the closely related area of service liability, with special emphasis given to the liability of accountants. By understanding the law of product and service liability, you may be less likely to take actions that would lead you and your company into costly litigation.

Theories of Recovery in Product Liability Cases

Product liability law is based primarily on tort law. The most commonly used theories of recovery in product liability cases are **negligence** and **strict product liability**. **Misrepresentation** is another theory that is sometimes used as a basis for product liability claims. A contract based theory of liability, **breach of warranty**, can also be used to bring an action when a plaintiff is injured by a defective product. This theory is discussed in Chapter 24. A plaintiff may bring a lawsuit based on as many of these theories of liability as will fit the plaintiff's factual situation, although a suit based on strict product liability is usually the easiest to prove.

Negligence

Negligence is the oldest theory on which a product liability case can be based. To win a case based on negligence, the plaintiff must prove the four elements of negligence explained in Chapter 8: (1) the defendant manufacturer or seller owed a duty of care to the plaintiff; (2) the defendant breached that duty of care; (3) this breach of duty caused the plaintiff's injury; (4) and the plaintiff suffered actual injury.

Prior to the landmark 1916[3] case of *MacPherson v. Buick Motor Co.*, negligence was rarely used as a theory of recovery for an injury caused by a defective product because of the difficulty of establishing the element of duty. Until that case, the courts said that a plaintiff who was not the purchaser of the defective product could not establish a duty of care, because one could not owe a duty to someone with whom they were not "in privity of contract." Being "in privity of contract" means being a party to a contract. Because most consumers do not purchase goods directly from the manufacturers, product liability cases against manufactures were rare before the *MacPherson* case.

In *MacPherson v. Buick Motors*, New York's high court held the remote manufacturer of an automobile with a defective wheel liable to the plaintiff automobile owner when the wheel broke and the plaintiff was injured. Judge Cardozo stated in that case that the presence of a sale does not control the duty if the elements of a product are such that it is harmful to individuals if negligently made, and if the manufacturer knows that the product will be used by others than the purchaser without new tests, then "irrespective of contract, the manufacturer of this thing is under a duty to make it carefully." Other state courts quickly followed Justice Cardozo's lead, and negligence soon became a common theory of liability used in cases where people were injured as a result of a lack of due care on the part of a manufacturer or seller of a product.

---

[2] Greg Winter, *Defective-Product Suits Raking In Large Sums,* Deseret News, January 30, 2001, at B-6.

[3] 111 N.E. 1050 (1916).

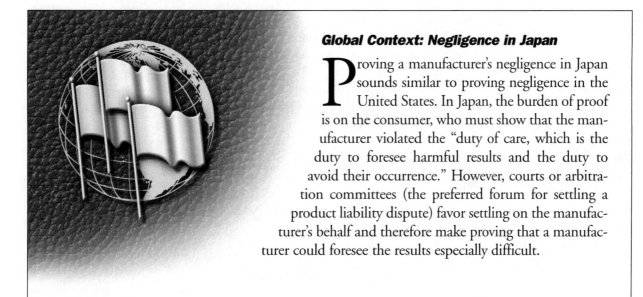

Global Context: Negligence in Japan

Proving a manufacturer's negligence in Japan sounds similar to proving negligence in the United States. In Japan, the burden of proof is on the consumer, who must show that the manufacturer violated the "duty of care, which is the duty to foresee harmful results and the duty to avoid their occurrence." However, courts or arbitration committees (the preferred forum for settling a product liability dispute) favor settling on the manufacturer's behalf and therefore make proving that a manufacturer could foresee the results especially difficult.

There are now a number of negligent acts or omissions that typically give rise to negligence-based product liability actions, which are listed in Exhibit 9-1 below. It is somewhat easy to figure out what types of negligent act could lead to negligence-based product liability cases. All you have to do is think about what a reasonable manufacturer or seller would need to do to ensure that the company's product did not pose an unreasonable risk to consumers. As you read about the different types of negligent actions, think about which types of negligent actions apply to the Donna Bailey case at the beginning of the chapter.

EXHIBIT 9-1

Common Negligent Actions Leading to Product Liability Cases

1. Negligent failure to warn.
2. Negligent provision of an inadequate warning.
3. Negligent manufacture.
4. Negligent testing or failure to test.

When thinking about the activities where a defendant risks incurring liability for negligent behavior, it becomes clear that the defendant has a duty to use reasonable care in designing a product, in selecting appropriate materials for the construction of the product, and in testing the product.

The activity that has given rise to the greatest number of negligence-based actions, however, is a negligent failure to provide an adequate warning.

To bring a successful case based on negligent failure to warn, the plaintiff must demonstrate that the defendant knew or should have known that without a warning, the product would be dangerous in its ordinary use, or in any *reasonably foreseeable* use, yet the defendant failed to provide a warning. No duty to warn exists for dangers arising from unforeseeable misuses of a product or from obvious dangers. A producer, for example, need not give a warning that a razor blade may cut someone. Courts often consider the likelihood of the injury, the seriousness of the injury, and the ease of warning when deciding whether a manufacture was negligent in failing to warn.

When providing a warning, the manufacturer must ensure that the warning will reach those who are intended to use the product. For example, if parties other than the original purchaser will be likely to use the product, the warning should be placed directly on the product itself, not just in a manual that comes with the product. Picture warnings may be required if children, or those who are illiterate, are likely to come into contact with the product and risk harm from its use.

Products such as drugs and cosmetics, which come into intimate bodily contact, are often the basis for actions based on negligent failure to warn, because the use of these products frequently causes adverse reactions. When the user of a cosmetic or an over-the-counter drug has a reaction to that product, many courts find that there is no duty to warn unless the plaintiff proves: (1) that the product contained an ingredient to which an appreciable number of people would have an adverse reaction; (2) that the defendant knew or should have known, in the exercise of ordinary care, about the existence of this group; and (3) that the plaintiff's reaction was due to his or her membership in this abnormal group.[4]

Other courts, however, use a balancing test to determine negligence in these cases. They weigh the degree of danger to be avoided with the ease of warning. For example, in 1994, a jury awarded over $8.8 million to a man who suffered permanent liver damage as a result of drinking a glass of wine with a Tylenol capsule. (The award was reduced to $350,000 pursuant to a statutory cap.) As early as 1977, the company knew that combining a normal dose of Tylenol with a small amount of wine could cause massive liver damage in some people, but the company failed to put a warning to that effect on the label because such a reaction was rare.[5] But using the balancing test, the degree of potential harm was substantial, and it would have been relatively easy to place a warning on the product label.

Negligence Per Se

As you know from Chapter 8, the violation of a statute that causes the harm that the statute was enacted to prevent, constitutes *negligence per se*. This doctrine is also applicable to product liability cases based on negligence. When a law establishes labeling, design, or content requirements for products, those statutory standards must be met. Failure by the manufacturer to meet those standards means that the manufacturer has breached his duty of reasonable care. If the plaintiff can establish that the failure to meet that standard caused injury, the plaintiff can recover under *negligence per se*. For example, if the defendant produced children's pajamas that failed to meet the Flammable Fabrics Act of 1953, and the plaintiff's daughter was burned because she was wearing pajamas made by the defendant, and they caught on fire, the plaintiff would be able to recover damages under a theory of *negligence per se*.

Damages

Damages that are recoverable in negligence-based product liability cases are the same as those in any action based on negligence: compensatory damages and punitive damages. As you should recall from Chapter 7,

compensatory damages are those designed to make the plaintiff whole again, and would include items such as medical bills, lost wages, and compensation for pain and suffering. While this list of recoverable harms may seem "obvious" to us, not all countries allow such extensive recovery. For example, in German product liability cases, consumers do not have a right to recover damages for pain and suffering or for emotional distress. Punitive damages are meant to punish the defendant for extremely harmful conduct. The amount of the punitive damages award is determined by the wealth of the defendant and the maliciousness of the action.

Defenses to a Negligence-Based Product Liability Action

The defenses to negligence discussed in the previous chapter are available in product liability cases based on negligence. A common defense in such cases is that the plaintiff's own failure to act reasonably contributed to the plaintiff's own harm. This negligence on the part of the plaintiff will allow the defendant to raise the defense of **contributory**, **pure comparative**, or **modified comparative negligence**, depending on which defense is accepted by the state where the case arose. Remember that in a state that allows the contributory negligence defense, proof of any negligence by the plaintiff is an absolute bar to recovery. In a state where the defense of pure comparative negligence is allowed, the plaintiff can recover for only that portion of the harm attributable to the defendant's negligence. In a modified comparative negligence state, the plaintiff can recover the percentage of harm caused by the defendant, as long as the jury finds the plaintiff's negligence responsible for less than 50% of the harm.

A closely related defense is **assumption of the risk**. This defense arises when a consumer knows that a defect exists, but still proceeds unreasonably to make use of the product, creating a situation where the consumer has voluntarily assumed the risk of injury from the defect and thus cannot recover. To decide whether the plaintiff did indeed assume the risk, the trier of fact may consider such factors as the plaintiff's age, experience, knowledge, and understanding, as well as the obviousness of the defect and the danger it poses. When a plaintiff knows of a danger, but does not fully appreciate the magnitude of the risk, the applicability of the defense is a question for the jury to determine.

Another common defense is *misuse* of the product. The misuse must be unreasonable or unforeseeable.

---

[4]W. Page et al., PROSSER AND KEETON ON TORTS, 5th ed. (St. Paul: West Publishing Co., 1984) 687.

[5] *Benedi v. McNeil Consumer Products Co.,* 1994 WL 729052 (LRP Jury).

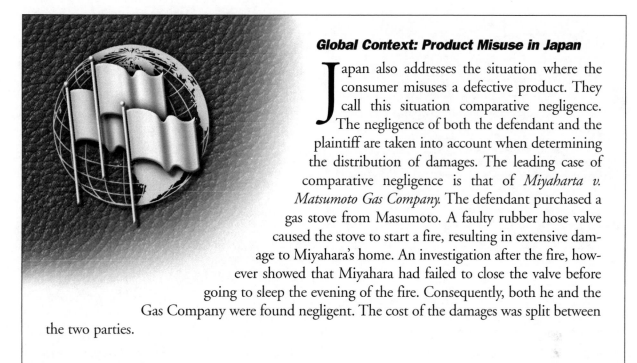

Global Context: Product Misuse in Japan

Japan also addresses the situation where the consumer misuses a defective product. They call this situation comparative negligence. The negligence of both the defendant and the plaintiff are taken into account when determining the distribution of damages. The leading case of comparative negligence is that of *Miyaharta v. Matsumoto Gas Company.* The defendant purchased a gas stove from Masumoto. A faulty rubber hose valve caused the stove to start a fire, resulting in extensive damage to Miyahara's home. An investigation after the fire, however showed that Miyahara had failed to close the valve before going to sleep the evening of the fire. Consequently, both he and the Gas Company were found negligent. The cost of the damages was split between the two parties.

When a defendant raises the defense of product misuse, what the defendant is really arguing is that the harm was caused not by the defendant's negligence, but by the plaintiff's failure to properly use the product.

The *state-of-the-art defense* is used by a defendant to demonstrate that their alleged negligent behavior was reasonable, given the available scientific knowledge existing at the time the product was sold or produced. If a case is based on the defendant's negligent defective design of a product, the state-of-the-art defense refers to the technological feasibility of producing a safer product at the time the product was manufactured. In cases of negligent failure to warn, the state-of-the-art defense refers to the scientific knowability of a risk associated with a product at the time of its production. This is a valid defense in a negligence case because the focus is on the reasonableness of the defendant's conduct. Given the state of scientific knowledge at the time, and demonstrating that there was no feasible way to make a safer product, does not always preclude liability. The court may find that the defendant's conduct was still unreasonable because even in its technologically safest form, the risks posed by the defect in the design so outweighed the benefits of the product, that the reasonable person would not have produced a product of that design.

An earlier section revealed that failure to comply with a safety standard may lead to the imposition of liability. An interesting question is whether the converse is true. Does compliance with safety regulations constitute a defense? There is no clear answer to this question. Sometimes, however, compliance with federal laws may lead to the defense that use of state tort law is preempted by a federal statute designed to ensure the safety of a particular class of products. The following case illustrates one situation in which the court accepted the preemption argument and found that compliance with a federal statute designed to regulate medical devices relieved a manufacturer from potential tort liability.

Case 9-1

**Irene M. Green and Martin Green,
Appellants**

v.

**Richard L. Dolsky, M. D. and
Collagen Corporation
Superior Court Of Pennsylvania
641 A. 2d 600 (1994)**

*P*laintiff Irene Green developed an auto-immune disease after she was treated with zyderm collagen implant. Zyderm in injected under the skin to fill in wrinkles, and is regulated as a Class III medical device under the Medical Device Amendments Act of 1976 (MDA). When Plaintiff Green sued Defendants Collagen Corporation and the doctor who treated her based on theories of negligence, strict liability, and breach of warranty, the defendants filed a motion for summary judgment on the grounds that the MDA preempted the Green's state tort claims. The trial court agreed and granted the motion. Plaintiffs appealed to the Pennsylvania Court of Appeals.

JUDGE JOHNSON

Under the supremacy clause of the United States Constitution, federal law is "the supreme Law of the Land; and the Judges in every State shall be bound thereby, any Thing in the Constitution or Laws of any State to the Contrary notwithstanding." As a result, all conflicts between federal and state laws must be resolved in favor of federal law. In determining whether a conflict between state and federal law exists, a court looks to congressional intent.

Generally, preemption may be express or implied, and it is compelled whether Congress' command is explicitly stated in the statute's language or implicitly contained in its structure and purpose. When Congress is silent on the matter, state law will be preempted by federal law "when (a) compliance with both state and federal law is impossible or, (b) when state law stands as an impediment to a federal purpose."

Pursuant to the MDA, the FDA classifies all medical devices into one of three categories. Class III devices, such as Zyderm, are subject to the most extensive controls "to provide reasonable assurance of…safety and effectiveness." Class III devices must obtain pre-market approval from the FDA because they "present a potential unreasonable risk of illness or injury."

Thus, the extensive pre-market approval process requires a manufacturer to submit a detailed application to the FDA, including information pertaining to product specifications, intended use, manufacturing methods, and proposed labeling. An appointed panel of experts conducts a comprehensive review of the application and prepares a report and recommendation. Within six months of receipt of the application, the FDA must either approve the device for sale, or reject it for additional information or testing. The MDA also imposes extensive post-approval regulations to keep the FDA apprised of any new information or safety findings relating to Class III devices. The FDA may withdraw approval of the product permanently, or suspend its approval temporarily if it determines that the device has become unsafe or its labeling inadequate. In enacting the MDA, Congress was not only interested in protecting the individual use, but it was also interested in encouraging research and development and allowing new and improved medical devices to be marketed without delay. In the MDA, Congress included an express preemption provision.

State requirements which, in effect, establish new substantive requirements for a medical device in a regulated area, such as labeling, are preempted. Since Congress has provided an express preemption provision in the MDA, we must determine whether the Green's state law tort claims fall within the scope of that provision by imposing requirements in addition to or different from those mandated by the FDA.

In *King v. Collagen Corp.* (a similar case), the plaintiff, Jane King, contracted an auto-immune disease after receiving a test dose of Zyderm. King filed suit against Collagen, the manufacturer, alleging strict liability, breach of warranty of merchantability, negligence....Collagen filed a motion for summary judgment on the basis that the MDA preempted King's claims. The United States District Court for the District of Massachusetts agreed.

The First Circuit Court of Appeals affirmed after finding that (1) the extensive pre-market approval process and the similarly extensive post-approval regulations were indications that the FDA had established specific "requirements" within the meaning of § 360k of the MDA and (2) King's state law tort claims would impose additional or different requirements than those mandated by the FDA, in contravention of § 360k.

In *Stamps v. Collagen Corp* (another similar case), guided by the express language of §360k(a), the Fifth Circuit Court of Appeals determined that Stamps' claims were preempted by federal law because first, the state tort law claims would constitute requirements in addition to or different from the MDA, and, second, these requirements would relate to either the safety or effectiveness of Zyderm and Zyplast. "State tort causes of action-to the extent they relate to safety, effectiveness, or other MDA requirements-constitute requirements 'different from, or in addition to' the Class III process; they are, therefore, preempted."

In the present case, the Greens claim that the district court erred in granting summary judgment on the basis that the MDA preempted their state tort law claims. Here, we are constrained to agree with the rationale in King, and Stamps, and we conclude that a finding in favor of the Greens on any of their alleged state tort law claims would impose additional or different requirements on Collagen, whose product, Zyderm, has already received FDA approval. Such requirements are in conflict with the MDA and thus, the Greens' state law claims are therefore preempted.

REVERSED, In favor of defendants.

1. Critical Thinking: Identify the three main reasons the Superior Court concluded that state law claims were preempted.

2. Ethical Decision-Making: Based on the explanation by Judge Johnson, under what theory of ethics did Congress enact the MDA?

The court's decision in the previous case turned to a great extent on the intent of Congress in passing the legislation that set the standards. Each preemption case requires careful scrutiny of the purpose of the statute, and the opposite result often occurs. For example, in *Tebbetts v. Ford Motor Co.,*[6] the plaintiff alleged that the 1988 Ford Escort was defectively designed because it did not have a driver's side air bag. Ford raised the preemption defense, arguing that it had complied with federal safety regulations under the National Traffic and Motor Vehicle Safety Act (NTMVSA), and that such compliance preempted recovery under state product liability laws. The court analyzed the legislative history of the act, as well as the language of the law itself. Finding a clause in the law that stated that "[c]ompliance with any Federal motor vehicle safety standard issued under this act does not exempt any person from any liability under common law," the court found that Tebbetts was not preempted from bringing the product liability action.

Certain statutory defenses are also available in negligence based product liability cases. To ensure that there will be sufficient evidence from which a trier of fact can make a decision, states have *statutes of limitations* that limit the time within which all types of civil actions may be brought. In most states, the statute of

---

[6] 665 A. 2d 345 (N.H. 1995).

limitations for tort actions, and thus for negligence-based product liability cases, is from one to four years from the date of injury.

Statutes of repose provide an additional statutory defense by barring actions arising more than a specified number of years after the product was purchased. Statutes of repose are usually much longer than statutes of limitations, generally running at least ten years.

From the foregoing discussion of negligence, it is apparent that negligence is a valid theory on which to base a product liability case. However, from a plaintiff's perspective, it offers too many defenses to the manufacturer.

Misrepresentation

A less commonly used theory of liability is misrepresentation. But a consumer who is injured as a result of relying on misrepresentations that were made about the quality of a product may be successful in recovering damages for their injuries under this theory.

To bring a successful product liability case based upon misrepresentation, the consumer must prove that the misrepresentation: (1) was made by a party engaged in the business of selling goods of the kind purchased; (2) was made to the public by advertising, labels, or other similar means; (3) concerned a material fact about the good that caused the injury, and (4) was actually and justifiably relied upon by the consumer.

A case based upon misrepresentation may also be made if the seller actively conceals a defect in the goods. As you might imagine, sellers are rarely going to affirmatively misrepresent a characteristic about a good that would cause harm or actively conceal a defect, so this type of product liability case is rare.

Strict Product Liability

In the 1963 case of *Greenman v. Yuba Power Products Co.*,[7] the Supreme Court of the State of California became the first state to impose strict liability in tort on the manufacturers of defective products. Since that time, strict product liability has become the dominant theory of product liability. The requirements for proving strict product liability can be found in Section 402A of the *Second Restatement of Torts*. This section reads as follows:

(1) One who sells any product in a defective condition, unreasonably dangerous to the user or consumer or his family is subject to liability for

physical harm, thereby, caused to the ultimate user or consumer, or to this property, if

   (a) the seller is engaged in the business of selling such a product, and

   (b) it is expected to and does reach the consumer or user without substantial change in the condition in which it was sold.

(2) The rule stated in Subsection (1) applies although

   (a) the seller has exercised all possible care in the preparation and sale of his product, and

   (b) the user or consumer has not bought the product from or entered into any contractual relation with the seller.

Under this theory, the manufacturer, distributor, or retailer may be held liable to any reasonably foreseeable injured party. Unlike causes of action based on negligence or misrepresentation, which focus on the actions of the manufacturer or seller, actions based on strict product liability focus on the *product*. The degree of care exercised by the defendant is not relevant in these cases. The issue in such cases is whether the product was in a "defective condition, unreasonably dangerous" when sold. To succeed in a strict liability action, the plaintiff must prove that:

1. The product was defective when sold;
2. The defective condition rendered the product unreasonably dangerous; and
3. The product was the cause of the plaintiff's injury.

The most difficult part of the case for the plaintiff to establish is usually the defect. A product may be defective because of: (1) some flaw or abnormality in its construction or marketing that led to its being more dangerous than it otherwise would have been; (2) missing or inadequate instructions or warnings that could have reduced or eliminated foreseeable risks posed by the product; or (3) a design that is defective.

A defect in manufacture or marketing is usually alleged when the product does not meet the manufacturer's specifications. Proof of such a defect is generally provided by (1) experts who testify as to the type of flaw that could have caused the accident that led to the plaintiff's injury and/or (2) evidence of the circumstances surrounding the accident that would lead the jury to infer that the accident must have been caused by a defect in the product. The following case illustrates how circumstances can provide a reasonable basis for such an inference.

---

[7] 59 Cal. 2d 57 (1963).

Case 9-2

Welge

v.

Planters Lifesavers Co.
Court of Appeals for the Seventh Circuit
17 F. 3d 209, 1994 U.S. App. Lexis 3081,
Cch Prod. Liab. Rep. P 13,784 (1994)

*R*ichard Welge, who boarded Karen Godfrey, with G loved to sprinkle peanuts on his ice cream sundaes. Godfrey bought a 24-ounce vacuum-sealed plastic-capped jar of Planters peanuts for him at a K-Mart. To obtain a $2 rebate, Godfrey needed proof of her purchase from the jar of peanuts. So she used an Exacto knife to remove the part of the label that contained the bar code. She then placed the jar on top of the refrigerator for Welge. A week later, Welge removed the plastic seal from the jar, uncapped it, took some peanuts, replaced the cap, and returned the jar to the top of the refrigerator. A week after that, he took down the jar, removed the plastic cap, spilled some peanuts into his left hand to put on his sundae, and replaced the cap with his right hand. As he pushed the cap down on the open jar, it shattered. His hand was severely cut, and became permanently impaired.

Welge filed products liability actions against K-Mart, the seller of the product; Planters, the manufacturer of the product (filled the glass jar with peanuts and sealed and capped it); and Brockway, the manufacturer of the glass jar. Defendants filed a motion for summary judgment after discovery. The district judge granted the motion on the ground that the plaintiff had failed to exclude possible causes of the accident other than a defect introduced during the manufacturing process. The plaintiff appealed.

JUSTICE POSNER

No doubt there are men strong enough to shatter a thick glass jar with one blow. But Welge's testimony stands uncontradicted that he used no more than the normal force that one exerts in snapping a plastic lid onto a jar. So the jar must have been defective. No expert testimony and no fancy doctrine are required for such a conclusion. A nondefective jar does not shatter when normal force is used to clamp its plastic lid on. The question is when the defect was introduced. It could have been at any time from the manufacture of the glass jar by Brockway (for no one suggests that the defect might have been caused by something in the raw materials out of which the jar was made) to moments before the accident. But testimony by Welge and Godfrey…excludes all reasonable possibility that the defect was introduced into the jar after Godfrey plucked it from a shelf in the K-Mart store. From the shelf she put it in her shopping cart. The checker at the check out counter scanned the bar code without banging the jar. She then placed the jar in a plastic bag. Godfrey carried the bag to her car and put it on the floor. She drove directly home, without incident. After the bar code portion of the label was removed, the jar sat on top of the refrigerator except for the two times Welge removed it to take peanuts out of it. Throughout this process it was not, so far as anyone knows, jostled, dropped, bumped, or otherwise subjected to stress beyond what is to be expected in the ordinary use of the product. Chicago is not Los Angeles; there were no earthquakes. Chicago is not Amityville either; no supernatural interventions are alleged. So the defect must have been introduced earlier, when the jar was in the hands of the defendants.

But, they argue, this overlooks two things. One is that Karen Godfrey took a knife to the jar. And no doubt, one can weaken a glass jar with a knife. But nothing is more common or, we should have thought, more harmless than to use a knife or a razor blade to remove a label from a jar or bottle. People do this all the time with the price labels on bottles of wine. Even though mishandling or misuse, by the consumer or by anyone else (other than the defendant itself), is a defense…to a products liability suit…and even if, as we greatly doubt, such normal mutilation as occurred in this case could be thought a species of mishandling or misuse, a defendant cannot defend against a products liability suit on the basis of a misuse that he invited. The Alka-Seltzer promotion to which Karen Godfrey was responding when she removed a portion from the label of the jar of Planters peanuts was in the K-Mart store. It was there, obviously, with K-Mart's permission. By the promotion, K- Mart invited its peanut customers to remove a part of the label on each peanut jar bought, in order to be able to furnish the maker of Alka-Seltzer with proof of purchase. If one just wants to efface a label, one can usually do that by scraping it off with a fingernail, but to remove the label intact requires the use of a knife or a razor blade. Invited misuse is no defense to a products liability claim. Invited misuse is not misuse…

Even so, the defendants point out, it is always possible that the jar was damaged while it was sitting unattended on the top of the refrigerator, in which event they are not responsible. Only if it had been securely under lock and key when not being used could the plaintiff and Karen Godfrey be certain that nothing happened to damage it after she brought it home. That is true-there are no metaphysical certainties-but it leads nowhere. Elves may have played ninepins with the jar of peanuts while Welge and Godfrey were sleeping; but elves could remove a jar of peanuts from a locked cupboard. The plaintiff in a products liability suit is not required to exclude every possibility, however fantastic or remote, that the defect which led to the accident was caused by someone other than one of the defendants. The doctrine of *res ipsa loquitur* teaches that an accident that is unlikely to occur, unless the defendant was negligent, is itself circumstantial evidence that the defendant was negligent. The doctrine is not strictly applicable to a products liability case because, unlike an ordinary accident case, the defendant in a products case has parted with possession and control of the harmful object before the accident occurs.…But the doctrine merely instantiates the broader principle, which is as applicable to a products case as to any other tort case, that an accident can itself be evidence of liability.…If it is the kind of accident that would not have occurred but for a defect in the product, and if it is reasonably plain that the defect was not introduced after the product was sold, the accident is evidence that the product was defective when sold. The second condition (as well as the first) has been established here, at least to a probability sufficient to defeat a motion for summary judgment. Normal people do not lock up their jars and cans lest something happens to damage these containers while no one is looking. The probability of such damage is too remote. It is not only too remote to make a rational person take measures to prevent it; it is too remote to defeat a products liability suit should a container prove dangerously defective.

Of course, unlikely as it may seem that the defect was introduced into the jar after Karen Godfrey bought it, if the plaintiffs' testimony is believed, other evidence might make their testimony unworthy of belief-might even show, contrary to all the probabilities, that the knife or some mysterious night visitor caused the defect after all. The fragments of glass into which the jar shattered were preserved and were examined by experts for both sides. The experts agreed that the jar must have contained a defect, but they could not find the fracture that had precipitated the shattering of the jar, and they could not figure out when the defect that caused the fracture that caused the collapse of the jar had come into being. The defendants' experts could neither rule out, nor rule in, the possibility that the defect had been introduced at some stage of the manufacturing process. The plaintiff's expert noticed what he thought was a preexisting crack in one of the fragments, and he speculated that a similar crack might have caused the fracture that shattered the jar. This, the district judge ruled, was not enough.

But if the probability that the defect which caused the accident arose after Karen Godfrey bought the jar of Planters peanuts is very small-and on the present state of the record we are required to assume that it is-then the probability that the defect was introduced by one of the defendants is very high.

....The strict-liability element in modern products liability law comes precisely from the fact that a seller, subject to that law, is liable for defects in his product even if those defects were introduced, without the slightest fault of his own for failing to discover them, at some anterior stage of production....So the fact that K-Mart sold a defective jar of peanuts to Karen Godfrey would be conclusive of K-Mart's liability, and since it is a large and solvent firm there would be no need for the plaintiff to look further for a tortfeasor. This point seems to have been more or less conceded by the defendants in the district court—the thrust of their defense was that the plaintiff had failed to show that the defect had been caused by any of them.

...Evidence of K-Mart's care in handling peanut jars would be relevant only to whether the defect was introduced after sale; if it was introduced at any time before sale—if the jar was defective when K-Mart sold it—the source of the defect would be irrelevant to K-Mart's liability. In exactly the same way, Planters' liability would be unaffected by the fact, if it is a fact, that the defect was due to Brockway rather than to itself. To repeat an earlier and fundamental point, a seller who is subject to strict products liability is responsible for the consequences of selling a defective product even if the defect was introduced without any fault on his part by his supplier or by his supplier's supplier.

...Here we know to a virtual certainty (always assuming that the plaintiff's evidence is believed, which is a matter for the jury) that the accident was not due to mishandling after purchase, but to a defect that had been introduced earlier.
REVERSED AND REMANDED, IN FAVOR OF THE PLAINTIFF.

1. Critical Thinking: Unlike many other opinions, Justice Posner does not rely on prior case law in his opinion. What are his reasons for reversing the decision? Do you find his reasons compelling?

2. Ethical Decision Making: Suppose the defect had been introduced by Brockway and that corporate management had been aware of the defect, but believed the chances of someone's being hurt were small enough as to be negligible. Therefore, they did not inform Planters of the defect. Should they have informed Planters?

In the previous case, the defect was in the manufacture of the product. It is sometimes more difficult to prove that a design is defective. States are not all in agreement as to how to establish a design defect, and two different tests have evolved to determine when a product is so defective as to be unreasonably dangerous. The first test, set out in the Restatement 2nd of Torts, is the **consumer expectations test**. This test asks the question, did the product meet the standards that would be expected by the reasonable consumer? This test relies on the experiences and expectations of the ordinary consumer, and thus is not answered by the use of expert testimony about the merits of the design.

The second is the **feasible alternatives test**, sometimes referred to as the risk-utility test. In applying this test, the court focuses on the usefulness and safety of the design, and compares it to an alternative design. The exact factors that the court examines are detailed in the following case, which makes explicit the differences between the two tests.

Case 9-3

Sperry-New Holland, A Division of Sperry Corporation

v.

John Paul Prestage and Pam Prestage

Supreme Court of Mississippi

617 So. 2d 248 (1993)

*M*r. Prestage's foot and lower leg were caught in a combine manufactured by defendant-appellant Sperry-New Holland. He and his wife sued defendant for damages arising out of the accident. Their first cause of action was based on the theory of strict product liability. A jury awarded John $1,425,000 for his injuries and Pam $218,750 for loss of consortium (the ability to engage in sexual relations with one's spouse). Defendant appealed.

JUDGE PRATHER

…Two competing theories of strict liability in tort can be extrapolated from our case law. While our older decisions applied a "consumer expectations" analysis in products cases, recent decisions have turned on an analysis under "risk-utility." We today apply a "risk-utility" analysis and write to clarify our reasons for the adoption for that test.

Section 402A is still the law in Mississippi. How this Court defines the phrases "defective conditions" and "unreasonably dangerous" used in 402A dictates whether a "consumer expectations" analysis or a "risk-utility" analysis will prevail. Problems have arisen because our past decisions have been unclear and have been misinterpreted in some instances.

"Consumer Expectations" Analysis

…In a "consumer expectations" analysis, "ordinarily the phrase 'defective condition' means that the article has something wrong with it, that it did not function as expected." Comment g of Section 402A defines "defective condition" as "a condition not contemplated by the ultimate consumer, which will be unreasonable dangerous to him." Thus, in a "consumer expectations" analysis, for a plaintiff to recover, the defect in a product which causes his injuries must not be one which the plaintiff, as an ordinary consumer, would know to be unreasonably dangerous to him. In other words, if the plaintiff, applying the knowledge of an ordinary consumer, sees a danger and can appreciate that danger, then he cannot recover for any injury resulting from that appreciated danger.

"Risk-Utility" Analysis

In a "risk-utility" analysis, a product is "unreasonably dangerous" if a reasonable person would conclude that the danger-in-fact, whether foreseeable or not, outweighs the utility of the product. Thus, even if a plaintiff appreciates the danger of a product, he can still recover for any injury resulting from the danger, provided that the utility of the product is outweighed by the danger that the product creates. Under the "risk-utility" test, either the judge or the jury can balance the utility and danger-in-fact, or risk, of the product.

A "risk-utility" analysis best protects both the manufacturer and the consumer. It does not create a duty on the manufacturer to create a completely safe product. Creating such a product is often impossible or prohibitively expensive. Instead, a manufacturer is charged with the duty to make its product reasonably safe, regardless of whether the plaintiff is aware of the product's dangerousness....In balancing the utility of the product against the risk it creates, an ordinary person's ability to avoid the danger by exercising care is also weighed.

Having here reiterated this Court's adoption of a "risk-utility" analysis for products liability cases, we hold, necessarily, that the "patent danger" bar is no longer applicable in Mississippi. Under a "risk-utility" analysis, the "patent danger" rule does not apply. In "risk-utility," the openness and obviousness of a product's design is simply a factor to consider in determining whether a product is unreasonably dangerous.

There is sufficient evidence to show that Prestage tried his case under a "risk-utility" analysis. It is also clear from the record that the trial court understood "risk-utility" to be the law in Mississippi and applied that test correctly.

AFFIRMED, IN FAVOR OF PLAINTIFF.

1. Critical Thinking: Why was the risk-utility test viewed as the best method of evaluating this case?

2. Ethical Decision Making: The risk-utility test allows products to pose a danger to consumers so long as they are reasonably safe. Under which ethical theory would producing such a product be ethical? Under which theory would such production not be ethical?

Impact of the Restatement 3rd of Torts

Section 402A of the Restatement of Torts 2nd is generally the foundation of modern product liability law. But that section has been subject to considerable criticism. And those criticisms led, in 1997, to the adoption of the American Law Institute's "Restatement of the Law (3rd), Torts: Product Liability", which is intended to replace Section 402A.

Under the Restatement (3rd), "[O]ne engaged in the business of selling or otherwise distributing products who sells or distributes a defective product is subject to liability for harm to persons or property caused by the defect." The section departs from the Restatement (2d) by holding the seller to a different standard of liability, depending on whether the defect in question is a manufacturing defect, a design defect, or a defective warning.

It is only a manufacturing defect that results in strict liability. A manufacturing defect arises when "the product departs from its intended design," and liability is imposed regardless of the care taken by the manufacturer.

The Restatement (3rd) applies a reasonableness standard to design defects, stating, "a product is defective in design when the foreseeable risks of the harm posed by the product could have been reduced or avoided by the adoption of a reasonable alternative design by the seller...and the omission of the alternative design renders the product not reasonably safe." Comments in the Restatement (3rd) list a number of factors the court can use to determine whether a reasonable alternative design renders the product not reasonably safe, including: "the magnitude and probability of the foreseeable risks of harm, the instructions and warnings accompanying the product, and the nature and strength of consumer expectations regarding the product, including expectations arising from product portrayal and marketing...the relative advantage and disadvantages of the product as designed and as it alternatively could have been designed...the likely effects of the alternative design on product longevity, maintenance, repair and esthetics, and the range of consumer choice among products..." Thus, the Restatement (3rd) has in effect shifted to a risk-utility test.

The Restatement (3rd) has likewise adopted a reasonableness standard for defective warnings. "A product is defective because of inadequate instructions or warnings when the foreseeable risks of harm posed by the product could have been reduced or avoided by the provision of reasonable instructions or warnings by the seller...and the omission of the warnings renders the product not reasonably safe."

The potential effects of changes brought about by the newest Restatement have yet to be fully felt. As of 2001, the Restatement (3d) had not been widely adopted.

Liability to Bystanders

We have been looking thus far at liability to those who are in lawful possession of the defective product. The question arises as to whether strict product liability can be used by someone other than the owner or user of the product. Note that in the case described in the beginning of this chapter, Donna Bailey was a passenger in the car and therefore a bystander. The following case provides the rationale of one court that chose to allow recovery by a bystander.

Case 9-4

James A. Peterson, Adm'r of the Estate of Maradean Peterson, et al.

v.

Lou Backrodt Chevrolet Co.,
Appellate Court of Illinois
307 N.E. 2d 729 (1974)

*D*efendant Lou Backrodt Chevrolet sold an automobile with a defective brake system. The defective brakes failed, causing the driver to strike two minors, killing one and injuring the other. The deceased minor's estate brought this product liability action against the seller of the defective automobile. The trial court dismissed the action against the defendant on the grounds that bystanders did not have a cause of action. The plaintiff appealed.

JUSTICE GUILD

The question of whether a bystander can employ the doctrine of strict liability in a lawsuit has been thoroughly considered by reviewing courts and legal commentators. These authorities indicate that permitting the bystander to maintain an action based on strict tort liability is the more enlightened approach. This has been the result when this issue has been considered in light of Illinois law.

The rationale behind this result is best expressed by this statement of the California Supreme court in *Elmore v. American Motors Corp.*

"If anything, bystanders should be entitled to greater protection than the consumer or user where injury to bystanders from the defect is reasonably foreseeable. Consumer and users, at least, have the opportunity to inspect for defects and to limit their purchases to articles manufactured by reputable manufacturers and sold by reputable retailers, whereas the bystander ordinarily has no such opportunities. In short, the bystander is in greater need of protection from defective products which are dangerous, and if any distinction should be made between bystanders and users, it should be made…to extend greater liability in favor of the bystanders.

…[T]he doctrine of strict liability in tort is available in an action for personal injuries by a bystander against the manufacturer and the retailer."

We agree with the California Supreme Court's cogent reasoning and hold that it is equally applicable when directed to those in the business of selling used cars.

REVERSED AND REMANDED, IN FAVOR OF PLAINTIFF.

1. Critical Thinking: What reason does the California court give for affording bystanders more protection? Do you find this reason compelling? Why or why not?

2. Ethical Decision Making: Might Lou Backrodt Chevrolet have acted differently in withholding information about the brakes if the corporation had applied the Golden Rule test to its actions?

Defenses to a Strict Product Liability Action

Most of the defenses to a negligence-based product liability claim are available in a strict product liability case. These defenses include product misuse, assumption of the risk, and the lapse of time under statutes of limitations and statutes of repose.

One defense that may not be available in all states, however, is the state-of-the-art defense. Courts have rejected the use of this defense in most strict liability cases, reasoning that the issue in such cases is not what the producers knew at the time the product was produced, but whether the product was defective, and whether the defect caused it to be unreasonably dangerous. For example, the Supreme Court of Missouri, in a case involving an asbestos claim, said that the state of the art has no bearing on the outcome of a strict liability claim because the issue is the defective condition of the product, not the manufacturer's knowledge, negligence, or fault.[8]

The refusal of most courts to allow the state-of-the-art defense in strict liability cases is consistent with the social policy reasons for imposing strict liability. A reason for imposing strict liability is that the manufacturers or producers are best able to spread the cost of the risk; this risk-spreading function does not change with the availability of scientific knowledge. The counterargument is that if the manufacturer has indeed done everything as safely and carefully as available data allows, it seems unfair to impose liability on the defendant. After all, how else could they have manufactured the product?

Market Share Liability

In most cases, the plaintiff knows who produced the defective product that caused the injury at issue. Sometimes, however, injuries resulting from defective products begin showing up decades after exposure to the product. By this time, plaintiffs cannot trace the product to any particular manufacturer. Often, a number of manufacturers produced the same product, and the plaintiff would have no idea whose product had been used. A plaintiff may have even used more than one manufacturer's product.

Prior to the 1980's, plaintiffs in this situation would have been unable to recovery for their injuries. However, recovery may be possible today because of the *market share theory*, created by the California Supreme Court in the case of *Sindell v. Abbott Laboratories*.[9]

In the Sindell case, the plaintiffs' mothers had all taken a drug known as diethylstibestrol (DES) during pregnancies that had occurred before the drug was banned in 1973. Because the drug had been produced twenty years before the plaintiffs suffered any effects from the drug their mothers had taken, it was impossible to trace the defective drug back to each manufacturer who had produced the drug causing each individual's problems. To balance the competing interests of the victims who had suffered injury from the drug, and the defendants, who did not want to be held liable for a drug they did not produce, the court allowed the plaintiffs to sue all of the manufacturers who had produced the drug at the time that the plaintiffs' mothers had used the drug. Then the judge apportioned liability among the defendant-manufacturers based upon the share of the market they had held at the time that the drug had been produced.

This theory has since been used by some other courts, primarily in drug cases. Courts using the theory generally require the plaintiffs to prove: (1) all defendants are tortfeasors; (2) the allegedly harmful products are identical and share the same defective qualities; (3) plaintiff is unable to identify which defendant caused her injury through no fault of her own; and (4) the manufacturers of substantially all of the defective products in the relevant area and during the relevant time are named as defendants.[10]

Some states have modified this approach. Others have adopted modifications of this theory. At least one court has held[11] that the plaintiff need sue only one maker of the allegedly defective drug. If the plaintiff can prove that the defendant manufactured a drug of the type taken by the plaintiff's mother at the time of the mother's pregnancy, that defendant can be held liable for all damages. However, the defendant may join other defendants and the jury may apportion liability among all defendants.

While the utility of this theory for drug cases is evident, plaintiffs have also not been very successful in extending the theory to products other than drugs. For example, in 2001, plaintiffs who were unable to identify the maker of the guns that were used to kill their family members were unsuccessful in their attempt to sue a group of manufacturers for negligent marketing under the theory of market share liability.[12] Thus it appears to be a theory of limited utility.

---

[8] 673 S.W. 2d 434 (MO. 1984).
[9] 607 P. 2d 924 (1980).

[10] *Erlich v. Abbott Lab.*, 5 Phila. 249 (1981).
[11] 342 N.W. 2d 37 (Sic. 1984).
[12] *Hamilton v. Beretta,*

Liability of Accountants & Other Professionals

Just as the manufacturers and sellers of defective products may be liable for harm caused by their products, professionals who provide substandard services may likewise be liable for the harm they cause. Actions brought against attorneys, lawyers, real estate brokers, doctors, architects, and other professionals are referred to as **malpractice** actions. Just as product liability cases are based on different legal theories, so are malpractice actions. Most malpractice cases are based upon theories of negligence, breach of contract, or fraud.

The professional whose malpractice most businesspersons are most likely to encounter is the accountant, and so we will focus on accountant's liability. Prior to February of 2002, most people had probably not given much thought to questions about the extent to which accountants should be held liable for their failure to properly perform their professional responsibilities. However, after a significant amount of the responsibility for the bankruptcy of the Enron Corporation was placed on the firms who provided accounting services for the corporation, the role of these professionals and their accountability became a question of significant public interest.

Liability Based on Breach of Contract

About half the states allow lawsuits against an accountant based on breach of contract. In a breach of contract claim, the plaintiff may assert that the accountant failed to comply with the terms of the contract and perform the agreed upon tasks within the agreed upon time frame. The defendant would then be liable for the provable, foreseeable damages that resulted from the professional's failure to uphold the terms of the contract.

Negligence

An accountant is liable to his/her client for negligence if he/she fails to exercise the care of a competent, reasonable professional when that failure causes loss or injury to the client. To prove negligence on the part of the accountant, the plaintiff establishes the basic elements of negligence as discussed in Chapter 8: duty, breach of duty, causation, and damages.

At minimum, the duty of care of the accountant entails compliance with Generally Accepted

Accounting Principles (GAAP), established by the Financial Accounting Standards Board (FASB), and the Generally Accepted Auditing Standards (GAAS), established by the American Institute of Certified Public Accountants (AICPA). While failure to comply with GAAP and GAAS will almost certainly constitute a breach of duty, compliance does not automatically mean that the duty of care has been met. In some circumstances, a reasonable, competent accountant would do more than GAAS or GAAP require.

Generally, unless engaged to do so, an accountant is not a fraud detector unless fraud would be uncovered by the exercise of reasonable care and skill. An accountant is, likewise, not required to have perfect judgment, and will not be held liable simply for errors in judgment that were made in good faith, while operating in accordance with GAAS and GAAP.

An important issue in accountant's liability that has not been decided in the same way by all states, is whether third parties have any claim against the accountant based on their reliance on negligently prepared financial statements. This issue was the focus of the most famous case involving accountant legal liability, *Ultramares v. Touche*.[13]

In that case, Justice Benjamin Cardozo, writing for the highest state court in New York, took a narrow view of what third parties were permissible plaintiffs. Because of concern that a more liberal rule would subject accountants to a liability of, "an indeterminate amount, for an indeterminate time, to an indeterminate class" Cardozo held an accountant liable in negligence only to those with whom they had privity of contract, meaning the client and anyone for whose "primary benefit" the accounting statements were prepared. The New York courts have fundamentally continued the *Ultramares* approach by requiring that the accountant be aware of the particular use for their work product, that there be known reliance on the work product by an identified third party, and that there be conduct by the accountant recognizing their awareness of such reliance. This has been referred to as the "near-privity" or "primary benefit" test and only a few states utilize it because it is viewed as too restrictive.

About half the states have adopted a somewhat more expansive approach to accountant liability for negligence to third parties. This test is referred to as the "Restatement" test. It holds an accountant liable to known third party users of the accountant's work product and also to those in the limited class whose reliance on the work was specifically foreseen by the accountant.

For example, assume a client has an accountant certify financial statements as part of a loan application of Third State Bank. The accountant, who is aware of this purpose, negligently audits the statements, which overvalue inventory and undervalue liabilities. The client not only uses the financials at Third State Bank but also uses them in a loan application at Federal State Bank, which makes the loan. When the client defaults on the loan because of too much indebtedness, Federal State can properly sue the accountant for negligence because the bank's use of the financial statements for loan considerations was foreseen, even if the specific institution was not. The Restatement test requires that the user be specifically known to the accountant or be of the limited class of foreseen users who utilize the accountant's work product in the contemplated manner. It is viewed as a "middle ground" test between the very restrictive, pro-accountant primary benefit test represented by *Ultramares* and the liability expanding "reasonably foreseeable users" test discussed next.

Very few states have adopted a general negligence standard of third party liability for accountants called the "reasonably foreseeable user" test. It holds an accountant liable to any third party that was or should have been foreseen as a possible user of the accountant's work product and who, in fact, did use and rely on that work product for a proper business purpose. The justification for this expanded accountant liability was succinctly stated by the New Jersey Supreme Court in a case subsequently overruled by statute:

"The responsibility of a public accountant is not only to the client who pays his fee, but also to investors, creditors, and others who may rely on the financial statements which he certifies…The auditor's function has expanded from that of a watchdog for management to an independent evaluator of the adequacy and fairness of financial statements issued by management to stockholders, creditors and others."[14]

The court justified its protection of reasonably foreseeable users on the policy grounds that it would encourage accountants to be more careful and thorough and that the cost of the increased liability risk, through insurance or otherwise, could be spread among all the accountant's clients. Courts used similar reasoning as justification for imposing strict product liability.

The *Bily* decision excerpted below contains some very good discussions of the three theories of the accountant's legal liability to third parties.

---

[13] 174 N.E. 441 (1931).

[14] *Rosenbloom, Inc. v Adler*, 461 A. 2d 138 (1983).

Case 9-5

Bily (Plaintiff/Respondent)
v.
Arthur Young & Company
(Defendant/Appellant)
Supreme Court of California
834 P. 24, 745 (1992)

*P*laintiffs purchased stock warrants (rights to purchase) for blocks of stock of Osborne Computer Corp., the manufacturer of the first mass market portable personal computer. Because of an inability to produce a new product line with sufficient speed and the entry of IBM-compatible software into the personal computer market, Osborne filed for bankruptcy shortly after the warrants were issued. Plaintiffs, thus, received nothing for their investment.

Arthur Young had audited Osborne's financial statements for the two years preceding the issuance of the warrants and had issued unqualified opinions on their fairness and compliance with Generally Accepted Accounting Principles. Plaintiffs sued Arthur Young for fraud, negligence, and negligent misrepresentation. After a thirteen week trial in which the plaintiff's expert witness alleged forty deficiencies in Arthur Young's audit and its noncompliance with Generally Accepted Auditing Standards the jury found Arthur Young liable for professional negligence. Arthur Young appealed based on the jury instructions regarding its liability to third parties.

CHIEF JUSTICE LUCAS

The AICPA's professional standards refer to the public responsibility of auditors: "A distinguishing mark of a profession is acceptance of its responsibility to the public. The accounting profession's public consists of clients, credit grantors, governments, employers, investors, the business and financial community, and others who rely on the objectivity and integrity of certified public accountants to maintain the orderly functioning of commerce. This reliance imposes a public interest responsibility on certified public accountants." (2 AICPA Professional Standards (CCH 1988) § 53.01.)

[The Court then discussed different state's approaches to the issue of accountant liability to third parties.]

A. *Privity of Relationship*

The New York Court of Appeals restated the law in light of *Ultramares, White v. Guarente*, and other cases in *Credit Alliance v. Arthur Andersen & Co.* (1985) 65 N.Y. 2d 536 [493 N.Y.S. 2d 435, 483 N.E. 2d 110]. *Credit Alliance* subsumed two cases with different factual postures: in the first case, plaintiff alleged it loaned funds to the auditor's client in reliance on audited financial statements which overstated the client's assets and net worth; in the second, the same scenario occurred, but plaintiff also alleged the auditor knew plaintiff was the client's principal lender and communicated directly and frequently with plaintiff regarding its continuing audit reports. The court dismissed plaintiff's negligence claim in the first case, but sustained the claim in the second.

The New York court promulgated the following rule for determining auditor liability to third parties for negligence: "Before accountants may be held liable in negligence to noncontractual parties who rely to their detriment on inaccurate financial reports, certain prerequisites must be satisfied: (1) the accountant must have been aware that the financial reports were to be used for a particular purpose or purposes; (2) in the furtherance of which a known party or parties was intended to rely; and (3) there must have been some conduct on the part of the accountants linking them to that party or parties, which evinces the accountants' understanding of that party or parties' reliance." *Credit Alliance v. Arthur Andersen & Co.*, supra, 483 N.E. 2d at p. 118.)

Discussing the application of its rule to the cases at hand, the court observed the primary, if not exclusive, "end and aim" of the audits in the second case was to satisfy the lender. The auditor's "direct communications and personal meetings [with the lender] result[ed] in a nexus between them sufficiently approaching privity. In contrast, in the first case, although the complaint did allege the auditor knew or should have known of the lender's reliance on its reports: "There was no allegation of either a particular purpose for the reports' preparation or the prerequisite conduct on the part of the accountants. . . [nor] any allegation [the auditor] had any direct dealings with plaintiffs, and agreed with [the client] to prepare the report for plaintiffs' use or according to plaintiffs' requirements, or had specifically agreed with [the client] to provide plaintiffs with a copy [of the report] or actually did so."

B. *Foreseeability*

Arguing that accountants should be subject to liability to third persons on the same basis as other tortfeasors, Justice Howard Wiener advocated rejection of the rule of *Ultramares* in a 1983 law review article. In its place, he proposed a rule based on foreseeability of injury to third persons. Criticizing what he called the "anachronistic protection" given to accountants by the traditional rules limiting third person liability, he concluded: "Accountant liability based on foreseeable injury would serve the dual functions of compensation for injury and deterrence of negligent conduct. Moreover, it is a just and rational judicial policy that the same criteria govern the imposition of negligence liability, regardless of the context in which it arises. The accountant, the investor, and the general public will in the long run benefit when the liability of the certified public accountant for negligent misrepresentation is measured by the foreseeability standard." Under the rule proposed by Justice Wiener, "[f]oreseeability of the risk would be a question of fact for the jury to be disturbed on appeal only where there is insufficient evidence to support the finding."

C. *The Restatement: Intent to Benefit Third Persons*

Section 552 of the Restatement Second of Torts covers "Information Negligently Supplied for the Guidance of Others." It states a general principle that one who negligently supplies false information "for the guidance of others in their business transactions" is liable for economic loss suffered by the recipients in justifiable reliance on the information. But the liability created by the general principle is expressly limited to loss suffered: "(a) [B]y the person or one of a limited group of persons for whose benefit and guidance he intends to supply the information or knows that the recipient intends to supply it; and (b) through reliance upon it in a transaction that he intends the information to influence or knows that the recipient so intends or in a substantially similar transaction." To paraphrase, a supplier of information is liable for negligence to a third party only if he or she intends to supply the information for the benefit of one or more third parties in a specific transaction or type of transaction identified to the supplier.

The authors of the Restatement Second of Torts offer several variations on the problem before us as illustrations of section 552. For example, the auditor may be held liable to a third party lender if the auditor is informed by the client that the audit will be used to obtain a $50,000 loan, even if the specific lender remains unnamed or the client names one lender and then borrows from another. However, there is no liability where the auditor agrees to conduct the audit with the express understanding the report will be transmitted only to a specified bank and it is then transmitted to other lenders. Similarly, there is no liability when the client's transaction (as represented to the auditor) changes so as to increase materially the audit risk, e.g., a third person originally considers selling goods to the client on credit and later buys a controlling interest in the client's stock, both in reliance on the auditor's report.

Under the Restatement rule, an auditor retained to conduct an annual audit and to furnish an opinion for no particular purpose generally undertakes no duty to third parties. Such an auditor is not informed "of any intended use of the financial statements; but…knows that the financial statements, accompanied by an auditor's opinion, are customarily used in a wide variety of financial transactions by the [client] corporation and that they may be relied upon by lenders, investors, shareholders, creditors, purchasers and the like, in numerous possible kinds of transactions. [The client corporation] uses the financial statements and accompanying auditor's opinion to obtain a loan from [a particular] bank. Because of [the auditor's] negligence, he issues an unqualifiedly favorable opinion upon a balance sheet that materially misstates the financial position of [the corporation] and through reliance upon it [the bank] suffers pecuniary loss." Consistent with the text of section 552, the authors conclude: "[The auditor] is not liable to [the bank]."

Analysis of Auditor's Liability to Third Persons for Audit Opinions
A. Negligence
In permitting negligence liability to be imposed in the absence of privity, we outlined the factors to be considered in making such a decision: "The determination whether in a specific case the defendant will be held liable to a third person not in privity is a matter of policy and involves the balancing of various factors, among which are the extent to which the transaction was intended to affect the plaintiff, the foreseeability of harm to him, the degree of certainty that the plaintiff suffered injury, the closeness of the connection between the defendant's conduct and the injury suffered, the moral blame attached to the defendant's conduct, and the policy of preventing future harm.

Viewing the problem before us in light of the factors set forth above, we decline to permit all merely foreseeable third party users of audit reports to sue the auditor on a theory of professional negligence. Our holding is premised on three central concerns: (1) Given the secondary "watchdog" role of the auditor, the complexity of the professional opinions rendered in audit reports, and the difficult and potentially tenuous causal relationships between audit reports and economic losses from investment and credit decision, the auditor exposed to negligence claims from all foreseeable third parties faces potential liability far out of proportion to its fault; (2) the generally more sophisticated class of plaintiffs in auditor liability cases (e.g., business lenders and investors) permits the effective use of contract rather than tort liability to control and adjust the relevant risks through "private ordering"; and (3) the asserted advantages of more accurate auditing and more efficient loss spreading relied upon by those who advocate a pure foreseeability approach are unlikely to occur; indeed, dislocations of resources, including increased expense and decreased availability of auditing services in some sectors of the economy, are more probable consequences of expanded liability.

For the reasons stated above, we hold that an auditor's liability for general negligence in the conduct of an audit of its client's financial statements is confined to the client, i.e., the person who contracts for or engages the audit services. Other persons may not recover on a pure negligence theory.

There is, however, a further narrow class of persons who, although not clients, may reasonably come to receive and rely on an audit reports and whose existence constitutes a risk of audit reporting that may fairly be imposed on the auditor. Such persons are specifically intended beneficiaries of the audit report who are known to the auditor and for whose benefit it renders the audit report. While such persons may not recover on a general negligence theory, we hold they may, for the reasons stated in part IV(B) post, recover on a theory of negligent misrepresentation.

1. Critical Thinking: If you were a justice sitting on the supreme court of a state that had yet to decide which of the three rules to follow in determining the extent of liability of auditors to third parties, which of the rules would you adopt? Why?

2. Ethical Decision Making: Which stakeholders would primarily benefit from each of the three alternatives?

Defenses To Negligence

When sued for negligence, the accountant can raise the same defenses that one would raise in any negligence claim. First, defendant could argue that any of the elements of negligence were not proven by the plaintiff. Alternatively, the defendant could raise either the defense of contributory or comparative negligence, depending on which of those defenses is accepted in the state where the suit is filed. Finally, an auditor may be able to escape liability if the basis for the action is an opinion letter that had been qualified or contained a disclaimer. When an opinion contains a specific disclaimer or qualifier, whatever is qualified or disclaimed cannot be the basis for holding the auditor liable. For example, if an opinion is qualified by a statement that there is uncertainty about the outcome of litigation in which the firm is involved, the auditor will not be held liable when it turns out that the firm's net worth is significantly lower because the losses from the lawsuit end up being substantial.

Fraud

Cases of common law fraud against accountants are less common than negligence suits because fraud cases require proof that the accountant acted with an intention to deceive. This intention to deceive is called "scienter." In addition to these instances of so-called actual fraud, accountants can also be liable for fraud if they act recklessly. Recklessness involves more than mere negligence but does not require intent. It could be described as deliberate indifference or carelessness. Reckless conduct is said to constitute constructive fraud. While courts are split on who may be a proper plaintiff in a case of alleged negligence by an accountant, there is a fairly high degree of uniformity that in cases of actual or constructive fraud, an accountant is liable to any foreseeable user of the accountant's work product that is injured by the accountant's conduct. This more expansive view of potential liability is reflective of the greater blameworthiness attached to the accountant's behavior.

Often a claim of fraud will be combined with other claims. For example, in conjunction with the Enron bankruptcy case, Connecticut attorney general Richard Blumenthal brought suit against Enron's accountant, Arthur Andersen, arguing that because Andersen failed to address Enron's hiding debt, the accounting firm was responsible for Connecticut Resources Recovery Authority's $220 million loss in a deal with Enron. Blumenthal's lawsuit accuses Andersen of fraud, negligence, and recklessness, stating that the Connecticut Resources Recovery Authority relied on the misrepresentations of Enron's financial condition. Because Andersen failed to remedy Enron's serious misrepresentation of its financial condition, Blumenthal argues that Andersen is liable for damages to his client.

Liability of Accountants Under the Federal Securities Laws

In addition to being held liable like other professionals under the theories of breach of contract, negligence, and fraud, accountants face the additional possibility of being found liable under the federal securities laws, the Securities Act of 1933 and the Securities Exchange Act of 1934. These laws, discussed in detail in Chapter 40, were enacted to protect the investing public. The chosen method of protection is to require companies to disclose all relevant information about the company and its securities to the potential buyer so they can assess its merits. Companies are also required to file periodic reports with the Securities and Exchange Commission (SEC) so that current, relevant information about the company and its issued securities are available to potential buyers and sellers of those securities. An important component of the disclosed information under both the '33 and '34 Acts are audited financial statements. Inaccuracies in those statements create potential liabilities for the attesting accountant. Liability under these acts is discussed in greater detail in Chapter 40.

Ford and Bridgestone/Firestone Wrap-Up

Donna Bailey settled her case, with one of the stipulations being public disclosure of the documents involved with the Ford and Bridgestone/Firestone investigations. Any information from tire recalls will have to be publicly disclosed as part of her settlement. By now, much of the personal injury litigation has been settled by the companies. However, the ramifications of product liability continue to be felt. In May 2001, Ford announced that it was recalling even more Firestone tires, including those that were given to customers as replacements during the previous recall. Ford's CEO said that Ford did not have "enough confidence in the future performance" of the tires to continue to use the tires on Ford vehicles. Bridgestone/Firestone's CEO disputed the claim, noting that the real problem was with the safety of the Ford Explorer. The replacements will cost Ford about $3 billion and has prompted further Congressional investigations of Bridgestone/Firestone and Ford.

One day before Ford made its announcement, Bridgestone/Firestone announced that they will no longer sell tires to Ford. This leaves Bridgestone/Firestone free to call into question the safety of the Ford Explorer, without fear of losing Ford as a customer. Soon after the announcement, Bridgestone/Firestone released evidence from Venezuela that Ford Explorers,

equipped with Goodyear tires, had rolled over in that country. The last of this story has probably not been heard, with several investigations pending.[15]

---

[15] Sources: MSNBC Staff and Wire Reporters, *"Settlement Reached in Lawsuit Against Ford and Bridgestone/Firestone,"* FIRESTONE TIRES: IN THE NEWS, January 8, 2001, <http://www.elslaw.com/firestone_news_settlement.htm> (May 23, 2001); Keith Bradsher, *Ford Intends to Replace 13 Million Firestone Wilderness Tires,* THE NEW YORK TIMES, May 23, 2001.

	Summary
Theories of Recovery in Product Liability Cases	**Negligence** is proven by establishing four elements: 1. duty of care; 2. breach of said duty; 3. breach caused injury to plaintiff; and 4. plaintiff has actual, compensable injury. Common negligent acts leading to liability include: **Negligent failure to warn**—defendant knew product was dangerous and failed to warn plaintiff accordingly. **Negligent design**—risk of harm outweighs the utility of the product as designed. Defenses to negligence include: **Contributory negligence**—no recovery for plaintiff. **Pure comparative negligence**—recover portion of harm attributable to defendant's negligence. **Modified comparative**—recover percentage of harm so long as plaintiff's negligence is less than 50%. **Assumption of risk**—voluntary encounter with risk by plaintiff. **Product misuse**—harm not caused by defendant's negligence, but by the plaintiff's misuse of the product. **State-of-the-art defense**—negligence was reasonable given state of knowledge at that time **Misrepresentation** requires the following elements: 1. misrepresentation made by party engaged in selling of good; 2. made to public; 3. concerned a material fact about the product; and 3. actually relied upon by customer. **Strict product liability** requires the following elements: 1. product was defective when sold; 2. defective condition rendered product unreasonably dangerous; and 3. product caused the injury to plaintiff.

Summary (continued)	
Theories of Recovery in Product Liability Cases (continued)	The tests for defective condition are: **Consumer expectations rest**—Did the product meet the standards that would be expected by the reasonable consumer? **Feasible alternatives rest** —Danger-in-fact outweighs the utility of the product. **Bystander liability**—Bystander is justified in receiving damages. Defenses to strict product liability: 1. Product misuse. 2. Assumption of risk. 3. State-of-the-art defense—probably will not be allowed.
Market Share Liability	**Market Share Theory**—allows plaintiffs to recover for damages from product with uncertain manufacturer by splitting damages among producers based on their market share at time of production.

Review Questions and Case Problems

1. Explain what privity is and what impact it had on the development of product liability law.

2. Explain the elements one would have to prove to bring a successful product liability case based on negligence.

3. Explain the defenses one can raise in a product liability case based on negligence.

4. Why would a defendant rather be found to have produced a product that was defectively manufactured rather than defectively designed?

5. How does the consumer expectations test differ from the feasible alternatives test?

6. Explain the defenses available in a case based on a theory of strict product liability.

7. Boutte fell asleep at the wheel while driving his car, struck a cement wall, and broke both of his ankles. He sued Nissan Motor Corp. alleging that the improper placement of the lap belt constituted negligent design. In testimony, the plaintiff's expert explained that a proper seat belt is positioned over the pelvis. Boutte's seat belt was positioned over his thighs, and the improper placement allowed him to slide forward and injure his ankles. The expert also explained that a passive restraint system, which was used by other manufacturers, would have kept the lap belt in the correct position. The expert for the manufacturer disagreed and argued that even with a passive restraint system Boutte would have sustained the same injuries. Initially, the jury attributed 84% of the fault to the plaintiff. On appeal, the defendants argued that Boutte's injuries were not a result of the seat belt placement and argued that the plaintiff's expert testimony should not have been considered in the trial court. How do you think the appellate court ruled in this case and why? *Boutte v.*

Nissan Motor Corp., 3d Cir. (1995) 48 ALR 5th 86.

8. Douglas Martin had been drinking when he went to see his friend Marcel Nadeau. As the two were leaving to get more beer, Martin saw Nadeau's .38 Colt Mustang pistol. Nadeau removed the magazine and handed the gun to Martin. Nadeau turned away briefly, and when he turned back around, Martin had the gun in his hand, pointed toward his head. Nadeau heard the gun discharge; Martin died not long after. Valerie-Ann Bolduc, acting as administrator of Martin's estate, sued Colt's Manufacturing Company, Inc., for negligent design. In Massachusetts, for a plaintiff to prevail in a negligent design case, she must show both that the defendant failed to exercise reasonable care to eliminate avoidable or foreseeable dangers to the user, and that there is a functional alternative design that would reduce the product's risk. Bolduc alleged that neither Martin nor Nadeau knew that the gun would fire with the magazine removed. She also alleged that there is an alternative design that includes a feature to stop the gun from firing when the magazine is disconnected. Thus, it appears that Bolduc satisfied both prongs of the Massachusetts test. Yet the District Court ruled that Bolduc could not prevail on the claim and dismissed the case. What are possible reasons the District Court used to find that Colt had not negligently designed the product? *Valerie-Ann Bolduc v. Colt's Manufacturing Company, Inc.*, 968 F. Supp. 16 (1997).

9. National Fulfillment Services was a tenant in an office building owned by Holmes Corporate Center. A fire in the building on February 4, 1992, damaged National Fulfillment's offices. National Fulfillment filed suit against the providers of fire and burglar alarm services, referred to as ADT, to recover uninsured losses. Among other claims, National Fulfillment alleged strict liability and negligence, claiming that ADT's alarm failed to alert fire fighters in a timely manner; thus, more damage was sustained than National Fulfillment had insurance for. ADT noted that

its contract was with Holmes Corporate Center, not with National Fulfillment, and that Holmes had a duty to defend ADT against any lawsuit filed by a nonparty to the agreement. The District Court granted summary judgment for ADT. National Fulfillment appealed. Did the Court of Appeals grant National Fulfillment's claims of strict liability and negligence, or did it affirm the decision of the District Court? Why? *Krueger Associates, Inc., Individually and Trading as National Fulfillment Services v. The American District Telegraph Company of Pennsylvania and ADT Security Systems, Inc.*, 247 F. 3d 61 (2001).

10. Finley, an office worker, sued NCR Corporation after she developed carpal tunnel syndrome. Arguing that the defectively designed keyboard caused her injury, Finley claimed that NCR had a duty to warn her about the possibility of carpal tunnel syndrome. The defendants argued that carpal tunnel syndrome is developed through overuse and depends on personal characteristics, not the characteristics of the keyboard. Further, NCR claimed that they did not have a duty to warn since a computer keyboard is safe for its intended use without a warning. The court granted the defendant's request for summary judgment. Do you think NCR was negligent in failing to provide an adequate warning about carpal tunnel syndrome? Why or why not? *Finley v. NCR Corp.*, 964 F. Supp. 882 (1996) 59 ALR 5th 479.

11. Plaintiff's son was given St. Joseph's Aspirin for Children when he had the flu. The aspirin triggered Reye's Syndrome, leaving the child a quadriplegic, blind, and mentally retarded. The aspirin contained a warning, approved by the food and Drug Administration, about the dangers of giving aspirin to children with the flu. The product was advertised in Spanish in the Los Angeles area, but the warning was not in Spanish. The child's guardians could not read English. Do you believe the court imposed liability on the company for failure of their duty to warn? Why or why not? *Ramirez v. Plough, Inc.*, 25 Cal Rptr. 2d (1993).

12. Plaintiff Darren Traub was playing basketball and tried to dunk the ball. Trying to execute the dunk, his hand hit the rim, and he fell down and hurt both wrists. He sued the manufacturer and the university, claiming that the rigid rim caused his injury or made it worse. The defendants filed a motion for summary judgment. Do you think it should have been granted? *Traub v. Cornell*, 1998 WL 187401 (N.D. N.Y.) (1998).

13. In 1991, three-year-old Douglas Moore was playing with one of BIC's lighters. While playing with the lighter, he started a fire that severely injured his seventeen month-old brother. BIC Manufacturers Inc. placed several child-safety warning labels on their lighters. These labels identified the risk of fire or injury as a result of misusing the product. The lighter provided warnings to adults to "keep out of reach of children" or "Keep away from children." The BIC corporation had knowledge that their lighters could be manipulated by children, but felt to include safety features would significantly increase the cost of the lighter. The Moore family brought a strict liability suit against BIC. Explain why or why not strict liability

should be applicable in this case. *Price v. BIC Corp.*, 702 A. 2d 330 (Sup. Ct., N.H. 1997).

14. Mr. Claude Swope was employed by Columbian Chemical Company as a maintenance worker. Columbian produced a product that required the use of ozone in its manufacturing. For this manufacturing Columbian used ozone generators purchased from Emory Inc. Mr. Swope brought a product liability suit against these two companies claiming he was completely and permanently disabled as a result of these ozone generators. He claimed, "that Columbian knew to a substantial certainty that its continual exposures of Mr. Swope to harmful amounts of ozone without providing him with any respiratory protection would cause repeated damage to his lungs." He alleged that the companies should be liable due to the inherently dangerous design and failure to warn of that danger. Construct an argument for the defense or plaintiff in this case. *Swope v. Columbian*, 2002 U.S. App. LEXIS 934.

15. Mr. McClaran was severely burned and injured when a steel-melting furnace he was stationed at exploded. Union Carbide manufactured the furnace. McClaran brought suit against Union Carbide for product liability. In the suit, the cause of the explosion was examined. The investigation revealed that water leaked from the roof of the furnace into the molten steel causing the explosion. Union Carbide designed the roof to be sprayed when necessary to reduce the temperature. The system had a vacuum to remove the water once dispensed and a backup drain on one side in case the vacuum failed. In addition to these features, the system had visual inspection points from which water could drain. At the time of the explosion, the vacuum line had a hole that prevented it from working and the unit was tilted to the opposite side of the drain. The inspection hatches were covered with dust and debris that prevented any drainage. McClaran did not make connections or allegations to the defective nature of the product when it left Union Carbide. How do you believe the court ruled? Explain your reasoning. *McClaran v. Union Carbide*, 2002 U.S. App. LEXIS 942.

16. In the early 1980's Jeffrey Canty created Canty Roofing and Sheetmetal Inc. (CRS). The company was primarily in the business of installing roofing and other sheetmetal products. During the existence of the company most of the financial work had been prepared and executed by Dias & Lapalme (D&L). By law, roofers in Massachusetts are required to carry bond insurance for their work to bid on certain projects. In accordance with this statute, Canty occasionally carried such insurance. One of these providers was North American Specialty Insurance Co. (NASI). However, before NASI provided bond coverage they required financial information from an outside auditor. They received the information from D&L. In 1995, Canty decided to sell his business to outside investors. The sale was executed on December 29, 1995. In the D&L's financial statements for 1995 that were released shortly after the sale, significant errors were discovered. This statement, issued by D&L on March 25, 1996, lacked specific information about the change in ownership. "To make matters worse, the notes to the financial statement contained

three arguably misleading comments that implied Canty's continuing participation as CRS's sole shareholder." In early January, NASI underwrote bonds totaling over $800,000 to CRS. Under the new agreement that was not outlined in the financial statements issued by D&L, CRS defaulted on its bonds and NASI was forced to pay. These payments cost NASI over $2,000,000. NASI sued D&L for negligent misrepresentation. "NASI grounded its complaint on the assertion that, but for the accountants' omission of accurate ownership information in the 1995 financial statement, it would not have continued furnishing bonds for CRS (and, therefore, would have avoided the ensuing losses)." The district court granted summary judgment in the defendants' favor. How do you believe the appellate court ruled? Why would D&L be liable or not? *North American Specialty Insurance Co. v. David Lapalme*, 258 F. 3d 35, 2001 U.S. App. LEXIS 17141.

17. KPMG Peat Marwick, LLP (Peat) audited the financial statements of Gulf Resources & Chemical Corp. (Gulf). Gulf had been the subject of two recent unsuccessful takeover attempts. Nycal Corp., thereafter, negotiated the purchase of a controlling interest in Gulf and in the process relied on Peat's audit reports. Peat was aware of the unsuccessful takeover attempts but was not aware of the Nycal purchase until it was nearly completed. The audit report in question had been done prior to the beginning of the Nycal/Gulf negotiation. Nycal alleges that the audit was negligently performed and has sued Peat for alleged material errors in the financial statements. Will Nycal prevail in a state using the Restatement test of accountant liability to third parties? *Nycal Corp. v. KPMG Peat Marwick LLP*, 688 N.E. 2d 1368 (1998).

Assignment on the Internet

Find a recent case or news story involving product liability. Identify the facts of the case, i.e., how the injured party was hurt and for what they are suing. Then identify the issue, reasons, and conclusion in the case or news story. Do you agree with the reasoning? Why or why not? Do you agree with the conclusion? Why or why not?

On the Internet

http://www.findlaw.com/01topics/22tort/ sites.html *Here is a good starting point for research about product liability law.*

http://www.consumerlawpage.com *This site contains information on legal aid and practical law for product liability cases and several articles summarizing recent product liability issues.*

http://www.ljx.com/practice/productliability/ index.html *This site contains recent news on product liability cases and editorials.*

http://www.law.cornell.edu/topics/products_ liability.html *This site provides a nice summary of product liability law and several outside sources.*

http://www.gis.net/chinalaw/prelaw.htm *Provides a general summary of the accounting law of the Peoples Republic of China.*

www.aicpa.org/assurance/scas/majtheme/ svcliob/index.htm *Discusses the litigation risk model for assurance services provided by the American Institute of CPA's.*

www.aicpa.org/statas/uaaltort.htm *Discusses tort reform issues of privity, joint and several liability and statutes of limitation.*

CHAPTER 10

Random House, Warner Brothers, and the "Bird Girl"

Random House commissioned photographer Jack Leigh to take a photograph for the cover of its book, *Midnight in the Garden of Good and Evil*. After Leigh photographed a statue, "Bird Girl," on a cemetery plot, he gave Random House permission to use the photo but retained a copyright on the photograph.

When Warner Brothers created a film based on the book, they decided to use the Bird Girl statue both in the movie as well as on the movie posters and advertisements. At the time Warner Brothers was making the movie, the family that owned the cemetery plot removed the Bird Girl statue. Consequently, Warner Brothers made a replica of the Bird Girl statue and used photos and film footage of the replica in the movie and movie advertisements. When Leigh discovered that Warner Brothers was taking pictures of a replica of the statue, he sued Warner Brothers for infringement of his intellectual property rights.[1]

1. If you were a business manager for Warner Brothers, would you have believed that your company was infringing on Leigh's rights to the picture of the statue? Why or why not?
2. If, during the creation of the movie, you were a Warner Brothers business manager and were told that there was a possibility that you might be infringing on Leigh's rights, what would you do? Would you decide to continue using the picture? How would you make this decision?

---

[1] For a discussion of this case, see *Question of 'Substantial Similarity' is One for Jury, Rules 11th Circuit*, 6 INTELLECTUAL PROPERTY LITIGATION REPORTER 3 (June 21, 2000).

CHAPTER 10

Intellectual Property

Trademark Protection

Copyright Protection

Patent Protection

Trade Secret Law Protection

International Protection of Intellectual Property

As suggested by the Warner Brothers scenario, intellectual property consists of property that is primarily the result of mental, rather than physical, effort. The various types of intellectual property are protected by trademarks, trade secrets, patents, and copyrights, all of which are discussed in this chapter. When you are reading each of the sections in this chapter, consider whether Leigh might have a case under each form of intellectual property protection.

Trademark Protection

A **trademark** is a distinctive "word, name, symbol, or device, or any combination thereof,"[2] which a producer attaches to a good so that consumers will identify the good with its producer. A wide range of characteristics have been protected as trademarks, including the nonfunctional shape of a product and its packaging. As one district court judge stated in the recent trademark infringement case of *Albecrombie & Fitch v. American Outfitters*,[3] "because we can conceive of no 'thing' inherently incapable of carrying meaning, any 'thing' can come to distinguish goods in commerce and thus constitute a mark within the meaning of the Lanham Act."

Yet, there has still been a significant amount of litigation over which features of a good can be protected by a trademark. In the following case, the United States Supreme Court agreed to determine whether a color could be a trademark.

[2] 15 U.S.C.A. § 1127.
[3] 2002 WL 226195 (6th Cir. , Ohio).

Case 10-1

Qualitex Co.

v.

Jacobson Products Co.
United States Supreme Court
514 U.S. 159 (1995)

Plaintiff, Qualitex Co., had colored the dry cleaning press pads it manufactured a special shade of green-gold since it had started making them in the 1950's. In 1991, after Defendant Jacobson Products, a competitor, started coloring its pads the same shade of green-gold, Qualitex obtained a registered trademark on its color, and sued the defendant for trademark infringement. The defendant challenged the trademark, arguing that color alone should not qualify for registration as a trademark.

The District Court found in favor of the plaintiff, but the Ninth Circuit reversed, holding that color alone could not be registered as a trademark. The plaintiff appealed to the United States Supreme Court.

JUSTICE BREYER

The Lanham Act gives a seller or producer the exclusive right to "register" a trademark, to prevent his or her competitors from using that trademark. Both the language of the Act and the basic underlying principles of trademark law would seem to include color within the universe of things that can qualify as a trademark. The language of the Lanham Act describes that universe in the broadest of terms. It says that trademarks "includ[e] any word, name, symbol, or device, or any combination thereof." Since human beings might use as a "symbol" or "device" almost anything at all that is capable of carrying meaning, this language, read literally, is not restrictive. The courts and the Patent and Trademark Office has authorized for use as a mark a particular shape (of a Coca-Cola bottle), a particular sound (of NBC's three chimes) and even a particular scent (of plumeria blossoms on sewing thread). If a shape, a sound, and a fragrance can act as symbols why, one might ask, can a color not do the same?

A color is also capable of satisfying the more important part of the statutory definition of a trademark, which requires that a person "us[e]" or "inten[d] to use" the mark.

"To identify and distinguish his or her goods, including a unique product, from those manufactured or sold by others and to indicate the source of the goods, even if that source is unknown."

True, a product's color is unlike "fanciful," "arbitrary," or "suggestive" words or designs, which almost automatically tell a customer that they refer to a brand. The imaginary word "Suntost," or the words "Suntost Marmalade," on a jar of orange jam immediately would signal a brand or a product "source"; the jam's orange color does not do so. But, over time, customers may come to treat a particular color on a product or its packaging (say, a color that in context seems unusual such as pink on a firm's insulating material or red on the head of a large industrial bolt) as signifying a brand. And, if so, that color would have come to identify and distinguish the goods—i.e. "to indicate" their "source"—much in the way that descriptive words on a product (say, "Trim" on nail clippers or "Car-Freshener" on deodorizer) can come to indicate a product's origin. In this circumstance, trademark law says that the word (e.g., "Trim"), although not inherently distinctive, has developed "secondary meaning." ("Secondary meaning" is acquired when "in the minds of the public, the primary significance of a product feature...is to identify the source of the product rather than the product itself".) Again, one might ask, if trademark law permits a descriptive word with secondary meaning to act as a mark, why would it not permit a color, under similar circumstances, to do the same?

It would seem, then, that color alone, at least sometimes, can meet the basic legal requirements for use as a trademark. It can act as a symbol that distinguishes a firm's goods and identifies their source, without serving any other significant function. The green-gold color acts as a symbol. Having developed secondary meaning (for customers identified the green-gold color as Qualitex's), it identifies the press pads' source. And, the green-gold color serves no other function. Accordingly, unless there is some special reason that convincingly militates against the use of color alone as a trademark, trademark law would protect Qualitex's use of the green-gold color on its press pads.

REVERSED, IN FAVOR OF PLAINTIFF.

1. Critical Thinking: Why did the court rule that color meets the basic legal requirements for use as a trademark? Are you persuaded by this reasoning? Why or why not?

2. Ethical Decision Making: Suppose you are the business manager at Jacobson's products. Knowing that your main competitor's products are a green-gold color, you decide to color your product green-gold. If the universalization rule guides your behavior, how might your decision be different?

Global Context: Software Piracy in China

A constant source of tension between the United States and China has been China's lax enforcement of intellectual property laws. A study released in July 1999 found that 95% of the business software installed in China during 1998 was pirated.[4]

As an indication that China is now attempting to crack down on software piracy, in July 1999 (the same year the report was released), that country handed down its first criminal sentence for software piracy. Wang Antao was sentenced to four years in prison, fined 20,000 yuan ($2,400), and required to pay the software owner 280,000 ($33,800) for selling a slightly modified version of a company's software without permission.

Registering A Mark

State common law protects a trademark used *intrastate*. To be protected in *interstate* use, the trademark, sometimes referred to as simply a mark, must be registered with the United States Patent and Trademark Office (USPTO) under the Lanham Act of 1947. This act protects the several types of marks defined in Exhibit 10-1.

EXHIBIT 10-1

Types of Marks Protected Under the Lanham Act

1. Product trademarks—affixed to a good, its packaging, or its labeling.
2. Service marks—used to identify a service provider.
3. Collective marks—used to identify the producers as belonging to a larger group, such as a trade union.
4. Certification marks—licensed by a group that has established certain criteria for use of the mark, such as the "U. L. Tested."

The holder of a registered mark may recover damages from an infringer who uses it to pass off goods as those of the mark owner. The owner may also obtain an injunction prohibiting the infringer from using the mark. The only remedy available to the holder of an unregistered mark is an injunction.

To register a mark with the USPTO, one must submit a drawing of the mark and indicate how and when it was first used in interstate commerce and how it is used. After verifying the facts in the submission, the USPTO will register a trademark as long as it is not generic, descriptive, immoral, deceptive, the name of the person whose permission has not been obtained, or substantially similar to another's trademark.

Determining whether a mark is generic has become more difficult in this era of increasing globalization. For example, can a foreign word that would be generic in its country of origin be used as a trademark in this country? The court grappled with that issue in the following case.

---

[4] The study was conducted by the U.S. Business Software Alliance and Software & Information Industry Association.

Case 10-2

Otokoyama Co. Ltd., a Japanese Corporation

v.

Wine of Japan Import, Inc.
United States Court of Appeals,
Second Circuit
175 F. 3d 783 (1999)

*O**tokoyoma Co. Ltd, a Japanese brewer that imported its "Otokoyama" sake into the United States, brought a trademark infringement action against a competitor, Wine of Japan Import, Inc., which imported "Mutsu Otokoyama" sake, claiming that the defendant had infringed on his trademark "Otokoyama." The plaintiff sought an injunction prohibiting the defendant from using the term.*

The defendant counterclaimed, seeking to cancel the plaintiff's trademarks. The United States District Court for the Southern District of New York granted a preliminary injunction for the plaintiff, finding it highly likely that the plaintiff would be able to successfully prove its case on the merits. The defendant appealed.

CIRCUIT JUDGE LEVAL

…Generic terms are not eligible for protection as trademarks; everyone may use them to refer to the goods they designate.…This rule protects the interest of the consuming public in understanding the nature of goods offered for sale, as well as a fair marketplace among competitors by insuring that every provider may refer to his goods as what they are.…

The same rule applies when the word designates the product in a language other than English. This extension rests on the assumption that there are (or someday will be) customers in the United States who speak that foreign language. Because of the diversity of the population of the United States, coupled with temporary visitors, all of whom are part of the United States marketplace, commerce in the United States utilizes innumerable foreign languages. No merchant may obtain the exclusive right over a trademark designation if that exclusivity would prevent competitors from designating a product as what it is in the foreign language their customers know best. Courts and the USPTO apply this policy, known as the doctrine of "foreign equivalents"…to make generic foreign words ineligible for private ownership as trademarks.

This rule, furthermore, does not apply only to words that designate an entire species. Generic words for subclassifications or varieties of a good are similarly ineligible for trademark protection. See, e.g.,…"fontina" held generic for a type of cheese"…"bundt" held generic for variety of ring-shaped coffee cake. A word may also be generic by virtue of its association with a particular region, cultural movement, or legend.

The defendant contended in the district court that the word "otokoyama" falls within the generic category. It claimed that in Japanese, otokoyama has long been understood as designating a variety of "dry, manly sake" that originated more than 300 years ago. If otokoyama in Japanese signifies a type of sake, and one United States merchant were given the exclusive right to use that word to designate its brand of sake, competing merchants would be prevented from calling their product by the word which designates that product in Japanese. Any Japanese-speaking customers and others who are familiar with the Japanese terminology would be misled to believe that there is only one brand of otokoyama available in the United

States...Consumers would be forced either to spend additional time and money investigating the characteristics of competing goods or to pay a premium price to the seller with trademark rights in the accepted generic term.

The meaning of otokoyama in Japanese, and particularly whether it designates sake, or a type or category of sake, was therefore highly relevant to whether plaintiff may assert the exclusive right to use that word as a mark applied to sake. Defendant should have been allowed to introduce evidence of otokoyama's meaning and usage in Japan to support its claim that the mark is generic and therefore ineligible for protection as a trademark. In light of this error, the district court's finding that plaintiff is likely to succeed on the merits cannot be sustained.

REVERSED, IN FAVOR OF THE DEFENDANT.

1. Critical Thinking: Are you satisfied with the evidence the judge used to support his conclusion in this case? Why or why not?

2. Ethical Decision Making: Think about the WPH Process of Ethical Decision making. What was the purpose of the *Otokoyama* decision? In other words, what value was guiding the court's reasoning?

Once the mark is registered, the registration must be renewed between the fifth and sixth years. After that initial renewal, the mark holder must renew their registration every ten years. (If the mark was initially registered prior to 1990, however, renewal is necessary only every twenty years.)

Trademark Infringement

It is sometimes difficult to determine whether a trademark will be issued. And once the trademark is issued, it is not always easy to predict when a similar mark will be found to infringe upon the registered trademark. The following case demonstrates a typical analysis used in a trademark infringement suit.

Case 10-3

Toys "R" Us, Inc.
v.
Canarsie Kiddie Shop, Inc.
District Court of the Eastern District of New York
559 F. Supp. 1189 (1983)

*B*eginning in 1960, plaintiff Toys-"R"-Us, Inc., sold children's clothes in stores across the country. The firm obtained a registered trademark and service mark for Toys "R" Us in 1961 and aggressively advertised and promoted their products using these marks. In the late 1970s, defendant Canarsie Kiddie Shop, Inc., opened two kids' clothing stores within two miles of a Toys "R" Us Shop, and contemplated opening a third. The owner of Canarsie Kiddie Shop, Inc., called the stores Kids "r" Us. He never attempted to register the name. Toys "R" Us sued for trademark infringement in the federal district court.

JUDGE GLASSER

In assessing the likelihood of confusion and in balancing the equities, this Court must consider the now classic factors....

1. Strength of the Senior User's Mark

..."[t]he term 'strength' as applied to trademarks refers to the distinctiveness of the mark, or more precisely, its tendency to identify goods sold under the mark as emanating from the particular, although possibly anonymous, source." A mark can fall into one of four general categories which, in order of ascending strength, are: (1) generic; (2) descriptive; (3) suggestive; and (4) arbitrary or fanciful. The strength of a mark is generally dependent both on its place upon the scale and on whether it has acquired secondary meaning.

A generic term "refers, or has come to be understood as referring to the genus of which the particular product is a species." A generic term is entitled to no trademark protection whatsoever, since any manufacturer or seller has the right to call a product by its name.

A descriptive mark identifies a significant characteristic of the product, but is not the common name of the product. A mark is descriptive if it "informs the purchasing public of the characteristics, quality, functions, uses, ingredients, components, or other properties of a product, or conveys comparable information about a service." To achieve trademark protection, a descriptive term must have attained secondary meaning, that is, it must have "become distinctive of the applicant's goods in commerce."

A suggestive mark is one that "requires imagination, thought, and perception to reach a conclusion as to the nature of the goods." These marks fall short of directly describing the qualities or functions of a particular product or service, but merely suggest such qualities. If a term is suggestive, it is entitled to protection without proof of secondary meaning.

Arbitrary or fanciful marks require no extended definition. They are marks which in no way describe or suggest the qualities of the product.

...Because I find that through the plaintiff's advertising and marketing efforts the plaintiff's mark has developed strong secondary meaning as a source of children's products, it is sufficient for purposes of this decision to note merely that the plaintiff's mark is one of medium strength, clearly entitled to protection, but falling short of the protection afforded an arbitrary or fanciful mark.

2. Degree of Similarity Between the Two Marks

...[T]he key inquiry is...whether a similarity exists which is likely to cause confusion....[I]t must be determined whether "the impression which the infringing [mark] makes upon the consumer is such that he is likely to believe the product is from the same source as the one he knows under the trademark."

Turning to the two marks involved here, various similarities and differences are readily apparent. The patent similarity between the marks is that they both employ the phrase, "R Us." Further, both marks employee the letter "R" in place of the word "are," although the plaintiff's mark uses an inverted capitalized "R," while the defendants generally use a noninverted lower case "r" for their mark.

The most glaring difference between the marks is that in one the phrase "R Us" is preceded by the word "Toys," while in the other it is preceded by the word "Kids." Other differences include the following: plaintiff's mark ends with an exclamation point, plaintiff frequently utilizes the image of a giraffe alongside its mark, plaintiff's mark is set forth in stylized lettering, usually multi-colored, and plaintiff frequently utilizes the words, "a children's bargain basement" under the logo in its advertising.

...While the marks are clearly distinguishable when placed side by side, there are sufficiently strong similarities to create the possibility that some consumers might believe that the two marks emanated from the same source. The similarities in sound and association also create the possibility that some consumers might mistake one mark for the other when seeing or hearing the mark alone.

3. Proximity of the Products

Where the products in question are competitive, the likelihood of consumer confusion increases.

...both plaintiff and defendants sell children's clothing;...the plaintiff and defendants currently are direct product competitors.

4. The Likelihood that Plaintiff Will "Bridge the Gap"

..."bridging the gap" refers to two distinct possibilities; first, that the senior user presently intends to expand his sales efforts to compete directly with the junior user, thus creating the likelihood that the two products will be directly competitive; second, that while there is no present intention to bridge the gap, consumers will assume otherwise and conclude, in this era of corporate diversification, that the parties are related companies...I find both possibilities present here.

5. Evidence of Actual Confusion

Evidence of actual confusion is a strong indication that there is a likelihood of confusion. It is not, however, a prerequisite for the plaintiff to recover.

6. Junior User's Good Faith

The state of mind of the junior user is an important factor in striking the balance of the equities. In the instant case, Mr. Pomeranc asserted at trial that he did not recall whether he was aware of the plaintiff's mark when he chose to name his store Kids 'r' Us in 1977.

I do not find this testimony to be credible. In view of the proximity of the stores, the overlapping of their products, and the strong advertising and marketing effort conducted by the plaintiff for a considerable amount of time prior to the defendants' adoption of the name Kids 'r' Us, it is difficult to believe that the defendants were unaware of the plaintiff's use of the Toys "R" Us mark.

The defendants adopted the Kids 'r' Us mark with knowledge of plaintiff's mark. A lack of good faith is relevant not only in balancing the equities, but also is a factor supporting a finding of a likelihood of confusion.

7. Quality of the Junior User's Product

If the junior user's product is of a low quality, the senior user's interest in avoiding any confusion is heightened. In the instant case, there is no suggestion that the defendants' products are inferior, and this factor therefore is not relevant.

8. Sophistication of the Purchasers

The level of sophistication of the average purchaser also bears on the likelihood of confusion. Every product, because of the type of buyer that it attracts, has its own distinct threshold for confusion of the source or origin.

The goods sold by both plaintiff and defendants are moderately priced clothing articles, which are not major expenditures for most purchasers. Consumers of such goods, therefore, do not exercise the same degree of care in buying as when purchasing more expensive items. Further, it may be that the consumers purchasing from the plaintiff and defendants are influenced in part by the desires of their children, for whom the products offered by plaintiff and defendants are meant.

9. Junior User's Goodwill

[A] powerful equitable argument against finding infringement is created when the junior user, through concurrent use of an identical trademark, develops goodwill in their mark. Defendants have not expended large sums advertising their store or promoting its name. Further, it appears that most of the defendants' customers are local "repeat shoppers," who come to the Kids 'r' Us store primarily because of their own past experiences with it. In light of this lack of development of goodwill, I find that the defendants do not have a strong equitable interest in retaining the Kids 'r' Us mark.

Conclusion on Likelihood of Confusion

[T]he defendants use of the Kids 'r' Us mark does create a likelihood of confusion for an appreciable number of consumers.

In reaching this determination, I place primary importance on the strong secondary meaning that the plaintiff has developed in its mark, the directly competitive nature of the products offered by the plaintiff and defendants, the plaintiff's substantially developed plans to open stores similar in format to those of the defendants', the lack of sophistication of the purchasers, the similarities between the marks, the defendants' lack of good faith in adopting the mark, and the limited goodwill the defendants have developed in their mark.

JUDGEMENT FOR THE PLAINTIFF.

1. Critical Thinking: The court is pretty clear about its reasons for its decisions. Can you think of any alternative reasons that the court might have used to come to the same conclusion? Can you create at least one reason that might have persuaded the court to reach a different conclusion?

2. Ethical Decision Making: Suppose you were a business manager at Kids 'r' Us a year after the company was created. You are aware of the Toys 'r' Us stores, and based on your business law knowledge, you think that your store might be infringing on their trademark. What would you do? Now, suppose that your decision is guided by the Golden Rule. Is your decision altered at all under the Golden Rule?

The potential for consumer confusion seems to be a very important consideration in a trademark infringement case. A recent case where consumer confusion was an issue arose in London when an American fast food chain argued that a Chinese restauranteur was infringing on its trademark. Frank Yeun opened two Chinese restaurants in London, calling them McChina. He claimed that the public would recognize that the Mc prefix meant "son of." McDonald's, in its attempt to prohibit the use of the McChina name, introduced evidence that it had commissioned a study in 1996 in which thirty percent of consumers thought that McChina was part of McDonald's. Despite McDonald's evidence, however, the High Court in London ruled that the name would not deceive or cause confusion among consumers, adding that McDonald's appeared to be trying to monopolize all names or words with the prefix Mc or Mac in the food service industry.[5]

Return to the Warner Brothers case discussed at the beginning of the chapter. Do you think Leigh could have brought a claim under trademark infringement? Actually, he did. Think about the holding in the Toys "R" Us case. Do you think Leigh was successful in his trademark infringement claim? We will return to this question at the end of the chapter.

Trade Dress

The term trade dress refers to the overall appearance and image of a product. For example, in the case of *Two Pesos v. Taco Cabana*,[6] the court found that Mexican restaurant Taco Cabana's trade dress consisted of "a festive eating atmosphere having interior dining and patio areas decorated with artifacts, bright colors, paintings and murals;" "a patio that has interior and exterior areas with the interior patio capable of being sealed off from the outside patio by overhead garage doors;" a stepped exterior of the building that has "a festive and vivid color scheme using top border paint and neon stripes;" and "bright awnings and umbrellas."

Trade dress is entitled to the same protection as a trademark. To succeed on a claim of trade dress infringement, a party must prove three elements: (1) the trade dress is primarily nonfunctional; (2) the trade dress is inherently distinctive or has acquired a secondary meaning; and (3) the alleged infringement creates a likelihood of confusion. Thus, when Two Pesos opened a series of competing Mexican restaurants that mimicked the trade dress features of Taco Cabana almost perfectly, the court found them to be guilty of trade dress infringement. Functionality was not an issue in this case; the previously described elements were distinctive; and when copied so closely, were likely to cause consumer confusion.

Trade dress infringement cases usually focus on whether or not there is likely to be consumer confusion. For example, in the case of *Pebble Beach Co. v. Tour 18 I, Ltd.*,[7] the defendant, a golf course, copied golf holes from famous golf courses without permission of the

---

[5] *McChina Wins Trademark Fight with McDonald's,* CHICAGO TRIBUNE, November 28, 2002 at 11.

[6] 112 S.Ct. 2753 (1994).

[7] *Pebble Beach Co. v. Tour 18 I, Ltd.,* 942 F. Supp. 1513.

Technology: Trademarks and Domain Names

If a business has a very strong trademark, what better domain name to have for your website than that trademark? Unfortunately, the same trademark may be owned by two companies selling noncompeting goods, yet there can be only one user of any single domain name. For example, apple is a trademark owned by both a computer company and the company that produces the Beatles' records. Both cannot establish a site identified as apple.com.

Domain names are important because they are the way people and business are located on the Web. A domain name is made up of a series of domains separated by periods. Most websites have two domains. The top level is the last domain name found in the address. There are two types of top level domains: country codes and generic names. The generic are descriptive of the type of site. Originally, all of the top level domains were generic. These original generic domain names were: .gov, for U.S. government sites; .edu, for sites sponsored by an educational institution; .com for commercial sites; .net for organizations involved in Internet infrastructure activities, and .org for nonprofit organizations.

In late 2000, seven new top level generic domain names were added: .aero, for the air-transport industry; .biz, for businesses; .coop, for cooperative; .museums, for museums; .name, for individuals; .pro, for professionals, such as doctors, accountants, and lawyers; and .info, for unrestricted use.

Top level country code domain names (ccTLDs) are two letter domains, such as .uk, .us, and .jp, that correspond to a country, territory, or other geographic location. The rules and policies for registering domain names in the ccTLDs vary significantly and some are reserved for use by citizens of the corresponding country.

The second level domain is usually the name of whoever maintains the site. For a college, for example, it would be an abbreviation of the college, as in bgsu. Businesses will generally want to use their firm name or some other trademark associated with their product, because that name will obviously make it easier for their customers to find them.

So how does a firm go about securing a domain name that reflects its trademark? Today, the Internet Corporation for Assigned Names and Numbers (ICANN), is the nonprofit corporation that is responsible for internet protocol (IP) address space allocation, protocol parameter assignment, domain name system management, and root server system management functions. They have allocated responsibility for registering addresses under each of the domain names to particular registrars, who may charge different fees for their services.

So, to register a domain name, a business or individual would go to the InterNIC Registrar Directory on the ICANN website (http://www.internic.net/regist.html) and find the names of registrars for the appropriate top level domain, and contact one of the appropriate registrars. Once the registrar is contacted, registration can usually be done over the Internet. Each registrar has the flexibility to offer initial and renewal registrations in one-year increments, with a total registration period limit of ten years. Because each registrar may offer different prices, and different ancillary services and means of registering, it makes sense to check a couple of different registrars before selecting the one to use to register your domain name.

When a trademark holder is unable to use the trademark for a domain name because some other party is already using it, the holder may use the dispute resolution process established by ICAAN. Under this process, a holder of trademark rights initiates the administrative procedure by filing a complaint with an approved dispute-resolution service provider alleging: (1) another's domain name is identical or confusingly similar to a trademark or service mark in which the complainant has rights; (2) a party has no rights or legitimate interests in respect of a registered domain name; or (3) a domain name has been registered and is being used in bad faith. If the administrative body finds for the complainant, the domain name in question may be cancelled and/or transferred to the complaining party. Despite the availability of this administrative proceeding however, parties may still take their dispute over who should be entitled to own the name to the court. Chapter 11 discusses the issue of conflicts over the use of domain names in greater detail.

course owners. Harbour Town Hole 19, a distinctive hole from one of the most famous courses in the country, was one of the holes they copied and featured prominently in their advertising. In duplicating this hole, they even copied the Harbour Town Lighthouse, the distinctive feature of that hole. When the operator of the Harbour Town course sued Tour 18 for trade dress infringement, the court agreed, and made Tour 18 remove the lighthouse and disclaim in its advertising any affiliation with the owner of the Harbour Town course.

One of the key issues in trade dress cases is often the question of whether an aspect of the trade dress is functional. This question is especially likely to arise when the trade dress involves the appearance or design of a product. If a part of the product's design had formerly been protected by a utility patent, can the design still be protected as trade dress? The Circuit Courts were split on the issue until the Supreme Court resolved it in the following case.

Case 10-4

TrafFix Devices, Inc.
v.
Marketing Displays Inc.
U.S. Supreme Court
532 U.S. 23 (2001)

*A*n inventor named Robert Sarkisian obtained two utility patents for a mechanism built upon two springs (the dual-spring design) to keep outdoor signs upright in heavy winds. These patents were transferred to Marketing Displays, Inc. (MDI), which established a successful business in the manufacture and sale of sign stands incorporating the patented feature. MDI's stands for road signs were recognizable to buyers and users (it says) because the dual-spring design was visible near the base of the sign.

After the patent expired, a competitor, TrafFix, had the MDI product reverse-engineered, and began producing and selling similar sign stands. MDI sued to enjoin TrafFix's sales of its signs on a number of *theories, including trade dress infringement, based on the copied dual-spring design. The lower court ruled against MDI on the trade dress question, finding that no reasonable finder of fact could conclude that MDI had established secondary meaning in the look of its dual-spring design. The District Court also determined the dual-spring design was functional, so it did not really matter whether secondary meaning had been established. The Court of Appeals reversed, saying that the exclusive use of a feature as part of a trade dress must significantly hinder the competition before trade dress protection is lost.*

Noting that there was a conflict among the circuits as to whether the existence of an expired utility patent over part of the trade dress foreclosed trade dress protection, the Supreme Court agreed to hear the case.

JUSTICE KENNEDY

It is well established that trade dress can be protected under federal law. The design or packaging of a product may acquire a distinctiveness which serves to identify the product with its manufacturer or source; and a design or package which acquires this secondary meaning, assuming other requisites are met, is a trade dress which may not be used in a manner likely to cause confusion as to the origin, sponsorship, or approval of the goods....Congress confirmed this statutory protection for trade dress by amending the Lanham Act to recognize the concept. Title 15 U. S. C. § 1125(a)(3) (1994 ed., Supp. V) provides: "In a civil action for trade dress infringement under this chapter for trade dress not registered on the principal register, the person who asserts trade dress protection has the burden of proving that the matter sought to be protected is not functional." This burden of proof gives force to the well-established rule that trade dress protection may not be claimed for product features that are functiona....

Trade dress protection must subsist with the recognition that in many instances there is no prohibition against copying goods and products. In general, unless an intellectual property right such as a patent or copyright protects an item, it will be subject to copying. As the Court has explained, copying is not always discouraged or disfavored by the laws which preserve our competitive economy....Allowing competitors to copy will have salutary effects in many instances. "Reverse engineering of chemical and mechanical articles in the public domain often leads to significant advances in technology."

The principal question in this case is the effect of an expired patent on a claim of trade dress infringement. A prior patent, we conclude, has vital significance in resolving the trade dress claim. A utility patent is strong evidence that the features therein claimed are functional. If trade dress protection is sought for those features, the strong evidence of functionality based on the previous patent adds great weight to the statutory presumption that features are deemed functional until proved otherwise by the party seeking trade dress protection. Where the expired patent claimed the features in question, one who seeks to establish trade dress protection must carry the heavy burden of showing that the feature is not functional, for instance by showing that it is merely an ornamental, incidental, or arbitrary aspect of the device.

In the case before us, the central advance claimed in the expired utility patents (the Sarkisian patents) is the dual-spring design; and the dual-spring design is the essential feature of the trade dress MDI now seeks to establish and to protect. The rule we have explained bars the trade dress claim, for MDI did not, and cannot, carry the burden of overcoming the strong evidentiary inference of functionality based on the disclosure of the dual-spring design in the claims of the expired patents.

The dual-springs shown in the Sarkisian patents were well apart...while the dual springs at issue here are close together.... The point is that the springs are necessary to the operation of the device....

The rationale for the rule that the disclosure of a feature in the claims of a utility patent constitutes strong evidence of functionality is well illustrated in this case. The dual-spring design serves the important purpose of keeping the sign upright even in heavy wind conditions; and, as confirmed by the statements in the expired patents, it does so in a unique and useful manner....The dual-spring design affects the cost of the device as well; it was acknowledged that the device "could use three springs but this would unnecessarily increase the cost of the device." These statements made in the patent applications and in the course of procuring the patents demonstrate the functionality of the design. MDI does not assert that any of these representations are mistaken or inaccurate, and this is further strong evidence of the functionality of the dual-spring design....

As we have noted, even if there has been no previous utility patent, the party asserting trade dress has the burden to establish the nonfunctionality of alleged trade dress features. MDI could not meet this burden. Discussing trademarks, we have said "[i]n general terms, a product feature is functional, and cannot serve as a trademark, if it is essential to the use or purpose of the article or if it affects the cost or quality of the article."...It is proper to inquire into a "significant nonreputation-related disadvantage" in cases of aesthetic functionality, the question involved in Qualitex. Where the design is functional...there is no need to proceed further to consider if there is a competitive necessity for the feature....

The Court has allowed trade dress protection to certain product features that are inherently distinctive....In the instant case, beyond serving the purpose of informing consumers that the sign stands are made by MDI (assuming it does so), the dual-spring design provides a unique and useful mechanism to resist the force of the wind. Functionality having been established, whether MDI's dual-spring design has acquired secondary meaning need not be considered.

Because the dual-spring design is functional, it is unnecessary for competitors to explore designs to hide the springs, say by using a box or framework to cover them, as suggested by the Court of Appeals....

In a case where a manufacturer seeks to protect arbitrary, incidental, or ornamental aspects of features of a product found in the patent claims, such as arbitrary curves in the legs or an ornamental pattern painted on the springs, a different result might be obtained. There the manufacturer could perhaps prove that those aspects do not serve a purpose within the terms of the utility patent....No such claim is made here, however.

1. Critical Thinking: What was the primary reason for the Supreme Court's decision in this case?

2. Ethical Decision Making: Thinking of all the stakeholders who have an interest in the outcome of this case, who benefits most from this decision, beyond the immediate party who won the case, and why?

Federal Trademark Dilution Act of 1995

Under the Lanham Act, trademark owners were protected from the unauthorized use of their marks on only competing goods or related goods where the use might lead to consumer confusion. Consequently, a mark might be used without permission on completely unrelated goods, thereby potentially diminishing the value of the mark. In response to this problem, a number of states passed trademark dilution laws, which prohibited the use of "distinctive" or "famous" trademarks, such as McDonald's, even without a showing of consumer confusion.

In 1995, Congress made similar protection available at the federal level by passing the Federal Trademark Dilution Act of 1995. The act defines dilution as "the lessening of the capacity of a famous mark to identify and distinguish goods or services."[8]

According to Congressional testimony, it was the intent of the drafters of the statute that "dilution might result either from 'uses that blur the distinctiveness of [a famous] mark or [that] tarnish or disparage it.'"[9] Thus, when bringing a case under this act, the plaintiff need only prove that the defendant has weakened the link in a consumer's mind between the plaintiff's mark and its goods or services, thereby causing "blurring." Alternatively, the plaintiff may claim "tarnishment," meaning the use of this similar mark by the defendant is unsavory or unwholesome, thereby "tarnishing" the reputation of the plaintiff's product.[10]

In one of the first cases decided under this law, the court said that the protection available under this act

[8] 15 U.S.C. § 1125(c)(1).

[9] See H.R.Rep. No. 104-374, at 2 (1995), U.S. Code Cong. & Admin. News at 1029, 1029.

[10] Chris A Carr & Brian C Tietje, *When is famous not?* Mktg. Mgmt. Mag. 52 (2001 WL 23067993) September 1, 2001.

extended not just to identical marks, but also to similar marks. In that case, Ringling Brothers-Barnum & Bailey challenged Utah's use of the slogan "The Greatest Snow on Earth" as diluting their famous "The Greatest Show on Earth." In denying Utah's motion to dismiss because the slogans were not identical, the court said that the marks need not be identical. The plaintiffs' victory in that case, however, was short lived because they ultimately lost the case on the merits.[11]

One of the biggest challenges to successfully bringing a claim under the Federal Trademark Dilution Act (FTDA) is that the Act protects only "famous" marks, and it is not always easy to know how the courts will rule on that issue, even though we know that the court considers such factors as: 1) the degree of distinctiveness of the mark; 2) the duration and extent of use of the mark in connection with the goods or services with which the mark is used; 3) degree of recognition of the mark in the trading areas and channels of trade used by the mark's owner and the person against whom relief is sought; 4) the nature and extent of use of the same or similar marks by third parties ; and 5) whether the mark was registered.[12] In a decision that was surprising to many, the court found that the "Clue" trademark, held by Hasbro Corporation for its murder mystery game, was not strongly "famous" and therefore not entitled to protection under the FTDA. The circuit court affirmed the decision.[13]

Copyrights

The Copyright Act of 1976,[14] as amended, provides federal protection for any "idea, procedure, process, system, method of operation, concept, principle, or discovery" that is expressed in a fixed form. It protects creative works such as books, periodicals, musical compositions, plays, motion pictures, sound recordings, lectures, works of art, and computer programs. Remember, Leigh's photograph of the Bird Girl statue was copyrighted.

Under the Sony Bono Copyright Term Extension Act (CTEA) of 1998, works created after 1978 are automatically protected by federal copyright law for the life of the creator plus 70 years. If the owner of the copyright is a publisher, the copyright lasts for 95 years after the date of publication or 120 years after creation, whichever is longer. All works copyrighted before 1978

are protected for 95 years. Prior to passage of the CTEA, such works were protected for the life of the creator plus 50 years.

However, these new time limits are currently being challenged in the case of *Elred v. Ashcroft*, which the United States Supreme Court has agreed to hear. The plaintiff, the owner of a company that offers on-line access to works that are now in the public domain, is arguing that the CTEA exceeds congressional authority under the Copyright Clause of the U.S. Constitution. He also argues that the extension violates the First Amendment by burdening free speech without advancing any significant public interest. Elred lost in both the District Court and the Court of Appeals, so many commentators do not feel that he has a strong likelihood of success in the high court.

One may register a copyrighted work by filing a form with the Register of Copyright and providing two copies of the copyrighted materials to the Library of Congress. Printed works are no longer required to be published with the word *copyright* and the symbol © or the abbreviation copr.. However, a prudent copyright owner may still wish to identify their work as being copyrighted, just to deter potential infringers.

Criteria for Copyright Protection

To receive federal copyright protection, a work must meet certain criteria. First, it must be original. Therefore, mere compilations of publicly known facts in a nonoriginal manner are not copyrightable. However, if pre-existing data is compiled in an original way, it may receive protection. Second, it must fall into one of the following categories established by the act: (1) literary works; (2) musical works; (3) dramatic works; (4) pantomimes and choreographic works; (5) pictorial, graphic, and sculptural works; (6) films and other audiovisual works; and (7) sound recordings. Finally, it must be in fixed form; that is, it must be in some sort of medium from which it may be reproduced.

Certain works, primarily because they do not meet the criteria just described, cannot be protected by copyright. For example, short phrases, titles of books, government documents, and maps cannot be copyrighted.

Copyright Infringement

It is not always easy to determine whether a copyright has been infringed, even when two works are similar. After all, if we are talking about creative works, like photographs of a famous scene, two people might independently take a very similar picture at completely

---

[11] *Ringling Bros.-Barnum & Bailey v. Utah Division of Travel Development*, 170 F. 3d 449 (4th Cir. 1999).

[12] Carr, supra note 10.

[13] *Id.*

[14] 176 U.S.C. §§ 101 et. seq.

different times and without even knowing of the other's work. Think about the Bird Girl statue. In that case, the two parties took pictures of different statues at different times. The following case illustrates the court's reason- ing in a successful copyright infringement case. Think about how Leigh's copyright infringement claim might have been decided while you consider the court's reasoning in the *Ty* case.

Case 10-5

Ty, Inc.

v.

GMA Accessories, Inc.
U.S. Court of Appeals Seventh Circuit
45 U.S.P.Q. 1519 (1998)

Ty began selling the popular "Beanie Babies" line of miniature stuffed beanbag animals, including Squealer, the pig, in 1993. The popularity of this line led GMA to bring out its own line of beanbag stuffed animals three years later.

Ty filed an action to obtain a preliminary injunction under the Copyright Act against the sale by GMA of "Preston the Pig" and "Louie the Cow." These are beanbag animals manufactured by GMA that Ty contends are copies of its copyrighted pig ("Squealer") and cow ("Daisy").

The district court granted the injunction. GMA appealed the part of the injunction that enjoined the sale of Preston.

JUSTICE RICHARD POSNER

We have appended to our opinion five pictures found in the appellate record. The first shows Squealer (the darker pig, actually pink) and Preston (white). The second is a picture of two real pigs. The third and fourth are different views of the design for Preston that Janet Salmon submitted to GMA several months before Preston went into production. The fifth is a picture of the two beanbag cows; they are nearly identical. A glance at the first picture shows a striking similarity between the two beanbag pigs as well...

The two pigs are so nearly identical that if the second is a copy of the first, the second clearly infringes Ty's copyright. But identity is not infringement. The Copyright Act forbids only copying; if independent creation results in an identical work, the creator of that work is free to sell it....The practical basis for this rule is that unlike the case of patents and trademarks, the creator of an expressive work—an author or sculptor or composer—cannot canvass the entire universe of copyrighted works to discover whether his poem or song or, as in this case, "soft sculpture," is identical to some work in which copyright subsists, especially since unpublished, unregistered works are copyrightable....But identity can be powerful evidence of copying....The more a work is both like an already copyrighted work and—for this is equally important—unlike anything that is in the public domain, the less likely it is to be an independent creation. As is generally true in the law, circumstantial evidence—evidence merely probabilistic rather than certain—can confer sufficient confidence on an inference, here of copying, to warrant a legal finding.

The issue of copying can be broken down into two subissues. The first is whether the alleged copier had access to the work that he is claimed to have copied; the second is whether, if so, he used his access to copy...

Obviously, access does not entail copying...But copying entails access. If, therefore, two works are so similar as to make it highly probable that the later one is a copy of the earlier one, the issue of access need not be addressed separately, since if the later work was a copy, its creator must have had access to the original....

What...is not a factor here is that two works may be strikingly similar—may in fact be identical—not because one is copied from the other, but because both are copies of the same thing in the public domain....A similarity may be striking without being suspicious.

But here it is both. GMA's pig is strikingly similar to Ty's pig but not to anything in the public domain —a real pig, for example...The parties' beanbag pigs bear little resemblance to real pigs even if we overlook the striking anatomical anomaly of Preston—he has three toes, whereas real pigs have cloven hooves...

Real pigs are not the only pigs in the public domain. But GMA has not pointed to any fictional pig in the public domain that Preston resembles. Preston resembles only Squealer, and resembles him so closely as to warrant an inference that GMA copied Squealer. In rebuttal, all that GMA presented was the affidavit of the designer, Salmon, who swears...that she never looked at a Squealer before submitting her design. But it is not her design drawing that is alleged to infringe the copyright on Squealer; it is the manufactured Preston, the soft sculpture itself, which, as a comparison of the first with the third and fourth pictures in the appendix is much more like Squealer than Salmon's drawing is....A glance at the last picture in the appendix shows an identity between Louie the Cow and Ty's Daisy that is so complete (and also not explainable by reference to resemblance to a real cow or other public domain figure) as to compel an inference of copying. If GMA must have had access to Louie, it is probable, quite apart from any inference from the evidence of similarity, that it had access to Squealer as well.

Access (and copying) may be inferred when two works are so similar to each other and not to anything in the public domain, that it is likely that the creator of the second work copied the first, but the inference can be rebutted by disproving access or otherwise showing independent creation...

The granting of a preliminary injunction depends on proof of irreparable harm if the injunction is withheld, as well as on the likelihood of success on the merits when the case is fully tried...

We may assume that if Ty licensed all who want to make Beanie Babies, appropriate compensatory relief in this case would be to make GMA pay for the license at Ty's standard rate retroactive to the date on which GMA began selling Preston....GMA's infringement is not only depriving Ty of the income on some number of pigs, but also disrupting its scheme of distribution. The harm to its marketing plan cannot readily be monetized and so is appropriately described as irreparable....The harm is aggravated by differences in appearance and quality control (remember the defective Preston) that, while not big enough to rebut an inference of copying, could impair Ty's goodwill if customers buy Preston thinking it is a Beanie Baby rather than a knockoff. This is a type of loss more commonly associated with trademark cases, but it is applicable to copyright as well.

AFFIRMED IN FAVOR OF THE PLAINTIFF.

1. Critical Thinking: What type of information could the defendant GMA have submitted in the previous case that might have kept the court from issuing the injunction?

2. Ethical Decision Making: Suppose you are a business manager for Ty. You are angry that GMA is tricking consumers into buying GMA's products by making products that look like Beanie Babies. Explain why your anger could be motivated by your preference for security, efficiency, or justice. Which of these values does the court prefer?

Every reproduction of a copyrighted work is not an infringement. Under the fair use doctrine, for example, a portion of a copyrighted work may be reproduced for purposes of "criticism, comment, news reporting, teaching (including multiple copies for classroom use), scholarships, and research."

Typically, a party will reproduce a copyrighted work and the copyright holder will bring an action for infringement. The fair use doctrine will then be raised as a defense. Section 107 of the Copyright Act requires the court to weigh the following four factors to determine whether the fair use doctrine applies to the reproduction in question:

1. the purpose and character of the use, including whether such use is of a commercial nature or is for nonprofit educational purposes;
2. the nature of the copyrighted work;

3. the amount and substantiality of the portion used in relation to the copyrighted work as a whole; and
4. the effect of the use upon the potential market for or value of the copyrighted work.

The following case examines a typical situation where the issue of fair use arises: the college classroom.

Case 10-6

Princeton University Press

v.

Michigan Document Services, Inc.
United States Court of Appeals, Sixth Circuit
99 F. 3d 1381 (1996)

Defendant Michigan Document Services, Inc., is a commercial copyshop that reproduced subsubstantial segments of copyrighted works of scholarship, bound the copies into "coursepacks," and sold the coursepacks to students for use in fulfilling reading assignments given by professors at the University of Michigan. The copyshop did not obtain copyright owners' permission to duplicate their copyrighted works.

Princeton University Press and two other publishers whose works had been used without permission sued MDS for copyright infringement. The trial court ruled in favor of the copyright holders, and MDS appealed.

CIRCUIT JUDGE NELSON

"[T]o negate fair use," the Supreme Court has said "one need only show that if the challenged use 'should become widespread, it would adversely affect the potential market for the copyrighted work.'

"…Under this test, we believe, it is reasonably clear that the plaintiff publishers have succeeded in negating fair use.

…M]ost of the copyshops that compete with MDS in the sale of coursepacks pay permission fees for the privilege of duplicating and selling excerpts from copyrighted works. The three plaintiffs together have been collecting permission fees at a rate approaching $500,000 a year. If copyshops across the nation were to start doing what the defendants have been doing here, this revenue stream would shrivel and the potential value of the copyrighted works of scholarship published by the plaintiffs would be diminished accordingly.

…Although [the federal] Classroom Guidelines purport to "state the minimum and not the maximum standards of educational fair use," they do evoke a general idea, at least, of the type of educational copying Congress had in mind. The guidelines allow multiple copies for classroom use provided that: (1) the copying meets the test of brevity (1,000 words, in the present context); (2) the copying meets the test of spontaneity, under which "[t]he inspiration and decision to use the work and the moment of its use for maximum teaching effectiveness [must be] so close in time that it would be unreasonable to expect a timely reply to a request for permission;" (3) no more than nine instances of multiple copying take place during a term, and only a limited number of copies are made from the works of any one author or from any one collective work; (4) each copy contains a notice of copyright; (5) the copying does not substitute for the purchase of "books, publishers' reprints or periodicals;" and (6) the student is not charged any more than the actual cost of copying. The Classroom Guidelines also make clear that unauthorized copying to create "anthologies, compilations or collective works" is prohibited.

In its systematic and premeditated character, its magnitude, its anthological content, and its commercial motivation, the copying done by MDS goes well beyond anything envisioned by the Congress that chose to incorporate the guidelines in the legislative history. Although the guidelines do not purport to be a complete and definitive statement of fair use law for educational copying, and although they do not have the force of law, they do provide us general guidance. The fact that the MDS copying is light years away from the safe harbor of the guidelines weighs against a finding of fair use.

AFFIRMED, IN FAVOR OF PLAINTIFFS

1. Critical Thinking: Why does the court decide that MDS's copying goes beyond fair use? What evidence does the court offer in support of this decision? Are you persuaded by this reasoning?

2. Ethical Decision Making: What ethical issue did the managers of Michigan Document Service have to consider when they were deciding whether to require permissions for the materials they were copying? How would the application of the universalization test affect the way they would think about this decision?

Parody is also protected under fair use, although it is not easy to know when the court will find that the infringement is so significant that the fair use doctrine will not apply. An interesting illustration of the difficulty of determining whether a parody will be considered fair use is the 2001 case involving *Gone With the Wind*. The estate of the author of the first book sued to enjoin publication of *The Wind Done Gone*, an alleged parody of the original work that presented a tale of the Old South from a black perspective. The estate argued that the book infringed on the original work, taking its characters, scenes, settings, physical descriptions and plot.[15]

The Estate sought a preliminary injunction to keep the book from being published until a full trial on the merits of the case could be held. The District Court granted the preliminary injunction based on its findings that: (1) the works were substantially similar; (2) *The Wind Done Gone*'s purpose was to provide a sequel, not a parody; (3) the amount of the original work used by the second work was more than necessary for a parody; (4) the effect of the allegedly infringing use on the market value of the original work weighed in favor of the estate; (5) the owners had demonstrated a substan-

tial likelihood of success on the merits; (6) defendants did not rebut the presumption of irreparable harm to the original copyright owners; (7) the balance of harms weighed in favor of the owners; and (8) competing public interests weighed in favor of preserving the owners' copyright interests.[16]

The appellate court viewed the case differently, however, and overturned the issuance of the injunction, characterizing it as an unconstitutional prior restraint of speech under the First Amendment. The Court of Appeals found that the plaintiffs had not made a strong enough case that: (1) there was a substantial likelihood of success on the merits; (2) irreparable harm would result if no injunction were issued; (3) the threatened injury to the plaintiff of not granting the injunction outweighed the threatened injury to the defendants from granting the injunction; and (4) granting the injunction would be in the public interest, all of which the court said would be necessary for granting the preliminary injunction.[17]

The Wind Done Gone went on sale on June 28, 2001, with the following words circled on its cover: "An Unauthorized Parody." It then spent six weeks on the best seller list, and continues to be sold today.

---

[15] *Mitchell and Joseph Reynolds Mitchell v. Houghton Mifflin Co.*, 58 U.S.P. Q. 2d 1652 (2001).

[16] *Id.*

[17] *Id.*

Copyright Protection For Software

As new technology develops, the legal response to such developments is not always easy to forecast. When software was initially developed, there was some uncertainty as to whether it should be protected under patent or copyright law. In 1980, Congress addressed that issue by amending the Copyright Act of 1976 with the Computer Software Copyright Act, which extended copyright protection to software. The Act classifies software as a "literary work" and defines a computer program as a "set of statements or instructions to be used directly or indirectly in a computer in order to bring about a certain result."

Even passage of the Act, however, did not really solve the problem of how to protect software. It took a series of cases to determine that the law protected not just the part of the computer program that could be read by humans, but also the binary-language object code of computer programs that can be read only by the computer.[18] Subsequent cases extended protection to the overall structure, sequence, and organization of the program.[19] Copyright protection was not extended to the general appearance of the computer screen when using the program.[20]

---

[18] See *Apple Computer, Inc. v. Franklin Computer Corp.*, 714 F. 2d 1240 (3d Cir. 1983).

[19] See, e.g., *Whelan Associates, Inc. v. Jaslow Dental Laboratory, Inc,* 797 F. 2d 1222 (3rd Cir. 1986).

[20] *Lotus Development Corp. v. Borland International, Inc.*, 517 U.S. 843 (1996).

Global Context:
Computer Program Protection in the European Union (EU)

In May of 1991, the Council of European Communities implemented a directive for the purpose of protecting computer programs. The directive equated the protection of computer programs with the protection of literary works under the Berne Convention Standards. The protection is inclusive of all "preparatory design material" and the only parameter necessary for a program to be eligible is that it must be the intellectual creation of the author. If a program is developed by a group of individuals, then the rights are jointly held. If an employee, while fulfilling an employer's instructions, created a program, then the employer has exclusive rights over the program. These protections are guaranteed for life and seventy years after the author's death. The specific remedies against violators of the directive are left to the jurisdiction of each Member State.

In October of 1998, the Data Protection Directive enhanced the above directive. The Data Protection directive required each Member State to legally regulate the processing of personal data with the EU. Most importantly, the directive stated that personal data would only be permitted to travel outside of the EU if the destination country had an adequate level of protection for the subject of the data. This stipulation may effect the European Union's trading relations. The U.S., Canada, Japan, and Australia, for example, do not have comprehensive statutes that regulate information within the private sector. Other foreign countries have even less adequate protection for certain data. If these countries wish to receive the same amount of information from European countries as they have in the past, they may have to consider altering their regulations.

Patents

A **patent** protects a product, process, invention, machine, or plant produced by asexual reproduction. For example, Xerox Corp. invented and patented a line of handheld computers called "PalmPilots" that used a single-stroke system to recognize handwritten text.

Four criteria must be met before a patent will be issued. The object of the patent must be genuine, novel, useful, and not obvious. That simple list of criteria obscures the fact that it is often not easy to know whether a patent is going to be issued, especially in the area of patents for processes. Process patents have always given the patent office difficulty because in many cases the processes seem to simply be "principles of nature" that cannot be patented. Among the most questionable process patents have been so-called business process patents. A business process patent protects a method of doing business that meets the standards of a patent. Initially, such processes appeared to be unpatentable.

A significant holding for business managers concerned about business process patents came in the case of *State St. Bank & Trust v. Signature Fin. Group, Inc.*[21] This case arose over a patent entitled "Data Processing System for Hub and Spoke Financial Services Configuration." The process at issue keeps track of individual mutual fund investments ("spokes") which have been pooled into a single portfolio (a "hub"). The patented system generates numbers that represent (among other things) each spoke's share of profits, numbers that are needed to comply with a set of Internal Revenue Service (IRS) regulations. The judge district court judge held that the patent was invalid under both the "mathematical algorithm" and "business method" exceptions to patentable subject matter.[22] The Circuit Court, however, in upholding the patent, stated that any transformation of data that produces "a useful, concrete, and tangible result" can be protected by a patent. He also stated that business processes have been, and should be, subject to the same legal requirements for patentability as applied to any other process or method. Thus, after this case, business process patents can be protected in the United States.

Despite the Federal Circuit's ruling with respect to business method patents, many still question whether allowing the patenting of business methods is a good idea. They are concerned primarily about whether such patents will stifle competition. Secondly, they are concerned that many of the methods for which such patents will be sought really will not meet the criteria of originality and nonobviousness, but those who decide questions of patentability will not be familiar enough with business to recognize that indeed, those methods have been around in various forms for a long time. Controversy over business methods patents is not likely to end soon, especially in light of the fact that the European Union explicitly prohibits patent protection for business methods.

Once a patent is issued, its holder has the exclusive right to produce, sell, and use the object of the patent for twenty years from the date of filing the patent application if it is a patent for an invention. If it is a patent for a design, protection lasts for only fourteen years; whereas, if it is for a drug, the holder will have the right to extend protection for an additional five years. The holder of the patent may *license*, or allow others to manufacture and sell, the patented object. In most cases, patents are licensed in exchange for the payment of *royalties*, a sum of money paid for each use of the patented process.

Patent holders may not use the patent for illegal purposes, such as *tying arrangements* and *exclusive cross licensing*. A *tying arrangement* occurs when the holder issues a license to use the patented object only if the licensee agrees also to buy some nonpatented product from the holder. *Exclusive cross-licensing* occurs when two patent holders license each other to use their patents *only* on the condition that neither licenses anyone else to use his or her patent without the other's consent. Both of these activities are unlawful because they tend to reduce competition.

While an individual may file for copyright protection without legal assistance, the services of a patent attorney really are necessary when seeking to obtain a patent. The attorney will do a *patent search* to make sure that no other similar patent exists. If it does not, the attorney will fill out a patent application and file it with the Patent Office. The Patent Office will evaluate the application, and if the object meets the aforementioned criteria, a patent will be issued within approximately two years. While two years may seem like a long time, it is short compared to the six years it typically takes to secure a patent in Japan.

---

[21] 149 F.3d 1368, 1377 (Fed. Cir. 1998)

[22] *Id.* at 1372.

After a patent is issued, the holder may bring a patent infringement suit in a federal court against anyone who uses, sells, or manufacturers the patented invention without the permission of the patent holder. When the patent infringement case is filed, the plaintiff will initially seek a preliminary injunction, seeking to prohibit the alleged infringer from using the patented process until the court has an opportunity to determine whether infringement has occurred or not. The patent holder in such a case is entitled to a preliminary injunction if it can succeed in showing: (1) a reasonable likelihood of success on the merits; (2) irreparable harm if an injunction was not granted; (3) a balance of hardships tipping in its favor; and (4) the injunction's favorable impact on the public interest.[23]

As the court explained in *Amazon.Com v. Barnes & Noble*[24] (BN), reasonable success on the merits requires the moving party to demonstrate both a likelihood of infringement and a likelihood that the patent will not be successfully challenged. If the alleged infringer can demonstrate the ability to mount a substantial challenge to the patent, the preliminary injunction will not be granted. In the Amazon case, for example, Amazon

had obtained a patent for its "1-Click (R)" method and system for placing a purchase order over the Internet, and sought a preliminary injunction to prohibit BN's use of a feature of its website called "Express Lane." The District Court granted the preliminary injunction after finding a likelihood that Amazon would be able to prove infringement of certain aspects of its patent.

In overturning the District Court's injunction, the Court of Appeals did not deny those findings. However, they pointed out that if BN raised a substantial question concerning validity of the patent, the preliminary injunction should not have been issued. In this case, BN had introduced several references to prior art that called into question the validity of the patent. The District Court had assessed the references and determined that they did not undermine Amazon's patent. The Appellate Court said the lower court had gone too far and had made a factual determination as to the quality of the references, when it should have limited its review to whether the alleged infringer had raised a substantial question as to the validity of the patent, as they did by providing references to prior art. Thus, the order to issue the injunction was overturned.[25]

[23] 35 U.S.C.A. § 283.
[24] 57 U.S.P.Q. 2d 1747 (2001).

[25] *Ibid.*

Global Context: Patent Protection in India

India has failed to provide adequate patent protection for American and European commerce. The Indian Patents Act of 1970 is very exclusionary. It forbids patents to be given to products intended for use as a food, medicine, or drug. Substances developed through or by chemical processes are also prohibited from receiving patents. Another inadequacy of India's patent laws until recently has been that the length of protection is not specified. These weaknesses are a source of tension between India and other foreign countries.

As the international business market expands, India's poor patent protection regulations have become an increasingly troublesome issue. In 1994, India took a step to improving their regulations by agreeing to the concessions of the Uruguay Round General Agreement on Tariffs and Trade (GATT). This agreement mandates twenty year protection for all inventions. It also commits India to providing full patent protection by the year 2005. By signing the Uruguay Round Agreement, India shows that it recognizes the inadequacies of its patent protection laws and entreats their improvement.

As the Amazon case illustrates, patent litigation can be quite complex. And while a successful action may result in an injunction prohibiting further use of the patented item by the infringer and also an award of damages, an unsuccessful case may lead to the patent holder's loss of the patent. This loss would occur when the alleged infringer is able to prove that the Patent Office should not have issued the patent in the first place.

Trade Secrets

Any process, product, method of operation, invention, formula, design, or compilation of information that gives a businessperson an advantage over his or her competitors can be a **trade secret**. A trade secret is protected by the common law from unlawful appropriation by competitors as long as it is kept secret and is comprised of elements not generally known in the trade. For example, McDonald's Corp. was recently accused of stealing trade secrets from Thermodyne Food Service Products, who had created the oven technology for an oven called "Temperfect." Thermodyne argued that it lost from $57 to $97 million because of McDonald's Corp.'s actions.

To get an injunction prohibiting a competitor from continuing to use a trade secret and/or to recover damages caused by the use of the secret, a plaintiff must prove three elements. First the plaintiff must prove that a trade secret actually existed.

Proving the second element, that it was obtained through unlawful means, is usually the most difficult part of the case. Often, competitors will obtain the secret through lawful means, such as reverse engineering or by going on public tours of plants and observing the use of trade secrets, which means there is no longer a trade secret. Unlawful means would include theft of the secret from the plaintiffs' facility or obtaining the secret by misusing a confidential present or former employee of the plaintiff. The final element is proof that the defendant used the trade secret without the plaintiff's permission.

A common dilemma facing an inventor is whether to protect an invention through patent or trade secret law. If the inventor successfully patents and defends the patent, the patent holder has a guarantee of an exclusive monopoly on the use of the invention for twenty years, a substantial period of time. The problem is that once this period is over, the patented good goes into the public domain and everyone has access to it. There is also the risk that the patent may be successfully challenged and the protection lost prematurely.

Trade secret law, on the other hand, could protect the invention in perpetuity. The problem is that once someone discovers the secret lawfully, the protection is lost. Holders of trade secrets have, not surprisingly, thought of a number of ways to try to protect their trade secrets. For example, companies may require anyone who handles any aspect of the trade secret to sign a nondisclosure agreement.

International Protection of Intellectual Property

As trade among nations increases, and as the Internet allows us instant access to almost all parts of the globe, the international protection of intellectual property rights becomes more important. The primary international protection for intellectual property comes from multilateral conventions, a few of which are briefly discussed in the following sections. Many of these treaties are administered by the World Intellectual Property Organization (WIPO), a specialized agency of the United Nations (UN) to whom membership is open to all countries belonging to the UN. Currently, 175 member states belong to the WIPO. The objectives of the WIPO are to (1) promote the protection of intellectual property throughout the world through cooperation among States and, where appropriate, in collaboration with any other international organization, and (2) ensure administrative cooperation among Unions.

The Berne Convention

The Berne Convention, which came into force in 1887, was the first multinational treaty designed to create uniform international standards of copyright protection. It provides that if a work originates in one of the 175 signatory countries, it will be protected in all other signatory countries without any further formalities. Member nations still have the right to maintain formalities for works created within their borders.

In 1996, members of the World Intellectual Property Organization (WIPO) adopted the World Intellectual Property Organization Copyright Treaty, an agreement under the Berne Convention. The purpose of this treaty was to require nations to provide more safeguards against copyright infringement on the Internet. The United States implemented the terms of this agreement in a section of the Digital Millennium Copyright Act.

The Paris Convention of 1883

The Paris Convention now has 101 members, including the United States, who have agreed to protect so-called "industrial rights," such as inventions and trademarks. Unfair competition is also restricted under the Act.

The treaty has been revised several times, and not all members have signed all versions. The treaty is extremely complex, but it is designed around implementing three basic principles: (1) *national treatment*, which means that the same protections are given to the works of members of signatory nations as are given to members of the home state; (2) *the right of priority*, which allows a national of a member state twelve months after filing for a patent in his home nation (six months for a trademark) to file an application in any other member state, and have the date of application be considered the date of the filing in the home nation, and (3) *common rules*, which set out minimum standard of protection in all states. These common rules include such items as outlawing false labeling and protecting trade names of companies from member states even without registration.

Patent Cooperation Treaty

The benefits of the Patent Cooperation Treaty (PCT), an agreement administered by WIPO, are also available to Paris Convention member nations. Under the PCT, using a simplified procedure, a member of a signatory nation can file one international application and seek patent protection in any or all of the 109 nations that are parties to the treaty. When the application is filed in any member state, the application is then forwarded to an international search authority. The patent is provisionally protected for thirty months in all signatory nations upon application. During that time period, the patent holder may decide in which signatory nations he or she wishes to obtain longer term patent protection.

In the year 2000, a total of 90,448 such patent applications were filed.[26] Americans filed the greatest number, with 38,171 applications. The U.S. was followed by Germany, Japan, the United Kingdom, and then France. Among the developing countries, South Koreans filed the greatest number of applications, followed by the Chinese, and then South Africans.

---

[26] *U.S. Tops Annual List of International Patent Applicants*, FINDLAW LEGAL NEWS <wysiwyg://9/http:// news.findlaw.co… 20010213/manufacturingpatents.html> (February 13, 2001).

The 1994 Agreement on Trade-Related Aspects of Intellectual Property Rights (TRIPS)

One hundred forty two nations are now signatories to TRIPS, which established minimum international standards for the protection and enforcement of trademarks and other forms of intellectual property. The TRIPS Agreement obligates World Trade Organization (WTO) member countries to: (1) provide minimum intellectual property rights protection through domestic laws; (2) provide effective enforcement of those rights; and (3) agree to submit disputes to the WTO dispute settlement system.

Thus, under this agreement, each signatory nation is required to establish broad, minimum intellectual property protections and effective means for enforcement of these protections. No country can give its own citizens better intellectual property protections than those granted to members of other nations that were signatories to the agreement. However, countries are free to determine their own methods of compliance with TRIPS Agreement obligations, and they may provide more extensive protections than those mandated in the treaty.

While developing countries and least-developed countries were given more time to implement these commitments, none were exempt from the standards set forth in TRIPS. In order to assist the developing nations in meeting these standards, WIPO agreed to provide technical assistance to developing countries trying to meet their obligations under the TRIPS Agreement.

The TRIPS Agreement obligates WTO members to "provide procedures and remedies under their domestic law to ensure that intellectual property rights can be effectively enforced, by foreign right holders as well as by their own nationals," and makes WTO members responsible for implementing broader measures to prevent the export of infringing goods. Signatory countries must also ensure that criminal sanctions provide for "the seizure, forfeiture, and destruction of the infringing goods and of any materials and [instruments used] in the commission of the offence."

If countries are not living up to their obligations under TRIPS, any adversely affected nation can bring a claim under the dispute resolution mechanism established to resolve disputes arising under the WTO. Thus, this treaty has more power than many other multinational agreements.

Warner Brothers Wrap-up

Leigh brought claims of copyright and trademark infringement against Warner Brothers for their use of pictures and film footage of a replica of the Bird Girl statue. The district court ruled that certain elements (e.g., lighting, shading, timing, angle, and film) of Leigh's photograph were protected by copyright; however, Warner Brothers' use of the replica in the film footage was not substantially similar to those elements. Similarly, the district court ruled that no reasonable jury would find that the photos of the replica were substantially similar to Leigh's photo. In regard to the trademark infringement claim, the district court held that Leigh could not demonstrate that there was a likelihood of consumer confusion; they would not believe that Leigh was involved with the movie.

Leigh appealed the decision. The 11th Circuit court upheld all of the district courts' rulings except for the holding that no jury would find the photo of the replica substantially similar to Leigh's photograph.

If you were a Warner Brothers business manager who decided to use the pictures of the replica, you might have wished that you did not use the photos based on the legal costs associated with this case. However, the courts have basically decided in your favor; thus, you were likely correct in determining that you were not infringing on Leigh's rights. Perhaps, if the Warner Brothers managers had learned a little more about intellectual property protection, they could have altered the statute and would not have had to worry about a court case.

	Summary
Trademarks	**A trademark** is a distinctive mark, word, design, picture, or arrangement used by a seller in conjunction with a product and tending to cause the consumer to identify the product with the producer. **Trade Dress** refers to the overall image and appearance of a product . Entitled to the same protection as a trademark. **Federal Trademark Dilution Act of 1995**—extended trademark protection to similar marks, not just identical marks.
Copyrights	**Copyrights** protect the expression of creative ideas.
Patents	**Patents** protect a product, process, invention, machine, or plant that reproduces asexually.
Trade Secrets	**Trade secrets** are a process, product, method of operation, or compilation of information that gives a businessperson an advantage over his or her competitors.
International Protection of Intellectual Property	**The Berne Convention of 1886**—oldest treaty designed to protect artistic rights. **The Universal Copyright Convention**—permits members to establish formalities for protection and make exceptions to common rules. **The Paris Convention of 1883**—members agree to protect industrial rights such as inventions and trademarks. **The 1994 Agreement on Trade-Related Aspects of Intellectual Property Rights (TRIPS)**—each nation signing the agreement establishes broad intellectual property protections.

Review Questions and Case Problems

1. Why do we have federal law protecting intellectual property?

2. What factors would a person consider in deciding whether to trade secret protection or patent protection to protect a formula?

3. Miller Brewing produced a reduced calorie beer called "Miller Lite," which it began selling in the 1970s and spent millions of dollars advertising. In 1980, Falstaff Brewing Corporation started marketing a reduced calorie beer "Falstaff Lite." Miller filed an action seeking an injunction against Falstaff to prevent them from using the term "Lite." What was the outcome of the case? *Miller Brewing Co. v. Falstaff Brewing Corporation*, 655 F. 2d 5 (1987).

4. CMM brought suit against Ocean Coast Properties alleging federal copyright, trademark, and trade dress infringement. CMM ran radio promotional contests entitled "Payroll Payoff" and "Paycheck Payoff." Both were registered as service marks in 1991. The radio station announces a name, and if the person announced calls the station, they are "on the payroll" until replaced by the next listener. The promotion was not original to CMM; rather, the idea for the promotion came from another station's promotion called "Working Women's Wednesday." After learning that the promotion was not original, another station, WPOR, began to run a promotion entitled "Payday Contest." Both WPOR and CMM used direct mail to advertise their promotions. The brochures for the stations contained similar graphics and phrases. In arguing that the two promotions could create confusion, CMM testified that they were contacted several times by listeners asking if their promotion was connected to WPOR's promotion. Do you think the court ruled in favor of CMM? *CMM Cable Rep., Inc. v. Ocean Coast Properties Inc.*, 888 F. Supp. 192 (1995).

5. The plaintiff, Lone Star Steakhouse, operates over thirty "Lone Star Steakhouse & Saloon" restaurants in the United States. The trademarks "Lone Star Café" and "Lone Star Steakhouse & Saloon" are owned by Lone Star Steakhouse. Clothing and accessories with the logo are also sold in the restaurant. In 1991 the defendant, Alpha, opened a restaurant named "Lone Star Grill" in Arlington, Virginia. Alpha conducted extensive advertising in the Virginia and Washington D.C. area. The advertisements featured coupons with the words "Lone Star" and a five-pointed star similar to the one used by Lone Star Steakhouse. Lone Star Steakhouse operates four restaurants in Virginia and one restaurant in Washington D.C. They testified that on several occasions customers presented coupons for "Lone Star Grill." To prevent customer dissatisfaction, Lone Star Steakhouse would give customers free drinks, coupons, or meal discounts. Lone Star Steakhouse & Saloon Incorporated brought a trademark infringement action against "Lone Star Grill." How do you think the court decided and why? *Lone Star Steakhouse & Saloon v. Alpha of Virginia*, 43 F. 3d 922 (1995).

6. The Stop & Shop Supermarket and Big Y Foods are supermarkets offering the same services and competing for the same customers. In an advertisement introducing their new, easy to use scan saver cards, Stop & Shop Supermarket used the slogan "It's that Simple." The supermarket used the slogan in radio, television, and print advertisements. The service mark was licensed to the supermarket to use by plaintiff Fullerton, who owns the right to the service mark. After Stop & Shop started using the slogan, Big Y Foods began to use a similar slogan, "We Make Life Simple." Both service marks are always accompanied by the name of the store. Fullerton and Stop & Shop Supermarket brought an action alleging infringement of the service mark. Do you think that the court granted the injunction? Why or why not? *The Stop & Shop Supermarket Company and Fullerton Corp. v. Big Y Foods, Inc.*, 943 F. Supp. 120 (1996).

7. The operator of a martial arts school brought a trademark infringement and unfair competition action against a competitor, alleging infringement of his "Kuk Sool," "Kuk Sool Won," and "World Kuk Sool Association" marks. On motions for summary judgment, the District Court held that: (1) "Kuk Sool" was generic term for type of Korean martial art, and was not entitled to trademark protection. Explain how you believe the court ruled on this motion, and what principle the court used in making its decision. *Suh v. Yang*, (N.D. Cal 1997).

8. Nike, Inc., has trademarks for its name, a "swoosh" design, and a phrase, "just do it." These marks appear on Nike clothing, hats, shoes, and other athletic products. Mike and his daughter started, for a summer project, Just Did it Enterprises, to manufacture and sell through mail order, t-shirts and sweatshirts that had the name Mike and the swoosh emblazoned on them. The project lost money, and Nike sued them for trademark infringement. Discuss the likely outcome of Nike's suit. *Nike, Inc. v. Just Did It Enterprises*, 6 F. 3d 1225 (1993).

9. Superior Form Builders held a copyright for animal mannequins. The sculpted animal forms were used to mount animal skins. The owner of Superior Form Builders, Tommy Knight, considers the mannequins to be a form of artistic expression. The defendant, Dan Chase Taxidermy Supply Company, ordered four of Knight's mannequins from the Superior Form catalog. Chase, a competitor of Superior Form, ordered under a fictitious name. He used the mannequins to mount animal skins and made few changes to the forms. When Knight realized that Chase was using the Superior Form mannequins, he sued for copyright infringement. Chase argued that the copyright should never have been granted because the mannequins were useful and unoriginal. How do you think the court decided? *Superior Form Builders, Inc v. Chase Taxidermy Supply Co.*, 74 F. 3d 488 (4th Cir. 1996).

10. Plaintiff Colombia Pictures Industries Inc. brought a copyright infringement action against Miramax Films Corp. The successful motion picture "Men in Black," produced by Colombia Pictures, grossed over $250 million at the box office in 1997. In advertising the film, Columbia

produced a copyrighted "MIB Poster" and two copyrighted "MIB trailers" shown in theatres. The poster shows Will Smith and Tommy Lee Jones standing in front of the New York City skyline. They hold over-sized weapons, and the copy reads: "PROTECTING THE EARTH FROM THE SCUM OF THE UNIVERSE." The movie trailers use the same slogan and show a shadow of Smith and Jones superimposed over the letters MIB.

In 1998, Miramax Films Corporation produced the film "The Big One." This was a documentary concerning corporate America's quest for profits at the expense of jobs and plant closings. Prior to the release, Miramax also produced posters and movie trailers. The posters featured Michael Moore, the writer and director of the film, standing in front of the New York City skyline with an over-sized microphone. The copy reads: "PROTECTING THE EARTH FROM THE SCUM OF CORPORATE AMERICA." The slogan is used again in the movie trailer, and the trailer ends with a picture of Moore superimposed over the letters TBO.

The promotions for "The Big One" were pulled after Miramax received complaints from Colombia pictures. Columbia argued that Miramax used copyrighted material to generate profits for the film. Miramax contended that they were protected under the fair use doctrine and argued that the films were not similar in nature. Whom do you think the court decided in favor of? Why? *Columbia Pictures Industries, Inc. v. Miramax Films Corp.*, 11 F. Supp. 1179 (1998).

11. Louis Gaste, the composer of an obscure French song written nearly seventeen years earlier, sued the composer of a successful popular song, "Feelings", for copyright infringement. The jury found the composer liable for copyright infringement, and awarded the plaintiff both damages and an injunction against further infringement. The defendants contended that the evidence was not sufficient for a jury to find infringement.

The evidence Gaste introduced to support his claim included the following information: In 1956, Gaste, a resident of France, composed the music to a song entitled "Pour Toi" as part of the score of a motion picture *Le Feu aux Poudres*, which was released in France that same year. Worldwide revenues of "Pour Toi," which was not successful, amounted to less than $15,000. Nearly two decades later, the defendant composed and recorded the song "Feelings," which became a smash hit internationally, winning "gold records" in a number of countries. Through a complicated chain of events, defendant could have received access to "Pour Toi" because the plaintiff had sent it to the defendant's publisher when the plaintiff was trying to market the song in the 1950's.

Gaste's expert testimony was that "there is not one measure of 'Feelings' which...cannot be traced back to something which occurs in 'Pour Toi.' " He also pointed to a unique musical "fingerprint"—an "evaded resolution" that occurred in the same place in the two songs. The witness said that while modulation from a minor key to its relative major was very common, he had never seen this particular method of modulation in any other composi-

tions. Using the case, explain why you believe the court of appeals either upheld or reversed the trial court's decision in this case. *Louis Gaste v. Morris Kaisermann*, 863 F. 2d 1061 (1988).

12. GoTo.Com's logo features a green circle surrounded by a yellow background, with the words "Go" and "To" printed in the circle. Disney Corp. started to use its logo, a green circle surrounded by a yellow background with the word "Go" printed inside, on its GoNetwork's page. GoTo.Com filed suit against Disney Corporation, seeking an injunction. Do you think the court granted the injunction? What factors would they have considered in making their decision? *GoTo.Com, Inc. v. The Walt Disney Company*, 202 F. 3d 1199 (2000).

Assignment on the Internet

Your grandmother wants to copyright her famous recipe for pecan pie. After reading this chapter, what information can you give her? You should be able to explain the basic criteria for copyright protection and the benefits of copyright protection. For additional information, visit the United States Copyright Office's website at **www.loc.gov/copyright** and examine the procedures for registering a recipe. Write a brief note to her explaining the registration procedures. What criteria must her recipe meet for a copyright to be appropriate? How much does registration cost? Write similar memos explaining the registration procedures and criteria for three other works, such as motion pictures, photographs, or computer programs.

On the Internet

http://www.findlaw.com/01topics/ 23intellectprop/index.html *This site contains links to legal resources related to intellectual property, including mailing lists, message boards, discussion groups, articles, and summaries of this area of law. It is a good place to start researching an intellectual property problem.*

http://patent.womplex.ibm.com *This is the site of the Intellectual Property Network, a searchable database maintained by IBM.*

http://www.businessandlaw.com/ip.shtml *This site provides a collection of links to various intellectual property sites.*

www.internic.net *The InterNIC® website is a public information resource for Internet users worldwide. It provides information on the domain-name system, the domain-name registration process, and domain-name registrars.*

dnso.icann.org: *The website of ICANN's Domain Name Supporting Organization (DNSO), which develops recommendations for global policies concerning the Internet's domain-name system (DNS).*

aso.icann.org *The website of ICANN's Address Supporting Organization (ASO), which develops recommendations for global policies concerning allocation of IP addresses and autonomous system (AS) numbers.*

www.iana.org *The website of the Internet Assigned Numbers Authority (the IANA), which is responsible for technical coordination of the assignment of parameters in over 120 identifier spaces used on the Internet. These identifiers include MIME media types,*
port numbers, private enterprise numbers, and protocol numbers. This website contains information about existing assignments and how to obtain a new assignment. The IANA is also responsible for the technical aspects of assigning top-level domains (including ccTLDs) within the Internet's domain name system, for coordinating of the IP-address allocation system operated in conjunction with the Regional Internet Registries (APNIC, ARIN, and RIPE NCC), and for overseeing the technical operation of the Internet's root-nameserver system.

http://www.uspto.gov/web/menu/pats.html *Here is the home page of the U.S. Patent and Trademark Office.*

The De-Content Scramble System (DeCSS) Case[1]

In fall 1999, Eric Corley, publisher of online journal *2600: The Hacker Quarterly*, posted DeCSS (De-Content Scramble System) to the journal. This program allows individuals with technological expertise to decipher Content Scrambling System (CSS), the code the film industry has developed to prevent people from making copies of DVD movies. In addition to posting DeCSS, Corley included links that led site visitors to other sites that posted DeCSS (hyperlinks[2]).

Soon after Corley posted DeCSS and the hyperlinks, he found himself in trouble with the Hollywood studios: Universal Studios, Paramount Pictures, MGM-Time Warner, Disney, and Twentieth Century Fox. These studios are members of the Motion Picture Association of America (MPAA). They sued Corley/*2600* (Corley), asking a judge to issue an injunction prohibiting both the initial posting and the hyperlinks.

The Hollywood studios are looking out for their property rights. Congress has passed a piece of legislation, the Digital Millennium Copyright Act (DMCA), which intends to help artists and other copyright holders curb piracy. The DMCA prohibits the use of, or trafficking in, computer code that circumvents the encryption scheme that protects certain digital content. The DMCA makes it clear that the entertainment industry has the right to put copyright protection codes on a range of digital media, including DVD movies. The Hollywood studios are trying to stop pirates from making it possible for people to have access to films before they leave theaters. If piracy is allowed, who will purchase movie tickets or DVDs?

Corley, assisted by powerful supporters, Kathleen Sullivan, Dean of Stanford University's law school, and the Electronic Frontier Foundation (EFF), asserts that he is not a pirate. Instead, he and his company are protectors of free speech. Corley argues that the DMCA violates the rights of programmers and scientists to share software programs and computer code. He believes the First Amendment guarantees him the right to post DeCSS and the hyperlinks. Corley maintains that journalists, programmers, and scientists should be free to share information on the Web and should not be responsible if people use the information to engage in piracy. The case raises important questions, including:

1. Is the DMCA a valid exercise of the government's power?
2. Does the First Amendment give Corley the right to post DeCSS? What about the hyperlinks?

---

[1] The cite for the decision of the Second Circuit Court of Appeals is *Universal Studios, Inc. v. Corley*, 273 F. 3d 429 (2001).

[2] A hyperlink is a programmed image on a Web page that allows users to click on it, then jump to another website.

CHAPTER 11

Cyberlaw and Business

Cyberlaw and Business: How Law Changes as Society Changes

Intellectual Property Issues in Cyberspace

E-commerce Issues

Employment Law Issues in Cyberspace

The War Against Cybercrime

The lawsuit between the Hollywood studios and Corley illustrates one of many current struggles that pit key values against each other in the context of the ever-changing environment of technology. Businesses need to be aware of how the legal system is responding to changes brought about by the Internet and World Wide Web.

This chapter presents issues that fall under a wide range of legal topics, including a general discussion of how law changes as society changes, an overview of the new slant on intellectual property issues and e-commerce, an outline of issues related to privacy and online marketing, a summary of employment issues in cyberspace, and an explanation of how government regulators and law enforcement officers are battling the war against cybercrime. This chapter presents information that allows business people to know which legal issues in cyberspace are important, and how they can use legal rules and ethical principles to engage in sound decision making.

Cyberlaw and Business: How Law Changes as Society Changes

In Chapter 1, you learned about the flexible nature of law. In particular, you learned that as the business environment changes, the legal system adjusts to those changes. Currently, the legal system is adapting to the most important changes in the business environment brought about by technological developments. Legislators and judges are reaching decisions that often show their support for particular value priorities.

The Federal Government's Changing Roles

One of the biggest news stories of the early 2000's was the Department of Justice's pursuit of Microsoft on antitrust charges, and the subsequent nonbreakup of the company. Americans watched the case with interest, as the federal government decided how much power it would exert to ensure competitive markets. The case pitted two definitions of freedom against each other. Microsoft wanted to be able to act without restriction from rules imposed by the government, while Microsoft's competitors wanted the government to step in to protect free markets. The competitors wanted the Justice Department to enact measures that would allow them to operate in markets free from Microsoft's inappropriate use of monopoly power.[3]

We also watched as Congress passed key legislation in the late 1990's and early 2000's in response to societal changes related to cyberspace. For instance, Congress enacted the DMCA in 1998 to help artists and other copyright holders curb piracy (see the DeCSS case at the beginning of the chapter). In the same year, Congress passed a far different law, the Children's Online Protection Act of 1998 (COPA), which expanded the protections provided by the Child Pornography Protection Act of 1996 (CPPA). CPPA prohibited and criminalized trafficking in child pornography; COPA extended the law to include online transmissions by service providers and e-commerce site providers. The Communications Decency Act of 1996 (CDA) is another example of relatively new federal legislation. This law established criminal liability for the online transmission of indecent and patently offensive material to minors.[4]

In Case 11-1, the court decides the extent to which one of the provisions of the CDA preempts state common law. The case shows how law changes as society changes. Before Congress passed the CDA, it was possible for plaintiffs to pursue Internet Service Providers (ISPs) for some forms of negligence. Individuals were

---

[3] See the antitrust chapter for a more detailed description of the Microsoft case.

[4] The United States Supreme Court has ruled that some parts of this law are unconstitutional.

secure, knowing that if ISPs harmed them, they could seek compensation. In Case 11-1, the court decides whether the CDA prevents a plaintiff from suing America Online (AOL), Inc. based upon the theory that AOL negligently distributed defamatory material.

As you read the case, notice the public policy decisions the court endorses. The court supports Congress' interest in promoting innovation, even if a particular plaintiff will not have the chance to seek compensation from AOL.

Case 11-1

Kenneth M. Zeran, Plaintiff
v.
America Online, Inc., Defendant
United States District Court, E.D. Virginia, Alexandria Division
958 F. Supp. 1124 (1997)

*K*enneth Zeran (Zeran) was the victim of a malicious hoax. In the immediate aftermath of the bombing of the Alfred P. Murrah Federal Building in downtown Oklahoma City, a posting appeared on an Internet bulletin board announcing the availability for sale of "Naughty Oklahoma T-Shirts," bearing such slogans as, "Rack'em, Stack'em and Pack'em—Oklahoma 1995," and "Visit Oklahoma—it's a BLAST."
The posting was made by someone using the screen name "Ken ZZ03" and indicated that the shirts could be ordered by telephone. The number provided was Kenneth Zeran's business telephone number. Zeran had nothing to do with the posting.

An AOL official told Zeran the posting would be removed from the bulletin board, but that, in keeping with company policy, AOL would not post a retraction. The next day, April 26, an unknown person posted another message advertising the T-shirts. The message gave Zeran's phone number and said to ask for "Ken" and to "please call back if busy." Zeran received even more threatening phone calls. For the next four days, an unidentified person continued posting messages on AOL, offering more merchandise (key chains and bumper stickers) and more offensive slogans. In the meantime, Zeran continued to call AOL to complain. AOL assured him the company would close the account from which the messages were posted. By the end of April, Zeran's phone rang every two minutes, each time with an abusive message. In spite of Zeran's repeated calls to AOL, the postings remained on the Internet for at least a week.

AOL had provided the unique screen name "Ken ZZ03" to an individual who opened up a trial AOL membership. AOL maintains a database with the names, addresses, phone numbers, and credit card numbers of its members, searchable by screen name. However, AOL does not verify member information before allowing a new member to go online utilizing a trial membership. AOL disseminates trial memberships by the tens of thousands. The true identity of Ken ZZ03 remains unknown, since the account was opened with false information.

Zeran decided to sue AOL, Inc., alleging that the company negligently disseminated defamatory information that caused harm to his reputation. Here, the trial judge rules on AOL's motion to dismiss.

DISTRICT JUDGE ELLIS
...Section 230 of the CDA, titled "protection for private blocking and screening of offensive material," represents an initial federal effort to define the appropriate scope of federal regulation of the

Internet...Zeran's alleged cause of action is pursuant to a duty he claims state law imposes on distributors to refrain from distributing material they knew or should have known was defamatory. Thus, the question is whether the CDA preempts any state common law cause of action Zeran may have against AOL resulting from its role in the malicious hoax perpetrated via AOL's electronic bulletin board.

...Preemption is...required where state law conflicts with the express language of a federal statute...AOL points to § 230(c)(1), which states that [n]o provider or user of an interactive computer service shall be treated as the publisher or speaker of any information provided by another information content provider...[T]he preemption issue reduces to the question whether a state cause of action for negligent distribution of defamatory material directly conflicts with the CDA's prohibition against treating an Internet provider as a "publisher or speaker." Put another way, the question is whether imposing common law distributor liability on AOL amounts to treating it as a publisher or speaker. If so, the state law is preempted.

...[D]istributor liability treats a distributor as a "publisher" of third party statements where that distributor knew or had reason to know that the statements were defamatory. It follows that Zeran's attempt to impose distributor liability on AOL is, in effect, an attempt to have AOL treated as the publisher of the defamatory material. This treatment is contrary to § 230(c)(1) of the CDA and, thus, Zeran's claim for negligent distribution of the notice is preempted.

...An alternative basis for preemption exists if subjecting AOL to state law distributor liability would stand "as an obstacle to the accomplishment of the full purposes and objectives of Congress" in passing § 230 of the CDA...Congress' clear objective in passing § 230 of the CDA was to encourage the development of technologies, procedures, and techniques by which objectionable material could be blocked or deleted, either by the interactive computer service provider itself or by the families and schools receiving information via the Internet. If this objective is frustrated by the imposition of distributor liability on Internet providers, then preemption is warranted. Closely examined, distributor liability has just this effect...Internet providers subjected to distributor liability are less likely to undertake any editing or blocking efforts because such efforts can provide the basis for liability. For example, distributors of information may be held to have "reason to know" of the defamatory nature of statements made by a third party where that party "notoriously persists" in posting scandalous items...[D]istributor liability discourages Internet providers from engaging in efforts to review online content and delete objectionable material, precisely the effort Congress sought to promote in enacting the CDA.

In sum, although the CDA does not preempt all state law causes of action concerning interactive computer services, it does preempt Zeran's claim. This is so because his "negligence" cause of action conflicts with both the express language and the purposes of the CDA.

AOL'S MOTION IS GRANTED.

1. Critical Thinking. Identify one **ambiguous word or phrase** in the court's decision, and show how that ambiguity affects your ability to accept the court's conclusion.

2. Ethical Decision Making. Ordinarily, it is legally wise for a company to treat its customers and potential customers well. Here, however, common law principles provide a disincentive for ISPs to look out for people like Zeran. How so? How does the court's decision attempt to provide an incentive for ISPs to look out for people like Zeran? What **value** supports the policy of providing incentives for ISPs to review online content and delete objectionable material?

EXHIBIT 11-1

The USA Patriot Act

The September 11, 2001 attacks on America triggered more federal legislative changes. In October 2001, President Bush signed The Uniting and Strengthening America by Providing Tools Required to Intercept and Obstruct Terrorism Act of 2001 (the "USA Patriot Act").

This law addresses terrorism by enhancing domestic security and surveillance procedures, protecting U.S. borders, and removing obstacles to investigate terrorism.

Cyberlaw experts are reviewing this law carefully, especially because it includes important new rules about the government's access to individual users on the Internet. The law increases the government's power, limiting individuals' freedom, to promote increased national security.

Challenges to State Law Power

The *Zeran v. AOL, Inc.* case is just one example of a case that shows the importance of federal law in cyberspace. Another example focuses on challenges to states' traditional regulatory role. Traditionally, states have regulated the way consumers gain access to prescription drugs. Now, it is possible to obtain prescription drugs through e-commerce sites, and these sites are difficult to regulate using state law. Some health law attorneys believe states can no longer regulate effectively and that the federal government should step in and regulate.[5]

Recently, however, two state attorneys general have demonstrated a strong ability to look out for consumers that use the Internet to purchase prescription drugs. The attorneys general of Florida and Washington State have filed a lawsuit against an online pharmacy (Aprescribe.com) and a Florida physician who prescribed Cipro without examining or speaking to the customers seeking the drug.[6] Cipro is used to treat anthrax. The attorneys general are concerned that the website fails to provide information about the risks of using Cipro, and that, in addition to threatening people's health, the online pharmacy is trying to profit

from Americans' fears of bioterrorism.[7] The attorneys general pointed out that if states work together, they can put a stop to fraudulent Internet practices that cross state lines.

Intellectual Property Issues in Cyberspace

Trademarks

Domain Names as Trademarks

A **trademark** is a distinctive mark, word, design, picture, or arrangement used by the producer of a product that tends to cause consumers to identify the product with the producer. As individuals and businesses have increasingly relied on the World Wide Web to engage in business transactions, **domain names** have become trademarks that allow us to identify products with producers. For instance, you probably identify the domain name "www.victoriassecret" with a particular product (lingerie). Domain names represent more to businesses than mere addresses.

The Anticybersquatting Consumer Protection Act

As these domain names have become more valuable, they provided an opportunity for **cybersquatters** to engage in questionable acts to make a profit. Typically, cybersquatting occurs when an individual or business intentionally obtains a domain name registration for a company's trademark so it can sell the domain name back to the trademark owner; the individual "pirates" the domain name. For instance, Stephen Gregory has purchased domain names for numerous cities (e.g., www.baltimoremaryland.com) and has used these sites as pornographic websites.[8] He is holding the names of certain cities for $8,500 each, and purchasers must pay in cash. He has purchased a number of other domain names, e.g., prison.com (on sale for $20,000), highdefinitiontv.com ($200,000), and beijingchina.com ($350,000). Unfortunately, some names cannot be trademarked (e.g., geographic place names), so these Internet domain names were available, first-come, first-served. It is possible, however, for cities like Baltimore to ask the World Intellectual Property Organization (WIPO) to arbitrate a dispute over the domain name.

---

[5] Kenneth Korenchuk, *21st-Century Technology Meets 20th Century Laws: Tension Between Old Divisions of Federal and State Jurisdiction Impedes Growth of Web Rx Biz*, THE NATIONAL LAW JOURNAL, April 10, 2000, at B19.

[6] Tamar Lewin, *Anthrax Drug Sold Online Leads to Suit*, THE NEW YORK TIMES, January 12, 2002.

[7] *Id.*

[8] The examples in this paragraph come from Gady A. Epstein, *Web Site Owner Links City to Smut*, THE BALTIMORE SUN, January 14, 2002.

Global Context:
Anticybersquatting in Canada[9]

Cybersquatting occurs when a person or company registers a domain name with a bad faith intent to profit from a protected trademark. For example, a person or company would show bad faith if they knowingly diverted another company's customers to its own website.

In Canada, trademark owners use the theories of trademark infringement, trademark dilution, or unfair competition to protect their trademarks. Canadian courts are beginning to rule in cybersquatting cases. In two recent cases, courts have issued injunctions against defendants who have violated trademark laws. In one case, *Bell Actimedia, Inc. v. Puzo*, a Canadian federal court issued an interlocutory injunction against Puzo after finding that Puzo tried to "pass off" Bell Actimedia's wares, services, and business as its own.

Some lawyers believe countries like Canada need to go beyond reliance on trademark law to protect individuals and businesses from cybersquatting. Attorneys Katarzyna Buchen and Brian Belowich, U.S. intellectual property litigators, have urged Canada to consider adopting anticybersquatting legislation similar to U.S.'s Anticybersquatting Consumer Protection Act.

Another way to resolve cybersquatting issues is through international arbitration. The World Intellectual Property Organization (WIPO) has authority to arbitrate cybersquatting disputes both in the U.S. and internationally. The WIPO decided its first case in January 2000 when it considered a case brought by the World Wrestling Federation Entertainment Inc.

Another form of cybersquatting occurs when an individual or business registers a domain name that is the same or similar to a pre-existing trademark that belongs to someone else. The intent is to confuse the consumer. For example, a company called Victoria's Cyber Secret chose four Internet domain names similar to Victoria's Secret's name: victoriassexsecret.com, victoriassexysecret.com, victoriasexsecret.com, and victoriasexysecret.com.[10] The company bought the domain names, planning to use the sites for adult entertainment starring Playboy Playmate Victoria Silvstedt.

In November 1999, the United States became the first country to pass legislation aimed directly at preventing cybersquatting. The law, the Anticybersquatting Consumer Protection Act, responds to cases that allege both traditional piracy and intentional confusion. The Act gives courts the power to forfeit, cancel or transfer domain names. Cybersquatters may be required to pay both actual and statutory damages that range from $1,000 to $100,000 per domain name. Companies like Victoria's Secret, which have a trademark in their name, benefit from this legislation. Victoria's Cyber Secret recently lost a court battle with Victoria's Secret. The court, using the Anticybersquatting Consumer Protection Act, ordered Victoria's Cyber Secret to refrain from using the domain names it had created and purchased.[11]

---

[9] The facts for this text box came from Katarzyna A. Buchen & Brian T. Belowich, *Trademark Law: Global Anti-cybersquatting*, THE NATIONAL LAW JOURNAL, March 13, 2000 at B7. This article also offers information about cybersquatting in England and France.

[10] The facts about Victoria's Secret come from Sarah Van Cott, *Web Matters: Cybersquatters Have Ways of Circumventing the Law*, THE SANTA FE NEW MEXICAN, September 23, 2001, available at 2001 WL 24199522.

[11] *Id.*

Website Copyright Issues

Direct Infringement and Fair Use

Copyrights protect the *expression* of creative ideas. As you learned in Chapter 10, copyrights protect fixed forms of expression, not ideas themselves. Copyrights protect a diverse range of creative works, such as books, periodicals, music compositions, plays, motion pictures, sound recordings, lectures, works of art, and computer programs. The United States Constitution (Article I, Section 8, Clause 8) and federal legislation (The Copyright Act of 1976, the Lanham Act) provide the basis for copyright protection.

For a work to be copyrightable, it must be fixed (*i.e.,* set out in a tangible medium of expression), original, and creative. An individual who wants to make sure he or she can collect damages from a copyright infringer protects their work by registering it with the Register of Copyrights and providing two copies of the work to the Library of Congress.

Copyright infringement occurs when a person or business reproduces a substantial and material part of the plaintiff's protected work, without permission. If a person or business believes someone is infringing on a copyright, that person or business may ask a court to enjoin the infringer from reproducing the copyrighted work. They may also seek compensatory damages. In response, alleged infringers often assert the **fair use doctrine**, which provides that a copyrighted work may be reproduced for a range of purposes, including criticism, news reporting, and teaching. In case 11-2, the court considers what it means for a company to engage in direct copyright infringement, and what the company must assert to establish a defense based upon the fair use doctrine.

Case 11-2

A & M Records, Inc.

v.

Napster, Inc.
United States Court of Appeals for the Ninth Circuit (California)
239 F. 3d 1004 (2001)

*R*ecord companies and music publishers sued Napster. Napster is a free online music trading service. The company provides software that facilitates the transmission and retention of digital audio files (called MP3 files) by users. Users download Napster's MusicShare software, which allows them to access the directory and index on a Napster server to locate MP3 files on other users' hard drives. Users download MP3 files from other users' hard drives. Although the MP3 files do not transfer through Napster's servers, users must access Napster's system to get access to file names and routing data.[12]

The plaintiffs sought an injunction against Napster, asking a trial court to prohibit Napster from facilitating the copying, downloading, or distributing of thousands of plaintiffs' copyrighted musical compositions and sound recordings without the plaintiffs' permission. In May and July 2000, Judge Marilyn Hall Patel issued two opinions, both of which supported the injunction plaintiffs requested. She rejected several of Napster's claims, including claims that their service constituted fair use, that their service constituted valid sampling or space-shifting, and that the First Amendment protected the company's service. In the excerpt below, an appellate court decides whether the trial court applied the law correctly when deciding to issue the injunction. The excerpt focuses on direct copyright infringement and selected parts of the court's discussion of fair use.

[12] Other peer-to-peer technologies exist that do not store directories on a central server.

CIRCUIT JUDGE BEEZER

A. Infringement

Plaintiffs must satisfy two requirements to present a prima facie case of direct infringement: (1) they must show ownership of the allegedly infringed material and (2) they must demonstrate that the alleged infringers violate at least one exclusive right granted to copyright holders under 17 U.S.C. § 106…Plaintiffs have sufficiently demonstrated ownership. The record supports the district court's determination that "as much as eighty-seven percent of the files available on Napster may be copyrighted and more than seventy percent may be owned or administered by plaintiffs."

The district court further determined that plaintiffs' exclusive rights under § 106 were violated: "here the evidence establishes that a majority of Napster users use the service to download and upload copyrighted music…And by doing that, it constitutes—the uses constitute direct infringement of plaintiffs' musical compositions, recordings."…The district court also noted that "it is pretty much acknowledged…by Napster that this is infringement." We agree that plaintiffs have shown that Napster users infringe at least two of the copyright holders' exclusive rights: the rights of reproduction, § 106(1); and distribution, § 106(3). Napster users who upload file names to search the index for others to copy violate plaintiffs' distribution rights. Napster users who download files containing copyrighted music violate plaintiffs' reproduction rights. Napster asserts an affirmative defense to the charge that its users directly infringe plaintiffs' copyrighted musical compositions and sound recordings.

B. Fair Use

Napster contends that its users do not directly infringe plaintiffs' copyrights because the users are engaged in fair use of the material…Napster identifies three specific alleged fair uses: sampling, where users make temporary copies of a work before purchasing; space-shifting, where users access a sound recording through the Napster system that they already own in audio CD format; and permissive distribution of recordings by both new and established artists.

The district court considered factors listed in 17 U.S.C. § 107, which guide a court's fair use determination. These factors are: (1) the purpose and character of the use; (2) the nature of the copyrighted work; (3) the "amount and substantiality of the portion used" in relation to the work as a whole; and (4) the effect of the use upon the potential market for the work or the value of the work…The district court concluded that Napster users are not fair users. We agree.

[The court then agreed with the district court that the first three factors weigh against a finding of fair use.]

4. Effect of Use on Market

…Addressing this factor, the district court concluded that Napster harms the market in "at least" two ways: it reduces audio CD sales among college students and it "raises barriers to plaintiffs' entry into the market for the digital downloading of music." The district court relied on evidence plaintiffs submitted to show that Napster use harms the market for their copyrighted musical compositions and sound recordings…Notably, plaintiffs' expert, Dr. E. Deborah Jay, conducted a survey (the "Jay Report") using a random sample of college and university students to track their reasons for using Napster and the impact Napster had on their music purchases. The court recognized that the Jay Report focused on just one segment of the Napster user population and found "evidence of lost sales attributable to college use to be probative of irreparable harm for purposes of the preliminary injunction motion."… [The court then discusses additional studies offered by the plaintiffs.]

As for defendant's experts, plaintiffs objected to the report of Dr. Peter S. Fader, in which the expert concluded that Napster is *beneficial* to the music industry because MP3 music file-sharing stimulates more audio CD sales than it displaces. The district court found problems in Dr. Fader's minimal role in overseeing the administration of the survey and the lack of objective data in his report…[The court then concluded that the district court demonstrated a proper exercise of discretion in using the studies to reject a fair use defense. Then, the court considered Napster's sampling and space-shifting arguments and concluded that the district court did not abuse its discretion in finding that these uses do not constitute a fair use.]

AFFIRMED.

1. Critical Thinking. What kind of evidence might have convinced the court that Napster was not harming the market?

2. Ethical Decision Making. What ethical rule would Napster executives be likely to cite in defense of their behavior in creating a business based upon copyright infringement? Would the **universalization test** provide support for Napster?

Contributory Copyright Infringement

The court also ruled that it was likely that Napster had engaged in **contributory copyright infringement**. Contributory copyright infringement occurs when one, with knowledge of an infringing activity, induces, causes, or materially contributes to the infringing conduct of another. The court stated that liability exists if Napster engaged in conduct that encouraged or assisted infringers. The court ruled that Napster had facilitated transmission and retention of digital files by its users, and had actual knowledge that specific infringing material was available on its system. Napster had failed to remove infringing material.

Some legal scholars predict that the United States Supreme Court will be forced to issuing rulings that resolve clashes between copyright law and the First Amendment in cyberspace. The First Amendment of the United States Constitution provides varying degrees of protection to different forms of oral, written, and symbolic speech. Both the Napster case and DeCSS cases (see the chapter opener) raise questions about the First Amendment: To what extent is computer code speech? To what extent can the government regulate speech in an effort to protect the work of artists? In some situations, do copyright laws have a chilling effect on free speech?

Those who defend the music recording and motion picture industries argue that federal copyright laws have already done a good job of adapting to technological change. As one author put it, copyright laws have "maintain[ed] a careful balance between consumers' desire for access to creative works and creators' incentives for the creation and dissemination of them

in the first place."[13] It is possible that new technology does not call for sweeping change.

E-Commerce Issues

The increasing importance of e-commerce raises key legal issues, many of which remain unresolved. For example, the issue of whether and how states can collect taxes on sales transacted on the Internet remains unresolved. Courts and legislatures have, however, tentatively resolved some issues. In this section, you will learn about three significant topics that directly affect e-commerce transactions: privacy, online marketing, and cybersignatures.

Privacy and Information Security

When people express concerns about **privacy** in the context of cyberspace, they usually have two concerns. First, individuals are concerned about external **surveillance**. For example, people might be concerned that a marketing company can track which websites they visit and compile a profile that would be used for targeted marketing campaigns. Second, individuals want to be able to control their private **information**. For instance, people might be concerned about online banking because of the possibility that outsiders could tap into account information. Both federal and state laws protect individuals' privacy rights.

---

[13] Cowan, Liebowitz & Latman, PC, *United States: Gimme Some Music: The Place of Napster in Copyright History,* MONDAQ BUSINESS BRIEFING, June 15, 2001, 2001 WL 8987040.

Federal Statutes

In the 1970s, Congress started passing laws that restricted how the government could keep and use personal information they have gathered about American citizens and others. More recent legislation relates directly to privacy issues in cyberspace. For instance, Congress passed The Electronic Communications Privacy Act of 1986 (ECPA). The ECPA prohibits any person from knowingly revealing to any other person the contents of an electronic communication while that communication is in transmission or in electronic storage. This law provides a basis for individuals to sue Internet service providers and others who fail to protect e-mail and voice mail privacy.

A more recent statute is The Children's Online Protection Act of 1998 (COPA), which (1) requires websites that collect personal information from children to provide notice on the site of what information will be collected and how it will be used and (2) requires sites to obtain parental consent to collect infor-

mation from children under age thirteen. Another example of recent legislation related to privacy issues in cyberspace is the Financial Services Modernization Act of 1999 (FSMA). This law aims to provide Internet consumers more control over who has access to their banking information.

State Common Law

State common law also protects privacy. Although common law varies from state to state, most have recognized some kind of privacy tort. Three torts that are especially important with regard to e-commerce are **intrusion upon seclusion, misappropriation of the right to publicity and false light invasion of privacy.** Intrusion upon seclusion is defined as intentionally intruding on the solitude or private affairs of another person. Misappropriation of the right of publicity occurs when someone attempts to appropriate a living person's name or identity for commercial purposes. The next case, Case 11-3, defines false light invasion of privacy.

Case 11-3

Kenneth M. Zeran, Plaintiff-Appellant
v.
Diamond Broadcasting, Inc., Defendant-Appellant
303 F. 3d 714
10th Circuit Court of Appeals
(Oklahoma)(2000)

Recall from Case 11-1 that Kenneth Zeran (Zeran) was the victim of a malicious hoax soon after the bombing of the Federal Building in Oklahoma City in 1995. Someone posted his business phone number on an AOL bulletin board as a contact number for people who wanted to purchase "Naughty Oklahoma T-shirts." In addition to suing AOL for the damages he incurred, Zeran sued Diamond Broadcasting, Inc., owners of KRXO, a classic-rock radio station in Oklahoma City.

On April 29, 1995, an AOL member sent Mark ("Shannon") Fullerton an e-mail message that contained a copy of the original posting. Shannon, one of KRXO's on-air personalities, did not know the person who sent the posting. On May 1, Shannon went on air, and, in addition to discussing the posting, reading the slogans, and reading Zeran's telephone number, urged listeners to call Ken ZZO3 and tell him what they thought of him for offering the t-shirts with offensive slogans. Shannon pursued these actions after making one unsuccessful e-mail attempt to verify the information prior to airing it. In other words, he did not check to make sure Zeran was actually offering the products prior to making announce-

ments on air. As a consequence of Shannon's behavior, Zeran received approximately eighty angry, obscenity-laced calls from the Oklahoma City area. Most callers hung up before Zeran was able to speak, but he was able to figure out that the calls came after a KRXO broadcast.

Zeran suffered because of the calls. These calls included death threats. Zeran described May 1 as the worst day of his life. He subsequently called law enforcement officials, and sought treatment for anxiety from his family physician. The doctor prescribed an anti-anxiety drug. Zeran also called KRXO and asked that the station broadcast a retraction, which it did. Zeran does not know of anyone who knows him by the name Kenneth Zeran who saw the AOL postings, heard the broadcast, or associated him with "Ken Z" or the phone number on the AOL postings.

In this case, the judge considers whether Zeran can use tort law to seek compensation for a variety of injuries, including those caused by possible invasion of his privacy.

DISTRICT JUDGE ELLIS
…The district court granted Defendant's motion for summary judgment on all claims. "We review the granting of summary judgment *de novo*…"

1. Defamation
Defamation through an oral communication, or slander, is defined by statute in Oklahoma as a false and unprivileged communication that (1) charges a person with a crime; (2) accuses him of having an infectious, contagious, or loathsome disease; (3) maligns him with respect to his office, profession, trade, or business; (4) imputes to him impotence or want of chastity; or (5) by its natural consequences, causes actual damage.

The district court correctly pointed out that the only subdivision possibly applicable to the broadcast is the last one, slander *per quod*. Evidence of special damages was specifically required…

Emotional distress is not a form of special damages, and Plaintiff's *de minimus* medical expenses, consisting of one visit to his physician and one prescription drug purchase, are insufficient to support this cause of action…

Although Plaintiff suffered an injury, the district court correctly found that
Plaintiff did not suffer an injury to his reputation, which is the essence of an action for defamation…

Plaintiff's defamation fails because Plaintiff has not shown that any person thinks less of him, Kenneth Zeran, as a result of the broadcast. As the district court found, there was no evidence that anyone who called his number in response to the postings or the broadcast even knew his last name. In other words, under the facts of this case, there was an insufficient link between Plaintiff's business telephone number and Plaintiff himself for Plaintiff to have sustained damage to his reputation.

2. False Light Invasion of Privacy
Oklahoma has recognized false light invasion of privacy…:
One who gives publicity to a matter concerning another that places the other before the public in a false light is subject to liability to the other for invasion of privacy, if (a) the false light in which the other was placed would be highly offensive to a reasonable person, and (b) the actor had knowledge of or acted in reckless disregard as to the falsity of the publicized matter and the false light in which the other would be placed…

Mere negligence is insufficient to establish the requisite fault necessary to hold a defendant liable—the defendant must have "had a high degree of awareness of probable falsity or in fact entertained serious doubts as to the truth of the publication."…The district court granted summary judgment to Defendant on this claim on the ground that Plaintiff had failed to offer proof that Defendant's employees either knew the postings were fictitious or acted recklessly…We affirm on the same basis.

…The Oklahoma Supreme Court…rejected the arguments for a negligence standard in false light cases stating that it was "committed" to "a standard of knowing or reckless conduct to afford recovery to those who suffer mental anguish by reason of a false light invasion of privacy…"

In order to establish reckless disregard, Plaintiff must demonstrate actual knowledge of probable falsity…Plaintiff's expert could not possibly have personal knowledge concerning the relevant question, namely, whether Shannon…had an actual, subjective awareness that [what he was] repeating on the air was probably false. For this reason, we find that the district court did not abuse its discretion in denying Plaintiff's motion for a new trial and affirm the district court's dismissal of the claim.

3. Intentional Infliction of Emotional Distress

Oklahoma recognizes intentional infliction of emotional distress ("IIED")…:

One who by extreme and outrageous conduct intentionally or recklessly causes severe emotional distress to another is subject to liability for such emotional distress, and if bodily harm to the other results from it, for such bodily harm.

The district court granted summary judgment against Plaintiff on the ground that Plaintiff failed to present evidence sufficient to show that KRXO behaved in an extreme and outrageous way toward him and on the ground that Plaintiff failed to demonstrate that he suffered severe emotional distress as a result. We affirm on the same grounds.

…The conduct must be beyond all bounds of human decency or such as is regarded as utterly intolerable in a civilized society.

…The conduct on which Plaintiff's claim is based—the commentary of a radio talk show host concerning an offensive advertisement that appeared on the Internet, even if that host failed to first verify that the information contained in the advertisement was accurate—does not compare to the kinds of conduct that have sustained IIED claim…

…It is also the trial court's initial responsibility to determine whether the distress allegedly suffered by the plaintiff is severe emotional distress…the distress must be of such a character that "no reasonable person should be expected to endure it."…Again, we concur with the district court in his finding that the evidence the Plaintiff submitted fails to show that the level of distress he suffered was sufficiently severe to be actionable…the Court is…influenced by the lack of evidence showing that the distress [in this case] interfered with Plaintiff's ability to conduct his daily life affairs…

AFFIRMED.

1. Critical Thinking. For each of Zeran's three claims, change one fact in the case in a way that increases his chances of avoiding the summary judgment.

2. Ethical Decision Making. If you find yourself sympathetic to Zeran, what **value** underlies your rationale? What **value** underlies this court's decision to affirm the summary judgment?

As *Zeran v. Diamond Broadcasting, Inc.* shows, judges balance individuals' privacy rights with competing values, including freedom of speech (*e.g.,* talk show hosts should be free to act without restrictions imposed by others, as long as they are not reckless) and efficiency (*e.g.,* radio stations should not have to pay for someone's *de minimus* expenses related to anxiety).

Sometimes, individuals find themselves looking to other areas of law when tort law will not support their claim. In addition to tort law, contract law sometimes provides some remedies for individuals who believe their privacy rights have been violated. If the lawsuit is against a website, the plaintiff can look at the site's privacy policy, which is a contract, and see whether the site has breached the contract. Privacy policies vary widely in terms of what they offer a customer.

Online Marketing

The Internet provides opportunities and challenges for online marketers. In the preceding section, the text pointed out privacy issues that challenge marketers. In particular, marketers must address consumers' privacy concerns. Consumers do not want marketers to violate their privacy rights by collecting information about them without their knowledge and/or consent. Consumers are also nervous about the possibility that expert marketers will promote and commit fraud and promote scams via the Internet. Marketers are learning to balance their self-interest in using the Internet to gather important marketing research data with policies consistent with self-preservation.

In Case 11-4, the court considers an online marketing issue. In particular, the court considers whether companies that advertise prescription drugs directly to consumers on television and websites have a duty to warn them about the dangers of the drugs. With direct-to-consumer advertising of prescription drugs on the rise, more courts will be considering these types of marketing issues.

Case 11-4

Saray Perez, (Plaintiff-Appellant)

v.

Wyeth Laboratories, Inc., (Respondent)
Supreme Court of New Jersey
734 A. 2d 1245 (1999)

*P*laintiffs, consumers of Norplant, a surgically implanted contraceptive, filed a product liability action against the maker of the drug, Wyeth Laboratories. Wyeth filed for a summary judgment against the consumers, and a trial court granted that motion. The trial court relied on a legal principle known as the "learned intermediary doctrine" to grant the summary judgment.

In the following excerpt, appellate judge O'Hern considers the learned intermediary doctrine. In particular, he asks whether a drug manufacturer that markets its product directly to consumers has a duty to warn consumers directly of foreseeable risks associated with the drug. In prior cases, judges had accepted a legal standard that required drug manufacturers to communicate with physicians, rather than consumers, about product dangers. In this case, O'Hern considers whether changing doctor-patient relationships call for a change in legal standards. The learned intermediary doctrine made sense when consumers enjoyed traditional doctor-patient relationships in which doctors "knew best" and informed us of product dangers. Manufacturers communicated with doctors through product literature or labels that listed a drug's risks. Manufacturers escaped liability by educating prescribing physicians ("learned intermediaries"), who passed information along to consumers. The trial court found that Wyeth had met FDA requirements for educating prescribing physicians.

J. O'HERN

…We believe that when mass marketing of prescription drugs seeks to influence a patients' choice of drug, a pharmaceutical manufacturer that makes direct claims to consumers for the efficacy of its project should not be unqualifiedly relieved of a duty to provide proper warnings of the dangers or side effects of the product.

…Direct advertising of drugs to consumers alters the calculus of the learned intermediary doctrine…First, with rare and wonderful exceptions, the "'Norman Rockwell' image of the family doctor no longer exists." Informed consent requires a patient-based decision rather than the paternalistic approach of the 1970s. The decision to take a drug is "not exclusively a matter for medical judgment." ...Second, because managed care has reduced the time allotted per patient, physicians have considerably less time to inform patients of the risks and benefits of a drug...Third, having spent $1.3 billion on advertising in 1998, drug manufacturers can hardly be said to "lack effective means to communicate directly with patients when their advertising campaigns can pay off in close to billions in dividends. Consumer-directed advertising of pharmaceuticals thus belies each of the premises on which the learned intermediary doctrine rests.

...Prescription drug manufacturers that market their products directly to consumers should be subject to claims by consumers if their advertising fails to provide an adequate warning of the product's dangerous propensities. [We conclude that] the learned intermediary doctrine does not apply to the direct marketing of drugs to consumers...The direct marketing of drugs to consumers generates a corresponding duty requiring manufacturers to warn of defects in the product.

REVERSED.

1. Critical Thinking. What information would you need before deciding whether this particular case was a good one for deciding to reject the learned intermediary doctrine? For example, would you want to know more about Norplant?

2. Ethical Decision Making. Identify and explain one **value** that would have supported a decision to embrace the learned intermediary doctrine, even as the marketing of prescription drugs changes.

Technology:

According to some new companies, the best way to resolve e-commerce disputes is through alternative dispute resolution (ADR) available on the Internet. To get an idea of what electronic sources can do for an individual or a company, investigate Square Trade at **www. squaretrade.com**. This website's mission is "building trust in transactions." Square Trade offers impartial online mediators that help buyers and sellers reach fair, fast resolutions. The website came online in 1999. Currently, Square Trade limits its services to complaints that have occurred on eBay, which is an online trading community. Square Trade promises a convenient, cooperative, fair dispute resolution process. The website promises customers that the process is faster and cheaper than filing a lawsuit in the traditional court system. Additionally, all communication takes place through e-mail, so participants can communicate according to their schedules.

Another online alternative dispute resolution site is iCourthouse, which you can find at **www.i-courthouse.com**. This electronic ADR forum provides a broader range of services than Square Trade. This forum resolves e-commerce disputes, plus a wide range of small claims court disputes. Small claims disputes range from complaints about parking skirmishes, to questions about whether a guy should help pay for birth control pills. This website also allows "jury" trials. The site offers both peer and panel juries. That means you can sign up to serve as a juror and offer opinions to peers about how you believe a particular dispute should be resolved.

Electronic Signatures

In 2000, Congress passed the Electronic Signatures in Global and National Commerce Act, which is commonly referred to as E-SIGN. This legislation gives legal standing to the use of electronic signatures on legal agreements and commercial transactions. It also provides that records of electronic commerce (*e.g.,* contracts, mortgages, *etc.*) may be stored electronically, rather than in paper form. In essence, the law makes it easier for businesses to create valid contracts over the Internet.

E-SIGN outlines how businesses can create valid contracts electronically with methods that imitate the effect of written signatures on paper. E-SIGN allows a wide range of authentication possibilities, from low to high-tech. The law allows the use of information unique to a customer, such as a mother's maiden name.[14] It also outlines a variety of technologies that individuals and businesses can use to create digital signatures, ranging from a password to encryption software. Encryption software involves a third party who holds the identity of the two parties and can use software to make sure only the two parties involved in a contract can obtain and sign the document.

Employment Law Issues in Cyberspace

Privacy v. Employment-at-will

Privacy matters not only in the context of business-to-consumer and business-to-business transactions, but also in the context of employment. Increasingly, employees are concerned that their employers may be monitoring them. For example, some employers are monitoring their employees' keystrokes, looking for words like "union" and "strike."[15] Employers are also interested in knowing which websites their employees visit. Issues related to monitoring illustrate the clash between employees' right to privacy and employers' right to control what happens in the workplace. Once employers monitor employees and discover wrongdoing, the issue of employers' right to fire at will becomes relevant.

For example, in a recent court case, *Michael A. Smyth v. The Pillsbury Company,*[16] a Pennsylvania court ruled on the issue whether an employer's invasion of an employee's privacy rights could provide a basis for an employee's abusive discharge case. The employee, Smyth, alleged his employer, The Pillsbury Company, violated his privacy rights by reading his e-mail, then illegally fired him based upon the content of some of his messages.

In particular, Smyth had transmitted a message to his supervisor in which he expressed his opinion about the company's sales management team. He threatened to "kill the backstabbing bastards." He also referred to an upcoming company holiday party as the "Jim Jones Koolaid affair."[17]

The court granted The Pillsbury Company's motion to dismiss, ruling that Smyth did not have a reasonable expectation of privacy in e-mail communications he made voluntarily over the company e-mail. The court was unimpressed with Smyth's assertion that management had repeatedly assured employees it would not intercept e-mail messages. Ultimately, the court ruled that the employer's right to prevent inappropriate, unprofessional, and possibly illegal comments over its e-mail system outweigh an employee's privacy rights.

Harassment in Cyberspace

A New Jersey Court appellate has ruled that employers have a duty to remedy online harassment when they have notice that employees are engaged in a pattern of retaliatory harassment using a work-related online forum.[18] Airline pilot Tammy Blakey sued her former employer, Continental Airlines, for sexual harassment, and part of her claim focused on retaliatory harassment that took place on an electronic bulletin board, the "Crew Members Forum." In particular, Blakey's fellow pilots posted information on the bulletin board that, suggested Blakey was a poor pilot, a "feminazi," and that by filing a sexual harassment lawsuit, she was using the legal system "to get a quick buck."[19]

In ruling for the employee on the bulletin board issue, the court stated that although an electronic bul-

---

[14] Nancy R. Mandell, *ESIGN: Been There, Done That! Federal Electronic Signature Legislation Catches Up to Securities Industry Practices,* On Wall Street, Sunday, July 1, 2001, 2001 WL 2271745.

[15] Stephen Lesavich, *Keystroke Spies: Conflicting Rights,* The National Law Journal, May 22, 2000, at A23.

[16] 914 F. Supp. 97 (1996).

[17] Jim Jones is the cult leader whose followers committed mass suicide by drinking a poisoned drink in Jonestown, Guyana in 1978.

[18] *Blakey v. Continental Airlines,* 751 A. 2d 538 (N.J. 2000).

[19] *Blakey v. Continental Airlines, Inc.,* 2000 WL 703018.

letin board did not have a physical location within an airport terminal, hangar, or aircraft, it might nonetheless have been so closely related to the workplace environment and beneficial to the employer, that continued harassment on the forum should be regarded as part of the workplace.

This case shows that, in some situations, employers have a duty to monitor their employees' use of e-mail and the Internet. They cannot allow harassment, including retaliatory harassment on an online bulletin board. Employers can reduce their liability exposure by conducting sexual harassment training and outlining clear workplace policies that prohibit harassing behavior, including behavior that takes place in cyberspace.

The War Against Cybercrime

The Internet revolution brings both good and bad consequences for society. One negative consequence is that, as technology changes, criminals are finding new ways to harm the public. This section explains two new crimes and two old crimes, updated as technology has evolved.

New Technology, New Crimes

One new crime is the **denial-of-service attack,**[20] which occurs when hackers clog a website's equipment by sending too many requests for information. This clogging can slow the site's performance and/or crash the site. Law enforcement officers see this crime as a threat to the success of e-commerce, and are taking steps to combat this crime. Officers ask companies, Internet service providers, and telecommunications suppliers to work together to write programs to reject requests that are clogging equipment.[21]

Another new crime is **theft and Internet distribution of intellectual property**. Law enforcement officers have recently investigated corporate executives, computer network administrators, and college students at some of the country's top universities,[22] seeking evidence of high-tech piracy. Interestingly, the alleged high-tech pirates are described in ways that make them sound like readers of journals like Corley's *2600,* who put what they learn to criminal use.

Investigators allege that the accused have defeated codes used to protect digital products, including applications software and DVDs, and have then distributed them illegally through the Internet.[23] Some of the accused have placed movies on the Internet that only recently opened in theaters. The accused face possible five-year sentences under conspiracy and copyright statutes. If individuals are members of a group, such as a Warez group (see Exhibit 11-2), they could be charged under federal statutes that combat organized crime.[24]

EXHIBIT 11-2

Warez Groups

The term "warez" refers to "hacked, unlicensed copies of popular programs."[25] Warez groups ask members to contribute to the group by offering something hacked (*e.g.,* software, a cracked security code), or distributing warez. Federal officials refer to Warez groups as gangs, and believe they are responsible for 95% of websites that offer and distribute warez, and 60% of pirated high-end software.[26]

Federal agents recently targeted a Warez group that calls itself "DrinkorDie."[27] This group has allegedly distributed movies currently in theaters, including the popular "Harry Potter and the Sorcerer's Stone."

Old Crimes, New Twists

Cybercriminals have found creative ways to manipulate the stock market to their advantage. For instance, some criminals have discovered how easy it is to manipulate stock prices by posting false information on Internet bulletin boards.[28] Others have engaged in **insider trading** made possible with assistance from co-conspirator relationships developed through online chat rooms. Insider trading is the use of material,

---

[20] Ira Sager, *Cybercrime: First Yahoo! Then eBay. The Net's Vulnerability Threatens E-Commerce—and You,* BUSINESS WEEK 37, 40 (February 21, 2000).

[21] *Id.* at 39.

[22] *Id.*

[23] *Id.*

[24] *Id.*

[25] *Online Piracy,* THE GUARDIAN, January 7, 2002, 2002 WL 2894002.

[26] Frank James, *Raids Target Software, DVD Piracy,* CHICAGO TRIBUNE, December 12, 2001.

[27] Andy Sullivan, *U.S. Nabs Suspects in Antipiracy Raids,* REUTERS ENGLISH NEWS SERVICE, Monday, January 14, 2002.

[28] David E. Rovella, *Preparing for a New Cyberwar: Justice Dept. Seeks Lawyers, Revised Laws to Fight Net Crimes,* THE NATIONAL LAW JOURNAL, May 20, 2000 at A1, A9.

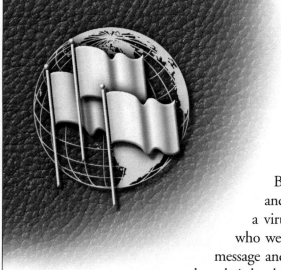

Global Context:
The "Love Bug" Puts the World on Notice

In May 2000, law enforcement officers and other actors in the legal system learned that computer vandals are acting in ways criminal and civil laws currently fail to proscribe, either nationally or internationally.[29]

Creators of a computer virus known as the Love Bug virus caused numerous problems for individuals and businesses around the world when they embedded a virus in a message labeled "ILOVEYOU." Recipients who were curious about who might love them opened the message and learned just how much damage a virus can cause when their hard drives were completely wiped out.

Victims of this virus probably became very interested in how criminal, civil and international law holds creators of viruses accountable for the damage they cause.

Unfortunately, it is possible the creators of the Love Bug, who live and work in the Philippines, will escape both civil and criminal liability because the Filipino government has not yet passed a cybercrime statute. The laws currently on the books fail to respond appropriately to the criminal acts like the one alleged in the case of the Love Bug. This case also provides an illustration of what happens when there is no Filipino law that resembles U.S. cybercrime statutes. That means no "dual criminality exists," which means law enforcement officers cannot bring the Love Bug creator to the United States for prosecution.

Even if Love Bug creators are caught, they do not appear to have assets that would allow them to compensate their victims for damages they incurred. In the meantime, those who were injured by the Love Bug are considering whom else they might sue—from insurance companies to companies that provided computer security services that could not prevent the Love Bug's damage.

One interesting—and ironic—feature of the Love Bug is that it likes to eat a variety of files, but one of its favorite snacks is MP3 files. Individuals who were trading songs on services like Napster when the Love Bug was active discovered that the "ILOVEYOU" worm can destroy a person's MP3 collection.

[29] See Bob Van Voris & David E. Rovella, *Love Bug Faster than the Law*, THE NATIONAL LAW JOURNAL, May 22, 2000, at A4, column 2. Facts in this text box are based upon facts contained in the Van Voris & Rovella article.

nonpublic information received from a corporate source by someone who has a fiduciary obligation to shareholders and potential investors and who benefits from trading on such information.

For example, John Freeman, an office temp who worked as a word processor at Goldman, Sachs & Company, was charged with insider trading after he and co-conspirators allegedly made $8.4 million on illegal tips.[30] Freeman used an America Online chat room to find conspirators, who helped him learn how to

[30] Christopher Drew, *19 Charged with Insider Trading Using the Internet and a Clerk*, THE NEW YORK TIMES, March 15, 2000, at C1. Freeman made $70,000 to $110,000. Robert Gearty, *Small Fish in Big Pond-Inside Trader Hooked*, NEW YORK DAILY NEWS, April 25, 2001, 2001 WL 17948886.

make money using sensitive information that crossed his desk. Freeman exchanged inside information for kickbacks with friends in both the real and virtual worlds. After he was arrested, Freeman cooperated with the FBI and testified against other defendants.

Another old crime with a new twist is **illegal gambling**, now possible on the Internet. Some states make gambling a crime and are quick to shut down gambling sites that operate through servers located in their states. However, even if a state bans companies in that state from providing access to gambling, they cannot control companies whose servers fall outside their jurisdiction. Some people argue that attempts to limit Internet gambling are inappropriate. They question why a person is allowed to physically travel to Las Vegas to gamble, but not allowed to travel to Las Vegas via the Internet to gamble.[31] Ultimately, Congress is likely to enact legislation to resolve new issues related to illegal gambling made possible by the Internet.

---

[31] *Committee on Cyberspace Law,* Cyberspace Law Developments —Annual Survey (St. Louis 1998 Spring Meeting) at 32.

DeCSS Wrap-Up

In August 2000, New York District Judge Lewis Kaplan issued a permanent injunction against Corley from posting DeCSS on his website or from knowingly linking via a hyperlink to any other website containing DeCSS. This injunction enforced the DMCA. Judge Kaplan ruled that the DMCA was a valid exercise of the government's power, and that the law did not violate Corley's First Amendment Rights.

On November 28, 2001, a three-judge panel of the United States Court of Appeals for the Second Circuit in Manhattan affirmed Kaplan's decision and reasoning. The appellate court panel agreed with Judge Kaplan's decision that computer code is content neutral speech, and that a narrowly tailored injunction did not burden substantially more speech than necessary to further the government's interest in preventing unauthorized access to copyrighted materials. Nothing about the DMCA or Judge Kaplan's injunction prevented fair use of copyrighted materials. The court pointed out that Corley did not claim to be making fair use of copyrighted materials.

Corley's lawyers have asked that the full appellate for the Second Circuit reconsider the panel's decision. Cyberlaw experts also believe it is likely that Corley and his attorneys will pursue the issues they raised with the United States Supreme Court. It is easy to find updates of this case online, but make sure you consider arguments on both sides of the case. Go to **www. 2600. com** and **www.mpaa.org**.

	Summary
Cyberlaw and Business: How Law Changes as Society Changes	**The flexibility of law**—The legal system adjusts to the changing needs of American citizens. The Internet and World Wide Web have raised important questions about how law should change. **The federal government's changing roles**—The federal government is enacting new legislation and also taking on stronger regulatory roles. **Challenges to state law power**—In some areas, legal experts believe the federal government can regulate the Internet more effectively than state governments.
Intellectual Property Issues in Cyberspace	A **trademark** is a distinctive mark, word, design, picture, or arrangement used by the producer of a product that tends to cause consumers to identify the product with the producer. **Domain names** on the World Wide Web have become trademarks that allow us to identify products with producers. The **Anticybersquatting Consumer Protection Act** outlines penalties for those who engage in cybersquatting. Cybersquatting occurs when an individual or business intentionally obtains a domain name registration for a company's trademark so it can sell the domain name back to the trademark owner. **Copyrights** protect the expression of creative ideas. They are protected under common law. A person who violates a copyright engages in **direct copyright infringement**. The **fair use doctrine** is a defense that allows people to use copyrighted work for certain purposes, including criticism, news reporting, and teaching. Some courts recognize the concept of **contributory copyright infringement,** which occurs when one who, with knowledge of an infringing activity, induces, causes, or materially contributes to the infringing conduct of another.
E-Commerce Issues in Cyberspace	**Privacy**—The growth of e-commerce depends in part upon how well federal and state law address consumers' privacy concerns. **Federal statutes** sometimes protect privacy and promote online security. Congress has supported the growth of e-commerce and consequently cares about some privacy issues. **State common law** also protects privacy. Individuals can use tort and contract law to assert privacy rights. **Online marketing** issues include issues related to direct-to-consumer advertising. **Electronic signatures** are now legally valid thanks to E-SIGN, a new federal statute. Records of electronic commerce may also be stored electronically instead of on paper.
Employment Law Issues in Cyberspace	**Employment-at-will** gives employers the freedom to fire employees who make inappropriate and unprofessional comments over a company e-mail system. Some courts have ruled that employees do not have a reasonable expectation of privacy in such communications. Employers cannot allow **harassment that occurs online**. Employers must stop hostile environments created through an e-mail system or Internet bulletin board used or accessed by employees.

Summary (continued)	
The War Against Cybercrime	**New Technology, New Crimes** **Denial of service attacks** occur when hackers use one computer to break into another, then clog a website's equipment by sending too many requests for information. Federal regulators are pursuing individuals who **steal and distribute intellectual property via the Internet**. **Old Crimes, New Twists** **Insider Trading** is on the rise now that the Internet has provided new ways for criminals to use material, nonpublic information received from a corporate source by someone who has a fiduciary obligation to shareholders and potential investors and who benefits from trading on such information. **Internet Gambling** is difficult to stop because states that have prohibited gambling cannot control companies whose servers fall outside their jurisdiction.

Review Questions And Case Problems

1. Explain how the conflict between copyright protection and the First Amendment has been exacerbated by the growth of the Internet.

2. Congress passed the Communications Decency Act (CDA) in 1996. This law included provisions that prohibited the knowing transmission of obscene or indecent messages to any recipient under eighteen years of age, and prohibited knowingly sending or displaying patently offensive messages in a manner that is available to a person under eighteen years of age. Several plaintiffs, including the American Civil Liberties Union and the Electronic Frontier Foundation, challenged these provisions as unconstitutional under the First Amendment. Were the plaintiffs correct? *Reno v. American Civil Liberties Union*, 521 U.S. 844 (1997).

3. Sidney Blumenthal sued Matt Drudge and America Online, Inc., after Drudge falsely accused Blumenthal of engaging in spousal abuse in the past. Drudge made this accusation in a gossip column called the Drudge Report, which he made available through AOL. Drudge had an agreement with AOL that allowed AOL to remove content from the Drudge Report if it violated AOL's standards. AOL moved for a summary judgment, based upon § 230 of the CDA. How is this case different from the Zeran lawsuit against AOL? Will AOL get a summary judgment, in spite of any differences you listed between this lawsuit and Zeran's? *Sidney Blumenthal v. Matt Drudge and America Online, Inc.*, 992 F. Supp. 44 (D.D.C. 1998).

4. The Hard Rock Café International, Inc. (HRCI), a restaurant chain, sued Peter A. Morton (Morton), owner of the Hard Rock Hotel, Inc. HRCI alleges that Morton's failure to convey the domain name "hardrock.com" constitutes trademark infringement, unfair competition, and trademark dilution in violation of both federal and state law. Will the court require Morton to convey the domain name "hardrock.com"? Why or why not? *Hard Rock Café International (USA) Inc. v. Morton*, 1999 WL 717995

(S.D.N.Y. 1999).

5. Bally Total Fitness Holding Corp. (Bally), a health club with a registered trademark to "Bally," brought a lawsuit against Faber for trademark infringement, trademark dilution, and unfair competition. Faber is a web page designer who used the "Bally" mark on a website entitled "Bally sucks." By entitling his site "Bally sucks," did Faber infringe on Bally's domain name? *Bally Total Fitness Holding Corp. v. Faber*, 29 F. Supp. 2d (C.D. Cal. 1998).

6. CoStar Group, Inc. sued LoopNet, Inc. alleging copyright infringement. In particular, CoStar, a real estate listing service, alleges that LoopNet, operator of a website, has taken over 300 of its copyrighted photographs of real estate (available online) and put them on their own website. CoStar accuses LoopNet of direct and contributory copyright infringement. How can LoopNet use the DMCA in its defense? Will the court grant either side's motion for summary judgment? *CoStar Group, Inc. v. LoopNet, Inc.*, 164 F. Supp. 2d 688 (D. Md. 2001).

7. Jerald and Sandra Tanner, who run Utah Lighthouse Ministry, Inc., posted on their website part of a guidebook for lay clergy of the Church of Jesus Christ of Latter-Day Saints. After a court granted a temporary restraining order requested by Intellectual Reserve, Inc. (IRD), which manages the church's intellectual property, the Tanners posted e-mail and text on their website that told users of other sites that had posted the handbook. Were the Tanners/Utah Lighthouse Ministry, Inc. engaging in contributory copyright infringement? *Intellectual Reserve, Inc. v. Utah Lighthouse Ministry, Inc.*, 75 F. Supp. 2d 1290 (1999).

8. Howard Stern, a controversial radio talk show host, sued Delphi Services Corporation (Delphi) after Delphi ran full-page ads in two New York newspapers promoting its online bulletin board. The online bulletin board was sponsoring a debate on Stern's candidacy for governor of the State of New York. Stern had announced his candidacy as a publicity stunt. The problem with the ads, according to Stern, was that they used a photograph of him without his permission. Delphi argues that it should be allowed to use

the photograph because news disseminators are allowed to use a person's photograph without permission if they are advertising or promoting newsworthy products. Is Delphi a news disseminator? Have Stern's privacy rights been violated? *Howard Stern v. Delphi Services Corporation*, 626 N.Y.S. 2d 694 (N.Y. Sup. Ct. 1995).

9. Linda Kelleher, clerk of the City Council for Reading, Pennsylvania, sued the City of Reading asserting several privacy-related theories after the City published allegedly private e-mails and information related to disciplinary actions the City took against her. The conflict arose after Kelleher took a stand regarding an ordinance to abolish the Reading Area Water Authority and her decision to set up a public information debate on a municipal trash collection ordinance. Kelleher asserts that, in retaliation for these acts, the City engaged in several acts of inappropriate behavior, including that they publicized private e-mail communications and other allegedly private information. Given that she lives in Pennsylvania and the court is sure to look at the Smyth case, what facts would be most helpful to Kelleher as she tries to distinguish her case from Smyth's? Her goal is to avoid a dismissal of the complaint. *Kelleher v. City of Reading*, 2001 WL 1132401 (E.D. Pa. decision dated September 24, 2001). This decision is reported only in Westlaw.

10. The Attorney General of the State of New York (Attorney General) sought an injunction against World Interactive Gaming Corporation (WIGC), seeking to enjoin them from offering a casino offshore to Internet users in New York. The state of New York has a law that represents the state's "deep-rooted policy…against unauthorized gambling." WIGC is a Delaware corporation that maintains corporate offices in New York. This corporation owns Golden Chips Casino, Inc. (GCC), which is an Antiguan subsidiary corporation that operates a land-based casino in Antigua and a website that allows Internet gambling that New York residents are able to view. Will the Attorney General be able to get the injunction? *People ex. rel. Vacco v. World Interactive Gaming Corp.*, 714 N.Y.S. 2d 844 (N.Y. Sup. 1999).

11. Dr. Stephen Martin, a reclusive California scientist, and Caryn Camp, a lonely Maine lab technician working for a veterinary products company called IDEXX, established a seven-month e-mail pen-pal relationship. Prosecutors alleged that this relationship was far more sinister: that the correspondence between the two mushroomed into a conspiracy to steal trade secrets and transport stolen property interstate, and that the two used e-mail and U.S. mails to further a scheme to defraud IDEXX. Dr. Martin was the CEO of Wyoming DNA Vaccine (WDV), a competitor to IDEXX. How did Martin and Camp get caught? What kind of evidence persuaded the jury to find Dr. Martin guilty of several crimes? How did Camp escape criminal conviction? *U.S. v. Martin*, 228 F. 3d 1 (C.A. 1 Me 2000).

Assignment on the Internet

This assignment asks you to investigate competing websites to determine the extent to which it is true that the Web has made it easier for college students to cheat. First, investigate the website **www.school-sucks.com**, which allows users to download essays and term papers for free. Then, investigate **www.plagiarism.org**, which refers professors to a user portal, **www.Turnitin.com**, which gives professors a tool to catch cheaters and restore integrity to the classroom. Write a two-page paper in which you present a description of the tools students can use to cheat, and the tools professors can use to catch cheaters. Your paper should provide an initial assessment of the situation. Which side has the upper hand in this battle? As a college student, which side are you applauding? Why? Compare your response to the responses of your peers. Did the "School Sucks" site have a paper on this topic?

On the Internet

http://www.2600.com *Check out the online journal Eric Corley publishes. In addition, you may want to look at the websites of the major film companies to see what the film companies post with regard to the lawsuit against Corley and 2600.*

http://www.nonprofit.net/hoax/hoax.html *This site is one of a variety of websites that track hoaxes. Sites like this one would have helped Zeran communicate the nature of the malicious hoax that caused his suffering.*

http://www.whototake.com *College students in favor of consumer review have created websites that allow students to review their professors. Professors have threatened lawsuits, but, from reading the chapter, you should be able to explain why they are not likely to win.*

http://www.musicnet.com *This site is one of two the major record labels have launched to offer music downloading services. Musicnet.com licenses its technology platform to companies that want to offer digital music subscription services. Musicnet includes the music catalogues of companies such as Bertelsmann, EMI Records, and AOL Time Warner. A competitor is a site called PressPlay.*

CHAPTER 12

Sharing Profits at Columbia Falls

Atlantic Richfield Company (Arco) owned and operated an aluminum processing plant in Columbia Falls, Montana, population 3,500. During the early 1980s the price of aluminum was depressed and the plant was losing money. Arco decided to bail out. In 1985 it sold the plant to one of the Company's executives for a symbolic $1, plus $3,000,000 for inventory.[1]

The new owner immediately began to cut costs. With the whole town behind him, he secured utility rate and tax reductions from governmental agencies.[2] He then turned to the plant's approximately 1,000 union and salaried employees, who agreed to a 21 percent pay cut.[3] In return, he allegedly promised to share half the plant's profits with employees.[4] A 50 percent profit-sharing plan also was referenced in a letter from Arco to the new owner.[5]

The price of aluminum rose, and in 1986 the profit-sharing arrangement nearly made up for the employees' reduced wages.[6] The following years were even better, as the price of aluminum continued to rise.

But not all was well in Columbia Falls. In 1989 the plant's chief financial officer voiced concerns that some of the firm's financial practices tended to reduce the profits shared with employees.[7] The matter surfaced again in 1991, when a young accountant raised similar concerns.[8] The new owner needed to know what, if any, action should be taken.

> 1. Assume you were the new owner and your accounting department informed you that problems existed in financial records causing an alleged failure to pay sufficient profits to the workers. What would you do when reminded of the alleged promise to the employees?
> 2. How would you determine if that alleged promise created a contract?

---

[1] Jim Robbins, *A Broken Pact and a $97 Million Payday*, NEW YORK TIMES, April 19, 1998.

[2] *Id.*

[3] Eric Sorensen, *Battle-Weary Workers Await a Big Payout, And So Does Town*, SEATTLE TIMES, April 1, 1998.

[4] Robert Berner and Scott Kilman, *Across America: Columbia Falls Workers Await a Windfall*, DETROIT NEWS, April 3, 1998.

[5] Jim Robbins, *A Broken Pact and a $97 Million Payday*, NEW YORK TIMES, April 19, 1998.

[6] *Id.*

[7] *Id.*

[8] *Id.*

Introduction To Contracts

The Importance of Contract Law

A Framework for Legal Contracting

The Role of Equity

The UCC and its Relationship to Contract Law

Classifications of Contracts

Virtually every aspect of business life depends on, or at least interacts with, contract law in some way. Businesses use many types of contracts including employment contracts, sales contracts, contracts with suppliers, shipping contracts, leases on rental property, and construction contracts. Other aspects of business law, such as corporate law, partnership law, and commercial paper, are grounded in contract law. In addition, misunderstandings about contract formation or interpretation can lead to costly mistakes, as the Columbia Falls example will demonstrate. Knowledge of contract law, then, is essential for effective management. The next seven chapters on contract law discuss how managers can create successful contracts and avoid contracting pitfalls.

This chapter introduces the basic principles of contract law, key concepts, and terminology. The chapter begins by discussing the importance of contract law in a market economy. It then introduces a framework for legal contracting, the role of equity, the relationship of the Uniform Commercial Code (UCC) to contract law, and classifications of contracts.

The Importance of Contract Law

In the *Wealth of Nations* (1776), Adam Smith reflected on how societies prospered, identifying a single factor—specialization. Smith observed that economic activities in wealthy nations were highly specialized, in poorer nations, less so. Specialization, he reasoned, required market exchanges. The easier exchanges were to consummate, the more prosperous was the nation.

Thus, Smith concluded, the law, including contract law, should seek to facilitate private market activities.

Contract rules reduce market costs in three important ways. First, by providing a clear and reliable sanction for breach, contract rules encourage the performance of mutually advantageous exchanges. Second, by prohibiting such things as fraud and duress, contract law seeks to assure that exchanges are meaningful and voluntary. And third, contract law provides a set of standard terms that become part of exchanges without the parties discussing them. This reduces the need for costly negotiations.

Taken collectively, these three functions of contract law explain the policies that underscore most, if not all, contract rules. Courts typically allow the parties themselves to determine the terms of their contracts, and require parties to perform in accordance with those terms or to compensate the other party for any breach. Courts will not, however, enforce contracts that are either too indefinite or procured through fraud or duress. This assures that parties are not forced to transfer property rights without their consent. Consent is inferred from both the words and actions of the parties and from the customary terms associated with the type of transaction. These customs are reflected in the standard terms supplied by the law in the event that the parties have not addressed a particular concern.

As we proceed through the contract chapters, note how Adam Smith's notion of cost reduction unifies the logic of most contract rules. The central idea is that a market economy needs to work efficiently. Efficiency, in turn, requires proper legal foundations, including a set of property rights protected by criminal and tort laws, and a set of contract rules that reduce the costs of conducting mutually beneficial trades.

A Framework for Legal Contracting

To manage effectively, a manager needs to know how to spot, organize, and answer contract issues. This section provides a framework. It identifies the four elements required to form a contract, outlines two defenses to contractual enforcement, and introduces the concept of contractual discharge. Taken collectively, this "Elements-Defenses-Discharge" framework helps organize the various contract rules that may apply to a managerial decision.

Elements of a Contract

The *Restatement (Second) of Contracts* defines a **contract** as "a promise or set of promises for the breach of which the law gives a remedy." A promise is a communication of intent to do or not do something in the future. When a promise is broken (breached), the law may order the breaching party to compensate the other party (provide a remedy). Contract law tells us which types of promises are legally enforceable and which are not.

Every contract must have *all four* of these elements:

1. *Agreement.* An agreement consists of an offer and an acceptance. One party offers to enter into a contract and the other party accepts the terms of that offer.

2. *Consideration.* Contracts must involve an exchange, or *quid pro quo* (Latin for "this for that"), where each party gives something of legal value to the other.

3. *Capacity.* All parties must have legal capacity to contract; that is, they must be of sound mind and of legal age (eighteen in most states).

4. *Legality.* The contract must not have an illegal effect, such as the commission of a tort or a crime, or violation of public policy.

If any element is missing, no contract is formed and you cannot safely rely on the promises made by others. For example, a promise by your current summer employer to rehire you next summer is probably an offer, but there is no agreement and no contract until you accept. A promise to give a gift does not involve an exchange of consideration, so no contract is formed. A seventeen-year-old lacks capacity to contract, so that person would not be legally held to their promises. A promise to pay a bribe is illegal, so it is not a contract. To have a contract, all four elements must be present.

Note how these elements help organize the legal issues presented in the Columbia Falls case outlined at the start of the chapter. It was alleged that management offered to share company profits and the employees accepted. The employees apparently gave consideration by agreeing to take a lower hourly wage. Both parties had legal capacity and there is nothing illegal about the transaction, so it appears that there may have been a contract. If, however, one of the elements is missing, management's promise is not enforceable.

Although these four elements are required to form a contract under U.S. law, this is not necessarily true elsewhere. As the Global Context feature demonstrates, it is important to understand which law applies and what the requirements of a foreign law are when contracting with a trading partner from another country.

Global Context:
Contractual Elements in Italy

Under Italian contract law, a legal contract can be formed without an exchange of consideration. Suppose a U.S. software consultant promises to give a seminar demonstrating the use of new software to the human resource managers at an Italian firm. The consultant is hoping to develop the firm as his customer for future consulting work, but he asks for no pay for the seminar. The firm accepts his offer and schedules the event. Under U.S. law, the consultant would not be bound to his promise to give the free seminar. He received no consideration in exchange for his promise, so no contract was formed. Italian law, by contrast, does not require an exchange of consideration to form a contract. So if the consultant cancels the engagement, he could be liable for breach of contract to the firm under Italian law.

Contract Defenses

Even if all four elements are present, a contract may not be enforceable. One or both parties may have a defense allowing them to rescind (get out of) the contract. Contract law recognizes two sets of defenses:

1. *Reality of Assent.* If a contract was agreed to because of a *misrepresentation, duress, undue influence, mutual mistake, or unconscionable conduct,* there is no true assent and the contract is not enforceable.

2. *Faulty Writing.* The law requires that some types of contracts be in writing. If a writing is required, and there is no writing, or the writing is incomplete, the contract is not enforceable.

The defenses arise during contract negotiations. For instance, suppose a seller offers to sell a computer for $300 and the buyer accepts (legal agreement). Both parties are adults and of sound mind (capacity); there is nothing illegal about selling computers (legality); and there is a *quid pro quo,* a promise of $300 in exchange for a promise to deliver a computer (consideration). All four elements are present, so a contract is formed. But suppose that the seller lied and the computer does not have the storage capacity promised. This misrepresentation would allow the buyer to rescind the contract. Chapter 16 on reality of assent gives the details of these and other contract negotiation defenses—duress, mutual mistake, undue influence, and unconscionability.

The second defense has to do with writings. Unless the parties agree otherwise, a writing is usually not required to form a contract. However, certain types of contracts do require a writing to be enforceable. If the law requires a writing and there is no writing, or the writing is incomplete, the contract is not enforceable. In Chapter 17 we learn which types of contracts (such as real estate sales contracts) must be in writing.

In sum, there are four elements to a contract and two defenses. A contract that has all four elements and to which neither defense applies is called **valid**. A **void** contract, in contrast, is no contract at all because one of the elements is missing. For instance, a contract to commit a crime lacks the element of legality and is void. If all four elements are present, but the contract fails for lack of a writing, it is called **unenforceable**. Contracts agreed to because of a misrepresentation or other negotiation impropriety are **voidable**. A voidable contract is enforceable by one party (for instance, the party who was lied to), but not by the other (the party who lied).

Contractual Discharge

The final component of our framework involves the issue of contractual discharge. To **discharge** a contract obligation means to terminate or end the obligation. Valid contracts can be discharged in one of five ways:

1. *Performance.* Once the promises have been fulfilled the contract is discharged.

2. *Breach.* If one party breaches the contract, the other party's promises are discharged.

3. *Operation of Law.* Sometimes the law releases a party from their promises, for example, with the running of a statute of limitations that bars a breach of contract action.

4. *Change of Circumstances.* Sometimes an unforeseen change of circumstances will so disrupt a contract that the contract will be discharged.

5. *Agreement of the Parties.* If the parties agree to terminate the contract, for example, by specifying in advance certain events that will discharge the contract, or by agreeing to settle a contract dispute once it has arisen, then the underlying contract is discharged.

The most common way to discharge a contract is by fulfilling or performing one's promises. Once a party has performed, the contractual obligations are terminated. In addition, when one party breaches the contract, the other party receives a discharge. The law can also discharge a contractual obligation when a person is declared bankrupt or the statute of limitations runs out.

Sometimes a change of circumstances can discharge a contract. For example, suppose that an opera singer contracts to sing at a concert, but the opera singer loses her voice, or alternatively, the opera house burns down before the performance date. The impossibility of fulfilling the contract would discharge the promises.

The parties can also agree to discharge a contract. For instance, most real estate sales contracts provide for a discharge if the buyer is unable to obtain financing. Depending on its wording, the contract may state that no contract is formed until financing is obtained or that the contract is discharged if financing is unavailable. In either case, the happening of the condition (failure to get financing) terminates contractual obligations. The law of discharge is fully discussed in Chapter 19.

A Checklist of Contract Issues

The "Elements-Defense-Discharge" framework just discussed provides a roadmap to what follows in the next seven chapters. As we proceed through these chapters, we examine the elements, defenses, and discharge concepts in detail. Contract law contains a lot of rules, exceptions to rules, and even some exceptions to the exceptions. This introductory framework is designed to keep these rules tractable. Exhibit 12-1 provides a checklist of contract issues.

Managers faced with a contract question can apply this framework to spot, organize, and answer contract law issues. For example, the new owner of Columbia Falls could have used this framework to decide if his promise to share profits was a contract, whether a defense applied, and whether his promise had been discharged.

EXHIBIT 12-1

Checklist of Contract Issues

Are the Four Elements Present?

- Was there an agreement between the parties? (Chapter 13)
- Did the parties bargain for an exchange of consideration? (Chapter 14)
- Did the parties have the capacity to contract? (Chapter 15)
- Does the agreement have a legal purpose? (Chapter 15)

Does a Defense Apply?

- Were the negotiations faulty? (Chapter 16) Misrpresentation, Duress, Mutual Mistake, Undue Influence, Unconscionability
- Was a required writing missing or faulty? (Chapter 17)

Was the Contract Discharged? (Chapter 19)

- By performance?
- Through a breach by the other party?
- Through operation of law?
- By an unforeseen changes of circumstances?
- By agreement of the parties?

The Role of Equity

The contract elements, defenses and rules of discharge discussed in the proceeding section helps managers gauge which contracts are enforceable and which are not. In some instances, however, the mechanical application of these legal rules can lead to unfair results. When this happens, the courts may turn to equity. Recall that equity is a doctrine that permits judges to make decisions based on fairness and ethics. Equity does not displace the law, but it supplements it in the name of justice. There are two equitable doctrines to consider in contractual settings: quasi contract and promissory estoppel.

Quasi Contract

A **quasi contract** (also called an **implied–in–law** contract or an **equitable contract**) arises when there is no valid legal contract, but fairness considerations dictate that a party should have a contract right. In such cases, a court may use the doctrine of quasi contract to grant a remedy under the doctrine of *quantum meruit* (Latin for "as much as he deserves").

Courts use quasi contracts to prevent unjust enrichment. To illustrate, consider an example. Suppose Able has a contract to paint Baker's barn, but paints Chan's barn by mistake. Chan is aware that Able is painting the wrong barn but says nothing. When Chan refuses to pay Able, Able sues for breach of contract. Because there was no agreement between Able and Chan, no contract was formed, and Able loses at law, but he wins in equity. An honest person would have cleared up the mistake before the work was begun, instead of trying to use the law to gain a benefit unfairly. The court orders Chan to pay the reasonable value of the benefit received (*quantum meruit*).

Note that the outcome would be different if Chan had been away on vacation while the work was being done, because Chan would not have known of Baker's mistake and could not have prevented it. If both parties have "clean hands"—that is, one makes a mistake and the other has no knowledge of the mistake—then the courts follow the law. Similarly, if Able had painted Chan's barn intentionally in an attempt to get paid for work that never was requested, equity would not disturb the legal result. Quasi contracts are based on fairness, with the courts looking to the totality of circumstances in determining what is fair. There are two elements of quasi contract based on unjust enrichment:

• A benefit is conferred from one party to another.

• It would be unfair to let the party who benefited enjoy the benefit without paying for it.

EXHIBIT 12-2:

Maxims of Equitable Contracting

Equity will not suffer a right to exist without a remedy. (If notions of justice and fair play indicate that a party should have a contract right, that party can win in a court of equity even if no legal contract exists.)

Equity looks to substance rather than to form. (Equity is concerned with justice, rather than with legal technicalities.)

One seeking the aid of an equity court must come to the court with clean hands. (Unless the party seeking to modify the legal rules was honest, the legal result will not be changed.)

When there is equal equity, the law must prevail. (If the parties were equally good or equally bad, then the courts will follow the rules of legal contracting and no equitable contract will be formed.)

Equity does justice by the wholes, not by the halves. (Courts of equity look at the totality of the situation in deciding a case.)

Exhibit 12-2 lists equitable maxims that guide the court in determining when to imply a quasi contract. Note how each clarifies the issue of fairness that underscores equitable relief.

Quasi contract relief is not limited to settings in which there is no agreement. In fact, the concept can be used to change the result dictated by any of the legal rules presented in our central framework. Suppose, for example, that Jane, a seventeen-year-old girl, brings a truck in for repair. Jane looks older than her true age and the repair shop never asks her age. The truck is repaired and a bill is presented, but Jane refuses to pay. Recall that to be held to your promises in contract law, you must be eighteen, so the contract is not enforceable in law. Would the court fashion a quasi-contract? Assuming that the garage was honest and that the young woman knew the rules of contract law and was trying to use the law to cheat the garage, the answer would be yes—Jane must pay the reasonable value of the repairs.

Case 12-1 raises the issue of unjust enrichment in yet another setting. Here the missing element is legality. The law of Tennessee requires a plumber to be licensed, and unlicensed plumbing contracts are illegal and void. Ask yourself why the court forms a *quasi contract.*

Case 12-1

Gene Taylor & Sons Plumbing Co.

v.

W & W Construction Co.

611 S.W. 2d 572 (Tenn. 1981)

W & W Construction (W & W) hired Gene Taylor & Sons (Taylor) to do some plumbing work on a townhouse development. A Tennessee statute required plumbers to be licensed. Taylor did not have a license. After the plumbing work was completed, Taylor submitted a final bill for $18,891. W & W refused to pay and Taylor sued. The trial court dismissed the case stating that the lack of license required by Tennessee law made the contract void. The Court of Appeals affirmed the dismissal. Taylor appealed the case to the Supreme Court of Tennessee.

JUDGE DROWOTA

The issue in this case is whether a subcontractor not licensed…can recover against a licensed general contractor and a property owner under a subcontract agreement.

At the time of entering into said contract…Plaintiff was not aware that a general contractor's license was required of it, nor was Plaintiff aware of said requirement at anytime during the performance of its contract. Plaintiff now has a general contractor's license which was acquired after the Complaint was filed in this case.

[In] *Santi v. Crabb*…the homeowner acted as his own general contractor and made an agreement with the plaintiff under which the plaintiff was to perform certain sheetrock work. The plaintiff was not licensed as a general contractor in his line of work as required by T.C.A. section 62-601. The plaintiff subsequently sued the homeowner for the value of his services, but this Court denied recovery.

…In *Santi*, this Court has recognized the general rule regarding the effect of noncompliance with licensing statutes on the enforceability of contracts…[T]he general rule need not be applied inflexibly without regard to the facts in a particular case… In the instant case, the appellant contends that the particular facts justify this Court in permitting recovery… [W]e agree.

In… [*Santi*], the unlicensed contractors were suing the owner of the property where the work was to be done. In the instant case, the appellant contracted with and brought suit against a construction company licensed as a general contractor. Other courts have recognized that the policies that bar recovery against a member of the general public do not apply in suits against licensed professionals in the same business…

In permitting recovery against W & W Construction Co. under a theory of *quantum meruit* [the value of the benefit conferred], we do not intend to approve unlawful conduct or to enforce an illegal contract…

Any recovery the appellant might have against W & W Construction company should be limited to actual expenses in the form of labor and materials expended on the project as shown by clear and convincing proof. These expenses should not include any amounts which constitute profit under the contract.
REVERSED AND REMANDED.

1. Critical Thinking: The court distinguishes the *Santi* case from this case, finding a quasi contract only in the latter. Do you think this distinction is justified based on the concept of fairness? Why or why not?

2. Ethical Decision Making: The court cites the theory of *quantum meruit* to determine the amount of money damages to be awarded in this case. Why would Gene Taylor deserve to recover its expenses, but not its lost profits? Is this limitation on damages fair? Why or why not?

Promissory Estoppel

Case 12-1 involved unjust enrichment. Equity can also intervene to address reliance concerns. Sometimes a promisor (the party who makes a promise) will make a promise with full knowledge that the promisee (the party to whom the promise is made) will rely on that promise. If the promisee takes action or forbears from action, and the promisor breaks the promise, courts can use the equitable doctrine of **promissory estoppel** to protect the promisee even though there was no valid contract.

To apply the doctrine of promissory estoppel, the court must find four elements:

• A clear and direct promise is made.
• The promisee reasonably relies on that promise.
• The promisor knows or has reason to know that the promisee will rely on the promise.
• It would be unfair to allow the promisor to break the promise without compensating the promisee.

Promissory estoppel often comes up in settings involving gifts. Suppose that a major corporation pledges a gift to a university. Relying on the pledge, the university begins construction of a new library. The corporation cancels the gift, even though it knows the university is relying on the gift to complete the project. Note that there is no contract because a necessary element (exchange of consideration) is missing. However, if the pledge is clear, and the university relies on it, then a court may use the doctrine of promissory estoppel to protect the university.

A similar result occurs in Japan, although under a different rationale. As the Global Context feature illustrates, in Japan a promise to give a gift is enforceable even without the doctrine of promissory estoppel. The case turns on the unfairness of allowing someone to take back a promise that they knew was being relied upon by someone else.

U.S. state courts are expanding their use of promissory estoppel. Today, it can be used to modify nearly every contract law rule. For example, in one well-known commercial case,[9] a prominent convenience-store chain promised to sell a particular franchise location to a buyer. The company encouraged the buyer to sell his current business at a loss and to secure housing for his family near the location of the franchise store. After the buyer did this, the company refused to go through with the deal as originally proposed. The court held that there was no valid contract because the offer and acceptance was too indefinite to constitute a legally binding agreement and certain things that had to be in writing were not. However, the buyer won in equity under promissory estoppel and received money damages to cover costs of selling his business and securing housing.

The practical lesson of promissory estoppel is that businesspeople should be careful of the promises they make. A manager who makes a promise and knows or should know that the promise is being relied upon, may be exposing their company to liability if the promise is broken. This can be true in equity even when no valid contract exists.

Assume, for the moment, that in the case described in the chapter opener, the alleged contract was not valid and that the workers agreed to the twenty-one percent pay cut on the basis of the company's promise that it would share profits. To apply the doctrine of promissory estoppel, a court would consider whether the profit-sharing promise was clear and direct, whether the employees reasonably relied on that promise, and whether the promisor knew or reasonably should have

---

[9] *Hoffman v. Red Owl Stores, Inc.,* 133 N.W. 2d 267 (Wis. 1965).

Global Context:
Promissory Estoppel in Japan

The Japanese do not apply the concept of promissory estoppel to gift settings, because they have no need for it. In Japan, a gratuitous promise is sufficient to create a binding contract, according to Japan's Civil Code, Section 549.

Sometimes, in Japan, an outright promise is not even necessary. In one case, a Japanese businessman gave a woman he had been dating his bank card. When she found out that he was married, she went to the bank and cleared out his bank account, which contained about 2.8 million yen. He sued to get his money back, but the court let her keep it. The court reasoned that if a man gives a woman a bank card, his act is the equivalent of promising her cash, and because a gift is as good as a bargained-for exchange, giving her the card was the equivalent of promising her the money she wanted.[10]

---

[10] *Kono v. Otsuyama,* 1048 Hanrei jiho 109 (Tokyo High Ct. Apr. 38, 1982).

known that the employees would rely on the promise. If each of these elements were present, the court might use equity to give the employees a share of profits even if no contract existed.

Although the use of promissory estoppel is growing, it is not without limits. Case 12-2 illustrates that for the doctrine to apply, the promise must be clear and direct and the reliance must be reasonable.

Case 12-2

Ypsilanti

v.

General Motors, Inc.
506 N.W. 2d 556 (Mich. Ct. App. 1993)

*G*eneral Motors (GM) operated the Willow Run plant in Ypsilanti, Michigan (township), for a number of years. The plant employed more than 4,000 workers. In 1984 GM applied for and the township granted a fifty percent property tax reduction on GM's $175 million investment to produce a new car. In April 1988, GM announced that it would produce its new car, the Chevrolet Caprice, at Willow Run. In December 1988, the township approved GM's application for additional tax abatement (reduction).

In December 1991, GM announced that it would be transferring some of the work done in the Willow Run plant to its plant in Arlington, Texas. GM stated that the consolidation was necessary because of the company's record losses and because the sales of the Caprice had been less than expected.

The town sued for breach of contract. The trial court found that there was no legal contract between the town and GM, but it did find that GM was bound in equity by promissory estoppel. The court enjoined GM from moving the production of the Caprice away from Ypsilanti for as long as GM produced the model. GM appealed.

Per Curiam

The trial court, relying on the background of GM's negotiations for abatements and principally on a statement by Willow Run plant manager Harvey Williams, found that a promise had been made…The trial court ruled:

"In the context of this background, when the plant manager, in the prepared statement on behalf of General Motors stated that, subject to "favorable market demand," General Motors would "continue production and maintain continuous employment" at Willow Run plant, *it was a promise.* The promise was clearly that if the Township granted the abatement, GM would make the Caprice at Willow Run and not just transfer that work somewhere else."

The elements of promissory estoppel are:

A promise, which the promisor should reasonably expect to induce action or forbearance on the part of the promisee or a third person which does induce such action or forbearance is binding if injustice can be avoided only by enforcement of the promise. The remedy granted for breach may be limited as justice requires. [*1 Restatement Contracts, 2d, section 90, p. 242*]

Promissory estoppel requires an actual, clear, and definite promise. Further, "reliance is reasonable only if it is induced by an actual promise."

The trial court's finding that GM promised to keep Caprice and station wagon production at Willow Run is clearly erroneous. First, the mere fact that a corporation solicits a tax abatement and persuades a municipality with assurances of jobs cannot be evidence of a promise. The very purpose of tax abatement legislation is to induce companies to locate and to continue business enterprises in the municipality. Second, representations of job creation and retention are a statutory prerequisite. An applicant for an industrial facilities exemption certificate must certify that "completion of the facility is calculated to have the reasonable likelihood to create employment, retain employment, prevent a loss of employment, or produce energy in the community in which the facility is situated."

Third, the fact that a manufacturer uses hyperbole and puffery in seeking an advantage or concession does not necessarily create such a promise. Turning to the case at bar, almost all the statements were, instead, expressions of GM's hopes or expectations of continued employment at Willow Run....The acts cited by the trial court were acts one would naturally expect a company to do in order to introduce and promote an abatement proposal to a municipality. The acts showed only efforts to take advantage of statutory opportunity. They did not constitute assurances of continued employment.

Even if the finding of a promise could be sustained, reliance on the promise would not have been reasonable. It has never been held that an abatement carries a promise of continued employment. Indeed, the history of this case shows that persons involved in the 1988 Willow Run abatement understood that GM was not promising continued employment. In short, GM made no promises.
REVERSED AND INJUNCTION VACATED.

1. Critical Thinking: Do you think that the town could reasonably rely on the assertions made by GM? Why or why not?

2. Ethical Decision Making: Note that the trial court felt that the GM's behavior was unfair, whereas the appellate court did not. When, if ever, is it ethical to make a promise and then to renege on that promise? Explain your reasoning.

As illustrated by the holding of the trial court in _Ypsilanti_, the courts have authority to decide contract disputes in accord with both legal rules _and_ equitable maxims. Typically, the plaintiff will allege a legal right to hold the defendant liable for breach of contract. The plaintiff will also "argue in the alternative"; that is, the plaintiff will claim that even if he or she loses in law, the plaintiff should win in equity so as to prevent injustice. The plaintiff claims to have both legal rights and equitable fairness on their side, and courts review both the legal rules and equitable principles before resolving contract disputes.

The UCC and its Relationship to Contract Law

Thus far, we have been discussing the rules of contract law and the maxims of equity that have been developed in state courts. There is, however, an additional source of contract law. Enacted in the early 1960s, Article 2 of the _Uniform Commercial Code_ (UCC) provides the rules for contracts for the sale of goods. The UCC is a state statute that is largely uniform, or common, to all the states.

The sale of goods forms a substantial portion of commercial activity. A **sale** is a transfer of title from seller to buyer for a price (UCC 2-106). A **good** is tangible personal property (UCC 2-105). A **tangible** property is one that has a corporeal (physical) presence, like inventory or a fleet of cars. Personal property is anything other than land or things attached to land, like an office building or a warehouse. The common law applies to all contracts other than the sale of goods, including rental agreements, services contracts, sales of real property, and sales of intangibles like corporate securities.

The distinction between the UCC and the common law is illustrated in Case 12-3. If the UCC applies, the defendant wins. If the common law applies, the plaintiff wins. The issue in the case is whether computer software is a "good."

Case 12-3

Advent Systems Ltd.

v.

Unisys Corporation

925 F. 2d 670 (3d Cir. 1991)

A British company, Advent Systems Unlimited (Advent) entered into a contract with Unisys Corporation whereby Unisys promised to promote and to market in the U.S. computer software developed by Advent. The agreement was to last two years. Unisys terminated the agreement early and Advent sued for breach of contract. Unisys filed a motion to dismiss arguing, among other things, that the writing used by the parties was not adequate because it failed to state the quantity term as required by UCC Section 2-201. The trial court ruled that the UCC did not apply in the case; therefore, it refused to grant the motion to dismiss. The case proceeded to trial and the jury awarded Advent $4,550,000. Advent appealed.

JUDGE WEIS

The increasing frequency of computer products as subjects of commercial litigation has led to controversy over whether software is a "good" or intellectual property. The Code does not specifically mention software.

Our court has addressed computer package sales in other cases, but has not been required to consider whether the UCC applied to software per se. Computer programs are the product of an intellectual process, but once implanted in a medium are widely distributed to computer owners. An analogy can be drawn to a compact disc recording of an orchestral rendition. The music is produced by the artistry of musicians and in itself is not a "good," but when transferred to a laser-readable disc becomes a readily merchantable commodity. Similarly, when a professor delivers a lecture, it is not a good, but, when transcribed as a book, it becomes a good.

That a computer program may be copyrightable as intellectual property does not alter the fact that once in the form of a floppy disc or other medium, the program is tangible, moveable and available in the marketplace….The topic has stimulated academic commentary with the majority espousing the view that software fits with the definition of a "good" in the UCC.

Applying the UCC to computer software transactions offers substantial benefits to litigants and the courts. The Code offers a uniform body of law in computer software disputes: implied warranties, consequential damages, disclaimers of warranties, disclaimers of liability, the statute of limitations, to name a few. The importance of software to the commercial world and the advantages to be gained by the uniformity inherent in the UCC are strong policy arguments favoring inclusion. The contrary arguments are not persuasive, and we hold that software is a "good" within the definition of the Code.

REVERSED AND REMANDED

1. Critical Thinking: The court drew an analogy between computer software and an electronic recording of music. Do you think that this analogy is valid? Why or why not?

2. Ethical Decision Making: Unisys argued that computer software is a good. Do you think that Unisys would have made the same argument if it were not in its economic interests to do so? When is it ethical to form your legal arguments so as to advance your economic interests? Explain your reasoning.

In Case 12-3, the UCC writing requirement was stricter (more things had to been in writing for the contract to be enforceable) than that of the common law.

A manager must remember that there is one source of law for contracts for the sale of goods and another for other types of contracts.

As the following Technology feature illustrates, model legislation has been proposed to treat certain types of computer transactions under yet another set of specialized rules.

Part Three of this text addresses the UCC in detail. In the contract chapters, we highlight sections that arise most commonly in business life. Exhibit 12-3 provides a list. For each topic there is one rule under the common law and another under the UCC. Unless otherwise stated, it is safe to assume that UCC rules largely conform to the common law. [and see Appendix B for the UCC, Article 2, in detail].

EXHIBIT 12-3

Key Sections of UCC Article 2

SECTION NUMBER	TOPIC
§2-201	When Must a Contract Be in Writing to Be Enforceable?
§2-204	How Definite Do Negotiations Have to Be Before Courts Will Say There Is an Agreement?
§2-205	When Can an Offeror Take Back an Offer?
§2-209	Are Promises to Modify Contracts Enforceable Without an Exchange of Consideration?
§2-314	When Do Courts Assume That a Contract Comes With a Warranty?

Technology: Emerging Legislation on Electronic Commerce

Law needs to be continually updated to address changes in societal norms and technology. The UCC was one such update. The common law took shape during the eighteenth and nineteenth centuries. At that time most contracting took place face to face and many contracts were individually negotiated. With the growth of big business, however, more and more contracts were entered into through a nonnegotiable form drafted by the stronger party. The UCC reflects these newer realties.

Today, the challenge comes from the explosion of contracting over the Internet, with billions of dollars of commerce being consummated by the click of a mouse. Two uniform acts promulgated by the National Conference of Commissioners on Uniform State Laws (a group of lawyers, judges, and legal scholars) seek to update contract rules to address the new technology. The Uniform Electronic Transactions Act (UETA) applies to all contracts between parties who have agreed to conduct their transaction by electronic means. The Uniform Computer Information Transaction Act (UCITA) applies to the contracts involving computer information transactions such as the selling or licensing of computer software and databases. UCITA has been adopted in full by only Virginia and Maryland, but many scholars project that with minor modifications, UCITA may be adopted by more states. UETA may also gain wide acceptance.

Managers need to remain abreast of this rapidly changing aspect of contract law. As we proceed through the remaining contract chapters, we will consider how UCITA and UETA address the issues outlined in our central framework for legal contracting.

Classifications of Contracts

Contracts are classified according to various characteristics, such as method of formation and the degree to which they have been performed. We close this chapter by introducing three classifications: (1) express and implied contracts, (2) unilateral and bilateral contracts, and (3) executory and executed contracts. This terminology will be used in the remaining contract chapters.

Express and Implied Contracts

An **express contract** is one in which all the essential terms of the agreement are fully stated in words, either orally or in writing. A detailed commercial lease is an example, as is a purchase of catalogue merchandise over the telephone.

When one or more of the essential terms of an agreement is inferred from the conduct of the parties, rather than from their words, an **implied contract** (also called an implied-in-fact contract) is formed. For example, when a customer pumps gasoline into the tank of their car, no words are spoken, but a contract to pay for the gas is inferred from the conduct.

Most contracts involve a mix of express and implied terms. For example, suppose a delivery contract expressly states the items to be delivered, price to pay, and time of delivery, but it fails to address which party bears the risk if the items are lost in transit. This con-tract is express (the essential terms are in words), but it contains an implied term.

Courts infer implied terms from industry customs, so managers need to learn these customs. For example, in the shipping industry it is customary for the seller to retain title (and risk of loss) until the items reach the buyer's door. By contrast, in real estate, the risk of damage to a home customarily transfers to the buyer who receives a deed, rather than when possession occurs. The following Global Context feature reminds us that customs differ not only between industries, but also between nations.

Bilateral and Unilateral Contracts

Every contract has at least two parties. One party (the offeror) makes an offer and the other party (the offeree) accepts. The offeror is free to specify the way in which its offer must be accepted. Most offers can be accepted with a return promise. For example, a wholesaler offers to deliver goods with payment on delivery and the retailer accepts. This exchange of promises forms a bilateral contract. No actual performance, such as delivery or payment, is needed to form a **bilateral contract**.

Sometimes the offeror specifies that an offer can only be accepted through an action. This is an offer to form a **unilateral contract**. For example, a homeowner promises to pay a salvage company $200 to remove

Global Context: Implied Terms in Hungary

The Hungarian Civil Code organizes its contract provisions into two parts. The first addresses issues common to any type of contract: the elements of a contract, contract defenses, and modes of discharge. As in the United States, the central terms of the contract can be inferred either from the words of the parties (express contract) or from their actions (implied contract).

The second part of the Hungarian Code provides implied terms. In Hungary, there are implied terms for about twenty-five types of contracts, including sales contracts, construction contracts, transportation contracts, and leases of real property. The reliance on statutory terms reflects a general civil law reliance on the legislative as opposed to judicial branch of government. Before entering a contract in Hungary, managers need to become familiar with the Hungarian Civil Code.

household rubbish. Once the rubbish is removed, a unilateral contract is formed. If the offer is ambiguous as to the way it can be accepted, the courts infer that acceptance can be either through an action or through a return promise.

Executory and Executed Contracts

Once both parties have fully performed their contractual obligations, the contract is said to be **executed**. Before full performance by both parties, the contract is **executory**. The term "executed" is also commonly used to refer to a contract that has been reduced to a signed writing.

Note that a contract may be described with more than one of these classifications. For example, suppose a retailer sends a purchase order to a manufacturer specifying needed inventory. The manufacturer acknowledges the order and promises prompt delivery. Before delivery, this contract is valid, express, bilateral, and executory.

Columbia Falls Wrap-Up

In 1992 a class action lawsuit was filed on behalf of employees against their employer, Columbia Falls Aluminum Company and it's new owners, alleging that the defendants had breached a contract in failing to distribute company profits.[11] A trial court ruled that an enforceable profit sharing contract existed, and a trial date was set to determine the amount owing.[12] A few weeks before that trial and almost six years after the case was filed, the defendants settled the dispute, agreeing to pay $97 million dollars, or an average of $100,000 per union employee and $150,000 for each salaried employee.[13]

---

[11] Jim Robbins, *A Broken Pact and a $97 Million Payday,* NEW YORK TIMES, April 19, 1998 http://www:nytimes.com/library. financial/Sunday/archives
[12] *Id.*
[13] *Id.*

	Summary
Framework of Legal Contracting	**Definition of contract**—A promise or set of promises that, in the event of a breach, the law gives a remedy.
Elements of Contract	Every contract has four elements. **Agreement**—one party makes an offer and the other party accepts. **Consideration**—the agreement was induced by a bargain for exchange of value. **Capacity**—each party is of sound mind and legal age. **Legality**—the agreement is not tortious, nor criminal, nor violates public policy.
Contract Defenses	**Reality of Assent**—a contract procured by misrepresentation, duress, undue influence, mutual mistake, or unconscionablity is voidable. **Faulty Writing**—if the contract must be in writing and there is no writing, or the writing is faulty, the contract is unenforceable.
Contractual Discharge	Contract duties can be terminated by performance, breach of the other party, operation of law, changed circumstance, or agreement of the parties.
Role of Equity	**Quasi Contract**—an obligation inferred by the courts to prevent unjust enrichment. **Promissory Estoppel**—an obligation inferred by the courts to protect justifiable reliance.
The Relationship of UCC to Contract Law	Contracts for the sale of goods are governed by UCC Article 2. **Sale**—transfer of title from buyer to seller for a price. **Goods**—tangible personal property.
Classification of Contracts	Contracts can be classified in a variety of ways. **Express and Implied Contracts** **Express contract**—all essential terms of contract have been stated in words. **Implied-in-Fact contract**—at least one essential term of contract is inferred from the actions of the parties. **Bilateral and Unilateral Contracts** **Bilateral contract**—a contract formed through an exchange of promises. **Unilateral contract**—a contract formed through an exchange of a promise for an act. **Executory and Executed Contracts** **Executory contract**—a contract that has not been fully performed by both parties. **Executed contract**—a contract that has been fully performed by both parties.

Review Questions and Case Problems

1. One of the purposes of contract law is to facilitate private market exchanges between business actors. Identify three ways contract law achieves this. Explain.

2. List four elements of a contract, two defenses, and five modes of contractual discharge. Use this framework to identify the legal issues presented in the case opener—Columbia Falls.

3. Identify the elements of a quasi contract. Construct an example that illustrates your understanding of this equitable doctrine.

4. Identify the elements of promissory estoppel. When will the equitable principles of estoppel modify the rules of legal contracting? Explain.

5. Distinguish between void, voidable, unenforceable and valid contracts. Does it make any sense to say that a contract exists but it is unenforceable? Explain.

6. To what type of contracts do the rules of Article 2 of the UCC apply?

7. Give an example of a contract that is bilateral, express, executory and valid.

8. Courts infer implied contract terms from the past dealing of the parties and industry customs. Give an example of two business customs that would automatically become part of a contract.

9. A manufacturer of golf tee mats had a long-term relationship with its supplier of artificial turf. The turf was used to make the mats. The supplier began to manufacture mats itself, resulting in a reduced amount of turf being supplied to the manufacturer. The manufacturer sued the turf supplier for breach of contract. The court held for the supplier. Identify the issues that might explain this result. What elements are needed for contract? What defenses may have applied in this case? How could the supplier's obligation have been discharged? *Major Mat Co. v. Monsanto Co.*, 969 F. 2d 579 (7th Cir. 1992).

10. A grandfather was distressed because his granddaughter had to work in a store. He encouraged her to quit her job and gave her a promissory note stating that he would give her $2,000 so she could quit. She quit, but before she received the money, her grandfather died. The executor of the estate did not know if the estate should pay the granddaughter the $2,000. What would you advise the executor? What element of a legal contract is missing? Would your advice have been different a century ago as compared to today? *Ricketts, Executor v. Scothorn*, 77 N.W. 365 (Neb. 1898).

11. The town of Old Orchard Beach, Maine, owned a minor league baseball stadium. The town contracted to sell that stadium to Stadium Partners Inc. Stadium Partners hired Aladdin Electric Associates to fix the electrical wiring in the stadium. Aladdin did the work and submitted a bill to Stadium Partners for $5,791. The work was done well, but Stadium Partners did not pay the the bill. In fact, Stadium Partners backed out of the deal with the town and did not buy the stadium. Aladdin had done the work at the request of Stadium Partners and had no direct dealings with town officials. Aladdin sued the town for breach of contract and the court found that there was no legal contract. Which element was missing? Explain. *Aladdin Electric Associates v. Town of Old Orchard Beach*, 645 A. 2d 1142 (Maine 1994)

12. An automobile manufacturer promised to award a dealership to a prospective dealer. Relying on the promise, the prospective dealer spent $232,131 in out-of-pocket expenses. The manufacturer then refused to grant the dealership and the prospective dealer sued for breach of contract? Is there a valid legal contract in this case? What additional information would you need to answer this question? *Walser v. Toyota Motor Sales, U.S.A., Inc.*, 43 F. 3d 396 (8th Cir. 1994).

13. Members of a religious movement resided on land located in Utah. The members had a deed to the land that they thought gave them a legal right to occupy the land for the rest of their lives. The deed was defective and a trial court declared that the members were merely tenants-at-will (could be evicted by the owners of property). The members had made numerous improvements to the land and sought to be reimbursed for these improvements. Which legal or equitable rule would most help the members? What else would the court need to know before deciding who wins? *Jeffs v. Stubbs*, 970 P. 2d 1234 (Utah 1998).

14. A liquor supplier contracted with a distributor giving the distributor exclusive rights to distribute liquor in a given geographic area. A term of the written contract stated that the relationship could be terminated by either party on due notice. The supplier orally assured the distributor that the exclusive distributorship would continue so long as the distributor's sales continued to meet the supplier's expectations, and so long as there were no changes in market conditions. Relying on the supplier's assurances, the distributor turned down an attractive offer from a third party to buy the distributor's assets. The supplier, then, suddenly terminated the distributorship and the distributor sued. Does this case raise the issue of unjust enrichment or promissory estoppel? What must the distributor prove to be able to win its case in equity? *D & G Stout, Inc. v. Bacardi Imports, Inc.*, 805 F. Supp. 1434 (N.D. Ind. 1992).

15. A general contractor bid on a construction project with the U.S. government. The government granted the contract to the contractor. The bid had been based on price quotes that the contractor had received from various subcontractors. One subcontractor, a distributor of fans, refused to sell the general contractor fans at the quoted price and the general contractor sued the subcontractor on the basis of promissory estoppel. What would the general contractor have to prove to win its case in equity? Explain. *Foley Co. v. Warren Engineering, Inc.*, 804 F. Supp. 1540 (D. Ga. 1992).

16. A patient received a blood transfusion as part of a necessary surgery. The blood was tainted with the hepatitis virus and the patient contracted the disease and died.

The deceased's estate sued the hospital for, among other things, breach of a contractual warranty that the blood would be pure. Whether there was a warranty or not depended on whether a blood transfusion was a service (the common law gives no implied warranty) or a sale of goods (UCC provides a warranty). Make an argument that a blood transfusion is a service. Make an argument that a blood transfusion is a sale of goods. Assuming that this is a "gray area case," whom would you want to win? Does your desire for one party or the other to win play any role in determining whether you think a blood transfusion is a service or a good? Should it? *Lovett v. Emory University, Inc.* (Ga. App. 1967).

17. A woman received a hair-coloring treatment at a beauty show. The treatment caused acute dermatitis and loss of hair. The woman sued for breach of implied warranty under Section 2-314 of the UCC. Does the UCC apply in this case? Why? *Epstein v. Giannattasio*, 197 A. 2d 342 (Conn. Sup. 1963).

18. A general contractor hired a carpet company to provide and install carpet in a hotel. The contract was formed when the carpet company submitted a bid that was accepted by the general contractor. Prior to any performance by either party, how would you classify this contract: express or implied? Bilateral or unilateral? Executed or executory? Is the contract void, voidable, valid or unenforceable? What else to you need to know to be able to answer these questions? Explain. *Flooring Systems, Inc. v. Radisson Group, Inc.*, 772 P. 2d 578 (Ariz. 1989).

Assignment on the Internet

F indlaw's directory offers various links to contract law matters. Click on the index of legal subjects under the term "Contracts" and you will find links to such subjects as "Layman's Guide to Drafting and Signing Contracts" and contract law in cyberspace. The site also provides sample form contracts. Findlaw's URL is http://findlaw.com/. List a set of practical tips for assuring that you can rely on the promises made by others.

On the Internet

http://lectlaw.com *Provides information on contracting, including the elements of contract and contractual defenses.*

http://www.lawschool.org *Includes bar review outlines for studying contract law.*

http://thelawoffice.com *Contains, among other things, a series of form contracts*

http://www.law.cornell.edu/topics/ contracts.html *Provides links to legal matters generally, including contract law.*

http://www.usalaw.com *Contains articles addressing various aspects of contracting.*

CHAPTER 13

Renegotiating an NFL Contract

The Seattle Seahawks made Ohio State wide receiver Joey Galloway the eighth pick in the 1995 NFL draft, signing him to a five-year rookie contract totaling more than $7 million. Galloway quickly became one of the best wide receivers in the league and in July 1999, prior to the start of his fifth year, the Seahawks offered to extend Galloway's contract for an additional seven years for $35 million including a $7 million signing bonus.[1] Communicating through his agent, Eric Metz, Joey seemingly rejected the Seahawks' offer in August 1999, suggesting that $25 million over five years with a $10 million bonus would be a more suitable sum.[2] In September, the Seahawks withdrew their offer stating that Galloway must play under his existing rookie contract if he were to play at all.[3]

1. Assume you were Joey Galloway and the Seahawks offered you $35 million dollars to play football. How long would this offer remain open? If you made a counteroffer, would that terminate the Seahawks offer?

2. How does communicating through a sports agent modify the rules of offer and acceptance?

---

[1] Jim Cour, *Seahawks Coach Won't Trade Holdout Joey Galloway*, The Detroit News, (September 9, 1999) www.detroitnews.com/1999/sports/9909/09/090901112.htm.

[2] *Id.*

[3] CNNSI.COM, *Keeping Their Money: Galloway Contract Negotiations Called Off by Seahawks* http://channel.cnnsi.com/football/nfl/news/1999/09/27/galloway_seahawks_ap/, (September 27, 1999).

CHAPTER 13

Agreement

Creating an Offer

Terminating an Offer

Irrevocable Offers

Accepting an Offer

At the heart of every contract lies an agreement, which is a manifestation of assent by two or more parties to be bound by a contract. Agreement indicates an end to preliminary negotiations, signals that a final bargain has been made, establishes the essential contract terms, and imposes a legal duty of performance. In general, the courts grant the parties wide latitude to shape their own agreements and tend to enforce whatever the parties agree to and no more. By refusing to find a contract where the parties did not agree to one, the courts embrace a principle of freedom of contract that is central to a free society and promotes an efficient market economy.

The courts have developed a number of principles designed to distinguish legal agreements from preliminary negotiations and other communications that do not amount to a contract. These principles are embodied in the rules of offer and acceptance. In simplest terms, those rules dictate that agreement occurs at the moment one party accepts an offer from another party. If the other three elements are present—consideration, capacity, and legality—the agreement establishes a legal contract.

This chapter explores the rules of creating and terminating an offer and the concept of irrevocable offers. It also examines the rules of acceptance. These rules will help us understand the case of Joey Galloway and the Seahawks and the legal effect of contract negotiations generally.

Creating an Offer

To create an offer, three elements must be present:
• Intent of the offeror to enter into a contract,
• Communication of that intent to the offeree, and
• Definiteness as to the central terms that are being offered.

To determine whether an offer has been created, the courts look to the totality of the circumstances, including the words and actions of the offeror and the surrounding business customs. They also examine the circumstances to allow contracting parties the flexibility of negotiating through an exchange of letters, multiple conversations, or other means. The first question courts consider is whether, given the totality of the circumstances, the offeror manifested an intent to enter into a contract.

Intent—Objective and Subjective Theories

When courts assess the intent of the parties, they distinguish between subjective intent and objective intent. **Subjective intent**, which refers to what the parties were actually thinking, might include hidden motives and concerns not revealed to the other party. **Objective intent**, in contrast, refers to what a reasonable listener would infer that party was thinking, given what was said and done. The courts use an objective intent standard. That is, they consider the totality of the circumstances and ask what a reasonable offeree would infer that the offeror had intended. The objective standard avoids the problems of proving what each party was actually thinking and provides a more predictable outcome as compared to the subjective standard. The practical lesson is that business people must take care, because their words and actions can have unintended legal consequences.

The fact that courts look for objective manifestations of intent does not necessarily mean they interpret spoken or written words literally. For example, offers or acceptances spoken in jest or in the heat of the moment may not manifest an objective intent to contract. This is illustrated in Case 13-1, where the parties negotiated the sale of a family farm while joking at a Christmas party.

Case 13-1

Lucy

v.

Zehmer

84 S.E. 2d 516 (Va. 1954)

W.O. Lucy had been trying for several years to buy a farm, known as the Ferguson farm, from A.H. and Ida Zehmer, but the Zehmers had always refused. One Saturday night in December, Lucy visited a restaurant operated by the Zehmers. A Christmas party was in progress and both Lucy and A.H. Zehmer began drinking whiskey. The conversation soon turned to the sale of the farm. Lucy said to Zehmer, "I bet you wouldn't take $50,000 for that place." Zehmer replied, "Yes I would too; you wouldn't give fifty." Zehmer then wrote on the back of a restaurant receipt: "I do hereby agree to sell to W.O. Lucy the Ferguson Farm for $50,000 complete." Lucy convinced Zehmer to change the wording to "we" and to have Zehmer's wife sign it, too. After this had been done, Lucy took the writing from the table, put it in his pocket, and handed Zehmer five dollars as a down payment. Zehmer refused to take the money, stating that he and his wife were only joking.

When Zehmer refused to tender a deed to the property, Lucy sued for specific performance. Zehmer testified that he, at no time, had any intention to sell the farm and that he had whispered to his wife that he was just "needling" Lucy, that it was only a joke. Zehmer also testified that at the time of the transaction he was as "high as a Georgia pine" and that the whole thing was "just a bunch of two doggoned drunks bluffing to see who could talk the biggest and say the most." The trial court found that no contract had been formed, and ruled for Zehmer. Lucy appealed.

JUDGE BUCHANAN

The defendants insist that the evidence was ample to support their contention that the writing they sought to be enforced was prepared as a bluff or dare to force Lucy to admit that he did not have $50,000; that the whole matter was joke; that the writing was not delivered to Lucy; and, no binding contract was ever made between the parties.

The record is convincing that Zehmer was not intoxicated to the extent of being unable to comprehend the nature and consequences of the instrument he executed, and hence that instrument is not to be invalidated on that ground.

In the field of contracts, as generally elsewhere, we must look to the outward expression of a person as manifesting his intention rather than to his secret and unexpressed intention. The law imputes to a person an intention corresponding to the reasonable meaning of his words and acts.

The mental assent of the parties is not requisite for the formation of a contract. If the words or other acts of one of the parties have but one reasonable meaning, his undisclosed intention is immaterial, except when an unreasonable meaning which he attaches to his manifestations is known to the other party. So a person cannot set up that he was merely jesting when his conduct and words would warrant a reasonable person in believing that he intended a real agreement.

Whether the writing signed by the defendants and now sought to be enforced by the complainants was the result of a serious offer by Lucy and a serious acceptance by the defendants, or was a serious offer by Lucy and an acceptance in jest by the defendants, in either event it constituted a binding contract of sale between the parties.

There was no fraud, no misrepresentation, no sharp practice, and no dealing between unequal parties. The farm had been bought for $11,000 and was assessed for taxation at $6,300. The purchase price was $50,000. Zehmer admitted that it was a good price.

The complainants are entitled to have specific performance of the contract.

REVERSED.

1. Critical Thinking: Identify the objective facts that seem to prove that the Zehmers intended to offer their farm for sale as well as the facts that seem to prove they did not. Would you make the Zehmers hand over the farm? Why or why not?

2. Ethical Decision Making: The court's decision to uphold the contract reflects certain values. Identify those values and then identify values that conflict with those upheld in the court's reasoning. Which set of values do you find most compelling?

Global Context:
Offers and Acceptances in Poland

The rules of offer and acceptance employed in centrally-planned countries, such as Poland before the fall of Communism, looked much like those found in Western European countries, such as France. In fact, comparing the agreement provisions in the Civil Code of Poland under communism with the Civil Codes of France, one finds few differences. The similarities can be deceiving, however. In a centrally-planned economy, the state owns the means of production (such as factories, business organizations, and real estate), so managers of these enterprises must follow the dictates of a state plan in deciding what contracts to offer and what offers to accept. Failure to make or accept an offer in accordance with the needs of the state plan can lead to liability. In addition, contracts are rewritten once they no longer conform to the needs of an evolving state plan.

In market economies, such as France's, individuals create their own mutually beneficial agreements and the state does not dictate what offers must be made or accepted. Once the parties enter an agreement, they create a corresponding duty to perform, which is equivalent to private law between the parties. Judicial respect for individual agreements provides an important legal foundation for decentralized market capitalism.

Poland and the other countries of the former Eastern Bloc have largely reformed their contract codes, and the notion of liability for failing to cooperate with the state plans is largely a relic of the past. In Poland, reformers have used the French Civil Law tradition as a guide. The newly written Polish laws, much like those in the West, require a manifestation of intent to form a contract before liability can be attached.

In applying an objective theory of intent, the court in the Zehmer case did not look at what Zehmer thought he had done; instead, it looked at what a reasonable observer would think Zehmer had done. The court was not persuaded by Zehmer's claim that Lucy should have known that he was joking. The fact that Zehmer might have had impaired capacity because he was intoxicated seemed to play little or no role in the court's decision.

Intent—the Role of Business Custom

Evidence of contractual intent is found primarily in the words and actions of the offeror, but business customs may also indicate intent. This is particularly true if the language of the offer is ambiguous. As a general rule, the courts interpret ambiguous language to be consistent with custom. Three examples illustrate how custom plays a role in determining contractual intent: advertising, bids, and auctions.

Advertising

According to business custom, most advertisements, including catalogs and price circulars, are invitations to contract, rather than offers.

Unless the ad is very specific and addresses certain issues, such as limited supply, it will not be considered an offer.

Consider this example. A car dealer places an ad to sell three specific cars. The ad lists the serial numbers, the makes and models of the cars, the exact price and credit terms, and states the cars will be sold on a first-come-first-served basis. The courts probably would consider this an offer because of the express language used in the ad. By contrast, if the ad had been less specific, the general rule would control and the ad would not be an offer.

Bids

Just as courts consider business custom when they assess ads, they also consider business custom when determining whether a bid is an effective offer. Customarily a bid is considered an offer because offerees typically rely on them. Construction is one industry that relies on bids. For instance, a general contractor who is bidding to build a school relies on the bids received from subcontractors such as plumbers, electricians, and excavators to assemble their bid. If the subcontractors were permitted to renege on their bids, the general contractor probably would not be able to build the school within the time and money parameters outlined in the bid. Consequently, the courts uphold this business custom, holding that such bids are offers.

Nevertheless, this custom, like the one surrounding advertisements, can be changed by the express language of the offeror. For instance, if the plumbing company expressly states that its bid is not an offer, but only an estimate, that language controls and the bid is not an offer. If the bid is ambiguous or silent with regard to intent, courts will usually find the bid is an offer.

Auctions

At an auction, the seller offers items for sale through an auctioneer. Unless stated otherwise, the offer to sell is made **with reserve**. This means that the seller retains the right to accept or reject the highest bid. An auction **without reserve** is one in which the seller agrees to accept the highest bid. Sometimes the seller specifies a minimum bid. In such cases, the seller has agreed to accept the highest bid at or above that minimum.

Auctions have become quite common over the internet. As the following technology box indicates, eBay, Amazon.com, and other auctioneers have transformed the traditional auction into a growing and dynamic business

Communication

The second element of an offer is communication. For an offer to be effective, it must be communicated to the offeree. As a general rule, sending an offer to the offeree's place of business constitutes effective communication, as does delivery of an offer to the offeree's authorized agent, such as an attorney. Joey Galloway communicated through his agents. So long as he authorized the agents to speak and receive communications on his behalf, the communications had the same legal effect as if they were from Galloway directly.

Communication can also occur through an action, such as posting a reward for return of a lost valuable. The courts are split on whether a reward can be claimed by someone who was not aware a reward was posted. Most courts would deny recovery in law because the offer was not communicated, while others would award damages in *quasi contract*, and still others would deny recovery on either law or equity.

The issue of communication can also arise in situations involving inconspicuous written terms, such as the liability disclaimers printed on the back of coat check receipts and parking garage tickets. For instance,

Technology: Auctions on the Internet

Traditional auctions typically required the physical presence of both the buyer and seller. The Internet has now made auctions possible in cyberspace. The industry leader was eBay, a "dot com" business who served as auctioneer for auctions conducted over the Internet. The company was not the seller or buyer, but simply the intermediary. The seller can post items for sale either with or without reserve. Upon a completed Internet sale, eBay took a six percent commission.

Although eBay pioneered Internet auctions, today many companies have become online auctioneers. For example, e-commerce leader Amazon.com conducts on line auctions for a wide range of products. So, too, does Sotheby's, the New York based auction house that specializes in high priced items such as jewelry, antiques, and works of art. Many companies have also started selling excess inventory and traditional business goods through Internet auctions. Auctions are no longer the sole province of the quirky antique and flea market collectible. In fact, business sales through online auctions now exceed nonbusiness sales.

suppose a customer leaves their coat at a coat check at the theater and it is gone when the customer returns to claim it. Even though the fine print on the back of the ticket says that the person cannot sue the theater, the courts may hold that the disclaimer was not effectively communicated and has no legal effect.

Definiteness of the Offer

The final element of an offer is definiteness. The courts require offers to be definite enough for the courts to be able to infer all of the express and implied terms of the offer. Recall that express terms are terms that the offeror puts into words and implied terms are unspoken terms derived from the past dealings of the parties and business custom. Typically, the courts will consider that an offer was made if the following terms are expressly stated:

- Identity of the parties to the contract.
- Goods or services to be exchanged.
- Quantity term.
- Price or other consideration to be paid.
- Time of performance.

If all of these terms are stated, the terms of the agreement will be fairly definite. The Seahawks' offer to Joey Galloway specified the parties (Galloway and the Seahawks), service to be performed (playing football), term of employment (seven years), price ($35 million), and time of performance (beginning with 1999 season). The court would not have to guess at the terms of the offer; they were specified by the offeror.

Agreements to Agree

The detail required by the common law can cause problems whenever it is difficult for the parties to specify in advance exactly what it is that they intend to do. Consider this example. A farmer has twenty acres of undeveloped land. A real estate developer proposes to develop the land as residential housing. The parties, however, cannot know exactly what is to be built nor what a fair split in the profits might be until money is spent on a marketing feasibility study, a civil engineering report, and an attorney who will seek a zoning variance. Neither party wants to proceed without a written agreement. The problem is that they cannot write their contract so that it clearly identifies the subject matter (are they going to build condominiums or single family dwellings?), price (what is a fair split?), and time of performance (how long will this take?).

This example highlights how the common-law contract requirement of definite terms poses difficulty when parties are organizing a business venture. In such cases, the parties may enter an "agreement to agree." They agree to cooperate with one another, and to spec-ify the exact terms of their agreement at a later time. An agreement to agree, however, may be too indefinite to constitute a valid contract. An alternative solution is to form a partnership or small corporation. The following Global Context feature illustrates that Japanese law is more receptive to agreements to agree.

Global Context: Agreements to Agree in Japan

The Japanese tend to see a contract as an ongoing relationship in which the parties agree to work with each other to smooth out any difficulties. Japanese business people can be suspicious of long, detailed agreements, particularly ones prepared by foreign firms. Japanese often prefer short contracts with flexible terms that will permit the parties to compromise if any difficulties arise. It is not surprising, then, to find an "agreement to agree" in Japan, with a number of terms left to be decided later. Such an agreement is typically bolstered with a "good faith clause" that requires the parties to resolve contractual disputes ethically and honestly.

Good faith clauses are also common in the U.S. Section 2-103 of the U.C.C. defines good faith as "honesty in fact and the observance of reasonable commercial standards of fair dealing." An obligation to act in good faith is an implied term of every contract. Yet, even with a good faith clause, an agreement to agree in the U.S. may be too indefinite to be unenforceable.

The parties in the following case find it difficult to agree to a long-term price in their contract, so they agreed to set the price at a later date. Note that the trial court, the appellate court, and the justices on New York's highest court split on whether this "agreement to agree" was enforceable.

Case 13-2

Martin

v.

Schumacher
417 N.E. 2d 541 (N.Y. 1981)

Schumacher rented a retail store from Martin. Their five-year lease specified an initial rent of $500 per month for the first year, escalating yearly to $650 per month in the fifth year. The lease also provided: "Tenant may renew this lease for an additional period of five years at annual rentals to be agreed upon." At the end of five years, Schumacher's business was doing well enough that he wanted to exercise his option for an additional five years. Martin insisted on a rent of $900 per month. Schumacher argued that $900 was not a fair rate, but Martin refused to take less. Schumacher sued Martin for specific performance of the renewal term at a "fair market rental value" to be determined by the court. The trial court dismissed the action, stating that the agreement to agree to a price was too indefinite to form a contract. Schumacher appealed and the appellate court reversed. Martin appealed to the New York Court of Appeals.

JUDGE FUCHSBERG

[B]efore the power of law can be invoked to enforce a promise, it must be sufficiently certain and specific so that what was promised can be ascertained. Otherwise, a court, in intervening, would be imposing its own conception of what the parties should or might have undertaken, rather than confining itself to the implementation of a bargain to which they have mutually committed themselves. Thus, definiteness as to material matters is of the very essence in contract law. Impenetrable vagueness and uncertainty will not do.

Dictated by these principles, it is rightfully well-settled in this State that a mere agreement to agree, in which a material term is left for future negotiations, is unenforceable. This is especially true of the amount to be paid for the sale or lease of real property.

This is not to say that the requirement for definiteness in the case before us now could only have been met by explicit expression of the rent to be paid. The concern here is with substance, not form. It certainly would have sufficed, for instance, if a methodology for determining rent was to be found within the four corners of the lease, for a rent so arrived at would have been the end product of agreement between the parties themselves....

But the renewal here.... speaks to no more than "annual rentals to be agreed upon." Its simple words leave no room for the legal construction or resolution of ambiguity. Neither tenant nor landlord is bound to any formula. There is not so much as a hint at a commitment to be bound by the "fair market rental value" or the "reasonable rent" the Appellate Division would impose, much less any definition of either....

For all these reasons, the order of the Appellate Division should be reversed....and the orders of the Supreme Court reinstated.

REVERSED.

JUDGE JASEN, DISSENTING

While I recognize that the traditional rule is that a provision of renewal of a lease must be "certain" in order to render it binding and enforceable, in my view the better rule would be that if the tenant can establish its entitlement to renewal under the lease, the mere presence of a provision calling for renewal at "rentals to be agreed upon" should not prevent judicial intervention to fix rent at a reasonable rate in order to avoid a forfeiture. Therefore, I would affirm the order of the Appellate Division.

1. Critical Thinking: Identify the reasons offered by Judge Fuchsberg. Why did Judge Jasen disagree? Which set of reasons do you find most compelling? Explain.

2. Ethical Decision Making: It would be very costly for Schumaker to move his store. Do you think Martin used this fact to his advantage in seeking a higher rent? Would it be ethical to do so? Why or why not?

The UCC Approach To Definiteness

Article 2 of the Uniform Commercial Code has modified the "definiteness" required by the common law. Section 2-204(3) states:

Even though one or more terms are left open, a contract for sale does not fail for indefiniteness if the parties have intended to make a contract and there is a reasonable certain basis for giving an appropriate remedy.

Under the Code, the courts are more willing to refer to past dealings of the parties, business customs, and notions of reasonableness to fill in the gaps in the express language of an agreement. There must still be an intent to contract, a communication of that intent, and enough definiteness in the agreement for the courts to reasonably infer the terms of the contract, but a contract will not fail simply because a particular term or terms have been left unstated. This lack of formality is typical of Code provisions. It also contrasts to the more formal requirements of contractual definiteness illustrated in the real estate developer example discussed above.

Terminating an Offer

To have an agreement, the offer must be open when it is accepted. An offer can terminate or close before it is accepted in any of these eight ways: (1) death of a party, (2) incapacity of a party, (3) destruction of subject matter, (4) supervening illegality, (5) lapse of time, (6) rejection, (7) counteroffer, and (8) revocation. The first five occur through operation of law; the last three derive from the actions of the parties.

Death or Incapacity

Death or incapacity of either the offeror or the offeree terminates an offer. In Galloway, if Joey had died or lost his capacity to contract prior to accepting the Seahawks' offer, then that offer would have terminated. Notice of death or incapacity is not required for operation of the rule. Death or incapacity does not terminate irrevocable offers.

Destruction of Subject Matter or Supervening Illegality

An offer is terminated if the subject matter is destroyed or there is supervening illegality. Consider this example. Jim offers to sell his boat to Lou. While the offer is still open, lightning strikes and the boat is destroyed. The destruction of the boat terminates Jim's offer. No notice is required. Similarly, if Galloway suffered a debilitating knee injury prior to accepting the Seahawks' offer, the offer would terminate by operation of law.

A similar result occurs if the proposed contract becomes illegal. For instance, during World War II, Congress passed a statute forbidding the production and sale of new cars. Congress wanted to put all the nation's resources into supplying tanks and munitions. This sudden illegality terminated any outstanding offers to buy or sell a new car.

Lapse of Time

An offer can also be terminated by a lapse of time. The time limit may be either express or implied. If the Seahawks had offered to extend Galloway's contract, stating that Galloway must accept prior to the first game of the 1999 season, any attempt to accept the offer after that time would be ineffective. If the offeror does not state a time limit, then the offer will terminate after a "reasonable length of time." What is reasonable will depend on the totality of the circumstances.

Rejections and Counteroffers

Rejections terminate offers. Suppose Cal offers to paint Sue's house for $400. Sue rejects Cal's offer. Later, Sue changes her mind and tries to accept. Sue's rejection terminated Cal's offer, so her "acceptance" is now a new offer, not an acceptance.

Offers are also terminated by counteroffers. Counteroffers contain implied rejections. The Seahawks offered Joey Galloway $35 million over seven years. Galloway, through his agent, countered with $35 million over five years. Suppose the Seahawks rejected the counteroffer, and Galloway then tried to accept the initial offer. Galloway's attempt to accept would be ineffective because his counteroffer terminated the Seahawks' offer.

A rejection or counteroffer must be definite. The courts draw a distinction between counteroffers and mere inquiries. Suppose that Sue, in the above example, responded to Cal's offer with "Would you be willing to take $300 to paint my house?" This would be an inquiry, not a counteroffer, and Cal's offer would remain open.

Revocation by the Offeror

Offers can be terminated if the offeror revokes the offer. Unless an offer is irrevocable, it can be revoked at any time before the offeree's acceptance. Thus, if the Seahawks changed their mind about offering Galloway $35 million, they could revoke the offer at any time before it was accepted simply by telling Galloway that the offer is closed.

Generally, this rule applies even if the offeror promises to give the offeree time to think about the offer. For example, suppose the Seahawks promised to give Galloway thirty days to consider their offer. Two days later, another wide receiver becomes available and the Seahawks no longer wish to hire Galloway. The Seahawks can safely contract with the other receiver once they communicate their intent to revoke to Galloway. The Seahawks are not legally held to their promise to give Galloway thirty days.

Exhibit 13-1

Methods of Terminating Offers

TERMINATION BY ACT OF LAW	TERMINATION BY ACT OF THE PARTIES
Death	Rejection
Incapacity	Counteroffer
Destruction of subject matter	Revocation
Supervening illegality	
Lapse of time	

Irrevocable Offers

The legal right to renege on one's promise (the promise to keep the offer open) can sometimes be unfair to the offeree. To prevent this, the offer is irrevocable in the case of:

- option contracts;
- firm offers;
- part performance of a unilateral contract; and
- promissory estoppel.

Option Contracts

In an **option contract**, the offeror promises to keep an offer open for a specific length of time and the offeree gives something of value, typically money, in exchange for that promise. In essence, the offeree pays for the right to think about the offer, so courts hold that the offer is irrevocable for the time stated. Option contracts arise under both the common law and Article 2 of the Uniform Commercial Code.

Option contracts, such as stock options, are common in business. For example, consider a stock option. Here's how they work. A stock is currently selling at $98. The owner of that stock offers to sell one share for $100 and promises to keep the offer open for ninety days. The offeree pays $5 for the option. If the value of the stock rises sufficiently, the offeree accepts the underlying offer and buys the stock at $100. If the price does not rise sufficiently or drops, the underlying offer is not accepted and is terminated through the lapse of time. The $5 payment is not refunded because it bought the right to think about the stock for ninety days.

Option payments should not be confused with down payments. A down payment occurs after a contract has been accepted; an option is the right to think about whether to accept the offer.

Firm Offers

Firm offers do not arise under the common law. The **firm offer** rule is found in UCC Section 2-205. Under this rule, if a **merchant** (someone who regularly deals in buying or selling the particular good) promises in a signed writing to keep an offer to buy or sell goods open, that offer is irrevocable for the time stated or for a reasonable time, if no time is stated. Under the Code, a firm offer cannot exceed three months and does not require any consideration from the offeree to be binding. Because giving someone time to think about an offer can be costly in terms of lost opportunities, the Code requires the promise be in writing to provide clear evidence that the merchant thought about and intended to bind itself to the promise. Note that the firm offer rule would not apply in Galloway because playing football is a service, not a sale of goods, and firm offers arise only under the UCC.

Part Performance of a Unilateral Contract

The offeror is free to specify the way in which its offer must be accepted. Sometimes the offeror specifies that an offer can only be accepted through an action. For example, suppose Jim offers to pay John $500 to remove rubbish from behind Jim's store. The offer states that the duty to pay the $500 arises only after the rubbish is fully removed. This is an offer to form a unilateral contract.

A problem arises if the offeror specifies that its offer can be accepted only through an action, the offeree begins to perform, and then the offeror tries to revoke its offer before the offeree finishes the work. To correct for this problem, once an offeree partially performs a unilateral contract, the offer becomes irrevocable until the offeree has a reasonable opportunity to complete its performance.

Promissory Estoppel

The fourth and final way an offer becomes irrevocable comes not from law, but from equity. A broken promise can result in unfairness, especially if the promisor knows or has reason to know that the promisee is relying on the promise and will be hurt if the offer is revoked. If extreme unfairness would result from reneging on a promise to hold an offer open, a court can use its equitable powers to insist that the offer be kept open for the time stated.

As Exhibit 13-2 illustrates, law provides three exceptions to the rule of revocability: option contracts, firm offers, and part performance of a unilateral contract. Equity can, on a rare occasion, provide a fourth exception through the doctrine of promissory estoppel.

Exhibit 13-2

When Are Offers Irrevocable?

Option Contract

1. Offeror promises to keep an offer open.
2. Offeree pays consideration for the right to consider the offer.

Firm Offer

1. Offeror promises to keep an offer open.
2. Offeror is a merchant.
3. The promise is in writing signed by the offeror.
4. The offer is to buy or sell goods.

Part Performance of a Unilateral Contract

1. Offeror specifies that the offer must be accepted through performance.
2. Offeree begins to perform.

Promissory Estoppel

1. Offeror promises to keep an offer open.
2. Offeree reasonably relies on the promise.
3. Offeror has reason to know that the offeree is relying on the promise.
4. Offeree would be hurt if the offer were revoked.
5. It would be unfair to let the offeror take back its promise.

Global Context: Revoking Offers in Germany or Mexico

In contrast to U.S. law, civil law countries such as Germany and Mexico, hold that if an offeror promises to hold an offer open, that offer is irrevocable without regard to whether the offeree pays money, the promise is in writing, the offeror is a merchant, or the offeror knows or has reason to know that the offeree relied on the promise and would be hurt by the revocation.

In Germany, for example, all written offers are irrevocable for the time promised. If no time is promised, the offer is irrevocable for a reasonable time. Most oral offers must be accepted immediately. However, if the offeror orally promises to keep the offer open for a specified time, the offer is irrevocable for that time.

Mexican law is similar. If the offeror does not specify a time limit, the offer remains open for three days plus the time necessary for a mailed acceptance to arrive. If the offeror promises to give time to the offeree to think about the offer, the offer is irrevocable for the time stated.

Technology: "Shrink-Wrap" and "Click-Through" Agreements

Today the issue of contractual silence often arises in the context of "shrink-wrap" agreements associated with sale of computer software. The consumer agrees to purchase software. When the software is downloaded, a previously unread licensing agreement is attached. The question is whether the buyer's failure to respond to the agreement manifests an intent to be bound to its terms. The typical answer is that if the buyer objects in a timely fashion, then the software contract can be cancelled. After a reasonable length of time passes, failure to object constitutes a valid acceptance of the attached terms.

A related issue arises when a consumer clicks on the "I agree" or "I accept" button on web pages offering a desired product. These buttons reference web pages typically filled with arcane legal language. Most consumers do not read the legal language and the terms are not negotiable. Lawyers refer to shrink-wrap and click-through agreements as "contracts of adhesion," likening them to rental car forms and airline tickets. Although there is little legal precedent testing the enforceability of shrink-wrap and click-through agreements, most scholars agree that such contracts are binding, as long as the provisions are not unreasonable.

Accepting an Offer

Courts assessing whether an acceptance has occurred consider the same three elements—intent, communication, and definiteness of terms—that are examined for offers. The central question is whether the offeree has objectively manifested and communicated to the offeror a definite intent to form a contract. Once effective, an acceptance binds the parties to a contract.

The offeror can specify the means of acceptance, such as requiring the offeree to do a specific act or to use a particular form. An offer that does not specify means can be accepted in any reasonable manner.

Contractual Intent and Silence as an Acceptance

The offeree generally indicates intent to form a contract with words or actions. Occasionally, however, the failure to respond can be viewed as acceptance. For example, suppose Kathy receives an unsolicited letter stating that, "If we do not hear from you in ten days, we will enroll you in Acme Book Club." No contract will be formed if Kathy does not respond. However, if Kathy had authorized the club to send her books, returning those she did not want, and paying for the ones she did not object to, her prior agreement established that silence would be an acceptance.

Silence can also be an acceptance based on the past dealings between the parties. For example, suppose a farmer ships unsolicited produce to a wholesaler and is paid one week later. The parties follow the same routine four times without incident. On the fifth occasion, the wholesaler does not want the produce and he places it in a back room where it rots. Given the past dealings between the parties, the wholesaler's silence constitutes an acceptance, and he would have to compensate the farmer for the loss.

Communication and the Mailbox Rule

An acceptance cannot be effective unless it is communicated to the offeror. Usually, acceptances are communicated through words. In the case of a unilateral offer, however, acceptance can be communicated by performance of the specified action. The courts assume that the offeror will know of the performance, so no additional communication of the acceptance of a unilateral contract is necessary.

Timing can affect the result, particularly if the terms are not explicit. Suppose a firm prepares a written offer and states that this offer will only be open for ten days. What does this mean? Does the deadline begin when the offer is mailed by the offeror or received by the offeree? Must the offeree mail an acceptance within the ten days or must the offeror receive the acceptance within that time? These questions are answered by the **mailbox rule**.

The mailbox rule states that acceptances are effective on dispatch. Offers, revocations, rejections, and counteroffers are effective on receipt. To "dispatch" an acceptance, the acceptance must leave the control of the offeree. The acceptance is dispatched the moment it has been put in the mailbox, handed to a courier, sent by e-mail, or faxed.

An offer, revocation, rejection, or counteroffer is "received" once it arrives at the addressee's authorized address, or when the addressee has reason to know of the offer, revocation, rejection or counteroffer, whichever comes first. In the above example, the offeree would have ten days to dispatch an acceptance, from the date the offer is received.

The mailbox rule tends to favor offerees at the expense of offerors. Suppose Frank writes a letter to Sue offering to sell his refrigerator to her for $350. While Frank is waiting for a reply, Tommy offers Frank $375. Can Frank sell the refrigerator to Tommy? Remember, he does not know whether Sue has already mailed an acceptance. If she has, then a contract will have been formed and Frank will breach that contract by selling to Tommy. Frank can try to first revoke his offer to Sue, but the revocation will only be effective on receipt. If he waits, Tommy may lose interest. Frank faces a tough decision.

Two exceptions lessen the harshness of the mailbox rule. First, for the "acceptance effective on dispatch" rule to help the offeree, the means of communication the offeree uses must be authorized. Customarily, a means of acceptance is authorized if it is as fast or faster than that used to communicate the offer. If Frank had made his offer to Sue in person, or via fax, Sue could not use the mailbox rule to bind Frank by mailing her letter. Her acceptance would only be effective when actually received by Frank.

Second, and perhaps more importantly, the mailbox rule can be changed by the terms of the offer. If Frank's letter had been written so that Sue's acceptance was only effective on receipt and that any revocation would be effective on dispatch, he could quickly dispatch a revocation to Sue and safely accept Tommy's offer. The mailbox rule applies only if the offer does not specify otherwise. Consequently, offerors who are aware of the mailbox rule typically specify otherwise.

The primary policy objective of the mailbox rule is to provide certainty for the parties. As Case 13-3 illustrates, the potential for harm is always present when letters cross in the mail. If the rules are clear, however, and the parties know the rule, then each can take steps to reduce any harm caused by crossed communications.

Case 13-3

Okosa
v.
Hall
718 A. 2d 1223 (N.J. Super. 1998)

*O*kosa had an automobile insurance policy with a premium due on February 28. The policy had a fifteen-day grace period. On March 1, Okosa's insurance company sent him a letter stating that the premium was overdue and that the policy would lapse unless a premium payment was received by 12:01 a.m. on March 16. Okosa mailed his payment on March 15. The next day, Okosa was in an automobile accident with Hall. Hall was not insured.

Okosa filed a "claim" with his own insurance company, but it refused to honor his policy. Okosa sued for breach of contract. The trial court held that the policy had lapsed and entered summary judgment in favor of the insurance company. Okosa appealed.

JUDGE KIMMELMAN

Plaintiffs were insured under an automobile insurance policy which required a quarterly premium payment to be made on February 28, 1994.... [T]he carrier directed a letter to plaintiffs which was posted on March 1, 1994, that advised plaintiffs that they had failed to pay the $347.50 installment then due and that their policy would be automatically cancelled at 12:01 a.m. on March 16, 1994, unless payment was made by that date. The letter advised plaintiffs:

If we receive payment on or before the cancellation date, we will continue your policy with no interruption in the protection it affords. *If you've recently mailed your payment, please disregard this notice.*

On March 15, 1994, while the policy was still in effect, plaintiffs mailed, by certified mail, a check for the required payment. As indicated, the automobile accident with the uninsured defendant occurred on the next day. It is not known exactly when plaintiff's check was received, but it is known that the carrier deposited and "cashed" the check on March 22, 1994....

Generally speaking, the Mailbox Rule sanctions the formation or completion of a contractual undertaking upon the act of mailing where the use of the mail is authorized by the other party as the medium for response.... Its letter of February 28, 1994, posted March 1, 1994, invited plaintiff's response with payment by mail. In so responding, plaintiffs did so by means of certified mail. The use of certified mail by plaintiffs was perspicacious [wise] because it insured proof of mailing and its use avoided the thorny issue which would arise from a fraudulent response by them that post-dated the accident.

...We have completely reviewed the record and are satisfied that by authorizing the use of mail as a means of paying premiums, the carrier constituted the postal authorities as its agent. Accordingly, the decision in this matter is controlled by the Mailbox Rule. As a consequence, the entry of summary judgment in favor of the carrier is reversed.

REVERSED AND REMANDED.

1. Critical Thinking: The company's letter stated that the policy would continue "if we receive payment" by the cancellation date. Do you think the case would come out differently if the company had specified that the policy would continue "**only if** we receive payment" by the cancellation date? Would this slight change in the language of the offer change the outcome of the case? Why or why not?

2. Ethical Decision Making: If there had been no accident, do you think that the company would have provided a partial refund to Okosa for the time when he was not insured? Is it ethical to keep the policy in effect when there is no accident, and claim it lapsed when there is an accident?

Definiteness of Terms and the Mirror Image Rule

The final element of an acceptance is definiteness of terms. Recall that the common law typically requires the offer to expressly state all material terms: parties, subject matter, quantity, price, and time. Because the offer already has all these terms, all the offeree need say is, "I accept," and an agreement will be formed.

Problems can arise when the offeree says, "I accept," and then specifies terms that vary from those of the offer. The **mirror image rule** states that unless the acceptance mirrors all the material terms in the offer, no contract will be formed. Hence, the safest way to accept an offer is to say: "Received your offer of September 1, and I hereby accept the same."

This rule is intended to protect offerors from offerees who thrust terms into a contract to which the offeror never agreed. Courts consider an "acceptance" containing terms that differ from those in the offer as a counteroffer that the original offeror can now accept or reject. In Case 13-4 the court must determine whether a movie star accepted a contract or made a counteroffer. Note that it is the offeree, not the offeror, who seeks to assert the mirror image rule.

Case 13-4

Hollywood Fantasy Corp.

v.

Gabor
151 F. 3d 203 (5th Cir. 1998)

*H*ollywood Fantasy Corporation provided one-week "fantasy vacation" packages that included an opportunity to "make a movie" with a well-known movie star. Hollywood Fantasy advertised one such vacation for San Antonio, Texas, with Zsa Zsa Gabor to serve as the star. Before advertising the vacation, Mr. Leonard Saffir, chief executive officer of Hollywood Fantasy, sent Ms. Gabor a letter specifying the terms of his offer to have her appear as the movie star in a vacation package. Gabor made three handwritten changes to the letter, signed it, and returned it to Saffir. When Gabor cancelled her appearance, Hollywood Fantasy sued her for breach of contract. Gabor claimed that her changes to the written offer were material and should be treated as a counteroffer that Hollywood Fantasy never accepted. The trial court found for Hollywood Fantasy. Ms. Gabor appealed.

JUDGE ROSENTHAL

The case began with a letter Hollywood Fantasy sent Zsa Zsa Gabor.... The letter set out the terms and conditions of Ms. Gabor's appearance in fourteen numbered paragraphs....

Ms. Gabor made three handwritten changes to this letter before signing and returning to Mr. Saffir. She inserted the word "one" into the sentence stating that she would make herself available for media interviews; inserted the words "two bedroom" above the sentence describing the hotel suite that was to be provided in San Antonio; and added the words "wardrobe to be supplied by Neiman Marcus" to the paragraph outlining the perquisites....Ms. Gabor signed the letter in a signature blank above the words "Agreed and accepted," and sent it back to Leonard Saffir who had already signed as the chief executive officer for Hollywood Fantasy.

The general rule is that "an acceptance must not change or qualify the terms of the offer. If it does, the offer is rejected." Under this "mirror image" rule, a modification of an offer qualifies as a rejection and counteroffer only if the modification is "material." Ms. Gabor asserts that by making the three handwritten changes to the March 4, 1991 letter, she rejected Hollywood Fantasy's offer and made a counteroffer, which Mr. Saffir did not accept before Ms. Gabor revoked it. Hollywood Fantasy asserts that the changes were not material and that Ms. Gabor accepted the offer and entered into a contract, which was breached.

The cases in which courts find modifications to be material under Texas law generally involve significant increases in a party's financial obligation for exposure, or in a party's duties under a proposed contract.... Applying these criteria to the changes Ms. Gabor made, [we find] that the changes were not material....

This court also notes that to apply the mirror image rule in this factual context would lead to a result inconsistent with the purpose of that rule. The rule requiring an acceptance of the terms of the original offer generally serve to protect the original offeror, "the master of the offer." Texas cases generally apply the rule defensively, when an original offeror seeks to avoid more onerous demands sought by the offeree. In this case, by contrast, Ms. Gabor, the offeree, seeks to use the mirror image rule offensively, arguing that her own additional demands prevented the formation of a contract.

We affirm the district court's judgment with respect to Ms. Gabor's liability for breach of contract.

AFFIRMED

1. Critical Thinking: Typically, it is the offeror who asserts the mirror image rule. Here it was the offeree. Given the policies that underlie the rule, should this make a difference? Why or why not?

2. Ethical Decision Making: When is it ethical to use a technical legal rule to avoid performing on a moral obligation such as a promise? Explain

Galloway Wrap-Up

Galloway sat out the first eight games of the 1999 season, returning in game nine under his original rookie contract. In February 2000, the Seahawks agreed to trade Galloway to the Dallas Cowboys for two first-round draft choices.[4] The trade was conditioned on the Cowboys being able to quickly sign Galloway to a contract. Cowboy owner, Jerry Jones, reached a preliminary agreement with agent Metz only to find that Galloway had switched agents, hiring agent Leigh Steinberg instead.[5] Jones was able to finalize an agreement with Steinberg, making Galloway the highest paid wide receiver in the league. The new deal totaled $42 million over seven years, including a $12.5 million bonus.[6] In Joey's first game as a Cowboy, he tore a ligament in his knee disabling him for the remainder of the 2000 season.

[4] Jean-Jacques Taylor, *Galloway Talks had Anxious Moments,* THE DALLAS MORNING NEWS, February 13, 2000.

[5] *Id.*

[6] *Id.*

	Summary
Definition of an Agreement	One of four elements of a legal contract. An agreement requires a valid offer and acceptance.
Creating an Offer:	Every offer has three elements: **Objective Intent**—given the words and actions of the offeror and surrounding business customs, a reasonable listener would infer that the offeror intends to create a contract. Customarily, advertisements are not offers, bids are offers, and auctions are with reserve. **Communication**—the offeror must communicate the offer to the offeree for it to be effective. **Definiteness**—under the common law the offer typically must state: (1) the parties, (2) price, (3) subject matter, (4) quantity, and (5) time of performance. Section 2-204 of the UCC requires less detail.
Terminating an Offer	Offers can be terminated by death or incapacity of a party, destruction of subject matter, supervening illegality, lapse of time, rejection, counteroffer, or by revocation.
Irrevocable Offers	Offers become irrevocable in one of four ways: • Option contracts. • Firm offers. • Part performance of a unilateral contract. • Promissory estoppel.
Accepting an Offer	Unless otherwise specified by the offeror, acceptance can be by any reasonable means. There are three elements of a valid acceptance: **Objective Intent**—given the words and actions of the offeree and the surrounding business customs, a reasonable listener would infer that the offeree intends to accept an offer. Ordinarily, failure to respond to an offer does not constitute an acceptance. **Communication**—the offeree must effectively communicate the acceptance to the offeror for it to be effective. Ordinarily, a mailed acceptance is effective on dispatch. **Definiteness**—the acceptance must match all the material terms of the offer.

Review Questions And Case Problems

1. Distinguish between objective and subjective intent. Give an example that illustrates the difference.

2. When is an advertisement an offer? When is a bid an offer? Explain.

3. What terms must be expressly stated by the offeror in order for an offer to be created? Does the answer depend on whether the contract involves the sale of goods?

4. What are the differences between an option contract and a firm offer? List the elements of each.

5. Clem promises to pay Jimmy $500 if Jimmy walks across the Brooklyn Bridge. Jimmy walks three quarters of the way over the bridge and Clem yells to Jimmy "I revoke my offer." Is Clem's offer revocable?

6. Suppose Fred offers in writing to sell his refrigerator to Sue for $350. The next day, while the offer to Sue is still open, Fred sells his refrigerator to Tommy. Sue learns of the sale when she sees Tommy loading the refrigerator on his truck. She immediately sends Fred a written acceptance before Fred can tell her that his offer is revoked. Under the mailbox rule, did Sue's letter form an agreement? Why or why not?

7. A surplus store ran an advertisement in the newspaper. The ad stated "2 Brand New Pastel Mink Scarfs Selling for $89.50. Out they go Saturday. Each $1.00. First Come, First Served." Mr. Lefkowitz was the first to claim the scarfs on Saturday morning, but the store refused to sell them to him. The store told Mr. Lefkowitz that the scarfs could only be claimed by a woman and that the ad was not an offer, but rather it was merely an invitation to negotiate. Mr. Lefkowitz sued the store for

breach of contract. Who do you think won? *Lefkowitz v. Great Minneapolis Surplus Store*, 86 N.W. 2d 689 (Minn. 1957).

8. In February, an employee sued her employer for sex discrimination. In March, the employer made a written offer to settle the case for $60,000. The employee responded in a letter that characterized the offer as "insulting and demeaning." In June a summary judgment hearing was held. The judge indicated an intention to dismiss the employee's claim, but reserved judgment while he studied the matter more closely. The judge said that a final decision would be forthcoming the next day. Immediately after this hearing, the employee faxed a letter accepting the March offer to settle the case for $60,000. Was the offer of March still open? What additional facts would you need to know to better answer the question? *Guzman v. Visalia Community Bank*, 84 Cal. Rptr. 2d 581 (Cal. App. 1999).

9. A commissioned employee was offered a bonus package. For all sales above a particular quota, the employee was promised a bonus that would be paid at the end of the year. The bonus plan was spelled out in detail in a twelve page manual prepared by the employer. By April, the employee had met her quota and was beginning to earn credits toward the bonus. In June, the company announced that it was changing the bonus plan. The changes would hurt the employee's bonus and the employee sued. The court characterized the bonus plan as an offer to form a unilateral contract. Given this characterization of the issue, whom do you think won? *Holland v. Graves*, 46 F. Supp. 2d 681 (E.D. Mich. 1998).

10. The owners of a chain of lumber yards were having difficulty making a profit, so they sold the chain. The new owners closed several yards, acquired a few new yards, and shifted employees between yards. Overall, about twenty-five percent of the workforce was dismissed, and the business began to show a profit. During the reorganization, a manager at a particular yard was asked to move to another yard. The manager expressed a concern that the new yard might be closed and that he might lose his job. The new owners assured him that "good employees are taken care of." The manager agreed to the transfer. A few weeks later this new yard was closed and he was fired. Was the new owner's statement about taking care of good employees sufficiently definite to become part of an enforceable agreement? Who should win, and why? *Rudd v. Great Plains Supply*, 526 N.W. 2d 369 (Minn 1995).

11. A major corporation hired an employee. At the time the employee was hired, he signed a statement acknowledging the he was an "at-will" employee who could be fired at any time without notice or cause. He was also handed an employee handbook. The preface stated that the handbook did not constitute a contract between the employee and the employer. The handbook contained a detailed procedure, including opportunities to be heard

and rights of appeal, in the event that the corporation intended to fire an employee. The employee was then fired without any of the procedures being followed. The employee sued for breach of contract. What is the legal issue in the case? If you were on the court, how would you rule? *Phipps v. IASD Health Services*, 558 N.W. 2d 198 (Iowa 1997).

12. Two computer programmers developed a software system useful to insurance companies in assessing damage to cars. The program relied on a database on which the programmers held a license. After extended negotiations, the programmers agreed to sell their system. The buying firm prepared a proposal specifying a payment of $900,000 and promising to employ the two programmers for five years. The buying firm paid the programmers $200,000 in cash as a down payment and the programmers came to work for the buying firm. A month later, the license to the database came under a legal dispute and the acquiring firm fired the two programmers and sought reimbursement of the $200,000. Was the proposal an offer? Can an offer be accepted through an action? Who do you think won? *Adjustrite Systems v. GAB Business Services*, 145 F. 3d 543 (2nd Cir. 1998).

13. Plaintiff was a "jobber" or middleman in the New York garment industry. A large manufacturer of clothes hangers promised to sell hangers to Plaintiff at a discounted bulk rate. The manufacturer promised in writing to "provide a seven percent rebate on all dollars invoiced in excess of $225,000 in a month." A few months later the manufacturer discontinued the rebate system. Was the offer to give a rebate revocable? What additional facts would strengthen the Plaintiff's case? What additional facts would strengthen the manufacturer's case? *S.O. Textiles Co. v. A & E Plastics*, 18 F. Supp. 2d 232 (E.D.N.Y. 1998).

14. The Jewish War Veterans of the United States offered a reward of $500 for information leading to the "conviction of the persons guilty of the murder of Maurice L. Bernstein." The reward was announced in the newspaper. Mary Glover gave police information without knowing of the reward. Is she entitled to the award? What are the legal and equitable issues in the case? *Glover v. Jewish War Veterans of the United States, Post No. 58*, 68 A. 2d 233 (D.C. App. 1949).

15. A lumber yard had some timber it wanted to sell. It solicited bids from potential buyers, and several were submitted. The lumber yard then changed its mind and did not sell the timber. The buyer who had placed the highest bid sued for breach of contract. Customarily, is a bid a preliminary negotiation, an offer, or an acceptance? Was there a contract in this case? *Eames v. James*, 549 P. 2d 1152 (Wash. App. 1984).

16. Rudy Turilli operated the "Jesse James Museum" in Stanton, Missouri. Turilli claimed that Jesse James had not been killed as reported in song and legend, but rather James had retired from his outlaw ways, and lived out a

long life with Turilli in Stanton, Missouri under the alias J. Frank Dalton. In an effort to promote his museum, Turilli appeared on television stating that he would pay $10,000 to anyone whom could prove his claims wrong. Stella James, a relative of Jesse James, provided affidavits of several people related to Jesse James who swore that Jesse James died as reported and never lived with Turilli. Turilli refused to pay the $10,000 and Stella sued for breach of contract. Who wins? *James v. Turilli,* 473 S.W. 2d 757 (Mo. App. 1972).

17. In 1979, a tenant entered a five-year lease with an option to renew for an additional five years. The renewal provision stated that notice of an intent to renew must be made by certified or registered mail on or before August 1, 1983. On July 29, 1983, the tenant sent a notice to renew by certified mail. The U.S. Postal Service lost the notice and it was never delivered to the landlord. The landlord refused to extend the lease for the additional five years and the tenant sued. Was the notice renewing the lease effective? *Jenkins v. Tuneup Masters,* 235 Cal. Rptr. 214 (Cal. App. 1987).

18. A construction company hired a draftsman to produce some engineering drawings. The draftsman stated that he would charge "street rates" and the construction company agreed. Street rates in the drafting industry meant $35 per hour for normal work, $40 per hour overtime. The draftsman presented two invoices that were paid. Thereafter, the construction company insisted that more work be done, but it complained that the drawings seemed too expensive. They refused to pay the draftsman's next four invoices, demanding that the price be adjusted to something more reasonable. The draftsman sued for breach of contract. What is the role of custom in inferring contractual intent? Were the negotiations definite enough to infer that an offer was made and accepted? *Anglin v. Barry,* 912 S.W. 2d 633 (Mo. App. 1995).

Assignment on the Internet

Duhaime's Canadian Contract Law Centre provides a general summary of Canadian contract law, both from the common law and equity. Visit the site at **www.duhaime.org/ca-conl.htm** and determine whether or not Canadian law embraces the mirror image rule.

On the Internet

http://www.ssrn.com/update/lsn/ cyberspace/csl papers.html
For information on cyberlaw questions generally, see Cyberspace Law Abstracts, edited by Professor Larry Lessig of Harvard Law School, containing summaries of leading academic papers on cyberlaw with links to the full length articles.

www.hg.org *Heiros Gamos provides links to 12 legal directories, 400 discussion groups.*

www.lawrunner.com *Lawrunner provides on opportunity to narrow research topics, offering more than one thousand "advanced query topics" to make legal research on the Web more efficient.*

www.law.harvard.edu/library *Most, if not all, law schools maintain an online catalogue. Browse the catalogue for the law library nearest you. The online catalogue for Harvard Law School can be found here.*

www.yahoo.com/Law *For a wide reaching legal search, use Yahoo.com. The site provides links to a variety of legal topics including law schools, legal ethics, taxation, and lawyer jokes.*

CHAPTER 14

Applying Law to Business Decisions: Exclusive Dealership Rights to a Manhattan Icon

Al Hirschfeld, 96, an artist whose witty caricatures of stage and screen stars have delighted readers of the New York Times for decades, recently sued his partner, gallery owner Margo Feiden, to annul a contract linking the two since 1974.[1] The contract gave Feiden exclusive rights to exhibit and sell Hirschfeld's drawings. At the time of the complaint, Feiden's Madison Avenue gallery exhibited more than 1,000 Hirschfeld drawings, each typically selling for $10,000 or more. Hirschfeld's work also graces the permanent collections of prestigious museums such as the Metropolitan Museum of Art, the National Portrait Gallery, and the Whitney Museum of American Art.

A dispute between the partners arose in 1999 when the Academy of Motion Picture Arts and Sciences offered to mount an exhibition in Hollywood supported by a new book called "Hirschfeld's Hollywood." Hirschfeld alleged that the exhibition and book deal collapsed when Feiden refused to cooperate with the California exhibitors. Hirschfeld asked the court to declare the contract void on the grounds that it unfair because (1) it gave Feiden the right to purchase Hirschfeld drawings "at unreasonably low prices," and resell them at much higher prices and (2) provided that Feiden could terminate the agreement without cause but allowed no such escape for Hirschfeld.[2] Hirschfeld claimed that the one-sided nature of the contract rendered it null and void.

1. Assume that you were Hirschfeld. Is there any way to regain control of the way your art is exhibited and sold?

2. How would you determine if the dealership contract were valid and enforceable?

---

[1] Judith H. Bobrzynski, *Al Hirschfeld Sues Gallery, Asserting It Cheated Him*, NEW YORK TIMES, May 17, 2000, at Section E, p.1.
[2] *Id.*

Consideration

Consideration, the second element of contract formation, distinguishes between agreements that are enforceable and those that are not. To be enforceable, an agreement must involve an exchange of legal value. That exchange of legal value is called consideration.

Consideration can be found in an act, forbearance (failure to act), or a promise. In the case of a unilateral contract, a promise is given in exchange for an act or forbearance. In a bilateral contract, each party makes a promise in exchange for a return promise. Without an exchange of consideration, no legal contract will be formed.

Because of the consideration rule certain promises are not legally enforceable. For example, a promise to give a social gift which is not given in exchange for anything, lacks consideration, and is not legally enforceable.

We will learn that the primary policy goal of the consideration doctrine is to provide evidence to the court that the promisor carefully considered their promise and intended to be bound by it. The presence of a bargained-for-exchange provides such evidence.

The issue of consideration arises frequently in business settings, as the opening scenario shows. The artist claimed that the price (consideration) paid for his art was inadequate. He also claimed that the dealer had not really promised to do anything because she could end the relationship without cause at anytime. In this chapter we discover whether these and similar claims can render a contract void.

The chapter begins by examining the two elements of consideration—legal value and bargained-for-exchange. It then discusses three common situations where contracts fail for lack of consideration—illusory promises, the preexisting duty rule, and past consideration. The chapter closes with a discussion of agreements that are enforceable without consideration.

Defining Consideration

Consideration is commonly defined as "legal value, bargained for and given in exchange for an act or a promise." Consideration has two elements: (1) legal value and (2) bargained-for-exchange. We consider each.

Legal Value

Courts will not enforce a promise unless the promisee has given up something of **legal value** in exchange for that promise. The requirement of legal value is satisfied anytime the promisee (1) does or promises to do something that he or she did not already have a legal duty to do or (2) forbears or promises to forbear from doing something that he or she has a legal right to do. Note that the definition of legal value does not require that the act or promise have any monetary (economic) value. Anytime a party gives up a legal right or assumes a legal duty in exchange for a promise, the first element of consideration, legal value, will be met.

The courts sometimes speak of legal value as residing in either a legal detriment (harm) to the promisee or a legal benefit to the promisor. Typically, consideration involves both. For example, when a consumer promises to pay for a product, that promise is both a harm to the consumer and a benefit to the seller. Legal value can be found in either the detriment suffered or in the benefit conferred.

The following classic case illustrates the issue of legal value. An uncle promised to pay his nephew $5,000 if the nephew refrained from various vices such as smoking tobacco and drinking alcohol. The court noted that refraining from such activities did not harm the nephew (the promisee) nor directly benefit the uncle (the promisor). At the time the case was decided, the nephew had a legal right to both smoke tobacco and to drink alcohol. The question became whether refraining from such activities constituted legal value.

Case 14-1

Hamer

v.

Sidway

27 N.E. 256 (N.Y. Ct. App. 1891)

*I*n the presence of a family members and guests, William Story promised to pay his nephew $5,000 if he would refrain from drinking alcohol, using tobacco, swearing, and gambling until his twenty-first birthday. The nephew fully performed and the uncle acknowledged that he did. Instead of giving the money to his nephew, the uncle offered to keep the money while it accumulated interest, promising to deliver the money anytime the nephew asked for it. The nephew agreed to this arrangement. The nephew then transferred his rights to the money to Hamer. Eight years later, the uncle died, never having delivered the money.

The executor of Story's estate, Sidway, did not know whether he should give the money to Hamer because it was unclear whether the uncle's promise was given in exchange for legal value or was a promise to give a gift, which is a legally unenforceable promise. The trial court held that the uncle's promise was a contract, and ordered the executor to give the money to Hamer. The appellate court reversed. Hamer appealed to New York's highest court.

JUDGE PARKER

The defendant contends that the contract was without consideration to support it, and therefore invalid. He asserts that the promisee, by refraining from the use of liquor and tobacco, was not harmed, but benefited; that that which he did was best for him to do, independently of the uncle's promise—and insists that it follows that, unless the promisor was benefited, the contract was without consideration....Such a rule could not be tolerated, and is without foundation in the law....Courts will not ask whether the thing which forms the consideration does in fact benefit the promisee or a third party, or is of any substantial value to any one. It is enough that something is promised, done, forborne, or suffered by the party to whom the promise is made....In general, a waiver of any legal right at the request of another party is sufficient consideration for a promise.

[A]pplying this rule to the facts before us, the promisee used tobacco, occasionally drank liquor, and he had a legal right to do so. That right he abandoned for a period of years upon the strength of the promise of [his uncle] that for such forbearance he would give him $5,000. We need not speculate on the effort which may have been required to give up the use of those stimulants. It is sufficient that he restricted his lawful freedom of action within certain prescribed limits upon the faith of his uncle's agreement, and now, having fully performed the conditions imposed, it is of no moment whether such performance actually proved a benefit to the promisor, and the court will not inquire into it.

REVERSED.

1. Critical Thinking: The court seeks to adopt a fairly broad definition of legal value. Which is better, a broad or narrow definition? Why?

2. Ethical Decision Making: When, if ever, is it ethical to renege on a promise? Do law and ethics differ on this point?

Although decided more than a century ago, the holding in *Hamer* is still good law. The case illustrates that the courts adopt a broad interpretation for what constitutes legal value. Anytime a party gives up or promises to give up a legal right, the requirement of legal value is met. The nephew had the right to smoke tobacco and drink alcohol so his forbearance constituted legal value.

Adequacy Of Value

It is important to keep the issue of legal value distinct from the question of the adequacy of that value. The *Restatement (Second) of Contracts* states: "If the requirement of consideration is met, there is no additional requirement of…. equivalence in the values exchanged." This means that courts do not inquire into the relative adequacy (monetary worth) of the consideration exchanged, leaving the parties to determine their own contract terms.

For example, suppose that Jerry has a farm that recently appraised at $200,000. He agrees to sell the farm to Dave for $50,000. Courts adhering to the general rule will enforce the agreement without assessing whether the price is adequate. The unusual price might be evidence of fraud, duress, or other unconscionable conduct (see Chapter 16), but the imbalance in the price, standing alone, will not invalidate the contract.

The issue of adequacy of consideration also arose in the Hirschfeld case. The artist claimed, among other things, that the price set on his drawings, although perhaps fair some twenty years ago, had

Global Context:
Consideration Under Talmudic Law

Rabbis study the Talmud, a holy scripture of the Jewish faith. Based on this study, many Talmudic experts conclude that the doctrine of consideration should be used to ensure a rough equivalence in an exchange. Talmudic experts split on how one-sided an exchange must be before it should be invalid, but generally agree that the profit margin must be no more than one-sixth of the value received. Thus, an agreement to sell grain that has a fair market value of $600 should be enforced only if the profit or loss to the seller is $100 or less ($600 x 1/6 = $100). Interestingly, these Talmudic experts assume that any price that varies from this standard must have been a product of an honest mistake, so they would not punish the offending party. Rather, they would modify the contract and hold the parties to the fair price.[3]

In the seventeenth and eighteenth centuries, U.S. courts often cited the Bible in deciding legal cases.[4] Like the Talmud, the Bible can be read as requiring a rough equivalence of consideration in commercial transactions, and judges responded with what is commonly called the "fair price doctrine," refusing to enforce contracts where the price appeared to the court to be unfair. Over time, however, the common law rule was changed to let the will of the parties, not the hand of the court, determine whether an exchange is fair, and the fair price doctrine is no longer the law in the United States. Today, U.S. courts will not inquire into the fairness of consideration as an independent means of invalidating a contract.

[1] Arthur Gross Schaefer, *Differing Concepts of Adequate Consideration from Common Law and Talmudic Law*, National Jewish Law Review, Vol. II, 79-95 (1987).

[2] Morton J. Horwitz, The Transformation of American Law 1780-1860 (Harvard University Press: 1977).

become inadequate. As a general rule, courts are not receptive to such claims and the doctrine of consideration does not permit a party to escape from contracts simply because they made a bad deal. As the following feature illustrates, however, this embrace of freedom of contract principles has not always been the common law norm.

By refusing to inquire into the adequacy of consideration, the courts embrace a notion of freedom of contract. The parties themselves, rather than the courts, determine the contents of a contract. Such a rule tends to promote predictability and thereby reduces the need to go to court to enforce a contract. As the following feature demonstrates, this same principle guides transactions consummated on the Internet.

Bargained-For-Exchange

The other element of consideration, in addition to legal value, is a "bargained-for-exchange." Section 71 of the *Restatement (Second) of Contracts* provides: "To constitute consideration, a performance or a return promise must be bargained for." In other words, consideration must reflect a *quid pro quo* ("this for that") where each promisor is induced to make their promise in anticipation of a return performance.

Courts insist that this bargain be a true one. If consideration is a mere pretense, no contract will be formed. For example, suppose Samir promises to sell his farm to his niece for one dollar. The dollar, called **nominal consideration**, reflects an attempt by the parties to transform what is essentially a gratuitous promise into a contract. Most courts would hold that no contract is formed. Although courts do not inquire into the adequacy of consideration, they do require that a true bargain be struck.

Common Law and Civil Law Compared

The law of consideration is unique to common law countries. Countries that follow civil law, by contrast, do not require consideration to form a contract. All Continental European and South American nations as well as most nations in Asia and Africa follow civil law. As illustrated in the following feature, a gratuitous promise in a civil law country, such as Japan, is fully enforceable.

Global Context:
Promises To Give Gifts In Japan

Like most civil law countries, Japan does not require an exchange of consideration to form a contract. But in Japan, a contract without consideration is only enforceable if it is in writing. For example, oral promises to give gifts are not enforceable. Note that putting a contract in writing provides evidence of contractual intent and forces the parties to more carefully consider the legal implications of their promises. These are the same functions provided by consideration. Because the policy reasons underlying the writing and consideration rules are the same, the two can often substitute for one another. In Japan, oral contracts require consideration, written contracts do not.

This same pattern appears in the U.S. treatment of irrevocable offers (see Chapter 13). Recall that an option contract requires consideration, but typically does not require a writing. A firm offer requires a writing but no consideration. The concern in both Japan and the United States is with proving that a contract was seriously intended. This concern can be addressed either by requiring a writing or by requiring an exchange of consideration. In Japan you need one or the other, but not both. In common law countries, you need consideration.

Technology: The Doctrine of Consideration Moves to the Internet

The Uniform Electronic Transactions Act (UETA) promulgated by the National Conference of Commissioners on Uniform State Laws and adopted by many states, applies to transactions between parties who have agreed to conduct their transaction by electronic means. Whether the parties have agreed to conduct their transaction electronically is determined by the totality of the circumstances, including actions of the parties and whether the customer initiated the business contact through Internet communications. When the UETA and common law conflict, the UETA controls.

The UETA addresses a variety of contract issues. For example, it specifies that an electronic record can suffice as a writing where a writing is required (writings are addressed in Chapter 18). The Act, however, does not address all contract law issues. When the UETA is silent, the common law controls. In particular, the UETA does not modify the common law rules of consideration. Thus, to form a contract over the Internet, a manager needs to be alert to common law rules and be sure that any agreement is supported by consideration.

There are two explanations why U.S. law requires consideration. The first is purely historical. The United States adopted English law, as did Canada, Australia, South Africa, and India, and English law requires consideration. The second explanation is one of policy: the primary policy goal of consideration is to provide *evidence* of contractual intent. U.S. courts recognize that it is generally *unethical* to renege on a promise, particularly if the other party relied on that promise. However, before enforcing a promise, U.S. courts insist on an exchange of consideration as evidence that the promisor fully intended to be legally bound by its promise. In civil law countries, by contrast, courts will often accept other forms or evidence, such as a formal writing, to substitute for consideration.

We now turn to three common business settings in which consideration issues arise—illusory promises, the preexisting duty rule, and past consideration. We beginning with the problem posed by illusory promises.

Agreements Lacking Legal Value— Illusory Promises

An **illusory promise** is a statement that is in the form of a promise but imposes no obligation on the maker of the statement. Illusory promises occur when a promisor retains so much discretion that the individual did not really promised anything. The promisor has not relinquished a legal right nor accepted a legal duty. The promise is an "illusion." Because illusory promises lack legal value, they are not good consideration, and no contract is formed. This section begins with a few examples of illusory promises, and then considers particular business settings where the issue commonly arises—conditional contracts and output and requirement contracts.

Illusory Promises In General

Suppose Cheryl promises to come to Anil's house every Tuesday to do household chores for Anil since he is too old to do for himself. In return, Anil promises to consider giving Cheryl money in his will.

Anil's promise is illusory because he retains too much discretion in deciding whether to give Cheryl an inheritance, and if so, how much. If Anil decided to give Cheryl nothing, she would not have grounds to complain. Anil's statement, though in the form of a promise, does not impose any legal duty on Anil. Because Anil's promise is illusory, Cheryl would not be held to her return promise to help Anil.

The typical illusory promise is more difficult to spot. Consider the well-known case of *Wood v. Lady Duff-Gordon*.[5] The Lady wanted to promote a brand of lingerie carrying her name. She entered into an agreement with Wood, an entrepreneur, promising exclusive rights to her name in exchange for a return promise of half the profits. The agreement looked like a contract, but Wood's promise was illusory. An exclusive right to the Lady's name had value, so Lady Duff-Gordon had given consideration, but Wood had not really promised to do anything. According to the language of the agreement, he could sit back and do nothing, not promote the lingerie at all, and still deny the Lady use of her name. The court invalidated the contract.

Illusory promises arise in business more often than one might expect. For example, in the Hirschfeld case the artist noted that Feiden could terminate her dealership agreement at anytime without notice or cause. He argued that this made her promise to exhibit and sell his drawings illusory. Managers should make sure they have promised something of value and should carefully scrutinize the language of an agreement to make sure that the trading partner has promised something of legal value.

Illusory Promises In Conditional Contracts

Illusory promises often arise in conditional contracts. A **condition** is an event or state of the world that affects the rights and duties of the parties to a contract. There are three types of conditions. With the first, **condition precedent,** the particular event must occur for a contract to be formed. With the other two, **conditions subsequent** and **conditions concurrent**, the particular event will excuse performance of the contract.

Conditions precedent arise out of the express language of the parties; a condition concurrent is an implied term. For example, it is an implied term of every contract that if one party breaches their contract, the other party is excused from performance. Each party's duties are concurrently conditioned on the other

party's willingness to perform. Implied conditions do not raise illusory promises.

Consideration problems arise when one of the parties retains too much power in determining whether that condition has occurred. Consider these examples. Simon has applied to transfer to a school in a different state. He is concerned about the availability of affordable housing in the new state, so he decides to look for an apartment even before he is admitted to the school. When he finds what he is seeking, he offers to lease the apartment on the condition that he is admitted to the new school. The landlord accepts Simon's offer. This is a valid conditional contract based on an *express condition precedent*. If Simon is not admitted, no contract is formed. If he is admitted, the contract is formed.

Consideration problems would only arise if Simon retains too much power in determining whether the condition occurs. For example, suppose Simon offered to lease the apartment if he (1) was admitted to the school and (2) decided to attend. Here, Simon retains so much control over the condition that his promise is illusory and no contract is formed.

Illusory promises can also arise with conditions subsequent. For example, Tucker agrees to lease an apartment in another state without first seeing the apartment. As part of the agreement with the landlord, the parties agree that if on Tucker's arrival he is *not satisfied* with the apartment, then the contract is null and void. At first glance, this agreement appears to create a contract subject to a condition subsequent (dissatisfaction terminates the contract), but Tucker's promise is illusory and no contract is formed. A contract would exist if the parties had defined the term satisfaction, perhaps with reference to a rent appraisal by a third party expert. But mere "satisfaction," standing alone, is generally held to be illusory because it is too vague.

Illusory Promises In Requirement And Output Contracts

Illusory promises can arise with reference to the quantity term of an agreement. For example, a producer of breakfast cereals wants to secure the price of a certain grade and quality grain for fall delivery. In July, a grain dealer promises to sell and the producer promises to buy all the grain the producer requires at $5 per bushel. The parties have addressed all the central terms (see Chapter 13) of their agreement—parties, subject matter, quantity, price, and time—but the quantity ("all the producer requires") is somewhat vague. Is the

---

[5] 118 N.E. 214 (1917).

promise illusory? The answer depends on whether one can reasonably estimate the amount of grain that producer will require.

If the producer has been in the cereal business for a few years and can project a reasonable estimate of the quantity of grain needed this fall, then a contract is formed. Such an agreement, which is called a **requirement contract**, is recognized under both the common law and the UCC. However, if the producer retains too much discretion in determining exactly how much is required, including the right to require no grain at all,

then the promise is illusory and no contract is formed.

The same concern arises if the producer had promised to sell its entire output of cereal to a particular wholesaler. If the parties can reasonably estimate the likely output of the producer, they have formed a valid **output contract**. But if the amount that is going to be produced remains totally within one party's discretion, then the quantity term is too vague and the consideration is illusory.

Case 14-2 involves a requirement contract that the defendant argued was illusory.

Case 14-2

Oscar Schlegel Co.
v.
Peter Cooper's Glue Factory
132 N.E. 148 (N.Y. 1921)

Oscar Schlegel Company agreed to buy all the glue it required from Peter Cooper's Glue Factory for nine cents per pound. The factory promised to keep the price open for one year. During that year, the market price for glue rose to twenty-four cents per pound and the factory refused to deliver glue to Schlegel at the stated price. Schlegel sued for breach of contract. The trial court found for Schlegel and the appellate court affirmed that judgment. The factory appealed to New York's highest court.

JUDGE MCLAUGHLIN

[T]he parties entered into a written agreement by which the defendants agreed to sell and deliver to the plaintiff, and the plaintiff agreed to purchase from the defendant, all its "requirements" of special BB glue for the year 1916, at the price of nine cents per pound....

The plaintiff at the time was engaged in no manufacturing business in which glue was used or required, nor was it then under any contract to deliver glue to any third parties at a fixed price or otherwise. It was simply a jobber, selling, among other things, glue to such customers as might be obtained by sending out salesmen to solicit orders....The plaintiff, it will be observed, did not agree to refrain from doing anything. It was not obligated to sell a pound of defendant's glue or to make any effort in that direction. It did not agree not to sell other glue in competition with defendants. The only obligation assumed by it was to pay nine cents per pound for such glue as it might order. Whether it should order any at all rested entirely with it. If it did not order any glue, then nothing was to be paid....Unless both parties to a contract are bound, so that either can sue the other for breach, neither is bound.

The price of glue having risen during the year 1916 from nine to twenty-four cents per pound, it is quite obvious why orders for glue increased correspondingly. Had the price dropped below nine cents, it may fairly be inferred such orders would not have been given. In that case, if the interpretation put upon the agreement be the correct one, plaintiff would not have been liable to the defendant for damage for a breach, since he had not agreed to sell any glue.

REVERSED.

1. Critical Thinking: How much glue do you think would Oscar Schlegel have ordered if the price of glue dropped to three cents per pound? Does your answer suggest that Schlegel's promise was illusory?

2. Ethical Decision Making: Schlegel's glue order increased dramatically once the price of glue increased. Do you think it was ethical for Schlegel to seek to enforce the literal language of the contract? Why or why not?

The Schlegel opinion, though written in 1921, remains good law. It illustrates how difficult illusory promises can be to identify. The promise to buy glue at a set price appeared ordinary enough. Upon closer inspection, however, the quantity term was too imprecise, the promise was illusory and no consideration was present.

Agreements Lacking Legal Value— The Preexisting Duty Rule

A second common scenario in which consideration problems arise involves the preexisting duty rule. The rule states that doing something, or promising to do something, that one already has a duty to do is not valid consideration and will not support a contract. Similarly, refraining, or promising to refrain, from doing something that one has no legal right to do is also not consideration. This rule relates to the concept that giving consideration means exchanging something of legal value.

The issue of a preexisting duty is easiest to understand in the case of promising to perform a public duty. The issue also arises in a variety of business settings when parties agree to modify preexisting contractual duties.

Promises To Perform Preexisting Public Duties

Promising to perform a preexisting public duty is not valid consideration. Suppose, for example, a house is ablaze and a distraught mother promises to pay a fireman $5,000 if he saves her trapped son. The fireman saves the son. Because the fireman already had a public duty to save the child (given the nature of his job), he gave no valid consideration, and the mother is not held to her promise. The case would be different if our hero had been a stranger under no preexisting duty to save the child. In that instance, the mother would have to pay the $5,000.

Refraining or promising to refrain from doing something that one has no legal right to do is also not

consideration. Suppose the uncle in *Hamer v. Sidway* promised to pay his nephew $5,000 if he refrained from smoking marijuana (an illegal act). Because the nephew has no legal right to smoke marijuana (he has a duty to follow the law), his forbearance is not valid consideration and his uncle would not have to pay. For an act, forbearance, or promise to be consideration, one must do something or promise to do something that he or she had no preexisting duty to do.

Promises To Modify Preexisting Contractual Duties

The preexisting duty rule also applies to contract modifications. Here the preexisting duty arises not from public law, but from a preexisting contract. We consider several settings in which the issue of contract modifications might arise.

Settlement Of Claims

Consideration issues often surface in debtor-creditor settings where a creditor agrees to accept a partial payment to settle a claim. For example, suppose a debtor borrows money and then defaults on the payments. The debtor admits that he owes the money, but simply does not pay. To settle the claim, the debtor promises to pay half of the loan if the creditor will forgive the other half. The creditor agrees. Is the creditor held to its promise? No. The borrower already had a preexisting duty (established by the initial loan agreement) to pay the money, so his promise to pay half was not valid consideration. The creditor can take the first half and then sue for the balance.

In addressing settlement of claims, the courts draw a distinction between liquidated and unliquidated debts. A **liquidated debt** is one that is not disputed as to existence or amount. A creditor's promise to take less money on a liquidated debt, such as in the previous example, is gratuitous and is not enforceable. In contrast, an **unliquidated debt** is disputed. For example, the creditor claims that the debt is $5,000 and the debtor claims it is only $1,000. An agreement to settle the dispute for $3,000 would be fully enforceable. Both parties have given something of value: The creditor can no longer insist on $5,000 and the debtor cannot insist on $1,000.

Unilateral Versus Bilateral Modifications

It is important to note that the preexisting duty rule applies *only if* the contractual modification is unilateral, not bilateral. In a unilateral modification, only one party changes his promise. In a bilateral modification, both parties agree to do something different. Managers always should consider whether the modification is unilateral or bilateral. If it is unilateral, a consideration problem arises and the agreement to modify may not be enforceable.

To avoid potential problems, it may be best to revise contracts through a **mutual rescission**, which is an agreement to cancel a preexisting contract. A mutual rescission is a separate contract; hence, to be effective, it must be supported by consideration. When the original contract is executory (not performed by either party), each party gives consideration by agreeing to call the deal off. A mutual rescission discharges the original contract (contractual discharge is discussed in Chapter 19), leaving the parties free to agree to a new contract.

Note that unlike the common law, the UCC does not require an exchange of consideration to modify a preexisting contract. UCC Section 2-209 provides that an agreement to unilaterally modify a contract is fully enforceable, provided other requirements are met.

Contract Modifications Due To Unforeseeable Difficulties

Some business problems are not foreseeable by the parties and are really no one's fault. When an agreement to modify a contract is prompted by such unforeseeable difficulties, the court will consider the modification bilateral and enforce the agreement to modify.

Suppose a real estate developer hires a construction company to excavate a building site. The company takes core samples to test the land and offers to do the work for $15,000. The developer accepts. The company begins to dig and discovers that beneath the surface lies an old school building complete with tangled iron and rusted beams. Excavating the site will prove much more difficult than envisioned. It is no one's fault that the school refuse was not found in advance. The construction company asks for an additional $10,000 and the developer agrees to the price increase. Is the promise to pay the extra $10,000 enforceable? On the one hand, if the presence of the school were truly unforeseeable, the agreement to pay more would be enforced. On the other hand, if the construction company knew or should have known of the potential difficulty, the modification is unilateral and the promise to pay more is not enforced. Distinguishing between foreseeable and unforeseeable difficulties is not always easy. Consider the facts in of Case 14-3 and see whether you agree with the court that the events that occurred were unforeseeable.

Case 14-3

Angel
v.
Murray
322 A. 2d 630 (R.I. 1974)

*T*he city of Newport, Rhode Island hired Maher to collect the city's garbage. The contract was for five years at $137,000 per year. By the end of the third year, the town had grown faster than anticipated and Maher asked for an additional $10,000. The city council paid the additional sum. Maher made a similar request at the end of the fourth year, and the city council again paid an additional $10,000.

Angel, a concerned taxpayer, filed suit against Murray, the director of finances for *the city, claiming that the city council exceeded its legal authority in agreeing to the price increases. Angel argued that a contract to collect garbage was in place at $137,000 per year and any agreement to pay more was essentially an illegal gift. The trial court agreed with Angel and ordered Maher to repay the $20,000. Maher appealed to the Rhode Island Supreme Court.*

JUDGE ROBERTS

The modern trend away from a rigid application of the preexisting duty rule is reflected by section 89(D) of the American Law Institute's Restatement (Second) of the Law of Contracts, which provides: "A promise modifying a duty under a contact not fully performed on either side is binding (a) if the modification is fair and equitable in view of circumstances not anticipated by the parties when the contract was made...."

We believe that section 89D(a) is the proper rule of law and find it applicable to the facts of this case. It not only prohibits modifications obtained by coercion, duress, or extortion, but also fulfills society's expectation that agreements entered into voluntarily will be enforced by the courts. Section 89D(a), of course, does not compel modifications of an unprofitable or unfair contract; it only enforces a modification if the parties voluntarily agree and if: (1) the promise modifying the original contract was made before the contract was fully performed on either side, (2) the underlying circumstances which prompted the modification were unanticipated by the parties, and (3) the modification is fair and equitable.

Having determined the voluntariness of this agreement, we turn our attention to the three criteria delineated above....First the modification was made....at a time when the five-year contract had not been fully performed by either party. Second, although the contract provided that Maher collect all the refuse generated within the city, it appears this contract was premised on Maher's past experience that the number of refuse-generating units would increase at a rate of twenty to twenty-five per year. Furthermore, the evidence is uncontradicted that the 1967-1968 increase of 400 units "went beyond any previous expectation." Clearly, the circumstances which prompted the city council to modify the 1964 contract were unanticipated. Third, although the evidence does not indicate what proportion of the total this increase comprised, the evidence does indicate that it was a "substantial" increase. In light of this, we cannot say that the council's agreement to pay Maher the $10,000 increase was not fair and equitable in the circumstances.

REVERSED.

1. Critical Thinking: If the town population had decreased and Maher had agreed to take less money, would that agreement be enforceable? Does your answer depend on whether the decrease in population was foreseeable?

2. Ethical Decision-Making: Refusal to remove trash can cause a health concern. Given this health issue, would it be ethical for Maher to threaten to stop removing trash unless the City agreed to pay more money?

Maher was entitled to enforce the city's promise to pay more money because the court ruled that the growth in demand for trash collection was unforeseeable. Distinguishing between foreseeable and unforeseeable contingencies is not necessary in civil law countries such as France or Italy. Because no consideration is required to bind someone to a promise under civil law, a promise to unilaterally modify a contract is fully enforceable, as illustrated in the following feature.

Global Context: Contract Modifications In France

Unlike U.S. common law, under French law a promise to modify a contract does not need consideration to be binding. The French have a civil law tradition that does not require consideration in any contract setting. But which approach is better—the U.S. approach or the French?

Consider the following case. A fishing company hires a crew of seamen to hunt salmon off the Northwest Pacific Coast. The crew agrees to work for $50 per day. Once out on the high seas, the crew demands twice that sum. The ship's captain knows that if he refuses, the salmon run will end before he can return to port and secure a new crew. The captain reluctantly agrees to the wage increase. Under the common law approach, the captain's promise would not be enforceable because the contract modification was unilateral.

Interestingly, French courts would reach a similar result, but would use a different rationale. In France, the captain's promise to pay more would be a contract, but that contract would not be enforceable because it was agreed to under duress. It seems that both common law and civil law countries are concerned with coerced contract modifications, but common law countries use consideration to address the issue, whereas civil law countries use the doctrine of duress.

Agreements Lacking a Bargained-For-Exchange—Past Consideration

A final set of consideration problems, beyond illusory promises and the preexisting duty rule, involves the doctrine of past consideration. This doctrine provides that a promise given after performance has been completed will not form a contract. For consideration to be valid, it must be bargained for in exchange for the promise. Notwithstanding its name, past consideration is not valid consideration.

For example, suppose Juan has some extra firewood and out of the goodness of his heart he fills Anita's rack while she is at school. When Anita returns, she expresses her gratitude by promising to pay Juan $50. Her promise is not legally enforceable. Juan had already given her the wood before she made her promise and past consideration is not valid.

Some states have modified the past consideration rule. Under the common law of Alabama, for example, a promise made to satisfy a preexisting moral obliga-

tion is enforceable. For example, in one Alabama case,[6] a man injured himself while saving the life of another. The man who had been saved promised to help pay the medical expenses of the injured hero. The Alabama Supreme Court noted that this was an example of past consideration, but nonetheless found a contract and enforced the promise. Although the past consideration doctrine remains the common law in most states, the *Restatement (Second) of Contracts* recommends that a promise made to satisfy moral obligations should be enforced, so the Alabama approach is likely to gain wider acceptance.

A few states have modified the past consideration rule by statute. For example, past consideration, whether based on a moral obligation or not, will support a written promise in New York. In the following Ohio case, by constrast, no such statute applies. Ohio follows the majority common law rule that past consideration is never valid consideration.

---

[6] McGowin v. Mobile, 4 So. 2d 161 (Ala. 1941).

In Case 14-4, the company's promise was both specific and in writing. It is also evident that Jan Carlise relied on that promise. Nonetheless, the promise was not enforceable under the common law. The next section suggests that when a promise is clear and the promisee relies, the courts may bypass the doctrine of consideration and turn to the equitable doctrine of promisorry estoppel to grant relief.

Case 14-4

Carlisle
v.
T & R Excavating
704 N.E. 2d 39 (Ohio App. 1997)

Jan and Tom Carlisle married in 1988. Tom was the president of T & R Excavating and Jan did bookkeeping for the company. Tom offered to pay Jan for her bookkeeping services, but she refused.

In 1992 Jan asked Tom for assistance in building a preschool. Tom helped Jan to secure a site for the school and promised to use the resources of T & R to build the school without charging Jan for labor or profit. Work began in January 1993. In March 1993, Jan and Tom separated in anticipation of divorce. T & R stopped working on the school project in June 1993. Jan sued T & R for breach of contract. The trial court found for Jan, awarding $35,790, the cost to complete the school. T & R appealed.

JUDGE DICKINSON

On September 25, 1992, T & R presented a "Proposal" to Ms. Carlisle in which it proposed the following:

We hereby propose to do all the excavation and site work at the above new location....All labor, equipment costs, overhead and profit, necessary for the completion of the this project, totaling $40,000 will be provided at no cost to Wishing Well Preschool, Inc. The $29,800 allotted for materials will be billed to Wishing Well Preschool at T & R Excavating's cost.

On that same date, Ms. Carlisle signed an "Acceptance of Proposal," which was printed at the bottom of the Proposal.

T & R [claims] that the trial court incorrectly found that there was a contract between the parties, because their agreement lacked sufficient consideration....

The trial judge, at one point, stated his opinion that Mr. Carlisle made this promise because he was "a nice guy who wanted to help Ms. Carlisle out," that the consideration for his promise was the "relationship," that they both hoped to benefit from the preschool. A desire to help cannot be consideration for a contract; rather, it is merely a motive....

Consideration was also not shown by Ms. Carlisle's testimony that Mr. Carlisle promised her, after she had refused payment for her bookkeeping services to T & R, that he would help her with her building. If Mr. Carlisle made the statement after Ms. Carlisle had done the work for T & R, her services were "past consideration" and could not support a contract.

Ms. Carlisle failed to establish that there was consideration for T & R's promise to do free excavation and site work for the preschool, or that she relied to her detriment on the promise. The promise, therefore, was not legally binding.

REVERSED.

1. Critical Thinking: Explain why you think this case would or would not come out differently in a civil law country. Is one approach better than the other?

2. Ethical Decision Making: What ethical values guided the court's decision? Identify alternative values that may have generated a different legal result.

Promissory Estoppel as a Substitute For Consideration

The rule of consideration has begun to erode in the United States. Modern courts still require consideration to form a legal contract, but courts are increasingly willing to uphold contracts based on promissory estoppel, an equitable doctrine, when the legal rules of consideration seem unfair. The promissory estoppel doctrine has four elements:

- The promisor must make a clear and definite promise.
- The promisee must reasonably rely on that promise.
- The promisor must know or have reason to know about the promisee's reliance.
- Severe injustice would occur if the promisor reneged on the promise.

The doctrine of promissory estoppel recognizes that making a promise creates a moral obligation and that sometimes it is reasonable for the promisee to rely on gratuitous promises. However, a court will not abandon the rule of consideration in favor of equitable reasoning unless it is convinced that the promise was definite and that reliance was reasonable.

U.S. courts use estoppel principles in diverse cases. For example, donors are typically held liable when they breach pledges made to charities. Suppose a firm promises to give money to a hospital. Relying on the pledge, the hospital begins to build a new wing. The promise is breached even though the managers know that the hospital is relying on the promise. Most courts would hold the firm liable under the promissory estoppel doctrine.

The doctrine of promissory estoppel is also used in employment settings. Suppose a firm promises to give a retired executive a pension. The promise is made after the executive has already retired and no pension had been promised previously. After a few months, a new board of directors seeks to terminate the pension. The executive argues that he has begun to rely on the pension as a source of income, and that it would be unfair to take back the promise. A court might agree, and even though the executive had given nothing in exchange for the promise, the promise could be enforceable in equity.

Keep in mind that promissory estoppel is a growing doctrine, but it still is the exception rather than the rule. The rule is that a promise is not enforceable unless it is given in exchange for consideration. As a result, if someone promises to do something for your firm, it is unsafe to rely on that promise unless your firm gives something of value in exchange. Prudent managers must be sensitive to equitable concerns and aware of common law requirements.

Hirschfeld Wrap-Up

Hirschfeld and Feiden settled their dispute. First, they agree to mutually rescind their original contract, with each party agreeing to forgo his or her rights under that contract.[7] They then agreed to a new contract. In a letter to the editor printed in the New York Times, Hirschfeld said that the new contract gave him much more control over the ways in which his art will be exhibited.[8] Feiden noted that when the relationship started in the 1970s, Hirschfeld "was famous, but illustrations did not sell."[9] Feiden retains the rights to sell Hirschfeld's works under the new contract.

---

[7] Celestine Bohlen, *Al Hirschfeld Drops Suit and Renews Ties with Gallery*, New York Times, October, 14, 2000 at Section B, p. 12.

[8] Robin Finn, *Public Lives: She's Happy, Hirschfeld's Happy, The Secret?*, October 24, 2000 (quoting Margo Feiden), at Section B, p. 7

[9] *Id.*

	Summary
Defining Consideration	A necessary element of a contract, consideration can be defined as a bargained-for-exchange of legal value. **Legal value**—doing or promising to do something that one does have a legal duty to do, or refraining or promising to refrain from doing something that one has a legal right to do. **Adequacy of consideration**—as a general rule, courts do not inquire into the relative economic worth of the consideration exchanged. **Bargained-for-exchange**—the exchange of legal value, or quid pro quo must reflect a true bargain agreed to by the parties, not mere sham or pretense. **Policy**—the primarily policy goal of the law of consideration is to provide the courts with evidence of contractual intent. **Civil law contrasted**—civil law does not require consideration to have a contract.
Common Consideration Problems	**Illusory promises**—a statement that is in the form of a promise but imposes no obligation on the maker. Most commonly arises in conditional contracts and requirement and output contracts. An illusory promise lacks legal value and is not valid consideration **The preexisting duty rule**—promising to perform in accordance with a preexisting public or contractual duty lacks legal value and is not valid consideration. **Settlement of claims**—for an agreement to settle a claim to be enforceable, each party must give up something of legal value. **Contact modifications**—under the common law, agreements to bilaterally modify contracts are enforceable, unilateral modifications are not. Under Article Two of the UCC, both bilateral and unilateral modifications will be enforced, provided other contractual requirements are met. **Past consideration**—promises made in recognition of consideration given in the past are not enforceable. Past consideration is invalid consideration.
Promissory Estoppel	An equitable obligation inferred by the courts to protect justifiable reliance on a promise. Promissory estoppel can render a promise enforceable without consideration when the following elements are present: • The promisor made a clear and direct promise. • The promisee reasonably relied on the promise. • The promisor knew or had reason to know of the promisee's reliance. • Severe injustice would occur if the promisor reneged on the promise.

Review Questions and Case Problems

1. Distinguish between the policies that underlie the common law and civil law treatment of consideration.

2. What is a conditional contract? Give an example of how an illusory promise might arise in a conditional contract.

3. What is a requirement contract? What is an output contract? Give an example of how an illusory promise might arise in a requirement and in an output contract.

4. What is the difference between a liquidated and unliquidated debt? When will a creditor's promise to forgive part of a liquidated debt be enforceable? Explain.

5. Distinguish between the common law and the UCC rules with regard to agreements to unilaterally modify contracts.

6. Past consideration is not good consideration. Explain.

7. Michelle Michalski worked for Circuit City. While she was employed, Circuit City instituted a new dispute resolution program that required employment-related disputes to be settled by arbitration. Circuit City later fired Ms. Michalski, and she claimed that her termination was due to her pregnancy. Ms. Michalski filed suit in U.S. District Court for employment discrimination. Circuit City filed a motion to dismiss, seeking to move the dispute to arbitration. Ms. Michalski claimed that she never promised to submit her claims to arbitration, and even if she had, her promise was not supported by consideration. Who do you think won? *Michalski v. Circuit City Stores, Inc.*, 177 F. 3d 634 (7th Cir. 1999).

8. Members of Prestwick Golf Club had a contract guaranteeing them a reduced fee at a public golf course. The members complained that the course owners were favoring nonmembers who paid higher fees, and that it was getting too difficult for members to schedule a convenient tee time. The course owners promised to reserve certain times for the club members, and to increase those reservations as the club membership grew. The club agreed to this arrangement. Later, the club continued to grow, but the reserved times did not. The club sued the golf course asking the court to force the owners to give the club more convenient tee times. Who should win? *Prestwick Golf Club v. Prestwick Limited Partnership*, 503 S.E. 2d 184 (S.C. App. 1998).

9. Webb was working in the loft of a textile mill when he saw a large wooden block begin to fall to the mill floor below. Directly beneath the path of the block stood Webb's coworker, McGowin. Webb threw himself on the block, deflecting its path. McGowin was saved. Webb suffered debilitating head and back injuries. In recognition of his moral debt to Webb, McGowin promised to pay him $15 every two weeks. Payments continued for several years and then McGowin died. The executor of McGowin's estate did not know if he had the authority to continue the payments. He petitioned the court for declaratory judge-

ment. Does this case raise an issue of past consideration? Might the doctrine of promissory estoppel apply? Explain. *McGowin v. Mobile*, 4 So. 2d 161 (Ala. 1941).

10. John DiMario served as trainer to Runaway Groom, a thoroughbred racehorse. After Runaway Groom won the "Prince of Wales" race, his owners promised to pay DiMario a bonus. They again promised DiMario a bonus after Runaway Groom won the "Travers Stakes." No bonuses were ever paid. DiMario sued for breach of contract. Who do you think won? *DiMario v. Coppola*, 10 F. Supp. 2d 213 (E.D.N.Y. 1998).

11. A reward was posted for information leading to the arrest and conviction of several notorious bank robbers. When the robbers were found and convicted, several people sought to claim the reward. Claimants included bank employees who were very helpful in describing the robbers to police, an off-duty policeman who had spotted the suspects and called the arresting officers, and the arresting officers themselves. Who among these claimants is entitled to a portion of the reward? *Denney v. Reppert*, 432 S.W. 2d 647 (Ky. App. 1968).

12. A dispute arose over a contract to sell blueberries. A seller promised to deliver its entire crop of blueberries but did not specify the price. The seller shipped the berries and the buyer accepted them. The buyer then sent the seller a check, together with a letter, stating that cashing the check would constitute a final settlement of any dispute over the contract price. The buyer cashed the check and then sued for additional money. Did cashing the check establish an enforceable settlement that would bar the lawsuit? *E.S. Herrick Co. v. Maine Wild Blueberries Co.*, 670 A. 2d 944 (Maine 1996).

13. McInerney served as a sales representative for Charter Golf, a company who sells golf apparel and supplies. Hickey-Freeman, an elite clothier in direct competition with Charter Golf, approached McInerney and offered him a sales job that included, among other things, an eight percent commission. When McInerney informed his employer of the offer, Charter Golf offered him a ten percent commission and guaranteed a job for life. McInerney stayed with Charter Golf. A few months later, McInerney was fired. McInerney sued. Who won and why? *McInerney v. Charter Golf, Inc.*, 680 N.E. 2d 1347 (Ill. 1997).

14. Mrs. Eichelbaum had over the years been very generous to the Virginia School of the Arts, donating close to $500,000. In October 1993, the school asked her for an additional "challenge gift" that would encourage others to donate as well. In Mrs. Eichelbaum's letter to the school pledging $100,000, she did not mention the challenge gift, nor state any conditions on the pledge. The school advertised the gift to other donors. Its advertisements stated that the school "must match this challenge gift by the end of the year." Mrs. Eichelbaum died on January 14, 1994 without having delivered the $100,000 gift. The school raised only $67,000 from other donors during the fiscal year. Should Mrs. Eichelbaum's executor pay the school the money? *Virginia School of the Arts v. Eichelbaum*, 493 S.E. 2d 510 (Va. 1997).

15. When a pastor of a church retired, the congregation unanimously voted to award him a lifetime pension. No pension had previously been mentioned. The promise of the pension was put in writing. The retired pastor continued to give an occasional sermon and he enjoyed the use of a church office. He also counseled the new pastor as he adjusted to his new job. Two years later, the church refused to continue pension payments. The pastor sued his former congregation. The church claimed that any consideration that had been given by the former pastor was inadequate consideration. Who do you think won and why? *Brads v. First Baptist Church of Germantown*, 624 N.E. 2d 737 (Ohio App. 1993).

16. Rodney and Donna Mathis filed a malpractice suit alleging negligent medical treatment provided by St. Alexis Hospital. After consulting with a doctor who assured the Mathises that no negligence could be sued, they entered into a settlement with the hospital in which the Mathises agreed to drop their lawsuit and the hospital agreed to not seek reimbursement of attorney fees spent in defending the suit. A few months later, the Mathises filed a malpractice suit against the hospital, raising the same issues as in the first suit. The hospital claimed that the suit was barred by the settlement agreement. The Mathises claimed that a mere promise not to seek attorney fees was inadequate to bind them to their promise to dismiss the suit. Who do you think won? *Mathis v. St. Alexis Hospital*, 650 N.E. 2d 141 (Ohio App. 1994).

17. Harold and Joe were buddies for twenty-five years. They had established a weekly habit of going together to a liquor store and buying a "package." The package included a half-pint of vodka, orange juice, two cups, and two lottery tickets. Typically, each buddy would pay half the total amount of the bill before the bottles were opened or the tickets "scratched." Sometimes the tickets yielded a small winning. When this happened, the two buddies would "plow back" the winnings into a purchase of more tickets. On the date their dispute arose, Harold did not have any money with him, so Joe paid. Before Joe scratched the cards he looked at Harold and asked "Are you in on it?" Harold nodded his assent. One of the cards Joe scratched was worth $20,000. Joe refused to share the money, and Harold sued. Joe claimed that because Harold did not pay for the tickets, he had no right to the proceeds. Is Harold right? *Pearsall v. Alexander*, 572 A. 2d 113 (D.C. App. 1990).

18. Jill was approached by a columnist for a popular magazine. The columnist was writing a story on patients who were sexually abused by their therapists. Jill had had such an experience and she agreed to tell the columnist about it, but only if the columnist promised to keep Jill's identity out of any story that would appear in print. The columnist promised. The magazine article recounted Jill's experience, and although Jill was referred to with a pseudonym, the story told enough details about her to reveal her identity to anyone who knew her. Jill sued under a theory of promissory estoppel. Who do you think won? *Ruzicka v. Conde Nast Publications*, 999 F. 2d 1319 (8th Cir. 1993).

Assignment on the Internet

Nothing distinguishes the contract law of the United States from that of its trading partners more than the law of consideration. In most countries of the world, an exchange of consideration is not necessary to have a contract. Recall that common law countries require consideration as evidence that the parties intended to enter into a contract. A writing can serve the same purpose. Check to see if the laws of France, Germany, and Italy require a promise to give a gift to be in writing. For information on European contract requirements visit **http://www.ljx.com/practice.internat/euro k.html**.

On The Internet

http://www.loc.gov/ *The Library of Congress provides links to a large array of legal topics including contract law.*

http://www.state.nh.us/org/cpb.html *The New Hampshire Consumer's Sourcebook provides contract law information from a consumer's perspective.*

http://www.law.upenn.edu/bll/ulc/uccita/uctast84.htm *The Uniform Electronics Transactions Act discussed in this chapter can be found online.*

www.law.cornell.edu/uscode/41 *Title 41 of the United States Code provides federal rules governing public contracts. The Cornell Law School reprints the Code online.*

www.virtualchase.com *For a set of annotated links to legal information arranged by information type go to this site.*

Troubles between MCI and Telmex

Long Distance International (LDI) and Star Marketing Services (SMS) brought suit against Telefonos de Mexico (Telmex) and SBC International (SBI), alleging that the defendants committed acts of tortious interference with contractual relations, tortious interference with prospective relations, conspiracy to commit tortious interference, breach of contract, antitrust, and Texas Deceptive Trade Practices Act violations. The trial court granted a summary judgment for Telmex and SBI on all claims. Thereafter, the court of appeals affirmed, stating that because LDI/SMS were in violation of Mexican law, their claims could not be maintained.[1]

Telmex is a company that provides communications service in Mexico. When calls destined for the U.S. originate in Mexico, Telmex's wires carry the call up to the border. There, the call is transferred via a United States carrier's line, in this case MCI. When a call is made from Mexico to the U.S., Telmex bills the customer in Mexico and reimburses MCI for carrying the call in the U.S. The reverse occurs when a call originates in the U.S., with MCI billing the American customer and reimbursing Telmex.

MCI contracted with SMS to receive 800 numbers that were supplied to LDI. MCI also had customers that included phone companies engaging in "callback" services. These companies provide Mexican callers with 800 numbers; the calls were then linked to a caller identification system. When a Mexican customer called the 800 number, the call would not be answered, but the phone number would be recorded. Thereafter, the Mexican would receive a callback, being provided with a dial tone that would allow the customer to place a call anywhere in the United States. Because the initial call was not answered, neither the phone company nor the caller paid Telmex for the unanswered call. Telmex was instead paid only for the Mexican leg of the callback, which is the standard payment procedure for calls originating in the U.S.

Consequently, Telmex sent MCI a letter, in which they explained that "resale" was illegal under Mexican law. Additionally, Telmex requested that MCI provide a list of all customers providing resale, which Telmex would disconnect. MCI responded with a letter requesting specific laws regarding resale, because they claimed that they did not understand Mexico's definition of "resale." After MCI refused to supply the customer list under the claim that such a disclosure of information was illegal under U.S. law, Telmex consulted with SBI, and thereafter disconnected the 800 numbers that they thought were being used for resale.

Therefore, the case was brought before the Supreme Court of Texas.[2] The court examined whether the plaintiffs' contracts with Mexican customers were made in violation of Mexican law. After you have studied this chapter, you will have a better understanding of two important elements in forming contracts—capacity and legality. The case involving Telmex provides an illustration that should enlighten you on the concept of legality.

1. *If you were negotiating contracts for MCI with other phone companies that you knew were providing resale benefits, what ethical concerns might you have?*

2. *Why did the court of appeals not maintain the claims of the plaintiffs? Think about how this legal issue affects the formation and enforcement of contracts as you read the chapter.*

---

[1] *Long Distance International, Inc. v. Telefonos De Mexico*, 2002WL 381436 (Tex. App.-San Antonio).

[2] *Long Distance International, Inc. v. Telefonos De Mexico*, 49 S.W. 3d 347, 44 Tex. Su.Ct. 894 (2001).

CHAPTER 15

Capacity and Legality

Contracting with a Minor

Contracting with the Mentally Incompetent

Contracting with Intoxicated People

Legality

In this chapter we explore the final two elements of a legal contract—capacity and legality. To form a legal contract, the parties must have contractual capacity. This means that each party must have reached the **age of majority** (eighteen in most states) and be of sound mind. As a general rule, an agreement with a minor, an insane person, or a person who is so intoxicated that they cannot comprehend the nature of the agreement, is not a contract. The purpose behind the rule is to protect the weak and immature from those who might take advantage of them.

Business managers who contract with a customer who might lack capacity must be careful. They must also be cautious when contracting with an unseen trading partner, such as transactions that take place via mail or the Internet. The final contract element, legality, places a limit on the notion of freedom to contract. Agreements that violate the law or are contrary to public policy are not enforceable. Obviously, courts will not enforce a contract that calls for the commission of a crime, such as bribery or murder. Other forms of illegality may be less obvious. For example, to install plumbing, one needs a license; to run a restaurant, one must meet health regulations; and to build a condominium, one's land must be properly zoned. We examine the legal effect of contracting in violation of a growing number of regulatory requirements.

The chapter closes by examining two contract clauses common in business. Each may, at times, violate public policy, and hence be unenforceable. The first,

the **exculpatory clause**, is used by a business to excuse itself from its tort liabilities. Examples include contracts in which a consumer waives the right to sue for a defective product or where an employee agrees not to sue his employer for injuries on the job. The second, the **non-competition clause**, is used by a business to protect its investment in training employees, in customer lists, and in trade secrets. In this situation, the employee agrees to "not compete" with the employer on leaving employment. Because some exculpatory and non-competition clauses are enforceable and some are not, managers should be aware of which ones a court will enforce.

Contracting with a Minor

Under U.S. common law, a contract between an adult and a minor is voidable. This means that the minor has the option to **ratify** (enforce) the contract with the adult; or alternatively, to **disaffirm** (cancel) the contract.

Ratifying a Contract

A minor who enters into a contract and then decides after reaching the age of majority to remain in that contract, has the power to do so. This power is called ratification. A party can only ratify after reaching the age of majority because before that age, the minor lacks capacity, so any attempt to ratify would be ineffective.

A ratification can be express (put into words) or can be inferred from an action or inaction. For example, a minor buys a car and enters a contract to make monthly payments. If the minor makes a payment or two after reaching the age of majority, the contract will be ratified. Most often, however, a ratification is accomplished through silence and inaction. A minor who does not seek to disaffirm a contract for a reasonable length of time after reaching the age of majority will ratify that contract through inaction and silence. Once ratified, a contract is fully enforceable by either party.

Global Context: The Age of Majority in the United Kingdom

The age of majority should not be confused with the legal drinking age, driving age, voting age, or the age for serving in the military. The term "age of majority" refers only to the age necessary to enter into a legal contract. The age is typically set by state statute, with eighteen years being most common.

In the United Kingdom, by way of contrast, there is no hard-and-fast age of majority. British courts will not enforce contracts with immature minors, but whether a person is too immature to contract is decided on a case-by-case basis. That is, if the court considers a person under the age of eighteen mature enough to protect themselves in contract negotiations, the contract will not be voided. Hence, the statutory approach in the United States is "over-inclusive." It gives protection to those who do not need it. But U.S. law is also "under-inclusive." Many people over the age of majority lack sufficient maturity to contract wisely. These people are not protected in the United States.

The British seek to avoid the problem of over-inclusiveness and under-inclusiveness by looking at the maturity level of the young person in each case. Often, the fairness of the exchange can signal maturity. A one-sided contract favoring the adult gives evidence that the young person lacked maturity. A fair contract suggests they did not.

Disaffirming a Contract

A minor has the option of disaffirming a contract any time prior to reaching the age of majority or for a reasonable time thereafter. On disaffirmation, a contract is rescinded and restitution is made. Recall that to rescind a contract means essentially to tear it up and destroy any remaining obligations under the contract. To make **restitution** means that the parties give back what they have received from the other party.

Suppose that John, a minor, buys a used Toyota from Sammie's Auto Sales. John gives $500 in cash and agrees to pay $100 per month for the next two years to Sammie. John takes the car home and then a week later changes his mind. He disaffirms by bringing the Toyota back to Sammie's. Sammie's tears up the promissory note and gives John his $500 back.

Problems arise when the minor seeks to make restitution and the goods have depreciated or have been damaged. Suppose, in the previous example, that John parked the Toyota on the street and a hit-and-run driver crashed into it. The car is now worth much less than it was when John bought it. In most states, John can still disaffirm and get a full refund, and John does not have to pay to repair the car. In Case 15-1, the court examines a situation involving a minor who wishes to disaffirm a contract.

Case 15-1

Swalberg

v.

Hannegan
883 P. 2d 931 (Utah App. 1994)

*T*odd Hannegan, a minor, purchased a 1974 Ford Truck from Larry Swalberg for $2,500. Hannegan gave $640 in cash and agreed to pay the remaining $1,860 three months later. Hannegan took possession of the truck. A few days later the truck was damaged and Hannegan sought to disaffirm. Swalberg claimed that the truck was now worth only $700. He accepted the truck when it was returned by Hannegan, but then sued for the balance owing on the promissory note. The trial court found for Swalberg (the plaintiff) and ordered Hannegan (the defendant) to pay $1,160—the remaining balance on the note minus the value of the truck in its returned condition. Hannegan appealed.

JUDGE BENCH

The dispositive issue on appeal is whether a minor who disaffirms a contract is required to restore the full value of the property received under the contract. Defendant argues that Utah law does not require a disaffirming minor to restore the other party to his or her precontractual status. We agree.

Utah Code Ann. Sec. 15-2-2 (1986) provides:

A minor is bound...for his contracts, unless he disaffirms them before or within a reasonable time after he obtains his majority and restores to the other party all money or property received by him by virtue of said contracts and remaining within his control at any time after attaining his majority.

This statute requires only that the property remaining within the minor's control be returned to the other party. The trial court held, however, that defendant was required to return the property in its original condition or be liable for the difference in value. This holding is clearly contrary to the provisions of this unamended nineteenth century statute, as interpreted by controlling Utah case law.

...Section 15-2-2 requires that a disaffirming minor must only return the property remaining within the minors control. The Utah Supreme Court has interpreted this statute to allow a minor to effectively disaffirm the underlying contract without restoring the full value of the property received under the contract. Although we do not necessarily believe in the wisdom of this approach, we are not in a position to hold contrary to controlling case law under the doctrine of stare decisis. If a contracting and disaffirming minor is to be held responsible for waste of property received under a contract, it is for the legislature to so provide. Alternatively, the Supreme Court might...overrule existing case law.

REVERSED.

1. Critical Thinking: Examine the court's reasoning that it used to arrive at its conclusion to reverse the decision of the trial court. Do you agree with the court's reasoning? Why or why not?

2. Ethical Decision Making: Suppose you were in Hannegan's position. If your decision to disaffirm without paying the balance were guided by the golden rule, would you have behaved differently than Hannegan?

Misrepresentation of Age

The law of capacity is intended to protect a weak, immature minor from adults who might take advantage of the unequal bargaining situation. However, not all minors are immature and vulnerable. Suppose a young person knows the rules of capacity, lies about one's age, enters a contract, and later seeks to disaffirm without compensating the adult for any depreciation in the value of the goods. Here the law of capacity is being used as a sword, not a shield, and the law does not permit it.

Most states will allow a minor to disaffirm a contract even when the minor misrepresented the age, but these states will require the minor to make full restitution. This means that the minor must compensate the adult for any depreciation or damage done to the items being returned. In some states, courts do not allow the minor who misrepresents one's age to disaffirm. They use the equitable doctrine of estoppel to protect the adult who reasonably believed that the minor was of age. Still, other states allow the minor to win in contract law, but hold the minor liable for the tort of fraud. Although minors are not liable for breach of contracts, they are liable for torts. Thus, in all states, the minor must compensate the adult for any damages caused by the misrepresentation of age.

The Equitable Doctrine of Necessaries

The law of capacity is intended to help minors, but can harm them at times. Suppose a seventeen-year old has moved away from his or her parents, married, taken employment, and started a family. Will anyone lease the young man or woman an apartment, or sell them a refrigerator? Given the law of capacity, a merchant would be reluctant to do so.

To address this problem, the law provides that a contract with an **emancipated minor** for the purchase of a **necessary** is enforceable so long as it is fair. A minor is "emancipated" if the minor no longer is supported financially by their parents. What is considered a "necessary" varies a bit by context, but typically includes reasonable food, shelter, clothing, and medical attention. In some settings, reasonable transportation may also be a necessary.

The law of necessaries comes from equity. In most states, a minor can still disaffirm a legal contract for a necessary, but the minor will be held to a quasi contract for the fair value of the necessary. Typically, the contract price and the reasonable value are the same. Under equity, sums exceeding the contract price are not recoverable.

Case 15-2 illustrates that not all contracts entered into by emancipated minors are enforceable. The contract must involve a necessary.

Case 15-2

Mitchell
v.
Mitchell
963 S.W. 2d 222 (Ky. App. 1998)

*S*herri Mitchell, age 17, was injured in an auto accident while riding in a car driven by her husband, Michael Mitchell. Sherri filed a claim with Michael's insurance company, State Farm Insurance. Sherri signed a release of all claims against State Farm in exchange for $2,500. She then sought to disaffirm the settlement contract, return the $2,500, and pursue her personal injury claim in court.

The trial court held that since Sherri was emancipated, she could not disaffirm her contract. Sherri appealed.

JUDGE EMBERTON

Marriage of the infant emancipates the minor; it does not, however, make the minor sui juris [capable of legally contracting]. In *Bensinger's Coex'rs*, the court declined to hold that an emancipated child must be bound by his contracts and followed the general rule that:

Although parental emancipation may free the infant from parental control, it does not remove all the disabilities of infancy. It does not, for example, enlarge or affect the minor's capacity or incapacity to contract...

We cannot adopt a rule that marriage by the minor somehow classifies him as more mature and intelligent than his unmarried counterpart. We...find that logic and common sense would not encourage such a result since marriage by a minor too frequently may itself be indicative of a lack of wisdom and maturity.

REVERSED.

1. Critical Thinking: What do you think about the reasoning offered in support of the court's conclusion? Are you persuaded by this reasoning?

2. Ethical Decision Making: What values were guiding the judge's decision to reverse the trial court's conclusion?

Contracting with the Mentally Incompetent

The rules regarding contracting with mental incompetents, such as the senile, delusional, retarded, and insane are similar to those involving minors. There are two classifications for insane people. If a court has previously declared the person insane and a guardian has been appointed, any contract with that previously **adjudicated insane** person is void and cannot be enforced by either party.

If the court did not make the declaration of insanity before the contract was formed, the contract is voidable. Like a minor, the insane person can either ratify or disaffirm such a contract upon regaining mental competence. On disaffirmation, the insane person typically must make full restitution, including compensating the other party for any damage or depreciation of goods received. Also, like the minor, an insane person will be liable in quasi contract for the fair value of any necessary.

Legal definitions of mental incompetence vary from state to state. Some states inquire into whether the insane person was capable of *understanding* the nature and consequences of the transaction. Other states ask whether the person could *control* their actions. Still other states look to the *fairness* of the transaction as proof of competency.

Contracting with Intoxicated People

Intoxication caused by taking drugs or drinking alcohol can also make a person lack capacity to contract. The legal tests for intoxication, like those for insanity, vary from state to state. Some states ask whether the intoxicated party understood the transaction. Others ask whether the party did *control* his or her actions. Others look at the *fairness* of the transaction. If intoxication is found, the contract will be voidable. When competency is regained, the person may either ratify or disaffirm the contract.

Note that the previous rule regarding intoxication applies *only if the other party has no reason to know of the intoxication*. This is obviously rare. The more common case involves a situation in which the sober party knows of the intoxication and tries to take unfair advantage. Such cases are treated in the law under the doctrines of fraud, duress, unconscionability, and undue influence—topics that are addressed in the next chapter.

Legality

The final element of a contract is legality. To have a valid contract, the terms of that contract must not violate the criminal law, call for a commission of an intentional tort, or violate public policy. If the subject matter of the contract is illegal, then the contract is void.

For example, the Supreme Court of Texas examined the legality of resale contracts in the case between LDI/SMS and Telmex. The court focused on AT&T's challenge to the FCC in Via USA for approving licenses for international callback services. The FCC responded with their reasons for favoring international resale, stating that international resale "advances the public interest, convenience, and necessity by promoting competition in international markets and driving down international phone rates. We believe it is in the best interests of consumers and eventually of economic growth around the world." However, if any foreign country has declared callback services illegal, the FCC requested documentation with the illegal restrictions for its country. Mexico was not one of the fifty-seven countries that had declared callback services illegal. Additionally, a clause in Telmex's concession with Mexico's government indicates that for the first six years, Telmex may allow its users to resell Telmex's surplus capacity, but they are not required to do so. In other words, the Mexican government gave Telmex the option of allowing MCI to resell Telmex's services. Therefore, the court determined that LDI/SMS's resale of Mexican telecommunications was not in violation of Mexican law and the contract was not considered void.

Effect of Illegality

A court will not grant a legal remedy for the breach of a void contract. Suppose a person accused of a crime promises to pay a juror $5,000 if that juror votes to acquit. The accused gives the juror $2,000 in advance and promises the remaining $3,000 after acquittal. If the juror breaches (votes to convict), the accused cannot get his $2,000 back. Similarly, if the juror votes to acquit, and the accused refuses to pay the final $3,000, the courts will not hold the accused to the illegal promise.

There are exceptions to the rule that courts will not touch illegal transactions. The exceptions arise in equity to prevent unjust enrichment and to protect reasonable reliance interests.

First, in the bribery example, both parties knew that their transaction was illegal. They stood **pari delicto** (Latin for "equally at fault"). In contrast, when one party is less at fault than the other, courts may use equity to assure that justice is done in the particular case. This is particularly true if there has been part performance and the more guilty party seems to be unjustly enriched. For example, in one case, a dairyman was coerced to pay an illegal "kickback" to secure a much needed contract. The court permitted the relatively innocent dairyman to recover the payment because he did not stand pari delicto with the extortioner.

Equity also recognizes the doctrine of **excusable ignorance**. If one party did not know that a transaction was illegal, courts may use equity to protect that party's reliance on the contract. For example, suppose a general contractor promised to build a house as a bribe for a favorable vote by a city councilman. The general contractor hires an electrician to do part of the work, and the electrician does not know of the illegal nature of the contract. The electrician would still be able to collect for the work completed.

According to the letter that MCI mailed to Telmex, MCI was unaware of the laws in Mexico regarding resale. Suppose the trial and appellate courts both ruled correctly in determining that resale was indeed an illegal practice in Mexico. If the court determined that the actions of the plaintiffs were categorized under the doctrine of excusable ignorance, the court may have ruled in favor of the plaintiffs' interests.

A third situation permitting recovery on an illegal contract involves the doctrine of **severability**. Sometimes courts will sever, or split, illegal contracts in two, enforcing the legal part and refusing to enforce the illegal.

An example will illustrate the doctrine of severability. Most states have **usury** laws that limit the interest rate that can be legally charged on a particular type of loan. Suppose a state allows a ten percent interest on a construction loan. A bank loans $100,000 to a builder who agrees to repay the principle plus fifteen percent interest. The contract is illegal because it violates the usury laws. If the builder has already received the loan, most courts would **reform** (rewrite) the contract requiring the borrower to repay the $100,000 (to prevent a windfall), but not allowing the bank to recover any interest (to provide the bank with an incentive to reduce the interest charged to future customers). In essence, the court would sever the legal portion of the contract (to repay principle) from the illegal (to repay usurious interest).

Whether a court will sever an illegal contract or otherwise rewrite the contract for the parties can be difficult to predict. In Case 15-3, the court reasons that both parties were aware of the illegal nature of the contract, so it refuses to offer any legal or equitable relief.

Case 15-3

Wilson

v.

Adkins

941 S.W. 2d 440 (Ark. App. 1997)

Georgia Adkins was in dire need of a bone marrow transplant. Georgia's sister, Alta, agreed to "donate" her marrow to her sister in exchange for $101,500. After the operation, Georgia died and Georgia's heir, Ronnie Adkins, refused to pay Alta. Alta sued. The trial court, citing a federal statute making it illegal to sell body organs, including bone marrow, dismissed Plaintiff's case. Plaintiff appealed.

JUDGE CRABTREE

The complaint artfully characterizes the agreement as an exchange of $101,500 for the risk, difficulties, and insurance consequences of appellant's marrow donation. While appellant's attorney goes to great lengths to disguise the nature of the contract, it is, as the trial court noted, "so intertwined and commingled that [it] cannot be separated," and clearly falls under the rubric of federal law on the sale of human organs.

Title 42 of the United States Code section 274(e) provides the following:

a) Prohibition

It shall be unlawful for any person to knowingly acquire, receive, or otherwise transfer any human organ for valuable consideration for use in human transplantation....

c) Definitions

The term "valuable consideration" does not include the reasonable payments associated with the removal, transportation, implantation, processing, preservation, quality control, and storage of a human organ or the expenses of travel, housing, and lost wages incurred by the donor of a human organ in connection with the donation of the organ.

While this statute does allow "reasonable payments" for the cost of the procedures and incidental expenses, it is clear that the $101,500 is not payment for reasonable incidental expenses incurred in the organ donation, but is an illegal sale of an organ specifically prohibited by federal law....Where an illegal contract has been made, neither the courts of law nor the courts of equity will interpose to grant any relief to the parties, but will leave them where it finds them, if they have been equally cognizant of the illegality.

AFFIRMED.

1. Critical Thinking: What ambiguous statute must the court examine to make a judgment? Do you agree with the manner in which the court interpreted the statute based on the reasoning provided?

2. Ethical Decision Making: Suppose you were in Alta's position. If your decision to donate bone marrow were guided by the universalization test, what would you have done differently? Why?

Contracts that Violate Licensing Regulations

Many trades and professions require a state-approved license. A question arises as to the status of contracts where one of the parties does not have the license necessary to perform under the contract.

The answer depends on the reason the state passed the licensing requirement. Most licensing requirements are designed to protect the public. Examples include licenses for the practice of medicine, law, real estate sales, and construction work that raise health and safety issues. In such cases, there is a strong policy to encourage practitioners to obtain licenses. For instance, public policy dictates that an unlicensed physician who performs surgery on a patient should not be able to collect a fee for those services. This policy provides an incentive for physicians to earn a license.

Other types of licenses are passed less to protect the public, and more to simply raise revenues for the state. In such instances, courts will overlook the licensing requirements. To illustrate, consider the case of a man who won a fishing contest in which first prize was a $14,000 fishing boat. The winner, however, did not produce a valid fishing license, and the sponsor of the contest refused to give him the boat. The court held that since the purpose of a fishing license is primarily to raise revenue for the state, the absence of a valid fishing license did not negate the fisherman's right to collect his prize.

Exculpatory Clauses

An exculpatory clause is a clause in a contract that says one party will not be liable to another for torts committed during performance of the contract. Such clauses are quite common. For example, suppose Spiro joins a health club. The written membership agreement says in plain English and boldface print that Spiro agrees to not sue the club if he is injured while using the club's facilities. Spiro separately signs that portion of the written contract. Later, while Spiro is using the club's whirlpool, an electrical short in the pool system causes Spiro a severe shock and skin burns. Can Spiro sue the

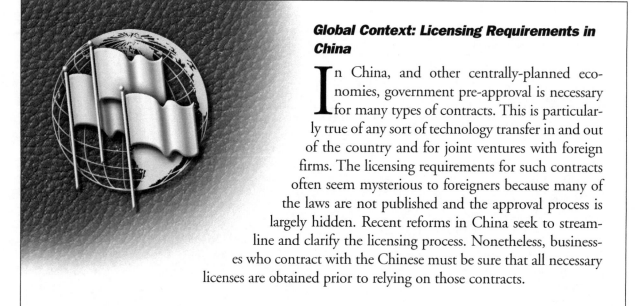

Global Context: Licensing Requirements in China

In China, and other centrally-planned economies, government pre-approval is necessary for many types of contracts. This is particularly true of any sort of technology transfer in and out of the country and for joint ventures with foreign firms. The licensing requirements for such contracts often seem mysterious to foreigners because many of the laws are not published and the approval process is largely hidden. Recent reforms in China seek to streamline and clarify the licensing process. Nonetheless, businesses who contract with the Chinese must be sure that all necessary licenses are obtained prior to relying on those contracts.

health club for his injuries even though he signed the exculpatory clause?

Some tort liabilities can be excused by agreement of the parties and some cannot. As a general rule, exculpatory clauses in the context of recreational activities are enforceable. But the club, or any other business for that matter, cannot exculpate (excuse) itself for gross and wanton negligence, for recklessness, or for willful and intentional torts. In other words, exculpatory clauses can excuse relatively minor acts of negligence,

but they cannot excuse more severe forms. In Spiro's case, the negligence of the health club seems extreme, so the clause would probably not prevent Spiro from suing.

Drawing a line between relatively minor acts of negligence and more aggravated forms of "gross negligence" or "recklessness" is not always easy. In Case 15-4 the Ohio Supreme Court addressed this distinction in a case involving a child's injury following a soccer practice.

Case 15-4

Zivich
v.
Mentor Soccer Club
696 N.E. 2d 201 (Ohio 1998)

*P*amela Zivich registered her seven-year-old son, Bryan, to play soccer in a league run by Mentor Soccer Club. Mentor is a nonprofit corporation managed and run by volunteers. After a winning soccer scrimmage, Bryan climbed, unsupervised, onto a soccer goal to celebrate. The goal collapsed and Bryan was injured. The Ziviches sued the Club for negligence for failing to supervise Bryan's activities. The Ziviches also claimed that the Club acted with "wilfull and wanton" disregard for Bryan's safety by failing to adequately secure the goal to the ground. The Club moved for summary judgment on the basis of an exculpatory clause signed by Pamela. The trial court granted the Club's motion. The Ohio Court of Appeals affirmed. The Ziviches appealed to the Ohio Supreme Court.

JUDGE SWEENY

The Club's registration form, signed by Mrs. Zivich, contained the following language:

Recognizing the possibility of physical injury associated with soccer and for the Mentor Soccer Club, and the USYSA [United States Youth Soccer Association] accepting the registrant for its soccer programs and activities, I hereby release, discharge and/or otherwise indemnify the Mentor Soccer Club, and the USYSA, its affiliated organizations and sponsors, their employees, and associated personnel, including the owners of the fields and facilities utilized by the Soccer Club, against any claim on the behalf of the registrant as a result of the registrant's participation in the Soccer Club.

[T]he general rule is that releases from liability for injuries cased by negligent acts arising in the context of recreational activities are enforceable. These holdings recognize the importance of individual autonomy and freedom of contract…

When Mrs. Zivich signed the release she did so because she wanted Bryan to play soccer. She made an important family decision and she assumed the risk of physical injury on behalf of the family as a whole. Thus, her decision to release the volunteer on behalf of her child simply shifted the cost of injury to the parents. Apparently, she made the decision that the benefits to her child outweighed the risk of physical injury. Mrs. Zivich did her best to protect Bryan's interests and we will not disturb her judgment.

It should not come as any great surprise for a parent to learn that, during a period of inactivity at a soccer practice, their child fiddled with loose equipment, climbed on nearby bleachers, or scaled the goal. It should be equally clear that the coaches supervising the practices will not be able to completely prevent such unauthorized activity, as some degree of bedlam is unavoidable, when children of tender years are brought together to play a game, and when their emotions are aroused.

[W]e hold that parents have the authority to bind their children to exculpatory agreements in favor of volunteers and where cause of action sounds in negligence…

As a separate ground for recovery, appellants also contend that the injury was caused by the Club's willful and wanton misconduct. This court [has] defined "willful" misconduct as conduct involving "an intent, purpose, or design to injure." "Wanton" misconduct was defined as conduct where one "fails to exercise any care whatsoever toward those to whom he owes a duty of care, and this failure occurs under circumstances in which there is a great probability that harm will result." We have held that while a participant in recreational activities can contract with the proprietor to relieve the proprietor from any damages or injuries he may negligently cause, the release is invalid as to willful and wanton misconduct.

Even accepting as true the appellants' claim that the club officials knew about the safety problems [of unanchored goals] but failed to act, this action does not amount to willful and wanton misconduct. As noted by the appellate court, "Park officials testified that the City never had anchored the goals in the past, and, apparently, of the thousands of young boys and girls playing soccer in the youth league throughout the years, no other child had been injured in this manner." Thus, reasonable minds could not conclude that the risk posed by the unanchored goal was so great as to require immediate remedial action.

AFFIRMED.

1. Critical Thinking: What evidence does the court offer to affirm the conclusion of both the trial and appellate courts? How strong is this evidence?

2. Ethical Decision Making: Suppose you were an ethical manager for the Mentor Soccer Club. Using the public disclosure test as your guideline, what action would you take to maintain a positive public image following the litigation processes?

An exculpatory clause sets up a conflict between the principles that underlie tort law and the principles that underlie contract law. Tort law says that a person should be liable when it is his or her *fault* that another person has been hurt. Contract law says that courts should enforce voluntary *agreements* entered into by competent adults. The question becomes whether the courts should follow the tort notion of *fault* or the contract notion of *agreement*.

Some exculpatory clauses are always held to be unenforceable. First, as discussed earlier, exculpatory clauses cannot be used to excuse recklessness or other forms of gross misconduct. Second, exculpatory clauses cannot excuse the tort liability owed by an employer to its employee for injuries sustained by the employee while on the job. Third, a merchant of a defective good cannot excuse itself for liabilities for personal injuries caused by the defect and sustained by the purchaser of that good. And fourth, liability cannot be excused in certain contracts affected with a public interest. Examples of this last category include contracts with common carriers (such as taxis, airlines, trains, and buses), with utility companies, and with financial institutions such as banks. In each of these four categories, the courts will not allow the parties to shift liability through an exculpatory clause. Such clauses are **per se unenforceable**, as summarized in Exhibit 15-1.

Exculpatory clauses that are not in one of the four "per se" categories will be enforceable so long as there is sufficient evidence that the injured party was aware of

EXHIBIT 15-1
Exculpatory Clauses that Are Per Se Unenforceable

1. Clauses that seek to excuse gross negligence, recklessness, or intentional torts.
2. Clauses in employer-employee contracts.
3. Warranty disclaimers by merchants sellers for personal injuries caused by defective products.
4. Clauses in contracts affected with a public interest.

the exculpatory language and agreed to assume the risks of injury and loss. For example, assume Lisa leaves her coat at a coatcheck counter at a music hall. A large sign posted at the counter reads: "MANAGEMENT IS NOT RESPONSIBLE FOR LOST OR STOLEN ITEMS." When Lisa returns, her coat has been stolen. Since this exculpatory language is conspicuous, management would not be liable if they committed minor acts of negligence that caused the coat to be stolen. By way of contrast, suppose there were no sign, but instead, the back of Lisa's coatcheck stub contained the exculpatory language in small print. As a general rule, exculpatory language that is not conspicuous is not enforced so the management would probably remain liable if they were negligent in taking reasonable precautions to protect Lisa's coat.

In Case 15-5, a clause on the reverse side of a form contract stated that a funeral home would not be liable for failing to carefully perform its duties. When the funeral home failed to deliver the deceased body, the court had to decide whether this exculpatory language violated public policy.

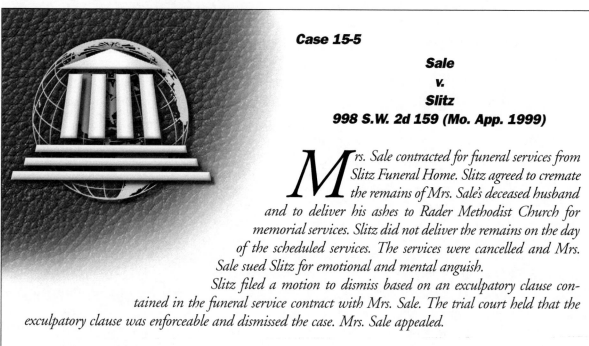

Case 15-5

Sale
v.
Slitz
998 S.W. 2d 159 (Mo. App. 1999)

*M*rs. Sale contracted for funeral services from Slitz Funeral Home. Slitz agreed to cremate the remains of Mrs. Sale's deceased husband and to deliver his ashes to Rader Methodist Church for memorial services. Slitz did not deliver the remains on the day of the scheduled services. The services were cancelled and Mrs. Sale sued Slitz for emotional and mental anguish.

Slitz filed a motion to dismiss based on an exculpatory clause contained in the funeral service contract with Mrs. Sale. The trial court held that the exculpatory clause was enforceable and dismissed the case. Mrs. Sale appealed.

JUDGE PREWITT

Plaintiff's claim against Defendants arises from the Defendant's failure to produce and deliver her deceased husband's cremated remains. Plaintiff alleges in her petition that because of Defendant's failure to perform their duties she…was unable to have memorial services…Plaintiff also contends that Defendants' conduct was "willful, wanton, and malicious and with total disregard to the consequences of their acts."

The agreement signed by Plaintiff was entitled "FUNERAL PURCHASE CONTRACT." A clause on the first of its two pages, above the signature lines, stated: "SEE OTHER SIDE FOR THE TERMS AND CONDITIONS OF THIS AGREEMENT, INCLUDING DISCLAIMER OF WARRANTIES AND LIMITATION OF REMEDIES, THAT ARE PART OF THIS AGREEMENT…" Plaintiff stated that she did not read the back of the contract; she was not told to read the back of it; she was not told that she was waiving any rights by signing the contract; and she was told that she "was required by law to sign the contract." On the second, or reverse side, the language upon which Defendants rely is in the fifth of fifteen paragraphs:

LIMITATIONS OF DAMAGES AND REMEDIES: By signing this Agreement, you expressly waive, and you agree that you shall not be entitled to recover damages or losses of any kind, whether direct or consequential, based on negligence.

It is clear that if Plaintiff can prove, as she alleged, that the Defendants' conduct was willful and wanton, this provision will not bar her claim. In Atlack, the [Missouri Supreme] Court stated that "there is no question that one may never exonerate oneself from future tort liability for intentional torts or for gross negligence, or for activities involving the public interest."

We now consider whether this provision bars a claim for negligence. Although disfavored and strictly construed, releases of future negligence are not void as against public policy. To release a party from its own future negligence, exculpatory language must be clear, unambiguous, unmistakable, and conspicuous…The exculpatory language must effectively notify a party that he or she is releasing the other party from claims arising from the other party's negligence.

Here, Plaintiff was anticipating the death of her husband, which occurred the next day. The language in question, or the effect of it, was not expressly brought to her attention. The exculpatory clause is on the reverse side of the contract and is located among fourteen other paragraphs…The location of the clause leads us to conclude that the purported release was not conspicuous.

We conclude that the petition stated a claim for which relief can be granted. Further, we decide that the exculpatory clause in the contract does not bar such a claim.

REVERSED AND REMANDED.

1. Critical Thinking: Evaluate the judge's reasoning for reversing the decision of the trial court. Based on the quality of the reasoning, do you agree with the court's decision? What unanswered questions, if any, do you have regarding the evidence used to support the judge's conclusion?

2. Ethical Decision Making: When Slitz included the exculpatory clause in his contract for services, he was trying to protect himself. Can you think of a better way for Sliltz to have protected himself while acting in a more ethical fashion?

Agreements Not-to-Compete

The law recognizes a strong public policy favoring free and fair competition between businesses. At times, businesses agree not-to-compete with one another. As Exhibit 15-2 highlights, such agreements are enforceable only if: (1) there is a *legitimate business purpose* for the noncompetition agreement; (2) the agreement is *reasonable* in terms of time, geography, and subject matter; and (3) the agreement is *ancillary* to, or part of, a larger transaction. In short, some agreements not-to-compete are enforceable, whereas some are not.

To illustrate, suppose Rachel sells her ice cream

EXHIBIT 15-2

Is an Agreement To-Not-Compete Enforceable?

1. There must be a legitimate business purpose for the agreement.
2. The agreement must be reasonable as to
   a. time,
   b. geography, and
   c. subject matter.
3. The agreement must be ancillary to a larger transaction.

---

shop to Rudy. A clause in their contract states that Rachel agrees to not open a competing ice cream store within thirty miles of the existing store for the following two years. Even though there is a strong public policy to promote free and fair competition, most courts would hold Rachel to her promise not to compete with Rudy.

First, note that there is a legitimate business purpose for Rachel's noncompetition clause. Rachel developed loyal customers over the years. Her trade name has value, as does her unique brand of ice cream. When she sells her business to Rudy, she is selling the **goodwill** associated with her shop. The value of this goodwill was reflected in the price Rudy paid for the store. In fact, Rudy may have been unwilling to buy the store without the non-competition agreement. Without the clause, Rachel could open another store just down the street and take many of her customers back.

Second, the time (two years) and geographic (30 miles) limits seem reasonable, as does the fact that Rachel promised to not open a competing ice-cream shop (subject matter). If Rachel had promised Rudy not to open any form of restaurant anywhere in the United States for the rest of her life, the agreement would not be reasonable and would not be enforceable in court.

And finally, the common law draws a distinction between ancillary and nonancillary agreements. **An ancillary** agreement is one that is part of a longer contract. Rachel's agreement not-to-compete is only one clause in a larger transaction to sell a business, so it is ancillary.

In Case 15-6, an otherwise valid agreement not-to-compete is somewhat vague and ambiguous. Because public policy disfavors restraints on competition, the court reads the clause as not restricting the activities of the party who promised not to compete.

Case 15-6

Sheehy

v.

Sheehy

702 N.E. 2d 200 (Ill. App. 1998)

John and James Sheehy are identical twins who worked together in the funeral business for twenty-seven years. James then sold his share in the business to John for $213,500. As part of the sale, James agreed to not compete with John within a ten-mile radius of the Sheehy funeral home for a period of four years.

One year later, James took employment with a competing funeral home. Although James worked at a branch more than ten miles from John's business, James' employer had a branch funeral home within the ten-miles radius. In addition, James occasionally conducted services at cemeteries within ten miles of his brother's business, and attended business meetings within the ten-mile radius. John sued James for breach of the agreement not-to-compete. The trial court found for James. The plaintiff appealed.

JUDGE COUSINS

The present case involves a covenant ancillary to the sale of a business. The enforceability of such a restraint depends on the reasonableness of the restraint as to time and territory as judged by the circumstances in a particular case…[T]he restraint as to time and as to territory must be necessary in its full extent for the protection of the purchaser, but must, at the same time, not be oppressive on the seller, and must not be injurious to the interests of the public.

The language of the covenant precludes defendant from participating with a funeral home business or otherwise competing with plaintiff's business within a ten-mile radius; however, if we were to interpret the covenant as precluding defendant's employment by *any* funeral home that has branches within the restricted zone, the covenant's proscription would be too broad.

Moreover, we agree with the trial court regarding the effect of defendant attending continuing education classes and business meetings within the ten-mile restricted zone. In our view, no adverse effect has been shown by plaintiff as a result of defendant's attendance at the classes and meetings.

It is undisputed that defendant, in his capacity as funeral director employed by SCI/Blake-Lamb, attended burials…at cemeteries within the ten-mile radius. However, due to the nature of funerals, the place of the burial is determined by the family members rather than the undertaker.

Defendant testified that he never conducted funerals from funeral homes with the ten-mile radius, nor did he conduct funerals for any decedent who lived within the ten-mile radius. He further acknowledged that he did not solicit any business from any families within the ten-mile radius. Consequently, no loss has been identified by plaintiff indicating a threatened business interest.

We agree with the trial court that any preclusion of defendant from entering cemeteries within a ten-mile radius should have been stated within the covenant. Restrictive covenants are strictly construed.

AFFIRMED.

1. Critical Thinking: Identify the various reasons why the court found for James. As you look at those reasons, evaluate what the court was trying to accomplish and why you think "restrictive covenants are strictly construed."

2. Ethical Decision Making: If you were in James' position and your decision were guided by the ethics of care, what would you have done to maintain good relations with John and possibly avoid litigation?

Technology: Agreement Not-to-Compete and Tech Industry Employees

Rapid technological advances require skilled tech employees. Because these employees are such valuable assets to firms, firms are understandably alert to the likelihood that a trained employee will abandon them for a better job elsewhere. When a high-tech employee leaves one firm, the knowledge possessed by this person could benefit the firm's competitors. Firms try to protect what they see as their property by restrictive agreements requiring former employees not-to-compete with their former employer when they take a new position.

Some scholars argue that time limitations, specified in these agreements, should be reduced for high-tech industries because the current technology loses its value so quickly. In light of the rapid changes in these industries, a month, or even several days, could render former technology obsolete. Therefore, these scholars propose that reducing the time limitations for "non-compete" agreements would best accommodate the context of high-tech industries.

Other scholars emphasize the importance of broadening geographical restrictions in agreements not-to-compete. As the Internet continues to reduce communication barriers and expand global markets, traditional boundaries would not reasonably fit the global reach of certain tech industries. Therefore, these scholars feel that noncompetition clauses should contain broad geographical restrictions. Several cases reflect the arguments for modifying agreements not-to-compete for high-tech industries. For example, in *EarthWeb, Inc. v. Schlack*, the court removed a time restriction in a non-competition clause on the grounds that it was too broad. Schlack was hired as Vice President for Worldwide Content by EarthWeb. For the eleven months that Schlack worked for EarthWeb, he was responsible for the firm's websites. After his resignation, Schlack began working for a competing Internet company. EarthWeb claimed that Schalck was in violation of a one year non-competition agreement. However, the court invalidated the agreement, stating, "When measured against the information technology industry in the Internet environment, a one year hiatus from the work force is several generations, if not an eternity."

Thus, high-tech industries are being encouraged by some scholars and several courts to begin modifying noncompetition clauses to fit the nature of a rapidly changing industry, by reducing time limitations and broadening geographical restrictions.

Non-competition clauses are not limited to settings involving the sale of businesses. They are also quite common in employment contracts. Many employers make significant investments in training new employees and share trade secrets, customer lists, and other valuable information with employees. To protect these investments, many business have employees sign agreements in which the employee agrees not to compete with their former employer on leaving the firm. These agreements are enforceable only if there is a legitimate business purpose and the limitation is reasonable in terms of time, geography, and subject matter. Because of the inequality of bargaining power in employment settings, courts are reluctant to enforce broad prohibitions on the ability of an employee to find new employment.

Wrap-Up

The Supreme Court of Texas examined the case between LDI/SMS and Telmex, which involved two issues. First, the court had to determine whether the plaintiff's contracts with Mexican customers were in violation of Mexican law. Second, if the contracts were illegal under Mexican law, the court had to determine whether that illegality is a defense to the plaintiff's assertions. Because the court found that the contracts were not in violation of Mexican law, the second issue was ignored. Therefore, the decision made by the court of appeals was reversed and remanded by the Supreme Court of Texas. This case demonstrates the importance of understanding legal rights and responsibilities not only in the U.S., but also, given the global scope of contemporary business, the rights and responsibilities provided to business by the law of other countries.

	Summary
Capacity	Each party must have reached the **age of majority** (eighteen in most states) and be of sound mind. Generally, an agreement with a minor, an insane person, or a person who is so intoxicated that he or she cannot comprehend the nature of the agreement, is not a contract. The purpose behind the rule is to protect the weak and immature from those who might take advantage of them.
Contracting with a Minor	**Ratifying a contract**—a minor who enters into a contract and then decides to remain in that contract has the power to do so. Once ratified, a contract is fully enforceable by either party. **Disaffirming a contract**—a minor has the option of disaffirming a contract any time prior to reaching the age of majority or for a reasonable time thereafter. On disaffirmation, a contract is rescinded and restitution is made. **Misrepresentation of age**—minors must compensate the adult for any damages caused by misrepresentation of age. **The equitable doctrine of necessaries**—a contract with an emancipated minor for the purchase of a necessary is enforceable so long as it is fair.
Contracting with the Mentally Incompetent	Two classifications for insane people: 1) One who has previously been declared insane—any contract with a previously adjudicated insane person is void and unenforceable. 2) One who has not been declared insane prior to forming the contract—the insane person can either ratify or disaffirm such a contract upon regaining mental competence.
Contracting with Intoxicated People	If intoxication is found, the contract will be voidable. When competency is regained, the person may either ratify or disaffirm the contract. This rule applies only if the other person had no reason to know of intoxication.
Legality	**Effect of illegality**—a court will not provide a legal remedy to a void contracts However, there are three exceptions in which a court may intervene in an illegal contract: 1) both parties do not stand *pari delicto* 2) excusable ignorance, and 3) the doctrine of severability. **Contracts that violate licensing regulations**—many trades and professions require a state-approved license. The status of the contract in which one of the parties does not have the required license depends on the reasons for the establishment of the license. **Exculpatory clauses**—a contract that says one party will not be liable to another for torts committed during performance of the contract. **Agreements not-to-compete**—sometimes, businesses agree not-to-compete with one another. Such agreements are enforceable only if: (1) there is a legitimate business purpose for the noncompetition agreement; (2) the agreement is reasonable in terms of time, geography, and subject matter; and (3) the agreement is ancillary to, or part of, a larger transaction.

Review Questions and Case Problems

1. To what does the "age of majority" refer? Is this the same as the legal voting age? Explain.

2. When will intoxication cause a contract to be unenforceable?

3. What is the legal effect of contracting with a mentally incompetent person? Distinguish between situations where the incompetent has been adjudicated insane from those where he or she has not.

4. Exculpatory clauses set up a tension between tort law and contract law. Explain this statement.

5. Do you think that a court would be more or less reluctant to enforce a non-compete clause in an employment contract as opposed to a contract for the sale of a business? Why?

6. Create a hypothetical situation where a person enters into a contract without the necessary license, but is able to win dollar damages under principles of equity and unjust enrichment.

7. Philip Talley, a minor, bought a car from Value Auto. When the car developed difficulties, Talley sued Value Auto for breach of a warranty. The sales contract contained a clause that Talley had separately initialed. The clause stated that any disputes over the sale must be submitted to arbitration. Talley seeks to disaffirm the arbitration agreement but to keep the remainder of the contract intact. Should Talley be able to disaffirm part of his contract while ratifying the rest? Explain. *Value Auto Credit, Inc. v. Talley, 727 So. 2d 61 (Ala. 1999).*

8. Fletcher and Marshall were housemates. They both signed a lease with the landlord. Fletcher was at all times over the age of majority (eighteen in Illinois). Marshall signed the lease a month prior to his eighteenth birthday. Two weeks after his birthday Marshall moved in. Six weeks later, he moved out. Marshall never paid any rent. Fletcher sued Marshall for his share of the unpaid rent. Marshall claimed that by moving out he had disaffirmed his lease. Fletcher claimed that by moving in, Marshall had ratified the lease. Who should win? Is the legal conclusion to this case the same as the ethical one? *Fletcher v. Marshall, 632 N.E. 2d 1105 (Ill. App. 1994).*

9. A hospital provided needed medical care for Thomas, a nine-year-old boy. Thomas had been injured in an auto accident. Thomas' parents were poor and they agreed to seek government (Medicaid) assistance in paying for the medical services. The medical bill was about $16,000. Thomas' parents did not succeed in securing Medicaid for Thomas and the bill went unpaid. Five years later, the hospital sued Thomas (now fourteen) for the balance due. Should Thomas have to pay for the reasonable value of the necessaries he received from the hospital? Would your answer be any different if you were told that Thomas received an insurance settlement of $25,000 because of his injuries? Should that matter? *North Carolina Baptist Hospitals v. Franklin, 405 S.E. 2d 814 (N.C. App. 1991).*

10. Quincy had nine children. During Quincy's lifetime he placed his son Armnees's name on his bank account. Armnee had the authority to write checks for Quincy. At times, Quincy would have bouts with hallucinations and delusions. At other times, Quincy would be perfectly competent and lucid. When Quincy died, Armnee claimed the $72,000 in the bank account as his own. His brothers and sisters complained to the court, claiming that Quincy lacked the capacity to make an effective transfer of the funds to Armnee. Armnee pointed out that Quincy was often quite aware that Armnee had sole access to the funds. Must Armnee share the proceeds with his siblings? *Coleman v. Coleman, 955 S.W. 2d 713 (Ark. App. 1997).*

11. Kimberly, a minor, worked for Frank's Nursery & Crafts. She signed a contract that stated all employment claims she had against Frank's would be submitted to arbitration. When she was fired by Frank's, she filed a complaint with the Equal Employment Opportunity Commission arguing that she had been discriminated against because of her gender. Frank's sought to have the case moved to arbitration? Is Kimberly's promise to arbitrate enforceable? Should it be? *Sheller v. Frank's Nursery & Crafts, 957 F. Supp. 150 (N.D. Ill. 1997).*

12. Dr. Farber was an employee of a Valley Medical, a professional corporation. He was also an internist who, among other things, treated AIDS patients. A clause in Dr. Farber's employment contract stated that on leaving Valley Medical, Dr. Farber would not practice medicine within five miles of Valley Medical's offices for three years. Dr. Farber claimed that noncompetition clauses should not be enforceable against doctors because of the unique public interest in having readily available medical care. Do you agree? *Valley Medical Specialists v. Farber, 982 P. 2d 1277 (Ariz. 1999).*

13. According to NCAA rules, once a college athlete enters into a contract with a professional sports agent, that athlete loses his or her amateur status and can no longer play in intercollegiate games. A college football player signs an agency contract in the fall of 1985. The contract is postdated "January 2, 1986," one day after the final college football game of the young athlete's career. At the time that the contract is signed, the agent loans the athlete $4,000. The loan is to be repaid to the agent once the athlete signs an NFL contract. The athlete later refuses to pay back the loan and the agent sues. Did the loan violate public policy? Should the courts enforce it? Why or why not? *Walters v. Fullwood, 675 F. Supp. 155 (S.D.N.Y. 1987).*

14. Gambling is illegal in Georgia. In Kentucky, it is legal to gamble on the state lottery. Two men in Georgia agree to pool their money and buy lottery tickets in Kentucky. They agree to split any winnings. One of the two men travels to Kentucky and uses the combined funds to purchase tickets. One of the tickets is a winner with a significant cash prize. The man with the winning ticket refuses to share the proceeds with the other man. Will a state court in Georgia enforce a contract to share gambling pro-

ceeds won in Kentucky? Should it? *Talley v. Mathis, 453 S.E. 2d 704 (Ga. 1995).*

15. Randy Rose suffered serious injuries when his tractor, an 1800 horsepower, turbo-charged behemoth, rolled over on top of him. His injury occurred while participating in a contest sponsored by the National Tractor Pullers Association (NTPA). Prior to the contest, Randy had signed an exculpatory clause waiving his rights to sue the NTPA for injuries sustained in the competition. Randy, nonetheless, sued the NTPA in tort. Randy argued that the NTPA should be liable for setting unsafe rules of competition. The NTPA filed a motion to dismiss, citing the exculpatory clause. Is the exculpatory clause enforceable? What additional facts would be important in determining whether the clause bars Randy's tort claim? *Rose v. National Tractor Pullers Ass'n, 33 F. Supp. 757 (W.D. Wis. 1998).*

16. Republic Bank purchased eight residential lots at a foreclosure sale. Previously, the plaintiff Modular One had improved the lots by building modular homes on them. After completing the work, Plaintiff filed mechanics liens on the properties for the value of the improvements made. Plaintiff, however, did not have the legally required builder permits when it did the construction work. Republic Bank asked the court to declare the liens invalid. Does Plaintiff have a legal right to collect on the value of the modular homes? Does Plaintiff have an equitable right? Explain. *Republic Bank v. Modular One, 591 N.W. 2d 335 (Mich. App. 1998).*

17. Brian Guest worked as a carpet installer for Brunswick Floors. A clause in his employment contract stated that Brian would not, for a period of two years following termination of employment, "engage in floor covering installation, or in floor covering services, directly or indirectly, as an individual, partner, adviser, stockholder, director, officer, clerk, principal, agent, or employee, within an eighty (80) mile radius from his Employer's location." Does this clause violate public policy? Is it enforceable? What additional facts might be important in making your decision? *Brunswick Floors v. Guest, 506 S.E. 2d 670 (Ga. App. 1998).*

18. Ron and Lynn Quiring were involved in a rather messy divorce. In settling there property disputes, Ron agreed to give Lynn full rights to their house in exchange for Lynn's promise not to report her allegations of Ron's sexual improprieties with their child to state officials. Later, Ron sought to invalidate their agreement on the grounds that the agreement violated public policy. Do you think that the property settlement was binding on Ron? Why or why not? *Quiring v. Quiring, 944 P. 2d 695 (Idaho 1997).*

Assignment on the Internet

Most states have usury statutes specifying the legally permissible rate of interest that can be charged on various loans. Sometimes courts rewrite usurious agreements and sometimes they do not. Use the Internet to look up the usury statutes in your state. Is the penalty for usury specified in your state's statutes? You can find state statutes through http://www.findlaw.com.

On the Internet

http://www.sylaw.org/documents/minor-contracts.htm *This site details the nature of contracting with minors.*

http://www.wld.com/conbus/weal/wcontra3.htm *This page contains more information of capacity.*

http://www.mckennalaw.com/ARTICLES/marr2.htm *This article examine how exculpatory clauses affect court decisions.*

http://www.mobar.org/journal/1998/mayjun/corrigan.htm *This site provides an explanation about noncompete agreements.*

CHAPTER 16

Allstate: What Is Assent?

A driver covered by Allstate Insurance Company was involved in an automobile accident with Allen and Darlene Kramer. After several failed attempts at arbitration, the case went to trial and the jury found for the plaintiffs, but awarded them zero damages.[1] Shortly afterwards, the Allstate adjuster who originally handled the case took a leave, and another adjuster took over the case. This new adjuster, unaware of the jury's decision, offered a $3,500 settlement for damages to the Kramers. The Kramers' attorney accepted the offer.[2]

A week later, the new adjuster discovered her mistake and contacted the Kramer's attorney, stating that Allstate would stand by the jury's verdict and refuse to pay the $3,500. She argued that the offer she had made was a mistake.[3]

1. *If you were on a jury hearing this case, would you decide to force Allstate to pay the $3,500?*
2. *Suppose you were a manager at Allstate. What would you do to prevent this kind of situation from happening again?*

---

[1] *Kramer v. Leeson*, Case No. 99-2047 (Superior Court 1999).

[2] *Kramer v. Allstate*, 201 Ariz. 322 (2000).

[3] *Id.*, 324.

CHAPTER 16

Legal Assent

When two people talk to each other in the hope that an exchange will take place, all kinds of things can go wrong. Global business needs dependability. Just imagine what it would be like if "YES" meant "MAYBE" or "I'M LISTENING"! Deals would be closed and then reopened again and again. The costs of all purchases would soar. Businesses would be forced to charge extra to pay for all the extra time they had to spend to finally get to the point where "YES" really means "YES." As a manager you are going to need a thorough understanding of when courts will enforce contracts.

The major theme of this chapter is that "best practice" firms aim for legal assent in their contracts. This chapter shows how. It explains the major obstacles to legal assent: **mistake, misrepresentation, undue influence, duress, and unconscionability.** As noted in Chapter 12, one way to think of these obstacles is that their existence can be raised as a defense to the claim that a contract exists. By knowing about these potential problems, future business managers will be more aware of when their assents will constitute legal assent.

The Importance of Legal Assent

To make business transactions more smooth and dependable, the law has developed rules about when an assent to buy or sell is a legal assent. We will mean by **legal assent**, a promise to buy or sell that the courts will require the parties to obey. The reason why there needs to be such an idea is to distinguish it from other kinds of assent that courts see as not reaching the level of legal assent. Something is wrong with those other kinds of assent. Thus, courts do not require parties to follow through on them. The point here is that courts see some forms of assent as just more genuine or real than others.

Learning the difference among these kinds of assent is the major purpose in this chapter. For example, notice the additional complexity in understanding assent indicated in the Tech Box. Why does it matter? When one person thinks he has sold his boat to another, the contract may be **voidable**, a circumstance that can cost businesses major profits when the sale is of a much larger scope than a single boat. When a contact is voidable, it may be **rescinded**. In other words, when a contract is voidable, it can be canceled. All the work in making the original deal was wasted.

For example, recently, a school district in Pennsylvania rescinded a "pour contract" with Coca-Cola.[4] This contract stated that Coke would have exclusive distribution rights in the school district in exchange for a new stadium and wrestling room for the high school. The school board argued that some of the members did not have time to review the specific elements of the agreement before they voted to accept the contract. Thus, if the recission is upheld, any work on the stadium or wrestling room would have to be stopped.

The cancellation of a contract permits the person who canceled the contract to require the return of everything he gave the other party. At the same time, persons who rescind contracts must themselves return whatever they have received from the other party. An enormous waste of time and an unnecessary cost of doing business may result.

---

[4] This information was discussed in Donna Dudick, *Central Bucks School District Coke Contract Rescinded*, THE LEGAL INTELLIGENCER, December 8, 1999, at p. 6.

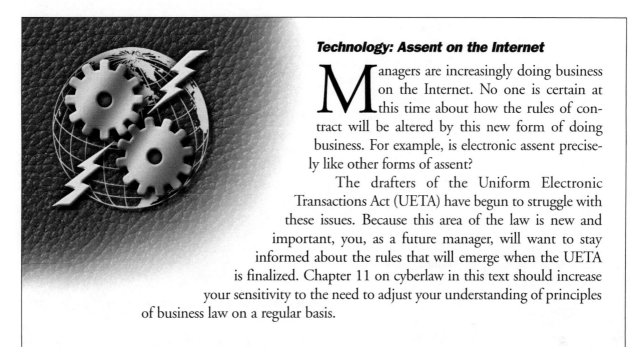

Technology: Assent on the Internet

Managers are increasingly doing business on the Internet. No one is certain at this time about how the rules of contract will be altered by this new form of doing business. For example, is electronic assent precisely like other forms of assent?

The drafters of the Uniform Electronic Transactions Act (UETA) have begun to struggle with these issues. Because this area of the law is new and important, you, as a future manager, will want to stay informed about the rules that will emerge when the UETA is finalized. Chapter 11 on cyberlaw in this text should increase your sensitivity to the need to adjust your understanding of principles of business law on a regular basis.

Mistake and Its Effect on Assent

When people agree to buy or sell, they do so with a particular understanding about the nature of the good or service they are about to exchange. One or both parties may think they consented to exchange a particular thing, only to find out later that no meeting of the minds had occurred. People may misunderstand either some fact about the deal or the value of what is being exchanged. We will focus on misunderstandings about facts because they are the only ones that raise the potential of recission in American courts.

But European courts take a different approach to mistakes *about the value of performance* of the contract. In general, they agree with the reluctance of American courts to interfere with a contract just because the value of the item in question has changed since the agreement. American courts assume that when parties form a contract they accepted the risk that the value might change later. However, European courts permit recission of the contract for a mistake of value *when the mistake is more than fifty percent of the value at the time of the contract.*

Legal assent is absent when a legal **mistake** occurs. A **mistake** in contract law is different from the ordinary use of the term. A mistake in contract law is an erroneous belief about the material facts of the contract *at the time the contract is formed.*

Mistakes may be **unilateral**, the result of an error by one party about a material fact, i.e., one that is important in the context of this particular contract, or, they may be **mutual**, i.e., shared by both parties to the agreement. This distinction is important in determining which contracts are voidable. Which kind of mistake do you think occurred in the case discussed at the beginning of this chapter?

Unilateral Mistake

In general, a unilateral mistake does not void a contract. The courts are hesitant to interfere with a contract in a situation where one of the parties is found to have had a correct understanding of the material facts of the agreement. For instance, a widow seeking to rescind her and her husband's decision to have his retirement benefits paid out over *his life* was not permitted to receive survivor's pension benefits. The court held that representatives of the retirement system had provided sufficient information to the plaintiff and her husband before they elected that particular form of payout.[5]

The Allstate opening vignette is certainly an example of a unilateral mistake. One party, the Kramers, knew that they had received zero damages from a jury. But the new Allstate adjuster did not at first know of that jury award. The adjuster acted on his mistaken understanding of a material fact about the agreement with the Kramers.

---

[5] *Ricks v. Missouri Local Government Employees Retirement System,* 1999 WL 663217 (MO. App. WD).

But sometimes, recission is permitted for even unilateral mistakes. Because their economic well-being depends so heavily on the certainty of contracts, business managers want to be aware when unilateral mistakes permit recission. Any of the following conditions would permit a court to invalidate a contract on grounds of unilateral mistake:

1. One party has made a mistake about a material fact, and the other party either knew or had reason to know about the mistake.

2. The mistake was caused by a clerical error that did not result from gross negligence.

3. The mistake is so serious that the contract would be unconscionable, i.e., so unreasonable that it is outrageous.

Although these situations are rare, they are important because any recission can be costly in terms of time and lost business opportunities.

Case 16-1 provides an example of an attempt to use unilateral mistake as grounds to rescind a contract. As you read this case, think about the Allstate case discussed at the start of this chapter. Is there any similarity between the Allstate claim manager and Mr. Phillips? Why or why not?

Case 16-1

Mary W. Scott, (Respondent-Appellant)
v.
Mid-Carolina Homes, Inc.,
(Appellant-Respondent)
Court of Appeals of South Carolina
293 S.C. 191 (1987)

*O*n March 23, 1985, Scott and her husband visited Mid-Carolina's sales lot in Hartsville, South Carolina, looking for a mobile home to purchase. One of the salesmen, Neal Phillips, invited Scott to see a repossessed 1984 mobile home priced at about $5,600.00. When the Scotts returned to the Hartsville lot on Saturday, March 30, Phillips was not there, but Ashley Hardwick, another salesman, offered to show them the mobile home. While examining the mobile home, they discussed its purchase with Hardwick. He told them the purchase price was $5,644.00, to be paid in full before delivery. Mrs. Scott then decided to purchase the home for the stated price. She gave Hardwick a check for $2,913.71, agreeing to pay the balance before April 30. Before the Scotts left the lot, Hardwick filled out a form entitled, "A Plain Language Purchase Agreement." Mrs. Scott signed her name as buyer in the lower right corner.

During the following week, the Scotts received a telephone call from Phillips telling them to meet him the following Saturday, April 6. Accordingly, the Scotts drove to the lot on Saturday. There, Phillips told them he was unable to sell them the mobile home because it had a bent frame. The Scotts offered to take the home anyway and sign a release for the frame, but Phillips said the South Carolina Manufactured Housing Board would not permit him to sell the home with a bent frame.

On April 12, 1985, another couple signed a Form 500 to purchase the same trailer from Mid-Carolina for $9,220.00. An officer of Mid-Carolina signed the form, and the purchase was completed.

On May 28, 1985, Mrs. Scott filed a complaint alleging Mid-Carolina had breached a contract to sell her the mobile home. The jury awarded Mrs. Scott $3,600.00 actual damages and $6,400.00 punitive damages for breach of contract accompanied by a fraudulent act and $3,000.00 actual damages for violation of the Act. The circuit judge upheld the jury's verdict, awarded Scott costs and attorney's fees for the statutory violation, and denied Scott's motion to treble the damages under the Act.

JUDGE BELL

Mid-Carolina argues it is entitled to rescind the contract because its sales personnel were acting under a mistake of fact when they told Mrs. Scott the purchase price.

Unilateral mistake is not by itself ground for rescinding a contract. A contract may be rescinded for unilateral mistake only when the mistake has been induced by fraud, deceit, misrepresentation, concealment, or imposition of the party opposed to the rescission, without negligence on the part of the party claiming rescission, or when the mistake is accompanied by very strong and extraordinary circumstances which would make it a great wrong to enforce the agreement. Mid-Carolina has not demonstrated the presence of any of the circumstances that would permit rescission for unilateral mistake.

Relying on *Hester v. New Amsterdam Casualty Co.*, 268 F. Supp. 623 (D.S.C. 1967), Mid-Carolina asserts it is entitled to rescission because Mrs. Scott should have been put on notice by the amount of the price, that Mid-Carolina was acting under a mistake of fact. In *Hester*, however, the Court was careful to observe that the parties lacked equal knowledge of the facts and that the party opposing rescission was aware of the fact about which the other party was mistaken. In this case, Mid-Carolina was in a superior position to know the intended price of the mobile home. Mid-Carolina set the price, was in possession of the documents listing the price, and was in the business of selling mobile homes. Nothing Mrs. Scott said or did induced Mid-Carolina's mistake, if there was one. Nor is there evidence she knew of the mistake and sought to take unfair advantage of it. The Hester rule is, therefore, inapplicable to the facts of this case, and Mid-Carolina is not entitled to rescission.

AFFIRMED.

1. Critical Thinking: What reasons did the court give for its decision? Do you think these reasons were good reasons? Why or why not?

2. Ethical Decision Making: Suppose you were the manager at Mid-Carolina. Using the universalization test as your ethical guideline, how would you have behaved after Mary Scott signed the agreement to purchase the mobile home for $5,400?

Mutual Mistake

In situations where both parties to a contract are mistaken about either a current or past material fact, either can choose to rescind the contract. In such an instance, any agreement would be an illusion. An ambiguity in some key fact prevented the parties from any genuine agreement.

Raffles v. Wichelhaus[6] has taught generations of students the importance of clearly defining the material facts in any contract. In *Raffles*, the parties to the contract had agreed that the vessel Peerless would deliver a cargo of cotton. Unfortunately for them, there were two ships named Peerless, and each of the parties had a different ship in mind when the deal was made. The ships were scheduled to sail at materially different times. So the court rescinded the contract.

WARNING: Excellent managers anticipate ambiguity in the material facts and clarify them in advance to save themselves headaches later.

For a mutual mistake to interfere with legal consent it must involve all of the following elements:

1. A basic assumption about the subject matter of the contract, i.e., the existence, quality, or quantity of the items to be exchanged;

2. A material effect on the agreement, i.e. the mistake must go to the essence of the agreement; and

3. An adverse effect on a party who did not agree to bear the risk of mistake at the time of the agreement.

The third condition is necessary to protect those who bargain with someone who has agreed to bear the risk of mistake at the time of the agreement, and then later wishes to avoid that risk when the contract does

---

[6] 159 ENG. REP. 375 (1864).

not work out as well as they had planned. An illustration would be where the adversely affected party had already agreed in the contract to accept the items "as is." Courts will not void contracts for reason of mutual mistake if even one of the preceding factors is missing.

Misrepresentation

Misrepresentations are similar to mistakes in that in both cases at least one of the parties is in error about a fact material to the agreement. However, a **misrepresentation** is an untruthful assertion by one of the parties about a material fact. The important thing is that one party said something that prevented the parties from the mental agreement necessary for legal assent.

The courts are insistent that there must be a meeting of the minds for a valid contract. Thus, they might rescind a contract even though the person making the false assertion may be entirely innocent of any intentional deception.

Innocent Misrepresentation

An **innocent misrepresentation** results from a false statement about a fact that is material to an agreement that the person making the statement believed to be true. In other words, the person who made the false statement had no **scienter**, that is, the person had no knowledge of the falsity of the claim.

Innocent misrepresentations permit the party who was misled by the false statement to rescind the contract, but the aggrieved party cannot sue for damages because the party who made the false statement had no intent to mislead. The reasoning in these cases has the appearance of the arguments in a mutual mistake case.

Case 16-2 gives a clear sense of the various elements the plaintiff must prove when trying to rescind a sales contract on grounds of innocent misrepresentation. As a prospective business person, the case should increase your awareness of the need to listen to and explain material facts *while the terms of the contract are being created.*

Case 16-2

Mark and Pam Siech, Plaintiffs-Respondents
v.
Erv's Sales & Service, Defendant-Appellant
Court of Appeals of Wisconsin
223 Wis. 2d 802, 598 N.W. 2d 456

The Sieches ordered a custom-made boat from Erv's Sales and Service after the sales agent had represented that, after delivery, they could add at least a forty-five-inch live well to the boat. The Sieches ordered the boat based upon this representation. They subsequently discovered that the live well could not be added because it would substantially compromise the boat's structural integrity, as well as void the manufacturer's warranty on the boat. After making this discovery, the Siech's refused delivery of the boat, and asked for their deposit to be returned. When the defendant refused to return their deposit, the plaintiffs sued in small claims court. The small claims court held that a recission of the contract was appropriate and ordered the defendant to return the $2,000 down payment. Defendant appealed.

JUDGE WEISEL

Rescission of a contract is an appropriate remedy when a person's manifestation of assent to the contract is induced by a fraudulent or material misrepresentation made by another person which the recipient is justified in relying upon. An innocent misrepresentation can form the basis for contract rescission. A nonfraudulent misrepresentation does not make a contract voidable unless it is material. Therefore, to demonstrate a claim for rescission of the sales contract based upon an innocent misrepresentation, the Sieches must show that: (1) Erv's made a misrepresentation of fact; (2) the misrepresentation was material; (3) the Sieches reliance on the misrepresentation induced them to enter the contract; and (4) the Sieches were justified in relying on the representation.

A misrepresentation of fact is an assertion that is not in accordance with the facts as they exist. In this instance, the trial court found that the representation of fact Erv's agent made was that at least a forty-five-inch live well could be added to the boat the Sieches ordered. The evidence reflects that, in fact, this representation was untrue. The trial court found that the proposed modification would significantly compromise the boat's structural integrity [and thus] voided the manufacturer's warranty for the boat. The representation that the modification was a feasible alternative to meet the Sieches desires was erroneous because the modification would have voided the warranty.

The trial court concluded that the installation of the well was material to the purchasers at the time of the order. A misrepresentation is material if it is likely to induce a reasonable person to manifest his assent by the misrepresentation, or if the maker knows that it is likely that the recipient will be induced to manifest his assent by the misrepresentation. Because Siech intended to use the boat for muskie tournament fishing, the lack of a sufficiently-sized live well rendered the boat unfit for his intended use. The necessity of the live well was fully disclosed to the sales agent, who fully understood that such a well was of critical importance to the Sieches. Notwithstanding such information, the agent represented that post-manufacturer modification creating a forty-five-inch live well was possible when, in fact, such modification ultimately turned out to be unfeasible. The trial court, therefore, properly concluded that the existence of at least a forty-five-inch live well was material to the purchaser entering into a contract for the purchase of this custom boat.

The trial court concluded that [Siech] was induced to enter into the contract for the purchase of the boat based upon the representation that a post-sales modification of the boat was possible. Siech testified that he wanted the boat for a particular purpose and that the representation the boat could be modified to meet that purpose substantially contributed to his decision to make the contract. The evidence is sufficient to support the element of reliance required for the rescission of the contract.

Finally, there is no basis in the record establishing that the Siech's reliance on the agent's misrepresentation was unjustified. The agent's assertion was not of peripheral importance, but rather was directed at the core issue of the sale, purchasing a boat conducive to muskie fishing. Further, there are no factual circumstances evident in the record indicating that the Siech's should not have taken this representation seriously.

Erv's contends that it is entitled to retain the $2,000 deposit because the Sieches breached the contract without justification, resulting in damages to Erv's, despite Erv's efforts to mitigate. We have determined that the trial court correctly concluded that the Sieches did not breach but were justified in rescinding the contract.

AFFIRMED.

1. Critical Thinking: What reasons did the court give for its decision that the Sieches were justified in rescinding the contract? Do you think there are alternative omitted reasons that would support the court's conclusion? What might those reasons be?

2. Ethical Decision Making: What was the ultimate purpose of the decision? In other words, what values are guiding the court's reasoning? How did the court's values conflict with Erv's values?

Negligent Misrepresentation

In some contract negotiations, one party negligently asserts a material fact that he or she thinks is true. A **negligent misrepresentation** occurs when the party making the statement would have known the truth about the fact had he or she used reasonable care to discover or reveal the fact. For example, a group of consumers recently brought a class action suit against Verizon Wireless for negligent misrepresentation because the quality of Verizon cellular service was poorer than landline phone service. Moreover, the consumer class group alleged that Verizon charged callers by rounding time to the full minute and billed airtime from the time the consumer hit the "send" button to the time the consumer hit the "end" button. The consumers argued that they would not have entered into the service contracts if they had been aware of these facts.[7]

Even though there was no actual intent to deceive, the party making the false statement is treated in contract law as if the intent were present. If this standard seems unfair, remember that the courts find negligent misrepresentation only when the party making the false statement should have known the truth had he used the skills and competence required of a person in the position or profession. The impact of negligent misrepresentation is identical to that of knowing misrepresentations, our next category.

To see the ethical justification for this legal rule, ask yourself how business would be affected if one of the parties to a bargain for a shipment of cloth knew that the law would protect her negligent representations. Would that knowledge increase or decrease the number of misrepresentations?

Fraudulent Misrepresentation

Any fraud on the part of a party to the contract provides a basis for recission. A **fraudulent misrepresentation** is a false representation of a material fact that is consciously false and intended to mislead the other party. Fraudulent misrepresentation is **intentional misrepresentation**. Here scienter is clear. The party making the misrepresentation either knows or believes that the factual claim is false, or knows that there is no basis for the assertion.

How can the parties be said to have assented when one of the parties was tricked into the "agreement" by a fraudulent misrepresentation? Thus, the agreement was not voluntary and can be rescinded on the grounds that there was no meeting of the minds.

Most, if not all, cultures have little sympathy for those who consciously mislead others in commercial activities. Even in countries like Mainland China, which are trying to encourage joint ventures and global commercial activity, fraudulent claims can end their hospitality to agreements with outsiders.[8] Accusations of fraudulent misrepresentation have resulted in heavy fines and even refusals to allow the fraudulent party to enter into any more agreements with Chinese firms.

To help see the requirements for a finding of fraudulent misrepresentation, start with the two elements from the definition:

1. A false statement about a past or existing fact that is either material to the contract or fraudulent. The false statement can be either an actual assertion, nondisclosure, or concealment.
2. Intent to deceive. Intent can be inferred from the particular circumstances.

Then add a third necessary element.

3. Justifiable reliance on the false statement by the innocent party to the agreement. Justifiable reliance is generally present unless the injured party knew, or should have known by the extravagance of the claim, that the false statement was indeed false. For example, a party could not justifiably rely on a claim by one party that a pea on her plate, while worth $1,000, was actually for sale at a price of $10. The extravagance of this claim about the value of a pea prevents justifiable reliance.

Finally, if damages are sought, the false statement must be material, and the defrauded party must have been injured by the misrepresentation.

Each of these elements can become a source of debate in any attempt to rescind a contract on grounds of fraudulent misrepresentation. Thus, it is your responsibility as a person who will be involved with dozens of contracts in your business activities to know these elements. A rescinded contract is a time consuming and expensive business opportunity that has gone wrong. *And don't forget that businesses can collect damages only from parties they can locate.*

Before we go into greater detail, consider Case 16-3, which looks at the elements of fraudulent misrepresentation. Follow the court's reasoning as they think through the elements of this attempt to rescind a contract.

---

[7] Jeffrey Silva, *Verizon Wireless Reaches Settlement in Consumer Class-Action Lawsuit*, RCR Wireless News, March 19, 2001, at 73.

[8] Charles D. Paglee, *Contracts and Agreements in the People's Republic of China* <http://www.qis.net.chinalaw/explan1.htm> (March 6, 1998).

Case 16-3

Gary W. Cruse and Venita R. Cruse

v.

Coldwell Banker/Graben Real Estate, Inc.
Supreme Court of Alabama
667 SO. 2d 714 (1995)

*M*r. and Mrs. Cruse sued Mr. and Mrs. Harris, Coldwell Banker, and Graben Real Estate, Inc., alleging defective workmanship in the construction of a house that they had bought from the Harrises, and alleging that the defendants had fraudulently misrepresented and/or suppressed material facts about the condition of the house.

When the Cruses began looking for a home, they contacted Graben Real Estate, and a Graben Real Estate agent took them to see the Harrises house. Randy Harris, a building contractor, had built the house for sale, and he and his wife were occupying it at that time. Graben Real Estate listed that house as "new" in its real estate advertisements, and the agent told the Cruses that it was new. She also told the Cruses that the house was comparable to, or even better than, the other houses in the neighborhood; that it was a good buy; and that if they purchased the house they could look forward to years of convenient, trouble-free living.

The Cruses signed a contract on November 11, 1992, to purchase the house from the Harris's. When they told the agent they wanted to hire an independent contractor to assess its condition, she told them that it was not really necessary to do so because Randy Harris was a contractor and because the house was well-built.

The Cruses signed an "Acceptance Inspection Contract," which stated that they had inspected the property or waived the right to do so and accepted it in "as is" condition, and that they based their decision to purchase on their own inspection and not on any representations by the broker.

Plaintiffs took possession of the residence in mid-December 1992 and, soon thereafter, they began noticing many defects in the structure and in its electrical wiring. They contacted Graben Real Estate, who sent an agent to remedy the problems. The defects continued and multiplied, so they sued. At the trial, defendants moved for summary judgment, which was granted. Plaintiffs appealed.

JUSTICE BUTTS

To establish fraudulent misrepresentations, the Cruses are required to show that Graben Real Estate made a false representation concerning a material fact and that they relied upon that representation, to their detriment. The Cruses contend that Graben Real Estate represented to them that the house was new; that, in reliance on that representation, they decided not to hire a contractor to inspect the house and discover its defects; and that reliance resulted in damage to them.

The unequivocal term "new," when applied to real estate, is not merely descriptive. It is a definite legal term that carries with it the implied warranty of habitability and prevents the realtor from invoking the protection of the doctrine of *caveat emptor*. Graben Real Estate marketed the house as "new," both in print and in direct response to the Cruses queries. In so doing, Graben Real Estate made statements that went beyond the patter of sales talk and became representations of material fact. Moreover, Gary Cruse testified…that he relied upon this representation in failing to hire a contractor to inspect the house before he bought it.

Graben Real Estate argues that even if it did misrepresent the newness of the house, the Cruses could not have justifiably believed the misrepresentation and relied upon it to the point that they would not closely inspect the house before buying it. Graben Real Estate relies heavily on the fact that the Cruses knew that the house was being occupied by the Harris's at the time of the sale, and concludes that this alone should have proved to the Cruses that the house was not actually new.…We do not agree that the mere knowledge of the Harrises prior occupancy so wholly contradicted the printed and spoken representations of Graben Real Estate that the Cruses could not, as a matter of law, have justifiably relied upon them.

Graben Real Estate also argues that, regardless of whether the house was new or was used, the Cruses cannot recover because they signed an "as is" agreement at the time of the sale, thereby, Graben Real Estate says, accepting the condition of the house without a prior inspection. Graben Real Estate relies on *Hope v. Brannan*, wherein this Court held that buyers of a 58-year-old house who signed a statement accepting the house "as is," without independently inspecting it for defects, could not maintain an action for fraud arising from the seller's statements concerning the condition of the house.

Graben Real Estate's reliance on *Hope* is misplaced; in *Hope*, the house was not new, nor was it represented to be new. A buyer's failure to inspect the premises of a 58-year-old house before signing an "as is" agreement is hardly the equivalent of the Cruses failure to inspect the premises of a house that their realtor had represented to be new.

The evidence establishes that Graben Real Estate misrepresented a material fact and creates a jury question as to whether the Cruses could have justifiably relied upon this misrepresentation in deciding not to closely inspect the house before buying it. The fact that the Cruses knew the house was occupied by a third party before they bought it, along with the fact that they signed an "as is" agreement, separate from the purchase contract, for a house they claim to have regarded as new, are elements for the jury to consider.

REVERSED AND REMANDED.

1. Critical Thinking: The court considers one case that is analogous to the case at hand. In the court's eyes, how does this case affect the Cruse case? Do you agree with the court's interpretation of how this analogous case fits with the Cruse case?
2. Ethical Decision Making: Who are the relevant stakeholders affected by this decision?

Let's now revisit each of the elements of fraudulent misrepresentation. While the elements may have seemed relatively straightforward when they were presented, they become more complicated in the context of actual disagreements among parties to a contract.

Suppose that in the case discussed at the start of this chapter, the second Allstate adjuster argued that the Kramers' attorney had engaged in fraudulent misrepresentation with regard to the settlement agreement. How difficult would it have been for Allstate to demonstrate this fraudulent misrepresentation?

False Assertion of Fact

For fraudulent misrepresentation to be the basis for a contract recission, the statement of fact does not have to be an actual assertion. Either **concealment** or **nondisclosure** can be treated as the equivalent of an actual assertion. Concealment involves the *active* hiding of the truth about a material fact, e.g., removing 20,000 miles from the odometer on a car before selling it. Nondisclosure is different because it refers to a failure to provide pertinent information about the projected contract. Under ordinary situations associated with a legal bargain, there is no obligation for a party to bring up any and all facts one might possess. Each individual is, to a large extent, treated as a responsible decision maker. Until recently, the courts have been hesitant to use nondisclosure as a basis for rescinding a contract because it is a passive form of misleading conduct. Now, however, courts treat nondisclosure as having the same legal effect as an actual false assertion if:

1. A relationship of trust exists between the parties to the contract. In these situations the relationship provided a reasonable basis for one party's expectation that the other would never act to defraud him or her.

2. There is failure to correct assertions of fact that are no longer true in light of events that have occurred since the initial consent to the terms of the agreement. For example, suppose you agree to purchase a "rust-free" car next month. The seller fails to tell you that there now is rust on the car.

Nondisclosure is especially likely to provide the basis for recission when one party has information about a basic assumption of the deal that is unavailable to the other party. *As a result of this logic, sellers have a special duty to disclose because they know more about the structural make-up of the item being purchased.* As the Global Context feature indicates, other countries may have different understandings of the amount of information for which it is reasonable to hold the buyer responsible.

Intent to Deceive

Scienter is present when the party accused of making the fraudulent assertion believed that the assertion was false or made the claim without any regard for whether it was true or false. Alternatively, intent to deceive is present when the party making the false statement claims or implies personal knowledge of the accuracy of the assertion. Any resulting assent is not legal because the injured party was not allowed to join the mind of the deceiving party. The party with scienter wanted the contract to be fulfilled on the basis of a falsehood.

Justifiable Reliance on the False Assertion

What responsibilities does an injured party have in instances where a false assertion was made by the other party? As we said earlier, the injured party has no justifiable claim of fraud when the party relied on assertions that should have been obviously false. Anyone who pays for a house in reliance on the claim that it was "built before the founding of our country" cannot, later, try to rescind the contract on grounds of fraudulent misrepresentation.

In addition, parties to contracts cannot successfully claim they justifiably relied on a false assertion of fact when the error in the statement would have been clear to anyone who had inspected the item being exchanged. However, even this duty to inspect is declining in modern contract law. Increasing responsibility is being placed on the person who made the erroneous assertion.

Undue Influence

When legal assent is present, both parties to the agreement are assumed to have made their own choices based on complete freedom to consent to or reject the terms of the bargain. But many factors in our lives can work together to make our choices anything but free. **Undue influence** refers to those special relationships where one party has taken advantage of their dominant position in a relationship to unduly persuade the other party. The persuasive efforts of the dominant party must have interfered with the ability of the other party to freely make a decision. When people are bargaining with their attorney, doctor, guardian, relative, or any relationship involving a high degree of trust, they can be persuaded by unusual pressures unique to those relationships.

The assent that results may not be legal consent. The courts may see the undue relationship as interfering with the free choice required of an enforceable contract. Whatever contracts result from undue influence can be voided.

Not all contracts among parties where undue influence might arise are likely to be rescinded. The courts look to (1) the mental condition of the person who would ordinarily rely on the guidance of the dominant party and (2) the extent to which the dominant party used their persuasive powers to "produce" the assent of the other party.

The following factors enter into the finding of undue influence:

- Was the dominant party rushing the other party to consent?
- Did the dominant party gain undue enrichment from the agreement?
- Was the nondominant party isolated from other advisors at the time of the agreement?
- Is the contract unreasonable in the sense that the results of the exchange overwhelmingly benefit the dominant party?

The more these factors are present in a particular agreement, the more likely courts will be to rescind the contract on grounds of undue influence.

For example, a recent undue interest case against Disney[9] will eventually be decided on the basis of the set of circumstances that led to a dying Disney executive's surrendering $2 million in benefits on his deathbed. The Ninth Circuit Court of Appeals reinstated the lawsuit based on the circumstances of a hospital meet-

---

[9] *Rothberg v. Disney,* 168 F. 3d 501, 1999 WL 51495. (9th Cir. (Cal.)).

Global Context:
Consumer Contracts Law in Japan

In 1997, the Japanese Social Policy Council, an advisory body to the Prime Minister, after studying the application of civil law in the country, recognized that the job of consumers is growing more complicated and that there is a significant gap between consumers and businesses in their access to information and knowledge, as well as in their negotiating power. Because it cannot honestly be said that consumers and businesses are equal, as contracting parties are presumed to be under the country's Civil Code, the Council developed a special Consumer Contracts Law. This legislation places consumers and businesses on a more equal footing.

Under the Consumer Contracts Law, if a business fails to provide a consumer with information or makes misrepresentations concerning basic or other important contractual matters that are necessary for the consumer to make a judgment about the contract, and if the consumer would not have entered into the contract had the information been provided or the misrepresentation not been made, the consumer may cancel the contract. This provision is said to be applicable whenever a business, in trying to induce a consumer to enter into a contract (1) fails to provide information about the contents of the contract; (2) fails to provide important information necessary for the consumer to make the decision to enter into the contract; or (3) makes misrepresentations. In many of these cases, the consumer would not have been entitled to relief under the civil code because of its strict requirements for the application of fraud.

---

ing in which a Disney financial officer obtained the signed waiver of benefits. The plaintiff's illness plus the $2 million gain that Disney and its insurer stood to gain was enough to take the case to a jury.

Duress

Duress is a much more visible and active interference with free will than is undue influence. **Duress** is found when one party was forced to consent to the agreement by the wrongful act of another.

The wrongful act may come in various forms. Any of the following would trigger a successful request for recission on grounds of duress:

- The threat of physical harm or extortion to gain consent to a contract.
- The threat to file a criminal lawsuit unless consent is given to the terms of the contract. (Threats to bring civil cases against a party does not constitute duress unless the suit is frivolous.)

- Economic duress has been established; a person's economic interests have been threatened. (Examples of economic duress could include such things as a requirement to sign a second agreement before completing the terms of the initial contract, requiring a higher price than was contained in the original agreement, etc.)

The injured party makes the case for duress by demonstrating that the threat left no reasonable alternatives to signing the contract. Their point is that the free will necessary for legal consent was removed by the specifics of the threat. Notice in the Global Context feature—later in the chapter—that Australia has a special form of duress that it recognizes.

When a party has entered into an agreement under duress, the party can argue that the duress should cause the contract to be voided. For example, suppose you were pressured verbally for an hour to sign a contract with a dating service; then, you eventually signed the agreement. Do you think that you could later claim that the contract should be voided because you signed the agreement under duress? Why or why not?

Consider the extent to which the threat in Case 16-4 left the plaintiff no reasonable options other than signing the agreement.

Case 16-4

Elizabeth Curran

v.

Ho Sung Kwon
United States 7th Circuit Court of Appeals
153 F. 3d 481 (7th Cir. 1998)

*I*n 1982, Ho Sung Kwon tried to develop a relationship with Elizabeth Curran, a professional model who was not interested in Kwon. In an attempt to gain Curran's interest, Kwon fabricated a modeling contest sponsored by Revlon. After Curran won the fabricated contest in New York, Kwon, the "supervisor" of the contest, accompanied her to Paris for the next stage of the contest. However, when Curran discovered she was suppose to share a hotel room with Kwon, she refused to stay in the room. Kwon left the room, but he left his passport and $1,200 in cash with Curran.

The next morning, Curran tried to fly back to New York. When Kwon discovered that his passport and money were missing, he reported the theft. Curran was arrested at the airport and held overnight. Although Kwon did not want to press charges, the French prosecutor set a trial for two days later. She sought the advice of legal counsel in Paris, and her father also flew to Paris for support. Curran was acquitted, and one day later she signed a release in which she was paid $10,260 so that Kwon and Revlon could be released from any claim which might be brought by Curran regarding the fabricated modeling contest. She left Paris the same day she signed the release.

However, soon after she returned to the United States, Curran disavowed the release and returned payment to Kwon. Approximately one year later, she filed suit against Kwon and Revlon, alleging negligence, fraudulent misrepresentation, and false arrest. Kwon filed for summary judgment, citing the release Curran signed in Paris. However, Curran claimed she signed the release under duress; thus, the release was voidable. She stated that she was "tired, confused, and fearful during her stay in Paris," and she argued that she was afraid that she would not be able to leave the country if she did not sign the release. The District Court ruled that the release was not signed under duress and was not voidable.

JUDGE RIPPLE

Curran makes no claim that she can meet the high standard of proof required under French law to prove the "violence" that would justify vitiating the contract. Nor, assuming Illinois law did apply, do we believe that she could show the type of coercion contemplated by the governing Illinois cases…(defining duress as "a condition where one is induced by a wrongful act or threat of another to make a contract under circumstances which deprive him of the exercise of his free will, and it may be conceded that a contract executed under duress is voidable"). Put simply, she cannot, on this record, demonstrate that her execution of the release was not the product of her free will.

As the district court noted, Curran had endured some difficult circumstances in the days before the execution of the release. Nevertheless, it is undisputed that, at the time she executed the document, she had been exonerated of any criminal charges under French law and had been assured that she was free to leave France. The claim that her freedom was contingent on her signing the release is simply not supported by the record. Indeed, she had rejected a settlement offer prior to the disposition of those charges. Moreover, at the time that she executed the release, she had the advice of both her French and American counsel and had familial support through the presence of her father. Under these circumstances, the record simply would not support a determination by the trier of fact that she executed the release under duress. She was not "bereft of the quality of mind essential to the making of a contract."

AFFIRMED.

1. Critical Thinking: Think about the court's conclusion and reasons. What do you think about the evidence that support's the court's argument? Does this evidence persuade you? Why or why not?

2. Ethical Decision Making: Suppose you are a business manager for Revlon. Your company's role was quite peripheral in this case; however, your name was involved. If your company is guided by the public exposure test, would you take any kind of action in this case? If so, what would you do?

Global Context: Duress in Australia

Australia recognizes a special category of duress that we do not acknowledge in the United States: *duress of goods*. Duress of goods occurs whenever an illegitimate threat is made to hold onto goods unless a payment is made or an agreement is entered into. This situation can be contrasted to a situation where someone legitimately holds onto goods when money is owed to them or they have been used as security for a loan.

Australia also recognizes *economic duress*, which is the unacceptable use of economic power to place the victim in a situation where the victim has no practical alternative but to submit to the accompanying demand.

To prove economic duress, a plaintiff must establish that: (1) pressure was used to procure plaintiff's assent to an agreement or to the payment of money; (2) that the pressure was illegitimate in the circumstance; (3) the pressure in fact contributed to the person assenting to the transaction; and (4) the person's assent to the transaction was reasonable in the circumstances.

Just as with economic duress in the United States, it is often unclear when pressure is illegitimate. A threat to do something unlawful is almost always undue pressure. A threat to use the civil legal process is usually considered lawful, unless the contemplated legal action would clearly be an abuse of process. "Driving a hard bargain" or refusing to do any more business with someone in the future is not generally regarded as economic duress, however.

Unconscionability

The appropriateness of consent may also be questioned whenever one of the parties has so much more bargaining power than the other, that the stronger party dictates the terms of the agreement. Such an agreement can be rescinded on grounds of **unconscionability**. The disproportionate amount of power possessed by the one party to the contract has made a mockery of the idea of free will, a necessity for legal consent. To enforce an unconscionable agreement would make the court a partner in an unfair exchange.

Consider this example of possible unconscionability. All contracts signed by Wal-Mart and its vendors

[10] This information was discussed in *Wal-Mart Headed To Trial Over Vendor Contract*, 34 DISCOUNT STORE NEWS, January 2, 1995 at 4.

include a standard clause, providing Wal-Mart the right to unilaterally and arbitrarily cancel its orders, at any stage of production prior to shipment.[10] Does Wal-Mart's size and power relative to that of any of its vendors make the clause unconscionable?

Although unconscionability has traditionally been limited to the sale of goods under the Uniform Commercial Code, many courts are becoming more comfortable with extending the idea when they see business contracts written by one party and then presented to the other party with the threat to "take it or leave it." Such contracts are referred to as adhesion contracts.

Follow the judge's reasoning in Case 16-5 to review the type of reasoning that makes up a claim for unconscionability.

Case 16-5

Orville and Maxine Arnold. Plaintiffs

v.

United Companies Lending & Michael T. Searls, Defendants

Supreme Court of Appeals of West Virginia
204 W. Va. 229 (1998)

On September 17, 1996, Michael Searls came to the residence of Orville and Maxine Arnold, an elderly couple. He offered to arrange a loan for the Amolds, acting as a loan broker. He procured a loan for them. Out of the loan proceeds, a mortgage broker fee of $940 was paid to Searls and/or Accent Financial Services, with which Searls is affiliated.

At the loan closing, United Lending had the benefit of legal counsel, while the Arnolds apparently did not. During the course of the transaction, the Arnolds were presented with more than twenty-five documents to sign. Among these documents were a promissory note, reflecting a principal sum of $19,300 and a yearly interest rate of 12.990%; a Deed of Trust, giving United Lending a security interest in the Arnolds real estate; and a two-page form labeled "Acknowledgment and Agreement to Mediate or Arbitrate," which stated that all legal controversies arising out of the loan would be resolved through non-appealable, confidential arbitration, and that all damages would be direct damages, with no punitive damages available. However, this agreement to not arbitrate did not limit the lender's right to pursue legal actions in a court of law relating to collection of the loan.

On July 10, 1997, the Arnolds filed suit against United Lending and Searls, seeking a declaratory judgment adjudging the arbitration agreement to be void and unenforceable. On August 11, 1997, United Lending moved to dismiss the entire action on the basis of the compulsory arbitration agreement. The circuit court certified three questions to the state supreme court.

JUSTICE McCUSKEY

We reformulate the question as follows: Whether an arbitration agreement entered into as part of a consumer loan transaction containing a substantial waiver of the consumer's rights, including access to the courts, while preserving for all practical purposes the lender's right to a judicial forum, is void as a matter of law.

The drafters of the Uniform Consumer Credit Code explained that the [basic test] of unconscionability is whether…the conduct involved is, or the contract or clauses involved are so one sided as to be unconscionable under the circumstances existing at the time the conduct occurs or is threatened or at the time of the making of the contract.

…[T]his Court stated:

[W]here a party alleges that the arbitration provision was unconscionable, or was thrust upon him because he was unwary and taken advantage of, or that the contract was one of adhesion, the question of whether an arbitration provision was bargained for and valid is a matter of law for the court to determine by reference to the entire contract…"[a] determination of unconscionability must focus on the relative positions of the parties, the adequacy of the bargaining position, the meaningful alternatives available to the plaintiff, and 'the existence of unfair terms in the contract.'"

Applying the rule…leads us to the inescapable conclusion that the arbitration agreement between the Arnolds and United Lending is "void for unconscionability" as a matter of law.…The relative positions of the parties, a national corporate lender on one side and elderly, unsophisticated consumers on the other, were "grossly unequal." In addition, there is no evidence that the loan broker made any other loan option available to the Arnolds. In fact, the record does not indicate that the Arnold's were seeking a loan, but rather were solicited by defendant Searls. Thus, the element of "a comparable, meaningful alternative" to the loan from United Lending is lacking. Because the Arnolds had no meaningful alternative to obtaining the loan from United Lending, and also did not have the benefit of legal counsel during the transaction, their bargaining position was clearly inadequate when compared to that of United Lending.

Given the nature of this arbitration agreement, combined with the great disparity in bargaining power, one can safely infer that the terms were not bargained for and that allowing such a one-sided agreement to stand would unfairly defeat the Arnolds legitimate expectations.

Finally, the terms of the agreement are "unreasonably favorable" to United Lending. United Lending's acts or omissions could seriously damage the Arnolds, yet the Arnolds only recourse would be to submit the matter to binding arbitration. At the same time, United Lending's access to the courts is wholly preserved in every conceivable situation where United Lending would want to secure judicial relief against the Arnolds. The wholesale waiver of the Arnolds rights, together with the complete preservation of United Lending's rights, "is inherently inequitable and unconscionable because in a way it nullifies all the other provisions of the contract."

JUDGMENT FOR PLAINTIFF.

1. Critical Thinking: Why does the court believe that the arbitration agreement is unconscionable? Do you agree with the court's ruling?

2. Ethical Decision Making: What value seems to be guiding the court's decision in the Arnold case? What value(s) is in conflict with the court's preferred value? Why?

Allstate Wrap-up

At trial, a superior court ruled that Allstate had to honor the $3,500 settlement agreement. The court stated that Allstate's unilateral mistake was not due to misrepresentation of the Kramers' attorney. Therefore, Allstate's mistake was not grounds for recision of the agreement.

Perhaps you think that a simple mistake occurred, and Allstate should not have been required to pay. Suppose that the facts of the case were changed such that Allstate made an agreement to purchase a large number of items from a manufacturer. After the manufacturer completes production of these items, Allstate argues that the agreement was made by mistake and refuses to pay. The manufacturer is stuck with the items.

The courts want to offer predictability to contracts; consequently, they would probably require Allstate to adhere to the agreement to purchase the items from the manufacturer and accept the items. Similarly, in the Allstate case at the start of the chapter, the court was offering predictability to settlement agreements by forcing Allstate to pay.

	Summary
Importance of Assent	Without legal assent, there is little predictability to contracts.
Mistake	**Definition**—erroneous belief about the material facts of the contract at the time the agreement is made. **Unilateral mistake**—an error by one party about a material fact in a contract. **Mutual mistake**—both parties to a contract are mistaken about either a current or past material fact.
Misrepresentation	**Definition**—intentional untruthful assertion by one of the parties about material fact. **Innocent misrepresentation**—when the party making the false assertion believed it to be true. **Negligent misrepresentation**—the party making the statement would have known the truth about the false assertion had he used reasonable care to discover or reveal the fact. **Fraudulent misrepresentation**—a false representation of a material fact that is consciously false and intended to mislead the other party. Elements of fraudulent misrepresentation: 1. False assertion of fact. 2. Intent to deceive. 3. Justifiable reliance on false assertion.
Undue Influence	**Definition**—persuasive efforts of a dominant party who has used a special relationship with the injured party to interfere with his or her free choice of the terms of the contract.
Duress	**Definition**—one party threatens the other with a wrongful act unless assent is given.
Unconscionability	**Definition**—one party has so much relative bargaining power that he or she, in effect, dictates the terms of the contract.

Review Questions and Case Problems

1. Explain why it is important to know the difference between a unilateral and bilateral mistake.

2. Explain the differences among innocent, negligent, and intentional misrepresentation.

3. Explain the elements needed to prove duress and undue influence.

4. Olga Mestrovic, the wife of an internationally known sculptor and artist, died owning a number of his works of art. Her will directed all the artwork to be sold with the proceeds split among the surviving family members. She also owned real estate that, likewise, was to be sold. The executor, 1st Source Bank, sold the real estate to Wilkins, along with specified pieces of personal property that were in the house, such as the refrigerator and the stove. When Wilkins took possession of the property, he complained to the bank that the property was a mess. The bank said they would either hire a rubbish removal service, or allow the Wilkins to clean it up and the bank would pay him for doing so.

In the process of cleaning up, Wilkins discovered eight drawings and one sculpture done by the artist. Wilkins claimed that he owned these items under his agreement with the bank, but the bank sought to recover them. The probate court ruled that there was no contract for the sale of the works of art. What argument do you think that Wilkins made on appeal? How do you think the court ruled? Why? *Wilkins v. 1st Source Bank*, 548 N.E. 2d 170 (Ind. Ct. App. 1990).

5. Appellant Independent School District No. 622, preparing to move into a new building one block away, called three movers to get bids for the cost of moving the school's property. They received bids of $19,854, $59,880, and $83,972. Because the lower bid was so much lower than the other bids, an employee of the school district contacted the company to make sure the bid was correct. The firm that made the low bid assured him that the company was "comfortable with the bid."

Prior to the move, the parties discussed the terms of the agreement and the dates. The contract was issued January 1997. The parties discussed various details of the move on six additional occasions. On the first day of the move, appellant received a requested invoice for the move, on which the estimate of $20,000 was listed. Midway through the move, appellant was presented with an invoice for $16,686, which he paid. At the end of the move, appellant received a second invoice for $49,854. He paid $3,168, which was the amount remaining on the original bid. Respondent sued for breach of contract, and sought damages of $45,991, the unpaid portion of the second invoice.

At the trial court, summary judgment was given to the School District. What argument do you think the Appellant made as to why he was entitled to the full amount of the second invoice? Look carefully at the facts surrounding the making of the contract. Why do you think the respon-

dent was or was not successful? *A.A. Metcalf v. North St. Paul -Maplewood-Oakdale Schools*, 587 N.W. 2d 311 (1998).

6. In December 1992, Koontz entered into an agreement with Tatum & Denziger (T & D), an architectural firm, whereby the firm was to design a residence for Koontz at a price of ten percent of the actual cost of construction. When the parties entered into the agreement, the firm estimated that the entire process, from design through final construction, should be able to be completed in less than twenty-four months. Koontz received the first plans in January 1993, sent them back for modification, and got the second set back on June 10, 1993. At that time, T & D estimated that the cost of construction would be $800,000. Koontz took bids for construction from three preselected contractors, and the bids he received ranged from $983,000 to $1.2 million. Koontz immediately terminated his contract with T & D, and asked that all architectural fees paid through the date of the termination be returned. T & D offered to continue working on the project and suggested revisions to lower costs, but Koontz refused. He ultimately hired a different architect, who designed a house that Koontz constructed for $870,000.

After the house was completed in 1996, Koontz sued the architect for, among other claims, negligent misrepresentation, alleging that T & D negligently represented how much the construction costs would be, the time frame of the design phase, and the amount of the architect's fees. T&D filed a motion for summary judgment, which was granted. What do you believe the outcome of Koontz's appeal was? Why? *Koontz v. Thomas and Denzinger*, 1999 WL 31459 (S.C. App.).

7. Audrey Vokes was a 51-year-old widow who wanted to become an "accomplished dancer." She was invited to attend a "dance party" at J. P. Davenports' School of Dancing, an Arthur Murray franchise. She subsequently signed up for dance classes, at which she received elaborate praise. Her instructor initially sold her eight half-hour dance lessons for $14.50 each, to be used one each month. She was continually told that she had excellent potential, and that she was developing into a beautiful dancer. Eventually, she purchased a total of 2,302 hours worth of dance lessons for a total of $31,090.45. When it finally became clear to Vokes that she was not developing her dance skills, in part because she had trouble even hearing the musical beat, she sued Arthur Murray. What was the basis of her argument? The trial court initially dismissed her case. What do you think the result of her appeal was? *Vokes v. Arthur Murray*, 212 So. 2d 906 (1968).

8. Arnold Olson and his now deceased spouse deeded their property to their five children in equal shares, and reserved for themselves a life estate in the property (a legal right to live on the property until they die). During a subsequent conversation with one son and the son's wife, held in the presence of two of the other children, he granted his son part of that property, which included the home and several buildings, as long as they promised not to sell

the property while he was alive, because he wanted to live in a trailer on the property.

Olson then executed a second deed conveying the property, but failed to include the life estate in this second deed. The father lived in his trailer on the property for four years. Then the son told him that he would have to move because the property was being sold. The father and other four children sued to have the contract reformed on the grounds of mistake. The trial court agreed, and reformed the contract to include the provision for the father's life estate. Why do you think the appellate court either affirmed or reversed the lower court's decision? *Olson v. Olson*, 1998 WL 170111.

9. Plaintiff Stirlen was the chief financial officer for Supercuts. On numerous occasions, he informed Lipson, to whom he reported directly, and other corporate officers, of various operating problems he felt had contributed to the general decline in Supercuts' retail profits and of "accounting irregularities" he feared might be in violation of state and federal statutes and regulations. After Stirlen brought his concerns to the company's auditor, Lipson allegedly reprimanded him, accused him of being a "troublemaker" and told him that if he did not reverse his position on the issues taken to the auditor he would no longer be considered a "member of the team." He was terminated the following month, and subsequently filed suit for wrongful discharge. Supercuts' general counsel moved to compel arbitration under the compulsory arbitration provision of the employment contract between the parties.

The contract provided that all claims arising out of the plaintiff's employment, including civil rights actions and tort claims, must be submitted to arbitration within one year of the date on which the dispute arose, or the plaintiff waives his right to pursue the claim. Damages that could be awarded through arbitration were limited to "a money award not to exceed the amount of actual damages for breach of contract, less any proper offset for mitigation of such damages, and the parties shall not be entitled to any other remedy at law or in equity, including, but not limited to, other money damages, punitive damages, specific performance, and/or injunctive relief." In addition, if an employee submitted a dispute to arbitration, the employee's employment would immediately cease, as would any claims he had to unpaid benefits, without any penalty to the company, pending the outcome of the arbitration.

The agreement did not totally prevent the use of the courts, however. It provided that the following need not be submitted to arbitration: "Any action initiated by the Company seeking specific performance or injunctive or other equitable relief in connection with any breach…of this Agreement." The trial court found that this agreement was unconscionable. How do you believe the appellate court ruled on this case? Why? *Stirlen v. Supercuts, Inc., et al.*, 51 Cal. App. 1519 (1997).

10. Paul Wurtz, president and sole stockholder of Hotel Luzern Inc., brought suit against William Fleischman, a real estate broker, for his refusal to convey nine and one half units of Lakeside Habitat Developments valued at $47,500 to him. Fleischman and Wurtz had agreed that Fleischman would purchase some property and trade it for Wurtz's hotel property, valued at $300,000. However, Fleischman had difficulty arranging the financing to purchase the hotel property. Consequently, the closing date for the property transaction was changed several times. Because the closing date was changed due to Fleischman's difficulties, Wurtz told him that he would have to increase the value of the property he was willing to exchange or Wurtz would withdraw the exchange offer. Thus, Fleischman offered the nine and a half units of Lakeside Habitat Developments as additional property that he would eventually convey to Wurtz when the transaction was completed. Fleischman then signed an agreement whereby he committed himself to transferring the units to Wurtz. Fleischman testified that he signed the agreement only to ensure that the larger deal would go through; he never intended to transfer the nine and a half units. Fleischman claimed that Wurtz made the demand for additional property the night before the original closing date. Consequently, Fleischman was afraid of financial ruin if the larger deal didn't close. What argument did Fleischman use to claim the contract should be revoked? Was he successful? Why or why not? *Wurtz v. Fleischman*, 293 N.W. 2d 155 (1980).

11. Rita McKnee sought to have her marriage annulled on an alleged basis of mistaken identity of the person she married. She married Bob McKnee in 1963. Rita discovered that Bob had a violent and uncontrollable temper. In 1971, Bob tried to run her over with an automobile and then tried to shoot her. They separated. Through the criminal proceedings against Bob, Rita learned that he had been convicted of robbery in 1952 and was sentenced to the state penitentiary for five years. Furthermore, Rita discovered that Bob's real name was Robert Allen Weaver. Rita wanted her marriage annulled, claiming that a mistake had occurred because she married a man under a false name. Do you think that Rita's claim was successful? Why or why not? *Rita Nell Foster McKnee v. Bob McKnee*, 262 So. 2d 111 (2nd Cir. 1972).

12. Mabayomije Alabi called DHL, a worldwide air express service for small packages and envelopes, and requested an envelope pickup for delivery to his cousin in London, England. He asked whether the envelope could be insured for $15,000 and was told that the insurance limit was $10,000. When the courier arrived, Alabi again asked whether the envelope could be insured for $15,000. He was again told that the limit was $10,000. Alabi paid $76 for the transfer of the envelope and insurance. The bill included a space where Alabi was asked to provide a description of the contents of the envelope. Alabi wrote "documents regarding school bills." DHL lost the envelope. DHL notified Alabi that the envelope was lost and conducted a search for the envelope. Alabi claimed that he had put $15,000 cash inside the envelope and brought suit. DHL moved for summary judgment, claiming that the contract was voidable because Alabi misrepresented the

contents of the envelope. How did the court rule? Why? *Mabayomije Alabi v. DHL Airways, Inc.*, 583 A. 2d 1358 (1990).

13. Ken and Carol began dating. In anticipation of marriage, they began to discuss a prenuptial agreement. Each had been previously married twice. They couldn't reach an agreement and split up. They reunited two years later and planned to get married. Again, they discussed the possibility of a prenuptial agreement. Ken consulted an attorney, who drafted an agreement. The wedding date was set for August 10, 1986. Ken insisted that the agreement be signed prior to the marriage although Carol was reluctant. However, on August 8, 1986, both parties signed the agreement, two days before their wedding.

In April 1987, they separated. Carol filed suit for dissolution of marriage. She argued that she had signed the prenuptial agreement under duress and undue influence by Ken. She claimed that she felt compelled to sign the document because Ken was insistent that the agreement was a prerequisite for marriage. However, Ken repeatedly asked Carol to obtain legal counsel regarding the agreement. Furthermore, Carol participated in some of the changes made to the draft agreement. Will Carol's claims be successful? Why or why not? *Carol M. Liebelt v. Kenneth H. Liebelt*, 118 Idaho 845 (1990).

Assignment on the Internet

Internet commerce is growing so rapidly that it is hard to even measure its growth with any accuracy. Many Internet sites are trying to get you to agree to make a purchase. Now that you understand what is necessary for legal assent, find a site that could benefit from your advice. List the steps you would urge them to take to avoid possible contract recission on grounds of mistake or misrepresentation.

On the Internet

http://law.anu.edu.au *Provides information about Australian contract law and related issues.*

http://www.law.cornell.edu/topics/ contracts.html *Contains references to recent contract law cases, international contract law, and other Internet sites where contract law is analyzed.*

http://www.lawrev.state.nj.us/contract.htm *Provides information about a New Jersey Law Revision regarding the unconscionability of standard contracts.*

http://www.zmlalaw.com/promise.htm *Examines how prenuptial agreements may be unconscionable.*

http://home.vicnet.net.au/~fcrc/crj/ 2_3a.htm *Considers the role of unconscionability, duress, and undue influences in contracts between married people.*

Oral Promises to Share Profits

Larry Johnson, aka Maurice Starr, served as a promoter for a musical group called New Kids on the Block. His contract entitled him to a share of New Kids' music royalties and other revenues. The New Kids proved to be a huge financial success, earning $74.1 million in 1990 and $115 million in 1991, and ranking as the highest paid 1991 performers according to Forbes Magazine.[1]

Jeffrey Furst alleged that he loaned Starr $115, 000 in the 1980's as "seed money" to help promote the New Kids, and that in return Starr orally promised to give Furst a 25 percent share in the music group.[2] Starr repaid the loan with interest but denied that an oral partnership agreement existed, claiming that the loan was for a mortgage and for personal expenses. Starr refused to share any New Kids profits with Furst.[3]

1. *Assume that you were Furst, how could you prove that a contract existed if that contract had never been put into writing?*
2. *Would Starr's profit-sharing agreement, even if proved, have to be in writing to be enforceable?*

---

[1] Judy Rakowsky, *New Kids' Profits on the Block*, BOSTON GLOBE, November 18, 1995 at p. 13, Metro/Region.

[2] Paul Sullivan, *Testimony Opens in Suit Against New Kids Founder*, BOSTON HERALD, News, page 17, November 15, 1995 at News, p. 17.

[3] Rakowsky, supra note 1.

CHAPTER 17

Contracts in Writing

Contracts that Must Be in Writing

Elements of a Writing

Maxims of Contract Interpretation

Parol Evidence Rule

Promissry Estoppel as a Substitute for a Writing

The preceding chapters examined the required elements of a contract, agreement, consideration, capacity, and legality, as well as the first defense to enforcing a contract, reality of assent. This chapter examines the second defense to contract enforcement: a missing or faulty writing. Certain types of contracts have to be in writing to be enforceable; others do not.

The writing requirement originated with a seventeenth-century English statute called the "Act for the Prevention of Fraud and Perjuries," commonly called the statute of frauds. The statute was enacted to prevent someone from falsely claiming that an oral contract existed, when in fact no contract was ever formed. Every state has adopted its own version of the statute that lists particular categories of contracts that must be in writing to be enforceable. A contract that must be in writing to be enforceable is said to fall within the statute of frauds. A contract that does not require a writing is said to be outside the statute of frauds, or simply, outside the statute.

The name of the statute may be a bit misleading because it has relatively little to do with fraud. The purpose of the statute is to provide evidence that a contract was intended and evidence of the terms of that contract. As illustrated in the Starr case, when contracts are not reduced to writings, the courts can be faced with disputes as to what was said and done between the parties. We will see that the requirement of a writing can be satisfied informally, perhaps through a collection of letters, invoices, memorandums, faxes, and e-mail correspondences. But for certain types of contracts, if there is no written evidence of the essential terms of the contract, together with the signatures of the parties, then

the contract is not enforceable.

This chapter explores the main categories of contracts that fall within the statute of frauds. It then examines what terms must be in writing, the signature requirement, rules of contract interpretation, and the parol evidence rule, which specifies when it is appropriate to look outside a written contract for additional contract terms. The chapter closes with a discussion of when principles of promissory estoppel can substitute for a writing. Understanding when a writing is required and how to write a contract so that it will be interpreted as intended are two of the most essential legal lessons managers should learn.

Contracts that Must Be in Writing

The general rule is that oral contracts are fully enforceable. The five main exceptions to this rule are numbered below. Each of these categories of contracts requires a writing. There are a few other, less common, types of contracts that also need a writing, and we consider these at the close of this section. Contracts that must be evidenced by a signed writing include:

1. Contracts for the sale of an interest in real property (land sales).
2. Contracts that cannot be performed in one year (one year rule).
3. Contracts for the sale of goods for $500 or more (UCC Sec. 2-201).
4. Contracts for the sale of intellectual property for $5,000 or more (UCC Sec. 1-206).
5. Contracts to answer for the debt of another (surety agreements).

Contracts for the Sale of an Interest in Real Property

The first category of contracts that fall within the statute of frauds involves real estate contracts. Real property is defined as "land and things attached to land" such as a buildings, trees, soil, and minerals. All other property is called personal property. Contracts to sell an interest in real property are enforceable only if they are in writing.

The inclusion of real estate contracts within the statute of frauds reflects the value society places on stability in land ownership. Historically, land provided the primary source of wealth in agrarian economies and the statute of frauds reduces disputes over title to land. The courts have interpreted this provision of the statute of frauds broadly, holding that contracts to sell any interest in land, such as a right to come upon the property to extract minerals or a real estate mortgage, fall within the statute. A lease (rental agreement) is an interest in real property too, but most states will enforce short-term leases (one year or less) even if there is no writing.

Full or Part Performance Exception

An oral contract to sell an interest in land that has been either fully performed by the seller or partly performed by the buyer is outside the statute. To understand this exception, recall that the purpose of the statute is to prevent fraudulent claims of oral contracts. If one party has already performed under a contract, it is less likely that the claims are fraudulent, and there is less need to insist on written evidence. Consequently, the statute of frauds does not apply to real estate contracts that have been fully performed, or performed sufficiently to indicate the existence of a contract.

For example, suppose Maggie orally contracts to buy a farm from Lawrence. They agree to hire a lawyer to prepare the "paperwork." Maggie pays Lawrence a down payment and moves into the farmhouse. She lays some needed gravel on an interior farm road and begins to work on the farm's drainage ditch. Lawrence then finds someone willing to pay more for the farm and he tries to cancel the deal with Maggie. Although a writing generally is required for the sale of a real estate, Maggie's *part performance* of the oral contract gives sufficient evidence of that contract, and Maggie can hold Lawrence to the oral contract. A similar result would occur if Lawrence, the seller, had tendered a deed to the farm (fully performed the contract), but Maggie had not yet made full payment. Either full performance by the sell-

Global Context:
No Statute of Frauds in Japan

The Japanese civil code does not have a general statute of frauds. Japanese law allows parties to sue on oral contracts, including real estate contracts, and to quarrel over both the existence and terms of that contract. Some experts believe that the willingness to consider oral contracts in Japan stems from the absence of juries. Courts in the U.S. maintain relatively strict rules of evidence, in part, because they do not trust juries to be able to discern the truth from a discordant symphony of conflicting testimony. Judges have more experience in such matters, and a judge is typically less persuaded by fraudulent claims of oral contracts.

Japanese courts understand that sensible business people put important contracts in writing. This is true even if a writing is not required by law. More importantly, the courts recognize the importance of ex ante incentives: that the economy will function more efficiently if parties put important agreements in writing and realize that Japanese courts will hold them to that text. With sophisticated judges addressing contract issues, Japanese courts do not need a general rule like the statute of frauds; rather, they can leave the issue open and trust the judge to take a sensible course in practice. Often this means that the judge will refuse to find that an oral contract exists when testimony and other evidence conflicts. As a result, parties that want their interest fully protected in Japan, should put real estate contracts in writing even though not required by Japanese law.

er or part performance by the buyer takes the contract outside the statute.

Case 17-1 resembles the Maggie-and-Lawrence example, but differences exist. The case illustrates that it is not always easy to tell when a buyer's performance is sufficient to bring a contract within the part performance exception.

Case 17-1

Gegg
v.
Kiefer
655 S.W. 2d 834 (Mo. App. 1983)

*F*ranco Gegg, the respondent in this case, leased and farmed land owned by Joe Kiefer. Over the years, Franco had cleaned the creek bed, cleared brush and weeds, and made improvements to the drainage system. Joe was pleased with the way Franco cared for Joe's land. On several occasions Joe told Franco, "Now, Franco, you take care of this land because someday it will be your own."
Joe became ill and called for Franco. Joe stated: "Franco, I want to sell you this farm; as soon as I get on my feet we'll take care of this." Joe and Franco agreed on a price of $45,000. Franco then bought a corn planter and applied for a $45,000 real estate loan. Before anything between Franco and Joe was put into writing, Joe died. The executor of Joe's estate refused to deliver a deed to Franco, and Franco sued. The trial court found in favor of Franco and the estate appealed.

JUDGE PUDLOWSKI

An oral contract to convey land falls within the literal ambit of the statute of frauds and so will not be enforced as law. However, equity will decree specific performance where a party has so far acted on the promise that to deny him the benefit of the agreement would be unjust. This resort to equity avails sparingly, and only upon clear and convincing proof of a definite agreement....

[R]ecent Missouri cases have recognized the legal principle that oral promises to convey real estate may be enforced, where the plaintiff has partially performed, or has done other acts in reliance on such promises, and thereby has changed his position so materially, that to invoke the statute to deny the performer the benefit of the agreement, would itself amount to a fraud...

We note that there is no showing of part performance by respondent to require enforcement of the contract. The initial occupancy of the farm by respondent was as a tenant under an oral agreement to pay an annual cash rental and with the obligation to maintain the property. Work performed on the property was necessary to make it productive and as previously stated, such work was self-beneficial. The act of purchasing the corn planter was not dispositive of a specific act arising from the agreement to purchase Kiefer's property. At the time of purchase, respondent was farming two additional parcels of land. Furthermore, respondent told the dealer that he only "thought" he was going to keep the Kiefer property. The evidence which revealed that he was arranging to borrow $45,000 from the bank was merely tentative...

It is the legislature and not Kiefer that has made this contract in this case unenforceable. We find no basis to remove the case from the operation of the statute of frauds.

REVERSED.

1. Critical Thinking: Courts make decisions based on the evidence presented. What additional information, if any, could Franco have provided that might have convinced the court to overlook the applicability of the statute of frauds in this case?

2. Ethical Decision Making: Do you think Kiefer's executor acted ethically when he asserted a technical legal defense like the statute of frauds? Why or why not?

As Case 17-1 illustrates, to prove partial performance, a party has to perform actions that he/she would not have done if there were no contract, and show that irreparable harm will occur if the statute is strictly applied. Gegg needed to improve Kiefer's land even if Gegg only rented it and he needed the new equipment for his other farming operations; thus, these actions did not prove that a contract existed. Consequently, the part performance exception did not apply.

Contracts that Cannot Be Performed within One Year

The second class of contracts within the statute of frauds involves long term contracts. Courts recognize that the memories of even honest people begin to fade with time. To address the problem of fading memories, a contract that cannot by its own terms be performed within one year must be evidenced by a writing to be enforceable.

Measuring the One-Year Timeframe

The "one-year" timeframe is measured from the date of the *agreement* until the earliest possible time that the contract could be fully performed. For example, suppose that on May 20, Theodore orally agrees to rent an apartment from Andrea. Theodore promises to move into the apartment on June 1 and to move out on May 31 of the following year. Even though the term of the lease is for one year, this contract is not enforceable. The one-year timeframe is dated from the date the agreement is reached (May 20), and by the terms of the agreement it cannot be completed until May 31 of the following year. In contrast, if Theodore and Andrea had agreed on the lease on June 1, the contract could be performed within one year and no writing would be necessary.

The one-year rule applies only to bilateral executory contracts. Once one of the parties has fully performed, the statute of frauds no longer applies. In the previous example, if Theodore had paid all his rent in advance, the lease would be enforceable, even if oral, and agreed to at the earlier date. Remember that the purpose of the statute of frauds is to provide evidence of a valid contract. If one party has performed and the other party has accepted that performance, there is little reason to suspect that the claim is fraudulent and the statute no longer applies.

Interpreting the One-Year Rule

Courts tend to interpret the one-year rule narrowly. In a gray-area case, a court is likely to rule that the contract does not need to be in writing. The contract terms themselves must make it impossible to complete the contract within one year. Suppose, for example, that a construction company orally contracts to build a bridge for a county. The company estimates the construction time at eighteen months and promises to complete the project within two years. It may look like this contract has to be in writing, but this is not the case. Because it is *possible*, though not probable, to complete the bridge within one year, most courts would say that the oral contract is enforceable.

To understand why courts tend to interpret this provision of the statute of frauds narrowly, consider the impact of finding that the statute applies. Assume for the moment that the company in our example can prove that an oral contract exists because it has several reliable witnesses who will testify to the promises made by county officials. Assume also that the construction company relies on the promises to buy materials that can only be used on this particular bridge, and cancels bids it has made on other projects to free up its schedule. Then the county reneges.

If the statute of frauds applies, the company's breach of contract case is dismissed without a trial. It does not matter what promises were made or if the company relied on those promises. If, however, the statute does not apply, we do not know who wins the case. All we know is that the court is willing to listen to an argument that an oral contract existed. The company must still prove in court that an oral contract was made (perhaps there was a written bid that was orally accepted) and what the terms of that agreement were. Courts are reluctant to deny a party his or her day in court.

The issue of one's right to a day in court arose in the Starr case discussed in at the beginning of this chapter. Furst, the plaintiff, filed a lawsuit alleging that Starr made an oral contract to pay him a share of the profits earned by the New Kids on the Block. Starr filed a motion to dismiss claiming that any such contract was within the statute because it could not be performed within one year. The trial court held that it was possible for the contract to be performed within one year (perhaps the New Kids' career would be short) and refused to dismiss the case on this grounds.[4]

Contracts for the Sale of Goods for $500 or More

The third category of contracts that must be in writing arises under UCC Article 2. Section 2-201 provides that a contract for the sale of goods for $500 or more must be in writing to be enforceable. Recall that a "good" is personal property (not land or houses) and is tangible. Tangible property has a physical body such as inventory or a fleet of cars. Recall also that a sale is distinct from a rental. According to the Code, any contract to buy or sell personal, tangible property where the contact price is $500 or more must be in writing to be enforceable.

Note that the $500 price level applies only to the Article 2 version of the statute of frauds. Real estate contracts and contracts that cannot be performed within one year must be in writing regardless of the price agreed to.

---

[4]*In Re Furst*, 914 F. Supp. 734 (D. Mass. 1996).

Agreements to modify a contract that brings the contract within the statute must also be in writing. For example, a seller orally contracts to sell certain goods for $490. The parties agree to modify the price, bringing the total to $510. The contract, as modified, is now within the statute and a writing would be required.

Specially Manufactured Goods Exception

There are two main exceptions to the UCC writing requirement. The first involves specially manufactured goods. To fall under this exception, the good must be manufactured at the request of a particular buyer and not be suitable for other buyers in the ordinary course of the seller's business. Examples include a contract to purchase a tailor-made suit, or a contract for ball bearings manufactured to the buyer's specifications. In such cases, it would be very unlikely that the seller would have produced the goods unless there were an oral contract to do so. In addition, the identity of the buyer in each example is unambiguous. Because the seller's conduct in such situations carries evidentiary weight, courts are less concerned with allegations of fraudulent oral contracts. As a result, the seller is allowed to prove the existence of a contract for specially manufactured goods without a writing. This specially manufactured good exception only applies if the seller, before the buyer repudiates, has changed his position substantially in reliance on the contract. Reliance can be shown either by a substantial beginning of manufacture or commitments for the procurement of labor and materials necessary for that manufacture.

In Case 17-2, the seller manufactured packaging materials carrying the logo of a particular buyer. When the buyer changed logos, the seller's inventory became obsolete, and the applicability of the specially manufactured goods exception to the statute of frauds became an issue.

Case 17-2

Webcor Packaging

v.

Autozone
158 F. 3d 354 (6th Cir. 1998)

*A*utozone retailed automotive parts under the brand name "Duralast." Autozone gave Webcor the specifications required for Autozone packaging, and Webcor manufactered cartons with the Duralast name and logo. Webcor sold these cartons to part suppliers who then sold packaged parts to Autozone. When Autozone announced its plan to change its brand name, Webcor had an inventory of cartons with the Duralast name totaling $101,736. Webcor alleged that Autozone had orally promised to buy obsolete inventory in the event of a name change. Autozone denied that such a promise had been made.

Webcor sued Autozone and Autozone raised the statute of frauds as a defense. Webcor argued that the statute did not apply because the goods were specially manufactured for a particular buyer. The trial court found for Autozone and Webcor appealed.

JUDGE JONES

Under the Michigan statute of frauds, a contract for the sale of goods priced over five hundred dollars must be in writing as a general matter. However, where a manufacturer produces special goods for a buyer, courts may permit evidence of the oral agreement at trial…The long accepted justification for this statutory rule lies in the assurance that, by virtue of the unique nature of the goods, the manufacturer would not have produced such unique goods absent an agreement with the alleged buyer…It is worth emphasizing that the statute of frauds is a rule of evidence. Thus, upon favorable judgment, a proponent party—one seeking to invoke the exception—may attempt to prove the validity of the alleged oral agreement.

In the present case, the application of the "look to the goods rule" presents the following problem. There is no question that the "Duralast" logo and coloring affixed to the cartons at issue conform to the packaging used by Autozone, the only retailer in the business of selling "Duralast" brake parts. Thus, in looking to the goods, this court might well have concluded that the rule favors Webcor. However, it is also true that numerous purchasers—the Autozone vendors—had an interest in purchasing "Duralast" cartons to fulfill their obligations to provide packaged brake parts to Autozone. Even though those Autozone vendors purchased the cartons with intentions to sell them to Autozone, their very presence complicates the question of whether Autozone can be implicated as the buyer in this case…The passage of the cartons through sale to Autozone vendors diminishes our usual assurance that production of special goods can be linked to the alleged buyer.

…[We hold that] because Webcor sold "Duralast" packaging to multiple buyers, the "specially manufactured" exception to the UCC's statute of frauds is not applicable to the facts before this court.

AFFIRMED.

1. Critical Thinking: Because of the presence of multiple buyers for the packaging materials, the court held that there was insufficient reason to assume the presence of an oral promise between Webcor and Autozone. Do you think the case would have come out differently if Webcor sold the packaging directly to Autozone? Why or why not?

2. Ethical Decision Making: Even if there were no oral contract between Webcor and Autozone, as Autozone asserted, would Autozone be under an ethical obligation to warn Webcor that it was considering changing its logo? Explain.

Case 17-2 illustrates that the specially manufactured good exception has two functions. It protects the reliance interests of the manufacturer and provides evidence of a particular contract. The presence of multiple buyers made it difficult, if not impossible, to identify who, if anyone made oral promises to the manufacturer, so the exception did not apply.

Part Payment or Part Delivery Exception

The other exception to the UCC statute of frauds involves partially performed contracts. Once goods have been delivered by the seller and accepted by the buyer, no writing is necessary to prove the existence of the contract. The same is true if the buyer has paid for the goods and the seller has accepted the payment. In either case, the actions of the parties provide sufficient evidence of an oral contract.

Note that there is a difference between the part performance exception under the common law and part payment or part delivery exception under the UCC. Recall that under the common law, part performance of a real estate contract permits the party to enforce the entirety of an oral contract. In our previous example, when Maggie paid a down payment on Lawrence's farm and made improvements to the drainage ditch and graveled the road, the entire contract became enforceable. By contrast, the UCC part performance provision states that the oral contract is only *enforceable up to the amount actually paid for or delivered.*

To illustrate the UCC approach, suppose there is an oral contract whereby a slaughterhouse promised to buy 1,000 head of cattle at $400 per head. A rancher delivered, and the slaughterhouse accepted, the first 200 head. The contract is now enforceable for the 200 delivered, not for the remaining 800 head. The same applies if the slaughterhouse had paid the rancher for two hundred head and the rancher had accepted payment. The oral contract would be enforceable only for the amount actually paid for (200 head).

Sales of Intellectual Property for $5000 or More

The fourth category of contracts within the statute arises under UCC Article 1. Section 1-206 provides that a contract to sell intellectual property, such as patents, copyrights, and royalties (these topics are addressed in Chapter 10), is not enforceable beyond $5,000 unless there is written evidence of that contract. This provision arose in the case set out at the beginning of the chapter, where Starr, the promoter, argued that even if an oral contract existed, it would be unenforceable because it involved the sale of music royalties in excess of $5,000. The court rejected this claim, holding instead that the alleged agreement did not create a right in music royalties directly, but rather was an agreement to share profits however derived. The court noted that such profit-sharing agreements are outside the statute.[5]

Recently, the question has arisen as to applicability of the statute of frauds to contracts to sell intellectual property rights to software or computer databases over the Internet. As the following technology box discusses, model legislation requires a writing if such contracts are for $5,000 or more. The legislation also provides that such writings be consummated via electronic means.

---

[5]*In Re Furst,* 914 F. Supp. 734 (D. Mass. 1996) (citing UCC Section 8-113).

Technology: UCITA and the Statute of Frauds

Owners of intellectual property rights such as computer software and information rights such as computer databases often wish to transfer limited rights to such property for specific purposes and limited duration. Such agreements are called licenses. The Uniform Computer Information Transactions Act (UCITA) provides contract rules to govern such transactions. UCITA becomes law when enacted by a state legislature. As of this writing, UCITA has been adopted in forty-four states and the remaining states are expect to follow suit. Once enacted, UCITA preempts state law that conflicts with UCITA provisions.

UCITA Section 2-201 addresses the statute of frauds. It states that if a license requires payment of a contract fee of $5,000 or more, the contract is enforceable against the licensor (the party selling the license) only if that party "authenticates a record." To authenticate a record under UCITA means either the signing of a written contract or executing an electronic symbol, sound, or message attached to, included in, or linking to a contract submitted electronically. So, for example, Hillary places an order over the Internet to license software for her computer from a licensor. Hillary uses licensor's website to place the order. The site asks her for a personal identification number which she enters. The site then asks her to verify that number with a second click. Once Hillary verifies, her contract is effectively in writing and the licensor will send an electronic copy of the software to Hillary's computer where it is installed. This licensing agreement is now fully enforceable.

Surety Agreements

The fifth category within the statute of frauds is the surety agreement. A surety is a person who promises to answer for the contractual obligation of another. For example, a parent may serve as a surety for an adult son who cannot afford legal services. The parent promises to pay the lawyer's fee if the son does not. The son is the primary obligor (the lawyer must seek his fee from the son first), but if the son does not pay then the secondary obligor (the parent) must. Although no writing is needed to hold the primary obligor to the contract, the surety's promise (secondary obligation) is only enforceable if it is in writing.

A surety is distinct from a co-obligor. A co-obligor can be sued without first suing the primary obligor (the son in our example). A surety may only be sued if the primary obligor is sued first. Unlike a surety agreement, a co-obligation is outside the statute of frauds. Whether an agreement involves a co-obligation or a surety arrangement depends on the intent of the parties. When an agreement is oral, it can be difficult to predict whether a court will call a particular person a co-obligor or a surety. The practical tip for managers is that when in doubt, put the agreement in writing.

Main Purpose Exception

There is an exception to the rule that surety agreements must be in writing. Note that in the previous example, the parent receives no direct economic benefit from guaranteeing the son's debt. When a surety receives no economic benefit in exchange for his or her promise, a writing is required. In contrast, if the surety receives consideration in the form of an economic benefit, the agreement does not have to be in writing. This is called the main purpose rule.

To illustrate the exception, suppose a major stockholder in a small corporation personally guarantees that his corporation will repay a loan. Relying on the promise, a bank loans money to the corporation. Note that the main purpose of the surety (the stockholder) is to generate a loan from which he or she will benefit. The fact that the surety is benefited gives evidence that the alleged oral promise was actually made, so the agreement would not have to be in writing. The following global feature illustrates a similar pattern under civil law. Although consideration is not an element of a civil law contract, when there is no consideration, civil law requires a writing.

Global Context: A Writing as a Substitute for Consideration Under Civil Law

Recall that an exchange of consideration is not necessary to form a contract in the civil law countries of the European continent. But when there is no exchange of consideration, European countries require that the promise must be in writing to be enforceable.

Note that this rule parallels the treatment of surety agreements in the United States. When the main purpose of the surety's promise is to secure a direct advantage to the surety, there is, in effect, an exchange of consideration and no writing is required. If the surety receives no direct benefit from the promise, however, then U.S. law requires that the promise be in writing to provide evidence that the promise was real and fully intended by the promisor.

The requirements of a writing and of consideration address similar policy concerns. Both an exchange of consideration and a writing give evidence that a promise was real and intended. If consideration exists there is less need for a writing. Conversely, if there is evidence of a writing, there is less need for an exchange of consideration.

EXHIBIT 17-1

Contracts within the Statute of Frauds

Contracts that Must Be in Writing	Exceptions
Contracts for the Sale of an Interest in Real Property	Part Performance
Contracts that Cannot Be Performed within One Year	Specially Manufactured Goods
Contracts for the Sale of Goods for $500 or More	Part Payment or Part Delivery
Contracts for the Sale of Intellectual Property for $5,000 or More	
Surety Agreements	Main Purpose Rule

Other Agreements that Must Be in Writing

The previous five categories capture most of the contracts that must be in writing to be enforceable. These provisions are summarized in Exhibit 17-1. There are a few other, less common, categories. An example is the prenuptial agreement, an agreement in which a bride and groom agree how to divide up property rights in the event of divorce. Some states refuse to enforce such contracts on public policy grounds. Most states enforce prenuptials but require that they be in writing.

Depending on the statute of frauds in a particular state, a writing can sometimes substitute for an exchange of consideration. Common examples include:

Promises to pay debts previously discharged in bankruptcy or by the operation of a statute of limitations.

- Promises by an executor of an estate to personally pay the debts of a deceased.
- Promises by a creditor to unilaterally modify the terms of a credit contract.
- Promises to leave property in a will.
- Promise by a merchant buyer or seller of goods

to keep an offer open for a stated period of time (this is the "firm offer rule" discussed in Chapter 13).

In each of the preceding examples, the promise is not given in exchange for consideration, but if there is a writing, the promise is still enforceable.

Elements of a Writing

Now that we know what contracts and promises must be in writing to be enforceable, the question becomes, what terms have to be in writing? To satisfy the statute of frauds, two things must be in writing: (1) the essential terms of the contract; and (2) the signature of the party against whom enforcement is sought. We consider these two elements in turn.

Essential Terms

To satisfy the statute of frauds, only the essential terms of a contract must be in writing. Recall from Chapter 13 that to have a contract under the common law the parties must expressly agree on five things: (1) *parties* to the contract; (2) *subject matter* to be exchanged; (3) *quantity*; (4) *price* or other consideration to be exchanged; and (5) *time* of performance. Although these essential terms vary by state (for instance, in some states price and time can be oral), generally these five terms are the essential terms that must be in writing to satisfy the common law statute of frauds.

The statute of frauds sections of the UCC require fewer written terms. Article 1, which applies to sales of intellectual property, requires that the writing must identify the parties, subject matter and price. Article 2, which applies to sales of goods, does not require that any particular term be in writing. It does, however, state

that an oral contract will only be enforced up to the *quantity* stated in writing. Exhibit 17-2 summarizes the essential terms required for a writing under the common law, UCC Article One and UCC Article Two.

EXHIBIT 17-2

Essential Terms for a Writing

Common Law	UCC Article 1	UCC Article 2
Parties	Parties	Parties
Subject Matter	Subject Matter	
Price	Price	
Quantity		
Time of Performance		

Multiple Document Rule

It may be tempting to think of a written contract as a single document with the names of the parties at the top, followed by the terms of the agreement, and concluding with signatures and dates. Though many contracts take this form, a single writing is not necessary to satisfy the writing requirement under either the common law or the UCC. A series of letters, invoices, payroll cards, checks, deeds, or other memorandum can be linked together to provide the essential terms of a writing. Courts have even used written admissions in court pleadings to provide either a signature or missing terms. This "multiple-document" rule is illustrated in Case 17-3.

Case 17-3

Simplex Supplies

v.

Abhe & Svoboda, Inc.
586 N.W. 2d 797 (Minn. App. 1998)

A bhe & Svoboda entered into a joint venture with Rainbow Inc. Rainbow successfully bid on a government construction project. As part of the bidding process, Rainbow was required to document that eleven percent of the work would be done by disadvantaged firms owned by women or minorities.

Simplex, owned by Sarah Stehly, was classified as a disadvantaged firm. Stehly claimed that Rainbow had accepted her proposal to provide a paint removal abrasive called Blastox. Her proposal listed Blastox at $145 per ton. It did not, however, state a quantity term. Rainbow never signed a formal contract with Simplex, but Rainbow referenced Simplex's price in the bid it submitted to the government. Rainbow also referenced Stehly's bid in the "disadvantaged firms" documents supplied to the government and in a supporting "affidavit of compliance" signed by Haagenson, CEO of Rainbow.

When Rainbow refused to buy Blastox from Simplex, Simplex sued. Rainbow raised the statute of frauds as a defense. The trial court found that no writing existed and ruled in favor of Rainbow. Simplex appealed.

JUDGE LANSING

On April 27, 1995, Simplex faxed the joint venture a proposal to provide Blastox at $145 per ton. The proposal listed the project number and contained a handwritten contract amount of $362,500. Stehly claims she met that same day with Michael DeBuhr, an industrial engineer for Rainbow, and that he agreed to Simplex's proposal…

A short time later, Rainbow submitted to the department a Request to Sublet [construction bid] that listed the project number, the $362,500 contract amount, and named Simplex as a subcontractor. The Request to Sublet contains a signature block that states: "I hereby certify that the proposed subcontractor's contract is in my office and contains language which refers to all the requirements thereof." Under the "Submitted By," Rainbow typed its name and address…

It is important to distinguish the statute of frauds' writing requirement from the issue of whether a contract exists. The writing required by the statute is not the contract itself, but only the written evidence of it…The statute of frauds does not require one writing containing both a signature and a quantity; several documents may be read together to satisfy the statute.

For writings to be effective against a party, the statute of frauds on the sale of goods requires that at least one writing contain the signature of the party to be charged. The signature can be found on any document and may consist of any symbol executed or adopted by a party with present intent to authenticate a writing…Haagenson's signature on his affidavit and Rainbow's typewritten signature on the Request to Sublet both satisfy the signature requirement.

In addition to a signature, at least one writing must contain the quantity to be charged against the party. The quantity may be derived from a dollar amount provided in the documents.…[A]ll four documents listed the $362,500 contract amount. Simplex's faxed proposal offered the joint venture Blastox at the price of $145 per ton. Dividing the $362,500 contract amount by $145 per ton results in a quantity of 2,500 tons...

Read together, the four documents satisfy the statute of frauds requirements relating to the sale of goods. Thus, we reverse the district court and remand for the determination on the disputed fact issue of whether an oral contract existed between Simplex and the joint venture.

REVERESED AND REMANDED.

1. Critical Thinking: Assume that you were the attorney representing Rainbow and make an argument that the multiple document should not apply.

2. Ethical Decision Making: Does the statute of frauds assist the ethical business manager, or does it serve as an impediment to ethical business? Is it ethical for Rainbow to assert the statute of frauds in this case? Why or why not?

The *Simplex* case reminds us that the statute of frauds is rule of evidence. If a series of documents provides sufficient evidence that the allegation of an oral contract is true, then there is little reason to deny a person a right to a day in court to prove the validity of that contract.

Signatures

The second element of a writing, beyond the essential terms, is a signature. Both the common law and the UCC require that before you can hold someone to a contract, the individual must first sign it. A "signature" is anything that the party intends to be his or her signature. Initials can suffice, as can an ink stamp, or other similar mark. A party can also authorize someone else to sign on the party's behalf.

Electronic Signatures

It is generally held that a contract entered into over the Internet can suffice as a written evidence of the

Global Context: Digital Signatures in the European Union

A recent directive from the European Union (EU) addressed the question of whether a digital signature passed through the Internet satisfies the signature requirement of the European Statute of Frauds. The directive answered with a definite "YES." A digital signature intended as a signature suffices. The EU directed member states to enact legislation conforming with the directive. Germany became one of the first European Union countries to do so, followed quickly by Ireland.

Although such legislation is spreading throughout the globe, it is not without its critics. For example, draft Thai e-commerce legislation is drawing criticism that it gives up too much national autonomy. The fear is that the global economy may facilitate the growth of a global governmental entity. In the Philippines, the concern is having the electronic infrastructure to implement the law into practice. Notwithstanding such concerns, the overwhelming trend is the adoption of legislation that facilitates electronic commerce rather than hinders it.

essential terms of the agreement. This is true because the parties can simply print out the terms of that agreement. Signatures, by contrast, are more troublesome, and the question arises as to how an electronic communication can be effectively signed.

On July 1, 2000, President Clinton signed federal legislation addressing the issue of electronic signatures. The new law, known as the E-Signature Act, recognizes the validity of a digital signature both for purposes of the statute of frauds and to authenticate e-contracts generally. A digital signature is an electronic identifier that employs encryption technology to assure the identity of the sender. The sender uses a private password, personal identification, or another form of symbol unavailable to others. Use of such technology produces a legally valid signature. The federal law preempts conflicting state law on the topic and provides a uniform federal standard with regard to electronic signatures. As the following Global feature indicates, similar legislation is being enacted in many nations of the world.

Confirming Memo Rule

As a general rule, if one party signs and the other party does not, only the party who has signed can be held to the contract under the statute of frauds. The signing party is estopped from raising the statute of frauds as a defense, but the nonsigning party is not. For example, if Juan contracts to sell his home to Francis but only Juan signs, then the contract is enforceable against Juan, but not against Francis.

There is an exception to this rule. Under UCC §2-201(2), if a merchant delivers a signed confirmation of an oral contract to another merchant, the receiving merchant may be bound to the contract even if he or she does not sign it. The receiving merchant has ten days to object to the writing and must have reason to know of its contents. If these two conditions are met, only one signature is needed to bind both parties. This exception is called the confirming memo exception to the statute of frauds. The purpose of the rule is to facilitate transactions between merchants. Exhibit 17-3 offers details about this rule.

In sum, to analyze the legal issues associated with a writing, ask first whether the type of contract falls within the statute of frauds peculiar to your state. If the answer is yes, then ask whether an exception applies. If no exception applies, then ask whether the essential terms and signatures are present. Remember that the terms and signatures can appear in more than one document. If the terms and signatures are present, then

---

EXHIBIT 17-3

Confirming Memo Rule

- Applies only to contracts for the sale of goods for $500 or more.
- Both buyer and seller must be merchants.
- Applies only if one party is *confirming* an existing oral contract.
- The writing must contain the quantity term, reference the oral contract, and be signed by the drafting party.
- The writing must be received within a reasonable time.
- The recipient must have reason to know of its contents.
- The recipient has not objected within ten days of receipt.

---

you have a writing and the contract is enforceable. If not, then any breach of contract case will be dismissed without a trial. We turn next to rules of contract interpretation.

Maxims of Contract Interpretation

Many important contracts do not need a writing to be enforceable. For example, contracts to hire a new employee at a high salary or to build a custom made (specially manufactured) yacht are enforceable without a writing. This does not mean that such contracts should be oral. To be able to enforce the contract, the parties must be able to prove that it exists and what its terms are. A writing typically provides the best evidence.

Prudent business people often agree not to bid themselves to a contract until everything is in writing. Remember that the hallmark of contracting is the agreement, so if parties agree to require a writing, one is required whether the contract falls within the statute of frauds or not. In addition, when business people put their agreements in writing, the contracts often contain more details than the essential terms identified by the statute of frauds. A written contract may be several pages long.

Anytime a contract is put in writing, care must be taken to ensure that the courts will interpret the writing to mean what it is intended to mean. Courts try to interpret contracts in accord with their plain meaning. But sometimes the writing is ambiguous or conflicted. When this occurs, courts use general rules of contract interpretation, or maxims, to guide their interpretation. We consider several such maxims.

Ambiguous Writings

Our first maxim states that if the contract is ambiguous, courts tend to *interpret the ambiguity against the drafting party.* For example, in one case an insurance contract covered a car owner for any liability sustained while "using" his car. The owner used the hood of his car as a gun rest to shoot at a passing deer. The bullet struck the car's roof, deflected into the car, and struck a passenger. The company argued that "use" meant *use as a vehicle.* The court found for the owner, stating that if the company had wanted this limitation, it should have drafted its contract more carefully.[6]

According to a second maxim of interpretation, courts will *interpret ambiguous language to make it consistent with business custom,* rather than contrary to it. In one case, a written contract specified "felt hats." The buyer objected when the hats that were delivered were only eighty percent felt. According to customary practice in the garment industry, the term "felt" included any material that is at eighty percent felt or more, so the buyer could not reject the delivery. The practical lesson, of course, is to understand the customs of the particular trade at issue in the contract.

All contracts contain both express and implied terms. Courts infer implied terms from past dealings between the parties and from business custom. If parties wish for their contract to exclude past dealings or business customs, they need to spell out this desire expressly. According to a third maxim, express language is given preference over past dealings, and past dealings are given preference over general business custom.

Conflicted Writings

Some contracts are preprinted, with blanks left to be filled in by the parties. Anytime a party scratches out preprinted language or fills in the blanks with a typewriter or with a pen, a problem of interpretation can arise. As a fourth general rule, courts will interpret conflicts in a writing so as to give handwritten language top priority, then typewritten, then preprinted. Courts also give spelled out numbers preference over conflicting Arabic numerals.

Conspicuous Terms

Finally, recall from Chapter 15 that clauses that tend to be disfavored by public policy often need to be printed in plain English with conspicuous type. Having

---

[6] *Payne v. Southern Guaranty Insurance Co.,* 282 S.E. 2d 711 (Ga. App. 1981).

such clauses separately initialed may be important in some situations. Exculpatory clauses, warranty disclaimers in consumer contracts, and agreements not-to-compete in employment contracts provide examples. Exhibit 17-4 summarizes these various maxims, or general rules, of contract interpretation.

EXHIBIT 17-4

Maxims of Contract Interpretation

- Ambiguous writings are interpreted against the party who drafted them.
- Ambiguities are interpreted to be consistent with business customs, rather than contrary to them.
- Express language is given preference over past-dealings between the parties and past-dealings between the parties are given preference over general business customs.
- Handwritten terms are given preference over typewritten terms and typewritten terms are given preference over preprinted terms.
- Numbers that are spelled out are given preference over conflicting Arabic numerals.
- Clauses disfavored by public policy may need to be conspicuous and written in plain English to be enforceable.

Parol Evidence Rule

The parol evidence rule is a particularly important rule of contract interpretation so we treat it in a separate section. The purpose of the rule is to make written contracts more reliable. The rule states that *parol evidence will not be admitted in court to contradict the terms of a written integrated contract.*

To *integrate* a contract means to agree to reduce the entirety of a contractual agreement to a single written document. Parties often engage in extended negotiations, exchanging offers and counteroffers, and discussing various terms. They then agree to put the entire agreement in a writing, to review the document, and to sign it. This is an integrated contract.

Parol evidence is evidence of negotiations that occurred at the time of, or prior to, signing the written integrated contract, but not referenced in the writing. Such evidence is not admissible in court to contradict the terms of an integrated contract. For example, Dan buys a used car from Acme Auto. Before signing a contract, the salesperson orally promises Dan a ninety-day warranty. The written sales contact, however, states that the car is sold "AS IS–NO WARRANTIES." Dan signs the contract. Most courts would not permit Dan to introduce evidence of the salesperson's oral promise.

Exceptions to the Parol Evidence Rule

The parol evidence rule does not exclude evidence of negotiations that occur *after* the contract is signed. If the salesperson had promised Dan a warranty after signing the contract, the parol evidence rule would not apply. Dan would simply argue that they had an integrated contract and then orally agreed to modify that contract.

Parol evidence is admissible to explain ambiguous writings or to fill in the gaps in a writing that is incomplete. If the contract did not mention warranties, or the written warranty was ambiguous (for example, an express warranty was given but the time limit was not mentioned), the salesperson's oral promise would be admissible. Similarly, parol evidence is permitted to prove that the contract was conditioned on an event not reflected in the writing. Parol evidence is also permitted to establish that the writing contains a clerical error, such as a mistake of arithmetic.

Finally, a party is also allowed to present parol evidence to establish that a contract is voidable on the grounds of incapacity or on grounds of reality of assent—fraud, duress, undue influence, mistake, or unconscionability. Notwithstanding this exception, most states would not allow Dan to prove a case of fraud with evidence of an oral promise that was squarely contradicted by the writing. This distinction is illustrated in Case 17-4.

Case 17-4

Columbia Gas Transmission
v.
Ogle
Court of Appeals, Southern District of Ohio
172 F. 3d 47 (S.D. Ohio, 1997)

*I*n 1976 Donna and Charles Ogle signed a written lease granting Columbia Gas the right to drill for gas on their land. In 1978 Columbia found gas on the Ogles' property and negotiated a second contract, specifying a right of way to lay gas pipelines. The Ogles claimed that in 1978 Hacker, the representative for Columbia, orally promised them that only one gas storage well would be drilled on their property. Neither the original 1976 lease nor the 1978 right-of-way agreement contained any express limitation on the number of wells. Hacker claimed that he never made such a promise.

Only one well was drilled before 1996. In 1996 Columbia sought to drill additional wells and the Ogles objected. Citing the parol evidence rule, the trial court refused to admit the Ogles' evidence regarding Hacker's oral promise. The trial court found for Columbia and the Ogles appealed.

JUDGE GRAHAM

According to the defendants, it had always been their preference that Columbia Gas be limited to the right to drill and maintain only one well on their property. Mrs. Ogle indicates that she and her husband believed that such a limitation was included in the original lease when they signed it. However, a cursory reading of the one page document reveals that no such limitation is included in the lease. The Ogles state that they learned this some time after signing the original lease, but before the time when Columbia Gas agreed to negotiate the laying of a pipeline to run near the Ogles' house. Defendants claim that they addressed this concern to Mr. Hacker when he came to negotiate the right-of-way agreement. According to defendants, Mr. Hacker responded with the oral representation that the language of the right-of-way agreement would make it clear that Columbia Gas was willing to be limited to only one gas storage well. The right-of-way agreement, signed on July 30, 1978, makes no reference to gas storage wells....

The parol evidence rule bars the Ogles from arguing that Columbia Gas made representations concerning the meaning of contract terms which were inconsistent with and refuted by the plain language of the right-of-way agreement. The Ogles were free to carefully read the one page right-of-way agreement and negotiate its terms before they signed it. The Ogles were also free to review the agreement with counsel....

A party in some cases may offer evidence of prior or contemporaneous representations to prove fraud in the execution or inducement of an agreement...However, Ohio law does not allow a party to prove fraud by claiming that the inducement to enter into an agreement was a promise which is squarely contradicted by the written terms of that agreement. When the terms of the writing itself directly contradict the parol agreement, then the party alleging the parol agreement cannot be heard to say that he relied on it.

AFFIRMED.

1. Critical Thinking: Review the discussion of exceptions to the parol evidence rule presented in the text prior to the case. Which of the exceptions might apply to the facts of this case? Explain.

2. Ethical Decision Making: Suppose that Hacker heard the Ogles say "We want only one well on our property." Would this create an ethical obligation upon Hacker to inform the Ogles that the writing they were about to sign contained no such limit? Why or why not?

The potential exists for managers to use oral statements to avoid confrontations in contract negotiations in order to get contracts signed, especially when unsophisticated and trusting parties are involved. This may have happened in the *Ogle* case. A manager who knows the parol evidence rule needs to consider the ethics of using the rule to achieve an unfair advantage with trusting parties. The primary exceptions to the parol evidence rule are listed in Exhibit 17-5.

EXHIBIT 17-5

Parole Evidence Is Admissible To:

1. Prove contract modifications made subsequent to the integrated writing.
2. Explain ambiguities in the writing.
3. Fill in the gaps of a writing that is incomplete.
4. Prove that the contract has a condition not reflected in the writing.
5. Establish that the writing contains a clerical error.
6. Prove that the contract is voidable for lack of capacity.
7. Prove that the contract is voidable on the grounds of reality of assent.

Promissory Estoppel as a Substitute for a Writing

The statute of frauds, which is designed to prevent injustice, can, at times, cause an injustice. The statute prevents injustice by refusing to hear claims of fictitious oral contracts. But it also allows parties to defeat real contracts. To illustrate, let us take some poetic license with the case we discussed at the beginning of this chapter. Suppose that Starr really had agreed to pay Furst a share of New Kids' profits, and that the existence and terms of that contract could be proven with reliable oral evidence. Suppose, also, that their contract was within the statute of frauds and there was writing but it was defective (e.g. missing the twenty-five percent term that was orally agreed to). In such a setting, Starr could use the statute to avoid his *bone fide* obligation. Reneging on a real contact is in many respects just as unjust as asserting a fictitious oral one.

In recent years, the courts in some states have begun to use the doctrine of promissory estoppel (discussed in Chapters 12 and 14) to allow a party to enforce an oral contract that would ordinarily be barred by the statute of frauds. In these states, when one party suffers sever hardship because of reliance on an oral contract, the other party is prohibited from asserting the statute of frauds as a defense. This use of promissory estoppel as a potential substitute for a writing has been embraced by the *Restatement (Second) of Contracts* so its use among the states is likely to grow. Section 139 of the *Restatement* provides that a promise that induces an action or forbearance is enforceable, notwithstanding the statute of frauds, if injustice can be avoided only by enforcement of the promise.

Using promissory estoppel principles to evade the statute of frauds is controversial, and many states do not permit it. Critics fear that a claim of reliance can be made in many, if not most, situations, and routine use of the promissory estoppel doctrine could essentially eliminate the writing requirement entirely. They also point out that the statute of frauds provides an incentive to put important contracts in writing, and that writings reduce the potential for misunderstandings that generate litigation. In this light, the statute of frauds is good for a productive economy.

Oral Promises Wrap-Up

The contract dispute between Maurice Starr and Jeffrey Furst wound up in federal court in 1995. The judge held that the statute of frauds did not apply and allowed the jury to consider conflicting testimony over the validity of an oral contract to pay a share of New Kids' profits to Furst.[7] The jury found for the plaintiff, with damages amounting to hundreds of millions of dollars.[8] Starr filed for bankruptcy protection, and as of summer of 1998, Furst reportedly had been unable to collect.[9] Furst is reported to be writing a book about his adventures and misadventures in promoting The New Kids on the Block.[10]

[7] *In re Furst,* 914 F. Supp. 734 (D. Mass. 1996)
[8] Tim Cornell, *Local Promoter Sees Stars Assets Frozen by the Court,* Boston Herald, December 2, 1995, at News, p. 11.
[9] *Ask the Globe,* Boston Globe, August 22, 1998, at p. A16.
[10] Gayle Fee and Laura Raposa, *The New Kids On The Block Are History, But the Lawsuits and Controversy Live On,* Boston Herald, March 11, 1997, at News, p. 15.

	Summary
Contracts that Must Be in Writing to Be Enforceable	**1. Contracts for the Sale of an Interest in Real Property** **Exception**—full performance by the seller or part performance by the buyer takes land sales contracts outside the statute. **2. Contracts that Cannot be Performed within One Year** **Measuring the One-Year Rule**—courts measure the one year from the time of the agreement until the earliest time that contract could be completed in accord with its terms. **Interpreting the One-Year Rule**—courts interpret this provision narrowly. **3. Contracts for the Sale of Goods for $500 or More** **Exception**—contracts for the sale of goods manufactured to the specifications of a particular buyer and not readily sellable within the manufacturer's ordinary business are outside the statute. **Exception**—part payment or part delivery takes the contract outside the statute to the amount actually paid for or delivered. **4. Contracts for the Sale of Intellectual Property for $5,000 or More** **Applicability**—applies to sales of patents, copyrights, royalty rights and to sales and licenses of computer software and databases. **5. Surety Agreements** **Applicability**—applies to promise to perform an obligation primarily owed by another. **Exception**—if the main purpose of the surety in making the promise is to receive a direct economic benefit, then the promise is outside the statute (main purpose rule).

	Summary (continued)
Elements of a Writing	**Essential Terms**—the essential terms of the contract must be evidenced in writing. The common law requires more terms than does the UCC. **Multiple Document Rule**—the essential terms may appear in a combination of more than one document. **Signatures**—the statute of frauds requires that the writing be signed by the party against whom enforcement of the contract is sought. **Electronic Signatures**—federal legislation provides that a signature may be submitted electronically. **Confirming Memo Rule**—when certain conditions are met, the UCC provides that the statute of frauds can be satisfied without a signature.
Maxims of Contract Interpretation	Courts interpret contracts in accord with their plain meaning. When writings are ambiguous or conflicted, the courts employ general maxims of construction to interpret the writing. Several important maxims are listed in Exhibit 17-4.
Parol Evidence Rule	Evidence of negotiations that occurred at the time of, or prior to, signing an intergrated contract is not admissible to contradict the terms of that contract. **Exceptions**—several important exceptions to the parol evidence are listed in Exhibit 17-5.
Promissory Estoppel as a Substitute for a Writing	Some states allow a party to enforce an oral contract that would ordinarily be barred by the statute of frauds if that party would suffer a sever hardship because of the reliance. Many states do not allow such equitable concerns to negate the statute.

Review Questions and Case Problems

1. List the five primary categories of contracts that must be in writing to be enforceable, together with the major exceptions to each category.

2. State the "multiple document rule" and construct an example of how it might affect the applicability of the statute of frauds.

3. To satisfy the statute of frauds, only the essential terms of a contract must be in writing. What terms are considered essential under the common law statute? Under UCC Article 1? Under UCC Article 2?

4. State the parol evidence rule and list the major exceptions to this rule.

5. When, if ever, can a party be bound to a contract that falls within the statute of frauds without signing that contract? Explain.

6. When, if ever, should the doctrine of promissory estoppel permit the enforcement of an oral contract that is within the statute of frauds? Explain.

7. Fernando orally promised Pando to share any winnings that Fernando won in a state lottery. Pando purchased tickets in Fernando's name. Fernando got lucky and won $2.8 million to be paid out over a ten-year period. Fernando refused to share the winnings and Pando sued for breach of contract. Fernando asserted the statute of frauds. Can this contract be performed within one year? Is it executory? Who do you think won? *Pando v. Fernandez*, 127 Misc. 2d 224, 485 N.Y.S. 2d 162 (1984).

8. Plaintiff and defendant entered into a binding contract by exchanging faxes. The plaintiff's fax contained a clause stating that it contained all of the terms of the parties' "written integrated contract." Differing terms appeared on the defendant's fax. When a dispute arose, plaintiff sought to use the parol evidence rule to limit the court's interpretation of the contract to the plaintiff's fax. The defendant sought to introduce evidence of prior dealings to explain the contract. Do you think that the defendant's parol evidence was excluded by the court? Why or why not? *B.N.E. Swedbank v. Banker*, 794 F. Supp. 1291 (S.D.N.Y. 1992).

9. Irwin and Samuels worked as partners in marketing products to oil companies. Although they never had a written partnership agreement, for seventeen years they shared profits equally. Each man later brought a son into the partnership. The sons encouraged their fathers to form a small corporation, and formal, written bylaws were adopted. Thereafter, relations between the two families declined. When they sued each other, the Irwin family sought to introduce evidence of the prior practice of sharing profits. The Samuels family tried to exclude that evidence under the parol evidence rule. Was the evidence admissible in court to help explain the corporate bylaws? *Ironite Products Co. v. Samuels*, 985 S.W. 2d 858 (Mo. App. 1998).

10. Adams orally agreed to sell steel reinforcing rods to help reinforce a retaining wall. About half of the rods were specially manufactured to meet the buyer's needs. The other half were to come from Adams' stock. When the buyer reneged on the deal, Adams sued. Is this oral contract enforceable? Why or why not? *Frank Adams & Co., Inc. v. Baker*, 439 N.E. 2d 953 (Ohio 1981).

11. Robert Lee, a big game hunter and collector of exotic cars, desperately wanted a particular Ferrari. This was no ordinary car; it had been specially manufactured for, and once owned by, King Leopold of France. The present owner, Wayne Golomb, of Springfield Illinois, asked for $275,000 and Lee initially counteroffered with $175,000. Although Lee owned twenty Ferraris, five Bentleys, four Rolls Royces, and twenty-one other exotic cars, he just had to have the "King Leopold Ferrari." Hence, Lee changed his mind, and informed Wayne that he would pay the $275,000 asking price. Wayne never signed anything. Can Lee bag his game and get the King Leopold Ferrari? For a lively rendition of the facts, see Judge Easterbrook's opinion. *Lee v. Boyles*, 11 UCC Rep. Serv. 2d 7 (7th Cir. 1990).

12. DaGrossa opened a restaurant in the Spring of 1986. In August of 1985, LaJaunie helped design necessary renovations. In exchange for LaJaunie's efforts, DaGrossa orally promised to give him an option to purchase one third of the restaurant's corporate stock if the restaurant proved profitable during its first year. Is this option contract within the statute of frauds? *LaJaunie v. DaGrossa*, 159 A.D. 2d 349, 552 N.Y.S. 2d 628 (1990).

13. Plaintiff paid $2,000 for a written option to purchase land owned by defendant. The option, entered into in December, gave plaintiff the right to buy the land for $43,000 anytime prior to July. In the spring, the parties orally agreed to modify their option contract. Defendant would seek other buyers, and if the property could be sold for more than $43,000, defendant would split any excess with plaintiff. In exchange for this promise, plaintiff agreed not to exercise its option. The property was sold in September for $195,000 and defendant refused to share the proceeds with plaintiff. Does the part performance exception to the statute of frauds apply to these facts? *B & B Land Acquistion v. Mandell*, 714 N.E. 2d 58 (Ill. App. 1999).

14. Franklin was a cotton farmer with a line of credit with UAP Agriculture Supply Company. Franklin's son, Sam, ran a separate farm. Franklin orally asked UAP to extend Sam credit on Franklin's account, and UAP did so. When the price of cotton dropped, Franklin's account fell into arrears and UAP sued. Franklin asserted that he should not be liable for loans made to Sam because any promise he made amounted to an unenforceable surety agreement. Do you agree? What additional facts would be helpful in deciding this case? *Franklin v. UAP/GA Ag. Chem., Inc*, 514 S.E. 2d 241 (Ga. App. 1999).

15. Levin and Lipton owned the San Diego Clippers NBA basketball team. They were negotiating a sale of the team to Knight. After extended negotiations, the parties reduced their agreement to a handwritten memorandum outlining the terms of the sale, including the parties, price, subject matter, and time. All three gentlemen initialed the memorandum. Two days later, Knight informed Levin and Lipton that he had decided not to buy the Clippers. Levin and Liption sued and Knight asserted the statute of frauds. Was a writing necessary in this case? If a writing were necessary, would the handwritten memo suffice? *Levin v. Knight*, 865 F. 2d 1271 (9th Cir. 1989).

16. Keeton and Stewart entered into a partnership. Stewart, on behalf of the partnership, opened a checking account. The checking account records and signature cards at the bank authorized Keeton, Stewart, and Rabinette to withdraw funds. Later, the bank informed Keeton that the funds in the account had been depleted and that the attached line of credit had been overdrawn by $34,000. Keeton sued the bank alleging that he had orally told the bank not to permit withdrawals from the checking account or the line of credit without his approval. The bank asserted the parol evidence rule. Is evidence of Keeton's oral instructions admissible in court? *Keeton v. First National Bank of Tuscaloosa*, 529 So. 2d 963 (Ala. 1988).

17. Unit Construction hired Wilson Floors to install floor materials in an office building. Pittsburgh National Bank held a mortgage on the building that secured a construction loan made to Unit. When Unit fell behind in its payments to Wilson, Wilson threatened to walk off the job. Pittsburgh National orally promised to pay Wilson if Unit did not. Relying on the bank's surety promise, Wilson completed the work. Is the Bank's oral promise enforceable? *Wilson Floors Co. v. Scioto Park, Ltd.*, 377 N.E. 2d 514 (Ohio 1978).

18. While plaintiffs were employed at Dun & Bradstreet Corp. (D & H), D & H reorganized, splitting into three separate companies. Plaintiffs' employment contract specified a set of bonuses based on performance. The contract stated that in the event of a reorganization, bonuses "shall immediately become payable in full, with the final value determined as though performance criteria and targets for the full award period had been achieved." A dispute arose as to how this language should be interpreted because the bonus plan had different "targets," with compensation depending on which target was achieved. D & H interpreted the clause to mean that all employees should receive the minimum bonus regardless of performance. Plaintiffs read the clause to mean that in the event of reorganization, each employee should receive the bonus they would have received if no reorganization had occurred. The difference between the two interpretations meant about two million dollars in collective bonuses. Applying the various maxims of contract interpretation, how would you decide the dispute? *Bourke v. Dun & Bradstreet Corp.*, 159 F. 3d 1032 (7th Cir. 1998).

Assignment on the Internet

Some, but not all states, allow principles of promissory estoppel to permit oral contracts that ordinarily would be barred by the statute of frauds, to be enforced. Go to the American Law Institute's website at **http://ali.org.** where you will find recent and planned revisions to the *Restatement (Second) of Contracts.* Click until you find the annotations to Section 139. These annotations stipulate when use of promissory estoppel should prevail over the statute and when it should not. Think about the kind of rule you would draft if you were a state legislator. When, if ever, would you permit estoppel to negate the writing requirement?

On the Internet

http://www.bcf.usc.edu/~ctalley/frauds.html
University of Southern California professor Eric Talley discusses the history and applicability of the statute of frauds both internationally and in the United States.

www.lib.uchicago.edu./~llou/mpoctalk.html
For information written by research librarian explaining why the Internet is useful for legal research and describing electronically available legal information, go to this site.

http://www.uchastins.edu/plri/fall94/ whippel.html *For a research project report on the enforceability of electronic contracts, go here.*

www.lawguru.com *The July 2000 enactment of the electronic signatures bill generated a lot of news coverage. Several sites link to general news including this one.*

www.legalresearch.ils.unc.edu *The University of North Carolina LibClient developed with the Association for Law Libraries provides a very useful research tool for contract law matters.*

Howdy Doody Puppet Problems

"The Howdy Doody Show," a popular children's television show broadcast on NBC from 1947 to 1960, starred Howdy Doody, a puppet who was operated by Rufus Rose and Robert "Buffalo Bill" Smith.[1] After the show ended, NBC and Rose began discussing the care and possession of the show puppets.

In a series of letters between NBC and Rose, NBC agreed to pay Rose to care for and store the "Howdy Doody" puppet, along with other show puppets. These letters stated that Rose could keep the other show puppets, but "Howdy Doody" would be turned over to the Detroit Institute for its "Puppetry in America" museum. Rose kept the puppet for a while and lent it to Smith. When Rose died, Smith decided to auction off the puppet and split the profits with Rose's son.

1. *Who do you think should get the puppet, Smith or the Detroit Institute? Why? Is there any additional information you want to know before deciding?*
2. *Suppose you are a manager at the Detroit Institute of Arts. You have been expecting to get the "Howdy Doody" puppet for the puppetry museum. What kind of action, if any, could you take to get the puppet?*

---

[1] *Detroit Institute of Arts v. Rose*, 127 F. Supp. 2d 117, 2001 U.S. Dist. LEXIS 1007 (D.Conn. 2001); Possession of 'Howdy Doody' puppet . . ., ENTERTAINMENT LAW REPORTER, May 2001, at ___.

CHAPTER 18

Third Party Rights

Third Party Beneficiary Contracts

Assigning Contract Rights

Anticipating and Avoiding Problems with Assignments

Delegating of Contract Duties

One way the Detroit Institute could attempt to get possession of "Howdy Doody" is to argue that it is a third party beneficiary. A **third-party beneficiary** is a third party that obtains contract rights when the original two parties to a contract intend that that third party will benefit from the contract.

Third parties acquire contract rights in one of two ways. The first is through the transfer of an existing contract. Third parties can also obtain contract rights when the original two parties to a contract intend that that third party will benefit from the contract. Such contracts are called "third-party beneficiary contracts."

In this chapter we examine first, third-party beneficiary contracts, distinguishing between intended and incidental beneficiaries. Then, we discuss assignments and analyze how to identify and avoid common pitfalls when assigning contracts. We close with a discussion of contract delegations.

Third-Party Beneficiary Contracts

In a third-party beneficiary contract, the two primary parties to the contract agree that a third party will obtain legal rights to enforce that contract. If the contract language demonstrates that the primary parties clearly intended for the third party to have contract rights, courts will uphold the third party's rights. For example, a court considering the "Howdy Doody" case would ask whether NBC and Rose clearly intended for the Detroit Institute to have possession of "Howdy Doody." If courts cannot determine whether a benefit is intended, they will not grant such rights. Because of the presumption that third parties do not have contract rights, courts insist that the language showing an intent

to benefit a third party be explicit and direct.

A life insurance contract illustrates this point. A father buys a contract that clearly names his son as the beneficiary of the proceeds when the father dies. The father pays premiums and the company promises to pay a sum of money to the son when the father dies. Even if the son did not know of the contract, when his father dies, the son will have a right to collect from the insurance company because he is a third-party beneficiary to his father's insurance contract.

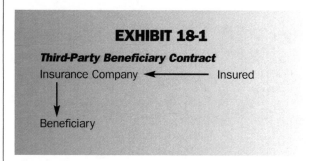

EXHIBIT 18-1

Third-Party Beneficiary Contract

Insurance Company ← Insured

Beneficiary

Vesting

Most life insurance contracts specify that the insured can change beneficiaries. As a result, the son's rights to the money will not mature, or **vest**, until his father dies with the son specified as the beneficiary, so if the father cancels the insurance policy, the son has no right to complain.

Sometimes the first two parties agree that the beneficiary cannot be changed. In such a case, third-party rights vest at the time that the contract is formed. If the contract does not mention vesting, there is a presumption that the rights are not vested. Some courts, however, infer that rights vest when a beneficiary learns of the contract, consents to it, and reasonably relies on it. To avoid misunderstandings, it is best to specify whether vesting is intended or not.

Intended Beneficiaries

If the parties to a contract intend that a third party will benefit from their agreement, the third party is an **intended beneficiary**. The two types of intended beneficiaries that we discuss are donee and creditor beneficiaries.

Donee Beneficiary

In the insurance example discussed earlier, the beneficiary pays no consideration because the father intends a gift. The son is called a **donee beneficiary**, a beneficiary to a contract in which the promisor intends to give a gift to the third-party beneficiary. Donee beneficiaries do not have to pay consideration to get contract rights. Would the Detroit Institute be considered a donee beneficiary in the "Howdy Doody" case?

Creditor Beneficiary

In other settings the intended beneficiary is not a recipient of a gift, but a creditor. Suppose that Jason wishes to take over a hardware store. This store owed $5,000 to a supplier. When Jason buys the store he promises to pay this debt. The supplier is called a **creditor beneficiary** and has rights to collect from Jason based on Jason's contract to buy the hardware store.

No particular words establish third-party rights. The courts look to the totality of the circumstances, including the words and actions of the parties and business customs. In addition, unless the statute of frauds or some other state statute specifies otherwise, no writing is necessary to establish a third-party beneficiary contract.

Incidental Beneficiaries

It is important to distinguish intended third-party beneficiaries from **incidental beneficiaries**. An incidental beneficiary is someone who benefits from a contract, but it is not the intent of the primary parties that the third party should benefit. Incidental beneficiaries do not have enforceable third-party rights.

For example, suppose a farmer contracts with a real estate promoter to build a shopping mall on the farmer's land. Neighboring businesses will benefit from the mall because the increased traffic flow promises to help their sales. Later, the farmer breaches his contract with the promoter and no mall is built. The neighboring businesses cannot sue the farmer for breach of contract because they are merely incidental beneficiaries, not intended beneficiaries.

In Case 18-1 the court analyzes whether the plaintiff is an intended or incidental beneficiary. The plain-

Global Context: Privity in Australia and the United Kingdom

The general rule throughout most of the world is that only the direct parties to a contract have rights pursuant to that contract. The notion that a third party can sue for breach of a contract for which he or she was not a party in Australia remains an exception.

This presumption against third parties' rights is called the doctrine of "privity." As a general rule, only a party who enjoys privity of contract can sue under contract law.

Privity as a means of avoiding liability is eroding in both Australia and the United Kingdom. For example, both the Queensland Court of Appeals and the British House of Lords have recently held solicitors (lawyers) liable to intended beneficiaries of wills where the wills have been produced in error. These findings are contrary to the traditional contract of privity: a solicitor acting on behalf of a client owed a duty of care to that client and not to third parties. The basis for the traditional rule was the third parties' lack of both privity and consideration in such situations. Allowing tort liability to third parties, absent privity and consideration, represents an invasion of fault-based tort principles into the province of contract law dependent on agreement and consideration. Although the privity requirement remains the rule in Australia and the United Kingdom, exceptions are growing.

tiff uses language in the contract to prove she was an intended beneficiary. Consider whether the language proves that the parties intended to give the plaintiff contract rights.

Case 18-1

Esquivel
v.
Murray Guard, Inc.
992 S.W. 2d 536 (Tex. App. 1999)

*D*ebbie Esquivel rented a hotel room at La Quinta Inn. She asked the clerk where she could park her U-Haul van. The clerk told her to park on the street adjacent to the hotel, assuring her that it would be safe because the hotel provided security. The next morning her car and the van containing her personal belongings were missing.

La Quinta had contracted with Murray Guard to provide security. Esquivel sued Murray Guard for negligence and for breach of a third-party beneficiary contract. The trial court dismissed the negligence action because the two-year statute of limitations had run out. Although the statute of limitations had not run out on Esquivel's contract claim, the court granted summary judgment for Murray Guard on that count. Esquivel appealed.

JUDGE FOWLER

[Esquivel] argues that she has a valid breach of contract claim…because she is a third party beneficiary of the contract between La Quinta and Murray Guard.

Esquivel bases her contention on the language of the contract, which states that Murray Guard shall furnish guards "for the purpose of securing persons and property of guests and employees of La Quinta." She contends this specifically identifies her as a party who was intended to be benefited by the contract…

Parties are presumed to contract only for their own benefit…There is a strong presumption against finding that a third party is a beneficiary of a contract. Any doubts are resolved against a finding of the existence of a third-party beneficiary.

Texas jurisprudence recognizes three types of third-party beneficiaries: donee, credit, and incidental. Only a donee or credit beneficiary may recover on a contract; an incidental beneficiary may not.

A person is a donee beneficiary if the performance of the contract inures to his benefit as a gift. An example is a prenuptial agreement in which a prospective bride promises to execute a will to benefit her prospective husband's children from a previous marriage. A donee beneficiary is not likely to be the intended beneficiary of a business agreement…

Since the contract between La Quinta and Murray Guard evidences a business relationship, before Esquivel can be an intended third-party beneficiary, she must qualify as a creditor beneficiary. Reviewing the contract, we find no evidence of an indebtedness, contractual relationship, or legally enforceable commitment, either actual or asserted, which would support Esquivel's contention that she is an intended third-party beneficiary…

Still, Esquivel contends that testimony of Patrick Devine, La Quinta's security director, establishes that she was an intended beneficiary. Mr. Devine testified that La Quinta intended to provide security for the benefit of its guests. Devine's testimony is irrelevant; we look only to the four corners of the agreement to determine the parties' intent…[T]he contract clearly shows that Esquivel is not a third party entitled to enforce the contract. Hence, there is no ambiguity, and summary judgment is appropriate. AFFIRMED.

1. Critical Thinking: What additional information about this contract would have been helpful in making the decision about whether Esquivel is a third-party beneficiary entitled to enforce the contract? Would additional information have altered the court's reasoning and decision in this case?

2. Ethical Decision Making: What values relating to third-party beneficiaries seem to influence the attitude of the Texas courts? What alternative values could lead another jurisdiction to establish rules about third-party beneficiaries that would accomplish a different ethical purpose?

Assigning Contract Rights

Contracts create both rights and duties. As a general rule, these rights and duties can be transferred to third parties. An **assignment** is a transfer of a contract right to a third party. A **delegation** is a transfer of a contract duty. Taken together, assignments and delegations provide a second means by which third parties can get rights and duties from a contract. In this section, we examine assignments in detail, including who the parties are, how to create an assignment, and which rights can and cannot be assigned.

Parties to an Assignment

As shown in Exhibit 18-2, the parties to an assignment are the *obligor, obligee, assignor, and assignee*. The person who is obligated to perform under a contract is called the **obligor**. The person who has the right to

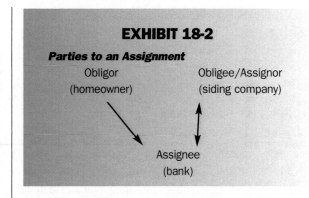

EXHIBIT 18-2
Parties to an Assignment

Obligor
(homeowner)

Obligee/Assignor
(siding company)

Assignee
(bank)

expect performance is called the **obligee**. When the obligee transfers (assigns) his or her contract right, he or she becomes the **assignor**. The person to whom the contract is assigned is called the **assignee**.

To illustrate the parties to an assignment, suppose that a home-improvement company contracts with a

Global Context: Assignability of Contract Rights in China

The free assignability of contract rights is a hallmark of a mature market economy. Assignability establishes capital accounts that enhance market efficiencies. In a centrally-planned economy, such as China, assignability is usually limited. Contract rights not directly involving the State can be assigned but only with the prior approval of the obligor. If a contract was originally created with State approval, the approval of the same State authority is required for an assignment, unless the original contract has terms to the contrary.

homeowner to install aluminum siding for $4,000. The homeowner pays $500 down and signs a promissory note agreeing to pay the siding company the balance with monthly installments. The company needs to pay its workers and its suppliers, so it assigns the right to collect on the homeowner's note to a bank. The bank pays a discounted rate, which is $3,100 for the $3,500 note. The homeowner now pays the installments to the bank, not to the siding company. As Exhibit 18-2 shows, the homeowner is the obligor, the siding company is the original obligee and the assignor, and the bank is the assignee.

An assignment differs from a third-party beneficiary contract because in an assignment there are two agreements, not one. The first agreement, which establishes the primary obligation, is between the homeowner and the company. The second is between the company and the bank. The second contract gives the third party assignee rights in the first contract between the homeowner and the siding company.

Creating an Assignment

To determine whether the parties have created an assignment, the court looks to the totality of the circumstances and asks whether the words and actions of the assignor indicate an intention to transfer rights to the assignee. A writing is not generally required for an assignment, though many states require that certain types of assignments be in writing. If the contract falls under the Statute of Frauds (Chapter 17)—a real estate contract, for instance—the assignment must be in writing.

In the typical case, such as the aluminum siding example, the assignee gives consideration and the assignment forms a contract that is not revocable. If the assignee does not give consideration, the assignment is generally revocable until the obligor performs.

Rights that Can and Cannot Be Assigned

Most contract rights can be assigned. We consider the four main exceptions to that general rule.

First, assignments that *increase the burden on the obligor* are not permitted without the consent of the obligor. In the siding example, transferring a right to collect money, called an **account receivable**, does not harm the obligor because it is just as easy for the homeowner to send the monthly payment to the bank as to the siding company. Hence, such an assignment does not require the approval of the homeowner.

If the assignment materially changes the obligation, however, it is ineffective. Suppose a concrete com-

pany in Philadelphia is obligated to deliver concrete to a local suburb. The obligee tries to assign the right to deliver the concrete to a company in Seattle. Because it is now more difficult to deliver the concrete, the assignment is ineffective. It is not fair to allow a subsequent assignment to materially change the original contract.

Second, some assignments *violate public policy* and are ineffective as a result. For instance, most states have a statute prohibiting or limiting the assignment of future wages. Such statutes are designed to protect wage earners from impoverishing themselves.

Third, *personal service contracts* are not assignable. For example, a homeowner may not assign a fire insurance policy to the buyer of his home. The insurance company based its policy on the personal characteristics of the original homeowner, so it would not be fair to allow the transfer of that policy without the approval of the company. Other examples of personal contracts include many employment contracts and contracts for professional services.

Fourth, if the *original contract prohibits assignments,* the contract is generally not assignable. For instance, real estate leases often contain clauses prohibiting subleasing—a form of assignment. There is an exception, however. Courts do not allow parties to prohibit the assignment of an account receivable. This limitation is based on a general public policy seeking to enhance assignability. It can also be found in Article 2 and Article 9 of the UCC discussed in later chapters.

EXHIBIT 18-3

Assignment of Contract Rights

Contract Rights Can Be Assigned Unless:

1. The assignment would materially change the obligor's duties.
2. The assignment is prohibited by public policy.
3. The rights assigned are personal in nature.
4. The original contract expressly prohibited assignments.
   (Exception: parties cannot expressly prohibit the assignment of a right to collect money.)

In Case 18-2, a client of a health club claimed that her selection of a club was based on its personal characteristics, including the expertise of its employees. When a second club bought the first, the client claimed that the exculpatory clause (discussed in Chapter 16) in her initial membership could not be assigned without her approval. The judges split on the issue of assignability.

Case 18-2

Petry
v.
Cosmopolitan Spa International, Inc.
641 S.W. 2d 202 (Tenn. App. 1982)

*S*hirley Petry signed a membership contract with Cosmopolitan Spa. A clause in that contract stated: "Member fully understands and agrees that in participating in one or more of the courses, or using the facilities maintained by Cosmopolitan, there is the possibility of accidental or other physical injury. Member further agrees to assume the risk of such injury and further agrees to indemnify Cosmopolitan from any and all liability to Cosmopolitan [resulting from] the use by the member of the facilities and instructions as offered by Cosmopolitan."
Cosmopolitan Spa sold its business to Holiday Spa, assigning its membership contracts on January 1. On February 25, Petry injured her back when an exercise machine collapsed under her. She sued both Holiday Spa and Cosmopolitan Spa. The trial court dismissed her action against both parties. Petry appealed.

JUDGE PARROT
Appellant contends that even if the exculpatory clause is valid, it does not protect appellee, Holiday, from liability because it could not be assigned. We must disagree. The exculpatory clause in this contract was a right of appellee Cosmopolitan. Generally, contractual rights can be assigned [unless]:

a) the substitution of a right of the assignee for the right of the assignor would materially change the duty of the obligor, or materially increase the burden or risk imposed on him by his contract, or materially impair his chance of obtaining return performance, or materially reduce its value to him, or

b) the assignment is forbidden by statute or is otherwise inoperative on grounds of public policy, or

c) assignment is validly precluded by contract.

None of the above exceptions to assignability can be successfully raised as to this exculpatory clause. Appellant contends that the assignment was invalid because the contract was of a personal nature and that she never consented to the assignment. We find this unpersuasive. This contract was primarily for the use of spa facilities and not of a personal nature…

In seems clear that the judge below was correct in his decision that appellant's suit was barred against appellee Holiday because it was appellee Cosmopolitan's assignee. That being the case, we must affirm the court below…
AFFRIMED.

JUDGE GODDARD, CONCURRING IN PART AND DISSENTING IN PART
I concur in the majority opinion insofar as it grants summary judgment in favor of Cosmopolitan Spa International, Inc., the original signator to the contract containing the exculpatory clause.

I do, however, respectfully dissent as to the dismissal of the assignee, Holiday Spa…I am of the opinion that there is a disputed fact whether the Plaintiff comes with the exception set out in Subsection (a) of the Restatement cited in the majority opinion…I believe it could be inferred that a change of personnel occurred from the time the assignment was made on January 1, until the accident happened on February 25, and that, absent a showing that the personnel of the assignee corporation was equally skilled in supervising the Plaintiff's exercise and in maintaining the equipment, reasonable minds could differ as to whether the Plaintiff's risk was materially increased.

1. Critical Thinking: The reasons that lead to legal conclusions often rely on a close reading of the facts. What factual dispute leads Judge Goddard to disagree with the majority in this case? Would the majority have necessarily agreed with Judge Goddard even if they had believed that there was a difference in the level of skill of Holiday and Cosmopolitan personnel?

2. Ethical Decision Making: Who are the relevant stakeholders in this case? Is it ethical to see the only relevant parties as just the three directly engaged in this dispute?

As illustrated in the Case 18-2, it is not always clear whether an assignment is personal in nature or increases the burden, including the risks imposed, on the obligor. To avoid misunderstandings, managers should address assignability in the initial contract—expressly stating that the contract may or may not be assigned.

Anticipating and Avoiding Problems with Assignments

As just discussed, distinguishing between assignments that are personal in nature and those that increase burdens on the obligor can be problematic. In this section we address two other potential problems with assignments. We look first at the rights and duties of the parties when the obligor does not perform. We then examine problems that can be avoided by promptly notifying the obligor of the assignment.

Rights and Duties of the Parties When the Obligor Does Not Perform

An assignment transfers contract rights from the original obligee to the assignee. But what happens if the obligor does not perform? Courts say "the assignee steps into the shoes of the assignor." This saying means that the assignee can sue the obligor directly. It also means that the assignee is subject to any defenses that the obligor could raise against the assignor.

Recall the aluminum siding example. Suppose that the homeowner does not pay the assignee bank. The bank sues the homeowner and the homeowner is able to prove that the siding company committed fraud in inducing the initial contract. Can the homeowner assert the fraud defense against the bank? The answer is yes, because the assignee bank "steps into the shoes" of

the siding company and obtains the rights of the siding company, its assignor—no more and no less. The company would not win against the homeowner, so neither does the bank. Note that the bank did not commit the fraud. Nonetheless, it cannot collect from the homeowner. To remedy this inequity, the bank can collect from the siding company if the company knew or should have known that the homeowner could assert fraud as a defense and did not inform the bank.

This remedy is available to assignees because assignors give an **implied warranty of assignability** stating that they do not know and have no reason to know of any defenses that the obligor can assert against the assignee. Potential defenses include arguing that the contract rights have not been previously assigned, lack of capacity, illegal nature of the contract; and lack of true assent due to fraud, duress, etc. The siding company clearly had reason to know of the fraud, so it breached its implied warranty and the bank will prevail in its suit against the company.

The implied warranty, however, does not guarantee payment. If the homeowner did not pay the bank because he subsequently lost his job and declared bankruptcy, the bank would recover from neither the homeowner nor the siding company.

Implied warranties also can be modified by express agreement. The siding company could have expanded its warranty by promising to pay the bank if the homeowner defaulted for any reason, including bankruptcy. The company could also have disclaimed the implied warranty. Such disclaimers, if not contrary to public policy, are enforceable.

In the following case the obligor did not pay the assignee, claiming that it had a "set-off" defense against the assignor. The obligor admitted owing money to the assignor, but claimed that the assignor owed it money on a separate account. The assignee sued the obligor and the obligor prevailed. Ask yourself whether the assignor breached an implied warranty of assignability. It may be helpful to draw a diagram to keep the status of the parties and legal issues clear.

Case 18-3

Hudson Supply & Equipment
v.
Home Factors Corp.
210 A. 2d 837 (D.C. 1965)

*O*n two occasions, Eastern Brick & Tile Company sold and delivered bricks to Hudson Supply & Equipment. Eastern then assigned its rights to collect for these sales to Home Factors Corporation. The accounts totaled $1,324.25. Home Factors demanded payment from Hudson and Hudson refused. Hudson argued that Eastern was indebted to it in an amount in excess of the amount sued for so it was entitled to a set-off defense for the amount claimed by Home Factors. The trial court did not allow Hudson to assert the set-off defense against Home Factors. Hudson appealed to the District of Columbia Court of Appeals.

JUDGE HOOD

At trial Hudson offered testimony that at the time of the assignment of the two accounts by Eastern to Home Factors, Hudson had claims of over $2,200 against Eastern growing out of other purchases.

The trial court ruled that there was a proper assignment from Eastern to Home Factors and that Home Factors was entitled to judgment for the full amount of its claim. However, the trial court stated "that the evidence indicated that the problem was between Hudson and Eastern, and that the defendant Hudson was entitled to credits of $229.22 and $172.31 from Eastern, and in addition had other claims or credits against Eastern—all of which indicated that Eastern and Hudson should litigate separately the issues between them."

The general rule here and elsewhere is that the assignee of a chose in action [contract] takes it subject to all defenses, including set-offs, existing at the time of the assignment. Since it is undisputed in this case that the asserted claims of Hudson existed at the time of the assignment, it is apparent that the trial court misconceived the law relating to assignments. When it was found that Hudson was entitled to certain credits, those credits should have been set off against the claim of Home Factors; and Hudson's "other claims for credits against Eastern" should have been determined, and, if established, should also have been set off against Home Factors' claim.

REVERSED AND REMANDED.

1. Critical Thinking: What ambiguity in the situation between Hudson and Eastern caused Home Factors to argue that Eastern and Hudson should litigate separately any obligations arising from their previous business interactions? Why was that ambiguity not persuasive to the court?

2. Ethical Decision Making: Would any particular values support a rule that would have freed the assignee from the requirement to take the contract, subject to all defenses existing at the time of the assignment?

Notice of Assignment

Although notice to the obligor is typically not necessary to create an assignment, notification can prevent many problems with an assignment. If the assignee in the previous case had notified the obligor of the assignment before paying the assignor, a lot of time, confusion, and litigation could have been avoided. Giving prompt notice also assures that the payments or other performance requirements are properly directed to the assignee, rather than to the assignor.

Notifying the obligor also protects the assignee in cases of multiple assignments. As shown in Exhibit 18-4, in a multiple assignment the assignor assigns a contract right to an assignee, and then *assigns the same contract right* to another assignee. Sometimes this is done by honest mistake. At other times it constitutes fraud.

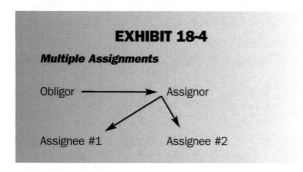

EXHIBIT 18-4

Multiple Assignments

An unscrupulous assignor might try to assign the same right to more than one person. When this happens, the obligor will pay only one of the assignees. Who is paid depends on the jurisdiction. Many states apply the *American rule*: the first assignee gets paid. Many others use the *English rule*: The first assignee to notify the obligor gets paid.

Of course, the losing assignee can always sue the assignor. But an unscrupulous assignor may be in jail, in bankruptcy court, in Acapulco under a false name, or all three. To safeguard business interests, managers should deal only with reputable assignors and promptly notify obligors of all assignments.

Now that we have discussed assignments, we examine delegation, the final means by which third parties can obtain rights and duties from a contract.

Delegating Contract Duties

One assigns contract rights and delegates contract duties. Often a given transaction will involve both an assignment and a delegation. For example, when a college student subleases her apartment for the summer, she assigns the right of occupancy and delegates the duty to pay the rent. Although people, including some lawyers, often speak of "assigning contracts," it is best to keep the issues of assignment and delegation separate. In this section, we discuss the parties to a delegation, how to create a delegation, and which duties can be delegated.

Parties to a Delegation

Like assignments, delegations involve two agreements. The first establishes a primary obligor and an obligee. The second involves a delegation of a duty from the obligor to a **delegatee**. The obligor becomes the **delegator** and the delegatee is obligated to perform on the behalf of the obligee. Exhibit 18-5 illustrates the parties to a typical delegation.

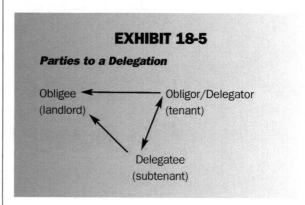

EXHIBIT 18-5

Parties to a Delegation

For example, assume Hannah has a one-year lease on her apartment. As the obligor Hannah is obligated to pay the rent. The landlord is the obligee. Hannah finds a subtenant, Macy, to take the apartment during the summer months. Macy agrees to pay the landlord the rent, and Hannah agrees to reimburse her for some of that rent. Macy, the subtenant, is the delegatee and Hannah is now the delegator.

A delegation differs from an assignment in one important respect. With an assignment, once the assignment is made, the assignor has no more rights with regard to the obligor. With a delegation, in contrast, the delegator is liable to the obligee if the delegatee does not perform. So, if Macy does not pay the landlord, the landlord can collect from Hannah.

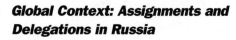

Global Context: Assignments and Delegations in Russia

The laws of assignments and delegations are fairly similar across most mature capitalist countries. In fact, comparing U.S. law with that of the United Kingdom, Germany, or France, one finds few distinctions. It seems that freely assigning contracts is essential to a credit-based market economy, and most nations seek to facilitate both assignments and delegations.

The United States expanded the freedom to assign contract rights and delegate contract duties in the late-eighteenth century to help support the industrial revolution. This trend continues today as contract rights are more freely assignable than ever.

Central planning in the former Soviet Union, by way of contrast, did not allow for free assignability. Recent reforms have largely changed that. The Russian Civil Code has been amended to reflect the German Code regarding freedom of assignment. Such legal changes are essential as Russia reforms its economic system from central planning to free market.

Creating a Delegation

As with assignments, no special words or actions are necessary to create a delegation. The courts look to the totality of the circumstances and ask whether a delegatee agreed to accept the duty to perform for the obligee. Unless the statute of frauds or other specialized state statute provides otherwise, no writing is necessary. Typically, the delegator will give the delegatee consideration, but no consideration is necessary to create a delegation.

Remember that a delegation of a duty to a delegatee does not release the delegator from potential liability to the obligee. In other words, if Macy, the subtenant, does not pay, the landlord can sue both the subtenant and Hannah, the primary obligor. For the obligor to be released from his or her obligation the obligee must agree. Such an agreement is called a *novation*.

A **novation** is an agreement to substitute one party to a contract for another. It essentially involves rescinding the first contract and creating a new contract with a substituted party. Hence, if the landlord had agreed to release Hannah from her lease and accept the subtenant under a new lease, Hannah would no longer be liable if the substitute tenant did not pay the rent. In contrast, if the landlord only consented to a delegation and assignment of the initial lease, Hannah would still be liable.

It is not always clear whether the parties intend a novation or a delegation. In the following case, no express novation occurred, but the North Dakota Supreme Court asked whether the actions of the parties indicated an intention to release the original obligor. Note that the parties may have avoided the litigation if they had made their intentions more clear.

Case 18-4

Rosenberg
v.
Son, Inc.
491 N.W. 2d 71 (N.D. 1992)

*I*n 1980 Mary Pratt contracted to buy a Dairy Queen restaurant from Harold and Gladys Rosenberg for $62,000. Pratt paid $10,000 down and agreed to pay the balance at ten percent interest over fifteen years. In 1982, Pratt assigned her rights and delegated her duties under this contract to Son, Inc. The contract between Pratt and Son contained a "Consent to Assignment Clause" signed by the Rosenbergs. The contract also had a clause stating that Son would indemnify Pratt in the event that Son failed to pay the Rosenbergs.

In 1984 Merit Corporation purchased the restaurant from Son, and the contract with the Rosenbergs was assigned a second time. The agreement with Merit did not contain a consent clause, but the Rosenbergs were fully aware of the transfer. In fact, the Rosenbergs received a $25,000 lump sum from Merit. Later, Merit filed bankruptcy and did not pay the $17,326 still owing to the Rosenbergs. The Rosenbergs sued both Pratt and Son. The trial court entered a summary judgment in favor of both defendants and the Rosenbergs appealed.

CHIEF JUSTICE ERICKSTAD

It is a well-established principle of contracts that the contracting party cannot escape its liability on the contract by merely assigning its duties and rights under the contract to a third party....

Thus, when Pratt entered into the "assignment agreement" with Son, a simple assignment alone was insufficient to release her from any further liability on the contact. It is not, however, a legal impossibility for a contracting party to rid itself of an obligation under a contract. It may seek the approval of the other original party for release, and substitute a new party in its place. In such an instance, the transaction is no longer called an assignment; instead, it is called a novation...

It is evident from the express language of the assignment agreement between Pratt and Son that only an assignment was intended, not a novation. The agreement made no mention of discharging Pratt from any further liability on the contract. To the contrary, the latter part of the agreement contained an indemnity clause holding Pratt harmless in the event of a breach by Son. Thus, it is apparent that Pratt contemplated being held ultimately responsible for performance of the obligation. Furthermore, the agreement was between Pratt and Son; they were the parties signing the agreement, not the Rosenbergs. An agreement between Pratt and Son cannot unilaterally affect the Rosenbergs' rights under the contract. The Rosenbergs did sign a consent to the assignment at the bottom of the agreement. However, by merely consenting to the assignment the Rosenbergs did not consent to a discharge of the principle obligor—Pratt. Nothing in the consent clause supports such an allegation...

The inquiry as to Pratt's liability does not end at this juncture. The trial court released Pratt from any liability on the contract due to the changes or alterations which took place following her assignment to Son. While it is true that Pratt cannot be forced to answer on the contract irrespective of events occurring subsequent to her assignment, it is also true that she cannot be exonerated for every type of alteration or change that may develop.

If the changes [second assignment] in the obligation prejudicially affect the assignor [Pratt], a new agreement has been formed between the assignee [Son] and the original contracting party [Rosenbergs]. More concisely, a novation has occurred and the assignor's original obligation has been discharged. Although we have previously determined that the terms of the assignment agreement between Pratt and Son did not contemplate a novation, there are additional methods of making a novation besides doing so in the express terms of an agreement. The question of whether or not there has been a novation is a question of fact. The trial court should not have granted summary judgment. There are questions of fact remaining as to the result of the changes in the contract. Thus, we reverse the summary judgement and remand for further proceedings.

REVERSED AND REMANDED.

1. Critical Thinking: The court says that there are factual issues that need to be decided before determining the contract rights in this case. What is this factual information that the court felt was important enough that a summary judgment by the trial court had been inappropriate?

2. Ethical Decision Making: Did the business managers of Merit Corporation behave ethically? Use the ethical guidelines outlined in Chapter 2 to assist you as you consider this question.

Duties that Can and Cannot Be Delegated

As a general rule, contract duties can be delegated with or without the permission of the obligor. Some duties, however, are not delegable unless the obligor consents.

The exceptions to the general rule resemble those discussed with assignments. If the contract is personal in nature, calling on the particular skill and expertise of the obligor, the duties cannot be delegated. Examples include contracts to paint portraits, to receive professional services, and most employment contacts. Thus, if you, as a business manager, hire an artist to paint your picture for your office, an attorney to represent you in court, or an employee to work in your office, the artist, attorney, or employee cannot transfer their duties to someone else unless you agree to the substitution.

Other duties, by contrast, are more routine. For example, a duty to water a lawn or to deliver newspapers requires no special expertise and hence is freely delegable. In addition, it is generally understood in the building industry that general contractors hire subcontractors to perform certain tasks such as laying carpet or installing plumbing. Given this custom, such duties can be delegated. Of course, delegations that violate public policy, such as delegating to an unlicensed subcontractor, are not valid.

Because it is not always clear whether a task is "personal" or "routine," it is a good idea to expressly address delegations in the primary contract. A clause stating that a "contract is assignable," or that "all rights under this contract are assignable," is interpreted to mean that both the rights are assignable and the duties can be delegated. Similar language prohibiting "assignments" will forbid both assignments and delegations.

"Howdy Doody" Wrap-Up

The Detroit Institute brought suit against Rose, asserting that the Institute was a third-party beneficiary of the agreement between Rose and NBC. One of the pieces of information, that might have been useful to know in your evaluation of the case, was if the letters between NBC and Rose specified a time that the puppet would be turned over to the Detroit Institute. The letters were silent about the time to hand over the puppet. Rose's estate argued that the puppet should not be turned over because Rose and Smith held the puppet for such a long period of time and the Detroit Institute delayed so long in asserting its right to the puppet. The court concluded that although a time to hand over the puppet was not specified, the Detroit Institute was a third-party beneficiary that was entitled to possession of the "Howdy Doody" puppet.

	Summary
Third Party Beneficiary Contracts	**Vesting**—when a party's right to a interest matures so that the party may take control of the interest. **Intended Beneficiaries**—two parties contract with the intention to benefit a third party. Donee Beneficiary Creditor Beneficiary **Incidental Beneficiaries**—third parties who benefit from a contract between primary parties who do not intend the third party to benefit.
Assigning Contract Rights	**Parties to an Assignment** Obligor—person who is obligated to perform under a contract. Obligee—person who has the right to expect performance. Assignor—obligee who transfers (assigns) his or her contract right. Assignee—person to whom the contract is assigned. **Creating an Assignment**—do the words and actions of the assignor indicate an intention to transfer rights to the assignee? **Rights that Cannot Be Assigned** Assignments that increase the burden on the obligor. Assignments violate public policy. Personal service contracts. When the original contract prohibits assignments.
Anticipating and Avoiding Problems with Assignments	**Rights and Duties of the Parties when the Obligor Does Not Perform**—assignors give an implied warranty of assignability. **Notice of Assignment**
Delegating Contract Duties	**Parties to a Delegation** Delegatee—one who takes on the duty to perform Delegator—one transferring the duty to perform **Creating a Delegation**—did a delegatee agreed to accept the duty to perform for the obligee? **Duties that Cannot Be Delegated** 1. Contracts for duties that are personal in nature. 2. Delegations that violate public policy.

Review Questions and Case Problems

1. Most contract rights can be assigned. List the exceptions.

2. Create an example of an incidental beneficiary and explain why that beneficiary does not get contract rights.

3. Define an assignor's *implied warranty of assignability*? What does this warranty include? What does it exclude?

4. What is the difference (if any) between a creditor beneficiary contract and a contract delegating a duty to pay a debt?

5. Your state legislature is considering legislation on the problem of multiple assignments. If you were a legislator, for which rule would you vote: the *American* or the *English*? Why?

6. A divorced wife brought a lawsuit against her ex-husband's former law firm partners to recover alimony and child support from the proceeds of the partnership's dissolution contract. Do you think that the divorced wife was given third-party contract rights in those proceeds? Why? *Micci v. Thomas*, 738 a. 2d 219 (Conn. App. 1999).

7. As part of a divorce settlement, the former husband promised to pay all reasonable college expenses for the children of the marriage. Four children attended col-

lege but the father failed to perform in accordance with his promise. Can the children sue their father for breach of contract? Under what theory? *Mitchell v. Combank/Winter Park,* 429 So. 2d 1319 (Fla. App. 1983).

8. In a classic case, Holly Fox owed Lawrence $300. Fox borrowed $300 from Holly and promised to repay the money to Lawrence. When Fox did not pay Lawrence, Lawrence sued Fox. Fox asserted both lack of privity and lack of consideration as defenses. Who won? Why would this be a classic case? *Lawrence v. Fox,* 20 N.Y. 268 (1859).

9. Allwaste, Inc. was considering merging with Philip Services Corporation. The board of directors for Allwaste contracted for consulting advice from Morgan Stanley Dean Witter. Morgan Stanley encouraged the transaction. After the merger, the stock price of Philip dropped. Holders of stock options in Philip sued Morgan Stanley for giving bad advice to Allwaste. Do you think that the option-holders won their third-party beneficiary claims? Why or why not? *Collins et al. V. Morgan Stanley Dean Witter,* 60 F. Supp. 2d 614 (S.D. Tex. 1999).

10. Terminal Freezing & Heating Company contracted to supply ice to W.C. Frederick, an ice-cream producer. The terms of the agreement specified that Frederick could order all the ice it "required" for a set price. Later, Crane Ice Cream, a much larger producer than Frederick, purchased all of Frederick's assets, including his contract rights. Terminal refused to deliver ice to Crane. Was Frederick's requirements contract assignable? *Crane Ice Cream v. Terminal Freezing & Heating,* 128 A. 280 (Md. 1925).

11. Patsy Ann Terry was killed in an automobile accident. Willie Terry, her husband, filed a wrongful death lawsuit. The case was settled with an insurance company promising to pay Willie monthly payments of $1,400 for a thirty years. The settlement contract contained a clause prohibiting assignment of those payments. Three years later, Willie bought some merchandise from Wentworth, paying for it by assigning one half ($700) of sixty future payments ($42,000). Two years later Willie filed bankruptcy, and Wentworth claimed that the assigned funds should be excluded from Willie's bankruptcy estate? Do you agree? *In re Terry, Case Number 99-12613-WHD, Lexis 141* (Bankr. N.D. Ga. 2000).

12. Thomas Hardee worked as a salesperson for Jordan Graphics. His employment contract contained a "non-competition" clause. When Reynolds & Reynolds Company purchased Jordan Graphics, Thomas ended his employment and began selling in competition with Reynolds. Reynolds sued, and Thomas contended that his employment contract, including the non-competition clause, was not assignable. Was Thomas correct? *Reynolds and Reynolds Co. v. Hardee,* 932 F. Supp. 149 (E.D. Va. 1996).

13. Superior Brassiere Company contracted to manufacture brassieres and corsets for Francbust, Inc. Francbust assigned all its accounts receivables for the sales of Superior's undergarments to Superior. Unfortunately for Superior, Francbust made a subsequent assignment of these same accounts to Finance Trust. The purchasers of the undergarments, who had no notice of any claims of Superior, paid Finance Trust. Superior sued Finance Trust. Who wins? Does your answer depend on whether the *American* or *English* rule is applied? *Superior Brassiere Co. v. Zimetbaum,* 212 N.Y.S. 467 (1925).

14. Magnum Enterprizes agreed to purchase the Diamond Ring Ranch from the Armstrong family for $10,800,000. After the contract was entered into, but before the real estate closing, Magnum agreed to let Berja, an investment group, buy the ranch. The Armstrongs agreed to accept Berja as the new buyer on the same terms as the original agreement. When Berja refused to go through with the closing, the Armstrongs sued Magnum. Magnum argued that the Armstrong's had agreed to a novation, discharging any duty owed by Magnum. The Armstrongs characterized the transaction between Magnum and Berja as an assignment and delegation. With whom do you agree? *Hagger v. Olfert,* 387 N.W. 2d 45 (S.D. 1986).

15. Pizza of Gaithersburg, Inc. contracted to have cold drink vending machines, owned by Virginia Coffee Services, placed in each of its restaurants. Macke Company later purchased Virginia. Pizza attempted to terminate the vending machine contracts. Pizza argued that it had prior dealings with Macke and had chosen Virginia because Pizza preferred the way Virginia serviced its contracts. Is the duty to service a vending machine of a "personal" nature? Can these duties be delegated even though the obligee objects? *Macke Company v. Pizza of Gaithersburg, Inc.,* 270 A. 2d 645 (Md. 1970).

Assignment on the Internet

In this chapter you learned the rights of third parties. There are many sites on the Internet that allow you to send an electronic greeting card to another person. E-Cards (www.ecards.com) is one such site. Is the recipient of an e-card a third-party beneficiary? What kind? What rights does a recipient of an e-card have against the company for any damage? Read the terms of use at E-Cards to answer these questions.

On the Internet

http://www.ladas.com/bulletins/2000/0600 Bulletin/UK_ThirdPartyBeneficiaries.html
Learn about the status of third party beneficiaries in the United Kingdom.

http://www.legalenglish.com/quiz3.html
Quiz yourself about the issues in this chapter at Legal-Ease International.

http://www.deanscourt.co.uk/legal/privity.html
Read about the United Kingdom's Rights of Third Parties Act of 1999. This act give additional context to the law regarding third party beneficiaries.

CHAPTER 19

First Islamic and Cirrus Holding Company

First Islamic Investment Bank created the Cirrus Holding Company for the sole purpose of aiding in the investments in Cirrus Industries, Inc. The Holding Company brought suit against Cirrus Industries, which is a corporation that manufactures small, single-engine aircraft, and also against AeroGlobal Capital Management, which is a limited liability company.

Although Cirrus is at the cutting-edge of the development of single-engine aviation aircraft, the company suffered from financial difficulties. Therefore, Cirrus explored fundraising opportunities, including investments from the Holding Company. The Holding Company and Cirrus made a nonbinding letter of agreement (LOA) on April 24, 2001, in which the Holding Company would receive sixty-one percent of the Cirrus's shares after investing $77.5 million. The LOA included details that restricted the amount of information that could be disclosed by Cirrus, and the LOA also prevented Cirrus from engaging in other negotiations or discussions that would be in competition with the agreement made between Cirrus and the Holding Company.[1]

As negotiations continued on the Stock Purchase Agreement (SPA), Cirrus stockholders expressed concerns, questioning their initial intent to sell their shares to the Holding Company. As the Holding Company was performing certain parts of the LOA, AeroGlobal expressed interest in dealing with Cirrus on May 16. After AeroGlobal submitted a proposal to Cirrus, the Holding Company claimed that Cirrus was not honoring the confidentiality sections of the LOA. Cirrus responded to the Holding Company's complaint, stating that the stockholders' vote would not be unanimously in favor of the Holding Company's proposal if AeroGlobal's proposal were not considered.[2]

Within the SPA between the Holding Company and Cirrus, the two parties made allowance for an "Open Window" (a ten-day period ending on June 17) during which Cirrus was permitted to consider proposals from other companies. If Cirrus found a "Superior Proposal," negotiations were allowable with another company if their proposal would be of greater benefit to Cirrus. The SPA also specified that the first seven days in the "Open Window" were for the consideration of other proposals and negotiations; the final three days were included for the purpose of allowing Cirrus to make a decision. During this "Open Window," Cirrus explored AeroGlobal's proposal and determined that an agreement made with AeroGlobal would be in the best interest of Cirrus. In other words, Cirrus stockholders unanimously viewed AeroGlobal's proposal as a "Superior Proposal" in accordance with the definition in the SPA. But the Holding Company argued that after June 16 at 11:59 p.m., the "Open Window" was unambiguously closed based on the SPA made with Cirrus. However, negotiations between Cirrus and AeroGlobal were still occurring in the morning of June 17, which the Holding Company argued was a breach of contract.[3]

---

[1] *Cirrus Holding Co. Ltd. v. Cirrus Industries and Aeroglobal Capital Management*, 2001 WL 846053 (Del. Ch.)

[2] *Id.*

[3] *Id.*

Therefore, the Holding Company filed for remedies that would oblige Cirrus to discontinue negotiations with AeroGlobal and force Cirrus to fulfill the obligations with the Holding Company that were established in the SPA.

1. *If you were negotiating contracts for Cirrus with AeroGlobal and the Holding Company, what ethical issues would concern you?*
2. *Do you think Cirrus should be permitted to contract with AeroGlobal, even though agreements were made after the "Open Window"? Why?*

CHAPTER 19

Performance, Discharge, Breach, and Remedies

Discharge by Performance

Discharge by Material Breach

Discharge by Agreement

Discharge by Operation of Law

Discharge by Changed Circumstances

Money Damages

Limitations on Money Damages

Equitable Remedies

In this chapter we consider the issues faced by parties such as the Holding Company and Cirrus. We begin with the issue of contractual discharge. Contractual obligations can be discharged, or terminated, in several ways: (1) by performance; (2) by material breach of the other party; (3) by agreement of the parties; (4) by operation of law; and (5) by a change in circumstances. We examine each of these discharge methods. In the second part of the chapter we examine the remedies courts can provide in the event a contract is breached.

Discharge by Performance

The most common way to discharge one's contractual duties is by performing them. If Andrea promises to sell you her bike for $50, she discharges her obligations by tendering the bike, and you discharge your duties by tendering the $50. Typically, performance must be exactly as promised. Tendering $49 for Andrea's bike will not discharge your duties; you must give $50.

Time of Performance

Some contracts have to be performed exactly on time; others do not. If the contract states that on-time performance is vital, or the court interprets time to be "of the essence," even a brief tardiness constitutes a material breach. If time is not essential, however, reasonable tardiness will not be a material breach and the obligor's duties will be discharged. The question here is

one of contractual intent, with the courts looking both to the express language of the contract and to the totality of the circumstances.

Substantial Performance

Some contracts are notoriously difficult to perform exactly as promised, such as those in the construction industry. In such settings, courts do not require exact performance, requiring **substantial performance** instead. Under this doctrine, a builder discharges its obligations if it makes a good faith effort to perform exactly as promised and provides the important and essential benefits of its promise. Minor discrepancies, then, do not constitute a material breach. The rule of substantial performance recognizes that building contracts contain numerous details, and it is almost impossible to meet every requirement exactly.

For example, suppose a builder places blue tile in the kitchen when the contract called for aqua, misplaces a bedroom wall by six inches, and completes the construction three weeks behind schedule. Many courts would find that the contract had been substantially performed, despite the discrepancies with the original agreement.

Because substantial performance is not complete performance, the other party is entitled to compensation for the reasonable costs to cure the defects. That is, the buyer must pay for the home, but would be permitted to deduct the cost of replacing the tile. If it would be impractical to correct the problem (moving the bedroom wall is probably impractical), the homeowner can deduct any loss in the value of the home caused by the problem. Unless the contract states otherwise, time is not of the essence in construction contracts. However, the buyer can deduct costs incurred by the three-week delay.

After Cirrus approved AeroGlobal's proposal after the Open Window, the Holding Company argued that this action constituted a breach of contract. Therefore, the Holding Company declared that the transaction between AeroGlobal and Cirrus must be terminated and Cirrus should be expected to perform in accordance with the SPA made with the Holding Company. The court acknowledged that Cirrus did make an agreement with AeroGlobal after the Open Window, but concluded that the agreement between AeroGlobal and Cirrus did not constitute a material breach because the agreement was made only several hours after the Open Window closed. In other words, although complete performance of the SPA did not occur, the court found that Cirrus substantially performed.

However, the doctrine of substantial performance is rarely applied outside of the construction industry. As illustrated in the following case, to discharge one's contractual obligations, performance usually has to be exactly as promised.

Case 19-1

Kichler's Inc.

v.

Persinger
265 N.E. 2d 319 (Ohio App. 1970)

*A*nn Persinger custom ordered two bedspreads, two valances, and two laminated shades from Kichler's Inc. to decorate her bedroom. The bedspreads were to reach from the top edge of the mattress to the floor, a distance of twenty-four inches. In addition, all materials were to come from the same bolt of cloth to ensure an exact match in color. Persinger gave a $40 down payment, leaving $82.54 due on delivery.

When the items arrived, the bedspreads were only twenty-two inches, not twenty-four, and Persinger claimed that the material used on the valances did not exactly match that used in the other items. Kichler's attempted to rectify the problem by adding a two-inch ruffle to the bedspreads, but Persinger refused to accept them, demanding a refund of her $40. Kichler's sued for breach of contract and Persinger filed a cross petition for her down payment. The trial court held that Kichler's had substantially performed and awarded it judgment. Persinger appealed.

JUDGE HESS

Substantial performance of a contact is interpreted to mean that mere nominal, trifling, or technical departures are not sufficient to breach a contract, and that slight departures, omissions, and inadvertences should be disregarded.

There is a great difference in performing an interior decorating contract wherein the purchaser of materials is concerned with the motif and décor of the premises and an ordinary building contract or service contract where slight variances in the use of materials do not change the appearance of the premises.

In the instant case, the trial court found the bedspreads, shades and valances did not harmonize in color, and that the bedspreads were not made in keeping with the "Mary Beth" spread the defendant purchased, and concluded that such disparity was "not of sufficient nature that is should have been objectionable to the defendant;" and further, that the addition of a ruffle did not "materially change to a substantial degree the type and design of bedspread."

It is not within the power of the court to determine whether the defendant should have been satisfied with the change in style and color of the bedspreads. The defendant was entitled to receive the style and color of furnishings in decorating her bedroom that she desired and specified. The plaintiff was obliged by his contract to provide the materials desired and ordered. It is common knowledge that color and style of interior decorations vary according to the desires and aesthetic pleasure of individuals. That which may be acceptable to one individual could be wholly unacceptable to another.

It is evident from the record in this case that there was a breach of contract by the plaintiff and the defendant should not be required to accept and pay for the materials described therein, and that the defendant is entitled to judgment on her cross petition.

REVERSED.

1. Critical Thinking: What is the key ambiguity in the application of the legal rule in this case?
2. Ethical Decision Making: What ethical values support a finding for the customer in this case? Do any ethical values justify Kichler's behavior in this case?

Discharge by Material Breach

The second rationale for discharging a contractual obligation is by the material breach of the other party. A **material breach** occurs when a party fails to substantially perform. When one party breaches, the other party's contractual obligations are discharged and he or she no longer has to perform. However, if the breach is minor, the nonbreaching party may sue for damages, but contractual obligations are not necessarily discharged. Once a minor breach is remedied, the nonbreaching party must continue to perform contractual duties.

Some contracts call for simultaneous performance, which means that the contract requires both parties to perform certain contractual duties at the same time. For example, suppose Andrea contracts to sell her bike with payment on delivery. Her performance (delivery of the bike) must be simultaneous with your performance (payment of $50). Because timely tendering of performance is a condition of the contract, a party must tender performance in a timely manner or the other party is discharged.

Anticipatory Repudiation

Generally, one cannot breach a contract before the time that performance is due. Sometimes, however, one party will know in advance that it will breach its contract and informs the other party. For example, Andrea promised to deliver her bike on May 10, but on May 8 she informs the buyer, or the buyer discovers, that she sold the bike to Tommy. This is called an **anticipatory repudiation**.

An anticipatory repudiation creates options for the nonbreaching party. That party may elect to rescind the contract and recover the value of any consideration rendered or to sue immediately for breach. He or she may

also choose to treat the contract as still binding and wait for the time of performance to sue. An anticipatory repudiation may be withdrawn any time before performance is due, unless the nonbreaching party has already sued or relied on the repudiation in some way.

Discharge by Agreement

The third way to discharge contractual duties is by agreement of the parties. This agreement to discharge duties can happen in several ways. Some key examples include the following: (1) express condition; (2) mutual rescission; (3) novation; or (4) accord and satisfaction.

Conditional Contracts

Parties sometimes agree to condition their promises on the happening of a particular event. If that event occurs, the contract is discharged. For example, most real estate contracts are conditioned on the buyer being able to acquire financing. The buyer and seller enter a binding contract, but agree that that contract will be discharged, or declared null and void, if the buyer cannot acquire financing following a good faith effort. The happening of the condition discharges the contract.

Parties are free to condition their contracts in any way they like. As discussed in Chapter 16, consideration problems arise if the happening of the condition is controlled by one of the parties. In such cases the promises may become "illusory" and no contract is formed.

Mutual Rescission

Parties sometimes agree to discharge one another even if the initial contract did not so provide. Suppose that Andrea contacts to sell her bike for $50 and later both the buyer and Andrea agree not to go through with the deal. The agreement to cancel the contract would be called a mutual rescission.

A mutual rescission is a separate contract, so to be effective it must have all the elements of contract, including an exchange of consideration. When the original contract is executory (not performed by either party), each party gives consideration in calling off the deal. If one party has already performed, however, then the mutual rescission will be effective only if that party receives some consideration in exchange for agreeing to discharge the other party. Assuming all contractual elements are present, mutual rescissions are fully enforceable and discharge the underlying contract.

Novation

A **novation** is an agreement to substitute one party in a contract for another. The exiting party is discharged. For example, you sell your home, while still owing money on it, to the bank. The bank agrees to release you from your debt and accept the new buyer in substitution. The novation discharges your obligation to the bank.

Accord and Satisfaction

A settlement contract, or *accord and satisfaction* (discussed in Chapter 16), will also discharge a contract. Here, the parties agree to substitute a settlement contract for the original contract. For example, a creditor claims that a debtor owes $7,000. The debtor claims the debt is only $3,000. They settle their dispute for $5,000. The contract to settle is an accord. Performing on the accord (paying the $5,000) is called a satisfaction. The satisfaction discharges both the settlement contract and the original contact. If the satisfaction is never performed, the other party may sue under either the original contract or for breach of the accord.

Discharge by Operation of Law

The fourth way that contractual duties can be discharged is through operation of law, such as through bankruptcy, running of the statute of limitations, or alteration. We explore these three topics next.

Bankruptcy

A debtor who has insufficient assets to meet his obligations may petition a federal court for bankruptcy protection. The aim of bankruptcy court proceedings is to distribute the debtor's remaining assets to creditors in a fair, timely manner. Most contractual obligations can be discharged in bankruptcy. Certain debts, such as taxes and child support payments, cannot. Although a debtor may later waive a discharge by following procedures in the Federal Bankruptcy Code, once a bankruptcy petition has been approved, a debtor's contractual obligations are discharged.

Statutes of Limitations

A statute of limitations states that a court action must be commenced within a specific time period or it is waived. The time period for suing on a contract varies from state to state. A typical state may give two or three years to initiate a suit for breach of an oral contract and maybe five years for breach of a written contract. Once the time period has run, the underlying contractual obligations are discharged.

Alteration

If one party to a contract willfully alters a written contract in a material way (such as adding a "zero" to change a number from 100 to 1000) without the consent of the other party, the contract will be discharged at the option of the innocent party.

Discharge by Changed Circumstances

The final way that a contract may be discharged is by an unforeseen change in circumstances. Sometimes, after a contract is entered but prior to performance, a disruptive event changes things so dramatically that it becomes either impossible or very impractical to perform. Such events may discharge a contract under one of three legal rules: (1) impossibility; (2) frustration of purpose; or (3) commercial impracticability.

Impossibility

At times a disruptive event may make performance literally impossible. Such events typically do not discharge contractual obligations. As a general rule, a promisor assumes the risk that performance will become impossible and must pay damages if failing to perform. There are three situations, however, in which impossibility of performance provides a legal excuse, discharging contractual obligations.

First, a personal service contract will be discharged by the *incapacity or death of an essential party*. Suppose Lilian, a famous diva, contracts to sing an opera. If Lilian suffers a sudden bout of laryngitis, or dies, her performance becomes impossible, and her (or her estate's) obligations are discharged. Although incapacity (or death) does not discharge most contractual duties, it does discharge personal service obligations when the promisor is an essential party.

Second, a sudden and *unanticipated change in the law* can also discharge a contract. For example, a construction contract to build an apartment building will be discharged if a zoning ordinance changes, making construction illegal.

Third, the *destruction of unique subject matter* of a contract creates a discharge. For example, Duncan contracts to sell a unique heirloom to Naomi. The night before delivery, fire destroys the heirloom. Since the heirloom was unique, performance is impossible and Duncan's obligations are discharged.

Courts tend to interpret the rules of impossibility rather narrowly. To receive a discharge, the disruptive event must not have been the fault of one of the parties. If a party is at fault, that party is liable. In addition, the event must not have been anticipated. If the parties anticipated the event and allocated the risk of loss to one of the parties, that allocation controls. Managers familiar with business law realize that they must be watchful for events that might disrupt a contract and then make certain that all contracts address those potential obstructions to smooth commercial exchanges.

The following global context contrasts the use of the doctrine of impossibility in the United States and Germany.

Global Context: Impossibility of Performance in Germany

In the United States, the doctrine of impossibility takes on an "all-or-nothing" quality. Courts will either declare that the doctrine applies and discharge the contract, or hold that the doctrine does not apply, finding the nonperforming party in breach. German courts, by way of contrast, are more willing to share the losses caused by a disruptive event.

For example, suppose that a U.S. shipping company operating in France promises to transport cars from a French production plant to buyers in India. The contract envisions shipment through the Suez Canal. A war breaks out in the Middle East, closing the Canal. Delivery, if it is to occur, must now be made around the horn of Africa. Does the impossibility of using the Canal discharge the shipping contracts? Who assumes the risk of war—the shippers in France or the buyers in India?

U.S. law either excuses the shippers completely or holds them strictly liable. The case probably turns on whether the contract specified a particular shipping route. If the contract did not specify the route, the shipper probably absorbs the increased shipping costs. If it did specify the route, the contract is probably discharged and the Indian buyers suffer the increased costs.

Under German law, in contrast, the court would be much more likely to split the losses between the two parties so they share the burden imposed by the disruptive event. Assuming that the contract was silent on the route issue, a German court would probably insist that the Indian buyers pay for part of the increased shipping costs, but not all.

Frustration of Purpose

Frustration of purpose is similar to impossibility. In such a case, performance of the contract is not impossible, but supervening events destroy the underlying purpose of the contract. The doctrine traces to a cancelled coronation procession for King Edward VII of England. Hotel rooms were rented along Pall Mall (the procession route) at exorbitant rates. When the procession was cancelled, the hotel owners tried to hold the renters to the contracts. The English Courts found for the renters, holding that the change of circumstances frustrated the mutual purpose of the parties and discharged the debts. U.S. courts have adopted this common law doctrine.

Commercial Impracticability

Courts also have the authority to discharge contracts when events render performance more expensive than originally intended. In one case, an aluminum processing plant promised to deliver aluminum at a fixed rate over a twenty-year period. The contract had an escalation clause allowing the price to increase in accord with the general inflation rate. But things changed, and the cost of producing aluminum increased much faster than general inflation. Citing commercial impracticability, the court allowed the plant to raise its prices so as to prevent an "unfair hardship" to the aluminum producer.

Care must be taken in employing the doctrine of commercial impracticability. First, the financial hardship must be extreme. Second, it must not be foreseeable. As a general rule, escalating prices or other events affecting the profitability of a contract will not generate a discharge. Nonetheless, commercial impracticability may discharge a contract to prevent an extreme injustice.

Although the United States has a general standard for determining what constitutes a commercial impracticability, other countries, such as Italy, have more specific rules to identify commercial impracticability. The following global context briefly examines the Italian approach.

Global Context:
Commercial Impracticability in Italy

Contract provisions in civil law countries, such as Italy, are typically organized in two parts. The first part addresses contract law generally, setting forth the elements and excuses applicable to any type of contract. The second provides a set of standard terms particular to various transaction types.

The Italian Code specifies the rules of commercial impracticability with regard to construction contracts. It states that a construction contractor must accept additional work caused by a change of circumstances anytime the additional work is less than one sixth of the value of the contract. The buyer must compensate the contractor for this additional work. In addition, if the cost of materials or labor changes (either up or down) by less than one tenth, no adjustment in the contract is made. If the costs change by more than one tenth, the aggrieved party must be compensated.

Comparing U.S. law with Italian law, U.S. courts are much less precise in specifying exactly what does and does not constitute commercial impracticability. Reflecting a common law tradition, each case is judged on its own merits.

Having discussed the ways that contractual duties can be discharged, which are summarized in Exhibit 19-1, we now turn to the remedies courts grant in the event of a material breach. We begin with a discussion of money damages and the limits on those damages. The chapter concludes with a discussion of non-monetary relief.

EXHIBIT 19-1

Method	Key Concepts
Discharge by Performance	Complete Performance Substantial Performance
Discharge by Material Breach	Anticipatory Repudiation
Discharge by Agreement	Conditional Contracts Mutual Rescission Novation Accord and Satisfaction
Discharge by Operation of Law	Bankruptcy Statute of Limitations Alteration
Discharge by Changed Circumstances	Impossibility Frustration of Purpose Commercial Impracticability

The common law remedy for a breach of contract is an award of **money damages**. The measure of damages is called an **expectation remedy**. The innocent party is awarded *the amount of money necessary to put him or her in the financial position he or she expected to be in if the contract were performed as promised.*

To illustrate, suppose Donnie promised to sell his canoe to Paula for $400. Donnie breaches. Paula then buys an essentially similar canoe for $475. Donnie must pay Paula $75. This payment would put Paula in the financial position she would have been in if Donnie had performed as promised. Paula would have a canoe, as expected, and would have paid a net of $400.

The order to pay $75 would be called a **compensatory damage** because it compensates Paula for the direct and usual consequences of the breach. Paula could also collect for any reasonable **incidental damages.** For example, suppose that because of the breach Paula ran an ad in the student newspaper reading "Canoe Wanted." The ad cost $10. Here, the court would order Donnie to pay Paula $85–$75 for direct compensatory damages plus $10 in reasonable incidental damages.

Contractual breaches can also cause more remote and unusual damages called **consequential damages.** For example, suppose Paula had intended to resell Donnie's canoe to a third party for $600. Although Paula was able to run an ad and get a similar canoe, the delay caused her to lose this sale and the $200 profit she expected. Consequential damages (also called **special damages**) for breach of contract are awarded only if reasonably foreseeable by the breaching party. Hence, Donnie would only be liable for the additional $200 if he knew or should have known of Paula's intent to resell. We return to this rule later in the chapter.

The following classic case, known as "The Case of the Hairy Hand," applies the expectation remedy to an unusual set of facts. The key to understanding the measure of damages is to ask where the innocent party is at the time of the breach, and then to award the dollars necessary to put the party in the position he or she expected to be in if there were no breach.

Case 19-2

Hawkins
v.
McGee
146 A. 641 (N.H. 1929)

*H*awkins touched an electric wire and burned the palm of his hand. Badly scarred, his hand remained useable, but lacked flexibility. *McGee, a physician, offered to operate using an experimental skin grafting technique. McGee guaranteed that the operation would make Hawkins' hand "one hundred percent perfect." After the operation, Hawkins' hand was worse, not better. The operation caused the motion of his hand to become so restricted that the hand was virtually useless. In addition, the grafting technique caused a "matted" and "unsightly growth"— presumably hair.*

Hawkins sued McGee for breach of contract. Although the jury found for Hawkins, Hawkins argued that the trial judge's instruction to the jury regarding money damages was in error. The Supreme Court of New Hampshire considered the issue of damages.

JUDGE FOWLER

The only substantial basis for the plaintiff's claim is the testimony that the defendant also said before the operation was decided upon, "I will guarantee to make the hand a hundred percent perfect hand" or "a hundred percent good hand." The plaintiff was present when these words were alleged to have been spoken, and if they are to be taken at their face value, it seems obvious that proof of their utterance would establish the giving of a warranty in accordance with his contention.

The substance of the charge to the jury on the question of damages appears in the following quotation: "If you find the plaintiff entitled to anything, he is entitled to recover for what pain and suffering he has been made to endure and for what injury he has sustained over and above what injury he had before." By it, the jury was permitted to consider two elements of damage, (1) pain and suffering due to the operation, and (2) positive ill effects of the operation upon the plaintiff's hand....[T]he forgoing instruction was erroneous.

The purpose of the law is to put the plaintiff in as good a position as he would have been in had the defendant kept his contract. The measure of recovery is based upon what the defendant should have given the plaintiff, not what the plaintiff has given the defendant or otherwise expended....

We therefore conclude that the true measure of the plaintiff's damage in the present case is the difference between the value to him of a perfect hand or a good hand, such as the jury found the defendant promised him, and the value of his hand in its present condition...

The extent of the plaintiff's suffering does not measure this difference in value. The pain, necessarily incident to a serious surgical operation, was a part of the contribution which the plaintiff was willing to make to his joint undertaking with defendant to produce a good hand. It was a legal detriment suffered by him which constituted a part of the consideration given by him for the contract.

It was also erroneous and misleading to submit to the jury as a separate element of damage any change for the worse in the condition of the plaintiff's hand resulting from the operation, although this error was probably more prejudicial to the plaintiff than to the defendant. Any such ill effect of the operation would be included under the true rule of damages set forth above, but damages might properly be assessed for the defendant's failure to improve the condition of the hand, even if there were no evidence that its condition was made worse as a result of the operation.

REMANDED ON THE ISSUE OF DAMAGES.

1. Critical Thinking: This case was remanded on the issue of damages. What reasons did the court provide for that decision? Can you explain the link between the court's reasoning and its conclusion?

2. Ethical Decision Making: The physician in this case did not provide what he promised. What missing information would enable you to determine whether he violated any of the classical ethical guidelines?

Limitations on Money Damages

In Case 19-2, the patient was entitled to the difference in value between a perfectly good hand and a motionless hand covered with unsightly hair. This expectation measure of damages applies in all contexts where there is a breach of an enforceable legal contract. There are, however, some limitations on common law damages. We consider several limitations in the sections that follow, beginning with the duty to mitigate.

Duty to Mitigate

After a breach, the nonbreaching party must take steps to mitigate, or lessen, the other party's damages. This limitation on common law damages, called a **duty to mitigate**, is based on a commonsense rule of fairness that prevents the nonbreaching party from taking advantage of the situation to accumulate damages.

For example, suppose Harry breaches his one-year apartment lease. Most states require Harry's landlord to make reasonable efforts to find a new tenant. If the landlord failed to take these steps, a court could reduce the level of damages owed by Harry by the amount the landlord would have received had the landlord found a substitute tenant.

A similar result occurs if an employer breaches an employment contact, firing an employee before the term of the contract expires. The fired employee must take reasonable steps to seek alternative employment and accept work of an essentially similar nature. Of course, the work must be similar. There is no duty to take a job that is not of the same type and rank.

The duty to mitigate is somewhat unique to common law systems. Most civil law countries do not recognize a clear duty to mitigate. For example, there is no provision in the French Civil Code requiring an employee to seek comparable employment on termination. In the United States, the duty to mitigate is routinely applied.

Nominal Damages

Sometimes a breach does not result in actual money losses. In such a case the courts grant one dollar, otherwise known as **nominal damages.** For example, suppose that Donnie breaches his contract to sell his canoe for $400 to Paula. Paula is able to buy an essen-tially similar canoe for $350. Although Donnie breached his contract, Paula did not suffer a money loss and she would receive a nominal damage award. Sometimes the award of nominal damages is important because the court may order the losing party to pay the court costs of the other party.

Nominal damages are also awarded when actual damages are too speculative. Parties must be able to prove damages with a reasonable degree of certainty or they will not be recoverable. For example, suppose a small start-up business contracts to advertise in a local monthly business magazine. The magazine breaches its contract and does not run the ad. Unless the business can prove actual losses caused by the failure to run the ad, it would receive a refund of any fees paid, if any, and only a nominal damage award.

Foreseeability

As stated earlier, consequential (special) damages can only be recovered if they were foreseeable by the breaching party at the time the contract was entered. Recall our example where Paula intends to buy Donnie's canoe and then resell it at a $200 profit. If Donnie had no reason to know of the resale, then he would not be liable for the $200 lost profit if he later breaches. In contract law, damages are awarded only for losses that could be reasonably foreseen.

To understand the rule of foreseeability, remember that the centerpiece of contracting is the agreement between the parties and that contracts allocate risks. If Paula wanted Donnie to accept the risk of special and unusual damages (the loss of the resale), she needed to inform him of that risk. Parties assume only those risks to which they objectively agreed, not to unforeseeable risks.

The rule of foreseeability traces to the classic case of *Hadley v. Baxendale.* In fact, the rule is commonly referred to as the "Rule of Hadley." Although *Hadley* involves a set of rather mundane facts, it is nonetheless the most famous contract case. The court focuses, in part, on whether it was customary in nineteenth-century England for mills to have backup crankshafts. In reading the case, consider what the mill could have done if it wanted to hold the shipper liable for the mill's lost profits.

Case 19-3

Hadley

v.

Baxendale
156 Eng. Rep. 143 (Court of Exchequer 1854)

*H*adley operated a mill in Gloucester, England. A crankshaft broke causing his mill to shut down. Hadley hired Baxendale to deliver the crankshaft to a repair shop in Greenwich. Baxendale guaranteed delivery in one day, but due to his neglect, delivery was delayed for several days. Hadley sued for the mill's lost profits caused by the delay in shipping. The jury found for Hadley. Baxendale appealed, arguing that the trial court erred by submitting the issue of lost profits to the jury. Baxendale contended that the lost profits were not foreseeable and should have been excluded from any damage award. The Court of Exchequer considered the appeal.

BARON ALDERSON

Where two parties have made a contract which one of them has broken, the damages which the other party ought to receive in respect of such breach of contract should be such as may fairly and reasonably be considered either arising naturally, i.e., according to the usual course of things, from such breach of contract itself, or such as may reasonably be supposed to have been in the contemplation of both parties, at the time they made the contract, as the probable result of the breach of it. Now, if the special circumstances under which the contract was actually made were communicated by the plaintiffs to the defendants, and thus known to both parties, the damages resulting from the breach of such a contract, which they would reasonably contemplate, would be the amount of injury which would ordinarily follow from a breach of contract under these special circumstances so known and communicated....[W]e find that the only circumstances here communicated by the plaintiffs to the defendants at the time the contract was made, were, that the article to be carried was the broken shaft of a mill, and that the plaintiffs were the millers of that mill. But how do these circumstances shew [show] reasonably that the profits of the mill must be stopped by an unreasonable delay in the delivery of the broken shaft by the carrier to the third person? Suppose the plaintiffs had another shaft in their possession put up or putting up at the time, and that they only wished to send back the broken shaft to the engineer who made it; it is clear that this would be quite consistent with the above circumstances, and yet the unreasonable delay in the delivery would have no effect upon the intermediate profits of the mill....But it is obvious that, in the great multitude of cases of millers sending off broken shafts to third persons by a carrier under ordinary circumstances, such consequences would not, in all probability, have occurred; and these special circumstances were here never communicated by the plaintiffs to the defendants. It follows, therefore, that the loss of profits here cannot reasonably be considered such a consequence of the breach of contract as could have been fairly and reasonably contemplated by both the parties when they made this contract.

REMANDED ON THE ISSUE OF DAMAGES.

1. Critical Thinking: What is the ambiguity associated with the concept of foreseeability? How should a court determine whether a particular consequence was foreseeable by the parties?

2. Ethical Decision Making: Did Baxendale behave ethically when he delayed delivery of the crankshaft? What stakeholders should be identified when considering the ethics of his behavior?

Liquidated Damages

Sometimes parties agree in advance on the amount of damages that will be paid in the event of a breach. Such agreements are called **liquidated damages**. A liquidated damage clause will be enforceable if it reflects a good faith effort to estimate the actual damages likely to result from a breach.

Punitive damages are never awarded for a breach of contract. The only exception is if the conduct constituting the breach is a tort (such as fraud) for which punitive damages are allowed. Care must be taken in drafting liquidated damage clauses to assure that they are not punitive. If a court determines that the liquidated damage does not reflect an honest attempt to estimate actual damages, courts will call it a penalty clause and refuse to enforce it because penalty clauses violate public policy.

For example, suppose a lease agreement states that a $1,000 security deposit will be forfeited if the tenant fails to clean the apartment at the end of the lease term. Even if this clause were labeled "liquidated damages" in the lease, it would still be a penalty because the $1,000 is not related to the costs of routine cleaning. Hence, the clause would not be enforceable. The clause must estimate a more reasonable cleaning sum to be enforceable as liquidated damages.

Oddly, parties often label liquidated damage clauses as "penalty clauses" in their contracts. Fortunately for these parties, courts pay little attention to labels, looking instead at the substance of the agreement. As illustrated in the following case, liquidated damage clauses are enforceable, whereas penalty clauses are not.

Case 19-4

Beasley
v.
Horrell
864 S.W. 2d 45 (Tenn. App. 1993)

William and Sarah Beasley owned two buildings out of which they ran a small business. The business was not doing well and the Beasleys needed cash. They sold the buildings to Henry Horrell under a sale and leaseback arrangement. Horrell paid $1,500,000 in cash and gave a $100,000 promissory note to the Beasleys. A cancellation provision in the note stated that if the Beasleys defaulted on any term in the lease, the $100,000 promissory note would be "null and void."

A year later, the Beasleys filed for bankruptcy and failed to make rent payments on the buildings. Citing the cancellation provision, Horrell refused to pay on the promissory note and the Beasleys sued. The trial court enforced the cancellation provision and entered a summary judgment for Horrell. The Beasleys appealed to the Tennessee Court of Appeals.

JUDGE LEWIS

Plaintiffs argue that the cancellation provision in the promissory note is an unenforceable penalty because it is not a reasonable estimation of the foreseeable damages from the failure to make payments required by the leases.

Parties to a contract may stipulate to an amount as liquidated damages. However, if the stipulated figure amounts to a penalty, it will not be enforced. A penalty is a sum inserted in a contract, not as the measure of compensation for its breach, but rather as a punishment for default. Liquidated damages is an amount determined by the parties to be just compensation for damages should a breach occur. In determining whether a particular provision constitutes liquidated damages or a penalty, the court must determine whether the amount stipulated was reasonable in relation to the amount of damages that could be expected to result from the breach....When there is doubt whether a provision is intended to be liquidated damages or a penalty, the court must construe it as a penalty.

From defendant Henry Horrell's testimony, it is clear that the note was intended to act as a spur to prevent the breach, and not as an estimate of damages resulting from the breach. Mr. Horrell described the note as a "good conduct" note and as a "carrot" and "reward for good behavior." A reading of the note shows that is also intended to be punishment if there is a default, no matter how slight the default.

In the instant case, plaintiffs would forfeit $100,000 for missing a payment required by the lease regardless of when, during the lease term, the breach occurred. We are, therefore, of the opinion that the defendants did not draft the cancellation provision with compensation in mind.
REVERSED.

1. Critical Thinking: The testimony of Horrell used the analogy between the promissory note and a carrot. How did that damage the reasoning on which Horrell was relying?

2. Ethical Decision Making: What ethical values and public policies is the Tennessee court upholding when it refuses to enforce a contract provision that serves as a penalty?

Restitution

Expectation damages are awarded for breach of an enforceable legal contract. When there has been part performance of an *unenforceable* contract, the remedy is **restitution**. The court requires each party to disgorge, or give back, the value of any benefit received. Where an expectation remedy puts the parties in the position they expected to be in, restitution returns them to their positions prior to contracting.

For example, suppose that Milan orally contracts to rent an apartment for two years. He gives a $500 down payment to seal the deal. The landlord then breaks the oral agreement and rents the apartment to someone else. Because of the statute of frauds (the contract cannot be performed within one year), Milan's agreement is not legally enforceable, so Milan will not get an expectation damage. However, Milan will get his $500 back to prevent unjust enrichment of the landlord.

Restitution is also the measure of damages under the equitable doctrine of **quantum meruit** for services rendered. For example, an unlicensed plumber contracts to do plumbing work. Although the contract is illegal (public policy requires a license), the plumber may receive the value of any work completed to prevent the unjust enrichment of the other party. The plumber would not, however, be given any profits or other expected gains.

Reliance Damages

A **reliance damage** is an alternative to measuring damages by the expectation rule. Like restitution, the goal of reliance damages is a return to the status quo. But unlike restitution, the intent is not to prevent unjust enrichment, but to protect the reliance interests of an innocent party. Reliance damages are most commonly given under the doctrine of promissory estoppel.

Recall that courts use promissory estoppel to form a quasi contract when: one party makes a promise knowing that the other party will rely; the other party reasonably relies to his or her detriment; yet no legal contract exists (Chapter 14). In such cases, the courts typically measure damages by the reliance damages suffered by the innocent party, not with reference to the benefit of the bargain.

For example, consider the case of *Hawkins v. McGee* presented earlier. The New Hampshire Supreme Court held that McGee breached a legal contract and awarded Hawkins an expectation damage—the difference in value between what he got (immobile hairy hand) and what he expected (hand as good as new). Under a reliance damage, by contrast, the court would restore Hawkins to his status before contracting with the doctor. This would be measured by the difference in value between what he got (immobile hairy hand) and what he had before he met the doctor (an inflexible hairless hand).

The following case was decided under the doctrine of promissory estoppel and the court discusses the issue of damages. Ask yourself if upon remand, the trial court will measure her lost wages with reference to the job that she quit, or with the job that she was promised. The former reflects a reliance damage; the latter is an expectation damage.

Case 19-5

Goff-Hamel

v.

Obstetricians & Gyn., P.C.
588 S.W. 2d 798 (Neb. 1999)

*G*off-Hamel worked for Hastings Family Planning for eleven years. On July 27, 1993, George Adam, a part owner of Obstetricians, offered her a job with him and she accepted. Goff-Hamel's first day of work was to be October 4, and she resigned from Hastings effective October 1. On October 3, she was told that she should not report to work at Obstetricians. Apparently, the wife of another part owner opposed the hiring of Goff-Hamel. Goff-Hamel was unable to find alternative work until April 1995, when she was employed part-time.

Goff-Hamel sued for breach of contract and under the doctrine of promissory estoppel. The trial entered a summary judgment for defendant on both counts. Goff-Hamel appealed to the Nebraska Supreme Court.

JUDGE WRIGHT

We have consistently held that when employment is not for a definite term and there are no contractual, statutory, or constitutional restrictions upon the right of discharge, an employer may lawfully discharge an employee whenever and for whatever cause it chooses. Therefore, the trial court correctly determined as a matter of law that Goff-Hamel could not bring a claim for breach of an employment contract.

Goff-Hamel's second cause of action was based upon promissory estoppel. The development of the law of promissory estoppel is an attempt by the courts to keep remedies abreast of increased moral consciousness of honesty and fair representations in all business dealings.

We have not specifically addressed whether promissory estoppel may be asserted as the basis for a cause of action for detrimental reliance upon a promise of at-will employment.…Other jurisdictions which have addressed the question.…have determined that when a prospective employer knows or should have known that a promise of employment will induce an employee to leave his or her current job, such employer shall be liable for the reliant's damages.…

[W]e conclude under the facts of this case that promissory estoppel can be asserted.…However, there remains a material issue of fact regarding the amount of damages sustained by Goff-Hamel. Promissory estoppel provides for the damages as justice requires and does not attempt to provide the plaintiff damages based upon the benefit of the bargain. For example, the damages sustained by an employee who quits current employment to accept another job are different than the damages sustained by an employee who had no prior employment but may have moved to a new location in reliance on a job offer. In the latter case, wages from prior employment are not considered in the determination of damages because the party did not give up prior employment in reliance on the new offer. In neither case are damages to be based upon the wages the employee would have earned in the prospective employment because the employment was terminable at-will.

REVERSED AND REMANDED ON THE ISSUE OF DAMAGES.

1. Critical Thinking: When damages are later determined in this case, what rival causes for Goff-Hamel's long unemployment should be examined? How do those rival causes affect the amount of damages?

2. Ethical Decision Making: The doctrine of promissory estoppel has ethical roots. How does the universalization principle assist us in understanding the growth of the doctrine?

Equitable Remedies

Although courts typically order money damages for breach of a contract, sometimes money cannot do full justice to the parties. When money proves inadequate, a court may grant an equitable remedy: (1) specific performance; (2) injunction; or (3) reformation.

Specific Performance

Specific performance is an order from a court to do a specific act other than pay money. When money damages seem an inadequate remedy, a court may order a party to perform exactly as promised under a contract.

Ordinarily, specific performance is not available when a seller breaches a contract to deliver goods because most goods can be purchased elsewhere in the market. When the good is unique, however, the court may order the breaching seller to deliver that good rather than to pay money. Heirlooms, antiques, and art objects might therefore be subject to an order of specific performance.

The most common use of the doctrine involves the seller's breach of a contract to sell land. Land is, by its very nature unique, so orders of specific performance are the norm in real estate transactions. The breaching seller is not ordered to pay money, but to tender the deed.

Global Context: Specific Performance in Germany and China

German law reverses the U.S. presumption of money damages as the most common contract remedy. In Germany, specific performance is the typical remedy for breach of contract and money damages are granted only after certain procedures are followed seeking specific performance.

Chinese law also emphasizes specific performance. In an economy in which many shortages of goods and services exist, money will often prove an inadequate remedy because alternatives are not available in the marketplace. Hence, the contract laws of centrally planned economies have historically relied on specific performance as a remedy, not dollar damages.

Injunction

Orders of specific performance are seldom given for breach of an employment or other personal service contract. Courts are reluctant to force people to work together under conditions where animosities may exist. The courts may, however, order an injunction in such settings. An **injunction** is an order from a court to *not* perform a specific act.

For example, suppose that a sports superstar is under contract with a team. A team in another league offers the star more money to play for it. If the current team cannot adequately be compensated with money (that is, the superstar has unique talents), the courts may grant an injunction, ordering the superstar to not play in the other league.

In the case involving agreements made with Cirrus, the Holding Company sought a preliminary injunction from the court that would prohibit Cirrus from fulfilling agreements made with AeroGlobal. Ultimately, the Holding Company hoped for specific performance, if the court ruled in their favor, which would require Cirrus's stockholders to vote on the proposal submitted by the Holding Company. On June 18, 2001, Cirrus provided the Holding Company with notice of termination (after the Open Window), and also paid the Holding Company a $5 million termination fee, which was required by the SPA. Upon payment of the termination fee, the SPA indicated that this fee would be the only remedy required by law for the Holding Company. Additionally, the SPA stated that the Holding Company could not seek additional equitable remedies, such as an injunction or specific performance, when the termination fee was paid. The court considered whether the Holding Company would suffer from excessive damages if the termination fee were the only remedy. Determining that the termination fee was unusually high, the court concluded that injunctive relief and specific performance were unnecessary remedies.

Reformation

On rare occasions, courts may elect to rewrite a contract for the parties and then enforce the contract as rewritten. This remedy, called a **reformation**, is used most commonly when a writing does not reflect the true intent of the parties. For example, if a land sale contract incorrectly describes the property to be sold, the court may reform the contract to reflect the true intent of the parties and then grant an order of specific performance. Reformation is often the most just way to remedy clerical errors in drafting contracts. In addition, some courts have used the power of reformation to limit the scope of noncompetition clauses that were drawn so broadly that they violated public policy.

Wrap-Up

The Court of Chancery of Delaware first concluded that Cirrus's negotiations made with AeroGlobal did not constitute a material breach. Therefore, when Cirrus gave notice of termination to the Holding Company on June 18, the court declared Cirrus' actions substantial performance. Accordingly, the court considered the termination fee of $5 million to be adequate for damages suffered by the Holding Company. Thus, the court denied the Holding Company's request for injunctive remedies and specific performance because the Holding Company could not demonstrate that damages would be excessive without additional remedies. This case illustrates that intricacies in contracts often lead to the implausibility of exact performance, and that consideration of remedies in case of a breach of contract should be included within contractual agreements.

	Summary
Discharge by Performance	**Time of Performance**—contracting parties determine whether there is a time that performance should occur. If time of performance is specified in the contract, and a party fails to perform by that specified time, a material breach has occurred. **Substantial Performance**—because it is nearly impossible to meet every requirement in a contract, substantial performance requires that parties show a good faith effort and meet most of the essential elements in a contract.
Discharge by Material Breach	**Anticipatory Repudiation**—when one party knows in advance that it will breach its contract and informs the other party, anticipatory repudiation has occurred.
Discharge by Agreement	**Conditional Contracts**—this term refers to contractual agreements based on the happening of a particular event, which discharge the contract. **Mutual Rescission**—both parties both agree to cancel the contract. **Novation**—this form of discharge refers to an agreement to substitute one party in a contract for another. **Accord and Satisfaction**—a discharge agreement between two parties to substitute a settlement contract for the original contract.
Discharge by Operation of Law	**Bankruptcy**—a debtor who has insufficient assets to meet his obligations may petition a federal court for bankruptcy protection. **Statute of Limitations**—this concept refers to the time limitations for when a party may sue for breach of a contract. **Alteration**—if a contract is materially altered by one party, the contract is discharged at the discretion of the other party.
Discharge by Changed Circumstances	**Impossibility**—an event may make performance impossible, but typically the promisor must pay damages for failing to perform. **Frustration of Purpose**—this discharge occurs when performance of the contract is not impossible, but supervening events destroy the underlying purpose of the contract. **Commercial Impracticability**—when performance creates extreme financial hardships that are not foreseeable, commercial impracticability may be implemented to prevent an extreme injustice.
Money Damages	The common law remedy for a breach of contract is to reward the amount of money necessary to the innocent party in the financial position he or she expected to be in if the contract were performed as promised.

	Summary (continued)
Limitations on Money Damages	**Duty to Mitigate**—this limitation is placed on the non-breaching party who promotes fairness by requiring the non-breaching party to reduce the other party's damages.
	Nominal Damages—this form of damages consists of a one dollar award to the non-breaching party when damages do not result in money loss.
	Foreseeability—damages are awarded only for those losses that are easily foreseen.
	Liquidated Damages—these agreements are made in advance, determining the amount of damages that will be paid in the event of a breach.
	Restitution—this remedy is for part performance of an unenforceable contract, which typically includes disgorging benefits received.
	Reliance Damages—this remedy provides an alternative to the expectation rule, returning parties to the status quo by protecting the reliance interests of the innocent party.
Equitable Remedies	**Specific Performance**—this remedy is an order from a court to do a specific act other than pay money.
	Injunction—an alternative equitable remedy is an order from a court to not perform a specific act.
	Reformation—another available remedy consists of rewriting a contract for the parties and then enforcing the contract as rewritten.

Review Questions and Case Problems

1. Review Exhibit 19-1. List the various ways that contractual duties can be discharged and discuss the key concepts associated with each.

2. Create three examples in which impossibility of performance will discharge a contractual obligation.

3. When a contract calls for simultaneous performance, each party must tender performance to maintain a right to sue for breach. Explain why.

4. A county hires a construction company to build a bridge for $100,000. The company expects to spend $50,000 on labor and $30,000 on materials. After the company has spent $20,000 on labor and $10,000 on materials, the county decides not to build the bridge and repudiates the deal. The company stops work immediately and sues for breach. The materials have a salvage value of $5,000. Using an expectation remedy, how many dollars will the court order the county to pay?

5. An anticipatory repudiation creates options for the nonbreaching party. That party may elect to sue immediately or to wait and sue later. What advantage does the breaching party receive by informing the other party that the contract will be breached?

6. French law does not recognize a duty to mitigate damages in the event of a breach of an employment contract by an employer. Law in the United States does. Which rule is better?

7. Baldwin agreed to build a house for Smith in accordance with certain building plans. The contract price was $31,000. When the house was completed, Smith refused to pay Baldwin because the fireplace contained a four-foot damper when the contract had specified a five-foot damper. The cost to cure the defect was $1,500. To what, if any, remedy is Baldwin entitled? *Baldwin v. Smith*, 586 S.W. 2d 624 (Tex. 1979).

8. Parker signed a contract for a series of dance lessons from Murray Dance Studios. The contract stated that it could not be cancelled and that no refunds would be made under the terms of a contract. Parker was seriously injured in an automobile accident and it became impossible for him to dance. Does this change of circumstances discharge Parker's contract with the Dance Studio? *Parker v. Arthur Murray, Inc.*, 295 N.E. 2d 487 (Ill. App. 1973).

9. A real estate sales contract stated that time was of the essence and called for closing on April 30, 1996. Like most such contracts, the contract contained a condition stating that the contract would be discharged in the event that the seller was unable to proved a clean title to the property. The seller delayed in obtaining title clearance and the closing deadline was missed. The buyer sued for specific performance of the sales contract. Was the contract discharged? Analyze. *English v. Muller*, 514 S.E. 2d 195 (Ga. 1999).

10. Cannarella purchased fish from Jay Cee Fish Company. Cannarella owed Jay Cee about $8,900. Cannarella informed Jay Cee that Cannarella was selling his business to Boan. Boan made several payments to Jay Cee on Cannarella's account and Jay Cee accepted these payments. Jay Cee then sued Cannarella for the amount

still owing? Analyze whether Cannarella's debt was discharged? *Jay Cee Fish Co. v. Cannarella*, 279 F. Supp. 67 (D.S.C. 1968).

11. An importer of sewing machines asked to be discharged from its contract because of a recent dramatic shift in the exchange rate between the U.S. dollar and the Swiss franc. The import contract permitted an adjustment in price in the event that costs of insurance, import fees, or shipping costs changed, but it did not mention fluctuating exchange rates. How much of a change in the exchange rate would be, or should be, necessary before a court will use commercial impracticability to discharge the obligor? *Bernina Distributors, Inc. v. Bernina Sewing Machine Co.*, 646 F. 2d 434 (10th Cir. 1981).

12. Gay Construction Company hired American Structural Systems as a subcontractor to do work on the San Jose Catholic Parish. The subcontract amount was $85,940. Structural performed some work and was paid $34,200. A dispute arose over whether Structural had agreed to supply a metal deck. Work stopped and Structural sued for recovery of the balance due on the contract. Gay filed a counterclaim for damages against Structural for breach of contract. The trial court found for Gay and ordered Structural to pay $47,353, the amount paid by Gay to complete the deck. Structural appealed, claiming that the trial did not correctly calculate damages. Do you agree? *American Structural Systems v. R.B. Gay Construction*, 619 So. 2d 367 (Fla. App. 1993).

13. Source Indirect, Inc. marketed various products, including vitamins. Donald Mantel, a physician, contracted to endorse the vitamins for a fee. Mantel later breached his contract and Source hired another physician at the same fee to endorse the vitamins. Source sued Mantel for breach of contract and won. Mantel argued that any damages caused by his failure to endorse the product were too speculative to be recoverable. Do you agree? *Source Direct, Inc. v. Mantel*, 870 P. 2d 686 (Kan. App. 1994).

14. John Bigda worked as general counsel and secretary of Fishbach Corporation. Victor Posner and his partners, Ivan Boskey and Michael Milikan, sought to acquire Fishbach. As part of the acquisition contract, Posner promised to retain the services of Bigda for a minimum of five years. The contract contained a liquidated damage clause guaranteeing Bigda a lump sum of triple his most recent annual salary in the event that Posner violated any term of the acquisition. Three weeks prior to the expiration of the five-year term, Bigda complained that Posner had never given Bigda the authority promised under the contract, sued Posner for breach, and demanded the triple salary in liquidated damages. Who do you think should win? Explain your answer. *Bigda v. Fishbach Corp.*, 849 F. Supp. 895 (S.D.N.Y. 1994).

15. Sullivan planned to open a restaurant and bookstore. He contacted a commercial leasing agent and asked if the owners of a property would make certain modifications to a particular site. After extensive negotiations, a commercial lease was signed. The landlord promised to make certain improvements. Sullivan spent many hours reading books on how to run a restaurant, testing recipes, obtaining financing, contracting to buy equipment, and performing myriad other tasks associated with a new business. When the landlord discovered that its promised structural expenses would be more than anticipated, it breached its lease and Sullivan sued and won. Because any lost profits were too speculative to be recoverable, the court awarded a reliance damage, rather than an expectation remedy. Which of the aforementioned expenses could Sullivan recover? Explain. *Sullivan v. Oregon Landmark-One, Ltd.*, 856 P. 2d 1043 (Or. App. 1993).

16. In 1970 Leona Fox entered into a revocable trust agreement with American State Bank. The primary asset of the trust was a large tract of land in Dearborn County, Indiana. The trust empowered the bank to sell the property and provided that any proceeds should be divided equally among Leona's four children upon Leona's death. In 1973 Leona executed a will stating that her son, Patrick, should receive only $100, with all other assets, including the trust, being divided equally among Leona's other three children. On April 9, 1984, Patrick died, survived by his widow, Anna. On June 2, 1984, the bank contracted to sell Leona's land to Pragar and Anna filed a lawsuit to block the sale. The lawsuit created a cloud on the title to the property. Leona died in 1985. In 1991, the Indiana Court of Appeals affirmed a trial court dismissal of Anna's claim. In 1993 the bank filed a petition requesting permission to sell the property at auction, and Pragar objected. Pragar sought specific performance of his 1984 contract. Did he wait too long to receive specific performance? *Wagner v. Estate of Fox*, 717 N.E. 2d 195 (Ind. App. 1999).

Assignment on the Internet

In this chapter, you learned about contract damages. Liquidated damages determine what the damages will be before the breach occurs. Contracts with athletic coaches commonly contain liquidated damage clauses. Due to the nature of coaching (coaches move on to better positions or are fired for failing to win), the contracts are often breached. These cases are usually settled without a trial. One such instance where a claim was litigated involved the former football coach of the University of Vanderbilt. (http://www.gatorsports.com/news/premium/articles/97/n_June_27_97_2476.html). Find press releases dealing with a coach's termination or resignation that discuss the details of the liquidated damages clause. Does the clause operate as a penalty? If you were a judge, would you enforce the clause?

On the Internet

http://www.flyingmag.com/FlightReports/ArticleDisplay.asp?ArticleID=31&page=1 *Flying Magazine's website includes an article about Cirrus Industries.*

http://www.judiciary.state.nj.us/charges/civil/412.htm *This site provides a definition of substantial performance and also includes a list of several cases related to substantial performance in construction.*

http://www.law.cornell.edu/ucc/2/2-610.html *Cornell's site contains the UCC code; this particular web page includes the UCC section about anticipatory repudiation.*

APPENDIX A

The Constitution of the United States

Preamble

We the People of the United States, in Order to form a more perfect Union, establish justice, insure domestic Tranquility, provide for the common defence, promote the general Welfare, and secure the Blessings of Liberty to ourselves and our Posterity, do ordain and establish this Constitution for the United States of America.

Article I

Section 1. All legislative Powers herein granted shall be vested in a Congress of the United States, which shall consist of a Senate and House of Representatives.

Section 2. The House of Representatives shall be composed of Members chosen every second Year by the People of the several States, and the Electors in each State shall have the Qualifications requisite for Electors of the most numerous Branch of the State Legislature.

No Person shall be a Representative who shall not have attained to the Age of twenty five Years, and been seven Years a Citizen of the United States, and who shall not, when elected, be an Inhabitant of that State in which he shall be chosen.

Representatives and direct Taxes shall be apportioned among the several States which may be included within this Union, according to their respective Numbers, which shall be determined by adding to the whole Number of free Persons, including those bound to Service for a Term of Years, and excluding Indians not taxed, three fifths of all other Persons. The actual Enumeration shall be made within three Years after the first Meeting of the Congress of the United States, and within every subsequent Term of ten Years, in such Manner as they shall by Law direct. The Number of Representatives shall not exceed one for every thirty Thousand, but each State shall have at Least one Representative; and until such enumeration shall be made, the State of New Hampshire shall be entitled to chuse three, Massachusetts eight, Rhode Island and Providence Plantations one, Connecticut five, New York six, New Jersey four, Pennsylvania eight, Delaware one, Maryland six, Virginia ten, North Carolina five, South Carolina five, and Georgia three.

When vacancies happen in the Representation from any State, the Executive Authority thereof shall issue Writs of Election to fill such Vacancies.

The House of Representatives shall chuse their Speaker and other Officers; and shall have the sole Power of Impeachment.

Section 3. The Senate of the United States shall be composed of two Senators from each State, chosen by the Legislature thereof, for six Years; and each Senator shall have one Vote.

Immediately after they shall be assembled in Consequence of the first Election, they shall be divided as equally as may be into three Classes. The Seats of the Senators of the first Class shall be vacated at the Expiration of the second Year, of the second Class at the Expiration of the fourth Year, and of the third Class at the Expiration of the sixth Year, so that one third may be chosen every second Year; and if Vacancies happen by Resignation, or otherwise, during the Recess of the Legislature of any State, the Executive thereof may make temporary Appointments until the next Meeting of the Legislature, which shall then fill such Vacancies.

No Person shall be a Senator who shall not have attained to the Age of thirty Years, and been nine Years a Citizen of the United States, and who shall not, when elected, be an Inhabitant of that State for which he shall be chosen.

The Vice President of the United States shall be President of the Senate, but shall have no Vote, unless they be equally divided

The Senate shall chuse their other Officers, and also a President pro tempore, in the Absence of the Vice President, or when he shall exercise the Office of President of the United States.

The Senate shall have the sole Power to try all Impeachments. When sitting for that Purpose, they shall be on Oath or Affirmation. When the President of the United States is tried, the Chief Justice shall preside: And no Person shall be convicted without the Concurrence of two thirds of the Members present.

Judgment in Cases of Impeachment shall not extend further than to removal from Office, and disqualification to hold and enjoy any Office of honor, Trust, or Profit under the United States: but the Party convicted shall nevertheless be liable and subject to Indictment, Trial, Judgment, and Punishment, according to Law.

Section 4. The Times, Places and Manner of holding Elections for Senators and Representatives, shall be prescribed in each State by the Legislature thereof, but the Congress may at any time by Law make or alter such Regulations, except as to the Places of chusing Senators.

The Congress shall assemble at least once in every Year, and such Meeting shall be on the first Monday in December, unless they shall by Law appoint a different Day.

Section 5. Each House shall be the judge of the Elections, Returns, and Qualifications of its own Members, and a Majority of each shall constitute a Quorum to do Business; but a smaller Number may adjourn from day to day, and may be authorized to compel the Attendance of absent Members, in such Manner, and under such Penalties as each House may provide.

Each House may determine the Rules of its Proceedings, punish its Members for disorderly Behavior, and, with the Concurrence of two thirds, expel a Member.

Each House shall keep a Journal of its Proceedings, and from time to time publish the same, excepting such Parts as may in their Judgment require Secrecy; and the Yeas and Nays of the Members of either House on any question shall, at the Desire of one fifth of those Present, be entered on the Journal.

Neither House, during the Session of Congress, shall, without the Consent of the other, adjourn for more than three days, nor to any other Place than that in which the two Houses shall be sitting.

Section 6. The Senators and Representatives shall receive a Compensation for their Services, to be ascertained by Law, and paid out of the Treasury of the United States. They shall in all Cases, except Treason, Felony and Breach of the Peace, be privileged from

Arrest during their Attendance at the Session of their respective Houses, and in going to and returning from the same; and for any Speech or Debate in either House, they shall not be questioned in any other Place.

No Senator or Representative shall, during the Time for which he was elected, be appointed to any civil Office under the Authority of the United States, which shall have been created, or the Emoluments whereof shall have been increased during such time; and no Person holding any Office under the United States, shall be a Member of either House during his Continuance in Office.

Section 7. All Bills for raising Revenue shall originate in the House of Representatives; but the Senate may propose or concur with Amendments as on other Bills.

Every Bill which shall have passed the House of Representatives and the Senate, shall, before it become a Law, be presented to the President of the United States; If he approve he shall sign it, but if not he shall return it, with his Objections to the House in which it shall have originated, who shall enter the Objections at large on their Journal, and proceed to reconsider it. If after such Reconsideration two thirds of that House shall agree to pass the Bill, it shall be sent together with the Objections, to the other House, by which it shall likewise be reconsidered, and if approved by two thirds of that House, it shall become a Law. But in all such Cases the Votes of both Houses shall be determined by Yeas and Nays, and the Names of the Persons voting for and against the Bill shall be entered on the Journal of each House respectively. If any Bill shall not be returned by the President within ten Days (Sundays excepted) after it shall have been presented to him, the Same shall be a Law, in like Manner as if he had signed it, unless the Congress by their Adjournment prevent its Return in which Case it shall not be a Law.

Every Order, Resolution, or Vote, to which the Concurrence of the Senate and House of Representatives may be necessary (except on a question of Adjournment) shall be presented to the President of the United States; and before the Same shall take Effect, shall be approved by him, or being disapproved by him, shall be repassed by two thirds of the Senate and House of Representatives, according to the Rules and Limitations prescribed in the Case of a Bill.

Section 8. The Congress shall have Power To lay and collect Taxes, Duties, Imposts and Excises, to pay the Debts and provide for the common Defence and general Welfare of the United States; but all Duties, Imposts and Excises shall be uniform throughout the United States;

To borrow Money on the credit of the United States;

To regulate Commerce with foreign Nations, and among the several States, and with the Indian Tribes;

To establish an uniform Rule of Naturalization, and uniform Laws on the subject of Bankruptcies throughout the United States;

To coin Money, regulate the Value thereof, and of foreign Coin, and fix the Standard of Weights and Measures;

To provide for the Punishment of counterfeiting the Securities and current Coin of the United States;

To establish Post Offices and post Roads;

To promote the Progress of Science and useful Arts, by securing for limited Times to Authors and Inventors the exclusive Right to their respective Writings and Discoveries;

To constitute Tribunals inferior to the supreme Court;

To define and punish Piracies and Felonies committed on the high Seas, and Offenses against the Law of Nations;

To declare War, grant Letters of Marque and Reprisal, and make Rules concerning Captures on Land and Water;

To raise and support Armies, but no Appropriation of Money to that Use shall be for a longer Term than two Years;

To provide and maintain a Navy;

To make Rules for the Government and Regulation of the land and naval Forces;

To provide for calling forth the Militia to execute the Laws of the Union, suppress Insurrections and repel Invasions;

To provide for organizing, arming, and disciplining, the Militia, and for governing such Part of them as may be employed in the Service of the United States, reserving to the States respectively, the Appointment of the Officers, and the Authority of training the Militia according to the discipline prescribed by Congress;

To exercise exclusive Legislation in all Cases whatsoever, over such District (not exceeding ten Miles square) as may, by Cession of particular States, and the Acceptance of Congress, become the Seat of the Government of the United States, and to exercise like Authority over all Places purchased by the Consent of the Legislature of the State in which the Same shall be, for the Erection of Forts, Magazines, Arsenals, dock—Yards, and other needful Buildings;—And

To make all Laws which shall be necessary and proper for carrying into Execution the foregoing Powers, and all other Powers vested by this Constitution in the Government of the United States, or in any Department or Officer thereof.

Section 9. The Migration or Importation of such Persons as any of the States now existing shall think proper to admit, shall not be prohibited by the Congress prior to the Year one thousand eight hundred and eight, but a Tax or duty may be imposed on such Importation, not exceeding ten dollars for each Person.

The privilege of the Writ of Habeas Corpus shall not be suspended, unless when in Cases of Rebellion or Invasion the public Safety may require it.

No Bill of Attainder or ex post facto Law shall be passed.

No Capitation, or other direct, Tax shall be laid, unless in Proportion to the Census or Enumeration herein before directed to be taken.

No Tax or Duty shall be laid on Articles exported from any State.

No Preference shall be given by any Regulation of Commerce or Revenue to the Ports of one State over those of another: nor shall Vessels bound to, or from, one State be obliged to enter, clear, or pay Duties in another.

No Money shall be drawn from the Treasury, but in Consequence of Appropriations made by Law; and a regular Statement and Account of the Receipts and Expenditures of all public Money shall be published from time to time.

No Title of Nobility shall be granted by the United States: And no Person holding any Office of Profit or Trust under them, shall, without the Consent of the Congress, accept of any present, Emolument, Office, or Title, of any kind whatever, from any King, Prince, or foreign State.

Section 10. No State shall enter into any Treaty, Alliance, or Confederation; grant Letters of Marque and Reprisal; coin Money; emit Bills of Credit; make any Thing but gold and silver Coin a Tender in Payment of Debts; pass any Bill of Attainder, ex post facto Law, or Law impairing the Obligation of Contracts, or grant any

Title of Nobility.

No State shall, without the Consent of the Congress, lay any Imposts or Duties on Imports or Exports, except what may be absolutely necessary for executing its inspection Laws: and the net Produce of all Duties and Imposts, laid by any State on Imports or Exports, shall be for the Use of the Treasury of the United States; and all such Laws shall be subject to the Revision and Controul of the Congress.

No State shall, without the Consent of Congress, lay any Duty of Tonnage, keep Troops, or Ships of War in time of Peace, enter into any Agreement or Compact with another State, or with a foreign Power, or engage in War, unless actually invaded, or in such imminent Danger as will not admit of delay.

Article II

Section 1. The executive Power shall be vested in a President of the United States of America. He shall hold his Office during the Term of four Years, and, together with the Vice President, chosen for the same Term, be elected, as follows:

Each State shall appoint, in such Manner as the Legislature thereof may direct, a Number of Electors, equal to the whole Number of Senators and Representatives to which the State may be entitled in the Congress; but no Senator or Representative, or Person holding an Office of Trust or Profit under the United States, shall be appointed an Elector.

The Electors shall meet in their respective States, and vote by Ballot for two Persons, of whom one at least shall not be an Inhabitant of the same State with themselves. And they shall make a List of all the Persons voted for, and of the Number of Votes for each; which List they shall sign and certify, and transmit sealed to the Seat of the Government of the United States, directed to the President of the Senate. The President of the Senate shall, in the Presence of the Senate and House of Representatives, open all the Certificates, and the Votes shall then be counted. The Person having the greatest Number of Votes shall be the President, if such Number be a Majority of the whole Number of Electors appointed; and if there be more than one who have such Majority, and have an equal Number of Votes, then the House of Representatives shall immediately chuse by Ballot one of them for President; and if no Person have a Majority, then from the five highest on the List the said House shall in like Manner chuse the President. But in chusing the President, the Votes shall be taken by States, the Representation from each State having one Vote; A quorum for this Purpose shall consist of a Member or Members from two thirds of the States, and a Majority of all the States shall be necessary to a Choice. In every Case, after the Choice of the President, the Person having the greater Number of Votes of the Electors shall be the Vice President. But if there should remain two or more who have equal Votes, the Senate shall chuse from them by Ballot the Vice President.

The Congress may determine the Time of chusing the Electors, and the Day on which they shall give their Votes; which Day shall be the same throughout the United States.

No person except a natural born Citizen, or a Citizen of the United States, at the time of the Adoption of this Constitution, shall be eligible to the Office of President; neither shall any Person be eligible to that Office who shall not have attained to the Age of thirty five Years, and been fourteen Years a Resident within the United States.

In Case of the Removal of the President from Office, or of his Death, Resignation or Inability to discharge the Powers and Duties of the said Office, the same shall devolve on the Vice President, and the Congress may by Law provide for the Case of Removal, Death, Resignation or Inability, both of the President and Vice President, declaring what Officer shall then act as President, and such Officer shall act accordingly, until the Disability be removed, or a President shall be elected.

The President shall, at stated Times, receive for his Services, a Compensation, which shall neither be increased nor diminished during the Period for which he shall have been elected, and he shall not receive within that Period any other Emolument from the United States, or any of them.

Before he enter on the Execution of his Office, he shall take the following Oath or Affirmation: "I do solemnly swear (or affirm) that I will faithfully execute the Office of President of the United States, and will to the best of my Ability, preserve, protect and defend the Constitution of the United States."

Section 2. The President shall be Commander in Chief of the Army and Navy of the United States, and of the Militia of the several States, when called into the actual Service of the United States; he may require the Opinion, in writing, of the principal Officer in each of the executive Departments, upon any Subject relating to the Duties of their respective Offices, and he shall have Power to grant Reprieves and Pardons for Offenses against the United States, except in Cases of Impeachment.

He shall have Power, by and with the Advice and Consent of the Senate to make Treaties, provided two thirds of the Senators present concur; and he shall nominate, and by and with the Advice and Consent of the Senate, shall appoint Ambassadors, other public Ministers and Consuls, Judges of the supreme Court, and all other Officers of the United States, whose Appointments are not herein otherwise provided for, and which shall be established by Law; but the Congress may by Law vest the Appointment of such inferior Officers, as they think proper, in the President alone, in the Courts of Law, or in the Heads of Departments.

The President shall have Power to fill up all Vacancies that may happen during the Recess of the Senate, by granting Commissions which shall expire at the End of their next Session.

Section 3. He shall from time to time give to the Congress Information of the State of the Union, and recommend to their Consideration such Measures as he shall judge necessary and expedient; he may on extraordinary Occasions, convene both Houses, or either of them, and in Case of Disagreement between them, with Respect to the Time of Adjournment, he may adjourn them to such Time as he shall think proper; he shall receive Ambassadors and other public Ministers; he shall take Care that the Laws be faithfully executed, and shall Commission all the Officers of the United States.

Section 4. The President, Vice President and all civil Officers of the United States, shall be removed from Office on Impeachment for, and Conviction of, Treason, Bribery, or other high Crimes and Misdemeanors.

Article III

Section 1. The judicial Power of the United States, shall be vested in one supreme Court, and in such inferior Courts as the Congress may from time to time ordain and establish. The Judges, both of the supreme and inferior Courts, shall hold their Offices during good Behaviour, and shall, at stated Times, receive for their

Services a Compensation, which shall not be diminished during their Continuance in Office.

Section 2. The Judicial Power shall extend to all Cases, in Law and Equity, arising under this Constitution, the Laws of the United States, and Treaties made, or which shall be made, under their Authority;—to all Cases affecting Ambassadors, other public Ministers and Consuls;—to all Cases of admiralty and maritime jurisdiction; —to Controversies to which the United States shall be a Party;—to Controversies between two or more States;—between a State and Citizens of another State;—between Citizens of different States;—between Citizens of the same State claiming Lands under Grants of different States, and between a State, or the Citizens thereof, and foreign States, Citizens or Subjects.

In all Cases affecting Ambassadors, other public Ministers and Consuls, and those in which a State shall be a Party, the supreme Court shall have original Jurisdiction. In all the other Cases before mentioned, the supreme Court shall have appellate Jurisdiction, both as to Law and Fact, with such Exceptions, and under such Regulations as the Congress shall make.

The Trial of all Crimes, except in Cases of Impeachment, shall be by Jury; and such Trial shall be held in the State where the said Crimes shall have been committed; but when not committed within any State, the Trial shall be at such Place or Places as the Congress may by Law have directed.

Section 3. Treason against the United States, shall consist only in levying War against them, or, in adhering to their Enemies, giving them Aid and Comfort. No Person shall be convicted of Treason unless on the Testimony of two Witnesses to the same overt Act, or on Confession in open Court.

The Congress shall have Power to declare the Punishment of Treason, but no Attainder of Treason shall work Corruption of Blood, or Forfeiture except during the Life of the Person attainted.

Article IV

Section 1. Full Faith and Credit shall be given in each State to the public Acts, Records, and judicial Proceedings of every other State. And the Congress may by general Laws prescribe the Manner in which such Acts, Records and Proceedings shall be proved, and the Effect thereof.

Section 2. The Citizens of each State shall be entitled to all Privileges and Immunities of Citizens in the several States.

A Person charged in any State with Treason, Felony, or other Crime, who shall flee from justice, and be found in another State, shall on Demand of the executive Authority of the State from which he fled, be delivered up, to be removed to the State having Jurisdiction of the Crime.

No Person held to Service or Labour in one State, under the Laws thereof, escaping into another, shall, in Consequence of any Law or Regulation therein, be discharged from such Service or Labour, but shall be delivered up on Claim of the Party to whom such Service or Labour may be due.

Section 3. New States may be admitted by the Congress into this Union; but no new State shall be formed or erected within the Jurisdiction of any other State; nor any State be formed by the Junction of two or more States, or Parts of States, without the Consent of the Legislatures of the States concerned as well as of the Congress.

The Congress shall have Power to dispose of and make all needful Rules and Regulations respecting the Territory or other Property belonging to the United States; and nothing in this Constitution shall be so construed as to Prejudice any Claims of the United States, or of any particular State.

Section 4. The United States shall guarantee to every State in this Union a Republican Form of Government, and shall, protect each of them against Invasion; and on Application of the Legislature, or of the Executive (when the Legislature cannot be convened) against domestic Violence.

Article V

The Congress, whenever two thirds of both Houses shall deem it necessary, shall propose Amendments to this Constitution, or, on the Application of the Legislatures of two thirds of the several States, shall call a Convention for proposing Amendments, which, in either Case, shall be valid to all Intents and Purposes, as part of this Constitution, when ratified by the Legislatures of three fourths of the several States, or by Conventions in three fourths thereof, as the one or the other Mode of Ratification may be proposed by the Congress; Provided that no Amendment which may be made prior to the Year One thousand eight hundred and eight shall in any Manner affect the first and fourth Clauses in the Ninth Section of the first Article; and that no State, without its Consent, shall be deprived of its equal Suffrage in the Senate.

Article VI

All Debts contracted and Engagements entered into, before the Adoption of this Constitution shall be as valid against the United States under this Constitution, as under the Confederation.

This Constitution, and the Laws of the United States which shall be made in Pursuance thereof; and all Treaties made, or which shall be made, under the Authority of the United States, shall be the supreme Law of the Land; and the Judges in every State shall be bound thereby, any Thing in the Constitution or Laws of any State to the Contrary notwithstanding.

The Senators and Representatives before mentioned, and the Members of the several State Legislatures, and all executive and judicial Officers, both of the United States and of the several States, shall be bound by Oath or Affirmation, to support this Constitution; but no religious Test shall ever be required as a Qualification to any Office or public Trust under the United States.

Article VII

The Ratification of the Conventions of nine States shall be sufficient for the Establishment of this Constitution between the States so ratifying the Same.

Amendment I [1791]

Congress shall make no law respecting an establishment of religion, or prohibiting the free exercise thereof; or abridging the freedom of speech, or of the press; or the right of the people peaceably to assembly, and to petition the Government for a redress of grievances.

Amendment II [1791]

A well regulated Militia, being necessary to the security of a free State, the right of the people to keep and bear Arms, shall not be infringed.

Amendment III [1791]

No Soldier shall, in time of peace be quartered in any house, without the consent of the Owner, nor in time of war, but in a manner to be prescribed by law

Amendment IV [1791]

The right of the people to be secure in their persons, houses, papers, and effects, against unreasonable searches and seizures, shall not be violated, and no Warrants shall issue, but upon probable cause, supported by Oath or affirmation, and particularly describing the place to be searched, and the persons or things to be seized.

Amendment V [1791]

No person shall be held to answer for a capital, or otherwise infamous crime, unless on a presentment or indictment of a Grand jury, except in cases arising in the land or naval forces, or in the Militia, when in actual service in time of War or public danger; nor shall any person be subject for the same offence to be twice put in jeopardy of life or limb; nor shall be compelled in any criminal case to be a witness against himself, nor be deprived of life, liberty, or property, without due process of law; nor shall private property be taken for public use, without just compensation.

Amendment VI [1791]

In all criminal prosecutions, the accused shall enjoy the right to a speedy and public trial, by an impartial jury of the State and district wherein the crime shall have been committed, which district shall have been previously ascertained by law, and to be informed of the nature and cause of the accusation; to be confronted with the witnesses against him; to have compulsory process for obtaining witnesses in his favor, and to have the Assistance of Counsel for his defence.

Amendment VII [1791]

In Suits at common law, where the value in controversy shall exceed twenty dollars, the right of trial by jury shall be preserved, and no fact tried by jury, shall be otherwise re-examined in any Court of the United States, than according to the rules of the common law.

Amendment VIII [1791]

Excessive bail shall not be required, nor excessive fines imposed, nor cruel and unusual punishments inflicted.

Amendment IX [1791]

The enumeration in the Constitution, of certain rights, shall not be construed to deny or disparage others retained by the people.

Amendment X [1791]

The powers not delegated to the United States by the Constitution, nor prohibited by it to the' States, are reserved to the States respectively, or to the people.

Amendment XI [1798]

The Judicial power of the United States shall not be construed to extend to any suit in law or equity, commenced or prosecuted against one of the United States by Citizens of another State, or by Citizens or Subjects of any Foreign State.

Amendment XII [1804]

The Electors shall meet in their respective states, and vote by ballot for President and Vice-President, one of whom, at least, shall not be an inhabitant of the same state with themselves; they shall name in their ballots the person voted for as President, and in distinct ballots the person voted for as Vice-President, and they shall make distinct lists of all persons voted for as President, and of all persons voted for as Vice-President, and of the number of votes for each, which lists they shall sign and certify, and transmit sealed to the seat of the government of the United States, directed to the President of the Senate; —The President of the Senate shall, in the presence of the Senate and House of Representatives, open all the certificates and the votes shall then be counted;—The person having the greatest number of votes for President, shall be the President, if such number be a majority of the whole number of Electors appointed; and if no person have such majority, then from the persons having the highest numbers not exceeding three on the list of those voted for as President, the House of Representatives shall choose immediately, by ballot, the President. But in choosing the President, the votes shall be taken by states, the representation from each state having one vote; a quorum for this purpose shall consist of a member or members from two-thirds of the states, and a majority of all states shall be necessary to a choice. And if the House of Representatives shall not choose a President whenever the right of choice shall devolve upon them, before the fourth day of March next following, then the Vice-President shall act as President, as in the case of the death or other constitutional disability of the President.—The person having the greatest number of votes as Vice-President, shall be the Vice-President, if such number be a majority of the whole number of Electors appointed, and if no person have a majority, then from the two highest numbers on the list, the Senate shall choose the Vice-President; a quorum for the purpose shall consist of two-thirds of the whole number of Senators, and a majority of the whole number shall be necessary to a choice. But no person constitutionally ineligible to the office of President shall be eligible to that of Vice-President of the United States.

Amendment XIII [1865]

Section 1. Neither slavery nor involuntary servitude, except as a punishment for crime whereof the party shall have been duly convicted, shall exist within the United States, or any place subject **to their jurisdiction.**

Section 2. Congress shall have power to enforce this article by appropriate legislation.

Amendment XIV [1868]

Section 1. All persons born or naturalized in the United States, and subject to the jurisdiction thereof, are citizens of the United States and of the State wherein they reside. No State shall make or enforce any law which shall abridge the privileges or immunities of citizens of the United States; nor shall any State deprive any person of life, liberty, or property, without due process of law; nor deny to any person within its jurisdiction the equal protection of the laws.

Section 2. Representatives shall be apportioned among the several States according to their respective numbers, counting the whole number of persons in each State, excluding Indians not taxed. But when the right to vote at any election for the choice of electors for President and Vice President of the United States, Representatives in Congress, the Executive and Judicial officers of a State, or the members of the Legislature thereof, is denied to any of the male inhabitants of such State, being twenty-one years of age, and citizens of the United States, or in any way abridged, except for participation in rebellion, or other crime, the basis of representation therein shall be reduced in the proportion which the number of such male citizens shall bear to the whole number of male citizens twenty-one years of age in such State.

Section 3. No person shall be a Senator or Representative in Congress, or elector of President and Vice President, or hold any office, civil or military, under the United States, or under any State, who having previously taken an oath, as a member of Congress, or as an officer of the United States, or as a member of any State legislature, or as an executive or judicial officer of any State, to support the Constitution of the United States, shall have engaged in insurrection or rebellion against the same, or given aid or comfort to the enemies thereof. But Congress may by a vote of two-thirds of each House, remove such disability.

Section 4. The validity of the public debt of the United States, authorized by law, including debts incurred for payment of pensions and bounties for services in suppressing insurrection or rebellion, shall not be questioned. But neither the United States nor any State shall assume or pay any debt or obligation incurred in aid of insurrection or rebellion against the United States, or any claim for the loss or emancipation of any slave; but all such debts, obligations and claims shall be held illegal and void.

Section 5. The Congress shall have power to enforce, by appropriate legislation, the provisions of this article.

Amendment XV [1870]

Section 1. The right of citizens of the United States to vote shall not be denied or abridged by the United States or by any State on account of race, color, or previous condition of servitude.

Section 2. The Congress shall have power to enforce this article by appropriate legislation.

Amendment XVI [1913]

The Congress shall have power to lay and collect taxes on incomes, from whatever source derived, without apportionment among the several States, and without regard to any census or enumeration.

Amendment XVII [1913]

Section 1. The Senate of the United States shall be composed of two Senators from each State, elected by the people thereof, for six years; and each Senator shall have one vote. The electors in each State shall have the qualifications requisite for electors of the most numerous branch of the State legislatures.

Section 2. When vacancies happen in the representation of any State in the Senate, the executive authority of such State shall issue writs of election to fill such vacancies: Provided, That the legislature of any State may empower the executive thereof to make temporary appointments until the people fill the vacancies by election as the legislature may direct.

Section 3. This amendment shall not be so construed as to affect the election or term of any Senator chosen before it becomes valid as part of the Constitution.

Amendment XVIII [1919]

Section 1. After one year from the ratification of this article the manufacture, sale, or transportation of intoxicating liquors within, the importation thereof into, or the exportation thereof from the United States and all territory subject to the jurisdiction thereof for beverage purposes is hereby prohibited.

Section 2. The Congress and the several States shall have concurrent power to enforce this article by appropriate legislation.

Section 3. This article shall be inoperative unless it shall have been ratified as an amendment to the Constitution by the legislatures of the several States, as provided in the Constitution, within seven years from the date of the submission hereof to the States by the Congress.

Amendment XIX [1920]

Section 1. The right of citizens of the United States to vote shall not be denied or abridged by the United States or by any State on account of sex.

Section 2. Congress shall have power to enforce this article by appropriate legislation.

Amendment XX [1933]

Section 1. The terms of the President and Vice President shall end at noon on the 20th day of January, and the terms of Senators and Representatives at noon on the 3d day of January, of the years in which such terms would have ended if this article had not been ratified; and the terms of their successors shall then begin.

Section 2. The Congress shall assemble at least once in every year, and such meeting shall begin at noon on the 3d day of January, unless they shall by law appoint a different day.

Section 3. If, at the time fixed for the beginning of the term of the President, the President elect shall have died, the Vice President elect shall become President. If the President shall not have been chosen before the time fixed for the beginning of his term, or if the President elect shall have failed to qualify, then the Vice President elect shall act as President until a President shall have qualified; and the Congress may by law provide for the case wherein neither a President elect nor a Vice President elect shall have qualified, declaring who shall then act as President, or the manner in which one who is to act shall be selected, and such person shall act accordingly until a President or Vice President shall have qualified.

Section 4. The Congress may by law provide for the case of the death of any of the persons from whom the House of Representatives may choose a President whenever the right of choice shall have devolved upon them, and for the case of the death of any of the persons from whom the Senate may choose a Vice President whenever the right of choice shall have devolved upon them.

Section 5. Sections 1 and 2 shall take effect on the 15th day of October following the ratification of this article.

Section 6. This article shall be inoperative unless it shall have been ratified as an amendment to the Constitution by the legislatures of three-fourths of the several States within seven years from the date of its submission.

Amendment XXI [1933]

Section 1. The eighteenth article of amendment to the Constitution of the United States is hereby repealed.

Section 2. The transportation or importation into any State, Territory, or possession of the United States for delivery or use therein of intoxicating liquors, in violation of the laws thereof, is hereby prohibited.

Section 3. This article shall be inoperative unless it shall have been ratified as an amendment to the Constitution by conventions in the several States, as provided in the Constitution, within seven years from the date of the submission hereof to the States by the Congress.

Amendment XXII [1951]

Section 1. No person shall be elected to the office of the President more than twice, and no person who has held the office of President, or acted as President, for more than two years of a term to which some other person was elected President shall be elected to the office of President more than once. But this Article shall not apply to any person holding the office of President when this Article was proposed by the Congress, and shall not prevent any person who may be holding the office of President, or acting as President, during the term within which this Article becomes operative from holding the office of President or acting as President during the remainder of such term.

Section 2. This article shall be inoperative unless it shall have been ratified as an amendment to the Constitution by the legislatures of three-fourths of the several States within seven years from the date of its submission to the States by the Congress.

Amendment XXIII [1961]

Section 1. The District constituting the seat of Government of the United States shall appoint in such manner as the Congress may direct:

A number of electors of President and Vice President equal to the whole number of Senators and Representatives in Congress to which the District would be entitled if it were a State, but in no event more than the least populous state; they shall be in addition to those appointed by the states, but they shall be considered, for the purposes of the election of President and Vice President, to be electors appointed by a state; and they shall meet in the District and perform such duties as provided by the twelfth article of amendment.

Section 2. The Congress shall have power to enforce this article by appropriate legislation.

Amendment XXIV [1964]

Section 1. The right of citizens of the United States to vote in any primary or other election for President or Vice President, for electors for President or Vice President, or for Senator or Representative in Congress, shall not be denied or abridged by the United States, or any State by reason of failure to pay any poll tax or other tax.

Section 2. The Congress shall have power to enforce this article by appropriate legislation.

Amendment XXV [1967]

Section 1. In case of the removal of the President from office or of his death or resignation, the Vice President shall become President.

Section 2. Whenever there is a vacancy in the office of the Vice President, the President shall nominate a Vice President who shall take office upon confirmation by a majority vote of both Houses of Congress.

Section 3. Whenever the President transmits to the President pro tempore of the Senate and the Speaker of the House of Representatives his written declaration that he is unable to discharge the powers and duties of his office, and until he transmits to them a written declaration to the contrary, such powers and duties shall be discharged by the Vice President as Acting President.

Section 4. Whenever the Vice President and a majority of either the principal officers of the executive departments or of such other body as Congress may by law provide, transmit to the President pro tempore of the Senate and the Speaker of the House of Representatives their written declaration that the President is unable to discharge the powers and duties of his office, the Vice President shall immediately assume the powers and duties of the office as Acting President.

Thereafter, when the President transmits to the President pro tempore of the Senate and the Speaker of the House of Representatives his written declaration that no inability exists, he shall resume the powers and duties of his office unless the Vice President and a majority of either the principal officers of the executive department or of such other body as Congress may by law provide, transmit within four days to the President pro tempore of the Senate and the Speaker of the House of Representatives their written declaration that the President is unable to discharge the powers and duties of his office. Thereupon Congress shall decide the issue, assembling within forty-eight hours for that purpose if not in session. If the Congress, within twenty-one days after receipt of the latter written declaration, or, if Congress is not in session, within twenty-one days after Congress is required to assemble, determines by two-thirds vote of both Houses that the President is unable to discharge the powers and duties of his office, the Vice President shall continue to discharge the same as Acting President; otherwise, the President shall resume the powers and duties of his office.

Amendment XXVI [1971]

Section 1. The right of citizens of the United States, who are eighteen years of age or older, to vote shall not be denied or abridged by the United States or by any State on account of age.

Section 2. The Congress shall have power to enforce this article by appropriate legislation.

Amendment XXVII [1992]

No law, varying the compensation for the services of the Senators and Representatives, shall take effect, until an election of Representatives shall have intervened.

APPENDIX B

The Uniform Commercial Code

Copyright 2000 by the American Law Institute and the National Conference of Commissioners on Uniform State Laws. Reproduced with permission.

(Adopted in fifty-two jurisdictions; all fifty States, although Louisiana has adopted only Articles 1, 3, 4, 7, 8, and 9; the District of Columbia; and the Virgin Islands.)

The Code consists of the following articles:

Art.
1. General Provisions
2. Sales
2A. Leases
3. Commercial Paper
4. Bank Deposits and Collections
4A. Funds Transfers
5. Letters of Credit
6. Bulk Transfers (including Alternative B)
7. Warehouse Receipts, Bills of Lading and Other Documents of Title
8. Investment Securities
9. Secured Transactions: Sales of Accounts and Chattel Paper
10. Effective Date and Repealer
11. Effective Date and Transition Provisions

Article 1

General Provisions

Part I Short Title, Construction, Application and Subject Matter of the Act

§ 1-101. Short Title.

This Act shall be known and may be cited as Uniform Commercial Code.

§ 1-102. Purposes; Rules of Construction; Variation by Agreement.

(1) This Act shall be liberally construed and applied to promote its underlying purposes and policies.

(2) Underlying purposes and policies of this Act are

   (a) to simplify, clarify and modernize the law governing commercial transactions;

   (b) to permit the continued expansion of commercial practices through custom, usage and agreement of the parties;

   (c) to make uniform the law among the various jurisdictions.

(3) The effect of provisions of this Act may be varied by agreement, except as otherwise provided in this Act and except that the obligations of good faith, diligence, reasonableness and care prescribed by this Act may not be disclaimed by agreement but the parties may by agreement determine the standards by which the performance of such obligations is to be measured if such standards are not manifestly unreasonable.

(4) The presence in certain provisions of this Act of the words "unless otherwise agreed" or words of similar import does not imply that the effect of other provisions may not be varied by agreement under subsection (3).

(5) In this Act unless the context otherwise requires

   (a) words in the singular number include the plural, and in the plural include the singular;

   (b) words of the masculine gender include the feminine and the neuter, and when the sense so indicates words of the neuter gender may refer to any gender.

§ 1-103. Supplementary General Principles of Law Applicable.

Unless displaced by the particular provisions of this Act, the principles of law and equity, including the law merchant and the law relative to capacity to contract, principal and agent, estoppel, fraud, misrepresentation, duress, coercion, mistake, bankruptcy, or other validating or invalidating cause shall supplement its provisions.

§ 1-104. Construction Against Implicit Repeal.

This Act being a general act intended as a unified coverage of its subject matter, no part of it shall be deemed to be impliedly repealed by subsequent legislation if such construction can reasonably be avoided.

§ 1-105. Territorial Application of the Act; Parties' Power to Choose Applicable Law.

(1) Except as provided hereafter in this section, when a transaction bears a reasonable relation to this state and also to another state or nation the parties may agree that the law either of this state or of such other state or nation shall govern their rights and duties. Failing such agreement this Act applies to transactions bearing an appropriate relation to this state.

(2) Where one of the following provisions of this Act specifies the applicable law, that provision governs and a contrary agreement is effective only to the extent permitted by the law (including the conflict of laws rules) so specified:

Rights of creditors against sold goods. Section 2-402.

Applicability of the Article on Leases. Sections 2A-105 and 2A-106.

Applicability of the Article on Bank Deposits and Collections. Section 4-102.

Governing law in the Article on Funds Transfers. Section 4A-507. Letters of Credit, Section 5-116.

Bulk sales subject to the Article on Bulk Sales. Section 6-103.

Applicability of the Article on Investment Securities. Section 8-106.

Perfection provisions of the Article on Secured Transactions. Section 9-103.

§ 1-106. Remedies to Be Liberally Administered.

(1) The remedies provided by this Act shall be liberally administered to the end that the aggrieved party may be put in as

good a position as if the other party had fully performed but neither consequential or special nor penal damages may be had except as specifically provided in this Act or by other rule of law.

(2) Any right or obligation declared by this Act is enforceable by action unless the provision declaring it specifies a different and limited effect.

§ 1-107. Waiver or Renunciation of Claim or Right After Breach.

Any claim or right arising out of an alleged breach can be discharged in whole or in part without consideration by a written waiver or renunciation signed and delivered by the aggrieved party.

§ 1-108. Severability.

If any provision or clause of this Act or application thereof to any person or circumstances is held invalid, such invalidity shall not affect other provisions or applications of the Act which can be given effect without the invalid provision or application, and to this end the provisions of this Act are declared to be severable.

§ 1-109. Section Captions.

Section captions are parts of this Act.

Part 2 General Definitions and Principles of Interpretation

§ 1-201. General Definitions.

Subject to additional definitions contained in the subsequent Articles of this Act which are applicable to specific Articles or Parts thereof, and unless the context otherwise requires, in this Act:

(1) "Action" in the sense of a judicial proceeding includes recoupment, counterclaim, set-off, suit in equity and any other proceedings in which rights are determined.

(2) "Aggrieved party" means a party entitled to resort to a remedy.

(3) "Agreement" means the bargain of the parties in fact as found in their language or by implication from other circumstances including course of dealing or usage of trade or course of performance as provided in this Act (Sections 1-205 and 2-208). Whether an agreement has legal consequences is determined by the provisions of this Act, if applicable; otherwise by the law of contracts (Section 1-103). (Compare "Contract".)

(4) "Bank" means any person engaged in the business of banking.

(5) "Bearer" means the person in possession of an instrument, document of tide, or certificated security payable to bearer or indorsed in blank.

(6) "Bill of lading" means a document evidencing the receipt of goods for shipment issued by a person engaged in the business of transporting or forwarding goods, and includes an airbill. "Airbill" means a document serving for air transportation as a bill of lading does for marine or rail transportation, and includes an air consignment note or air waybill.

(7) "Branch" includes a separately incorporated foreign branch of a bank.

(8) "Burden of establishing" a fact means the burden of persuading the triers of fact that the existence of the fact is more probable than its non-existence.

(9) "Buyer in ordinary course of business" means a person who in good faith and without knowledge that the sale to him is in violation of the ownership rights or security interest of a third party in the goods buys in ordinary course from a person in the business of selling goods of that kind but does not include a pawnbroker. All persons who sell minerals or the like (including oil and gas) at wellhead or minehead shall be deemed to be persons in the business of selling goods of that kind. "Buying" may be for cash or by exchange of other property or on secured or unsecured credit and includes receiving goods or documents of tide under a pre-existing contract for sale but does not include a transfer in bulk or as security for or in total or partial satisfaction of a money debt.

(10) "Conspicuous": A term or clause is conspicuous when it is so written that a reasonable person against whom it is to operate ought to have noticed it. A printed heading in capitals (as: NON-NEGOTIABLE BILL OF LADING) is conspicuous. Language in the body of a form is "conspicuous" if it is in larger or other contrasting type or color. But in a telegram any stated term is "conspicuous". Whether a term or clause is "conspicuous" or not is for decision by the court.

(11) "Contract" means the total legal obligation which results from the parties' agreement as affected by this Act and any other applicable rules of law. (Compare "Agreement".)

(12) "Creditor" includes a general creditor, a secured creditor, a lien creditor and any representative of creditors, including an assignee for the benefit of creditors, a trustee in bankruptcy, a receiver in equity and an executor or administrator of an insolvent debtor's or assignor's estate.

(13) "Defendant" includes a person in the position of defendant in a cross-action or counterclaim.

(14) "Delivery" with respect to instruments, documents of tide, chattel paper, or certificated securities means voluntary transfer of possession.

(15) "Document of title" includes bill of lading, dock warrant, dock receipt, warehouse receipt or order for the delivery of goods, and also any other document which in the regular course of business or financing is treated as adequately evidencing that the person in possession of it is entitled to receive, hold and dispose of the document and the goods it covers. To be a document of tide a document must purport to be issued by or addressed to a bailee and purport to cover goods in the bailee's possession which are either identified or are fungible portions of an identified mass.

(16) "Fault" means wrongful act, omission or breach.

(17) "Fungible" with respect to goods or securities means goods or securities of which any unit is, by nature or usage of trade, the equivalent of any other like unit. Goods which are not fungible shall be deemed fungible for the purposes of this Act to the extent that under a particular agreement or document unlike units are treated as equivalents.

(18) "Genuine" means free of forgery or counterfeiting.

(19) "Good faith" means honesty in fact in the conduct or transaction concerned.

(20) "Holder" with respect to a negotiable instrument, means the person in possession if the instrument is payable to bearer or, in the cases of an instrument payable to an identified person, if the identified person is in possession. "Holder" with respect to a document of title means the person in possession if the goods are deliverable to bearer or to the order of the person in possession.

(21) To "honor" is to pay or to accept and pay, or where a credit so engages to purchase or discount a draft complying with the terms of the credit.

(22) "Insolvency proceedings" includes any assignment for the benefit of creditors or other proceedings intended to liquidate or rehabilitate the estate of the person involved.

(23) A person is "insolvent" who either has ceased to pay his debts in the ordinary course of business or cannot pay his debts as they become due or is insolvent within the meaning of the federal bankruptcy law.

(24) "Money" means a medium of exchange authorized or adopted by a domestic or foreign government and includes a monetary unit of account established by an intergovernmental organization or by agreement between two or more nations.

(25) A person has "notice" of a fact when

    (a) he has actual, knowledge of it; or

    (b) he has received a notice or notification of it; or

    (c) from all the facts and circumstances known to him at the time in question he has reason to know that it exists.

A person "knows" or has "knowledge" of a fact when he has actual knowledge of it. "Discover" or "learn" or a word or phrase of similar import refers to knowledge rather than to reason to know. The time and circumstances under which a notice or notification may cease to be effective are not determined by this Act.

(26) A person "notifies" or "gives" a notice or notification to another by taking such steps as may be reasonably required to inform the other in ordinary course whether or not such other actually comes to know of it. A person "receives" a notice or notification when

    (a) it comes to his attention; or

    (b) it is duly delivered at the place of business through which the contract was made or at any other place held out by him as the place for receipt of such communications.

(27) Notice, knowledge or a notice or notification received by an organization is effective for a particular transaction from the time when it is brought to the attention of the individual conducting that transaction, and in any event from the time when it would have been brought to his attention if the organization had exercised due diligence. An organization exercises due diligence if it maintains reasonable routines for communicating significant information to the person conducting the transaction and there is reasonable compliance with the routines. Due diligence does not require an individual acting for the organization to communicate information unless such communication is part of his regular duties or unless he has reason to know of the transaction and that the transaction would be materially affected by the information.

(28) "Organization" includes a corporation, government or governmental subdivision or agency, business trust, estate, trust, partnership or association, two or more persons having a joint or common interest, or any other legal or commercial entity.

(29) "Party", as distinct from "third party", means a person who has engaged in a transaction or made an agreement within this Act.

(30) "Person" includes an individual or an organization (See Section 1-102).

(31) "Presumption" or "presumed" means that the trier of fact must find the existence of the fact presumed unless and until evidence is introduced which would support a finding of its non-existence.

(32) "Purchase" includes taking by sale, discount, negotiation, mortgage, pledge, lien, issue or re-issue, gift or any other voluntary transaction creating an interest in property.

(33) "Purchaser" means a person who takes by purchase.

(34) "Remedy" means any remedial right to which an aggrieved party is entitled with or without resort to a tribunal.

(35) "Representative" includes an agent, an officer of a corporation or association, and a trustee, executor or administrator of an estate, or any other person empowered to act for another.

(36) "Rights" includes remedies.

(37) "Security interest" means an interest in personal property or fixtures which secures payment or performance of an obligation. The retention or reservation of title by a seller of goods notwithstanding shipment or delivery to the buyer (Section 2-401) is limited in effect to a reservation of a "security interest". The term also includes any interest of a buyer of accounts or chattel paper which is subject to Article 9. The special property interest of a buyer of goods on identification of those goods to a contract for sale under Section 2-401 is not a "security interest, but a buyer may also acquire a "security interest" by complying with Article 9. Unless a consignment is intended as security, reservation of tide thereunder is not a "security interest," but a consignment is in any event subject to the provisions on consignment sales (Section 2-326).

Whether a transaction creates a lease or security interest is determined by the facts of each case; however, a transaction creates a security interest if the consideration the lessee is to pay the lessor for the right to possession and use of the goods is an obligation for the term of the lease not subject to termination by the lessee, and

    (a) the original term of the lease is equal to or greater than the remaining economic life of the goods,

    (b) the lessee is bound to renew the lease for the remaining economic life of the goods or is bound to become the owner of the goods,

    (c) the lessee has an option to renew the lease for the remaining economic life of the goods for no additional consideration or nominal additional consideration upon compliance with the lease agreement, or

    (d) the lessee has an option to become the owner of the goods for no additional consideration or nominal additional consideration upon compliance with the lease agreement.

A transaction does not create a security interest merely because it provides that

    (a) the present value of the consideration the lessee is obligated to pay the lessor for the right to possession and use of the goods is substantially equal to or is greater than the fair market value of the goods at the time the lease is entered into,

    (b) the lessee assumes risk of loss of the goods, or agrees to pay taxes, insurance, filing, recording, or registration fees, or service or maintenance costs with respect to the goods,

    (c) the lessee has an option to renew the lease or to become the owner of the goods,

    (d) the lessee has an option to renew the lease for a fixed rent that is equal to or greater than the reasonably predictable fair market rent for the use of the goods for the term of the renewal at the time the option is to be performed, or

(e) the lessee has an option to become the owner of the goods for a fixed price that is equal to or greater than the reasonably predictable fair market value of the goods at the time the option is to be. performed.

For purposes of this subsection (37):

(x) Additional consideration is not nominal if (i) when the option to renew the lease is granted to the lessee the rent is stated to be the fair market rent for the use of the goods for the term of the renewal determined at the time the option is to be performed, or (ii) when the option to become the owner of the goods is granted to the lessee the price is stated to be the fair market value of the goods determined at the time the option is to be performed. Additional consideration is nominal if it is less than the lessee's reasonably predictable cost of performing under the lease agreement if the option is not exercised;

(y) "Reasonably predictable" and "remaining economic life of the goods" are to be determined with reference to the facts and circumstances at the time the transaction is entered into; and

(z) "Present value" means the amount as of a date certain of one or more sums payable in the future, discounted to the date certain. The discount is determined by the interest rate specified by the parties if the rate is not manifestly unreasonable at the time the transaction is entered into; otherwise, the discount is determined by a commercially reasonable rate that takes into account the facts and circumstances of each case at the time the transaction was entered into.

(1) "Send" in connection with any writing or notice means to deposit in the mail or deliver for transmission by any other usual means of communication with postage or cost of transmission provided for and properly addressed and in the case of an instrument to an address specified thereon or otherwise agreed, or if there be none to any address reasonable under the circumstances. The receipt of any writing or notice within the time at which it would have arrived if properly sent has the effect of a proper sending.

(39) "Signed" includes any symbol executed or adopted by a party with present intention to authenticate a writing.

(40) "Surety" includes guarantor.

(41) "Telegram" includes a message transmitted by radio, teletype, cable, any mechanical method of transmission, or the like.

(42) "Term" means that portion of an agreement which relates to a particular matter.

(43) "Unauthorized" signature means one made without actual, implied or apparent authority and includes a forgery.

(44) "Value". Except as otherwise provided with respect to negotiable instruments and bank collections (Sections 3-303, 4-210 and 4-211) a person gives "value" for rights if he acquires them

(a) in return for a binding commitment to extend credit or for the extension of immediately available credit whether or not drawn upon and whether or not a chargeback is provided for in the event of difficulties in collection; or

(b) as security for or in total or partial satisfaction of a pre-existing claim; or

(c) by accepting delivery pursuant to a preexisting contract for purchase; or

(d) generally, in return for any consideration sufficient to support a simple contract.

(45) "Warehouse receipt" means a receipt issued by a person engaged in the business of storing goods for hire.

(46) "Written" or "writing" includes printing, typewriting or any other intentional reduction to tangible form.

§ I-202. Prima Facie Evidence by Third Party Documents.

A document in due form purporting to be a bill of lading, policy or certificate of insurance, official weigher's or inspector's certificate, consular invoice, or any other document authorized or required by the contract to be issued by a third party shall be prima facie evidence of its own authenticity and genuineness and of the facts stated in the document by the third party.

§ 1-203. Obligation of Good Faith.

Every contract or duty within this Act imposes an obligation of good faith in its performance or enforcement.

§ 1-204. Time; Reasonable Time; "Seasonably".

(1) Whenever this Act requires any action to be taken within a reasonable time, any time which is not manifestly unreasonable may be fixed by agreement.

(2) What is a reasonable time for taking any action depends on the nature, purpose and circumstances of such action.

(3) An action is taken "seasonably" when it is taken at or within the time agreed or if no time is agreed at or within a reasonable time.

§ 1-205. Course of Dealing and Usage of Trade.

(1) A course of dealing is a sequence of previous conduct between the parties to a particular transaction which is fairly to be regarded as establishing a common basis of understanding for interpreting their expressions and other conduct.

(2) A usage of trade is any practice or method of dealing having such regularity of observance in a place, vocation or trade as to justify an expectation that it will be observed with respect to the transaction in question. The existence and scope of such a usage are to be proved as facts. If it is established that such a usage is embodied in a written trade code or similar writing the interpretation of the writing is for the court.

(3) A course of dealing between parties and any usage of trade in the vocation or trade in which they are engaged or of which they are or should be aware give particular meaning to and supplement or qualify terms of an agreement.

(4) The express terms of an agreement and an applicable course of dealing or usage of trade shall be construed wherever reasonable as consistent with each other; but when such construction is unreasonable express terms control both course of dealing and usage of trade and course of dealing controls usage trade.

(5) An applicable usage of trade in the place where any part of performance is to occur shall be used in interpreting the agreement as to that part of the performance.

(6) Evidence of a relevant usage of trade offered by one party is not admissible unless and until he has given the other party such notice as the court finds sufficient to pre-vent unfair surprise to the latter.

§ 1-206. Statute of Frauds for Kinds of Personal Property Not Otherwise Covered.
(1) Except in the cases described in subsection of this section a contract for the sale of personal property is not enforceable by way of action or defense beyond five thou-sand dollars in amount or value of remedy unless there is some writing which indicates that a contract for sale has been made between the parties at a defined or stated price, reasonably identifies the subject matter, and is signed by the party against whom enforcement is sought or by his authorized agent.
(2) Subsection (1) of this section does not apply to contracts for the sale of goods (Section 2-201) nor of securities (Section 8-113) nor to security agreements(Section 9-203).

§ I-207. Performance or Acceptance Under Reservation of Rights.
(1) A party who with explicit reservation of rights performs or promises performance or assents to performance in a manner demanded or offered by the other party does not thereby prejudice the rights reserved. Such words as "with-out prejudice", "under protest" or the like are sufficient.
(2) Subsection (1) does not apply to an accord and satisfaction.

§ 1-208. Option to Accelerate at Will.
A term providing that one party or his successor in interest may accelerate payment or performance or require collateral or additional collateral "at will" or "when he, deems himself insecure" or in words of similar import shall be construed to mean that he shall have power to do so only if he in good faith believes that the prospect of payment or performance is impaired. The burden of establishing lack of good faith is on the party against whom the power has been exercised.

§ 1-209. Subordinated Obligations.
An obligation may be issued as subordinated to payment of another obligation of the person obligated, or a creditor may subordinate his right to payment of an obligation by agreement with either the person obligated or another creditor of the person obligated. Such a subordination does not create a security interest as against either the common debtor or a subordinated creditor. This section shall be construed as declaring the law as it existed prior to the enactment of this section and not as modifying it. Added 1966.
Note: This new section is proposed as an optional provision to make it clear that a subordination agreement does not create a security interest unless so intended.

Article 2
SALES

Part I Short Title, General Construction and Subject Matter

§ 2-101. Short Title.
This Article shall be known and may be cited as Uniform Commercial Code-Sales.

§ 2-102. Scope; Certain Security and Other Transactions Excluded From This Article.
Unless the context otherwise requires, this Article applies to transactions in goods; it does not apply to any transaction which although in the form of an unconditional contract to sell or present sale is intended to operate only as a security transaction nor does this Article impair or repeal any statute regulating sales to consumers, farmers or other specified classes of buyers.

§ 2-103. Definitions and Index of Definitions.
(1) In this Article unless the context otherwise requires
(a) "Buyer" means a person who buys or contracts to buy goods.
(b) "Good faith" in the case of a merchant means honesty in fact and the observance of reasonable commercial standards of fair dealing in the trade.
(c) "Receipt" of goods means taking physical possession of them.
(d) "Seller" means a person who sells or contracts to sell goods.
(2) Other definitions applying to this Article or to specified Parts thereof, and the sections in which they appear are:
"Acceptance". Section 2-606.
"Banker's credit". Section 2-325.
"Between merchants". Section 2-104.
"Cancellation". Section 2-106(4).
"Commercial unit". Section 2-105.
"Confirmed credit". Section 2-325.
"Conforming to contract". Section 2-106.
"Contract for sale". Section 2-106.
"Cover". Section 2-712.
"Entrusting". Section 2-403.
"Financing agency". Section 2-104.
"Future goods". Section 2-105.
"Goods". Section 2-105.
"Identification". Section 2-501.
"Installment contract". Section 2-612.
"Letter of Credit". Section 2-3 2 5.
"Lot". Section 2-105.
"Merchant". Section 2-104.
"Overseas". Section 2-323.
"Person in position of seller". Section 2-707.
"Present sale". Section 2-106.
"Sale". Section 2-106.
"Sale on approval". Section 2-326.
"Sale or return". Section 2-326.
"Termination". Section 2-106.
(3) The following definitions in other Articles apply to this Article:
"Check". Section 3-104.
"Consignee". Section 7-102.
"Consignor". Section 7-102.
"Consumer goods". Section 9-109.
"Dishonor". Section 3-507.
"Draft. Section 3-104.
(4) In addition Article I contains general definitions and principles of construction and interpretation applicable throughout this Article.

§ 2-104. Definitions: "Merchant"; "Between Merchants"; "Financing Agency".

(1) "Merchant" means a person who deals in goods of the kind or otherwise by his occupation holds himself out as having knowledge or skill peculiar to the practices or goods involved in the transaction or to whom such knowledge or skill may be attributed by his employment of an agent or broker or other intermediary who by his occupation holds himself out as having such knowledge or skill.

(2) "Financing agency" means a bank, finance company or other person who in the ordinary course of business makes advances against goods or documents of tide or who ordinary course to make or collect payment due or claimed under the contract for sale, as by purchasing or paying the seller's draft or making advances against it or by merely taking it for collection whether or not documents of title accompany the draft. "Financing agency" includes also a bank or other person who similarly intervenes between persons who are in the position of seller and buyer in respect to the goods (Section 2-707).

(3) "Between merchants" means in any transaction with respect to which both parties are chargeable with the knowledge or skill of merchants.

§ 2-105. Definitions: Transferability; "Goods";"Future" Goods; "Lot"; "Commercial Unit".

(1) "Goods" means all things (including specially manufactured goods) which are movable at the time of identification to the contract for sale other than the money in which the price is to be paid, investment securities (Article8) and things in action. "Goods" also includes the unborn young of animals and growing crops and other identified things attached to realty as described in the section on goods to be severed from realty (Section 2-107).

(2) Goods must be both existing and identified before any interest in them can pass. Goods which are not both existing and identified are "future" goods. A purported present sale of future goods or of any interest therein operates as a contract to sell.

(3) There may be a sale of a part interest in existing identified goods.

(4) An undivided share in an identified bulk of fungible goods is sufficiently identified to be sold although the quantity of the bulk is not determined. Any agreed proportion of such a bulk or any quantity thereof agreed upon by number, weight or other measure may to the extent of the seller's interest in the bulk be sold to the buyer who then becomes an owner in common.

(5) "Lot" means a parcel or a single article which is the subject matter of a separate sale or delivery, whether or not it is sufficient to perform the contract.

(6) "Commercial unit" means such a unit of goods as by commercial usage is a single whole for purposes of sale and division of which materially impairs its character or value on the market or in use. A commercial unit may be a single article (as a machine) or a set of articles (as a suite of furniture or an assortment of sizes) or a quantity (as a bale, gross, or carload) or any other unit treated in use or in the relevant market as a single whole.

§ 2-106. Definitions: "Contract"; "Agreement"; "Contract for Sale"; "Sale"; "Present Sale"; "Conforming" to Contract; "Termination"; "Cancellation".

(1) In this Article unless the context otherwise requires "contract" and "agreement" are limited to those relating to the present or future sale of goods. "Contract for sale" includes both a present sale of goods and a contract to sell goods at a future time. A "sale" consists in the passing of tide from the seller to the buyer for a price (Section 2-401). A "present sale" means a sale which is accomplished by the making of the contract.

(2) Goods or conduct including any part of a performance are "conforming" or conform to the contract when they are in accordance with the obligations under the contract.

(3) "Termination" occurs when either party pursuant to a power created by agreement or law puts an end to the contract otherwise than for its breach. On "termination" all obligations which are still executory on both sides are discharged but any right based on prior breach or performance survives.

(4) "Cancellation" occurs when either party puts an end to the contract for breach by the other and its effect is the same as that of "termination" except that the canceling party also retains any remedy for breach of the whole contract or any unperformed balance.

§ 2-107. Goods to Be Severed From Realty: Recording.

(1) A contract for the sale of minerals or the like (including oil and gas) or a structure or its materials to be removed from realty is a contract for the sale of goods within this Article if they are to be severed by the seller but until severance a purported present sale thereof which is not effective as a transfer of an interest in land is effective only as a contract to sell.

(2) A contract for the sale apart from the land of growing crops or other things attached to realty and capable of severance without material harm thereto but not described in subsection (1) or of timber to be cut is a contract for the sale of goods within this Article whether the subject matter is to be severed by the buyer or by the seller even though it forms part of the realty at the time of contracting, and the parties can by identification effect a present sale before severance.

(3) The provisions of this section are subject to any third party rights provided by the law relating to realty records, and the contract for sale may be executed and recorded as a document transferring an interest in land and shall then constitute notice to third parties of the buyer's rights under the contract for sale.

Part 2 Form, Formation and Readjustment of Contract

§ 2-20 1. Formal Requirements; Statute of Frauds.

(1) Except as otherwise provided in this section a contract for the sale of goods for the price of $500 or more is not enforceable by way of action or defense unless there is some writing sufficient to indicate that a contract for sale has been made between the parties and signed by the party against whom enforcement is sought or by his authorized agent or broker. A writing is not insufficient because it omits or incorrectly states a term agreed upon but the contract is not enforceable under this paragraph beyond the quantity of goods shown in such writing.

(2) Between merchants if within a reasonable time a writing in

confirmation of the contract and sufficient against the sender is received and the party receiving it has reason to know its contents, its satisfies the requirements of subsection (1) against such party unless written notice of objection to its contents is given within ten days after it is received.

(3) A contract which does not satisfy the requirements of subsection (1) but which is valid in other respects is enforceable

   (a) if the goods are to be specially manufactured for the buyer and are not suitable for sale to others in the ordinary course of the seller's business and the seller, before notice of repudiation is received and under circumstances which reasonably indicate that the goods are for the buyer, has made either a substantial beginning of their manufacture or commitments for their procurement; or

   (b) if the party against whom enforcement is sought admits in his pleading, testimony or otherwise in court that a contract for sale was made, but the contract is not enforceable under this provision beyond the quantity of goods admitted; or

   (c) with respect to goods for which payment has been made and accepted or which have been received and accepted (See. 2-606).

§ 2-202. Final Written Expression: Parol or Extrinsic Evidence.

Terms with respect to which the confirmatory memoranda of the parties agree or which are otherwise set forth in a writing intended by the parties as a final expression of their agreement with respect to such terms as are included therein may not be contradicted by evidence of any prior agreement or of a contemporaneous oral agreement but may be explained or supplemented

   (a) by course of dealing or usage of trade (Section1-205) or by course of performance (Section 2-208);and

   (b) by evidence of consistent additional terms unless the court finds the writing to have been intended also as a complete and exclusive statement of the terms of the agreement.

§ 2-203. Seals Inoperative.

The affixing of a seal to a writing evidencing a contract for sale or an offer to buy or sell goods does not constitute the writing a sealed instrument and the law with respect to sealed instruments does not apply to such a contract or offer.

§ 2-204. Formation in General.

(1) A contract for sale of goods may be made in any manner sufficient to show agreement, including conduct by both parties which recognizes the existence of such a contract.

(2) An agreement sufficient to constitute a contract for sale may be found even though the moment of its making is undetermined.

(3) Even though one or more terms are left open a contract for sale does not fail for indefiniteness if the parties have intended to make a contract and there is a reasonably certain basis for giving an appropriate remedy.

§ 2-205. Firm Offers.

An offer by a merchant to buy or sell goods in a signed writing which by its terms gives assurance that it will be held open is not revocable, for lack of consideration, during the time stated or if no time is stated for a reasonable time, but in no event may such period of irrevocability exceed three months; but any such term of assurance on a form supplied by the offeree must be separately signed by the offeror.

§ 2-206. Offer and Acceptance in Formation of Contract.

(1) Unless other unambiguously indicated by the language or circumstances

   (a) an offer to make a contract shall be construed as inviting acceptance in any manner and by any medium reasonable in the circumstances;

   (b) an order or other offer to buy goods for prompt or current shipment shall be construed as inviting acceptance either by a prompt promise to ship or by the prompt or current shipment of conforming or nonconforming goods, but such a shipment of nonconforming goods does not constitute an acceptance if the seller seasonably notifies the buyer that the shipment is offered only as an accommodation to the buyer.

(2) Where the beginning of a requested performance is a reasonable mode of acceptance an offer or who is not notified of acceptance within a reasonable time may treat the offer as having lapsed before acceptance.

§ 2-207. Additional Terms in Acceptance or Confirmation.

(1) A definite and seasonable expression of acceptance or a written confirmation which is sent within a reasonable time operates as an acceptance even though it states terms additional to or different from those offered or agreed upon, unless acceptance is expressly made conditional on assent to the additional or different terms.

(2) The additional terms are to be construed as proposals for addition to the contract. Between merchants such terms become part of the contract unless:

   (a) the offer expressly limits acceptance to the terms of the offer;

   (b) they materially alter it; or

   (c) notification of objection to them has already been given or is given within a reasonable time after notice of them is received.

(3) Conduct by both parties which recognizes the existence of a contract is sufficient to establish a contract for sale although the writings of the parties do not otherwise establish a contract. In such case the terms of the particular contract consist of those terms on which the writings of the parties agree, together with any supplementary terms incorporated under any other provisions of this Act.

§ 2-208. Course of Performance or Practical Construction.

(1) Where the contract for sale involves repeated occasions for performance by either party with knowledge of the nature of the performance and opportunity for objection to it by the other, any course of performance accepted or acquiesced in without objection shall be relevant to determine the meaning of the agreement.

(2) The express terms of the agreement and any such course of performance, as well as any course of dealing and usage of trade, shall be construed whenever reasonable as consistent with each other; but when such construction is unreasonable, express

terms shall control course of performance and course of performance shall control both course of dealing and usage of trade (Section 1-205).

(3) Subject to the provisions of the next section on modification and waiver, such course of performance shall be relevant to show a waiver or modification of any term inconsistent with such course of performance.

§ 2-209. Modification, Rescission and Waiver.

(1) An agreement modifying a contract within this Article needs no consideration to be binding.

(2) A signed agreement which excludes modification or rescission except by a signed writing cannot be otherwise modified or rescinded, but except as between merchants such a requirement on a form supplied by the merchant must be separately signed by the other party.

(3) The requirements of the statute of frauds section of this Article (Section 2-201) must be satisfied if the contract as modified is within its provisions.

(4) Although an attempt at modification or rescission does not satisfy the requirements of subsection (2) or (3) it can operate as a waiver.

(5) A party who has made a waiver affecting an executory portion of the contract may retract the waiver by reasonable notification received by the other party that strict performance will be required of any term waived, unless the retraction would be unjust in view of a material change of position in reliance on the waiver.

§ 2-2 10. Delegation of Performance; Assignment of Rights.

(1) A party may perform his duty through a delegate unless otherwise agreed or unless the other party has a substantial interest in having his original promisor perform or control the acts required by the contract. No delegation of performance relieves the party delegating of any duty to perform or any liability for breach.

(2) Unless otherwise agreed all rights of either seller or buyer can be assigned except where the assignment would materially change the duty of the other party, or increase materially the burden or risk imposed on him by his contract, or impair materially his chance of obtaining return performance. A right to damages for breach of the whole contract or a right arising out of the assignor's due performance of his entire obligation can be assigned despite agreement otherwise.

(3) Unless the circumstances indicate the contrary a prohibition of assignment of "the contract" is to be construed as barring only the delegation to the assignee of the assignor's performance.

(4) An assignment of "the contract" or of "all my rights under the contract" or an assignment in similar general terms is an assignment of rights and unless the language or the circumstances (as in an assignment for security) indicate the contrary, it is a delegation of performance of the duties of the assignor and its acceptance by the assignee constitutes a promise by him to perform those duties. This promise is enforceable by either the assignor or the other party to the original contract

(5) The other party may treat any assignment which delegates performance as creating reasonable grounds for insecurity

and may without prejudice to his rights against the assignor demand assurances from the assignee (Section 2-609).

Part 3 General Obligation and Construction of Contract

§ 2-301. General Obligations of Parties.

The obligation of the seller is to transfer and deliver and that of the buyer is to accept and pay in accordance with the contract.

§ 2-302. Unconscionable Contractor Clause.

(1) If the court as a matter of law finds the contract or any clause of the contract to have been unconscionable at the time it was made the court may refuse to enforce the contract, or it may enforce the remainder of the contract without the unconscionable clause, or it may so limit the application of any unconscionable clause as to avoid any unconscionable result.

(2) When it is claimed or appears to the court that the contract or any clause thereof may be unconscionable the parties shall be afforded a reasonable opportunity to present evidence as to its commercial setting, purpose and effect to aid the court in making the determination.

§ 2-303. Allocations or Division of Risks.

Where this Article allocates a risk or a burden as between the parties "unless otherwise agreed", the agreement may not only shift the allocation but may also divide the risk or burden.

§ 2-304. Price Payable in Money, Goods, Realty, or Otherwise.

(1) The price can be made payable in money or otherwise. If it is payable in whole or in part in goods each party is a seller of the goods which he is to transfer.

(2) Even though all or part of the price is payable in an interest in realty the transfer of the goods and the seller's obligations with reference to them are subject to this Article, but not the transfer of the interest in realty or the transferor's obligations in connection therewith.

§ 2-305. Open Price Term.

(1) The parties if they so intend can conclude a contract for sale even though the price is not settled. In such a case the price is a reasonable price at the time for delivery if
(a) nothing is said as to price; or
(b) the price is left to be agreed by the parties and they fail to agree; or
(c) the price is to be fixed in terms of some agreed market or other standard as set or recorded by a third person or agency and it is not so set or recorded.

(2) A price to be fixed by the seller or by the buyer means a price for him to fix in good faith.

(3) When a price left to be fixed otherwise than by agreement of the parties fails to be fixed through fault of one party the other may at his option treat the contract as cancelled or himself fix a reasonable price.

(4) Where, however, the parties intend not to be bound unless the price be fixed or agreed and it is not fixed or agreed there is no contract. In such a case the buyer must return any goods already received or if unable so to do must pay their reasonable value at the time of delivery and the seller must return any portion of

the price paid on account.

§ 2-306. Output, Requirements and Exclusive Dealings.

(1) A term which measures the quantity by the output of the seller or the requirements of the buyer means such actual output or requirements as may occur in good faith, except that no quantity unreasonably disproportionate to any stated estimate or in the absence of a stated estimate to any normal or otherwise comparable prior output or requirements may be tendered or demanded.

(2) A lawful agreement by either the seller or the buyer for exclusive dealing in the kind of goods concerned imposes unless otherwise agreed an obligation by the seller to use best efforts to supply the goods and by the buyer to use best efforts to promote their sale. § 2-307. Delivery in Single Lot or Several Lots. Unless otherwise agreed all goods called for by a contract for sale must be tendered in a single delivery and payment is due only on such tender but where the circumstances give either party the right to make or demand delivery in lots the price if it can be apportioned may be demanded for each lot.

§ 2-308. Absence of Specified Place for Delivery. Unless otherwise agreed

(a) the place for delivery of goods is the seller's place of business or if he has none his residence; but

(b) in a contract for sale of identified goods which to the knowledge of the parties at the time of contracting are in some other place, that place is the place for their delivery; and (c) documents of tide may be delivered through customary banking channels.

§ 2-309. Absence of Specific Time Provisions; Notice of Termination.

(1) The time for shipment or delivery or any other action under a contract if not provided in this Article or agreed upon shall be a reasonable time.

(2) Where the contract provides for successive performances but is indefinite in duration it is valid for a reason-able time but unless otherwise agreed may be terminated at any time by either party.

(3) Termination of a contract by one party except on the happening of an agreed event requires that reasonable notification be received by the other party and an agreement dispensing with notification is invalid if its operation would be unconscionable.

§ 2-310. Open Time for Payment or Running of Credit; Authority to Ship Under Reservation.

Unless otherwise agreed

(a) payment is due at the time and place at which the buyer is to receive the goods even though the place of shipment is the place of delivery; and

(b) if the seller is authorized to send the goods he may ship them under reservation, and may tender the documents of title, but the buyer may inspect the goods after their arrival before payment is due unless such inspection is inconsistent with the terms of the contract (Section 2-5 13); and

(c) if delivery is authorized and made by way of documents of title otherwise than by subsection (b) then payment is due at the time and place at which the buyer is to receive the documents regardless of where the goods are to be received; and(d) where the seller is required or authorized to ship the goods on credit the credit period runs from the time of shipment but post-dating the invoice or delaying its dispatch will correspondingly delay the starting of the credit period.

§ 2-311. Options and Cooperation Respecting Performance.

(1) An agreement for sale which is otherwise sufficiently definite (subsection (3) of Section 2-204) to be a contract is not made invalid by the fact that it leaves particulars of performance to be specified by one of the parties. Any such specification must be made in good faith and within limits set by commercial reasonableness.

(2) Unless otherwise agreed specifications relating to assortment of the goods are at the buyer's option and except as otherwise provided in subsections (1)(c) and (3) of Section 2-3 19 specifications or arrangements relating to shipment are at the seller's option.

(3) Where such specification would materially affect the other party's performance but is not seasonably made or where one party's cooperation is necessary to the agreed performance of the other but is not seasonably forthcoming, the other party in addition to all other remedies

(a) is excused for any resulting delay in his own performance; and

(b) may also either proceed to perform in any reasonable manner or after the time for a material part of his own performance treat the failure to specify or to cooperate as a breach by failure to deliver or accept the goods.

§ 2-312. Warranty of Title and Against Infringement; Buyer's Obligation Against Infringement.

(1) Subject to subsection (2) there is in a contract for sale a warranty by the seller that

• the title conveyed shall be good, and its transfer rightful; and

• the goods shall be delivered free from any security interest or other lien or encumbrance of which the buyer at the time of contracting has no knowledge.

(2) A warranty under subsection (1) will be excluded or modified only by specific language or by circumstances which give the buyer reason to know that the person selling does not claim title in himself or that he is purporting to sell only such right or title as he or a third person may have.

(3) Unless otherwise agreed a seller who is a merchant regularly dealing in goods of the kind warrants that the goods shall be delivered free of the rightful claim of any third person by way of infringement or the like but a buyer who furnishes specifications to the seller must hold the seller harmless against any such claim which arises out of compliance with the specifications.

§ 2-313. Express Warranties by Affirmation, Promise, Description, Sample.

(1) Express warranties by the seller are created as follows:

(a) Any affirmation of fact or promise made by the seller to the buyer which relates to the goods and becomes part of the basis of the bargain creates an express warranty that the goods shall conform to the affirmation or promise.

(b) Any description of the goods which is made part of the basis of the bargain creates an express warranty that the goods shall conform to the description.

(c) Any sample or model which is made part of the basis of the bargain creates an express warranty that the whole of the goods shall conform to the sample or model.

(2) It is not necessary to the creation of an express warranty that the seller use formal words such as "warrant" or "guarantee" or that he have a specific intention to make a warranty, but an affirmation merely of the value of the goods or a statement purporting to be merely the seller's opinion or commendation of the goods does not create a warranty.

§ 2-314. Implied Warranty: Merchantability; Usage of Trade.

(1) Unless excluded or modified (Section 2-316), a warranty that the goods shall be merchantable is implied in a contract for their sale if the seller is a merchant with respect to goods of that kind. Under this section the serving for value of food or drink to be consumed either on the premises or elsewhere is a sale.

(2) Goods to be merchantable must be at least such as

(a) pass without objection in the trade under the contract description; and

(b) in the case of fungible goods, are of fair average quality within the description; and

(c) are fit for the ordinary purposes for which such goods are used; and

(d) run, within the variations permitted by the agreement, of even kind, quality and quantity within each unit and among all units involved; and

(e) are adequately contained, packaged, and labeled as the agreement may require; and(f) conform to the promises or affirmations of fact made on the container or label if any.

(3) Unless excluded or modified (Section 2-316) other implied warranties may arise from course of dealing or usage of trade.

§ 2-315. Implied Warranty: Fitness for Particular Purpose.

Where the seller at the time of contracting has reason to know any particular purpose for which the goods are required and that the buyer is relying on the seller's skill or judgment to select or furnish suitable goods, there is unless excluded or modified under the next section an implied warranty that the goods shall be fit for such purpose.

§ 2-316. Exclusion or Modification of Warranties.

(1) Words or conduct relevant to the creation of an express warranty and words or conduct tending to negate or limit warranty shall be construed wherever reasonable as consistent with each other; but subject to the provisions of this Article on parol or extrinsic evidence (Section 2-202) negation or limitation is inoperative to the extent that such construction is unreasonable.

(2) Subject to subsection (3), to exclude or modify the implied warranty of merchantability or any part of it the language must mention merchantability and in case of a writing must be conspicuous, and to exclude or modify any implied warranty of fitness the exclusion must be by a writing and con-

spicuous. Language to exclude all implied warranties of fitness is sufficient if it states, for example, that "There are no warranties which extend beyond the description on the face hereof."

(3) Notwithstanding subsection (2)

(a) unless the circumstances indicate otherwise, all implied warranties are excluded by expressions like "as is", "with all faults" or other language which in common understanding calls the buyer's attention to the exclusion of warranties and makes plain that there is no implied warranty; and

(b) when the buyer before entering into the contract has examined the goods or the sample or model as fully as he desired or has refused to examine the goods there is no implied warranty with regard to defects which an examination ought in the circumstances to have revealed to him; and

(c) an implied warranty can also be excluded or modified by course of dealing or course of performance or usage of trade.,

(4) Remedies for breach of warranty can be limited in accordance with the provisions of this Article on liquidation or limitation of damages and on contractual modification of remedy (Sections 2-718 and 2-719).

§ 2-317. Cumulation and Conflict of Warranties Express or Implied.

Warranties whether express or implied shall be construed as consistent with each other and as cumulative, but if such construction is unreasonable the intention of the parties shall determine which warranty is dominant. In ascertaining that intention the following rules apply:

(a) Exact or technical specifications displace an inconsistent sample or model or general language of description.

(b) A sample from an existing bulk displaces inconsistent general language of description.

(c) Express warranties displace inconsistent implied warranties other than an implied warranty of fitness fora particular purpose.

§ 2-318. Third Party Beneficiaries of Warranties Express or Implied.

Note: If this Act is introduced in the Congress of the United States this section should be omitted. (States to select one alternative.)

Alternative A

A seller's warranty whether express or implied extends to any natural person who is in the family or household of his buyer or who is a guest in his home if it is reasonable to expect that such person may use, consume or be affected by the goods and who is injured in person by breach of the warranty. A seller may not exclude or limit the operation of this section.

Alternative B

A seller's warranty whether express or implied extends to any natural person who may reasonably be expected to use, consume or be affected by the goods and who is injured in person by breach of the warranty. A seller may not exclude or limit the operation of this section.

Alternative C

A seller's warranty whether express or implied extends to any person who may reasonably be expected to use, consume or be affected by the goods and who is injured by breach of the warranty. A seller may not exclude or limit the operation of this section with respect to injury to the person of an individual to whom the warranty extends. As amended 1966.

§ 2-319. F.O.B. and F.A.S. Terms.

(1) Unless otherwise agreed the term F.O.B. (which means "free on board") at a named place, even though used only in connection with the stated price, is a delivery term under which

(a) when the term is F.O.B. the place of shipment, the seller must at that place ship the goods in the manner provided in this Article (Section 2-504) and bear the expense and risk of putting them into the possession of the carrier; or

(b) when the term is F.O.B. the place of destination, the seller must at his own expense and risk transport the goods to that place and there tender delivery of them in the manner provided in this Article (Section 2-503);

(c) when under either (a) or (b) the term is also F.O.B. vessel, car or other vehicle, the seller must in addition at his own expense and risk load the goods on board. If the term is F.O.B. vessel the buyer must name the vessel and in an appropriate case the seller must comply with the provisions of this Article on the form of bill of lading (Section 2-32 3).(2)

(2) Unless otherwise agreed the term F.A.S. vessel (which means "free alongside") at a named port, even though used only in connection with the stated price, is a delivery term under which the seller must

(a) at his own expense and risk deliver the goods alongside the vessel in the manner usual in that port or on a dock designated and provided by the buyer; and

(b) obtain and tender a receipt for the goods in exchange for which the carrier is under a duty to issue a bill of lading.

(3) Unless otherwise agreed in any case falling within subsection (1)(a) or (c) or subsection (2) the buyer must seasonably give any needed instructions for making delivery, including when the term is F.A.S. or F.O.B. the loading berth of the vessel and in an appropriate case its name and sailing date. The seller may treat the failure of needed instructions as a failure of cooperation under this Article (Section 2-311). He may also at his option move the goods in any reasonable manner preparatory to delivery or shipment.

(4) Under the term F.O.B. vessel or F.A.S. unless otherwise agreed the buyer must make payment against tender of the required documents and the seller may not tender nor the buyer demand delivery of the goods in substitution for the documents.

§ 2-320. C.I.F. and C. & F. Terms.

(1) The term C.I.F. means that the price includes in a lump sum the cost of the goods and the insurance and freight to the named destination. The term C. & F. or C.F. means that the price so includes cost and freight to the named destination.

(2) Unless otherwise agreed and even though used only in connection with the stated price and destination, the term C.I.F.

destination or its equivalent requires the seller at his own expense and risk to

(a) put the goods into the possession of a carrier at the port for shipment and obtain a negotiable bill or bills of lading covering the entire transportation to the named destination; and

(b) load the goods and obtain a receipt from the carrier(which may be contained in the bill of lading) showing that the freight has been paid or provided for; and

(c) obtain a policy or certificate of insurance, including any war risk insurance, of a kind and on terms then current at the port of shipment in the usual amount, in the currency of the contract, shown to cover the same goods covered by the bill of lading and providing for payment of loss to the order of the buyer or for the account of whom it may concern; but the seller may add to the price the amount of the premium for any such war risk insurance; and

(d) prepare an invoice of the goods and procure any other documents required to effect shipment or to comply with the contract; and

(e) forward and tender with commercial promptness all the documents in due form and with any indorsement necessary to perfect the buyer's rights.

(3) Unless otherwise agreed the term C. & F. or its equivalent has the same effect and imposes upon the seller the same obligations and risks as a C.I.F. term except the obligation as to insurance.

(4) Under the term C.I.F. or C. & F. unless otherwise agreed the buyer must make payment against tender of the required documents and the seller may not tender nor the buyer demand delivery of the goods in substitution for the documents.

§ 2-321. C.I.F. or C. & F.: "Net Landed Weights"; "Payment on Arrival"; Warranty of Condition on Arrival.

Under a contract containing a term C.I.F. or C. & F.

(1) Where the price is based on or is to be adjusted according to "net landed weights", "delivered weights", "out turn" quantity or quality or the like, unless otherwise agreed the seller must reasonably estimate the price. The payment due on tender of the documents called for by the contract is the amount so estimated, but after final adjustment of the price a settlement must be made with commercial promptness.

(2) An agreement described in subsection (1) or any warranty of quality or condition of the goods on arrival places upon the seller the risk of ordinary deterioration, shrinkage and the like in transportation but has no effect on the place or time of identification to the contract for sale or delivery or on the passing of the risk of loss.

(3) Unless otherwise agreed where the contract provides for payment on or after arrival of the goods the seller must before payment allow such preliminary inspection as is feasible; but if the goods are lost delivery of the documents and payment are due when the goods should have arrived.

§ 2-322. Delivery "Ex-Ship".

1. Unless otherwise agreed a term for delivery of goods "ex-ship"

(which means from the carrying vessel) or in equivalent language is not restricted to a particular ship and requires delivery from a ship which has reached a place at the named port of destination where goods of kind are usually discharged.

2. Under such a term unless otherwise agreed
    (a) the seller must discharge all liens arising out of the carriage and furnish the buyer with a direction which puts the carrier under a duty to deliver the goods; and
    (b) the risk of loss does not pass to the buyer until the goods leave the ship's tackle or are otherwise properly unloaded.

§ 2-323. Form of Bill of Lading Required in Overseas Shipment; "Overseas".
(1) Where the contract contemplates overseas shipment and contains a term C.I.F. or C. & F. or F.O.B. vessel, the seller unless otherwise agreed must obtain a negotiable bill of lading stating that the goods have been loaded on board or, in the case of a term C.I.F. or C. & F., received for shipment.
(2) Where in a case within subsection (1) a bill of lading has been issued in a set of parts, unless otherwise agreed if the documents are not to be sent from abroad the buyer may demand tender of the full set; otherwise only one part of the bill of lading need be tendered. Even if the agreement expressly requires a full set
    (a) due tender of a single part is acceptable within the provisions of this Article on cure of improper delivery(subsection (1) of Section 2-508); and
    (b) even though the full set is demanded, if the documents are sent from abroad the person tendering an incomplete set may nevertheless require payment upon furnishing an indemnity which the buyer in good faith deems adequate.
(3) A shipment by water or by air or a contract contemplating such shipment is "overseas" insofar as by usage of trade or agreement it is subject to the commercial, financing or shipping practices characteristic of international deep water commerce.

§ 2-324. "No Arrival, No Sale" Term.
Under a term "no arrival, no sale" or terms of like meaning, unless otherwise agreed,
    (a) the seller must properly ship conforming good sand if they arrive by any means he must tender the non-arrival but he assumes no obligation that the goods will arrive unless he has caused the non-arrival; and
    (b) where without fault of the seller the goods are in part lost or have so deteriorated as no longer to con-form to the contract or arrive after the contract time, the buyer may proceed as if there had been casualty to identified goods (Section 2-613).

§ 2-325. "Letter of Credit" Tenn; "Confirmed Credit".
(1) Failure of the buyer seasonably to furnish an agreed letter of credit is a breach of the contract for sale.
(2) The delivery to seller of a proper letter of credit suspends the buyer's obligation to pay. If the letter of credit is dishonored, the seller may on seasonable notification to the buyer require payment directly from him.
(3) Unless otherwise agreed the term "letter of credit" or "banker's credit" in a contract for sale means an irrevocable credit issued by a financing agency of good repute and, where the shipment is overseas, of good international repute. The term "confirmed credit" means that the credit must also carry the direct obligation of such an agency which does business in the seller's financial market.

§ 2-326. Sale on Approval and Sale or Return; Consignment Sales and Rights Of Creditors.
(1) Unless otherwise agreed, if delivered goods may be returned by the buyer even though they conform to the contract, the transaction is
    (a) a "sale on approval" if the goods are delivered primarily for use, and
    (b) a "sale or return" if the goods are delivered primarily for resale.
(2) Except as provided in subsection goods held on approval are not subject to the claims of the buyer's creditors until acceptance; goods held on sale or return are subject to such claims while in the buyer's possession.
(3) Where goods are delivered to, a person for sale and such person maintains a place of business at which he deals in goods of the kind involved, under a name other than the name of the person making delivery, then with respect to claims of creditors of the person conducting the business the goods are deemed to be on sale or return. The provisions of this sub-section are applicable even though an agreement purports to reserve title to the person making delivery until payment or resale or uses such words as "on consignment" or "on memorandum". However, this sub-section is not applicable if the person making delivery
    (a) complies with an applicable law providing for a consignor's interest or the like to be evidenced by a sign, or
    (b) establishes that the person conducting the business is generally known by his creditors to be substantially engaged in selling the goods of others, or
    (c) complies with the filing provisions of the Article on Secured Transactions (Article 9).
(4) Any "or return" term of a contract for sale is to be treated as a separate contract for sale within the statute of frauds section of this Article (Section 2-201) and as contradicting the sale aspect of the contract within the provisions of this Article on parol or extrinsic evidence (Section2-202).

§ 2-327. Special Incidents of Sale on Approval and Sale or Return.
(1) Under a sale on approval unless otherwise agreed
    (a) although the goods are identified to the contract the risk of loss and the title do not pass to the buyer until acceptance; and
    (b) use of the goods consistent with the purpose of trial is not acceptance but failure seasonably to notify the seller of election to return the goods is acceptance, and if the goods conform to the contract acceptance of any part is acceptance of the whole; and
    (c) after due notification of election to return, the return is at the seller's risk and expense but a merchant buyer must follow any reasonable instructions.
(2) Under a sale or return unless otherwise agreed
    (a) the option to return extends to the whole or any com-

mercial unit of the goods while in substantially their original condition, but must be exercised seasonably; and
(b) the return is at the buyer's risk and expense.

§ 2-328. Sale by Auction.
(1) In a sale by auction if goods are put up in lots each lot is the subject of a separate sale.
(2) A sale by auction is complete when the auctioneer so announces by the fall of the hammer or in other customary manner. Where a bid is made while the hammer is falling in acceptance of a prior bid the auctioneer may in his discretion reopen the bidding or declare the goods sold under the bid on which the hammer was falling.
(3) Such a sale is with reserve unless the goods are in explicit terms put up without reserve. In an auction with reserve the auctioneer may withdraw the goods at any time until he announces completion of the sale. In an auction without reserve, after the auctioneer calls for bids on an article or lot, that article or lot cannot be withdrawn unless no bid is made within a reasonable time. In either case a bidder may retract his bid until the auctioneer's announcement of completion of the sale, but a bidder's retraction does not revive any previous bid.
(4) If the auctioneer knowingly receives a bid on the seller's behalf or the seller makes or procures such as bid, and notice has not been given that liberty for such bidding is reserved, the buyer may at his option avoid the sale or take the goods at the price of the last good faith bid prior to the completion of the sale. This subsection shall not apply to any bid at a forced sale.

Part 4 Title, Creditors and Good Faith Purchasers

§ 2-401. Passing of Title; Reservation for Security; Limited Application of This Section.
Each provision of this Article with regard to the rights, obligations and remedies of the seller, the buyer, purchasers or other third parties applies irrespective of title to the goods except where the provision refers to such tide. Insofar as situations are not covered by the other provisions of this Article and matters concerning tide became material the following rules apply:
(1) Title to goods cannot pass under a contract for sale prior to their identification to the contract (Section2-501), and unless otherwise explicitly agreed the buyer acquires by their identification a special property as limited by this Act. Any retention or reservation by the seller of the tide (property) in goods shipped or delivered to the buyer is limited in effect to a reservation of a security interest. Subject to these provisions and to the provisions of the Article on Secured Transactions (Article 9), tide to goods passes from the seller to the buyer in any manner and on any conditions explicitly agreed on by the parties.
(2) Unless otherwise explicitly agreed tide passes to the buyer at the time and place at which the seller completes his performance with reference to the physical delivery of the goods, despite any reservation of a security interest and even though a document of tide is to be delivered at a different time or place; and in particular and despite any reservation of a security interest by the bill of lading

(a) if the contract requires or authorizes the seller to send the goods to the buyer but does not require him to deliver them at destination, tide passes to the buyer at the time and place of shipment; but
(b) if the contract requires delivery at destination, title passes on tender there.
(3) Unless otherwise explicitly agreed where delivery is to be made without moving the goods,
(a) if the seller is to deliver a document of tide, title passes at the time when and the place where he delivers such documents; or
(b) if the goods are at the time of contracting already identified and no documents are to be delivered, title passes at the time and place of contracting.
(4) A rejection or other refusal by the buyer to receive or retain the goods, whether or not justified, or a justified revocation of acceptance revests title to the goods in the seller. Such revesting occurs by operation of law and is not a "sale".

§ 2-402. Rights of Seller's Creditors Against Sold Goods.
(1) Except as provided in subsections (2) and (3), rights of unsecured creditors of the seller with respect to goods which have been identified to a contract for sale are subject to the buyer's rights to recover the goods under this Article (Sections 2-502 and 2-716).
(2) A creditor of the seller may treat a sale or an identification of goods to a contract for sale as void if as against him a retention of possession by the seller is fraudulent under any rule of law of the state where the goods are situated, except that retention of possession in good faith and current course of trade by a merchant-seller for a commercially reasonable time after a sale or identification is not fraudulent.
(3) Nothing in this Article shall be deemed to impair the rights of creditors of the seller
(a) under the provisions of the Article on Secured Transactions (Article 9); or
(b) where identification to the contract or delivery is made not in current course of trade but in satisfaction of or as security for a pre-existing claim for money, security or the like and is made under circumstances which under any rule of law of the state where the goods are situated would apart from this Article constitute the transaction a fraudulent transfer or voidable preference.

§ 2-403. Power to Transfer; Good Faith Purchase of Goods; "Entrusting".
(1) A purchaser of goods acquires all title which his transferor had or had power to transfer except that a purchaser of a limited interest acquires rights only to the extent of the interest purchased. A person with voidable title has power to transfer a good title to a good faith purchaser for value. When goods have been delivered under a transaction of purchase the purchaser has such power even though
(a) the transferor was deceived as to the identity of the purchaser, or
(b) the delivery was in exchange for a check which is later dishonored, or
(c) it was agreed that the transaction was to be a "cash sale", or(d) the delivery was procured through fraud punish-

able as larcenous under the criminal law.

(2) Any entrusting of possession of goods to a merchant who deals in goods of that kind gives him power to transfer all rights of the entruster to a buyer in ordinary course of business.

(3) "Entrusting" includes any delivery and any acquiescence in retention of possession regardless of any condition expressed between the parties to the delivery or acquiescence and regardless of whether the procurement of the entrusting or the possessor's disposition of the goods have been such as to be larcenous under the criminal law.

(4) The rights of other purchasers of goods and of lien creditors are governed by the Articles on Secured Transactions (Article 9), Bulk Transfers (Article 6) and Documents of Title (Article 7).

Part 5 Performance

§ 2-501. Insurable Interest in Goods; Manner of Identification of Goods.

(1) The buyer obtains a special property and an insurable interest in goods by identification of existing goods as goods to which the contract refers even though the goods so identified are non-conforming and he has an option to return or reject them. Such identification can be made at any time and in any manner explicitly agreed to by the parties. In the absence of explicit agreement identification occurs

   (a) when the contract is made if it is for the sale of goods already existing and identified;

   (b) if the contract is for the sale of future goods other than those described in paragraph when goods are shipped, marked or otherwise designated by the seller as goods to which the contract refers;

   (c) when the crops are planted or otherwise become growing crops or the young are conceived if the contract is for the sale of unborn young to be born within twelve months after contracting or for the sale of crops to be harvested within twelve months or the next normal harvest season after contracting whichever is longer.

(2) The seller retains an insurable interest in goods so long as title to or any security interest in the goods remains in him and where the identification is by the seller alone he may until default or insolvency or notification to the buyer that the identification is final substitute other goods for those identified.

(3) Nothing in this section impairs any insurable interest recognized under any other statute or rule of law.

§ 2-502. Buyer's Right to Goods on Seller's Insolvency.

(1) Subject to subsection (2) and even though the goods have not been shipped a buyer who has paid a part or all of the price of goods in which he has a special property under the provisions of the immediately preceding section may on making and keeping good a tender of any unpaid portion of their price recover them from the seller if the seller becomes insolvent within ten days after receipt of the first installment on their price.

(2) If the identification creating his special property has been made by the buyer he acquires the right to recover the goods only if they conform to the contract for sale.

§ 2-503. Manner of Seller's Tender of Delivery.

(1) Tender of delivery requires that the seller put and hold conforming goods at the buyer's disposition and give the buyer any notification reasonably necessary to enable him to take delivery. The manner, time and place for tender are determined by the agreement and this Article, and in particular

   (a) tender must be at a reasonable hour, and if it is of goods they must be kept available for the period reasonably necessary to enable the buyer to take possession; but

   (b) unless otherwise agreed the buyer must furnish facilities reasonably suited to the receipt of the goods.

(2) Where the case is within the next section respecting shipment tender requires that the seller comply with its provisions.

(3) Where the seller is required to deliver at a particular destination tender requires that he comply with subsection (1) and also in any appropriate case tender documents as described in subsections (4) and (5) of this section.

(4) Where goods are in the possession of a bailee and are to be delivered without being moved

   (a) tender requires that the seller either tender a negotiable document of title covering such goods or procure acknowledgment by the bailee of the buyer's right to possession of the goods; but

   (b) tender to the buyer of a non-negotiable document of title or of a written direction to the bailee to deliver is sufficient tender unless the buyer seasonably objects, and receipt by the bailee of notification of the buyer's rights fixes those rights as against the bailee and all third persons; but risk of loss of the goods and of any failure by the bailee to honor the non-negotiable document of title or to obey the direction remains on the seller until the buyer has had a reasonable time to present the document or direction, and a refusal by the bailee to honor the document or to obey the direction defeats the tender.

(5) Where the contract requires the seller to deliver documents

   (a) he must tender all such documents in correct form, except as provided in this Article with respect to bills of lading in a set (subsection (2) of Section 2-323); and

   (b) tender through customary banking channels is sufficient and dishonor of a draft accompanying the documents constitutes non-acceptance or rejection.

§ 2-504. Shipment by Seller.

Where the seller is required or authorized to send the goods to the buyer and the contract does not require him to deliver them at a particular destination, then unless otherwise agreed he must

(a) put the goods in the possession of such a carrier and make such a contract for their transportation as may be reasonable having regard to the nature of the goods and other circumstances of the case; and

(b) obtain and promptly deliver or tender in due form any document necessary to enable the buyer to obtain possession of the goods or otherwise required by the agreement or by usage of trade; and

(c) promptly notify the buyer of the shipment. Failure to notify the buyer under paragraph (c) or to make a proper contract under paragraph (a) is a ground for rejection only if material delay or loss ensues.

§ 2-505. Seller's Shipment under Reservation.
(1) Mere the seller has identified goods to the contract by or before shipment:
   (a) his procurement of a negotiable bill of lading to his own order or otherwise reserves in him a security interest in the goods. His procurement of the bill to the order of a financing agency or of the buyer indicates in addition only the seller's expectation of transferring that interest to the person named.
   (b) a non-negotiable bill of lading to himself or his nominee reserves possession of the goods as security but except in a case of conditional delivery (subsection (2) of Section 2-507) a non-negotiable bill of lading naming the buyer as consignee reserves no security interest even though the seller retains possession of the bill of lading.
(2) When shipment by the seller with reservation of a security interest is in violation of the contract for sale it constitutes an improper contract for transportation within the preceding section but impairs neither the rights given to the buyer by shipment and identification of the goods to the contract nor the seller's powers as a holder of a negotiable document.

§ 2-506. Rights of Financing Agency.
(1) A financing agency by paying or purchasing for value a draft which relates to a shipment of goods acquires to the extent of the payment or purchase and in addition to its own rights under the draft and any document of tide securing it any rights of the shipper in the goods including the right to stop delivery and the shipper's right to have the draft honored by the buyer.
(2) The right to reimbursement of a financing agency which has in good faith honored or purchased the draft under commitment to or authority from the buyer is not impaired by subsequent discovery of defects with reference to any relevant document which was apparently regular on its face.

§ 2-507. Effect of Seller's Tender; Delivery on Condition.
(1) Tender of delivery is a condition to the buyer's duty to accept the goods and, unless otherwise agreed, to his duty to pay for them. Tender entitles the seller to acceptance of the goods and to payment according to the contract.
(2) Where payment is due and demanded on the delivery to the buyer of goods or documents of title, his right as against the seller to retain or dispose of them is conditional upon his making the payment due.

§ 2-508. Cure by Seller of Improper Tender or Delivery; Replacement.
(1) Where any tender or delivery by the seller is rejected because non-conforming and the time for performance has not yet expired, the seller may seasonably notify the buyer of his intention to cure and may then within the contract time make a conforming delivery.
(2) Where the buyer rejects a non-conforming tender which the seller had reasonable grounds to believe would be acceptable with or without money allowance the seller may if he season-

ably notifies the buyer have a further reasonable time to substitute a conforming tender.

§ 2-509. Risk of Loss in the Absence of Breach.
(1) Where the contract requires or authorizes the seller to ship the goods by carrier
   (a) if it does not require him to deliver them at a particular destination, the risk of loss passes to the buyer when the goods are duly delivered to the carrier even though the shipment is under reservation (Section 2-505); but
   (b) if it does require him to deliver them at a particular destination and the goods are there duly tendered while in the possession of the carrier, the risk of loss passes to the buyer when the goods are there duly so tendered as to enable the buyer to take delivery.
(2) Where the goods are held by a bailee to be delivered without being moved, the risk of loss passes to the buyer
   (a) on his receipt of a negotiable document of title covering the goods; or
   (b) on acknowledgment by the bailee of the buyer's right to possession of the goods; or
   (c) after his receipt of a non-negotiable document of title or other written direction to deliver, as provided in subsection (4)(b) of Section 2-503.
(3) In any case not within subsection (1) or (2), the risk of loss passes to the buyer on his receipt of the goods if the seller is a merchant; otherwise the risk passes to the buyer on tender of delivery.
(4) The provisions of this section are subject to contrary agreement of the parties and to the provisions of this Article on sale on approval (Section 2-3 27) and on effect of breach on risk of loss (Section 2-510).

§ 2-510. Effect of Breach on Risk of Loss.
(1) Where a tender or delivery of goods so fails to conform to the contract as to give a right of rejection the risk of their loss remains on the seller until cure or acceptance.
(2) Where the buyer rightfully revokes acceptance he may to the extent of any deficiency in his effective insurance coverage treat the risk of loss as having rested on the seller from the beginning.
(3) Where the buyer as to conforming goods already identified to the contract for sale repudiates or is otherwise in breach before risk of their loss has passed to him, the seller may to the extent of any deficiency in his effective insurance coverage treat the risk of loss as resting on the buyer for a commercially reasonable time.

§ 2-511. Tender of Payment by Buyer; Payment by Check.
(1) Unless otherwise agreed tender of payment is a condition to the seller's duty to tender and complete any delivery.
(2) Tender of payment is sufficient when made by any means or in any manner current in the ordinary course of business unless the seller demands payment in legal tender and gives any extension of time reasonably necessary to procure it.
(3) Subject to the provisions of this Act on the effect of an instrument on an obligation (Section 3-3 10), payment by check is conditional and is defeated as between the parties by dishonor of the check on due presentment.

§ 2-512. Payment by Buyer Before Inspection.

(1) Where the contract requires payment before inspection non-conformity of the goods does not excuse the buyer from so making payment unless

    (a) the non-conformity appears without inspection; or

    (b) despite tender of the required documents the circumstances would justify injunction against honor under the provisions of this Act (Section 5-114).

(2) Payment pursuant to subsection (1) does not constitute an acceptance of goods or impair the buyer's right to inspect or any of his remedies.

§ 2-513. Buyer's Right to Inspection of Goods.

(1) Unless otherwise agreed and subject to subsection (3),where goods are tendered or delivered or identified to the contract for sale, the buyer has a right before payment or acceptance to inspect them at any reasonable place and time and in any reasonable manner. When the seller is required or authorized to send the goods to the buyer, the inspection may be after their arrival.

(2) Expenses of inspection must be borne by the buyer but may be recovered from the seller if the goods do not conform and are rejected.

(3) Unless otherwise agreed and subject to the provisions of this Article on C.I.F. contracts (subsection (3) of Section 2-321), the buyer is not entitled to inspect the goods before payment of the price when the contract provides

    (a) for delivery "C.O.D." or on other like terms; or

    (b) for payment against documents of title, except where such payment is due only after the goods are to become available for inspection.

(4) A place or method of inspection fixed by the parties is presumed to be exclusive but unless otherwise expressly agreed it does not postpone identification or shift the place for delivery or for passing the risk of loss. If compliance becomes impossible, inspection shall be as provided in this section unless the place or method fixed was clearly intended as an indispensable condition failure of which avoids the contract.

§ 2-514. When Documents Deliverable on Acceptance;

When on Payment. Unless otherwise agreed documents against which a draft is drawn are to be delivered to the drawee on acceptance of the draft if it is payable more than three days after presentment; otherwise, only on payment.

§ 2-515. Preserving Evidence of Goods in Dispute.

In furtherance of the adjustment of any claim or dispute

(a) either party on reasonable notification to the other and for the purpose of ascertaining the facts and preserving evidence has the right to inspect, test and sample the goods including such of them as may be in the possession or control of the other; and

(b) the parties may agree to a third party inspection or survey to determine the conformity or condition of the goods and may agree that the findings shall be binding upon them in any subsequent litigation or adjustment.

Part 6 Breach, Repudiation and Excuse

§ 2-601. Buyer's Rights on Improper Delivery.

Subject to the provisions of this Article on breach in installment contracts (Section 2-612) and unless otherwise agreed under the sections on contractual limitations of remedy (Sections 2-718 and 2-719), if the goods or the tender of delivery fail in any respect to conform to the contract, the buyer may

    (a) reject the whole; or

    (b) accept the whole; or

    (c) accept any commercial unit or units and reject the rest.

§ 2-602. Manner and Effect of Rightful Rejection.

(1) Rejection of goods must be within a reasonable time after their delivery or tender. It is ineffective unless the buyer seasonably notifies the seller.

(2) Subject to the provisions of the two following sections on rejected goods (Sections 2-603 and 2-604),

    (a) after rejection any exercise of ownership by the buyer with respect to any commercial unit is wrongful as against the seller; and

    (b) if the buyer has before rejection taken physical possession of goods in which he does not have a security interest under the provisions of this Article (sub-section (3) of Section 2-711), he is under a duty after rejection to hold them with reasonable care at the seller's disposition for a time sufficient to permit the seller to remove them; but

    (c) the buyer has no further obligations with regard to goods rightfully rejected.

(3) The seller's rights with respect to goods wrongfully rejected are governed by the provisions of this Article on Seller's remedies in general (Section 2-703).

§ 2-603. Merchant Buyer's Duties as to Rightfully Rejected Goods.

(1) Subject to any security interest in the buyer (subsection (3) of Section 2-711), when the seller has no agent or place of business at the market of rejection a merchant buyer is under a duty after rejection of goods in his possession or control to follow any reasonable instructions received from the seller with respect to the goods and in the absence of such instructions to make reasonable efforts to sell them for the seller's account if they are perishable or threaten to decline in value speedily. Instructions are not reasonable if on demand indemnity for expenses is not forthcoming.

(2) When the buyer sells goods under subsection (1), he is entitled to reimbursement from the seller or out of the proceeds for reasonable expenses of caring for and selling them, and if the expenses include no selling commission then to such commission as is usual in the trade or if there is none to a reasonable sum not exceeding ten per cent on the gross proceeds.

(3) In complying with this section the buyer is held only to good faith and good faith conduct hereunder is neither acceptance nor conversion nor the basis of an action for damages.

§ 2-604. Buyer's Options as to Salvage of Rightfully Rejected Goods.

Subject to the provisions of the immediately preceding section on perishables if the seller gives no instructions within a reasonable time after notification of rejection the buyer may store the rejected goods for the seller's account or reship them to him or resell them for the seller's account with reimbursement as provided in the preceding section. Such action is not acceptance or conversion.

§ 2-605. Waiver of Buyer's Objections by Failure to Particularize.

(1) The buyer's failure to state in connection with rejection a particular defect which is ascertainable by reasonable inspection precludes him from relying on the unstated defect to justify rejection or to establish breach

    (a) where the seller could have cured it if stated seasonably; or

    (b) between merchants when the seller has after rejection made a request in writing for a full and final written statement of all defects on which the buyer proposes to rely.

(2) Payment against documents made without reservation of rights precludes recovery of the payment for defects apparent on the face of the documents.

§ 2-606. What Constitutes Acceptance of Goods.

(1) Acceptance of goods occurs when the buyer

    (a) after a reasonable opportunity to inspect the goods signifies to the seller that the goods are conforming or that he will take or retain them in spite of their non-conformity; or

    (b) fails to make an effective rejection (subsection (1)of Section 2-602), but such acceptance does not occur until the buyer has had a reasonable opportunity to inspect them; or

    (c) does any act inconsistent with the seller's owner-ship; but if such act is wrongful as against the seller it is an acceptance only if ratified by him.

(2) Acceptance of a part of any commercial unit is acceptance of that entire unit.

§ 2-607. Effect of Acceptance; Notice of Breach; Burden of Establishing Breach After Acceptance; Notice of Claim or Litigation to Person Answerable Over.

(1) The buyer must pay at the contract rate for any goods accepted.

(2) Acceptance of goods by the buyer precludes rejection of the goods accepted and if made with knowledge of anon-conformity cannot be revoked because of it unless the acceptance was on the reasonable assumption that the non-conformity would be seasonably cured but acceptance does not of itself impair any other remedy provided by this Article for nonconformity.

(3) Where a tender has been accepted

    (a) the buyer must within a reasonable time after he discovers or should have discovered any breach notify the seller of breach or be barred from any remedy; and

    (b) if the claim is one for infringement or the like(subsection (3) of Section 2-312) and the buyer issued as a result of such a breach he must so notify the seller within a reasonable time after he receives notice of the litigation or be barred from any remedy over for liability established by the litigation.

(4) The burden is on the buyer to establish any breach with respect to the goods accepted.

(5) Where the buyer is sued for breach of a warranty or other obligation for which his seller is answerable over

    (a) he may give his seller written notice of the litigation. If the notice states that the seller may come in and defend and that if the seller does not do so he will be bound in any action against him by his buyer by any determination of fact common to the two litigations, then unless the seller after seasonable receipt of the notice does come in and defend he is so bound.

    (b) if the claim is one for infringement or the like(subsection (3) of Section 2-312) the original seller may demand in writing that his buyer turn over to him control of the litigation including settlement or else be barred from any remedy over and if he also agrees to bear all expense and to satisfy any adverse judgment, then unless the buyer after seasonable receipt of the demand does turn over control the buyer is so barred.

(6) The provisions of subsections (3), (4) and (5) apply to any obligation of a buyer to hold the seller harmless against infringement or the like (subsection (3) of Section 2-312).

§ 2-608. Revocation of Acceptance in Whole or in Part.

(1) The buyer may revoke his acceptance of a lot or commercial unit whose non-conformity substantially impairs its value to him if he has accepted it

    (a) on the reasonable assumption that its nonconformity would be cured and it has not been seasonably cured; or

    (b) without discovery of such non-conformity if his acceptance was reasonably induced either by the difficulty of discovery before acceptance or by the seller's assurances.

(2) Revocation of acceptance must occur within a reasonable time after the buyer discovers or should have discovered the ground for it and before any substantial change in condition of the goods which is not caused by their own defects. It is not effective until the buyer notifies the seller of it.

(3) A buyer who so revokes has the same rights and duties with regard to the goods involved as if he had rejected them.

§ 2-609. Right to Adequate Assurance of Performance.

(1) A contract for sale imposes an obligation on each party that the other's expectation of receiving due performance will not be impaired. When reasonable grounds for insecurity arise with respect to the performance of either party the other may in writing demand adequate assurance of due performance and until he receives such assurance may if commercially reasonable suspend any performance for which he has not already received the agreed return.

(2) Between merchants the reasonableness of grounds for insecurity and the adequacy of any assurance offered shall be determined according to commercial standards.

(3) Acceptance of any improper delivery or payment does not prejudice the party's right to demand adequate assurance of future performance.

(4) After receipt of a justified demand failure to provide within a reasonable time not exceeding thirty days such assurance of due performance as is adequate under the circumstances of the particular case is a repudiation of the contract.

§ 2-610. Anticipatory Repudiation.

When either party repudiates the contract with respect to a performance not yet due the loss of which will substantially impair the value of the contract to the other, the aggrieved party may

(a) for a commercially reasonable time await performance by the repudiating party; or

(b) resort to any remedy for breach (Section 2-703 or Section 2-711), even though he has notified the repudiating party that he would await the latter's performance and has urged retraction; and

(c) in either case suspend his own performance or proceed in accordance with the provisions of this Article on the seller's right to identify goods to the contract notwithstanding breach or to salvage unfinished goods (Section 2-704).

§ 2-611. Retraction of Anticipatory Repudiation.

(1) Until the repudiating party's next performance is due he can retract his repudiation unless the aggrieved party has since the repudiation cancelled or materially changed his position or otherwise indicated that he considers the repudiation final.

(2) Retraction may be by any method which clearly indicates to the aggrieved party that the repudiating party intends to perform, but must include any assurance justifiably demanded under the provisions of this Article (Section 2-609).

(3) Retraction reinstates the repudiating party's rights under the contract with due excuse and allowance to the aggrieved party for any delay occasioned by the repudiation.

§ 2-612. "Installment Contract"; Breach.

(1) An "installment contract" is one which requires or authorizes the delivery of goods in separate lots to be separately accepted, even though the contract contains a clause 11 each delivery is a separate contract" or its equivalent.

(2) The buyer may reject any installment which is non-conforming if the non-conformity substantially impairs the value of that installment and cannot be cured or if the non-conformity is a defect in the required documents; but if the non-conformity does not fall within subsection (3) and the seller gives adequate assurance of its cure the buyer must accept that installment.

(3) Whenever non-conformity or default with respect to one or more installments substantially impairs the value of the whole contract there is a breach of the whole. But the aggrieved party reinstates the contract if he accepts a non-conforming installment without seasonably notifying of cancellation or if he brings an action with respect only to past installments or demands performance as to future installments.

§ 2-613. Casualty to Identified Goods.

Where the contract requires for its performance goods identified when the contract is made, and the goods suffer casualty without fault of either party before the risk of loss passes to the buyer, or in a proper case under a "no arrival, no sale" term (Section 2-324) then

(a) if the loss is total the contract is avoided; and

(b) if the loss is partial or the goods have so deteriorated as no longer to conform to the contract the buyer may nevertheless demand inspection and at his option either treat the contract as voided or accept the goods with due allowance from the

contract price for the deterioration or the deficiency in quantity but without further right against the seller.

§ 2-614. Substituted Performance.

(1) Where without fault of either party the agreed berthing, loading, or unloading facilities fail or an agreed type of carrier becomes unavailable or the agreed manner of delivery otherwise becomes commercially impracticable but a commercially reasonable substitute is available, such substitute performance must be tendered and accepted.

(2) If the agreed means or manner of payment fails because of domestic or foreign governmental regulation, the seller may withhold or stop delivery unless the buyer provides a means or manner of payment which is commercially a substantial equivalent. If delivery has already been taken, payment by the means or in the manner provided by the regulation discharges the buyer's obligation unless the regulation is discriminatory, oppressive or predatory.

§ 2-615. Excuse by Failure of Presupposed Conditions.

Except so far as a seller may have assumed a greater obligation and subject to the preceding section on substituted performance:

(a) Delay in delivery or non-delivery in whole or in part by a seller who complies with paragraphs (b) and (c) is not a breach of his duty under a contract for sale if performance as agreed has been made impracticable by the occurrence of a contingency the nonoccurrence of which was a basic assumption on which the contract was made or by compliance in good faith with any applicable foreign or domestic governmental regulation or order whether or riot it later proves to be invalid.

(b) Where the causes mentioned in paragraph (a) affect only a part of the seller's capacity to perform, he must allocate production and deliveries among his customers but may at his option include regular customers not then under contract as well as his own requirements for further manufacture. He may so allocate in any manner which is fair and reasonable.

(c) The seller must notify the buyer seasonably that there will be delay or non-delivery and, when allocation is required under paragraph (b), of the estimated quota thus made available for the buyer.

§ 2-616. Procedure on Notice Claiming Excuse.

(1) Where the buyer receives notification of a material or indefinite delay or an allocation justified under the preceding section he may by written notification to the seller as to any delivery concerned, and where the prospective deficiency substantially impairs the value of the whole contract under the provisions of this Article relating to breach of installment contracts (Section 2-612), then also as to the whole,

(a) terminate and thereby discharge any unexecuted portion of the contract; or

(b) modify the contract by agreeing to take his available quota in substitution.

(2) If after receipt of such notification from the seller the buyer fails so to modify the contract within a reasonable time not exceeding thirty days the contract lapses with respect to any deliveries affected.

(3) The provisions of this section may not be negated by agreement except. in so far as the seller has assumed a greater obli-

gation under the preceding section.

Part 7 Remedies

§ 2-701. Remedies for Breach of Collateral Contracts Not Impaired.

Remedies for breach of any obligation or promise collateral or ancillary to a contract for sale are not impaired by the provisions of this Article.

§ 2-702. Seller's Remedies on Discovery of Buyer's Insolvency.

(1) Where the seller discovers the buyer to be insolvent he may refuse delivery except for cash including payment for all goods theretofore delivered under the contract, and stop delivery under this Article (Section 2-70 5).

(2) Where the seller discovers that the buyer has received goods on credit while insolvent he may reclaim the goods upon demand made within ten days after the receipt, but if misrepresentation of solvency has been made to the particular seller in writing within three months before delivery the ten day limitation does not apply. Except as provided in this subsection the seller may not base a right to reclaim goods on the buyer's fraudulent or innocent misrepresentation of solvency or of intent to pay.

(3) The seller's right to reclaim under subsection (2) is subject to the rights of a buyer in ordinary course or other good faith purchaser under this Article (Section 2-403).Successful reclamation of goods excludes all other remedies with respect to them.

§ 2-703. Seller's Remedies in General.

Where the buyer wrongfully rejects or revokes acceptance of goods or fails to make a payment due on or before delivery or repudiates with respect to a part or the whole, then with respect to any goods directly affected and, if the breach is of the whole contract (Section 2-612), then also with respect to the whole undelivered balance, the aggrieved seller may

(a) withhold delivery of such goods;

(b) stop delivery by any bailee as hereafter provided(Section 2-705);

(c) proceed under the next section respecting goods still unidentified to the contract;

(d) resell and recover damages as hereafter provided(Section 2-706);

(e) recover damages for non-acceptance (Section 2-708) or in a proper case the price (Section 2-709);

(f) cancel.

§ 2-704. Seller's Right to Identify Goods to the Contract Notwithstanding Breach or to Salvage Unfinished Goods.

(1) An aggrieved seller under the preceding section may

(a) identify to the contract conforming goods not already identified if at the time he learned of the breach they are in his possession or control;

(b) treat as the subject of resale goods which have demonstrably been intended for the particular contract even though those goods are unfinished.

(2) Where the goods are unfinished an aggrieved seller may in the exercise of reasonable commercial judgment for the purposes of avoiding loss and of effective realization either complete the manufacture and wholly identify the goods to the contract or cease manufacture and resell for scrap or salvage value or proceed in any other reasonable manner.

§ 2-705. Seller's Stoppage of Delivery in Transit or Otherwise.

(1) The seller may stop delivery of goods in the possession of a carrier or other bailee when he discovers the buyer to be insolvent (Section 2-702) and may stop delivery of carload, truckload, planeload or larger shipments of express or freight when the buyer repudiates or fails to make a payment due before delivery or if for any other reason the seller has a right to withhold or reclaim the goods.

(2) As against such buyer the seller may stop delivery until

(a) receipt of the goods by the buyer; or

(b) acknowledgment to the buyer by any bailee of the goods except a carrier that the bailee holds the goods for the buyer; or

(c) such acknowledgment to the buyer by a carrier by reshipment or as warehouseman; or

(d) negotiation to the buyer of any negotiable document of title covering the goods.

(3) (a) To stop delivery the seller must so notify as to enable the bailee by reasonable diligence to prevent delivery of the goods.

(b) After such notification the bailee must hold and deliver the goods according to the directions of the seller but the seller is liable to the bailee for any ensuing charges or damages.

(c) If a negotiable document of title has been issued for goods the bailee is not obliged to obey a notification to stop until surrender of the document.

(d) A carrier who has issued a non-negotiable bill of lading is not obliged to obey a notification to stop received from a person other than the consignor.

§ 2-706. Seller's Resale Including Contract for Resale.

(1) Under the conditions stated in Section 2-703 on seller's remedies, the seller may resell the goods concerned or the undelivered balance thereof Where the resale is made in good faith and in a commercially reasonable manner the seller may recover the difference between the resale price and the contract price together with any incidental damages allowed under the provisions of this Article (Section 2-710), but less expenses saved in consequence of the buyer's breach.

(2) Except as otherwise provided in subsection or unless otherwise agreed resale may be at public or private sale including sale by way of one or more contracts to sell or of identification to an existing contract of the seller. Sale may be as a unit or in parcels and at any time and place and on any terms but every aspect of the sale including the method, manner, time, place and terms must be commercially reasonable. The resale must be reasonably identified as referring to the broken contract, but it is not necessary that the goods be in existence or that any or all of them have been identified to the contract before the breach.

(3) Where the resale is at private sale the seller must give the

buyer reasonable notification of his intention to resell.

(4) Where the resale is at public sale
(a) only identified goods can be sold except where there is a recognized market for a public sale of futures in goods of the kind; and
(b) it must be made at a usual place or market for public sale if one is reasonably available and except in the case of goods which are perishable or threaten to decline in value speedily the seller must give the buyer reasonable notice of the time and place of the resale; and
(c) if the goods are not to be within the view of those attending the sale the notification of sale must state the place where the goods are located and provide for their reasonable inspection by prospective bidders; and
(d) the seller may buy.

(5) A purchaser who buys in good faith at a resale takes the goods free of any rights of the original buyer even though the seller fails to comply with one or more of the requirements of this section.

(6) The seller is not accountable to the buyer for any profit made on any resale. A person in the position of a seller (Section 2-707) or a buyer who has rightfully rejected or justifiably revoked acceptance must account for any excess over the amount of his security interest, as hereinafter defined (subsection (3) of Section 2-711).

§ 2-707. "Person. in the Position of a Seller".
(1) A "person in the position of a seller" includes as against a principal an agent who has paid or become responsible for the price of goods on behalf of his principal or anyone who otherwise holds a security interest or other right in goods similar to that of a seller.
(2) A person in the position of a seller may as provided in this Article withhold or stop delivery (Section 2-705) and resell (Section 2-706) and recover incidental damages (Section 2-7 10).

§ 2-708. Seller's Damages for Non-Acceptance or Repudiation.
(1) Subject to subsection (2) and to the provisions of this Article with respect to proof of market price (Section 2-723), the measure of damages for non-acceptance or repudiation by the buyer is the difference between the market price at the time and place for tender and the unpaid contract price together with any incidental dam-ages provided in this Article (Section 2-710), but less expenses saved in consequence of the buyer's breach.
(2) If the measure of damages provided in subsection (1) is inadequate to put the seller in as good a position as performance would have done then the measure of damages is the profit (including reasonable overhead) which the seller would have made from full performance by the buyer, together with any incidental damages provided in this Article (Section 2-7 10), due allowance for costs reasonably incurred and due credit for payments or proceeds of resale.

§ 2-709. Action for the Price.
(1) When the buyer fails to pay the price as it becomes due the seller may recover, together with any incidental damages under the next section, the price

(a) of goods accepted or of conforming goods lost or damaged within a commercially reasonable time after risk of their loss has passed to the buyer; and
(b) of goods identified to the contract if the seller is unable after reasonable effort to resell them at a reasonable price or the circumstances reasonably indicate that such effort will be unavailing.

(2) Where the seller sues for the price he must hold for the buyer any goods which have been identified to the contract and are still in his control except that if resale becomes possible he may resell them at any time prior to the collection of the judgment. The net proceeds of any such resale must be credited to the buyer and payment of the judgment entitles him to any goods not resold.

(3) After the buyer has wrongfully rejected or revoked acceptance of the goods or has failed to make a payment due or has repudiated (Section 2-610), a seller who is held not entitled to the price under this section shall nevertheless be awarded damages for non-acceptance under the preceding section.

§ 2-710. Seller's Incidental Damages.
Incidental damages to an aggrieved seller include any commercially reasonable charges, expenses or commissions incurred in stopping delivery, in the transportation, care and custody of goods after the buyer's breach, in connection with return or resale of the goods or otherwise resulting from the breach.

§ 2-711. Buyer's Remedies in General; Buyer's Security Interest in Rejected Goods.
(1) Where the seller fails to make delivery or repudiates or the buyer rightfully rejects or justifiably revokes acceptance then with respect to any goods involved, and with respect to the whole if the breach goes to the whole con-tract (Section 2-612), the buyer may cancel and whether or not he has done so may in addition to recovering so much of the price as has been paid
(a) "cover" and have damages under the next section as to all the goods affected whether or not they have been identified to the contract; or
(b) recover damages for non-delivery as provided in this Article (Section 2-713).

(2) Where the seller fails to deliver or repudiates the buyer may also
(a) if the goods have been identified recover them as provided in this Article (Section 2-502); or
(b) in a proper case obtain specific performance or replevy the goods as provided in this Article (Section 2-716).

(3) On rightful rejection or justifiable revocation of acceptance a buyer has a security interest in goods in his possession or control for any payments made on their price and any expenses reasonably incurred in their inspection, receipt, transportation, care and custody and may hold such goods and resell them in like manner as an aggrieved seller (Section 2-706).

§ 2-712. "Cover"; Buyer's Procurement of Substitute Goods.
(1) After a breach within the preceding section the buyer may "cover" by making in good faith and without unreasonable delay any reasonable purchase of or contract to purchase goods in substitution for those due from the seller.

(2) The buyer may recover from the seller as damages the difference between the cost of cover and the contract price together with any incidental or consequential damages as hereinafter defined (Section 2-715), but less expenses saved in consequence of the seller's breach.

(3) Failure of the buyer to effect cover within this section does not bar him from any other remedy.

§ 2-713. Buyer's Damages for Non-Delivery or Repudiation.

(1) Subject to the provisions of this Article with respect to proof of market price (Section 2-723), the measure of damages for non-delivery or repudiation by the seller is the difference between the market price at the time when the buyer learned of the breach and the contract price together with any incidental and consequential damages provided in this Article (Section 2-715), but less expenses saved in consequence of the seller's breach.

(2) (2) Market price is to be determined as of the place for tender or, in cases of rejection after arrival or revocation of acceptance, as of the place of arrival.

§ 2-714. Buyer's Damages for Breach in Regard to Accepted Goods.

(1) Where the buyer has accepted goods and given notification (subsection (3) of Section 2-607) he may recover as damages for any non-conformity of tender the loss resulting in the ordinary course of events from the seller's breach as determined in any manner which is reasonable.

(2) The measure of damages for breach of warranty is the difference at the time and place of acceptance between the value of the goods accepted and the value they would have had if they had been as warranted, unless special circumstances show proximate damages of a different amount.

(3) In a proper case any incidental and consequential damages under the next section may also be recovered.

§ 2-715. Buyer's Incidental and Consequential Damages.

(1) Incidental damages resulting from the seller's breach include expenses reasonably incurred in inspection, receipt, transportation and care and custody of goods right-fully rejected, any commercially reasonable charges, expenses or commissions in connection with effecting cover and any other reasonable expense incident to the delay or other breach.

(2) Consequential damages resulting from the seller's breach include

(a) any loss resulting from general or particular requirements and needs of which the seller at the time of contracting had reason to know and which could not reasonably be prevented by cover or otherwise; and

(b) injury to person or property proximately resulting from any breach of warranty.

§ 2-716. Buyer's Right to Specific Performance or Replevin.

(1) Specific performance may be decreed where the goods are unique or in other proper circumstances.

(2) The decree for specific performance may include such terms and conditions as to payment of the price, damages, or other relief as the court may deem just.

(3) The buyer has a right of replevin for goods identified to the contract if after reasonable effort he is unable to effect cover for such goods or the circumstances reasonably indicate that such effort will be unavailing or if the goods have been shipped under reservation and satisfaction of the security interest in them has been made or tendered.

§ 2-717. Deduction of Damages From the Price.

The buyer on notifying the seller of his intention to do so may deduct all or any part of the damages resulting from any breach of the contract from any part of the price still due under the same contract.

§ 2-718. Liquidation or Limitation of Damages; Deposits.

(1) Damages for breach by either party may be liquidated in the agreement but only at an amount which is reasonable in the light of the anticipated or actual harm caused by the breach, the difficulties of proof of loss, and the inconvenience or non-feasibility of otherwise obtaining an adequate remedy. A term fixing unreasonably large liquidated damages is void as a penalty.

(2) Where the seller justifiably withholds delivery of goods because of the buyer's breach, the buyer is entitled to restitution of any amount by which the sum of his payments exceeds

(a) the amount to which the seller is entitled by virtue of terms liquidating the seller's damages in accordance with subsection (1), or

(b) in the absence of such terms, twenty per cent of the value of the total performance for which the buyer is obligated under the contract or $500, whichever is smaller.

(3) The buyer's right to restitution under subsection (2) is subject to offset to the extent that the seller establishes

(a) a right to recover damages under the provisions of this Article other than subsection (1), and (b) the amount or value of any benefits received by the buyer directly or indirectly by reason of the con-tract.

(4) Where a seller has received payment in goods their reasonable value or the proceeds of their resale shall be treated as payments for the purposes of subsection (2); but if the seller has notice of the buyer's breach before reselling goods received in part performance, his resale is subject to the conditions laid down in this Article on resale by an aggrieved seller (Section 2-706).

§ 2-719. Contractual Modification or Limitation of Remedy.

(1) Subject to the provisions of subsections (2) and (3) of this section and of the preceding section on liquidation and limitation of damages,

(a) the agreement may provide for remedies in addition to or in substitution for those provided in this Article and may limit or alter the measure of damages recoverable under this Article, as by limiting the buyer's remedies to return of the goods and repayment of the price or to repair and replacement of non-conforming goods or parts; and

(b) resort to a remedy as provided is optional unless the remedy is expressly agreed to be exclusive, in which case it is the sole remedy.

(2) Where circumstances cause an exclusive or limited remedy to fail of its essential purpose, remedy may be had as provided in this Act.

(3) Consequential damages may be limited or excluded unless the limitation or exclusion is unconscionable. Limitation of consequential damages for injury to the per-son in the case of consumer goods is prima facie unconscionable but limitation of damages where the loss is commercial is not.

§ 2-720. Effect of "Cancellation" or "Rescission" on Claims for Antecedent Breach. Unless the contrary intention clearly appears, expressions of "cancellation" or "rescission" of the contract or the like shall not be construed as a renunciation or discharge of any claim in damages for an antecedent breach.

§ 2-72 1. Remedies for Fraud.

Remedies for material misrepresentation or fraud include all remedies available under this Article for non-fraudulent breach. Neither rescission or a claim for rescission of the contract for sale nor rejection or return of the goods shall bar or be deemed inconsistent with a claim for damages or other remedy.

§ 2-722. Who Can Sue Third Parties for Injury to Goods.

Where a third party so deals with goods which have been identified to a contract for sale as to cause actionable injury to a party to that contract

(a) a right of action against the third party is in either party to the contract for sale who has title to or a security interest or a special property or an insurable interest in the goods; and if the goods have been destroyed or converted a right of action is also in the party who either bore the risk of loss under the contract for sale or has since the injury assumed that risk as against the other;

(b) if at the time of the injury the party plaintiff did not bear the risk of loss as against the other party to the contract for sale and there is no arrangement between them for disposition of the recovery, his suit or settlement is, subject to his own interest, as a fiduciary for the other party to the contract;

(c) either party may with the consent of the other sue for the benefit of whom it may concern.

§ 2-723. Proof of Market Price: Time and Place.

(1) If an action based on anticipatory repudiation comes to trial before the time for performance with respect to some or all of the goods, any damages based on market price (Section 2-708 or Section 2-713) shall be determined according to the price of such goods prevailing at the time when the aggrieved party learned of the repudiation.

(2) If evidence of a price prevailing at the times or places described in this Article is not readily available the price prevailing within any reasonable time before or after the time described or at any other place which in commercial judgment or under usage of trade would serve as a reasonable substitute for the one described may be used, making any proper allowance for the cost of transporting the goods to or from such other place.

(3) Evidence of a relevant price prevailing at a time or place other than the one described in this Article offered by one party is not admissible unless and until he has given the other party such notice as the court finds sufficient to prevent unfair surprise.

§ 2-724. Admissibility of Market Quotations.

Whenever the prevailing price or value of any goods regularly bought and sold in any established commodity market is in issue, reports in official publications or trade journals or in newspapers or periodicals of general circulation published as the reports of such market shall be admissible in evidence. The circumstances of the preparation of such a report may be shown to affect its weight but not its admissibility.

§ 2-725. Statute of Limitations in Contracts for Sale.

(1) An action for breach of any contract for sale must be commenced within four years after the cause of action has accrued. By the original agreement the parties may reduce the period of limitation to not less than one year but may not extend it.

(2) A cause of action accrues when the breach occurs, regardless of the aggrieved party's lack of knowledge of the breach. A breach of warranty occurs when tender of delivery is made, except that where a warranty explicitly extends to future performance of the goods and discovery of the breach must await the time of such performance the cause of action accrues when the breach is or should have been discovered.

(3) Where an action commenced within the time limited by subsection (1) is so terminated as to leave available a remedy by another action for the same breach such other action may be commenced after the expiration of the time limited and within six months after the termination of the first action unless the termination resulted from voluntary discontinuance or from dismissal for failure or neglect to prosecute.

(4) This section does not alter the law on tolling of the statute of limitations nor does it apply to causes of action which have accrued before this Act becomes effective.

Article 2A
Leases

Part I General Provisions

§ 2A-101. Short Title.

This Article shall be known and may be cited as the Uniform Commercial Code-Leases.

§ 2A-102. Scope.

This Article applies to any transaction, regardless of form, that creates a 1ease.

§ 2A-103. Definitions and Index of Definitions.

(1) In this Article unless the context otherwise requires:

(a) "Buyer in ordinary course of business" means a person who in good faith and without knowledge that the sale to him [or her] is in violation of the ownership rights or security interest or leasehold interest of a third party in the goods buys in ordinary course from a per-son in the business of selling goods of that kind but does not include a pawnbroker. "Buying" may be for cash or by exchange of other property or on secured or unsecured credit and includes receiving goods or documents of title under a pre-existing contract for sale but does not include a transfer in bulk or as security for or in total or partial satisfaction of a money debt.

(b) "Cancellation" occurs when either party puts an end to the lease contract for default by the other party.

(c) "Commercial unit" means such a unit of goods as by commercial usage is a single whole for purposes of lease and division of which materially impairs its character or value on the market or in use. A commercial unit may be a single article, as a machine, or a set of articles, as a suite of furniture or a line of machinery, or a quantity, as a gross or carload, or any other unit treated in use or in the relevant market as a single whole.

(d) "Conforming" goods or performance under a lease contract means goods or performance that are in accordance with the obligations under the lease contract.

(e) "Consumer lease" means a lease that a lessor regularly engaged in the business of leasing or selling makes to a lessee who is an individual and who takes under the lease primarily for a personal, family, or household "purpose [, if " the total payments to be made under the lease contract, excluding payments for options to renew or buy, do not exceed . . . .

(f) "Fault" means wrongful act, omission, breach, or default.

(g) "Finance lease" means a lease with respect to which:

(i) the lessor does not select, manufacture or supply the goods;

(ii) the lessor acquires the goods or the right to possession and use of the goods in connection with the lease; and

(iii) one of the following occurs:

(A) the lessee receives a copy of the contract by which the lessor acquired the goods or the right to possession and use of the goods before signing the lease contract;

(B) the lessee's approval of the contract by which the lessor acquired the goods or the right to possession and use of the goods is a condition to effectiveness of the lease contract;

(C) the lessee, before signing the lease contract, receives an accurate and complete statement designating the promises and warranties, and any disclaimers of warranties, limitations or modifications of remedies, or liquidated damages, including those of a third party, such as the manufacturer of the goods, provided to the lessor by the person supplying the goods in connection with or as part of the contract by which the lessor acquired the goods or the right to possession and use of the goods; or

(D) if the lease is not a consumer lease, the lessor, before the lessee signs the lease contract, informs the lessee in writing (a) of the identity of the person supplying the goods to the lessor, unless the lessee has selected that person and directed the lessor to acquire the goods or the right to possession and use of the goods from that person, (b) that the lessee is entitled under this Article to any promises and war-

ranties, including those of any third party, provided to the lessor by the person supplying the goods in connection with or as part of the contract by which the lessor acquired the goods or the right to possession and use of the goods, and (c) that the lessee may communicate with the person supplying the goods to the lessor and receive an accurate and complete statement of those promises and warranties, including any disclaimers and limitations of them or of remedies.

(h) "Goods" means all things that are movable at the time of identification to the lease contract, or are fixtures (Section 2A-309), but the term does not include money, documents, instruments, accounts, chattel paper, general intangibles, or minerals or the like, including oil and gas, before extraction. The term also includes the unborn young of animals.

(i) "Installment lease contract" means a lease contract that authorizes or requires the delivery of goods in separate lots to be separately accepted, even though the lease contract contains a clause "each delivery is a separate lease" or its equivalent.

(j) "Lease" means a transfer of the right to possession and use of goods for a term in return for consideration, but a sale, including a sale on approval or a sale or return, or retention or creation of a security interest is not a lease. Unless the context clearly indicates otherwise, the term includes a sublease.

(k) "Lease agreement" means the bargain, with respect to the lease, of the lessor and the lessee in fact as found in their language or by implication from other circumstances including course of dealing or usage of trade or course of performance as provided in this Article. Unless the context clearly indicates otherwise, the term includes a sublease agreement.

(l) "Lease contract" means the total legal obligation that results from the lease agreement as affected by this Article and any other applicable rules of law. Unless the context clearly indicates otherwise, the term includes a sublease contract.

(m) "Leasehold interest" means the interest of the lessor or the lessee under a lease contract.

(n) "Lessee" means a person who acquires the right to possession and use of goods under a lease. Unless the context clearly indicates otherwise, the term includes a sublessee.

(o) "Lessee in ordinary course of business" means a person who in good faith and without knowledge that the lease to him [or her] is in violation of the owner-ship rights or security interest or leasehold interest of a third party in the goods, leases in ordinary course from a person in the business of selling or leasing goods of that kind but does not include a pawnbroker." Leasing" may be for cash or by exchange of other property or on secured or unsecured credit and includes receiving goods or documents of title under a preexisting lease contract but does not include a transfer in bulk or as security for or in total or partial satisfaction of a money debt.

(p) "Lessor" means a person who transfers the right to possession and use of goods under a lease. Unless the context clearly indicates otherwise, the term includes a sublessor.

(q) "Lessor's residual interest" means the lessor's interest in the goods after expiration, termination, or cancellation of the lease contract.

(r) "Lien" means a charge against or interest in goods to secure payment of a debt or performance of an obligation, but the term does not include a security interest.

(s) "Lot" means a parcel or a single article that is the subject matter of a separate lease or delivery, whether or not it is sufficient to perform the lease contract.

(t) "Merchant lessee" means a lessee that is a merchant with respect to goods of the kind subject to the ease.

(u) "Present value" means the amount as of a date certain of one or more sums payable in the future, discounted to the date certain. The discount is determined by the interest rate specified by the parties if the rate was not manifestly unreasonable at the time the transaction was entered into; otherwise, the discount is determined by a commercially reasonable rate that takes into account the facts and circumstances of each case at the time the transaction was entered into.

(v) "Purchase" includes taking by sale, lease, mortgage, security interest, pledge, gift, or any other voluntary transaction creating an interest in goods.

(w) "Sublease" means a lease of goods the right to possession and use of which was acquired by the lessor as a lessee under an existing lease.

(x) "Supplier" means a person from whom a lessor buys or leases goods to be leased under a finance lease.

(y) "Supply contract" means a contract under which a lessor buys or leases goods to be leased.

(`a) "Termination" occurs when either party pursuant to a power created by agreement or law puts an end to the lease contract otherwise than for default.

(2) Other definitions applying to this Article and the sections in which they appear are: "Accessions". Section 2A-310(l).
"Construction mortgage". Section 2A-309(l)(d).
"Encumbrance". Section 2A-309(l)(e).
"Fixtures". Section 2A-309(l)(a).
"Fixture filing". Section 2A-309(l)(b).
"Purchase money lease". Section 2A-309(l)(c).

(3) The following definitions in other Articles apply to this Article:
"Accounts". Section 9-106.
"Between merchants". Section 2-104(3).
"Buyer". Section 2-103(l)(a).
"Chattel paper". Section 9-105(l)(b).
"Consumer goods". Section 9-109(l).
"Document". Section 9-105(l)(fl.
"Entrusting". Section 2-403(3).
"General intangibles". Section 9-106.
"Good faith". Section 2-103(l)(b).
"Instrument". Section 9-105(l)(i).
"Merchant". Section 2-104(l).
"Mortgage". Section 9-105(l)(j).
"Pursuant to commitment". Section 9-105(l)(k).
"Receipt". Section 2-103(l)(c).
"Sale". Section 2-106(l).

"Sale on approval". Section 2-326.
"Sale or return". Section 2-3 26.
"Seller". Section 2-103(l)(d).

(4) In addition Article 1 contains general definitions and principles of construction and interpretation applicable throughout this Article.
As amended in 1990.

§ 2A-104. Leases Subject to Other Law.

(1) A lease, although subject to this Article, is also subject to any applicable:

(a) certificate of title statute of this State: (list any certificate of title statutes covering automobiles, trailers, mobile homes, boats, farm tractors, and the like);

(b) certificate of title statute of another jurisdiction (Section 2A-10 5); or

(c) consumer protection statute of this State, or final consumer protection decision of a court of this State existing on the effective date of this Article.

(2) In case of conflict between this Article, other than Sections 2A-105, 2A-304(3), and 2A-305(3), and a statute or decision referred to in subsection (1), the statute or decision controls.

(3) Failure to comply with an applicable law has only the effect specified therein. As amended in 1990.

§ 2A-105. Territorial Application of Article to Goods Covered by Certificate of Title.

Subject to the provisions of Sections 2A-304(3) and 2A-305(3), with respect to goods covered by a certificate of title issued under a statute of this State or of another jurisdiction, compliance and the effect of compliance or noncompliance with a certificate of title statute are governed by the law (including the conflict of laws rules) of the jurisdiction issuing the certificate until the earlier of (a) surrender of the certificate, or (b) four months after the goods are removed from that jurisdiction and thereafter until a new certificate of title is issued by another jurisdiction.

§ 2A-106. Limitation on Power of Parties to Consumer Lease to Choose Applicable Law and judicial Forum.

(1) If the law chosen by the parties to a consumer lease is that of a jurisdiction other than a jurisdiction in which the lessee resides at the time the lease agreement becomes enforceable or within 30 days thereafter or in which the goods are to be used, the choice is not enforceable.

(2) If the judicial forum chosen by the parties to a consumer lease is a forum that would not otherwise have jurisdiction over the lessee, the choice is not enforceable.

§ 2A-107. Waiver or Renunciation of Claim or Right After Default.

Any claim or right arising out of an alleged default or breach of warranty may be discharged in whole or in part without consideration by a written waiver or renunciation signed and delivered by the aggrieved party.

§ 2A-108. Unconscionability.

(1) If the court as a matter of law finds a lease contract or any clause of a lease contract to have been unconscionable at the time it was made the court may refuse to enforce the lease contract, or it may enforce the remainder of the lease contract

without the unconscionable clause, or it may so limit the application of any unconscionable clause as to void any unconscionable result.

(2) With respect to a consumer lease, if the court as a matter of law finds that a lease contract or any clause of a lease contract has been induced by unconscionable conduct or that unconscionable conduct, has occurred in the collection of a claim arising from a lease contract, the court may grant appropriate relief.

(3) Before making a finding of unconscionability under subsection (1) or (2), the court, on its own motion or that of a party, shall afford the parties a reasonable opportunity to present evidence as to the setting, purpose, and effect of the lease contract or clause thereof, or of the conduct.

(4) In an action in which the lessee claims unconscionability with respect to a consumer lease:(a) If the court finds unconscionability under subsection (1) or (2), the court shall award reasonable attorney's fees to the lessee.(b) If the court does not find unconscionability and the lessee claiming unconscionability has brought or maintained an action he [or she] knew to be ground-less, the court shall award reasonable attorney's fees to the party against whom the claim is made.(c) In determining attorney's fees, the amount of the recovery on behalf of the claimant under subsections(1) and (2) is not controlling.

§ 2A-109. Option to Accelerate at Will.

(1) A term providing that one party or his [or her] successor in interest may accelerate payment or performance or require collateral or additional collateral "at will" or "when he [or she] deems himself [or herself] insecure" or in words of similar import must be construed to mean that he [or she] has power to do so only if he [or she] in good faith believes that the prospect of payment or performance is impaired.

(2) With respect to a consumer lease, the burden of establishing good faith under subsection (1) is on the party who exercised the power; otherwise the burden of establishing lack of good faith is on the party against whom the power has been exercised. Part 2 Formation and Construction of Lease Contract

§ 2A-201. Statute of Frauds.

(1) A lease contract is not enforceable by way of action or defense unless:

(a) the total payments to be made under the lease contract, excluding payments for options to renew or buy, are less than $1,000; or

(b) there is a writing, signed by the party against whom enforcement is sought or by that party's authorized agent, sufficient to indicate that a lease contract has been made between the parties and to describe the goods leased and the lease term.

(2) Any description of leased goods or of the lease term is sufficient and satisfies subsection (1)(b), whether or not it is specific, if it reasonably identifies what is described.

(3) A writing is not insufficient because it omits or incorrectly states a term agreed upon, but the lease contract is not enforceable under subsection (1)(b) beyond the lease term and the quantity of goods shown in the writing.

(4) A lease contract that does not satisfy the requirements of subsection (1), but which is valid in other respects, is enforceable:

(a) if the goods are to be specially manufactured or obtained for the lessee and are not suitable for lease or sale to others in the ordinary course of the lessor's business, and the lessor, before notice of repudiation is received and under circumstances that reasonably indicate that the goods are for the lessee, has made either a substantial beginning of their manufacture or commitments for their procurement;

(b) if the party against whom enforcement is sought admits in that party's pleading, testimony or otherwise in court that a lease contract was made, but the lease contract is not enforceable under this provision beyond the quantity of goods admitted; or

(c) with respect to goods that have been received and accepted by the lessee.

(5) The lease term under a lease contract referred to in subsection (4) is:

(a) if there is a writing signed by the party against whom enforcement is sought or by that party's authorized agent specifying the lease term, the term so specified;

(b) if the party against whom enforcement is sought admits in that party's pleading, testimony, or otherwise in court a lease term, the term so admitted; or

(c) a reasonable lease term.

§ 2A-202. Final Written Expression: Parol or Extrinsic Evidence.

Terms with respect to which the confirmatory memoranda of the parties agree or which are otherwise set forth in a writing intended by the parties as a final expression of their agreement with respect to such terms as are included therein may not be contradicted by evidence of any prior agreement or of a contemporaneous oral agreement but may be explained or supplemented:

(a) by course of dealing or usage of trade or by course of performance; and

(b) by evidence of consistent additional terms unless the court finds the writing to have been intended also as a complete and exclusive statement of the terms of the agreement.

§ 2A-203. Seals Inoperative.

The affixing of a seal to a writing evidencing a lease contract or an offer to enter into a lease contract does not render the writing a sealed instrument and the law with respect to sealed instruments does not apply to the lease contract or offer.

§ 2A-204. Formation in General.

(1) A lease contract may be made in any manner sufficient to show agreement, including conduct by both parties which recognizes the existence of a lease contract.

(2) An agreement sufficient to constitute a lease contract may be found although the moment of its making is undetermined.

(3) Although one or more terms are left open, a lease contract does not fail for indefiniteness if the parties have intended to make a lease contract and there is a reasonably certain basis for giving an appropriate remedy.

§ 2A-205. Firm Offers.

An offer by a merchant to lease goods to or from another

person in a signed writing that by its terms gives assurance it will be held open is not revocable, for lack of consideration, during the time stated or, if no time is stated, for a reasonable time, but in no event may the period of irrevocability exceed 3 months. Any such term of assurance on a form supplied by the offeree must be separately signed by the offeror.

§ 2A-206. Offer and Acceptance in Formation of Lease Contract.
(1) Unless otherwise unambiguously indicated by the language or circumstances, an offer to make a lease contract must be construed as inviting acceptance in any manner and by any medium reasonable in the circumstances.
(2) If the beginning of a requested performance is a reasonable mode of acceptance, an offeror who is not notified of acceptance within a reasonable time may treat the offer as having lapsed before acceptance.

§ 2A-207. Course of Performance or Practical Construction.
(1) If a lease contract involves repeated occasions for performance by either party with knowledge of the nature of the performance and opportunity for objection to it by the other, any course of performance accepted or acquiesced in without objection is relevant to determine the meaning of the lease agreement.
(2) The express terms of a lease agreement and any course of performance, as well as any course of dealing and usage of trade, must be construed whenever reasonable as consistent with each other; but if that construction is unreasonable, express terms control course of performance, course of performance controls both course of dealing and usage of trade, and course of dealing controls usage of trade.
(3) Subject to the provisions of Section 2A-208 on modification and waiver, course of performance is relevant to show a waiver or modification of any term inconsistent with the course of performance.

§ 2A-208. Modification, Rescission and Waiver.
(1) An agreement modifying a lease contract needs no consideration to be binding.
(2) A signed lease agreement that excludes modification or rescission except by a signed writing may not be other-wise modified or rescinded, but, except as between merchants, such a requirement on a form supplied by a merchant must be separately signed by the other party.
(3) Although an attempt at modification or rescission does not satisfy the requirements of subsection (2), it may operate as a waiver.
(4) A party who has made a waiver affecting an executory portion of a lease contract may retract the waiver by reasonable notification received by the other party that strict performance will be required of any term waived, unless the retraction would be unjust in view of a material change of position in reliance on the waiver.

§ 2A-209. Lessee under Finance Lease as Beneficiary of Supply Contract.
(1) The benefit of the supplier's promises to the lessor under the supply contract and of all warranties, whether express or implied, including those of any third party provided in connection with or as part of the supply contract, extends to the lessee to the extent of the lessee's leasehold interest under a finance lease related to the supply contract, but is subject to the terms warranty and of the supply contract and all defenses or claims arising there from.
(2) The extension of the benefit of supplier's promises and of warranties to the lessee (Section 2A-209(l)) does not: (i) modify the rights and obligations of the parties to the supply contract, whether arising there from or otherwise, or (ii) impose any duty or liability under the supply contract on the lessee.
(3) Any modification or rescission of the supply contract by the supplier and the lessor is effective between the supplier and the lessee unless, before the modification or rescission, the supplier has received notice that the lessee has entered into a finance lease related to the supply con-tract. If the modification or rescission is effective between the supplier and the lessee, the lessor is deemed to have assumed, in addition to the obligations of the lessor to the lessee under the lease contract, promises of the supplier to the lessor and warranties that were so modified or rescinded as they existed and were available to the lessee before modification or rescission.
(4) In addition to the extension of the benefit of the supplier's promises and of warranties to the lessee under subsection (1), the lessee retains all rights that the lessee may have against the supplier which arise from an agreement between the lessee and the supplier or under other law. As amended in 1990.

§ 2A-210. Express Warranties.
(1) Express warranties by the lessor are created as follows:
    (a) Any affirmation of fact or promise made by the lessor to the lessee which relates to the goods and becomes part of the basis of the bargain creates an express warranty that the goods will conform to the affirmation or promise.
    (b) Any description of the goods which is made part of the basis of the bargain creates an express warranty that the goods will conform to the description.
    (c) Any sample or model that is made part of the basis of the bargain creates an express warranty that the whole of the goods will conform to the sample or model.
(2) It is not necessary to the creation of an express warranty that the lessor use formal words, such as "warrant" or "guarantee," or that the lessor have a specific intention to make a warranty, but an affirmation merely of the value of the goods or a statement purporting to be merely the lessor's opinion or commendation of the goods does not create a warranty.

§ 2A-211. Warranties Against Interference and Against Infringement; Lessee's Obligation Against Infringement.
(1) There is in a lease contract a warranty that for the lease term no person holds a claim to or interest in the goods that arose from an act or omission of the lessor, other than a claim by way of infringement or the like, which will interfere with the lessee's enjoyment of its leasehold interest.
2) Except in a finance lease there is in a lease contract by a lessor who is a merchant regularly dealing in goods of the kind a warranty that the goods are delivered free of the rightful claim of any person by way of infringement or the like.
3) A lessee who furnishes specifications to a lessor or a supplier

shall hold the lessor and the supplier harmless against any claim by way of infringement or the like that arises out of compliance with the specifications.

§ 2A-212. Implied Warranty of Merchantability.

(1) Except in a finance lease, a warranty that the goods will be merchantable is implied in a lease contract if the lessor is a merchant with respect to goods of that kind.

(2) Goods to be merchantable must be at least such as

    (a) pass without objection in the trade under the description in the lease agreement;

    (b) in the case of fungible goods, are of fair average quality within the description; \

    (c) are fit for the ordinary purposes for which goods of that type are used;

    (d) run, within the variation permitted by the lease agreement, of even kind, quality, and quantity within each unit and among all units involved;

    (e) are adequately contained, packaged, and labeled as the lease agreement may require; and

    (f) conform to any promises or affirmations of fact made on the container or label.

(3) Other implied warranties may arise from course of dealing or usage of trade.

§ 2A-213. Implied Warranty of Fitness for Particular Purpose.

Except in a finance of lease, if the lessor at the time the lease contract is made has reason to know of any particular purpose for which the goods are required and that the lessee is relying on the lessor's skill or judgment to select or furnish suitable goods, there is in the lease contract an implied warranty that the goods will be fit for that purpose.

§ 2A-214. Exclusion or Modification of Warranties.

(1) Words or conduct relevant to the creation of an express warranty and words or conduct tending to negate or limit a warranty must be construed wherever reasonable as consistent with each other; but, subject to the provisions of Section 2A-202 on parol or extrinsic evidence, negation or limitation is inoperative to the extent that the construction is unreasonable.

(2) Subject to subsection (3), to exclude or modify the implied warranty of merchantability or any part of it the language must mention "merchantability", be by a writing, and be conspicuous. Subject to subsection (3), to exclude or modify any implied warranty of fitness the exclusion must be by a writing and be conspicuous. Language to exclude all implied warranties of fitness is sufficient if it is in writing, is conspicuous and states, for example, "There is no warranty that the goods will be fit for a particular purpose".

(3) Notwithstanding subsection (2), but subject to subsection 4,

    (a) unless the circumstances indicate otherwise, all implied warranties are excluded by expressions like "as is" or "with all faults" or by other language that in common understanding calls the lessee's attention to the exclusion of warranties and makes plain that there is no implied warranty, if in writing and conspicuous;

    (b) if the lessee before entering into the lease contract has examined the goods or the sample or model as fully as

desired or has refused to examine the goods, there is no implied warranty with regard to defects that an examination ought in the circumstances to have revealed; and

    (c) an implied warranty may also be excluded or modified by course of dealing, course of performance, or usage of trade.

(4) To exclude or modify a warranty against interference or against infringement (Section 2A-211) or any part of it, the language must be specific, be by a writing, and be conspicuous, unless the circumstances, including course of performance, course of dealing, or usage of trade, give the lessee reason to know that the goods are being leased subject to a claim or interest of any person.

§ 2A-215. Cumulation and Conflict of Warranties Express or Implied.

Warranties, whether express or implied, must be construed as consistent with each other and as cumulative, but if that construction is unreasonable, the intention of the parties determines which warranty is dominant. In ascertaining that intention the following rules apply:

    (a) Exact or technical specifications displace an inconsistent sample or model or general language of description.

    (b) A sample from an existing bulk displaces inconsistent general language of description.

    (c) Express warranties displace inconsistent implied warranties other than an implied warranty of fitness for a particular purpose.

§ 2A-216. Third-Party Beneficiaries of Express and Implied Warranties.

Alternative A

A warranty to or for the benefit of a lessee under this Article, whether express or implied, extends to any natural person who is in the family or household of the lessee or who is a guest in the lessee's home if it is reasonable to expect that such person may use, consume, or be affected by the goods and who is injured in person by breach of the warranty. This section does not displace principles of law and equity that extend a warranty to or for the benefit of a lessee to other persons. The operation of this section may not be excluded, modified, or limited, but an exclusion, modification, or limitation of the warranty, including any with respect to rights and remedies, effective against the lessee is also effective against any beneficiary designated under this section.

Alternative B

A warranty to or for the benefit of a lessee under this Article, whether express or implied, extends to any natural person who may reasonably be expected to use, consume, or be affected by the goods and who is injured in person by breach of the warranty. This section does not displace principles of law and equity that extend a warranty to or for the benefit of a lessee to other persons. The operation of this section may not be excluded, modified, or limited, but an exclusion, modification, or limitation of the warranty, including any with respect to rights and remedies, effective against the lessee is also effective against the beneficiary designated under this section.

Alternative C

A warranty to or for the benefit of a lessee under this Article, whether express or implied, extends to any person who may reasonably be expected to use, consume, or be affected by the goods and who is injured by breach of the warranty. The operation of this section may not be excluded, modified, or limited with respect to injury to the person of an individual to whom the warranty extends, but an exclusion, modification, or limitation of the warranty, including any with respect to rights and remedies, effective against the lessee is also effective against the beneficiary designated under this section.

§ 2A-217. Identification.

Identification of goods as goods to which a lease contract refers may be made at any time and in any manner explicitly agreed to by the parties. In the absence of explicit agreement, identification occurs:

(a) when the lease contract is made if the lease contract is for a lease of goods that are existing and identified;

(b) when the goods are shipped, marked, or otherwise designated by the lessor as goods to which the lease contract refers, if the lease contract is for a lease of goods that are not existing and identified; or

(c) when the young are conceived, if the lease contract is for a lease of unborn young of animals.

§ 2A-218. Insurance and Proceeds.

(1) A lessee obtains an insurable interest when existing goods are identified to the lease contract even though the goods identified are nonconforming and the lessee has an option to reject them.

(2) If a lessee has an insurable interest only by reason of the lessor's identification of the goods, the lessor, until default or insolvency or notification to the lessee that identification is final, may substitute other goods for those identified.

(3) Notwithstanding a lessee's insurable interest under subsections (1) and (2), the lessor retains an insurable interest until an option to buy has been exercised by the lessee and risk of loss has passed the lessee.

(4) Nothing in this section impairs any insurable interest recognized under any other statute or rule of law.

(5) The parties by agreement may determine that one or more parties have an obligation to obtain and pay for insurance covering the goods and by agreement may determine the beneficiary of the proceeds of the insurance.

§ 2A-219. Risk of Loss.

(1) Except in the case of a finance lease, risk of loss is retained by the lessor and does not pass to the lessee. In the case of a finance lease, risk of loss passes to the lessee.

(2) Subject to the provisions of this Article on the effect of default on risk of loss (Section 2A-220), if risk of loss is to pass to the lessee and the time of passage is not stated, the following rules apply:

(a) If the lease contract requires or authorizes the goods to be shipped by carrier

(i) and it does not require delivery at a particular destination, the risk of loss passes to the lessee when the goods are duly delivered to the carrier; but

(ii) if it does require delivery at a particular destination and the goods are there duly tendered while in the possession of the carrier, the risk of loss passes to the lessee when the goods are there duly tendered as to enable the lessee to take delivery.

(b) If the goods are held by a bailee to be delivered without being moved, the risk of loss passes to the lessee on acknowledgment by the bailee of the lessee's right to possession of the goods.

(c) In any case not within subsection (a) or (b), the risk of loss passes to the lessee on the lessee's receipt of the goods if the lessor, or, in the case of a finance lease, the supplier, is a merchant; otherwise the risk passes to the lessee on tender of delivery.

§ 2A-220. Effect of Default on Risk of Loss.

(1) Where risk of loss is to pass to the lessee and the time of passage is not stated:

(a) If a tender or delivery of goods so fails to conform to the lease contract as to give a right of rejection, the risk of their loss remains with the lessor, or, in the case of a finance lease, the supplier, until cure or acceptance.

(b) If the lessee rightfully revokes acceptance, he [or she], to the extent of any deficiency in his [or her] effective insurance coverage, may treat the risk of loss as having remained with the lessor from the beginning.

(2) Whether or not risk of loss is to pass to the lessee, if the lessee as to conforming goods already identified to a lease contract repudiates or is otherwise in default under the lease contract, the lessor, or, in the case of a finance lease, the supplier, to the extent of any deficiency in his [or her] effective insurance coverage may treat the risk of loss as resting on the lessee for a commercially reasonable time.

§ 2A-221. Casualty to Identified Goods.

If a lease contract requires goods identified when the lease contract is made, and the goods suffer casualty without fault of the lessee, the lessor or the supplier before delivery, or the goods suffer casualty before risk of loss passes to the lessee pursuant to the lease agreement or Section 2A-219, then:

(a) if the loss is total, the lease contract is avoided; and

(b) if the loss is partial or the goods have so deteriorated as to no longer conform to the lease contract, the lessee may nevertheless demand inspection and at his [or her] option either treat the lease contract as avoided or, except in a finance lease that is not a consumer lease, accept the goods with due allowance from the rent payable for the balance of the lease term for the deterioration or the deficiency in quantity but without further right against the lessor.

Part 3 Effect Of Lease Contract

§ 2A-301. Enforceability of Lease Contract.

Except as otherwise provided in this Article, a lease contract is effective and enforceable according to its terms between the parties, against purchasers of the goods and against creditors of the parties.

§ 2A-302. Title to and Possession of Goods.

Except as otherwise provided in this Article, each provision of this Article applies whether the lessor or a third party has tide to the goods, and whether the lessor, the lessee, or a third party has possession of the goods, notwithstanding any statute or rule of law that possession or the absence of possession is fraudulent.

§ 2A-303. Alienability of Party's Interest Under Lease Contract or of Lessor's Residual Interest in Goods; Delegation of Performance; Transfer of Rights.

(1) As used in this section, "creation of a security interest" includes the sale of a lease contract that is subject to Article 9, Secured Transactions, by reason of Section 9-102(l)(b).

(2) Except as provided in subsections (3) and (4), a provision in a lease agreement which (i) prohibits the voluntary or involuntary transfer, including a transfer by sale, sublease, creation or enforcement of a security interest, or attachment, levy, or other judicial process, of an interest of a party under the lease contract or of the lessor's residual interest in the goods, or (ii) makes such a transfer an event of default, gives rise to the rights and remedies provided in subsection (5), but a transfer that is prohibited or is an event of default under the lease agreement is otherwise effective.

(3) A provision in a lease agreement which (i) prohibits the creation or enforcement of a security interest in an interest of a party under the lease contract or in the lessor's residual interest in the goods, or (ii) makes such a transfer an event of default, is not enforceable unless, and then only to the extent that, there is an actual transfer by the lessee of the lessee's right of possession or use of the goods in violation of the provision or an actual delegation of a material performance of either party to the lease contract in violation of the provision. Neither the granting nor the enforcement of a security interest in (i) the lessor's interest under the lease contract or (ii) the lessor's residual interest in the goods is a transfer that materially impairs the prospect of obtaining return performance by, materially changes the duty of, or materially increases the burden or risk imposed on, the lessee within the purview of subsection (5) unless, and then only to the extent that, there is an actual delegation of a material performance of the lessor.

(4) A provision in a lease agreement which (i) prohibits a transfer of a right to damages for default with respect to the whole lease contract or of a right to payment arising out of the transferor's due performance of the transferor's entire obligation, or (ii) makes such a transfer an event of default, is not enforceable, and such a transfer is not a transfer that materially impairs the prospect of obtaining return performance by, materially changes the duty of, or materially increases the burden or risk imposed on, the other party to the lease contract within the purview of subsection (5).

(5) (Subject to subsections (3) and (4):
  (a) if a transfer is made which is made an event of default under a lease agreement, the party to the lease contract not making the transfer, unless that party waives the default or otherwise agrees, has the rights and remedies described in Section 2A-501(2);
  (b) if paragraph (a) is not applicable and if a transfer is made that (i) is prohibited under a lease agreement or(ii) materially impairs the prospect of obtaining return performance by, materially changes the duty of, or materially increases the burden or risk imposed on, the other party to the lease contract, unless the party not making the transfer agrees at any time to the transfer in the lease contract or otherwise, then, except as limited by contract, (i) the transferor is liable to the party not making the transfer for damages caused by the transfer to the extent that the damages could not reasonably be prevented by the party not making the transfer and (ii)a court having jurisdiction may grant other appropriate relief, including cancellation of the lease contract or an injunction against the transfer.

(6) A transfer of "the lease" or of "all my rights under the lease; or a transfer in similar general terms, is a transfer of rights and, unless the language or the circumstances, as in a transfer for security, indicate the contrary, the transfer is a delegation of duties by the transferor to the transferee. Acceptance by the transferee constitutes a promise by the transferee to perform those duties. The promise is enforce-able by either the transferor or the other party to the lease contract.

(7) Unless otherwise agreed by the lessor and the lessee, a delegation of performance does not relieve the transferor as against the other party of any duty to perform or of any liability for default.

(8) In a consumer lease, to prohibit the transfer of an interest of a party under the lease contract or to make a transfer an event of default, the language must be specific, by a writing, and conspicuous. As amended in 1990.

§ 2A-304. Subsequent Lease of Goods by Lessor.

(1) Subject to Section 2A-303, a subsequent lessee from a lessor of goods under an existing lease contract obtains, to the extent of the leasehold interest transferred, the lease-hold interest in the goods that the lessor had or had power to transfer, and except as provided in subsection 2 and Section 2A-5 27(4), takes subject to the existing lease contract. A lessor with voidable title has power to transfer a good leasehold interest to a good faith subsequent lessee for value, but only to the extent set forth in the preceding sentence. If goods have been delivered under a transaction of purchase the lessor has that power even though:
  (a) the lessor's transferor was deceived as to the identity of the lessor;
  (b) the delivery was in exchange for a check which is later dishonored;
  (c) it was agreed that the transaction was to be a "cash sale"; or (d) the delivery was procured through fraud punishable as larcenous under the criminal law.

(2) A subsequent lessee in the ordinary course of business from a lessor who is a merchant dealing in goods of that kind to whom the goods were entrusted by the existing lessee of that lessor before the interest of the subsequent lessee became enforceable against that lessor obtains, to the extent of the leasehold interest transferred, all of that lessor's and the existing lessee's rights to the goods, and takes free of the existing lease contract.

(3) A subsequent lessee from the lessor of goods that are subject to an existing lease contract and are covered by a certificate of tide issued under a statute of this State or of another jurisdiction takes no greater rights than those provided both by this section and by the certificate of title statute. As amended in 1990.

§ 2A-305. Sale or Sublease of Goods by Lessee.

(1) Subject to the provisions of Section 2A-303, a buyer or sublessee from the lessee of goods under an existing lease contract

obtains, to the extent of the interest transferred, the leasehold interest in the goods that the lessee had or had power to transfer, and except as provided in subsection (2) and Section 2A-511(4), takes subject to the existing lease contract. A lessee with a voidable lease-hold interest has power to transfer a good leasehold interest to a good faith buyer for value or a good faith sublessee for value, but only to the extent set forth in the preceding sentence. When goods have been delivered under a trans-action of lease the lessee has that power even though:

(a) the lessor was deceived as to the identity of the lessee;

(b) the delivery was in exchange for a check which is later dishonored; or

(c) the delivery was procured through fraud punish-able as larcenous under the criminal law.

(2) A buyer in the ordinary course of business or a sub-lessee in the ordinary course of business from a lessee who is a merchant dealing in goods of that kind to whom the goods were entrusted by the lessor obtains, to the extent of the interest transferred, all of the lessor's and lessee's rights to the goods, and takes free of the existing lease contract.

(3) A buyer or sublessee from the lessee of goods that are subject to an existing lease contract and are covered by a certificate of title issued under a statute of this State or of another jurisdiction takes no greater rights than those provided both by this section and by the certificate of title statute.

§ 2A-306. Priority of Certain Liens Arising by Operation of law.

If a person in the ordinary course of his [or her] business furnishes services or materials with respect to goods subject to a lease contract, a lien upon those goods in the possession of that person given by statute or rule of law for those materials or services takes priority over any interest of the lessor or lessee under the lease contract or this Article unless the lien is created by statute and the statute provides otherwise or unless the lien is created by rule of law and the rule of law provides otherwise.

§ 2A-307. Priority of Liens Arising by Attachment or Levy on, Security Interests in, and Other Claims to Goods.

(1) Except as otherwise provided in Section 2A-306, a creditor of a lessee takes subject to the lease contract.

(2) Except as otherwise provided in subsections (3) and (4) and in Sections 2A-306 and 2A-308, a creditor of a lessor takes subject to the lease contract unless:

(a) the creditor holds a lien that attached to the goods before the lease contract became enforceable,

(b) the creditor holds a security interest in the goods and the lessee did not give value and receive delivery of the goods without knowledge of the security interest; or

(c) the creditor holds a security interest in the goods which was perfected (Section 9-303) before the lease contract became enforceable.

(3) A lessee in the ordinary course of business takes the leasehold interest free of a security interest in the goods created by the lessor even though the security interest is perfected (Section 9-303) and the lessee knows of its existence.

(4) A lessee other than a lessee in the ordinary course of business takes the leasehold interest free of a security interest to the extent that it secures future advances made after the secured party acquires knowledge of the lease or more than 45 days after the lease contract becomes enforceable, whichever first occurs, unless the future advances are made pursuant to a commitment entered into without knowledge of the lease and before the expiration of the 45-day period.

§ 2A-308. Special Rights of Creditors.

(1) A creditor of a lessor in possession of goods subject to a lease contract may treat the lease contract as void if as against the creditor retention of possession by the lessor is fraudulent under any statute or rule of law, but retention of possession in good faith and current course of trade by the lessor for a commercially reasonable time after the lease contract becomes enforceable is not fraudulent.

(2) Nothing in this Article impairs the rights of creditors of a lessor if the lease contract

(a) becomes enforceable, not in current course of trade but in satisfaction of or as security for a pre-existing claim for money, security, or the like, and

(3) is made under circumstances which under any statute or rule of law apart from this Article would constitute the transaction a fraudulent transfer or voidable preference.

(4) A creditor of a seller may treat a sale or an identification of goods to a contract for sale as void if as against the creditor retention of possession by the seller is fraudulent under any statute or rule of law, but retention of possession of the goods pursuant to a lease contract entered into by the seller as lessee and the buyer as lessor in connection with the sale or identification of the goods is not fraudulent if the buyer bought for value and in good faith.

§ 2A-309. Lessor's and Lessee's Rights When Goods Become Fixtures.

(1) In this section:

(a) goods are "fixtures" when they become so related to particular real estate that an interest in them arises under real estate law;

(b) a "fixture filing" is the filing, in the office where a mortgage on the real estate would be filed or recorded, of a financing statement covering goods that are or are to become fixtures and conforming to the requirements of Section 9-402(5);

(c) a lease is a "purchase money lease" unless the lessee has possession or use of the goods or the right to possession or use of the goods before the lease agreement is enforceable;

(d) a mortgage is a "construction mortgage" to the extent it secures an obligation incurred for the construction of an improvement on land including the acquisition cost of the land, if the recorded writing so indicates; and

(e) "encumbrance" includes real estate mortgages and other liens on real estate and all other rights in real estate that are not ownership interests.

(2) Under this Article a lease may be of goods that are fixtures or may continue in goods that become fixtures, but no lease exists under this Article of ordinary building materials incorporated into an improvement on land.

(3) This Article does not prevent creation of a lease of fixtures pursuant to real estate law.

(4) The perfected interest of a lessor of fixtures has priority over a conflicting interest of an encumbrancer or wrier of the real estate if

(a) the lease is a purchase money lease, the conflicting interest of the encumbrancer or owner arises before the goods become fixtures, the interest of the lessor is perfected by a fixture filing before the goods become fixtures or within ten days thereafter, and the lessee has an interest of record in the real estate or is in possession of the real estate; or

(b) the interest of the lessor is perfected by a fixture filing before the interest of the encumbrancer or owner is of record, the lessor's interest has priority over any conflicting interest of a predecessor in title of the encumbrancer or owner, and the lessee has an interest of record in the real estate or is in possession of the real estate.

(5) The interest of a lessor of fixtures, whether or not perfected, has priority over the conflicting interest of an encumbrancer or owner of the real estate if

(a) the fixtures are readily removable factory or office machines, readily removable equipment that is not primarily used or]eased for use in the operation of the real estate, or readily removable replacements of domestic appliances that are goods subject to a consumer lease, and before the goods become fixtures the lease contract is enforceable; or

(b) the conflicting interest is a lien on the real estate obtained by legal or equitable proceedings after the lease contract is enforceable; or

(c) the encumbrancer or owner has consented in writing to the lease or has disclaimed an interest in the goods as fixtures; or

(d) the lessee has a right to remove the goods as against the encumbrancer or owner. If the lessee's right to remove terminates, the priority of the interest of the lessor continues for a reasonable time.

(6) Notwithstanding paragraph (4)(a) but otherwise subject to subsections (4) and (5), the interest of a lessor of fixtures, including the lessor's residual interest, is subordinate to the conflicting interest of an encumbrancer of the real estate under a construction mortgage recorded before the goods become fixtures if the goods become fixtures before the completion of the construction. To the extent given to refinance a construction mortgage, the conflicting interest of an encumbrancer of the real estate under a mortgage has this priority to the same extent as the encumbrancer of the real estate under the construction mortgage.

(7) In cases not within the preceding subsections, priority between the interest of a lessor of fixtures, including the lessor's residual interest, and the conflicting interest of an encumbrancer or owner of the real estate who is not the lessee is determined by the priority rules governing conflicting interests in real estate.

(8) If the interest of a lessor of fixtures, including the lessor's residual interest, has priority over all conflicting interests of all owners and encumbrancers of the real estate, the lessor or the lessee may (i) on default, expiration, termination, or cancellation of the lease agreement but subject to the agreement and this Article, or (ii) if necessary to enforce other rights and remedies of the lessor or lessee under this Article, remove the goods from the real estate, free and clear of all conflicting interests of all owners and encumbrancers of the real estate, but the lessor or lessee must reimburse any encumbrancer or owner of the real estate who is not the lessee and who has not otherwise agreed for the cost of repair of any physical injury, but not for any diminution in value of the real estate caused by the absence of the goods removed or by any necessity of replacing them. A person entitled to reimbursement may refuse permission to remove until the party seeking removal gives adequate security for the performance of this obligation.

(9) Even though the lease agreement does not create a security interest, the interest of a lessor of fixtures, including the lessor's residual interest, is perfected by filing a financing statement as a fixture filing for leased goods that are or are to become fixtures in accordance with the relevant provisions of the Article on Secured Transactions (Article 9).
As amended in 1990.

§ 2A-310. Lessor's and Lessee's Rights When Goods Become Accessions.

(1) Goods are "accessions" when they are installed in or affixed to other goods.

(2) The interest of a lessor or a lessee under a lease con-tract entered into before the goods became accessions is superior to all interests in the whole except as stated in sub-section (4).

(3) The interest of a lessor or a lessee under a lease con-tract entered into at the time or after the goods became accessions is superior to all subsequently acquired interests in the whole except as stated in subsection (4) but is sub-ordinate to interests in the whole existing at the time the lease contract was made unless the holders of such interests in the whole have in writing consented to the lease or disclaimed an interest in the goods as part of the whole.

(4) The interest of a lessor or a lessee under a lease contract described in subsection (2) or (3) is subordinate to the interest of

(a) a buyer in the ordinary course of business or a lessee in the ordinary course of business of any interest in the whole acquired after the goods became accessions; or

(b) a creditor with a security interest in the whole perfected before the lease contract was made to the extent that the creditor makes subsequent advances without knowledge of the lease contract.

(5) When under subsections (2) or (3) and (4) a lessor or a lessee of accessions holds an interest that is superior to all interests in the whole, the lessor or the lessee may (a) on default, expiration, termination, or cancellation of the lease contract by the other party but subject to the provisions of the lease contract and this Article, or (b) if necessary to enforce his [or her] other rights and remedies under this Article, remove the goods from the whole, free and clear of all interests in the whole, but he [or she] must reimburse any holder of an interest in the whole who is not the lessee and who has not otherwise agreed for the cost of repair of any physical injury but not for any diminution in value of the whole caused by the absence of the goods removed or by any necessity for replacing them. A person entitled to reimbursement may refuse permission to remove until the party seeking removal gives

adequate security for the performance of this obligation.

§ 2A-311. Priority Subject to Subordination.

Nothing in this Article prevents subordination by agree-ment by any person entitled to priority.

As added in 1990.

Part 4 Performance Of Lease Contract: Repudiated, Substituted And Excused

§ 2A-401. Insecurity: Adequate Assurance of Performance.

(1) A lease contract imposes an obligation on each party that the other's expectation of receiving due performance will not be impaired.

(2) If reasonable grounds for insecurity arise with respect to the performance of either party, the insecure party may demand in writing adequate assurance of due performance. Until the insecure party receives that assurance, if commercially reasonable the insecure party may suspend any performance for which he [or she] has not already received the agreed return.

(3) A repudiation of the lease contract occurs if assurance of due performance adequate under the circumstances of the particular case is not provided to the insecure party within a reasonable time, not to exceed 30 days after receipt of a demand by the other party.

(4) Between merchants, the reasonableness of grounds for insecurity and the adequacy of any assurance offered must be determined according to commercial standards.

(5) Acceptance of any nonconforming delivery or payment does not prejudice the aggrieved party's right to demand adequate assurance of future performance.

§ 2A-402. Anticipatory Repudiation.

If either party repudiates a lease contract with respect to a performance not yet due under the lease contract, the loss of which performance will substantially impair the value of the lease contract to the other, the aggrieved party may:

(a) for a commercially reasonable time, await retraction of repudiation and performance by the repudiating party;

(b) make demand pursuant to Section 2A-401 and await assurance of future performance adequate under the circumstances of the particular case; or

(c) resort to any right or remedy upon default under the lease contract or this Article, even though the aggrieved party has notified the repudiating party that the aggrieved party would await the repudiating party's performance and assurance and has urged retraction. In addition, whether or not the aggrieved party is pursuing one of the foregoing remedies, the aggrieved party may suspend performance or, if the aggrieved party is the lessor, proceed in accordance with the provisions of this Article on the lessor's right to identify goods to the lease contract notwithstanding default or to salvage unfinished goods (Section 2A-5 24).

§ 2A-403. Retraction of Anticipatory Repudiation.

(1) Until the repudiating party's next performance is due, the repudiating party can retract the repudiation unless, since the repudiation, the aggrieved party has cancelled the lease contract or materially changed the aggrieved party's position or otherwise indicated that the aggrieved party considers the repudiation final.

(2) Retraction may be by any method that clearly indicates to the aggrieved party that the repudiating party intends to perform under the lease contract and includes any assurance demanded under Section 2A-401.

(3) Retraction reinstates a repudiating party's rights under a lease contract with due excuse and allowance to the aggrieved party for any delay occasioned by the repudiation.

§ 2A-404. Substituted Performance.

(1) If without fault of the lessee, the lessor and the supplier, the agreed berthing, loading, or unloading facilities fail or the agreed type of carrier becomes unavailable or the agreed manner of delivery otherwise becomes commercially impracticable, but a commercially reasonable substitute is available, the substitute performance must be tendered and accepted.

(2) If the agreed means or manner of payment fails because of domestic or foreign governmental regulation:

(a) the lessor may withhold or stop delivery or cause the supplier to withhold or stop delivery unless the lessee provides a means or manner of payment that is commercially a substantial equivalent; and

(b) if delivery has already been taken, payment by the means or in the manner provided by the regulation dis- charges the lessee's obligation unless the regulation is discriminatory, oppressive, or predatory.

§ 2A-405. Excused Performance.

Subject to Section 2A-404 on substituted performance, the following rules apply:

(a) Delay in delivery or non delivery in whole or in part by a lessor or a supplier who complies with paragraphs (b) and (c) is not a default under the lease contract if performance as agreed has been made impracticable by the occurrence of a contingency the nonoccurrence of which was a basic assumption, on which the lease contract was made or by compliance in good faith with any applicable foreign or domestic governmental regulation or order, whether or not the regulation or order later proves to be invalid.

(b) If the causes mentioned in paragraph (a) affect only part of the lessor's or the supplier's capacity to perform, he[or she] shall allocate production and deliveries among his[or her] customers but at his [or her] option may include regular customers not then under contract for sale or lease as well as his [or her] own requirements for further manufacture. He [or she] may so allocate in any manner that is fair and reasonable.

(c) The lessor seasonably shall notify the lessee and in the case of a finance lease the supplier seasonably shall notify the lessor and the lessee, if known, that there will be delay or non delivery and, if allocation is required under paragraph (b), of the estimated quota thus made available for the lessee.

§ 2A-406. Procedure on Excused Performance.

(1) If the lessee receives notification of a material or indefinite delay or an allocation justified under Section2A-405, the lessee may by written notification to the lessor as to any goods involved, and with respect to all of the goods if under an installment lease contract the value of the whole lease contract is substantially impaired(Section 2A-5 10):

    (a) terminate the lease contract (Section ZA-,505(2));or

    (b) except in a finance lease that is not a consumer lease, modify the lease contract by accepting the avail-able quota in substitution, with due allowance from the rent payable for the balance of the lease term for the deficiency but without further right against the lessor.

(2) If, after receipt of a notification from the lessor under Section 2A-405, the lessee fails so to modify the lease agreement within a reasonable time not exceeding 30 days, the lease contract lapses with respect to any deliveries affected.

§ 2A-407. Irrevocable Promises: Finance Leases.

(1) In the case of a finance lease that is not a consumer lease the lessee's promises under the lease contract become irrevocable and independent upon the lessee's acceptance of the goods.

(2) A promise that has become irrevocable and independent under subsection (1):

    (a) is effective and enforceable between the parties, and by or against third parties including assignees of the parties, and

    (b) is not subject to cancellation, termination, modification, repudiation, excuse, or substitution without the consent of the party to whom the promise runs.

(3) This section does not affect the validity under any other law of a covenant in any lease contract making the lessee's promises irrevocable and independent upon the lessee's acceptance of the goods.

As amended in 1990.

Part 5 Default

A. In General

§ 2A-501. Default: Procedure.

(1) Whether the lessor or the lessee is in default under a lease contract is determined by the lease agreement and this Article.

(2) If the lessor or the lessee is in default under the lease contract, the party seeking enforcement has rights and remedies as provided in this Article and, except as limited by this Article, as provided in the lease agreement.

(3) If the lessor or the lessee is in default under the lease contract, the party seeking enforcement may reduce the party's claim to judgment, or otherwise enforce the lease contract by self-help or any available judicial procedure or nonjudicial procedure, including administrative proceeding, arbitration, or the like, in accordance with this Article.

(4) Except as otherwise provided in Section 1-106(l) or this Article or the lease agreement, the rights and remedies referred to in subsections (2) and (3) are cumulative.

(5) If the lease agreement covers both real property and goods, the party seeking enforcement may proceed under this Part as to the goods, or under other applicable law as to both the real property and the goods in accordance with that party's rights and remedies in respect of the real property, in which case this Part does not apply.

As amended in 1990.

§ 2A-502. Notice After Default.

Except as otherwise provided in this Article or the lease agreement, the lessor or lessee in default under the lease contract is not entitled to notice of default or notice of enforcement from the other party to the lease agreement.

§ 2A-503. Modification or Impairment of Rights and Remedies.

(1) Except as otherwise provided in this Article, the lease agreement may include rights and remedies for default in addition to or in substitution for those provided in this Article and may limit or alter the measure of damages recoverable under this Article.

(2) Resort to a remedy provided under this Article or in the lease agreement is optional unless the remedy is expressly agreed to be exclusive. If circumstances cause an exclusive or limited remedy to fail of its essential purpose, or provision for an exclusive remedy is unconscionable, remedy may be had as provided in this Article.

(3) Consequential damages may be liquidated under Section 2A-504, or may otherwise be limited, altered, or excluded unless the limitation, alteration, or exclusion is unconscionable. Limitation, alteration, or exclusion of consequential damages for injury to the person in the case of consumer goods is prima facie unconscionable but limitation, alteration, or exclusion of damages where the loss is commercial is not prima facie unconscionable.

(4) Rights and remedies on default by the lessor or the lessee with respect to any obligation or promise collateral or ancillary to the lease contract are not impaired by this Article.

As amended in 1990.

§ 2A-504. Liquidation of Damages.

(1) Damages payable by either party for default, or any other act or omission, including indemnity for loss or diminution of anticipated tax benefits or loss or damage to lessor's residual interest, may be liquidated in the lease agreement but only at an amount or by a formula that is reasonable in light of the then anticipated harm caused by the default or other act or omission.

(2) If the lease agreement provides for liquidation of damages, and such provision does not comply with subsection (1), or such provision is an exclusive or limited remedy that circumstances cause to fail of its essential purpose, remedy may be had as provided in this Article.

(3) If the lessor justifiably withholds or stops delivery of goods because of the lessee's default or insolvency (Section 2A-5 2 5 or 2A-5 26), the lessee is entitled to restitution of any amount by which the sum of his [or her] payments exceeds:

    (a) the amount to which the lessor is entitled by virtue of terms liquidating the lessor's damages in accordance with subsection (1); or

    (b) in the absence of those terms, 20 percent of the then

present value of the total rent the lessee was obligated to pay for the balance of the lease term, or, in the case of a consumer lease, the lesser of such amount or $500.

(4) A lessee's right to restitution under subsection (3) is subject to offset to the extent the lessor establishes:

(a) a right to recover damages under the provisions of this Article other than subsection (1); and

(b) the amount or value of any benefits received by the lessee directly or indirectly by reason of the lease contract.

§ 2A-505. Cancellation and Termination and Effect of Cancellation, Termination, Rescission, or Fraud on Rights and Remedies.

(1) On cancellation of the lease contract, all obligations that are still executory on both sides are discharged, but any right based on prior default or performance survives, and the cancelling party also retains any remedy for default of the whole lease contract or any unperformed balance.

(2) On termination of the lease contract, all obligations that are still executory on both sides are discharged but any right based on prior default or performance survives.

(3) Unless the contrary intention clearly appears, expressions of "cancellation rescission," or the like of the lease contract may not be construed as a renunciation or discharge of any claim in damages for an antecedent default.

(4) Rights and remedies for material misrepresentation or fraud include all rights and remedies available under this Article for default.

(5) Neither rescission nor a claim for rescission of the lease contract nor rejection or return of the goods may bar or be deemed inconsistent with a claim for damages or other right or remedy.

§ 2A-506. Statute of Limitations.

(1) An action for default under a lease contract, including breach of warranty or indemnity, must be commenced within 4 years after the cause of action accrued. By the original lease contract the parties may reduce the period of limitation to not less than one year.

(2) A cause of action for default accrues when the act or omission on which the default or breach of warranty is based is or should have been discovered by the aggrieved party, or when the default occurs, whichever is later. A cause of action for indemnity accrues when the act or omission on which the claim for indemnity is based is or should have been discovered by the indemnified party, whichever is later.

(3) If an action commenced within the time limited by subsection (1) is so terminated as to leave available a remedy by another action for the same default or breach of warranty or indemnity, the other action may be commenced after the expiration of the time limited and within 6 months after the termination of the first action unless the termination resulted from voluntary discontinuance or from dismissal for failure or neglect to prosecute.

(4) This section does not alter the law on tolling of the statute of limitations nor does it apply to causes of action that have accrued before this Article becomes effective.

§ 2A-507. Proof of Market Rent: Time and Place.

(1) Damages based on market rent (Section 2A-519 or 2A-528) are determined according to the rent for the use of the goods concerned for a lease term identical to the remaining lease term of the original lease agreement and prevailing at the times specified in Sections 2A-519 and 2A-528.

(2) If evidence of rent for the use of the goods concerned for a lease term identical to the remaining lease term of the original lease agreement and prevailing at the times or places described in this Article is not readily available, the rent prevailing within any reasonable time before or after the time described or at any other place or for a different lease term which in commercial judgment or under usage of trade would serve as a reasonable substitute for the one described may be used, making any proper allowance for the difference, including the cost of transporting the goods to or from the other place.

(3) Evidence of a relevant rent prevailing at a time or place or for a lease term other than the one described in this Article offered by one party is not admissible unless and until he [or she] has given the other party notice the court finds sufficient to prevent unfair surprise.

(4) If the prevailing rent or value of any goods regularly leased in any established market is in issue, reports in official publications or trade journals or in newspapers or periodicals of general circulation published as the reports of that market are admissible in evidence. The circumstances of the preparation of the report may be shown to affect its weight but not its admissibility.

As amended in 1990.

A. Default by Lessor

§ 2A-508. Lessee's Remedies.

(1) If a lessor fails to deliver the goods in conformity to the lease contract (Section 2A-509) or repudiates the lease contract (Section 2A-402), or a lessee rightfully rejects the goods (Section 2A-509) or justifiably revokes acceptance of the goods (Section 2A-517), then with respect to any goods involved, and with respect to all of the goods if under an installment lease contract the value of the whole lease contract is substantially impaired (Section 2A-5 10), the lessor is in default under the lease contract and the lessee may:

(a) cancel the lease contract (Section 2A-505(l));

(b) recover so much of the rent and security as has been paid and is just under the circumstances;

(c) cover and recover damages as to all goods affected whether or not they have been identified to the lease contract (Sections 2A-518 and 2A-520), or recover damages for nondelivery (Sections 2A-519 and 2A-520);

(d) exercise any other rights or pursue any other remedies provided in the lease contract..

(2) If a lessor fails to deliver the goods in conformity to the lease contract or repudiates the lease contract, the lessee may also:

(a) if the goods have been identified, recover them (Section 2A-5 22); or

(b) in a proper case, obtain specific performance or replevy the goods (Section 2A-52 1).

(3) If a lessor is otherwise in default under a lease contract, the lessee may exercise the rights and pursue the remedies provided in the lease contract, which may include a right to can-

cel the lease, and in Section 2A-519(3).

(4) If a lessor has breached a warranty, whether express or implied, the lessee may recover damages (Section 2A-519(4)).

(5) On rightful rejection or justifiable revocation of acceptance, a lessee has a security interest in goods in the lessee's possession or control for any rent and security that has been paid and any expenses reasonably incurred in their inspection, receipt, transportation, and care and custody and may hold those goods and dispose of them in good faith and in a commercially reasonable manner, subject to Section 2A-527(5).

(6) Subject to the provisions of Section 2A-407, a lessee, on notifying the lessor of the lessee's intention to do so, may deduct all or any part of the damages resulting from any default under the lease contract from any part of the rent still due under the same lease contract.

As amended in 1990.

§ 2A-509. Lessee's Rights on Improper Delivery; Rightful Rejection.

(1) Subject to the provisions of Section 2A-510 on default in installment lease contracts, if the goods or the tender or delivery fail in any respect to conform to the lease contract, the lessee may reject or accept the goods or accept any commercial unit or units and reject the rest of the goods.

(2) Rejection of goods is ineffective unless it is within a reasonable time after tender or delivery of the goods and the lessee seasonably notifies the lessor.

§ 2A-5 10. Installment Lease Contracts: Rejection and Default.

(1) Under an installment lease contract a lessee may reject any delivery that is nonconforming if the nonconformity substantially impairs the value of that delivery and cannot be cured or the nonconformity is a defect in the required documents; but if the nonconformity does not fall within subsection (2) and the lessor or the supplier gives adequate assurance of its cure, the lessee must accept that delivery.

(2) Whenever nonconformity or default with respect to one or more deliveries substantially impairs the value of the installment lease contract as a whole there is a default with respect to the whole. But, the aggrieved party rein-states the installment lease contract as a whole if the aggrieved party accepts a nonconforming delivery without seasonably notifying of cancellation or brings an action with respect only to past deliveries or demands performance as to future deliveries.

§ 2A-511. Merchant Lessee's Duties as to Rightfully Rejected Goods.

(1) Subject to any security interest of a lessee (Section 2A-508(5)), if a lessor or a supplier has no agent or place of business at the market of rejection, a merchant lessee, after rejection of goods in his [or her] possession or control, shall follow any reasonable instructions received from the lessor or the supplier with respect to the goods. In the absence of those instructions, a merchant lessee shall make reasonable efforts to sell, lease, or otherwise dispose of the goods for the lessor's account if they threaten to decline in value speedily. Instructions are not reasonable if on demand indemnity for expenses is not forthcoming.

(2) If a merchant lessee (subsection (1)) or any other lessee (Section 2A-512) disposes of goods, he [or she] is entitled to reimbursement either from the lessor or the supplier or out of the proceeds for reasonable expenses of caring for and disposing of the goods and, if the expenses include no disposition commission, to such commission as is usual in the trade, or if there is none, to a reasonable sum not exceeding 10 percent of the gross proceeds.

(3) In complying with this section or Section 2A-512, the lessee is held only to good faith. Good faith conduct hereunder is neither acceptance or conversion nor the basis of an action for damages.(4) A purchaser who purchases in good faith from a lessee pursuant to this section or Section 2A-512 takes the goods free of any rights of the lessor and the supplier even though the lessee fails to comply with one or more of the requirements of this Article.

§ 2A-512. Lessee's Duties as to Rightfully Rejected Goods.

(1) Except as otherwise provided with respect to goods that threaten to decline in value speedily (Section 2A-511) and subject to any security interest of a lessee (Section 2A-508(5)):

(a) the lessee, after rejection of goods in the lessee's possession, shall hold them with reasonable care at the lessor's or the supplier's disposition for a reasonable time after the lessee's seasonable notification of rejection;

(b) if the lessor or the supplier gives no instructions within a reasonable time after notification of rejection, the lessee may store the rejected goods for the lessor's or the supplier's account or ship them to the lessor or the supplier or dispose of them for the lessor's or the supplier's account with reimbursement in the manner provided in Section 2A-5 11; but

(c) the lessee has no further obligations with regard to goods rightfully rejected.

(2) Action by the lessee pursuant to subsection (1) is not acceptance or conversion.

§ 2A-513. Cure by Lessor of Improper Tender or Delivery; Replacement.

(1) If any tender or delivery by the lessor or the supplier is rejected because nonconforming and the time for performance has not yet expired, the lessor or the supplier may seasonably notify the lessee of the lessor's or the supplier's intention to cure and may then make a conforming delivery within the time provided in the lease contract.

(2) If the lessee rejects a nonconforming tender that the lessor or the supplier had reasonable grounds to believe would be acceptable with or without money allowance, the lessor or the supplier may have a further reasonable time to substitute a conforming tender if he [or she] seasonably notifies the lessee.

§ 2A-514. Waiver of Lessee's Objections.

(1) In rejecting goods, a lessee's failure to state a particular defect that is ascertainable by reasonable inspection precludes the lessee from relying on the defect to justify rejection or to establish default:

(a) if, stated seasonably, the lessor or the supplier could have cured it (Section 2A-513); or

(b) between merchants if the lessor or the supplier after rejection has made a request in writing for a full and final written statement of all defects on which the lessee proposes to rely.

(2) A lessee's failure to reserve rights when paying rent or other consideration against documents precludes recovery of the payment for defects apparent on the face of the documents.

§ 2A-515. Acceptance of Goods.

(1) Acceptance of goods occurs after the lessee has had a reasonable opportunity to inspect the goods and(a) the lessee signifies or acts with respect to the goods in a manner that signifies to the lessor or the supplier that the goods are conforming or that the lessee will take or retain them in spite of their non-conformity; or(b) the lessee fails to make an effective rejection of the goods (Section 2A-509(2)).(2) Acceptance of a part of any commercial unit is acceptance of that entire unit.

§ 2A-516. Effect of Acceptance of Goods; Notice of Default; Burden of Establishing Default after Acceptance; Notice of Claim or Litigation to Person Answerable Over.

(1) A lessee must pay rent for any goods accepted in accordance with the lease contract, with due allowance for goods rightfully rejected or not delivered.

(2) A lessee's acceptance of goods precludes rejection of the goods accepted. In the case of a finance lease, if made with knowledge of a nonconformity, acceptance cannot be revoked because of it. In any other case, if made with knowledge of a nonconformity, acceptance cannot be revoked because of it unless the acceptance was on the reasonable assumption that the nonconformity would be seasonably cured. Acceptance does not of itself impair any other remedy provided by this Article or the lease agreement for nonconformity.

(3) If a tender has been accepted:
   (a) within a reasonable time after the lessee discovers or should have discovered any default, the lessee shall notify the lessor and the supplier, if any, or be barred from any remedy against the party notified;
   (b) except in the case of a consumer lease, within a reasonable time after the lessee receives notice of litigation for infringement or the like (Section 2A-211) the lessee shall notify the lessor or be barred from any remedy over for liability established by the litigation; and
   (c) the burden is on the lessee to establish any default.

(4) If a lessee is sued for breach of a warranty or other obligation for which a lessor or a supplier is answerable over the following apply:
   (a) The lessee may give the lessor or the supplier, or both, written notice of the litigation. If the notice states that the person notified may come in and defend and that if the person notified does not do so that person will be bound in any action against that person by the lessee by any determination of fact common to the two litigations, then unless the person notified after seasonable receipt of the notice does come in and defend that person is so bound.
   (b) The lessor or the supplier may demand in writing that the lessee turn over control of the litigation including settlement if the claim is one for infringement or the like (Section 2A-211) or else be barred from any remedy over.

If the demand states that the lessor or the supplier agrees to bear all expense and to satisfy any adverse judgment, then unless the lessee after seasonable receipt of the demand does turn over control the lessee is so barred.

(5) Subsections (3) and (4) apply to any obligation of a lessee to hold the lessor or the supplier harmless against infringement or the like (Section 2A-21 1).
As amended in 1990.

§ 2A-517. Revocation of Acceptance of Goods.

(1) A lessee may revoke acceptance of a lot or commercial unit whose nonconformity substantially impairs its value to the lessee if the lessee has accepted it:
   (a) except in the case of a finance lease, on the reasonable assumption that its nonconformity would be cured and it has not been seasonably cured; or
   (b) without discovery of the nonconformity if the lessee's acceptance was reasonably induced either by the lessor's assurances or, except in the case of a finance lease, by the difficulty of discovery before acceptance.

(2) Except in the case of a finance lease that is not a consumer lease, a lessee may revoke acceptance of a lot or commercial unit if the lessor defaults under the lease con-tract and the default substantially impairs the value of that lot or commercial unit to the lessee.

(3) If the lease agreement so provides, the lessee may revoke acceptance of a lot or commercial unit because of other defaults by the lessor.

(4) Revocation of acceptance must occur within a reasonable time after the lessee discovers or should have discovered the ground for it and before any substantial change in condition of the goods which is not caused by the nonconformity. Revocation is not effective until the lessee notifies the lessor.

(5) A lessee who so revokes has the same rights and duties with regard to the goods involved as if the lessee had rejected them.
As amended in 1990.

§ 2A-518. Cover; Substitute Goods.

(1) After a default by a lessor under the lease contract of the type described in Section 2A-508(l), or, if agreed, after other default by the lessor, the lessee may cover by making any purchase or lease of or contract to purchase or lease goods in substitution for those due from the lessor.

(2) Except as otherwise provided with respect to damages liquidated in the lease agreement (Section 2A-504) or otherwise determined pursuant to agreement of the par-ties (Sections 1-102(3) and 2A-503), if a lessee's cover is by lease agreement substantially similar to the original lease agreement and the new lease agreement is made in good faith and in a commercially reasonable manner, the lessee may recover from the lessor as damages (i) the present value, as of the date of the commencement of the term of the new lease agreement, of the rent under the new lease agreement applicable to that period of the new lease term which is comparable to the then remaining term of the original lease agreement minus the present value as of the same date of the total rent for the then remaining lease term of the original lease agreement, and (ii) any incidental or consequential damages, less expenses saved in consequence of the lessor's default.

(3) If a lessee's cover is by lease agreement that for any reason does not qualify for treatment under subsection (2), or is by purchase or otherwise, the lessee may recover from the lessor as if the lessee had elected not to cover and Section 2A-5 19 governs. As amended in 1990.

§ 2A-519. Lessee's Damages for Non-Delivery, Repudiation, Default, and Breach of Warranty in Regard to Accepted Goods.

(1) Except as otherwise provided with respect to damages liquidated in the lease agreement (Section 2A-504) or otherwise determined pursuant to agreement of the parties (Sections 1-102(3) and 2A-503), if a lessee elects not to cover or a lessee elects to cover and the cover is by lease agreement that for any reason does not qualify for treatment under Section 2A-518(2), or is by purchase or otherwise, the measure of damages for non-delivery or repudiation by the lessor or for rejection or revocation of acceptance by the lessee is the present value, as of the date of the default, of the then market rent minus the present value as of the same date of the original rent, computed for the remaining lease term of the original lease agreement, together with incidental and consequential damages, less expenses saved in consequence of the lessor's default.

(2) Market rent is to be determined as of the place for tender or, in cases of rejection after arrival or revocation of acceptance, as of the place of arrival.

(3) Except as otherwise agreed, if the lessee has accepted goods and given notification (Section 2A-516(3)), the measure of damages for non-conforming tender or delivery or other default by a lessor is the loss resulting in the ordinary course of events from the lessor's default as deter-mined in any manner that is reasonable together with incidental and consequential damages, less expenses saved in consequence of the lessor's default.

(4) Except as otherwise agreed, the measure of damages for breach of warranty is the present value at the time and place of acceptance of the difference between the value of the use of the goods accepted and the value if they had been as warranted for the lease term, unless special circumstances show proximate damages of a different amount, together with incidental and consequential damages, less expenses saved in consequence of the lessor's default or breach of warranty. As amended in 1990.

§ 2A-520. Lessee's Incidental and Consequential Damages.

(1) Incidental damages resulting from a lessor's default include expenses reasonably incurred in inspection, receipt, transportation, and care and custody of goods right-fully rejected or goods the acceptance of which is justifiably revoked, any commercially reasonable charges, expenses or commissions in connection with effecting cover, and any other reasonable expense incident to the default.

(2) Consequential damages resulting from a lessor's default include: (a) any loss resulting from general or particular requirements and needs of which the lessor at the time of contracting had reason to know and which could not reasonably be prevented by cover or otherwise; and (b) injury to person or property proximately resulting from any breach of warranty.

§ 2A-521. Lessee's Right to Specific Performance or Replevin.

(1) Specific performance may be decreed if the goods are unique or in other proper circumstances.

(2) A decree for specific performance may include any terms and conditions as to payment of the rent, damages, or other relief that the court deems just.

(3) A lessee has a right of replevin, detinue, sequestration, claim and delivery, or the like for goods identified to the lease contract if after reasonable effort the lessee is unable to effect cover for those goods or the circumstances reasonably indicate that the effort will be unavailing.

§ 2A-522. Lessee's Right to Goods on Lessor's Insolvency.

(1) Subject to subsection

(2) and even though the goods have not been shipped, a lessee who has paid a part or all of the rent and security for goods identified to a lease contract (Section 2A-217) on making and keeping good a tender of any unpaid portion of the rent and security due under the lease contract may recover the goods identified from the lessor if the lessor becomes insolvent within 10 days after receipt of the first installment of rent and security. (2) A lessee acquires the right to recover goods identified to a lease contract only if they conform to the lease contract.

A. Default by Lessee

§ 2A-523. Lessor's Remedies.

(1) If a lessee wrongfully rejects or revokes acceptance of goods or fails to make a payment when due or repudiates with respect to a part or the whole, then, with respect to any goods involved, and with respect to all of the goods if under an installment lease contract the value of the whole lease contract is substantially impaired (Section 2A-5 10), the lessee is in default under the lease contract and the lessor may:
  (a) cancel the lease contract (Section 2A-505(l));
  (b) proceed respecting goods not identified to the lease contract (Section 2A-524);
  (c) withhold delivery of the goods and take possession of goods previously delivered (Section 2A-52 5);
  (d) stop delivery of the goods by any bailee (Section 2A-526);
  (e) dispose of the goods and recover damages (Section 2A-527), or retain the goods and recover damages (Section 2A-528), or in a proper case recover rent (Section 2A-529)
  (f) exercise any other rights or pursue any other remedies provided in the lease contract.

(2) If a lessor does not fully exercise a right or obtain a remedy to which the lessor is entitled under subsection (1), the lessor may recover the loss resulting in the ordinary course of events from the lessee's default as determined in any reasonable manner, together with incidental damages, less expenses saved in consequence of the lessee's default.

(3) If a lessee is otherwise in default under a lease con-tract, the lessor may exercise the rights and pursue the remedies provided in the lease contract, which may include a right to can-

cel the lease. In addition, unless otherwise provided in the lease contract:

(a) if the default substantially impairs the value of the lease contract to the lessor, the lessor may exercise the rights and pursue the remedies provided in subsections(1) or (2); or

(b) if the default does not substantially impair the value of the lease contract to the lessor, the lessor may recover as provided in subsection (2).

As amended in 1990.

§ 2A-524. Lessor's Right to Identify Goods to Lease Contract.

(1) After default by the lessee under the lease contract of the type described in Section 2A-523(l) or 2A-523(3)(a) or, if agreed, after other default by the lessee, the lessor may:

(a) identify to the lease contract conforming goods not already identified if at the time the lessor learned of the default they were in the lessor's or the supplier's possession or control; and

(b) dispose of goods (Section 2A-527(l)) that demonstrably have been intended for the particular lease contract even though those goods are unfinished.(2) If the goods are unfinished, in the exercise of reason-able commercial judgment for the purposes of avoiding loss and of effective realization, an aggrieved lessor or the supplier may either complete manufacture and wholly identify the goods to the lease contract or cease manufacture and lease, sell, or otherwise dispose of the goods for scrap or salvage value or proceed in any other reasonable manner.

As amended in 1990.

§ 2A-525. Lessor's Right to Possession of Goods.

(1) If a lessor discovers the lessee to be insolvent, the lessor may refuse to deliver the goods.

(2) After a default by the lessee under the lease contract of the type described in Section 2A-523(l) or 2A-523(3)(a)or, if agreed, after other default by the lessee, the lessor has the right to take possession of the goods. If the lease contract so provides, the lessor may require the lessee to assemble the goods and make them available to the lessor at a place to be designated by the lessor which is reasonably convenient to both parties. Without removal, the lessor may render unusable any goods employed in trade or business, and may dispose of goods on the lessee's premises (Section 2A-527).

(3) The lessor may proceed under subsection (2) without judicial process if that can be done without breach of the peace or the lessor may proceed by action.

As amended in 1990.

§ 2A-526. Lessor's Stoppage of Delivery in Transit or Otherwise.

(1) A lessor may stop delivery of goods in the possession of a carrier or other bailee if the lessor discovers the lessee to be insolvent and may stop delivery of carload, truckload, planeload, or larger shipments of express or freight if the lessee repudiates or fails to make a payment due before delivery, whether for rent, security or otherwise under the lease contract, or for any other reason the lessor has a right to withhold or take possession of the goods.

(2) In pursuing its remedies under subsection (1), the lessor may stop delivery until

(a) receipt of the goods by the lessee;

(b) acknowledgment to the lessee by any bailee of the goods, except a carrier, that the bailee holds the goods for the lessee; or

(c) such an acknowledgment to the lessee by a carrier via reshipment or as warehouseman.

(3) (a) To stop delivery, a lessor shall so notify as to enable the bailee by reasonable diligence to prevent delivery of the goods.

(b) After notification, the bailee shall hold and deliver the goods according to the directions of the lessor, but the lessor is liable to the bailee for any ensuing charges or damages.

(c) A carrier who has issued a nonnegotiable bill of lading is not obliged to obey a notification to stop received from a person other than the consignor.

§ 2A-527. Lessor's Rights to Dispose of Goods.

(1) After a default by a lessee under the lease contract of the type described in Section 2A-523(l) or 2A-523(3)(a) or after the lessor refuses to deliver or takes possession of goods (Section 2A-525 or 2A-526), or, if agreed, after other default by a lessee, the lessor may dispose of the goods concerned or the undelivered balance thereof by lease, sale, or otherwise.

(2) Except as otherwise provided with respect to damages liquidated in the lease agreement (Section 2A-504) or otherwise determined pursuant to agreement of the par- ties (Sections 1-102(3) and 2A-503), if the disposition is by lease agreement substantially similar to the original lease agreement and the new lease agreement is made in good faith and in a commercially reasonable manner, the lessor may recover from the lessee as damages (i) accrued and unpaid rent as of the date of the commencement of the term of the new lease agreement, (ii) the present value, as of the same date, of the total rent for the then remaining lease term of the original lease agreement minus the present value, as of the same date, of the rent under the new lease agreement applicable to that period of the new lease term which is comparable to the then remaining term of the original lease agreement, and (iii) any incidental dam-ages allowed under Section 2A-5 30, less expenses saved in consequence of the lessee's default.

(3) If the lessor's disposition is by lease agreement that for any reason does not qualify for treatment under subsection (2), or is by sale or otherwise, the lessor may recover from the lessee as if the lessor had elected not to dispose of the goods and Section 2A-5 28 governs.

(4) A subsequent buyer or lessee who buys or leases from the lessor in good faith for value as a result of a disposition under this section takes the goods free of the original lease contract and any rights of the original lessee even though the lessor fails to comply with one or more of the requirements of this Article.

(5) The lessor is not accountable to the lessee for any profit made on any disposition. A lessee who has rightfully rejected or justifiably revoked acceptance shall account to the lessor for any excess over the amount of the lessee's security interest (Section 2A-508(5)).

As amended in 1990.

§ 2A-528. Lessor's Damages for Non-acceptance, Failure to Pay, Repudiation, or Other Default.

(1) Except as otherwise provided with respect to damages liquidated in the lease agreement (Section 2A-504) or otherwise determined pursuant to agreement of the parties (Section 1-102(3) and 2A-503), if a lessor elects to retain the goods or a lessor elects to dispose of the goods and the disposition is by lease agreement that for any reason does not qualify for treatment under Section 2A-527(2), or is by sale or otherwise, the lessor may recover from the lessee as damages for a default of the type described in Section 2A-523(l) or 2A-523(3)(a), or if agreed, for other default of the lessee, (i) accrued and unpaid rent as of the date of the default if the lessee has never taken possession of the goods, or, if the lessee has taken possession of the goods, as of the date the lessor repossesses the goods or an earlier date on which the lessee makes a tender of the goods to the lessor, (ii) the present value as of the date determined under clause (i) of the total rent for the then remaining lease term of the original lease agreement minus the present value as of the same date of the market rent as the place where the goods are located computed for the same lease term, and (iii) any incidental damages allowed under Section 2A-530, less expenses saved in consequence of the lessee's default.

(2) If the measure of damages provided in subsection (1) is inadequate to put a lessor in as good a position as performance would have, the measure of damages is the present value of the profit, including reasonable overhead, the lessor would have made from full performance by the lessee, together with any incidental damages allowed under Section 2A-530, due allowance for costs reasonably incurred and due credit for payments or proceeds of disposition. As amended in 1990.

§ 2A-5 29. Lessor's Action for the Rent.

(1) After default by the lessee under the lease contract of the type described in Section 2A-523(l) or 2A-523(3)(a) or, if agreed, after other default by the lessee, if the lessor complies with subsection (2), the lessor may recover from the lessee as damages:

(a) for goods accepted by the lessee and not repossessed by or tendered to the lessor, and for conforming goods lost or damaged within a commercially reasonable time after risk of loss passes to the lessee (Section 2A-219), (i) accrued and unpaid rent as of the date of entry of judgment in favor of the lessor (ii) the present value as of the same date of the rent for the then remaining lease term of the lease agreement, and (iii) any incidental damages allowed under Section 2A-5 30, less expenses saved in consequence of the lessee's default-and

(b) for goods identified to the lease contract if the lessor is unable after reasonable effort to dispose of them at a reasonable price or the circumstances reasonably indicate that effort will be unavailing, (i) accrued and unpaid rent as of the date of entry of judgment in favor of the lessor, (ii) the present value as of the same date of the rent for the then remaining lease term of the lease agreement, and (iii) any incidental damages allowed under Section 2A-530, less expenses saved in consequence of the lessee's default.

(2) Except as provided in subsection (3), the lessor shall hold for the lessee for the remaining lease term of the lease agreement any goods that have been identified to the lease contract and are in the lessor's control.

(3) The lessor may dispose of the goods at any time before collection of the judgment for damages obtained pursuant to subsection (1). If the disposition is before the end of the remaining lease term of the lease agreement, the lessor's recovery against the lessee for damages is governed by Section 2A-5 27 or Section 2A-5 28. and the lessor will cause an appropriate credit to be provided against a judgment for damages to the extent that the amount of the judgment exceeds the recovery available pursuant to Section 2A-527 or 2A – 528.

(4) Payment of the judgment for damages obtained pursuant to subsection (1) entities the lessee to the use and pos-session of the goods not then disposed of for the remaining lease term of and in accordance with the lease agreement.

(5) After default by the lessee under the lease contract of the type described in Section 2A-523(l) or Section 2A-52 3(3)(a) or, if agreed, after other default by the lessee, a lessor who is held not entitled to rent under this section must nevertheless be awarded damages for non-acceptance under Sections 2A-527 and 2A-528. As amended in 1990.

§ 2A-530. Lessor's Incidental Damages.

Incidental damages to an aggrieved lessor include any commercially reasonable charges, expenses, or commissions incurred in stopping delivery, in the transportation, care and custody of goods after the lessee's default, in connection with return or disposition of the goods, or otherwise resulting from the default.

§ 2A-531. Standing to Sue Third Parties for Injury to Goods.

(1) If a third party so deals with goods that have been identified to a lease contract as to cause actionable injury to a party to the lease contract

(a) the lessor has a right of action against the third party, and

(b) the lessee also has a right of action against the third party if the lessee:

(i) has a security interest in the goods;

(ii) has an insurable interest in the goods; or

(iii) bears the risk of loss under the lease contract or has since the injury assumed that risk as against the lessor and the goods have been converted or destroyed.

(2) If at the time of the injury the party plaintiff did not bear the risk of loss as against the other party to the lease contract and there is no arrangement between them for disposition of the recovery, his [or her] suit or settlement, subject to his [or her] own interest, is as a fiduciary for the other party to the lease contract.

(3) (3) Either party with the consent of the other may sue for the benefit of whom it may concern.

§ 2A-532. Lessor's Rights to Residual Interest.

In addition to any other recovery permitted by this Article or other law, the lessor may recover from the lessee an amount that will fully compensate the lessor for any loss of or damage to the lessor's residual interest in the goods caused by the default of the lessee.

As added in 1990.